Praise for *The Rails Way*

For intermediates and above, I strongly recommend adding this title to your technical bookshelf. There is simply no other Rails title on the market at this time that offers the technical depth of the framework than *The Rails™ 3 Way*.

—Mike Riley, *Dr. Dobb's Journal*

I highly suggest you get this book. Software moves fast, especially the Rails API, but I feel this book has many core API and development concepts that will be useful for a while to come.

—Matt Polito, software engineer and member of Chicago Ruby User Group

This book should live on your desktop if you're a Rails developer. It's nearly perfect in my opinion.

—Luca Pette, developer

The Rails™ 3 Way is likely to take you from being a haphazard poke-a-stick-at-it programmer to a deliberate, skillful, productive, and confident RoR developer.

—Katrina Owen, JavaRanch

I can positively say that it's the single best Rails book ever published to date. By a long shot.

—Antonio Cangiano, software engineer and technical evangelist at IBM

This book is a great crash course in Ruby on Rails! It doesn't just document the features of Rails, it filters everything through the lens of an experienced Rails developer—so you come out a pro on the other side.

—Dirk Elmendorf, cofounder of Rackspace Inc. and Rails developer

The key to *The Rails Way* is in the title. It literally covers the "way" to do almost everything with Rails. Writing a truly exhaustive reference to the most popular web application framework used by thousands of developers is no mean feat. A thankful community of developers that has struggled to rely on scant documentation will embrace *The Rails Way* with open arms. A tour de force!

—Peter Cooper, editor, *Ruby Inside: The Ruby Blog*

In the past year, dozens of Rails books have been rushed to publication. A handful are good. Most regurgitate rudimentary information easily found on the Web. Only this book provides both the broad and deep technicalities of Rails. Nascent and expert developers, I recommend you follow *The Rails Way*.

—Martin Streicher, chief technology officer, McClatchy Interactive, former editor in chief of *Linux Magazine*

Hal Fulton's *The Ruby Way* has always been by my side as a reference while programming Ruby. Many times I had wished there was a book that had the same depth and attention to detail, only focused on the Rails framework. That book is now here and hasn't left my desk for the past month.

—Nate Klaiber, Ruby programmer

I knew soon after becoming involved with Rails that I had found something great. Now, with Obie's book, I have been able to step into Ruby on Rails development coming from .NET and be productive right away. The applications I have created I believe to be a much better quality due to the techniques I learned using Obie's knowledge.

—Robert Bazinet, InfoQ.com, .NET, and Ruby community editor and founding member of the Hartford Ruby Brigade

Extremely well written; it's a resource that every Rails programmer should have. Yes, it's that good.

—Reuven Lerner, *Linux Journal* columnist

THE RAILS™ 4 WAY

THE RAILS™ 4 WAY

Obie Fernandez

Kevin Faustino

✦▾Addison-Wesley

Upper Saddle River, NJ • Boston • Indianapolis • San Francisco
New York • Toronto • Montreal • London • Munich • Paris • Madrid
Capetown • Sydney • Tokyo • Singapore • Mexico City

Many of the designations used by manufacturers and sellers to distinguish their products are claimed as trademarks. Where those designations appear in this book, and the publisher was aware of a trademark claim, the designations have been printed with initial capital letters or in all capitals.

The authors and publisher have taken care in the preparation of this book but make no expressed or implied warranty of any kind and assume no responsibility for errors or omissions. No liability is assumed for incidental or consequential damages in connection with or arising out of the use of the information or programs contained herein.

For information about buying this title in bulk quantities or for special sales opportunities (which may include electronic versions; custom cover designs; and content particular to your business, training goals, marketing focus, or branding interests), please contact our corporate sales department at corpsales@pearsoned.com or (800) 382-3419.

For government sales inquiries, please contact governmentsales@pearsoned.com.

For questions about sales outside the United States, please contact international@pearsoned.com.

Visit us on the web: informit.com/aw

Library of Congress Cataloging-in-Publication Data
Fernandez, Obie.
    The Rails 4 way / Obie Fernandez, Kevin Faustino.
        pages   cm
    Includes bibliographical references and index.
    ISBN-13: 978-0-321-94427-6 (pbk. : alk. paper)
    ISBN-10: 0-321-94427-5 (pbk. : alk. paper)
    1. Ruby on rails (Electronic resource) 2. Object-oriented programming
(Computer science) 3. Ruby (Computer program language) 4. Web site
development. 5. Application software—Development. I. Faustino,
Kevin. II. Title.
    QA76.64.F4725 2014
    005.1'17—dc23
                                                    2014012567

ISBN-13: 978-0-321-94427-6
ISBN-10: 0-321-94427-5
Text printed in the United States on recycled paper at Courier in Westford, Massachusetts.
Second printing, July 2015

Editor-in-Chief
Mark L. Taub

Acquisitions Editor
Debra Williams Cauley

Managing Editor
John Fuller

Full-Service Production Manager
Julie B. Nahil

Editorial Assistant
Kim Boedigheimer

Production Editor
Scribe Inc.

Copy Editor
Scribe Inc.

Indexer
Scribe Inc.

Proofreader
Scribe Inc.

Compositor
Scribe Inc.

Cover Designer
Chuti Prasertsith

Taylor, your hard work and dedication to your craft are an inspiration to me every day. I love you.

Contents

Foreword

A long time ago, I was an intern at a technology company. We had "deploy week," meaning that after deploying, we took an entire week to fight fires. Moving our code to the production environment would inevitably cause unexpected changes. One day, I read a blog post titled "Unit Testing with Ruby on Rails," and my life was forever changed. I excitedly went and told my team that we could write code to check whether our code worked before deploying, but they weren't particularly interested. A few months later, when a friend asked me to be the CTO of his startup, I said, "Only if I can do it in Ruby on Rails."

My story was fairly typical for that period. I didn't know anything about Ruby, but I *had* to write my application in Rails. I figured out enough Ruby to fake it and cobbled together an application in record time. There was just one problem: I didn't really understand how it actually *worked*. This is the deal everyone makes with Rails at the start. You can't think about the details too much because you're flying to the sky like a rocket.

This book, however, isn't about that. When I read *The Rails Way* for the first time, I felt like I truly understood Rails for the first time. All those details I didn't fully understand were now able to be grokked. Every time someone said, "Rails is magic," I would smile to myself. If Rails was magic, I had peered behind the curtain. One day, I decided that I should write some documentation to help dispel those kinds of comments. One commit became two; two became twenty. Eventually, I was a large contributor in my own right. Such a long way for someone who had just a few short years earlier never heard of a unit test!

As Rails has changed, so has *The Rails Way*. In fact, one criticism you could make of this book is that it's not actually "the Rails way"; after all, it teaches you HAML instead of ERb! I think that this criticism misses the mark. After all, it's not 2005 anymore. To see what I mean, go read the two forewords from the previous edition. They appear right after this one … I'll wait.

Done? David's foreword was quite accurate for both Rails 2 and *The Rails Way*. At that time, Rails was very much "not as a blank slate equally tolerant of every kind of expression." Rails was built for what I call the "Omakase Stack": you have no choice, you get exactly what Chef David wants to serve you.[1]

Yehuda's foreword was also quite accurate—but for Rails 3 and *The Rails™ 3 Way*. "We brought this philosophy to every area of Rails 3: flexibility without compromise." With Rails 3, you get the Omakase stack by default, but you are free to swap out components: if you don't like sushi, you can substitute some sashimi.

There was a lot of wailing and gnashing of teeth during the development of Rails 3. Jeremy Ashkenas called it "by far the worst misfortune to ever happen to Rails." Rails 3 was an investment in the future of Rails, and investments can take a while to pay off. At the release of Rails 3, it seemed like we had waited more than a year for no new features. Rails was a little better but mostly the same. The real benefit was where it couldn't be seen: in the refactoring work. Rails 1 was "red-green." Rails 2 was "red-green." Rails 3 was "refactor." It took a little while for gem authors to take advantage of this flexibility, but eventually, they did.

And that brings us to Rails 4 and *The Rails™ 4 Way*. This book still explains quite a bit about how Rails works at a low level but also gives you an alternate vision from the Omakase Stack, based on the experience and talent of Hashrocket. In many ways, *The Rails™ 4 Way*, *Agile Web Development with Rails*, and *Rails 4 in Action* are all "the Rails way." Contemporary Rails developers get the best of both worlds: They can take advantage of the rapid development of convention over configuration, but if they choose to follow a different convention, they can. And we have many sets of conventions to choose from. It's no longer "David's way or the highway," though David's way is obviously the default, as it should be.

It has been an amazing few years for Rails, and it has been a pleasure to take a part in its development. I hope that this book will give you the same level of insight and clarity into Rails as it did for me, years ago, while also sparking your imagination for what Rails will undoubtedly become in the future.

—Steve Klabnik

---

1. *Omakase* is a Japanese term used at sushi restaurants to leave the selection to the chef. To learn more about the Omakase stack, read `http://words.steveklabnik.com/rails-has -two-default-stacks`

Foreword to the Previous Edition

Rails is more than programming framework for creating web applications. It's also a framework for thinking about web applications. It ships not as a blank slate equally tolerant of every kind of expression. On the contrary, it trades that flexibility for the convenience of "what most people need most of the time to do most things." It's a designer straightjacket that sets you free from focusing on the things that just don't matter and focuses your attention on the stuff that does.

To be able to accept that trade, you need to understand not just how to do something in Rails but also why it's done like that. Only by understanding the why will you be able to consistently work with the framework instead of against it. It doesn't mean that you'll always have to agree with a certain choice, but you will need to agree to the overachieving principle of conventions. You have to learn to relax and let go of your attachment to personal idiosyncrasies when the productivity rewards are right.

This book can help you do just that. Not only does it serve as a guide in your exploration of the features in Rails, but it also gives you a window into the mind and soul of Rails. Why we've chosen to do things the way we do them and why we frown on certain widespread approaches. It even goes so far as to include the discussions and stories of how we got there—straight from the community participants that helped shape them.

Learning how to do Hello World in Rails has always been easy to do on your own, but getting to know and appreciate the gestalt of Rails, less so. I applaud Obie for trying to help you on this journey. Enjoy it.

—**David Heinemeier Hansson**
creator of Ruby on Rails

Foreword to the Previous Edition

From the beginning, the Rails framework turned web development on its head with the insight that the vast majority of time spent on projects amounted to meaningless sit-ups. Instead of having the time to think through your domain-specific code, you'd spend the first few weeks of a project deciding meaningless details. By making decisions for you, Rails frees you to kick off your project with a bang, getting a working prototype out the door quickly. This makes it possible to build an application with some meat on its bones in a few weekends, making Rails the web framework of choice for people with a great idea and a full-time job.

Rails makes some simple decisions for you, like what to name your controller actions and how to organize your directories. It also gets pretty aggressive and sets development-friendly defaults for the database and caching layer you'll use, making it easy to change to more production-friendly options once you're ready to deploy.

By getting so aggressive, Rails makes it easy to put at least a few real users in front of your application within days, enabling you to start gathering the requirements from your users immediately rather than spending months architecting a perfect solution only to learn that your users use the application differently than you expected.

The Rails team built the Rails project itself according to very similar goals. Don't try to overthink the needs of your users. Get something out there that works and improve it based on actual usage patterns. By all accounts, this strategy has been a smashing success, and with the blessing of the Rails core team, the Rails community leveraged the dynamism of Ruby to fill in the gaps in plugins. Without taking a close look at Rails, you might think that Rails' rapid prototyping powers are limited to the 15-minute blog demo but that you'd fall off a cliff when writing a real app. This has never been true. In fact, in Rails 2.1, 2.2, and 2.3, the Rails team looked closely at common usage patterns reflected in very popular plugins, adding features that would further reduce the number of sit-ups needed to start real-life applications.

By the release of Rails 2.3, the Rails ecosystem had thousands of plugins, and applications like Twitter started to push the boundaries of the Rails defaults. Increasingly, you might build your next Rails application using a nonrelational database or deploy it inside a Java infrastructure using JRuby. It was time to take the tight integration of the Rails stack to the next level.

Over the course of 20 months, starting in January 2008, we looked at a wide range of plugins, spoke with the architects of some of the most popular Rails applications, and changed the way the Rails internals thought about its defaults.

Rather than starting from scratch, trying to build a generic data layer for Rails, we took on the challenge of making it easy to give any ORM the same tight level of integration with the rest of the framework as Active Record. We accepted no compromises, taking the time to write the tight Active Record integration using the same APIs that we now expose for other ORMs. This covers the obvious, such as making it possible to generate a scaffold using DataMapper or Mongoid. It also covers the less obvious, such as giving alternative ORMs the same ability to include the amount of time spent in the model layer in the controller's log output.

We brought this philosophy to every area of Rails 3: flexibility without compromise. By looking at the ways that an estimated million developers use Rails, we could hone in on the needs of real developers and plugin authors, significantly improving the overall architecture of Rails based on real user feedback.

Because the Rails 3 internals are such a departure from what's come before, developers building long-lived applications and plugin developers need a resource that comprehensively covers the philosophy of the new version of the framework. *The Rails™ 3 Way* is a comprehensive resource that digs into the new features in Rails 3 and perhaps, more important, the rationale behind them.

—**Yehuda Katz**
Rails Core

Introduction

It's an exciting time for the Rails community. We have matured tremendously and our mainstream adoption continues to pick up steam. Nearly 10 years after DHH first started playing with Ruby, it's safe to say that Rails remains a relevant and vital tool in the greater web technology ecosystem.

Rails 4 represents a big step forward for the community. We shed a variety of vestigial features that had been deprecated in Rails 3. Security was beefed up and raw performance improved. Most everything in the framework feels, well, tighter than before. Rails 4 is leaner and meaner than its previous incarnations, and so is this edition of *The Rails Way*.

In addition to normal revisions to bring the text up to date with the evolution of Rails' numerous APIs, this edition adds a significant amount of new and updated material about security, performance, and caching; Haml; RSpec; Ajax; and the new Asset Pipeline.

About This Book

As with previous editions, this book is not a tutorial or basic introduction to Ruby or Rails. It is meant as a day-to-day reference for the full-time Rails developer. The more confident reader might be able to get started in Rails using just this book, extensive online resources, and his or her wits, but there are other publications that are more introductory in nature and might be a wee bit more appropriate for beginners.

Every contributor to this book works with Rails on a full-time basis. We do not spend our days writing books or training other people, although that is certainly something that we enjoy doing on the side.

This book was originally conceived for myself, because I hate having to use online documentation, especially API docs, which need to be consulted over and over again. Since the API documentation is liberally licensed (just like the rest of Rails), there are a few sections of the book that reproduce parts of the API documentation. In practically all cases, the API documentation has been expanded and/or corrected and supplemented with additional examples and commentary drawn from practical experience.

Hopefully you are like me—I really like books that I can keep next to my keyboard, scribble notes in, and fill with bookmarks and dog-ears. When I'm coding, I want to be able to quickly refer to API documentation, in-depth explanations, and relevant examples.

Book Structure

I attempted to give the material a natural structure while meeting the goal of being the best possible Rails reference book. To that end, careful attention has been given to presenting holistic explanations of each subsystem of Rails, including detailed API information where appropriate. Every chapter is slightly different in scope, and I suspect that Rails is now too big a topic to cover the whole thing in depth in just one book.

Believe me, it has not been easy coming up with a structure that makes perfect sense for everyone. Particularly, I have noted surprise in some readers when they notice that Active Record is not covered first. Rails is foremost a web framework and, at least to me, the controller and routing implementation is the most unique, powerful, and effective feature, with Active Record following a close second.

Sample Code and Listings

The domains chosen for the code samples should be familiar to almost all professional developers. They include time and expense tracking, auctions, regional data management, and blogging applications. I don't spend pages explaining the subtler nuances of the business logic for the samples or justifying design decisions that don't have a direct relationship to the topic at hand. Following in the footsteps of my series colleague Hal Fulton and *The Ruby Way*, most of the snippets are not full code listings—only the relevant code is shown. Ellipses (…) often denote parts of the code that have been eliminated for clarity.

Whenever a code listing is large and significant, and I suspect that you might want to use parts of it verbatim in your code, I supply a listing heading. There are not too many of those. The whole set of code listings will not add up to a complete working system, nor are there 30 pages of sample application code in an appendix.

The code listings should serve as inspiration for your production-ready work, but keep in mind that it often lacks touches necessary in real-world work. For example, examples of controller code are often missing pagination and access control logic, because it would detract from the point being expressed.

Some of the source code for my examples can be found at `https://github.com/obie/tr3w_time_and_expenses`. Note that it is not a working nor complete application. It just made sense at times to keep the code in the context of an application and hopefully you might draw some inspiration from browsing through it.

Concerning Third-Party RubyGems and Plugins

Whenever you find yourself writing code that feels like plumbing, by which I mean completely unrelated to the business domain of your application, you're probably doing too much work. I hope that you have this book at your side when you encounter that feeling. There is almost always some new part of the Rails API or a third-party RubyGem for doing exactly what you are trying to do.

As a matter of fact, part of what sets this book apart is that I never hesitate to call out the availability of third-party code, and I even document the RubyGems and plugins that I feel are most crucial for effective Rails work. In cases where third-party code is better than the built-in Rails functionality, I don't cover the built-in Rails functionality (pagination is a good example).

An average developer might see her productivity double with Rails, but I've seen serious Rails developers achieve gains that are much higher. That's because we follow the "don't repeat yourself" (DRY) principle religiously, of which "don't reinvent the wheel" (DRTW) is a close corollary. Reimplementing something when an existing implementation is good enough is an unnecessary waste of time that nevertheless can be very tempting, since it's such a joy to program in Ruby.

Ruby on Rails is actually a vast ecosystem of core code, official plugins, and third-party plugins. That ecosystem has been exploding rapidly and provides all the raw technology you need to build even the most complicated enterprise-class web applications. My goal is to equip you with enough knowledge that you'll be able to avoid continuously reinventing the wheel.

Recommended Reading and Resources

Readers may find it useful to read this book while referring to some of the excellent reference titles listed in this section.

Most Ruby programmers always have their copy of the "Pickaxe" book nearby, *Programming Ruby* (ISBN: 0-9745140-5-5), because it is a good language reference.

Readers interested in really understanding all the nuances of Ruby programming should acquire *The Ruby Way, Second Edition* (ISBN: 0-672-3288-4-4).

I highly recommend Peepcode Screencasts, in-depth video presentations on a variety of Rails subjects by the inimitable Geoffrey Grosenbach, available at `http://peepcode.com`.

Ryan Bates does an excellent job explaining nuances of Rails development in his long-running series of free webcasts available at `http://railscasts.com`.

Regarding David Heinemeier Hansson, a.k.a. DHH: I had the pleasure of establishing a friendship with David, creator of Rails, in early 2005, before Rails hit the mainstream and he became an international Web 2.0 superstar. My friendship with David is a big factor in my writing this book today. David's opinions and public statements shape the Rails world, which means he gets quoted a lot when we discuss the nature of Rails and how to use it effectively.

I don't know if this is true anymore, but back when I wrote the original edition of this book, David had told me on a couple of occasions that he hates the "DHH" moniker that people tend to use instead of his long and difficult-to-spell full name. For that reason, in this book I try to always refer to him as "David" instead of the ever-tempting "DHH." When you encounter references to "David" without further qualification, I'm referring to the one and only David Heinemeier Hansson.

There are a number of notable people from the Rails world that are also referred to on a first-name basis in this book. Those include the following:

- *Yehuda* Katz
- *Jamis* Buck
- *Xavier* Noria
- *Tim* Pope

Goals

As already stated, I hope to make this your primary working reference for Ruby on Rails. I don't really expect too many people to read it through to the end unless they're expanding their basic knowledge of the Rails framework. Whatever the case may be, over time, I hope this book gives you as an application developer/programmer greater confidence in making design and implementation decisions while working on your day-to-day tasks. After spending time with this book, your understanding of the fundamental concepts of Rails coupled with hands-on experience should leave you feeling comfortable working on real-world Rails projects, with real-world demands.

If you are in an architectural or development lead role, this book is not targeted to you but should make you feel more comfortable discussing the pros and cons of

Ruby on Rails adoption and ways to extend Rails to meet the particular needs of the project under your direction.

Finally, if you are a development manager, you should find the practical perspective of the book and our coverage of testing and tools especially interesting and hopefully get some insight into why your developers are so excited about Ruby and Rails.

Prerequisites

The reader is assumed to have the following knowledge:

- Basic Ruby syntax and language constructs such as blocks
- Solid grasp of object-oriented principles and design patterns
- Basic understanding of relational databases and SQL
- Familiarity with how Rails applications are laid out and function
- Basic understanding of network protocols such as HTTP and SMTP
- Basic understanding of XML documents and web services
- Familiarity with transactional concepts such as ACID properties

As noted in the section "Book Structure," this book does not progress from easy material in the front to harder material in the back. Some chapters do start out with fundamental, almost introductory material and push on to more advanced coverage. There are definitely sections of the text that experienced Rails developers will gloss over. However, I believe that there is new knowledge and inspiration in every chapter for all skill levels.

Required Technology

A late-model Apple MacBook Pro running Mac OS X should be fine—just kidding, of course. Linux is pretty good for Rails development also. Microsoft Windows—well, let me just put it this way: your mileage may vary. I'm being nice and diplomatic in saying that. We specifically do not discuss Rails development on Microsoft platforms in this book. It's common knowledge that the vast majority of working Rails professionals develop and deploy on non-Microsoft platforms.

Acknowledgments

The Rails™ 4 Way was very much a team effort. On behalf of myself and Kevin, I would like to thank Vitaly Kushner and Ari Lerner for their contributions and support throughout the life of the project. We'd also like to thank Mike Perham, Juanito Fatas, Phillip Campbell, Brian Cardarella, Carlos Souza, and Michael Mazyar for technical review and edits. I must thank my understanding business partner Trevor Owens and staff at Lean Startup Machine for their ongoing support. Of course, Kevin and I also thank our families for their patience as writing tasks quite often ate into our personal time with them.

As always, I'd also like to express a huge debt of gratitude to our executive editor at Pearson: Debra Williams Cauley. Without her constant support and encouragement throughout the years, the Professional Ruby Series would not exist.

—**Obie Fernandez**
December 2013

About the Authors

Obie Fernandez

Obie has been hacking computers since he got his first Commodore VIC-20 in the eighties. In the midnineties, he found himself in the right place and time as a programmer on some of the first Java enterprise projects. He moved to Atlanta, Georgia, in 1998 and founded the Extreme Programming (later Agile Atlanta) User Group and was that group's president and organizer for several years. In 2004, he joined world-renowned consultancy ThoughtWorks and made a name for himself tackling high-risk, progressive projects in the enterprise, including some of the first enterprise projects in the world utilizing Ruby on Rails.

As founder and CEO of Hashrocket, one of the world's best web design and development consultancies, Obie specialized in orchestrating the creation of large-scale, web-based applications, both for startups and mission-critical enterprise projects. In 2010, Obie sold his stake in Hashrocket and has been working with technology startups ever since. He's currently cofounder and CTO of Lean Startup Machine, where he leads an awesome technology team and is building recognition as a thought leader on lean startup topics.

Obie's evangelization of Ruby on Rails online via blog posts and publications dates back to early 2005, and it earned him quite a bit of notoriety (and trash talking) from his old friends in the Java open-source community. Since then, he has traveled around the world relentlessly promoting Rails at large industry conferences. The previous two editions of this book are considered the "bibles" of Ruby on Rails development and are bestsellers.

Obie still gets his hands dirty with code daily and posts regularly on various topics to his popular weblog at `http://blog.obiefernandez.com`. His next book, *The Lean Enterprise*, is scheduled to be published in spring 2014.

Kevin Faustino

Kevin is founder and chief craftsman of Remarkable Labs, based in Toronto, Canada. He believes that software should not just work but be well crafted. He founded Remarkable Labs because he wanted to build a company that he would be proud to work for and that other companies would love to work with.

Following his passion for sharing knowledge, Kevin also founded the Toronto Ruby Brigade, which hosts tech talks, hack nights, and book clubs. Kevin has been specializing in Ruby since 2008 and has been professionally developing since 2005.

CHAPTER 1

Rails Environments and Configuration

[Rails] gained a lot of its focus and appeal because I didn't try to please people who didn't share my problems. Differentiating between production and development was a very real problem for me, so I solved it the best way I knew how.

—David Heinemeier Hansson

Rails applications are preconfigured with three standard modes of operation: development, test, and production. These modes are basically execution environments and have a collection of associated settings that determine things such as which database to connect to and whether the classes of your application should be reloaded with each request. It is also simple to create your own custom environments if necessary.

The current environment can be specified via the environment variable RAILS_ENV, which names the desired mode of operation and corresponds to an environment definition file in the config/environments folder. You can also set the environment variable RACK_ENV, or as a last resort, you may rely on the default being development. Since this environment setting governs some of the most fundamental aspects of Rails, such as class loading, in order to really understand the Rails way, you should understand its environment settings.

In this chapter, we start by covering Bundler, a tool that manages gem dependencies for your Ruby application. It takes a gem manifest file and is able to fetch, download, and install the gems in the manifest and all child dependencies. Then we move on to how Rails starts up and handles requests, by examining scripts such as boot.rb and application.rb and the settings that make up the three standard environment settings (modes). We also cover some of the basics of defining your own environments and why you might choose to do so.

Note that this book is not written with absolute newcomers to Rails in mind. To make the most out of this book, you should already be at least somewhat familiar with how to bootstrap a Rails application and the meaning of MVC. If you are not, I recommend that you first take advantage of the excellent Ruby on Rails Tutorial website[1] by Michael Hartl, another Professional Ruby Series author.

1.1 Bundler

Bundler[2] is not a technology that is specific to Rails 4, but it *is* the preferred way to manage your application's gem dependencies. Applications generated with Rails 4 use Bundler automatically, and you should not need to install the `bundler` gem separately since it's a dependency of Rails itself.

Since we believe that you should use Bundler, figuring out how to not use Bundler is left as an exercise for adventurous and/or nonconformist readers.

One of the most important things that Bundler does is dependency resolution on the full list of gems specified in your configuration, all at once. This differs from the one-at-a-time dependency resolution approach employed by RubyGems and previous versions of Rails, which can (and often did) result in the following hard-to-fix problem:

Assume that your system had the following RubyGem versions installed.

```
activesupport 4.0.2
activesupport 3.2.11
activemerchant 1.29.3
rails 3.2.11
```

It turns out that `activemerchant 1.29.3` depends on `activesupport >= 2.3.14`; therefore, when you load it using the `gem` command (from the RubyGems library) like this,

```
gem 'activemerchant', '1.29.3'
```

it results in the loading of `activemerchant`, as well as the latest compatible versions of its dependencies, including the `activesupport 4.0.2` gem, since it is greater than or equal to version 2.3.14. Subsequently, trying to load Rails itself with

```
gem 'rails', '3.2.11'
```

results in the following exception at runtime:

---

1. http://ruby.railstutorial.org/
2. http://bundler.io

```
can't activate activesupport (= 3.2.11, runtime)
for ["rails-3.2.11"], already activated
activesupport-4.0.2 for ["activemerchant-1.29.3"]
```

The exception happens because activemerchant has a broader dependency that results in the activation of a version of Active Support that does not satisfy the more narrow dependency of the older version of Rails. Bundler solves this problem by evaluating all dependencies at once and figuring out exactly the right versions of gems to load.

For an interesting perspective concerning the way that Bundler was conceived, make sure to read Yehuda's blog post on the subject.[3]

1.1.1 `Gemfile`

Located in the root of your Rails project directory is a Ruby-based gem manifest file named `Gemfile`. The `Gemfile` specifies all dependencies of your Rails app, including the version of Rails being used. The basic syntax for the `Gemfile` is simple:

```
gem 'kaminari'
gem 'nokogiri'
```

To load a dependency only in a specific environment, place it in a group block specifying one or more environment names as symbols:

```
group :development do
  gem 'pry-rails'
end

group :test do
  gem 'capybara'
  gem 'database_cleaner'
end

group :development, :test do
  gem 'rspec-rails'
  gem 'factory_girl_rails'
end
```

Upgrading from Rails 3

If you're upgrading from Rails 3, note that Rails 4 no longer uses the assets group for Asset Pipeline–related gems. You will need to move all assets grouped gems inline.

---

3. http://yehudakatz.com/2010/04/21/named-gem-environments-and-bundler/

The gem directive takes an optional second argument describing the version of the RubyGem desired. Leaving the version argument off will simply get the latest available *stable* version, which may not be the latest version available. To include a release candidate or a prerelease gem, you'll need to specify the version explicitly.

The format of the version argument matches the RubyGem versioning scheme to which you should already be accustomed.

```
gem 'nokogiri', '1.5.6'
gem 'pry-rails', '> 0.2.2'
gem 'decent_exposure', '~> 2.0.1'
gem 'draper', '1.0.0.beta6'
```

You can find full instructions on how to craft a version string in the RubyGems documentation.[4]

Occasionally, the name of the gem that should be used in a require statement is different from the name of that gem in the repository. In those cases, the :require option solves this simply and declaratively right in the Gemfile.

```
gem 'webmock', require: 'webmock/rspec'
```

1.1.1.1 Loading Gems Directly from a Git Repository

Until now we have been loading our gems from https://rubygems.org. It is possible to specify a gem by its source repository as long as it has a .gemspec file in the root directory. Just add a :git option to the call to gem.

```
gem 'carrierwave',git:'git@github.com:carrierwaveuploader/carrierwave.git'
```

If the gem source repository is hosted on GitHub and is public, you can use the :github shorthand.

```
gem 'carrierwave', github: 'carrierwaveuploader/carrierwave'
```

Gemspecs with binaries or C extensions are also supported.

```
gem 'nokogiri', git: 'git://github.com/tenderlove/nokogiri.git'
```

If there is no .gemspec file at the root of a gem's Git repository, you must tell Bundler which version to use when resolving its dependencies.

```
gem 'deep_merge', '1.0', git: 'git://github.com/peritor/deep_merge.git'
```

---

4. http://docs.rubygems.org/read/chapter/16

It's also possible to specify that a Git repository contains multiple `.gemspec` files and should be treated as a gem source. The following example does just that for the most common Git repository that fits the criteria—the Rails codebase itself. (Note: You should never actually need to put the following code in a `Gemfile` for one of your Rails applications!)

```
git 'git://github.com/rails/rails.git'
gem 'railties'
gem 'action_pack'
gem 'active_model'
```

Additionally, you can specify that a Git repository should use a particular ref, branch, or tag as options to the `git` directive:

```
git 'git://github.com/rails/rails.git',
  ref: '4aded'

git 'git://github.com/rails/rails.git',
  branch: '3-2-stable'

git 'git://github.com/rails/rails.git',
  tag: 'v3.2.11'
```

Specifying a ref, branch, or tag for a Git repository specified inline uses the same option syntax.

```
gem 'nokogiri', git: 'git://github.com/tenderlove/nokogiri.git', ref: '0eec4'
```

1.1.1.2   Loading Gems from the Filesystem

You can use a gem that you are actively developing on your local workstation using the `:path` option.

```
gem 'nokogiri', path: '~/code/nokogiri'
```

1.1.2   Installing Gems

Every time you modify the `Gemfile`, or more specifically, if you introduce dependencies not yet installed, invoke the `install` command to ensure that all the dependencies in your `Gemfile` are available to your Rails application.[5]

---

5. rbenv allows you to easily install, manage, and work with multiple Ruby interpreters and it's a must-have tool for modern Rails developers: `https://github.com/sstephenson/rbenv`

```
$ bundle install
Fetching gem metadata from https://rubygems.org/.........
Fetching gem metadata from https://rubygems.org/..
Installing rake (10.1.0)
Installing i18n (0.6.9)
Installing minitest (4.7.5)
Installing multi_json (1.8.2)
Installing atomic (1.1.14)
Installing thread_safe (0.1.3)
Installing tzinfo (0.3.38)
Installing activesupport (4.0.2)
Installing builder (3.1.4)
Installing erubis (2.7.0)
Installing rack (1.5.2)
Installing rack-test (0.6.2)
Installing actionpack (4.0.2)
Installing mime-types (1.25.1)
Installing polyglot (0.3.3)
Installing treetop (1.4.15)
Installing mail (2.5.4)
Installing actionmailer (4.0.2)
Installing activemodel (4.0.2)
Installing activerecord-deprecated_finders (1.0.3)
Installing arel (4.0.1)
Installing activerecord (4.0.2)
Installing coffee-script-source (1.6.3)
Installing execjs (2.0.2)
Installing coffee-script (2.2.0)
Installing thor (0.18.1)
Installing railties (4.0.2)
Installing coffee-rails (4.0.1)
Installing hike (1.2.3)
Installing jbuilder (1.5.2)
Installing jquery-rails (3.0.4)
Installing json (1.8.1)
Installing bundler (1.3.5)
Installing tilt (1.4.1)
Installing sprockets (2.10.1)
Installing sprockets-rails (2.0.1)
Installing rails (4.0.2)
Installing rdoc (3.12.2)
Installing sass (3.2.12)
Installing sass-rails (4.0.1)
Installing sdoc (0.3.20)
Installing sqlite3 (1.3.8)
Installing turbolinks (1.3.1)
Installing uglifier (2.3.2)
Your bundle is complete!
Use `bundle show [gemname]` to see where a bundled gem is installed.
```

The `install` command updates all dependencies named in your `Gemfile` to the latest versions that do not conflict with other dependencies.

You can opt to install dependencies, except those in specified groups using the `--without` option.

```
$ bundle install --without development test
$ bundle install --without test
```

1.1.3   Gem Locking

Every time you run `bundle install` or `bundle update`, Bundler calculates the dependency tree for your application and stores the results in a file named `Gemfile .lock`. From that point on, Bundler will only load specific versions of gems that you are using at the moment that the `Gemfile` was locked—versions that you know will work well with your application.

Note

The `Gemfile.lock` file should always be checked into version control to ensure every machine running the application uses the exact same versions of gems.[6]

To illustrate the importance of this, imagine the `Gemfile.lock` is missing and the application is being deployed to production. Since the dependency tree is nonexistent, Bundler has to resolve all the gems from the `Gemfile` on that machine. This may install newer gem versions than you tested against, causing unforeseen issues.

1.1.4   Packaging Gems

You can package up all your gems in the `vendor/cache` directory inside of your Rails application.

```
$ bundle package
```

Running `bundle install --local` in an application with packaged gems will use the gems in the package and skip connecting to rubygems.org or any other gem sources. You can use this to avoid external dependencies at deploy time or if you depend on private gems that are not available in any public repository.

---

6. `http://yehudakatz.com/2010/12/16/clarifying-the-roles-of-the-gemspec-and -gemfile/`

1.1.4.1 Making Gem Dependencies Available to Non-Rails Scripts

Non-Rails scripts must be executed with `bundle exec` in order to get a properly initialized RubyGems environment.

```
$ bundle exec guard
```

As of Rails 4, generating a new application will result in the creation of binstubs for Rails executables, located in the `bin` folder. A *binstub* is a script containing an executable that runs in the context of the bundle. This means one does not have to prefix `bundle exec` each time a Rails-specific executable is invoked. Binstubs are also first class citizens in Rails 4 and should be added into your version control system like any other source code file.

By default, the following stubs are available on every new Rails 4 project:

- `bin/bundle`
- `bin/rails`
- `bin/rake`
- `bin/spring`

1.1.4.2 Upgrading from Rails 3

If you are upgrading from Rails 3 and have generated binstubs using Bundler in the past, you must upgrade your binstubs by running the following commands:

```
1 bundle config --delete bin # Turn off Bundler's stub generator
2 rake rails:update:bin # Use the new Rails 4 executables
3 git add bin # Add bin/ to source control
```

To add a *binstub* of a commonly used executable in your bundle, invoke `bundle binstubs some-gem-name`. To illustrate, consider the following example:

```
$ bundle binstubs guard
```

This example creates a binstub for `guard` in the `bin` folder.

```
1 #!/usr/bin/env ruby
2 #
3 # This file was generated by Bundler.
4 #
5 # The application 'guard' is installed as part of a gem, and
6 # this file is here to facilitate running it.
7 #
8
```

```
 9 require 'pathname'
10 ENV['BUNDLE_GEMFILE'] ||= File.expand_path("../../Gemfile",
11    Pathname.new(__FILE__).realpath)
12
13 require 'rubygems'
14 require 'bundler/setup'
15
16 load Gem.bin_path('guard', 'guard')
```

Using binstubs, scripts can be executed directly from the `bin` directory.

```
1 $ bin/guard
```

1.2 Startup and Application Settings

Whenever you start a process to handle requests with Rails (such as with `rails server`), one of the first things that happens is that `config/boot.rb` is loaded.

There are three files involved in setting up the entire Rails stack:

config/boot.rb Sets up Bundler and load paths.

config/application.rb Loads Rails gems and gems for the specified `Rails.env` and configures the application.

config/environment.rb Runs all initializers.

All three are run when you need the whole Rails environment loaded. That's what's done by `runner`, `console`, `server`, and so on.

1.2.1 `config/application.rb`

The file `config/application.rb` is home to your Rails application settings, and it's the only file required at the top of `config/environment.rb`.

Let's go step by step through the settings provided in the default `config/application.rb` file that you'll find in a newly created Rails application. By the way, as you're reading the following sections, make a mental note to yourself that changes to these files require a server restart to take effect.

The next lines of `config/application.rb` are where the wheels really start turning once `config/boot.rb` is loaded:

```
require File.expand_path('../boot', __FILE__)
```

Note that the boot script is generated as part of your Rails application, but you won't usually need to edit it.

Getting back to `config/application.rb`, we find the following line:

```
require 'rails/all'
```

You also have the ability to easily cherry-pick only the components needed by your application.

```
 1 # To pick the frameworks you want, remove 'require "rails/all"'.
 2 # and list the framework railties that you want:
 3 #
 4 # require "active_model/railtie"
 5 # require "active_record/railtie"
 6 # require "action_controller/railtie"
 7 # require "action_mailer/railtie"
 8 # require "action_view/railtie"
 9 # require "sprockets/railtie"
10 # require "rails/test_unit/railtie"
```

The main configuration of our application follows, which in Rails 4 gets its own module and class:

```
1 module TimeAndExpenses
2   class Application < Rails::Application
3     # Settings in config/environments/* take precedence over those
4     # specified here. Application configuration should go into files
5     # in config/initializers
6     # -- all .rb files in that directory are automatically loaded.
```

The creation of a module specifically for your application is part of the groundwork for supporting running multiple Rails applications in the same process.

1.2.1.1   Time Zones

The default time zone for Rails 4 applications is UTC (Coordinated Universal Time). If the business domain of your application is sensitive to knowing exactly what time zone the server is in, then you can use the following setting to override the default:

```
# Set Time.zone default to the specified zone and make Active Record
# autoconvert to this zone.
# Run "rake -D time" for a list of tasks for finding time zone names.
config.time_zone = 'Central Time (US & Canada)'
```

Juanito Says ...

---

rake `time:zones:all` will list all the time zones Rails knows about.

1.2.1.2   Localization

Rails features localization support via locale files and is covered in detail in Chapter 11, "All about Helpers," in the TranslationHelper and I18n API sections.

The default locale is :en and can be overridden in your configuration.

```
# The default locale is :en and all translations from
# config/locales/*.rb,yml are autoloaded.
# config.i18n.load_path += Dir[Rails.root.join('my', 'locales',
#  '*.{rb,yml}')]
# config.i18n.default_locale = :de
```

1.2.1.3   Generator Default Settings

Rails generator scripts make certain assumptions about your tool chain. Setting the correct values here means having to type less parameters on the command line. For instance, to use RSpec without fixtures and Haml as the template engine, our settings would look like the following:

```
# Configure generator's values. Many other options are available.
# Be sure to check the documentation.
config.generators do |g|
  g.template_engine :haml
  g.test_framework :rspec, fixture: false
end
```

Note that RubyGems such as rspec-rails and factory_girl_rails handle this for you automatically.

1.2.2   Initializers

Rails 2 introduced the concept of breaking out configuration settings into their own small Ruby files under the config/initializers directory, where they are automatically loaded at startup. You can add configuration settings for your own application by adding Ruby files to the initializers directory. The following seven initializers are included by default in all Rails applications.

1.2.2.1   Backtrace Silencers

Nobody likes long exception backtraces, except maybe Java programmers. Rails has a mechanism for reducing the size of backtraces by eliminating lines that don't really add anything to your debugging.

The backtrace_silencers.rb initializer lets you modify the way that backtraces are shortened. I've found it useful to remove backtrace entries for noisy libraries, but removing all silencers is usually never needed during normal application development.

```
1  # You can add backtrace silencers for libraries that you're using but
2  # don't wish to see in your backtraces.
3  Rails.backtrace_cleaner.add_silencer { |line| line =~ /my_noisy_library/}
4
5  # You can also remove all the silencers if you're trying to debug a
6  # problem that might stem from framework code.
7  Rails.backtrace_cleaner.remove_silencers!
```

1.2.2.2   Filter Parameter Logging

When a request is made to your application, by default Rails logs details such as the request path, HTTP method, IP address, and parameters. If an attacker somehow gained access to your logs, they may be able to view sensitive information, like passwords and credit card numbers.

The `filter_parameter_logging.rb` initializer lets you specify which request parameters should be filtered from your log files. If Rails receives a request parameter included in the `filter_parameters` collection, it will mark it as `[FILTERED]` in your logs.

```
# Configure sensitive parameters which will be filtered from the log file.
Rails.application.config.filter_parameters += [:password]
```

1.2.2.3   Inflections

Rails has a class named `Inflector` whose responsibility is to transform strings (words) from singular to plural, class names to table names, modularized class names to ones without, class names to foreign keys, and so on. (Some of its operations have funny names, such as `dasherize`.)

The default inflections for pluralization and singularization of uncountable words are kept in an interesting file inside the Active Support gem, named `inflections.rb`.

Most of the time the `Inflector` class does a decent job of figuring out the pluralized table name for a given class, but occasionally it won't. This is one of the first stumbling blocks for many new Rails users, but it is not necessary to panic. With a little ad hoc testing beforehand, it's easy to find out how `Inflector` will react to certain words. We just need to use the Rails console, which by the way is one of the best things about working in Rails.

You fire up the console from your terminal with the `rails console` command.

```
$ rails console
>> ActiveSupport::Inflector.pluralize "project"
=> "projects"
>> ActiveSupport::Inflector.pluralize "virus"
=> "viri"
>> "pensum".pluralize  # Inflector features are mixed into String.
   by default
=> "pensums"
```

As you can see in the example, `Inflector` tries to be smart, pluralizing *virus* as *viri*; but if you know your Latin, you have already noticed that the plural *pensum* should actually be *pensa*. Needless to say, the inflector does not know Latin.[7]

However, you can teach the inflector new tricks by adding new pattern rules, by pointing out an exception, or by declaring certain words unpluralizable. The preferred place to do that is inside the `config/initializers/inflections.rb` file, where a commented example is already provided:

```
1 ActiveSupport::Inflector.inflections(:en) do |inflect|
2   inflect.plural /^(ox)$/i, '\1en'
3   inflect.singular /^(ox)en/i, '\1'
4   inflect.irregular 'person', 'people'
5   inflect.uncountable %w( fish sheep )
6 end
```

The file `activesupport/test/inflector_test_cases.rb`[8] has a long list of pluralizations correctly handled by `Inflector`. I found some of them pretty interesting, such as the following:

```
1 "datum"        => "data",
2 "medium"       => "media",
3 "analysis"     => "analyses"
```

1.2.2.4   Custom MIME Types

Rails supports a standard set of MIME types (*/*, text/html, text/plain, text/javascript, text/css, text/calendar, text/csv, application/xml, application/rss+xml, application/atom+xml, application/x-yaml, multipart/form-data, application/x-www-form-urlencoded, application/json).

---

7. Comically, the Rails inflection of virus is also wrong. See `http://en.wikipedia.org/wiki/Plural_form_of_words_ending_in_-us#Virus`

8. `https://github.com/rails/rails/blob/master/activesupport/test/inflector_test_cases.rb`

Table 1.1   Custom MIME Types

Short name	`respond_to` symbol	Aliases and explanations
text/html	`:html`, `:xhtml`	application/xhtml+xml
text/plain	`:text`, `:txt`	
text/javascript	`:js`	application/javascript, application/x-javascript
text/css	`:css`	Cascading style sheets
text/calendar	`:ics`	iCalendar format for sharing meeting requests and tasks
text/csv	`:csv`	Comma-separated values
application/xml	`:xml`	text/xml, application/x-xml
application/rss+xml	`:rss`	Really Simple Syndication format for web feeds
application/atom+xml	`:atom`	Atom Syndication Format for web feeds
application/x-yaml	`:yaml`	text/yaml—the human-readable
		Data serialization format
application/x-www-form urlencoded	`:url_encoded_form`	The default content type of HTML forms
multipart/form-data	`:multipart_form`	Used for HTML forms that contain files, non-ASCII data, and binary data
application/json	`:json`	text/x-json, application/jsonrequest—JavaScript object notation

If your application needs to respond to other MIME types, you can register them in the `mime_types.rb` initializer:

```
# Add new MIME types for use in respond_to blocks:
# Mime::Type.register "text/richtext", :rtf
# Mime::Type.register_alias "text/html", :iphone
```

1.2.2.5   Session Store

As of Rails 4, session cookies are encrypted by default using the new encrypted cookie store. The `session_store.rb` initializer configures the session store of the application by setting its session store type and key.

```
Rails.application.config.session_store :cookie_store,
  key: '_example_session'
```

The session cookies are signed using the `secret_key_base` set in the `config/secrets.yml` configuration file. If you are really paranoid, you can change the secret key in `config/secrets.yml` or run `rake secret` to generate a new one automatically.

1.2.2.6 Wrap Parameters

Introduced in Rails 3.1, the `wrap_parameters.rb` initializer configures your application to work with JavaScript MVC frameworks, such as Backbone.js, out of the box.

```
# Be sure to restart your server when you modify this file.

# This file contains settings for ActionController::ParamsWrapper,
# which is enabled by default.

# Enable parameter wrapping for JSON. You can disable this by setting
# :format to an empty array.
ActiveSupport.on_load(:action_controller) do
  wrap_parameters format: [:json] if respond_to?(:wrap_parameters)
end

# To enable root element in JSON for ActiveRecord objects.
# ActiveSupport.on_load(:active_record) do
#  self.include_root_in_json = true
# end
```

When submitting JavaScript object notation (JSON) parameters to a controller, Rails will *wrap* the parameters into a nested hash, with the controller's name being set as the key. To illustrate, consider the following JSON:

```
{"title": "The Rails 4 Way"}
```

If a client submitted this JSON to a controller named `ArticlesController`, Rails would nest the `params` hash under the key "article." This ensures the setting of model attributes from request parameters is consistent with the convention used when submitting from Rails form helpers.

```
{"title": "The Rails 4 Way", "article" => {"title": "The Rails 4 Way"}}
```

1.2.3   Additional Configuration

That does it for the configuration options for which we get examples in the default `config/application.rb` and the standard initializers. There are additional options that you can add in additional initializer files.

1.2.3.1   Load Path Modifications

By default, Rails looks for code in a number of standard directories, including all nested directories under `app`, such as `app/models`. This is referred to collectively as the load path. You can add other directories to the load path using the following code:

```
# Custom directories with classes and modules you want to be autoloadable
# config.autoload_paths += %W(#{config.root}/extras)
```

In case you didn't know, the `%W` functions as a white space–delimited array literal and is used quite often in the Rails codebase for convenience.

1.2.3.2   Log-Level Override

The default log level is `:debug`, and you can override it if necessary.

```
# Force all environments to use the same logger level
# (by default production uses :info, the others :debug).
config.log_level = :debug
```

Use of the Rails logger is discussed in depth later on in this chapter.

1.2.3.3   Schema Dumper

Every time you run tests, Rails dumps the schema of your development database and copies it to the test database using an autogenerated `schema.rb` script. It looks very similar to an Active Record migration script; in fact, it uses the same API.

You might find it necessary to revert to the older style of dumping the schema using SQL if you're doing things that are incompatible with the schema dumper code (see the comment).

```
# Use SQL instead of Active Record's schema dumper when creating the
# test database. This is necessary if your schema can't be completely
# dumped by the schema dumper—for example, if you have constraints
# or db-specific column types.
config.active_record.schema_format = :sql
```

Remember how we said that the value of the `RAILS_ENV` environment variable dictates which additional environment settings are loaded next? Let's review the default settings for each of Rails's standard modes.

1.2.3.4   Console

New to Rails 4 is the ability to supply a block to `console`, a method that is only evaluated when the Rails environment is loaded through the console. This allows you to set console-specific configurations, such as using Pry over IRB. Put this in your `config/application.rb`:

```
1 console do
2   # This block is called only when running console,
3   # so we can safely require pry here.
4   require "pry"
5   config.console = Pry
6 end
```

Note that the `pry` gem must be included in your `Gemfile`.

1.2.4   Spring Application Preloader

As of version 4.1, Rails ships with an application preloader named Spring.[9] In doing so, during development, your application will remain running in the background. This speeds up development by eliminating the need to boot up Rails every time you execute tests or run a `rake` task.

While running, Spring monitors folders `config` and `initializers` for changes. If a file within those folders are changed, Spring will automatically restart your application. Spring will also restart if any gem dependencies are changed during development.

To demonstrate the speed increase Spring provides, let's run the same `rake` task in both Rails 4.0 and a preloaded 4.1 application:

```
1 # Rails 4.0
2 $ time bin/rake about
3   ...
4   bin/rake about  1.20s user 0.36s system 22% cpu 6.845 total
5
6 # Rails 4.1
7 $ time bin/rake about
8   ...
9   bin/rake about  0.08s user 0.04s system 32% cpu 0.370 total
```

9. https://github.com/rails/spring

The preloaded Rails environment using Spring provided a savings of more than six seconds.

1.3   Development Mode

Development is Rails's default mode and the one in which you will spend most of your time as a developer. This section contains an in-depth explanation of each setting.

```
# File: config/environments/development.rb
Rails.application.configure do
  # Settings specified here will take precedence over those in
  # config/application.rb.
```

1.3.1   Automatic Class Reloading

One of the signature benefits of using Rails is the quick feedback cycle whenever you're working in development mode. Make changes to your code, hit Reload in the browser, and Shazam! Magically, the changes are reflected in your application. This behavior is governed by the `config.cache_classes` setting:

```
# In the development environment, your application's code is reloaded on
# every request. This slows down response time but is perfect for
# development since you don't have to restart the web server when you
# make code changes.
config.cache_classes = false
```

Without getting into too much nitty-gritty detail, when the `config.cache_classes` setting is `true`, Rails will use Ruby's `require` statement to do its class loading, and when it is `false`, it will use `load` instead.

When you require a Ruby file, the interpreter executes and caches it. If the file is required again (as in subsequent requests), the interpreter ignores the require statement and moves on. When you load a Ruby file, the interpreter executes the file again, no matter how many times it has been loaded before.

Now it's time to examine the Rails class-loading behavior a bit more in depth, because sometimes you won't be able to get certain things to reload automatically, and it will drive you crazy unless you understand how class loading works!

1.3.1.1   The Rails Class Loader

In plain old Ruby, a script file doesn't need to be named in any particular way that matches its contents. In Rails, however, you'll notice that there's almost always a direct correlation between the name of a Ruby file and the class or module contained within. Rails takes advantage of the fact that Ruby provides a callback mechanism for missing constants. When Rails encounters an undefined constant in the code, it uses a class loader routine based on file-naming conventions to find and require the needed Ruby script.

How does the class loader know where to search? We already covered it earlier in the chapter when we discussed the role of `initializer.rb` in the Rails startup process. Rails has the concept of load paths, and the default load paths include the base directories of just about anywhere you would think of adding code to your Rails application.

Want to see the contents of your project's load path? Just fire up the console and type `$LOAD_PATH`:

```
$ rails console
Loading development environment.
>> $LOAD_PATH
=> ["/usr/local/lib/ruby/... # about 20 lines of output
```

I snipped the console output to save space. A typical Rails project load path will usually have 60 or more items in its load path. Try it and see.

1.3.1.2   Rails, Modules, and Autoloading Code

Normally in Ruby, when you want to include code from another file in your application, you have to include a require statement. However, Rails enhances Ruby's default behavior by establishing a simple convention that enables Rails to automatically load your code in most cases. If you've used the Rails console at all, you've already seen this behavior in action: You never have to explicitly `require` anything!

This is how it works: If Rails encounters a class or module in your code that is not already defined, Rails uses the following convention to guess which files it should require to load that module or class.

If the class or module is not nested, insert an underscore between the constant's names and require a file of this name. The following are some examples:

- `EstimationCalculator` becomes `require "estimation_calculator"`.
- `KittTurboBoost` becomes `require "kitt_turbo_boost"`.

If the class or module is nested, Rails inserts an underscore between each of the containing modules and requires a file in the corresponding set of subdirectories. The following are some examples:

- `MacGyver::SwissArmyKnife` becomes `require "mac_gyver/swiss _army_knife"`.

- `Example::ReallyRatherDeeply::NestedClass` becomes `require "example/really_rather_deeply/nested_class"`, and if not already loaded, Rails would expect to find it in a file called `nested_class .rb` in a directory called `really_rather_deeply`, itself in the directory `example`, which can be found somewhere in Ruby's load path (e.g., one of the app subdirectories, `lib`, or a plugin's `lib` directory).

The bottom line is that you should rarely need to explicitly load Ruby code in your Rails applications (using `require`) if you follow the naming conventions.

1.3.2 Eager Load

To speed up the boot time of starting a Rails server during development, code is no longer eager loaded. This behavior is governed by the `config.eager_load` setting:

```
# Do not eager load code on boot.
config.eager_load = false
```

In your production environment, you will want this set to `true`, as it copies most of your application in memory. This provides a performance increase to web servers that copy on write, such as Unicorn.

1.3.3 Error Reports

Requests from localhost, like when you're developing, generate useful error messages that include debugging information such as a line number where the error occurred and a backtrace. Setting `consider_all_requests_local` to true causes Rails to display those developer-friendly error screens, even when the machine making the request is remote.

```
config.consider_all_requests_local = true
```

1.3.4 Caching

You normally do not want caching behavior when you're in development mode. The only time you do want it is if you're actually testing caching.

```
config.action_controller.perform_caching = true
# for testing in development mode
```

Remember to set it back to `false` when you're done testing. Unexpected caching behavior can be very tricky to figure out.

1.3.5   Raise Delivery Errors

Rails assumes that you don't want Action Mailer to raise delivery exceptions in development mode, so based on the `config.action_mailer.raise_delivery_errors` settings, it will swallow them. Mailing capabilities don't necessarily work in an average development workstation, particularly on Windows and other platforms that lack `sendmail`.

```
# Don't care if the mailer can't send.
config.action_mailer.raise_delivery_errors = false
```

If you actually want to send mail while in development mode as part of debugging or ad hoc testing, then you probably want to toggle this setting.

Xavier Says ...

> I find it handy to set `config.action_mailer.perform_deliveries = false` in development. No delivery attempt is performed, but you can still see the mail in the log file to check that it looks good, copy account activation URLs, and so on.

1.3.6   Deprecation Notices

Deprecations warnings are very useful to let you know when you should stop using a particular piece of functionality. The configuration setting `config.active_support.deprecation` allows you to set how you would like to receive deprecation warnings. In development mode, by default all deprecation warnings will appear in the development log.

```
# Print deprecation notices to the Rails logger.
config.active_support.deprecation = :log
```

1.3.7   Pending Migrations Error Page

In previous versions of Rails, if pending migrations needed to be run, the web server would fail to start. As of Rails 4, a new error page is displayed instead, indicating to developers that they should run `rake db:migrate RAILS_ENV=development` to resolve the issue.

```
# Raise an error on page load if there are pending migrations
config.active_record.migration_error = :page_load
```

1.3.8   Assets Debug Mode

Rails 3.1 introduced us to the Asset Pipeline, a framework to concatenate and minify JavaScript and CSS assets. By default in development mode, JavaScript and CSS files are served separately in the order they were specified in their respective manifest files. Setting `config.assets.debug` to `false` would result in Sprockets concatenating and running preprocessors on all assets.

```
# Debug mode disables concatenation and preprocessing of assets.
config.assets.debug = true
```

The Asset Pipeline is covered in detailed in Chapter 20, "Asset Pipeline."

1.4   Test Mode

Whenever you run Rails in test mode—that is, the value of the RAILS_ENV environment value is `test`—then the following settings are in effect (reproduced here for reference purposes):

```
1  # File: config/environments/test.rb
2  Rails.application.configure do
3    # Settings specified here will take precedence over those in
4    # config/application.rb.
5
6    # The test environment is used exclusively to run your application's
7    # test suite. You never need to work with it otherwise. Remember that
8    # your test database is "scratch space" for the test suite and is wiped
9    # and recreated between test runs. Don't rely on the data there!
10   config.cache_classes = true
11
12   # Do not eager load code on boot. This avoids loading your whole
13   # application just for the purpose of running a single test. If you are
14   # using a tool that preloads Rails for running tests, you may have to set
15   # it to true.
16   config.eager_load = false
17
18   # Configure static asset server for tests with Cache-Control for
19   # performance.
20   config.serve_static_assets  = true
21   config.static_cache_control = "public, max-age=3600"
22
23   # Show full error reports and disable caching.
24   config.consider_all_requests_local       = true
25   config.action_controller.perform_caching = false
26
27   # Raise exceptions instead of rendering exception templates.
28   config.action_dispatch.show_exceptions = false
29
```

```
30   # Disable request forgery protection in test environment.
31   config.action_controller.allow_forgery_protection = false
32
33   # Tell Action Mailer not to deliver emails to the real world.
34   # The :test delivery method accumulates sent emails in the
35   # ActionMailer::Base.deliveries array.
36   config.action_mailer.delivery_method = :test
37
38   # Print deprecation notices to the stderr.
39   config.active_support.deprecation = :stderr
40 end
```

Most people get by without ever needing to modify their test environment settings.

Custom Environments

If necessary, you can create additional environments for your Rails app to run by cloning one of the existing environment files in the `config/environments` directory of your application. The most common use case for custom environments is in setting up additional production configurations, such as for staging and QA deployments. Do you have access to the production database from your development workstation? Then a triage environment might make sense. Use the normal environment settings for development mode, but point its database connection to a production database server. It's a potentially lifesaving combination when you need to quickly diagnose issues in production.

1.5   Production Mode

Finally, production mode is what you want your Rails application running in whenever it is deployed to its hosting environment and serving public requests. There are a number of significant ways that production mode differs from the other modes, not least of which is the speed boost you get from not reloading all your application classes for every request.

```
 1 # File: config/environments/production.rb
 2 Rails.application.configure do
 3   # Settings specified here will take precedence over those in
 4   # config/application.rb.
 5
 6   # Code is not reloaded between requests.
 7   config.cache_classes = true
 8
 9   # Eager load code on boot. This eager loads most of Rails and
10   # your application in memory, allowing both thread web servers
11   # and those relying on copy on write to perform better.
```

```
12    # Rake tasks automatically ignore this option for performance.
13    config.eager_load = true
14
15    # Full error reports are disabled and caching is turned on.
16    config.consider_all_requests_local       = false
17    config.action_controller.perform_caching = true
18
19    # Enable Rack::Cache to put a simple HTTP cache in front of your
20    # application.
21    # Add `rack-cache` to your Gemfile before enabling this.
22    # For large-scale production use, consider using a caching reverse proxy
23    # like nginx, varnish, or squid.
24    # config.action_dispatch.rack_cache = true
25
26    # Disable Rails's static asset server (Apache or nginx will
27    # already do this).
28    config.serve_static_assets = false
29
30    # Compress JavaScripts and CSS.
31    config.assets.js_compressor  = :uglifier
32    # config.assets.css_compressor = :sass
33
34    # Whether to fallback to assets pipeline if a precompiled
35    # asset is missed.
36    config.assets.compile = false
37
38    # Generate digests for assets URLs.
39    config.assets.digest = true
40
41    # Version of your assets, change this if you want to expire
42    # all your assets.
43    config.assets.version = '1.0'
44
45    # Specifies the header that your server uses for sending files.
46    # config.action_dispatch.x_sendfile_header = "X-Sendfile" # for apache
47    # config.action_dispatch.x_sendfile_header = 'X-Accel-Redirect'
48    # for nginx
49
50    # Force all access to the app over SSL, use Strict-Transport-Security,
51    # and use secure cookies.
52    # config.force_ssl = true
53
54    # Set to :debug to see everything in the log.
55    config.log_level = :info
56
57    # Prepend all log lines with the following tags.
58    # config.log_tags = [ :subdomain, :uuid ]
59
60    # Use a different logger for distributed setups.
```

```
61    # config.logger = ActiveSupport::TaggedLogging.new(SyslogLogger.new)
62
63    # Use a different cache store in production.
64    # config.cache_store = :mem_cache_store
65
66    # Enable serving of images, stylesheets, and JavaScripts from an
67    # asset server.
68    # config.action_controller.asset_host = "http://assets.example.com"
69
70    # Precompile additional assets.
71    # application.js, application.css, and all non-JS/CSS in app/assets
72    # folder are already added.
73    # config.assets.precompile += %w( search.js )
74
75    # Ignore bad email addresses and do not raise email delivery errors.
76    # Set this to true and configure the email server for immediate delivery
77    # to raise delivery errors.
78    # config.action_mailer.raise_delivery_errors = false
79
80    # Enable locale fallbacks for I18n (makes lookups for any locale fall
81    # back to the I18n.default_locale when a translation cannot be found).
82    config.i18n.fallbacks = true
83
84    # Send deprecation notices to registered listeners.
85    config.active_support.deprecation = :notify
86
87    # Disable automatic flushing of the log to improve performance.
88    # config.autoflush_log = false
89
90    # Use default logging formatter so that PID and timestamp
91    # are not suppressed.
92    config.log_formatter = ::Logger::Formatter.new
93  end
```

1.5.1   Assets

In production mode, assets are by default precompiled by the Asset Pipeline. All files
included in `application.js` and `application.css` asset manifests are compressed and concatenated into their respective files of the same name, located in the
`public/assets` folder.

If an asset is requested that does not exist in the `public/assets` folder, Rails
will throw an exception. To enable live asset compilation fallback on production, set
`config.assets.compile` to `true`.

The `application.js` and `application.css` manifest files are the only
JavaScript file and stylesheet included during the Asset Pipeline precompile step. To

include additional assets, specify them using the `config.assets.precompile` configuration setting.

```
config.assets.precompile += %w( administration.css )
```

Like most features in Rails, the usage of the Asset Pipeline is completely optional. To include assets in your project as it was done in Rails 3.0, set `config.assets.enabled` to `false`.

1.5.2   Asset Hosts

By default, Rails links to assets on the current host in the public folder, but you can direct Rails to link to assets from a dedicated asset server. The `config.action_controller.asset_host` setting is covered in detail in Chapter 11, "All about Helpers," in the "Using Asset Hosts" section.

1.6   Configuring a Database

The file `database.yml` found in the `config` folder specifies all the configuration settings required by Active Record to connect to a database. When a new application is generated, Rails automatically generates sections in the YAML for each environment.

The following is an example of a generated `database.yml` file configured to work with PostgreSQL.

```
1  # config/database.yml
2  default: &default
3    adapter: postgresql
4    encoding: unicode
5    # For details on connection pooling, see rails configuration guide:
6    # http://guides.rubyonrails.org/configuring.html#database-pooling
7    pool: 5
8    username: example
9    password:
10
11 development:
12   <<: *default
13   database: example_development
14
15   # Connect on a TCP socket. Omitted by default since the client uses a
16   # domain socket that doesn't need configuration. Windows does not have
17   # domain sockets, so uncomment these lines.
18   #host: localhost
19
20   # The TCP port the server listens on. Defaults to 5432.
21   # If your server runs on a different port number, change accordingly.
22   #port: 5432
```

```
23
24     # Schema search path. The server defaults to $user,public
25     #schema_search_path: myapp,sharedapp,public.
26
27     # Minimum log levels, in increasing order:
28     #   debug5, debug4, debug3, debug2, debug1,
29     #   log, notice, warning, error, fatal, and panic.
30     # Defaults to warning.
31     #min_messages: notice
32
33 # Warning: The database defined as "test" will be erased and
34 # re-generated from your development database when you run "rake".
35 # Do not set this db to the same as development or production.
36 test:
37   <<: *default
38   database: example_test
39
40 production:
41   <<: *default
42   database: example_production
```

A common best practice within the Rails community has been not to store `config/database.yml` in version control. First and foremost, if a hacker gained access to the application repository, they would have all the connection settings to your production database. Second, developers on the team could potentially have different development and test database settings. New to Rails 4.1 is the ability to configure Active Record with an environment variable `DATABASE_URL`. This allows each developer working on the project to have her own copy of `config/database.yml` that is not stored in version control. The production environment of the Rails application would just need to have `DATABASE_URL` set with a valid connection string to be configured correctly.

1.7   Configuring Application Secrets

Being introduced in Rails 4.1 is the `secrets.yml` file found within the `config` folder. This file is meant to store your application's sensitive data, such as access keys and passwords that are required for external APIs. At a minimum, Rails requires that `secret_key_base` is set for each environment of your application. In Rails 4.0, `secret_key_base` was set in the `secret_token.rb` initializer.

```
1 # config/secrets.yml
2
3 # Be sure to restart your server when you modify this file.
4
5 # Your secret key is used for verifying the integrity of signed cookies.
```

```
 6 # If you change this key, all old signed cookies will become invalid!
 7
 8 # Make sure the secret is at least 30 characters and all random,
 9 # nonregular words or you'll be exposed to dictionary attacks.
10 # You can use `rake secret` to generate a secure secret key.
11
12 # Make sure the secrets in this file are kept private
13 # if you're sharing your code publicly.
14
15 development:
16   secret_key_base: 7aed4bcb28...
17
18 test:
19   secret_key_base: a4b717a2a8...
20
21 production:
22   secret_key_base: 39a63892bd...
```

Kevin Says ...

I would strongly advise to not store any production secret values in version
control. Like database.yml, if a hacker gained access to the application
repository, they could use these values to exploit your application. Instead,
set all production secret values to environment variables. The environment
variables will only be set on your production machine.

```
# config/secrets.yml
...
production:
  secret_key_base: <%= ENV['SECRET_KEY_BASE'] %>
```

A hash of all the secrets defined in config/secrets.yml can be accessed
via Rails.application.secrets.

```
>> Rails.application.secrets
=> {:secret_key_base=>"7aed4bcb28..."}
   To access a specific secrets, pass X to
```

An accessor for each secret key is also provided. For example, to access the secret
for secret_key_base, invoke Rails.application.secrets.secret_key_base.
This will return the value of secret_key_base for the current environment.

```
>> Rails.env
=> "development"
>> Rails.application.secrets.secret_key_base
=> "7aed4bcb28..."
```

Secret Token

Certain types of hacking involve modifying the contents of cookies without the server knowing about it. By digitally signing all cookies sent to the browser, Rails can detect whether they were tampered with. Rails signs cookies using the value of `secret_key_base`, found in `config/secrets.yml`, which is randomly generated along with your app.

1.8   Logging

Most programming contexts in Rails (models, controllers, view templates) have a `logger` attribute, which holds a reference to a logger conforming to the interface of `Log4r` or the default Ruby 1.8+ `Logger` class. Can't get a reference to `logger` somewhere in your code? The `Rails.logger` method references a logger that you can use anywhere.

It's really easy to create a new `Logger` in Ruby, as shown in the following example:

```
 1  $ pry
 2  > require 'logger'
 3  => true
 4
 5  > logger = Logger.new STDOUT
 6  => #<Logger:0x00000106c795f0 @progname=nil, @level=0, ...>
 7
 8  > logger.warn "do not want!!!"
 9  W, [2013-11-02T18:34:30.281003 #54844]  WARN -- : do not want!!!
10  => true
11
12  > logger.info "in your logger, giving info"
13  I, [2013-11-02T18:34:57.186636 #54844] INFO --: in your logger, giving info
14  => true
```

Typically, you add a message to the log using the logger whenever the need arises, using a method corresponding to the severity of the log message. The standard logger's severities are the following (in increasingly severe order):

Debug Use the debug level to capture data and application state useful for debugging problems later on. This level is not usually captured in production logs.

Info Use info level to capture informational messages. I like to use this log level for timestamping nonordinary events that are still within the bounds of good application behavior.

Warn Use the warn level to capture things that are out of the ordinary and might be worth investigating. Sometimes I'll throw in a logged warning when guard clauses in my code keeps clients from doing something they weren't supposed to do. My goal is to alert whoever's maintaining the application about a malicious user or bug in the user interface, as in the following example:

```
1 def create
2   begin
3     group.add_member(current_user)
4     flash[:notice] = "Successfully joined #{scene.display_name}"
5   rescue ActiveRecord::RecordInvalid
6     flash[:error] = "You are already a member of #{group.name}"
7     logger.warn "A user tried to join a group twice. UI should
8                  not have allowed it."
9   end
10
11  redirect_to :back
12 end
```

Error Use the error log level to capture information about error conditions that don't require a server restart.

Fatal The worst case imaginable has happened—your application is now dead and manual intervention is necessary to restart it.

1.8.1   Rails Log Files

The `log` folder of your Rails application holds three log files corresponding to each of the standard environments. Log files can grow very large over time. A rake task is provided for easily clearing the log files:

```
$ rake log:clear  # Truncates all *.log files in log/ to zero bytes
```

The contents of `log/development.log` are very useful while you're working. Many Rails coders leave a terminal window open with a continuous tail of the development log open while they're coding:

```
$ tail -f log/development.log

  Article Load (0.2ms)  SELECT "articles".* FROM "articles" WHERE
    "articles"."id" = $1 LIMIT 1  [["id", "1"]]
```

All sorts of valuable information are available in the development log. For instance, every time you make a request, a bunch of useful information about it shows up in the log. Here's a sample from one of my projects:

```
 1 Started GET "/user_photos/1" for 127.0.0.1 at 2007-06-06 17:43:13
 2   Processing by UserPhotosController#show as HTML
 3   Parameters: {"/users/8-Obie-Fernandez/photos/406"=>nil,
 4   "action"=>"show", "id"=>"406", "controller"=>"user_photos",
 5   "user_id"=>"8-Obie-Fernandez"}
 6   User Load (0.4ms)   SELECT * FROM users WHERE (users.'id' = 8)
 7   Photo Load (0.9ms)   SELECT * FROM photos WHERE (photos.'id' = 406
 8   AND (photos.resource_id = 8 AND photos.resource_type = 'User'))
 9   CACHE (0.0ms)    SELECT * FROM users WHERE (users.'id' = 8)
10 Rendered adsense/_medium_rectangle (1.5ms)
11   User Load (0.5ms)    SELECT * FROM users WHERE (users.'id' = 8)
12   LIMIT 1
13   SQL (0.4ms)    SELECT count(*) AS count_all FROM messages WHERE
14   (messages.receiver_id = 8 AND (messages.'read' = 0))
15 Rendered layouts/_header (25.3ms)
16 Rendered adsense/_leaderboard (0.4ms)
17 Rendered layouts/_footer (0.8ms)
18 Rendered photos/show.html.erb within layouts/application.html.erb (38.9ms)
19 Completed in 99ms (Views: 37.4ms | ActiveRecord: 12.3ms) with 200
```

This is a list of all the data items contained in that chunk of log output:

- Controller and action that were invoked

- Remote IP address of the computer making the request

- Timestamp indicating when the request happened

- Session ID associated with the request

- Hash of parameters associated with the request

- Database request information, including the time and the SQL statement executed

- Query cache hit info, including time and the SQL statement triggering results from the cache instead of a round trip to the database

- Rendering information for each template involved in rendering the view output and time consumed by each

- Total time used in completing the request with corresponding request-per-second figures

- Analysis of the time spent in database operations versus rendering

- HTTP status code and URL of the response sent back to the client

1.8.2   Tagged Logging

Log files can contain an extensive amount of information, making tracking down issues or particular requests difficult. To alleviate this issue, Rails 3.2 introduced the ability to prepend information to each of your log messages.

To add "tagged" information to your logs, pass an array of one or many method names that respond to the `request` object to the `config.log_tags` configuration setting.

To illustrate, assuming we want to track the subdomain that each request is made from, we can achieve this by setting `config.log_tags` to `[:subdomain]`. When Rails writes to the log, it will prefix the output of `request.subdomain`, resulting in a log message like the following:

```
[some_subdomain] Started GET "/articles" for 127.0.0.1 at 2013-02-01 11:49:09 -0500
```

1.8.3   Log File Analysis

A number of informal analyses can be easily performed using just the development log output and some common sense.

Performance   One of the more obvious analyses would be a study of the performance of your application. The faster your requests execute, the more requests you can serve with a given Rails process. That's why performance figures are often expressed in terms of requests per second. Find the queries and rendering sections that are taking a long time and figure out why.

It's important to realize that the times reported by the logger are not accurate. In fact, they're wrong more often than not, if simply for the reason that it's very difficult to measure the timing of something from within itself. Add up the percentage of rendering and database times for any given request, and it will not always be close to 100 percent.

However, despite not being accurate in a purely objective sense, the reported times are perfect for making subjective comparisons within the same application. They give you a way of gauging whether an action is taking longer than it used to, whether it is relatively faster or slower than another action, and so on.

SQL Queries   Active Record not behaving as expected? The fact that SQL generated by Active Record is logged can often help you debug problems caused by complicated queries.

Identification of N+1 Select Problems Whenever you are displaying a record along
with an associated collection of records, there's a chance that you will have a
so-called N+1 select problem. You'll recognize the problem by a series of many
SELECT statements, with the only difference being the value of the primary key.

For example, here's a snippet of some log output from a real Rails application showing an N+1 select issue in the way that FlickrPhoto instances are being loaded:

```
1    FlickrPhoto Load (1.3ms)   SELECT * FROM flickr_photos WHERE
2    (flickr_photos.resource_id = 15749 AND flickr_photos.resource_type =
3    'Place' AND (flickr_photos.'profile' = 1)) ORDER BY updated_at desc
4    LIMIT 1
5    FlickrPhoto Load (1.7ms)   SELECT * FROM flickr_photos WHERE
6    (flickr_photos.resource_id = 15785 AND flickr_photos.resource_type =
7    'Place' AND (flickr_photos.'profile' = 1)) ORDER BY updated_at desc
8    LIMIT 1
9    FlickrPhoto Load (1.4ms)   SELECT * FROM flickr_photos WHERE
10   (flickr_photos.resource_id = 15831 AND flickr_photos.resource_type =
11   'Place' AND (flickr_photos.'profile' = 1)) ORDER BY updated_at desc
12   LIMIT 1
```

and so on, for pages and pages of log output. Look familiar?

Luckily, each of those database queries is executing very quickly (around 0.0015
seconds each). That's because (1) MySQL is extraordinarily fast for small SELECT
statements, and (2) my Rails process is on the same physical machine as the database.

Still, accumulate enough of those N queries and they add up quickly to eat away at
performance. Absent the mitigating factors I mentioned, I would have a serious performance problem to address. The problem would be especially severe if the database was
on a separate machine, giving me network latency to deal with on each of those queries.

N+1 select issues are not the end of the world. A lot of times all it takes is proper
use of the includes method on a particular query to alleviate the problem.

Separation of Concerns

A well-designed MVC application follows certain protocols related to the logical tier that does database operations (that would be the model) versus rendering tasks (the view). Generally speaking, you want your controller to cause the
loading of all the data that is going to be needed for rendering from the database. In Rails, this is accomplished by controller code that queries the model
for needed data and makes that data available to the view.

Database access during rendering is usually considered a bad practice. Calling database methods directly from template code violates proper separation of concerns and is a maintainability nightmare.[10]

However, there are plenty of opportunities for implicit database access during view rendering to creep into your codebase, encapsulated by the model and perhaps triggered by lazy loading of associations. Can we conclusively call it a bad practice? It's hard to say so definitively. There are cases (such as usage of fragment caching) where it makes sense to have database operations happening during view rendering.

Using Alternate Logging Schemes

It's easy! Just assign a class compatible with Ruby's Logger to one of the various `logger` class variables, such as `ActiveRecord::Base.logger`. A quick hack based on the ability to swap loggers is one demonstrated by David at various events, including his keynote at Railsconf 2007. During a console session, assign a new `Logger` instance pointing to `STDOUT` to `Active Record::Base.logger` in order to see the SQL being generated right in your console. Jamis has a complete write-up of the technique and more at `http://weblog.jamisbuck.org/2007/1/31/more-on-watching -activerecord`.

1.8.3.1 `Rails::Subscriber.colorize_logging`

This code tells Rails whether to use ANSI codes to colorize the logging statements. The colors make it much easier to read the logs (except on Windows) and may complicate matters if you use software like syslog. It defaults to `true`. Change to `false` if you view your logs with software that doesn't understand the ANSI color codes.

Here's a snippet of log output with the ANSI codes visible:

```
1  ^[[4;36;1mSQL (0.0ms)^[[0m  ^[[0;1mMysql::Error: Unknown table
2  'expense_reports': DROP TABLE expense_reports^[[0m
3    ^[[4;35;1mSQL (3.2ms)^[[0m  ^[[0mCREATE TABLE expense_reports ('id'
4  int(11) DEFAULT NULL auto_increment PRIMARY KEY, 'user_id' int(11))
```

Wilson Says ...

Almost nobody I meet seems to know how to display colorized logs in a pager. The `-R` option tells `less` to output "raw" control characters to the screen.

---

10. Practically every PHP application ever written has this problem.

Syslog

UNIX-like systems have a system service called `syslog`. For various reasons, it might be a better choice for production logging of your Rails applications.

- Finer-grained control over logging levels and content is offered.
- Consolidation of logger output for multiple Rails applications is possible.
- If you're using remote syslog capabilities of many systems, consolidation of logger output for multiple Rails application servers is possible. Contrast with having to handle individual log files on each application server box separately.

You can use Eric Hodel's SyslogLogger[11] to interface your Rails application to `syslog`.

1.9   Conclusion

We've kicked off our Rails journey by covering Bundler in fairly good detail and then reviewing the different environments in which Rails executes and how it loads its dependencies, including your application code. An in-depth look at `config/application.rb` and its per-mode variants revealed how we can customize Rails behavior to our taste.

---

11. `http://docs.seattlerb.org/SyslogLogger/`

CHAPTER 2

Routing

I dreamed a thousand new paths...I woke and walked my old one.

—Chinese proverb

The routing system in Rails is the system that examines the URL of an incoming request and determines what action should be taken by the application. And it does a good bit more than that. Rails routing can be a bit of a tough nut to crack. But it turns out that most of the toughness resides in a small number of concepts. After you've got a handle on those, the rest falls into place nicely.

This chapter will introduce you to the principal techniques for defining and manipulating routes. The next chapter will build on this knowledge to explore the facilities Rails offers in support of writing applications that comply with the principles of representational state transfer (REST). As you'll see, those facilities can be of tremendous use to you even if you're not planning to scale the heights of REST theorization. Both chapters assume at least a basic knowledge of the model-view-controller (MVC) pattern and Rails controllers.

Some of the examples in these two chapters are based on a small auction application. The examples are kept simple enough that they should be comprehensible on their own. The basic idea is that there are auctions and each auction involves auctioning off an item. There are users and they submit bids. That's it.

The triggering of a controller action is the main event in the life cycle of a connection to a Rails application. Therefore, it makes sense that the process by which Rails determines which controller and which action to execute must be very important. That process is embodied in the routing system.

The routing system maps URLs to actions. It does this by applying rules that you specify using a special syntax in the `config/routes.rb` file. Actually, it's just plain Ruby code, but it uses special methods and parameters, a technique sometimes referred to as an internal domain-specific language (DSL). If you're using Rails generators, code gets added to the routes file automatically, and you'll get some reasonable behavior. But it doesn't take much work to write custom rules and reap the benefits of the flexibility of the routing system.

2.1   The Two Purposes of Routing

The routing system does two things: It maps requests to controller action methods, and it enables the dynamic generation of URLs for you for use as arguments to methods like `link_to` and `redirect_to`.

Each rule—or to use the more common term, route—specifies a pattern, which will be used both as a template for matching URLs and as a blueprint for creating them. The pattern can be generated automatically based on conventions, such as in the case of REST resources. Patterns can also contain a mixture of static substrings, forward slashes (mimicking URL syntax), and positional *segment key* parameters that serve as "receptors" for corresponding values in URLs.

A route can also include one or more hard-coded segment keys, in form of key/value pairs accessible to controller actions in a hash via the `params` method. A couple of keys (`:controller` and `:action`) determine which controller and action gets invoked. Other keys present in the route definition simply get stashed for reference purposes.

Putting some flesh on the bones of this description, here's a sample route:

```
get 'recipes/:ingredient' => "recipes#index"
```

In this example, you find the following:

- HTTP verb constraining method (`get`)
- Static string (`recipes`)
- Slash (`/`)
- Segment key (`:ingredient`)
- Controller action mapping (`"recipes#index"`)

Routes have a pretty rich syntax—this one isn't by any means the most complex (nor the most simple)—because they have to do so much. A single route, like the one in this example, has to provide enough information both to match an existing URL and to manufacture a new one. The route syntax is engineered to address both of these processes.

2.2   The `routes.rb` File

Routes are defined in the file `config/routes.rb`, as shown (with some explanatory comments) in Listing 2.1. This file is created when you first create your Rails application and contains instructions about how to use it.

Listing 2.1   The Default `routes.rb` File

```
 1  Rails.application.routes.draw do
 2    # The priority is based on order of creation:
 3    # first created -> highest priority.
 4    # See how all your routes lay out with "rake routes".
 5
 6    # You can have the root of your site routed with "root":
 7    # root 'welcome#index'
 8
 9    # Example of regular route:
10    #   get 'products/:id' => 'catalog#view'
11
12    # Example of named route that can be invoked with
13    # purchase_url(id: product.id)
14    #   get 'products/:id/purchase' => 'catalog#purchase', as: :purchase
15
16    # Example resource route (maps HTTP verbs to controller
17    # actions automatically):
18    #   resources :products
19
20    # Example resource route with options:
21    #   resources :products do
22    #     member do
23    #       get 'short'
24    #       post 'toggle'
25    #     end
26    #
27    #     collection do
28    #       get 'sold'
29    #     end
30    #   end
31
32    # Example resource route with subresources:
33    #   resources :products do
34    #     resources :comments, :sales
35    #     resource :seller
36    #   end
37
```

```
38    # Example resource route with more complex subresources:
39    #   resources :products do
40    #     resources :comments
41    #     resources :sales do
42    #       get 'recent', on: :collection
43    #     end
44    #   end
45
46    # Example resource route with concerns:
47    #   concern :toggleable do
48    #     post 'toggle'
49    #   end
50    #   resources :posts, concerns: :toggleable
51    #   resources :photos, concerns: :toggleable
52
53    # Example resource route within a namespace:
54    #   namespace :admin do
55    #     # Directs /admin/products/* to Admin::ProductsController
56    #     # (app/controllers/admin/products_controller.rb)
57    #     resources :products
58    #   end
59  end
```

The whole file consists of a single call to the method `draw` of `Rails`
`.application.routes`. That method takes a block, and everything from the
second line of the file to the second-to-last line is the body of that block.

At runtime, the block is evaluated inside of an instance of the class `Action`
`Dispatch::Routing::Mapper`. Through it, you configure the Rails routing system.

The routing system has to find a pattern match for a URL it's trying to recognize
or a parameters match for a URL it's trying to generate. It does this by going through
the routes in the order in which they're defined—that is, the order in which they
appear in `routes.rb`. If a given route fails to match, the matching routine falls
through to the next one. As soon as any route succeeds in providing the necessary
match, the search ends.

2.2.1   Regular Routes

The basic way to define a route is to supply a URL pattern plus a controller class/
action method mapping string with the special `:to` parameter.

```
get 'products/:id', to: 'products#show'
```

Since this is so common, a shorthand form is provided:

```
get 'products/:id' => 'products#show'
```

David publicly commented on the design decision behind the shorthand form when he said that it drew inspiration from two sources:

> 1) the pattern we've been using in Rails since the beginning of referencing controllers as lowercase without the "Controller" part in `controller: "main"` declarations and 2) the Ruby pattern of signaling that you're talking about an instance method by using #. The influences are even part mixed. Main #index would be more confusing in my mind because it would hint that an object called Main actually existed, which it doesn't. MainController#index would just be a hassle to type out every time. Exactly the same reason we went with `controller: "main"` vs. `controller: "MainController"`. Given these constraints, I think `"main#index"` is by far the best alternative.[1]

2.2.2 Constraining Request Methods

As of Rails 4, it's recommended to limit the HTTP method used to access a route. If you are using the `match` directive to define a route, you accomplish this by using the `:via` option:

```
match 'products/:id' => 'products#show', via: :get
```

Rails provides a shorthand way of expressing this particular constraint by replacing `match` with the desired HTTP method (`get`, `post`, `patch`, etc.)

```
get 'products/:id' => 'products#show'
post 'products' => 'products#create'
```

If, for some reason, you want to constrain a route to more than one HTTP method, you can pass `:via` an array of verb names.

```
match 'products/:id' => 'products#show', via: [:get, :post]
```

Defining a route without specifying an HTTP method will result in Rails raising a `RuntimeError` exception. While strongly not recommended, a route can still match *any* HTTP method by passing `:any` to the `:via` option.

```
match 'products' => 'products#index', via: :any
```

---

1. Full comments at http://yehudakatz.com/2009/12/26/the-rails-3-router-rack-it-up

2.2.3   URL Patterns

Keep in mind that there's no necessary correspondence between the number of fields in the pattern string, the number of segment keys, and the fact that every connection needs a controller and an action. For example, you could write a route like the following:

```
get ":id" => "products#show"
```

This would recognize a URL like the following:

```
http://localhost:3000/8
```

The routing system would set `params[:id]` to 8 (based on the position of the `:id` segment key, which matches the position of 8 in the URL), and it would execute the `show` action of the `products` controller. Of course, this is a bit of a stingy route in terms of visual information. On the other hand, the following example route contains a static string, `products/`, inside the URL pattern:

```
match 'products/:id' => 'products#show'
```

This string anchors the recognition process. Any URL that does not contain the static string `products/` in its leftmost slot will not match this route.

As for URL generation, static strings in the route simply get placed within the URL that the routing system generates. The URL generator uses the route's pattern string as the blueprint for the URL it generated. The pattern string stipulates the substring `products`.

As we go, you should keep the dual purpose of recognition/generation in mind, which is why it was mentioned several times so far. There are two principles that are particularly useful to remember:

- The same rule governs both recognition and generation. The whole system is set up so that you don't have to write rules twice. You write each rule once, and the logic flows through it in both directions.

- The URLs that are generated by the routing system (via `link_to` and friends) only make sense to the routing system. The resulting URL (`http://example .com/products/19201`) contains not a shred of a clue as to what's supposed to happen when a user follows it—except insofar as it maps to a routing rule. The routing rule then provides the necessary information to trigger a controller action. Someone looking at the URL without knowing the routing rules won't know which controller and action the URL maps to.

2.2.4 Segment Keys

The URL pattern string can contain parameters (denoted with a colon), referred to as *segment keys*. In the following route declaration, `:id` is a segment key:

```
get 'products/:id' => 'products#show'
```

When this route matches a request URL, the `:id` portion of the pattern acts as a type of matcher and picks up the value of that segment. For instance, using the same example, the value of `id` for the following URL would be 4: `http://example.com/products/4`.

This route, when matched, will always take the visitor to the product controller's `show` action. You'll see techniques for matching controller and action based on segments of the URL shortly. The symbol `:id` inside the quoted pattern in the route is a segment key (that you can think of as a type of variable). Its job is to be latched onto by a value.

What that means in the example is that the value of `params[:id]` will be set to the string `"4"`. You can access that value inside your `products/show` action.

When you generate a URL, you have to supply values that will attach to the segment keys inside the URL pattern string. The simplest to understand (and original) way to do that is using a hash, like this:

```
link_to "Products",
  controller: "products",
  action: "show",
  id: 1
```

As you probably know, it's actually more common nowadays to generate URLs using what are called *named routes* versus supplying the controller and action parameters explicitly in a hash. However, right now we're reviewing the basics of routing.

In the call to `link_to`, we've provided values for all three parameters of the route. Two of them are going to match the hard-coded, segment keys in the route; the third, `:id`, will be assigned to the corresponding segment key in the URL pattern.

It's vital to understand that the call to `link_to` doesn't *know* whether it's supplying hard-coded or segment values. It just knows (or hopes!) that these three values, tied to these three keys, will suffice to pinpoint a route, a pattern string, and therefore a blueprint for generating a URL dynamically.

Hard-Coded Parameters

It's always possible to insert additional hard-coded parameters into route definitions that don't have an effect on URL matching but are passed along with the normal expected `params`.

```
get 'products/special' => 'products#show', special: 'true'
```

Mind you, I'm not suggesting that this example is a good practice. It would make more sense to me (as a matter of style) to point at a different action rather than inserting a clause. Your mileage may vary.

```
get 'products/special' => 'products#special'
```

2.2.5   Spotlight on the `:id` Field

Note that the treatment of the `:id` field in the URL is not magic; it's just treated as a value with a name. If you wanted to, you could change the rule so that `:id` was `:blah`, but then you'd have to do the following in your controller action:

```
@product = Product.find(params[:blah])
```

The name `:id` is simply a convention. It reflects the commonness of the case in which a given action needs access to a particular database record. The main business of the router is to determine the controller and action that will be executed.

The `id` field ends up in the `params` hash, already mentioned. In the common, classic case, you'd use the value provided to dig a record out of the database:

```
1 class ProductsController < ApplicationController
2   def show
3     @product = Product.find(params[:id])
4   end
5 end
```

2.2.6   Optional Segment Keys

Rails 3 introduced a syntax for defining optional parts of the URL pattern. The easiest way to illustrate this syntax is by taking a look at the *legacy default controller route*, found in the previous versions of Rails at the bottom of a default `config/routes.rb` file:

```
match ':controller(/:action(/:id(.:format)))', via: :any
```

Note that parentheses are used to define optional segment keys, kind of like what you would expect to see when defining optional groups in a regular expression.

2.2.7   Redirect Routes

It's possible to code a redirect directly into a route definition using the `redirect` method:

```
get "/foo", to: redirect('/bar')
```

The argument to `redirect` can contain either a relative URL or a full URI.

```
get "/google", to: redirect('https://google.com/')
```

The `redirect` method can also take a block, which receives the request params as its argument. This allows you to, for instance, do quick versioning of web service API endpoints.[2]

```
match "/api/v1/:api",
  to: redirect { |params| "/api/v2/#{params[:api].pluralize}" },
  via: :any
```

The `redirect` method also accepts an optional `:status` parameter.

```
match "/api/v1/:api", to:
  redirect(status: 302) { |params| "/api/v2/#{params[:api].pluralize}" },
  via: :any
```

The `redirect` method returns an instance of `ActionDispatch::Routing ::Redirect`, which is a simple Rack endpoint, as we can see by examining its source code.

```
1 module ActionDispatch
2   module Routing
3     class Redirect # :nodoc:
4       ...
5       def call(env)
6         req = Request.new(env)
7
8         # If any of the path parameters has an invalid encoding then
9         # raise since it's likely to trigger errors further on.
10        req.symbolized_path_parameters.each do |key, value|
11          unless value.valid_encoding?
12            raise ActionController::BadRequest,
13              "Invalid parameter: #{key} => #{value}"
14          end
15        end
```

---

2. Examples are drawn from Yehuda Katz's excellent blog post about generic actions in Rails 3 routes at http://yehudakatz.com/2009/12/20/generic-actions-in-rails-3/

Routes

```
16
17          uri = URI.parse(path(req.symbolized_path_parameters, req))
18          uri.scheme ||= req.scheme
19          uri.host   ||= req.host
20          uri.port   ||= req.port unless req.standard_port?
21
22          if relative_path?(uri.path)
23            uri.path = "#{req.script_name}/#{uri.path}"
24          end
25
26          body = %(<html><body>You are being
27            <a href="#{ERB::Util.h(uri.to_s)}">redirected</a>.</body></html>)
28
29          headers = {
30            'Location' => uri.to_s,
31            'Content-Type' => 'text/html',
32            'Content-Length' => body.length.to_s
33          }
34
35          [ status, headers, [body] ]
36        end
37        ...
38      end
39    end
40  end
```

2.2.8 The Format Segment

Let's revisit the legacy default route again:

```
match ':controller(/:action(/:id(.:format)))', via: :any
```

The `.:format` at the end matches a literal dot and a "format" segment key after the id field. That means it will match, for example, a URL like the following:

```
http://localhost:3000/products/show/3.json
```

Here, `params[:format]` will be set to `json`. The `:format` field is special; it has an effect inside the controller action. That effect is related to a method called `respond_to`.

The `respond_to` method allows you to write your action so that it will return different results, depending on the requested format. Here's a `show` action for the products controller that offers either HTML or JSON:

```
1 def show
2   @product = Product.find(params[:id])
```

```
3    respond_to do |format|
4      format.html
5      format.json { render json: @product.to_json }
6    end
7  end
```

The `respond_to` block in this example has two clauses. The HTML clause just consists of `format.html`. A request for HTML will be handled by the usual rendering of a view template. The JSON clause includes a code block; if JSON is requested, the block will be executed and the result of its execution will be returned to the client.

Here's a command-line illustration, using `curl` (slightly edited to reduce line noise):

```
$ curl http://localhost:3000/products/show/1.json -i
HTTP/1.1 200 OK
Content-Type: application/json; charset=utf-8
Content-Length: 81
Connection: Keep-Alive

{"created_at":"2013-02-09T18:25:03.513Z",
"description":"Keyboard",
"id":"1",
"maker":"Apple",
"updated_at":"2013-02-09T18:25:03.513Z"}
```

The `.json` on the end of the URL results in `respond_to` choosing the *json* branch, and the returned document is a JSON representation of the product.

Requesting a format that is not included as an option in the `respond_to` block will not generate an exception. Rails will return a `406 Not Acceptable` status to indicate that it can't handle the request.

If you want to set up an *else* condition for your `respond_to` block, you can use the any method, which tells Rails to catch any other formats not explicitly defined.

```
1 def show
2    @product = Product.find(params[:id])
3    respond_to do |format|
4      format.html
5      format.json { render json: @product.to_json }
6      format.any
7    end
8  end
```

Just make sure that you explicitly tell any what to do with the request or have view templates corresponding to the formats you expect. Otherwise, you'll get a `MissingTemplate` exception.

```
ActionView::MissingTemplate (Missing template products/show,
  application/show with {:locale=>[:en], :formats=>[:xml],
  :handlers=>[:erb, :builder, :raw, :ruby, :jbuilder, :coffee]}.)
```

2.2.9   Routes as Rack Endpoints

You'll see usage of the :to option in routes throughout this chapter. What's most interesting about :to is that its value is what's referred to as a *Rack endpoint*. To illustrate, consider the following simple example:

```
get "/hello", to: proc { |env| [200, {}, ["Hello world"]] }
```

The router is very loosely coupled to controllers! The shorthand syntax (like "items#show") relies on the action method of controller classes to return a Rack endpoint that executes the action requested.

```
>> ItemsController.action(:show)
=> #<Proc:0x01e96cd0@...>
```

The ability to dispatch to a Rack-based application, such as one created with Sinatra,[3] can be achieved using the mount method. The mount method accepts an :at option, which specifies the route the Rack-based application will map to.

```
1 class HelloApp < Sinatra::Base
2   get "/" do
3     "Hello World!"
4   end
5 end
6
7 Rails.application.routes.draw do
8   mount HelloApp, at: '/hello'
9 end
```

Alternatively, a shorthand form is also available:

```
mount HelloApp => '/hello'
```

2.2.10   Accept Header

You can also trigger a branching on respond_to by setting the Accept header in the request. When you do this, there's no need to add the .:format part of the URL. (However, note that out in the real world, it's difficult to get this technique to work reliably due to HTTP client/browser inconsistencies.)

---

3. http://www.sinatrarb.com

Here's a `curl` example that does not specify a `.json` format but does set the `Accept` header to `application/json`:

```
$ curl -i -H "Accept: application/json" http://localhost:3000/products/show/1
HTTP/1.1 200 OK
Content-Type: application/json; charset=utf-8
Content-Length: 81
Connection: Keep-Alive

{"created_at":"2013-02-09T18:25:03.513Z",
"description":"Keyboard",
"id":"1",
"maker":"Apple",
"updated_at":"2013-02-09T18:25:03.513Z"}
```

The result is exactly the same as in the previous example.

2.2.11 Segment Key Constraints

Sometimes you want not only to recognize a route but to recognize it at a finer-grained level than just what components or fields it has. You can do this through the use of the `:constraint` option (and possibly regular expressions).

For example, you could route all `show` requests so that they went to an error action if their `id` fields were nonnumerical. You'd do this by creating two routes, one that handled numerical ids and a fall-through route that handled the rest:

```
get ':controller/show/:id' => :show, constraints: {:id => /\d+/}
get ':controller/show/:id' => :show_error
```

Implicit Anchoring

The example constraint we've been using,

```
constraints: {:id => /\d+/}
```

seems like it would match `"foo32bar"`. It doesn't because Rails implicitly anchors it at both ends. In fact, as of this writing, adding explicit anchors `\A` and `\z` causes exceptions to be raised.

Apparently, it's so common to set constraints on the `:id` param that Rails lets you shorten our previous example to simply

```
get ':controller/show/:id' => :show, id: /\d+/
get ':controller/show/:id' => :show_error
```

Regular expressions in routes can be useful, especially when you have routes that differ from each other only with respect to the patterns of their components. But they're not a full-blown substitute for data-integrity checking. You probably still want to make sure that the values you're dealing with are usable and appropriate for your application's domain.

From the example, you might conclude that :constraints checking applies to elements of the params hash. However, you can also check a grab bag of other request attributes that return a string, such as :subdomain and :referrer. Matching methods of request that return numeric or boolean values are unsupported and will raise a somewhat cryptic exception during route matching.

```
# only allow users admin subdomain to do old-school routing
get ':controller/:action/:id' => :show, constraints: {subdomain: 'admin'}
```

If for some reason you need more powerful constraints checking, you have full access to the request object by passing a block or any other object that responds to call as the value of :constraints like the following:

```
# protect records with id under 100
get 'records/:id' => "records#protected",
   constraints: proc { |req| req.params[:id].to_i < 100 }
```

2.2.12   The Root Route

At around line 8 of the default config/routes.rb (refer to Listing 2.1), you'll see the following:

```
# You can have the root of your site routed with "root":
# root 'welcome#index'
```

What you're seeing here is the root route—that is, a rule specifying what should happen when someone connects to

```
http://example.com   # Note the lack of "/anything" at the end!
```

The root route says, "I don't want any values; I want nothing, and I already know what controller and action I'm going to trigger!"

In a newly generated routes.rb file, the root route is commented out, because there's no universal or reasonable default for it. You need to decide what this *nothing* URL should do for each application you write.

Here are some examples of fairly common empty route rules:

```
1 root to: "welcome#index"
2 root to: "pages#home"
3
4 # Shorthand syntax
5 root "user_sessions#new"
```

Defining the empty route gives people something to look at when they connect to your site with nothing but the domain name. You might be wondering why you see something when you view a newly generated Rails application that still has its root route commented out.

The answer is that if a root route is not defined, by default, Rails will route to an internal controller `Rails::WelcomeController` and render a welcome page instead.

In previous versions of Rails, this was accomplished by including the file index `.html` in the public directory of newly generated applications. Any static content in the public directory hierarchy matching the URL scheme that you come up with for your app results in the static content being served up instead of triggering the routing rules. Actually, the web server will serve up the content without involving Rails at all.

A Note on Route Order

Routes are consulted, both for recognition and for generation, in the order they are defined in `routes.rb`. The search for a match ends when the first match is found, meaning that you have to watch out for false positives.

2.3   Route Globbing

In some situations, you might want to grab one or more components of a route without having to match them one by one to specific positional parameters. For example, your URLs might reflect a directory structure. If someone connects to

`/items/list/base/books/fiction/dickens`

then you want the `items/list` action to have access to all four remaining fields. But sometimes there might be only three fields:

`/items/list/base/books/fiction`

Or sometimes there might be five:

`/items/list/base/books/fiction/dickens/little_dorrit`

So you need a route that will match (in this particular case) everything after the second URI component. You define it by *globbing* the route with an asterisk.

```
get 'items/list/*specs', controller: 'items', action: 'list'
```

Now the `products/list` action will have access to a variable number of slash-delimited URL fields, accessible via `params[:specs]`:

```
def list
  specs = params[:specs] # e.g., "base/books/fiction/dickens"
end
```

Globbing Key-Value Pairs

Route globbing might provide the basis for a general mechanism for fielding ad hoc queries. Let's say you devise a URI scheme that takes the following form:

```
http://localhost:3000/items/q/field1/value1/field2/value2/...
```

Making requests in this way will return a list of all products whose fields match the values, based on an unlimited set of pairs in the URL.

In other words, `http://localhost:3000/items/q/year/1939/material/wood` could generate a list of all wood items made in 1939. The route that would accomplish this would be the following:

```
get 'items/q/*specs', controller: "items", action: "query"
```

Of course, you'll have to write a `query` action like this one to support the route:

```
1 def query
2   @items = Item.where(Hash[*params[:specs].split("/")])
3   if @items.empty?
4     flash[:error] = "Can't find items with those properties"
5   end
6   render :index
7 end
```

How about that square brackets class method on `Hash`, eh? It converts a one-dimensional array of key/value pairs into a hash! Further proof that in-depth knowledge of Ruby is a prerequisite for becoming an expert Rails developer.

2.4 Named Routes

The topic of named routes almost deserves a chapter of its own. In fact, what you learn here will feed directly into our examination of REST-related routing in Chapter 3, "REST, Resources, and Rails."

The idea of naming a route is basically to make life easier on you, the programmer. There are no outwardly visible effects as far as the application is concerned. When you name a route, a new method gets defined for use in your controllers and views; the method is called `name_url` (with name being the name you gave the route), and calling the method, with appropriate arguments, results in a URL being generated for the route. In addition, a method called `name_path` also gets created; this method generates just the path part of the URL, without the protocol and host components.

2.4.1 Creating a Named Route

The way you name a route is by using the optional `:as` parameter in a rule:

```
get 'help' => 'help#index', as: 'help'
```

In this example, Rails will generate methods called `help_url` and `help_path` in controller and view contexts, which you can use wherever Rails expects a URL or URL components:

```
link_to "Help", help_path
```

And, of course, the usual recognition and generation rules are in effect. The pattern string consists of just the static string component `"help"`. Therefore, the path you'll see in the hyperlink will be the following:

```
/help
```

When someone clicks on the link, the `index` action of the `help` controller will be invoked.

Xavier Says ...

You can test named routes in the console directly using the special app object.

```
>> app.clients_path
=> "/clients"

>> app.clients_url
=> "http://www.example.com/clients"
```

Named routes save you some effort when you need a URL generated. A named route zeros in directly on the route you need, bypassing the matching process that would be needed other. That means you don't have to provide as much detail as you otherwise would, but you still have to provide values for any segment keys in the route's pattern string that cannot be inferred.

2.4.2 `name_path` versus `name_url`

When you create a named route, you're actually creating at least two route helper methods. In the preceding example, those two methods are `help_url` and `help_path`. The difference is that the `_url` method generates an entire URL, including protocol and domain, whereas the `_path` method generates just the path part (sometimes referred to as an *absolute path* or a *relative URL*).

According to the HTTP spec, redirects should specify a URI, which can be interpreted (by some people) to mean a fully qualified URL.[4] Therefore, if you want to be pedantic about it, you probably should always use the `_url` version when you use a named route as an argument to `redirect_to` in your controller code.

The `redirect_to` method works perfectly with the relative URLs generated by _path helpers, making arguments about the matter somewhat pointless. In fact, other than redirects, permalinks, and a handful of other edge cases, it's the Rails way to use `_path` instead of `_url`. It produces a shorter string and the user agent (browser or otherwise) should be able to infer the fully qualified URL whenever it needs to do so, based on the HTTP headers of the request, a base element in the document, or the URL of the request.

As you read this book and as you examine other code and other examples, the main thing to remember is that `help_url` and `help_path` are basically doing the same thing. I tend to use the `_url` style in general discussions about named route techniques but the `_path` style in examples that occur inside view templates (e.g., with `link_to` and `form_for`). It's mostly a writing style thing, based on the theory that the URL version is more general and the path version more specialized. In any case, it's good to get used to seeing both and getting your brain to view them as very closely connected.

Using Literal URLs

You can, if you wish, hard-code your paths and URLs as string arguments to `link_to`, `redirect_to`, and friends. For example, instead of

```
link_to "Help", controller: "main", action: "help"
```

4. `http://www.w3.org/Protocols/rfc2616/rfc2616-sec10.html`

you can write

```
link_to "Help", "/main/help"
```

However, using a literal path or URL bypasses the routing system. If you write literal URLs, you're on your own to maintain them. And in that case, I hope you're an expert with find and replace! You can of course use Ruby's string interpolation techniques to insert values, if that's appropriate for what you're doing, but really stop and think about whether you are reinventing Rails functionality if you go down that path.

2.4.3 What to Name Your Routes

As we'll learn in Chapter 3, "REST, Resources, and Rails," the best way to figure out what names you should use for your routes is to follow REST conventions, which are baked into Rails and simplify things greatly. Otherwise, you'll need to think top-down; that is, think about what you want to write in your application code and then create the routes that will make it possible.

Take, for example, this call to link_to:

```
link_to "Auction of #{item.name}",
  controller: "items",
  action: "show",
  id: item.id
```

The routing rule to match that path is (a generic route)

```
get "item/:id" => "items#show"
```

It sure would be nice to shorten that link_to code. After all, the routing rule already specifies the controller and action. This is a good candidate for a named route for items:

```
get "item/:id" => "items#show", as: "item"
```

Let's improve the situation by introducing item_path in the call to link_to:

```
link_to "Auction of #{item.name} ", item_path(id: item.id)
```

Giving the route a name is a shortcut; it takes us straight to that route, without a long search and without having to provide a thick description of the route's hard-coded parameters.

2.4.4   Argument Sugar

In fact, we can make the argument to `item_path` even shorter. If you need to supply an id number as an argument to a named route, you can just supply the number, without spelling out the `:id` key:

```
link_to "Auction of #{item.name}", item_path(item.id)
```

And the syntactic sugar goes even further: You can and should provide objects and Rails will grab the id automatically.

```
link_to "Auction of #{item.name}", item_path(item)
```

This principle extends to other segment keys in the pattern string of the named route. For example, if you've got a route like

```
get "auction/:auction_id/item/:id" => "items#show", as: "item"
```

you'd be able to call it

```
link_to "Auction of #{item.name}", item_path(auction, item)
```

and you'd get something like this as your path (depending on the exact id numbers):

```
/auction/5/item/11
```

Here, we're letting Rails infer the ids of both an auction object and an item object, which it does by calling `to_param` on whatever nonhash arguments you pass into named route helpers. As long as you provide the arguments in the order in which their ids occur in the route's pattern string, the correct values will be dropped into place in the generated path.

2.4.5   A Little More Sugar with Your Sugar?

Furthermore, it doesn't have to be the id value that the route generator inserts into the URL. As alluded to a moment ago, you can override that value by defining a `to_param` method in your model.

Let's say you want the description of an item to appear in the URL for the auction on that item. In the `item.rb` model file, you would override `to_params`; here, we'll override it so that it provides a "munged" (stripped of punctuation and joined with hyphens) version of the description, courtesy of the `parameterize` method added to strings in Active Support.

```
1 def to_param
2   description.parameterize
3 end
```

Subsequently, the method call `item_path(auction, item)` will produce something like

```
/auction/3/item/cello-bow
```

Of course, if you're putting things like "cello-bow" in a path field called `:id`, you will need to make provisions to dig the object out again. Blog applications that use this technique to create *slugs* for use in permanent links often have a separate database column to store the munged version of the title that serves as part of the path. That way, it's possible to do something like

```
Item.where(munged_description: params[:id]).first!
```

to unearth the right item. (And yes, you can call it something other than `:id` in the route to make it clearer!)

Courtenay Says ...

> Why shouldn't you use numeric ids in your URLs? First, your competitors can see just how many auctions you create. Numeric consecutive ids also allow people to write automated spiders to steal your content. It's a window into your database. And finally, words in URLs just look better. (Google "German tank problem" to learn about how serial numbers on German tanks helped the allies win World War II.)

2.5   Scoping Routing Rules

Rails gives you a variety of ways to bundle together related routing rules concisely. They're all based on usage of the `scope` method and its various shortcuts. For instance, let's say that you want to define the following routes for auctions:

```
1 get 'auctions/new' => 'auctions#new'
2 get 'auctions/edit/:id' => 'auctions#edit'
3 post 'auctions/pause/:id' => 'auctions#pause'
```

You could DRY up your `routes.rb` file by using the `scope` method instead:

```
1 scope controller: :auctions do
2   get 'auctions/new' => :new
3   get 'auctions/edit/:id' => :edit
4   post 'auctions/pause/:id' => :pause
5 end
```

Then you would DRY it up again by adding the `:path` argument to `scope`:

```
1 scope path: '/auctions', controller: :auctions do
2   get 'new' => :new
3   get 'edit/:id' => :edit
4   post 'pause/:id' => :pause
5 end
```

2.5.1 Controller

The scope method accepts a `:controller` option (or it can interpret a symbol as its first argument to assume a controller). Therefore, the following two scope definitions are identical:

```
scope controller: :auctions do
scope :auctions do
```

To make what's going on more obvious, you can use the `controller` method instead of `scope`, in what's essentially syntactic sugar:

```
controller :auctions do
```

2.5.2 Path Prefix

The scope method accepts a `:path` option (or it can interpret a string as its first parameter to mean a path prefix). Therefore, the following two scope definitions are identical:

```
scope path: '/auctions' do
scope '/auctions' do
```

New to Rails 4 is the ability to pass the `:path` option symbols instead of strings. The scope definition

```
scope :auctions, :archived do
```

will scope all routes nested under it to the "/auctions/archived" path.

2.5.3 Name Prefix

The scope method also accepts a `:as` option that affects the way that named route URL helper methods are generated. The route

```
1 scope :auctions, as: 'admin' do
```

```
2   get 'new' => :new, as: 'new_auction'
3 end
```

will generate a named route URL helper method called `admin_new_auction_url`.

2.5.4   Namespaces

URLs can be grouped by using the `namespace` method, which is syntactic sugar that rolls up module, name prefix, and path prefix settings into one declaration. The implementation of the `namespace` method converts its first argument into a string, which is why in some example code you'll see it take a symbol.

```
1 namespace :auctions, :controller => :auctions do
2   get 'new' => :new
3   get 'edit/:id' => :edit
4   post 'pause/:id' => :pause
5 end
```

2.5.5   Bundling Constraints

If you find yourself repeating similar segment key constraints in related routes, you can bundle them together using the `:constraints` option of the scope method:

```
1 scope controller: :auctions, constraints: {:id => /\d+/} do
2   get 'edit/:id' => :edit
3   post 'pause/:id' => :pause
4 end
```

It's likely that only a subset of rules in a given scope need constraints applied to them. In fact, routing will break if you apply a constraint to a rule that doesn't take the segment keys specified. Since you're nesting, you probably want to use the `constraints` method, which is just more syntactic sugar to tighten up the rule definitions.

```
1 scope path: '/auctions', controller: :auctions do
2   get 'new' => :new
3   constraints id: /\d+/ do
4     get 'edit/:id' => :edit
5     post 'pause/:id' => :pause
6   end
7 end
```

To enable modular reuse, you may supply the `constraints` method with an object that has a `matches?` method.

```
1 class DateFormatConstraint
2   def self.matches?(request)
3     request.params[:date] =~ /\A\d{4}-\d\d-\d\d\z/   # YYYY-MM-DD
4   end
5 end
6
7 # in routes.rb
8 constraints(DateFormatConstraint) do
9   get 'since/:date' => :since
10 end
```

In this particular example (`DateFormatConstraint`), if an errant or malicious user input a badly formatted date parameter via the URL, Rails will respond with a 404 status instead of causing an exception to be raised.

2.6   Listing Routes

A handy route listing utility is included in all Rails projects as a standard rake task. Invoke it by typing `rake routes` in your application directory. For example, here is the output for a routes file containing just a single `resources :products` rule:

```
$ rake routes
     products GET    /products(.:format)          products#index
              POST   /products(.:format)          products#create
 new_product GET    /products/new(.:format)      products#new
edit_product GET    /products/:id/edit(.:format) products#edit
      product GET    /products/:id(.:format)      products#show
              PATCH  /products/:id(.:format)      products#update
              PUT    /products/:id(.:format)      products#update
              DELETE /products/:id(.:format)      products#destroy
```

The output is a table with four columns. The first two columns are optional and contain the name of the route and HTTP method constraint, if they are provided. The third column contains the URL mapping string. Finally, the fourth column indicates the controller and action method that the route maps to plus constraints that have been defined on that routes segment keys (if any).

Note that the routes task checks for an optional `CONTROLLER` environment variable

```
$ rake routes CONTROLLER=products
```

would only lists the routes related to `ProductsController`.

Juanito Says ...

> While you have a server up and running on development environment, you could visit /rails/info/routes to get a complete list of routes of your Rails application.

2.7 Conclusion

The first half of the chapter helped you to fully understand the generic routing rules of Rails and how the routing system has two purposes:

- Recognizing incoming requests and mapping them to a corresponding controller action, along with any additional variable receptors

- Recognizing URL parameters in methods such as link_to and matching them up to a corresponding route so that proper HTML links can be generated

We built on our knowledge of generic routing by covering some advanced techniques such as using regular expressions and globbing in our route definitions, plus the bundling of related routes under shared scope options.

Finally, before moving on, you should make sure that you understand how named routes work and why they make your life easier as a developer by allowing you to write more concise view code. As you'll see in the next chapter, once we start defining batches of related named routes, we're on the cusp of delving into REST.

## CHAPTER 3

REST, Resources, and Rails

> Before REST came I (and pretty much everyone else) never really knew where to put stuff.
>
> —Jonas Nicklas on the Ruby on Rails mailing list

With version 1.2, Rails introduced support for designing APIs consistent with the REST style. Representational state transfer (REST) is a complex topic in information theory, and a full exploration of it is well beyond the scope of this chapter.[1] We'll touch on some of the keystone concepts, however. And in any case, the REST facilities in Rails can prove useful to you even if you're not a REST expert or devotee.

The main reason is that one of the inherent problems that all web developers face is deciding how to name and organize the resources and actions of their application. The most common actions of all database-backed applications happen to fit well into the REST paradigm.

3.1 REST in a Rather Small Nutshell

REST is described by its creator, Roy T. Fielding, as a network *architectural style*, specifically the style manifested in the architecture of the World Wide Web. Indeed, Fielding is not only the creator of REST but also one of the authors of the HTTP protocol itself. REST and the web have a very close relationship.

---

1. For those interested in REST, the canonical text is Roy Fielding's dissertation, which you can find at http://www.ics.uci.edu/~fielding/pubs/dissertation/top.htm. In particular, you'll probably want to focus on chapters 5 and 6 of the dissertation, which cover REST and its relation to HTTP. You'll also find an enormous amount of information—and links to more—on the REST wiki at http://rest.blueoxen.net/cgi-bin/wiki.pl

Fielding defines REST as a series of constraints imposed upon the interaction between system components. Basically, you start with the general proposition of machines that can talk to each other, and you start ruling some practices in and others out by imposing constraints that include (among others) the following:

- Use of a client-server architecture

- Stateless communication

- Explicit signaling of response cacheability

- Use of HTTP request methods such as GET, POST, PUT, and DELETE

The World Wide Web allows for REST-compliant communication. It also allows for violations of REST principles; the constraints aren't always all there unless you put them there. As for this chapter, the most important thing you have to understand is that REST is designed to help you provide services using the native idioms and constructs of HTTP. You'll find, if you look for it, lots of discussion comparing REST to, for example, SOAP—the thrust of the pro-REST argument being that HTTP already enables you to provide services, so you don't need a semantic layer on top of it. Just use what HTTP already gives you.

One of the allures of REST is that it scales relatively well for big systems, like the web. Another is that it encourages—mandates, even—the use of stable, long-lived identifiers (URIs). Machines talk to each other by sending requests and responses labeled with these identifiers. Messages consist of representations (manifestations in text, XML, graphic format, etc.), resources (high-level, conceptual descriptions of content), or simply HTTP headers.

Ideally at least, when you ask a machine for a JSON representation of a resource—say, Romeo and Juliet—you'll use the same identifier every time and the same request metadata indicating that you want JSON, and you'll get the same response. And if it's not the same response, there's a reason—like, the resource you're retrieving is a changeable one ("The current transcript for Student #3994," for example).

3.2   Resources and Representations

The REST style characterizes communication between system components (where a component is, say, a web browser or a server) as a series of requests to which the responses are representations of resources.

A resource, in this context, is a "conceptual mapping" (Fielding). Resources themselves are not tied to a database, a model, or a controller. Examples of resources include the following:

- The current time of day

- A library book's borrowing history

- The entire text of *The Little Prince*

- A map of Jacksonville Beach

- The inventory of a store

A resource may be singular or plural, changeable (like the time of day) or fixed (like the text of *The Little Prince*). It's basically a high-level description of the thing you're trying to get hold of when you submit a request.

What you actually do get a hold of is never the resource itself but a representation of it. This is where REST unfolds onto the myriad content types and actual deliverables that are the stuff of the web. A resource may, at any given point, be available in any number of representations (including zero). Thus your site might offer a text version of *The Little Prince* but also an audio version. Those two versions would be understood as the same resource and would be retrieved via the same identifier (URI). The difference in content type—one representation versus another—would be negotiated separately in the request.

3.3   REST in Rails

The REST support in Rails consists of methods to define resources in the routing system, designed to impose a particular style and order and logic on your controllers and, consequently, on the way the world sees your application. There's more to it than just a set of naming conventions (though there's that too). In the large scheme of things, the benefits that accrue to you when you use Rails' REST support fall into two categories:

- Convenience and automatic best practices for you

- A RESTful interface to your application's services for everyone else

You can reap the first benefit even if you're not concerned with the second. In fact, that's going to be our focus here: what the REST support in Rails can do for you in the realm of making your code nicer and your life as a Rails developer easier.

I don't mean to minimize the importance of REST itself nor the seriousness of the endeavor of providing REST-based services. Rather, it's an expedient; we can't talk about everything, and this section of the book is primarily about routing and how to do it, so we're going to favor looking at REST in Rails from that perspective.

Getting back to practical matters, the focus of the rest of this chapter will be showing you how REST support works in Rails, opening the door to further study and practice, including the study of Fielding's dissertation and the theoretical tenets of REST. We won't cover everything here, but what we do cover will be compatible with the wider topic.

The story of REST and Rails starts with CRUD.

3.4   Routing and CRUD

The acronym CRUD (create, read, update, and delete) is the classic summary of the spectrum of database operations. It's also a kind of rallying cry for Rails practitioners. Because we address our databases through abstractions, we're prone to forget how simple it all is. This manifests itself mainly in excessively creative names for controller actions. There's a temptation to call your actions `add_item` and `replace _email_address` and things like that. But we needn't, and usually shouldn't, do this. True, the controller does not map to the database the way the model does. But things get simpler when you name your actions after CRUD operations or as close to the names of those operations as you can get.

The routing system does not force you to implement your app's CRUD functionality in any consistent manner. You can create a route that maps to any action, whatever the action's name. Choosing CRUD names is a matter of discipline. Except when you use the REST facilities offered by Rails, it happens automatically.

REST in Rails involves standardization of action names. In fact, the heart of the Rails' REST support is a technique for creating bundles of named routes automatically—named routes that are bundled together to point to a specific, predetermined set of actions.

Here's the logic: It's good to give CRUD-based names to your actions. It's convenient and elegant to use named routes. The REST support in Rails gives you named routes that point to CRUD-based action names. Therefore, using the REST facilities gives you a shortcut to some best practices.

Shortcut hardly describes how little work you have to do to get a big payoff. If you put

```
resources :auctions
```

into your `config/routes.rb` file, you will have created four named routes, which, in a manner to be described in this chapter, connect to seven controller actions. And those actions have nice CRUD-like names, as you will see.

3.4.1   REST Resources and Rails

Like most of Rails, support for RESTful applications is "opinionated"; that is, it offers a particular way of designing a REST interface, and the more you play along, the more convenience you reap from it. Most Rails applications are database-backed, and the Rails take on REST tends to associate a resource very closely with an Active Record model or a model/controller stack.

In fact, you'll hear people using the terminology fairly loosely. For instance, they'll say that they have created a *book resource*. What they mean, in most cases, is that they have created a `Book` model, a book controller with a set of CRUD actions, and some named routes pertaining to that controller (courtesy of `resources :books`). You can have a `Book` model and controller, but what you actually present to the world as your resources, in the REST sense, exists at a higher level of abstraction: *The Little Prince*, borrowing history, and so on.

The best way to get a handle on the REST support in Rails is by going from the known to the unknown. In this case, from the topic of named routes to the more specialized topic of REST.

3.4.2   From Named Routes to REST Support

When we first looked at named routes, we saw examples where we consolidated things into a route name. By creating a route like

```
get 'auctions/:id' => "auction#show", as: 'auction'
```

you gain the ability to use nice helper methods in situations like

```
link_to item.description, auction_path(item.auction)
```

The route ensures that a path will be generated that will trigger the `show` action of the auctions controller. The attraction of this kind of named route is that it's concise and readable.

Now think in terms of CRUD. The named route `auction_path` is a nice fit for a `show` (the R in CRUD) action. What if we wanted similarly nicely named routes for the `create`, `update`, and `delete` actions?

Well, we've used up the route name `auction_path` on the `show` action. We could make up names like `auction_delete_path` and `auction_create _path`, but those are cumbersome. We really want to be able to make a call to `auction_path` and have it mean different things, depending on which action we want the URL to point to.

We could differentiate between the singular (`auction_path`) and the plural (`auctions_path`). A singular URL makes sense, semantically, when you're doing something with a single, existing auction object. If you're doing something with auctions in general, the plural makes more sense.

The kinds of things you do with auctions in general involve creating. The `create` action will normally occur in a form:

```
form_tag auctions_path
```

It's plural because we're not saying "perform an action with respect to a particular auction" but rather "with respect to the collection of auctions, perform the action of creation." Yes, we're creating one auction, not many. But at the time we make the call to our named route, `auctions_path`, we're addressing auctions in general.

Another case where you might want a plural named route is when you want an overview of all the objects of a particular kind, or at least some kind of general view, rather than a display of a particular object. This kind of general view is usually handled with an `index` action. These `index` actions typically load a lot of data into one or more variables, and the corresponding view displays it as a list or table (possibly more than one).

Here, again, we'd like to be able to say,

```
link_to "Click here to view all auctions", auctions_path
```

Already, though, the strategy of breaking `auction_path` out into singular and plural has hit the wall: We've got two places where we want to use the plural named route. One is create; the other is index. But they're both going to look like

```
/auctions
```

How is the routing system going to know that, when we use `auctions_path` as a link versus using it in a form, we mean the `create` action and not `index`? We need another qualifier, another flag, another variable on which to branch.

Luckily, we've got one.

3.4.3 Reenter the HTTP Verb

Form submissions are POSTs by default. Index actions are GETs. That means that we need to get the routing system to realize that

```
/auctions submitted in a GET request!
```

and

```
/auctions submitted in a POST request!
```

are two different things. We also have to get the routing system to generate the same URL—`/auctions`—but with a different HTTP request method, depending on the circumstances.

This is what the REST facility of Rails routing does for you. It allows you to stipulate that you want `/auctions` routed differently, depending on the HTTP request method. It lets you define named routes with the same name but with intelligence about their HTTP verbs. In short, it uses HTTP verbs to provide that extra data slot necessary to achieve everything you want to achieve in a concise way.

The way you do this is by using a special routing method: `resources`. Here's what it would look like for auctions:

```
resources :auctions
```

That's it. Making this one call inside `routes.rb` is the equivalent of defining four named routes. And if you mix and match those four named routes with a variety of HTTP request methods, you end up with seven useful—very useful—permutations.

3.5 The Standard RESTful Controller Actions

Calling `resources :auctions` involves striking a kind of deal with the routing system. The system hands you four named routes. Between them, these four routes point to seven controller actions, depending on HTTP request method. In return, you agree to use very specific names for your controller actions: index, create, show, update, destroy, new, and edit.

It's not a bad bargain, since a lot of work is done for you and the action names you have to use are nicely CRUD-like.

Table 3.1 summarizes what happens. It's a kind of "multiplication table" showing you what you get when you cross a given RESTful named route with a given HTTP request method. Each box (the nonempty ones, that is) shows you, first, the URL that the route generates and, second, the action that gets called when the route is recognized. (The table lists _path methods rather than _url ones, but you get both.)

Table 3.1 RESTful Routes Table Showing Helpers, Paths, and the Resulting Controller Action

Helper method	GET	POST	PATCH	DELETE
`client_path` `(client)`	/clients/1 show		/clients/1 update	/clients/1 destroy
`clients_path`	/clients index	/clients create		
`edit_client` `_path(client)`	/clients/1/edit edit			
`new_client` `_path`	/clients/new new			

REST

(The `edit` and `new` actions have unique named routes, and their URLs have a special syntax.)

Since named routes are now being crossed with HTTP request methods, you'll need to know how to specify the request method when you generate a URL, so that your GET'd `clients_url` and your POST'd `clients_url` don't trigger the same controller action. Most of what you have to do in this regard can be summed up in a few rules:

1. The default request method is GET.

2. In a `form_tag` or `form_for` call, the POST method will be used automatically.

3. When you need to (which is going to be mostly with PATCH and DELETE operations), you can specify a request method along with the URL generated by the named route.

An example of needing to specify a DELETE operation is a situation when you want to trigger a `destroy` action with a link:

```
link_to "Delete", auction_path(auction), method: :delete
```

Depending on the helper method you're using (as in the case of `form_for`), you might have to put the method inside a nested hash:

```
form_for "auction", url: auction_path(auction),
  html: { method: :patch } do |f|
```

That last example, which combined the singular named route with the PATCH method, will result in a call to the `update` action when submitting the form (as per row 2, column 4, of Table 3.1). You don't normally have to program this functionality specifically, because as we'll see later in the book, Rails automatically figures out whether you need a POST or PATCH if you pass an object to form helpers.

3.5.1 PATCH versus PUT

If you are coming from a previous version of Rails, you may be wondering why the update action of a RESTful route is mapped to the HTTP verb PATCH instead of PUT. In the HTTP standards document RFC 5789,[2] it outlines that a PUT request to a given resource is meant to completely replace it on the origin server. However, when updating a resource in Rails, rarely, if ever, do you replace an entire resource when performing an update. For example, when updating an

---

2. http://tools.ietf.org/html/rfc5789

Active Record model, Rails sets the attribute `updated_at` timestamp, not the requesting client.

To follow better HTTP semantics, Rails will be using the HTTP verb PATCH for updates. PATCH allows for both full and partial updates of a resource and is more suited to how Rails updates resources.

If you are upgrading an existing Rails application, the HTTP verb PUT will still map to the update action in RESTful routes, but it's recommended to use PATCH moving forward.

3.5.2   Singular and Plural RESTful Routes

As you may have noticed, some of the RESTful routes are singular and some are plural. The logic is as follows:

1. The routes for `show`, `new`, `edit`, and `destroy` are singular because they're working on a particular resource.

2. The rest of the routes are plural. They deal with collections of related resources.

The singular RESTful routes require an argument because they need to be able to figure out the id of the member of the collection referenced.

```
item_url(item)   # show, update, or destroy, depending on HTTP verb
```

You don't have to call the `id` method on `item`. Rails will figure it out (by calling `to_param` on the object passed to it).

3.5.3   The Special Pairs: **new/create** and **edit/update**

As Table 3.1 shows, `new` and `edit` obey somewhat special RESTful naming conventions. The reason for this has to do with `create` and `update` and how `new` and `edit` relate to them.

Typically, `create` and `update` operations involve submitting a form. That means that they really involve two actions—two requests—each:

1. The action that results in the display of the form

2. The action that processes the form input when the form is submitted

The way this plays out with RESTful routing is that the `create` action is closely associated with a preliminary `new` action, and `update` is associated with `edit`. These two actions, `new` and `edit`, are really assistant actions: All they're supposed to do is show the user a form as part of the process of creating or updating a resource.

Fitting these special two-part scenarios into the landscape of resources is a little tricky. A form for editing a resource is not, itself, really a resource. It's more like a *preresource*. A form for creating a new resource is sort of a resource if you assume that being new—that is, nonexistent—is something that a resource can do and still be a resource!

That line of reasoning might be a little too philosophical to be useful. The bottom line, as implemented in RESTful Rails, is the following: The `new` action is understood to be giving you a new, single (as opposed to plural) resource. However, since the logical verb for this transaction is GET, and GETting a single resource is already spoken for by the `show` action, `new` needs a named route of its own.

That's why you have to use

```
link_to "Create a new item", new_item_path
```

to get a link to the `items/new` action.

The `edit` action is understood not to be giving you a full-fledged resource, exactly, but rather a kind of edit *flavor* of the `show` resource. So it uses the same URL as `show` but with a kind of modifier, in the form of `/edit`, hanging off the end, which is consistent with the URL form for `new`:

```
/items/5/edit
```

The corresponding named route is `edit_item_url(@item)`. As with `new`, the named route for `edit` involves an extra bit of name information to differentiate it from the implied `show` of the existing RESTful route for GETting a single resource.

3.5.4   The PATCH and DELETE Cheat

We have just seen how Rails routes PATCH and DELETE requests. Some HTTP clients are able to use said verbs, but forms in web browsers can't be submitted using anything other than a POST. Rails provides a hack that is nothing to worry about, other than being aware of what's going on.

A PATCH or DELETE request originating in a browser, in the context of REST in Rails, is actually a POST request with a hidden field called `_method` set to either `"patch"` or `"delete"`. The Rails application processing the request will pick up on this and route the request appropriately to the `update` or `destroy` action.

You might say, then, that the REST support in Rails is ahead of its time. REST components using HTTP should understand all the request methods. They don't, so Rails forces the issue. As a developer trying to get the hang of how the named routes map to action names, you don't have to worry about this little cheat. And hopefully it won't be necessary someday.

3.5.5   Limiting Routes Generated

It's possible to add `:except` and `:only` options to the call to `resources` in order to limit the routes generated.

```
resources :clients, except: [:index]
resources :clients, only: [:new, :create]
```

3.6   Singular Resource Routes

In addition to `resources`, there's also a singular (or *singleton*) form of resource routing: `resource`. It's used to represent a resource that only exists once in its given context.

A singleton resource route at the top level of your routes can be appropriate when there's only one resource of its type for the whole application—perhaps something like a per-user profile.

```
resource :profile
```

You get almost the full complement of resource routes—all except the collection route (index). Note that the method name `resource`, the argument to that method, and all the named routes generated are in the singular.

```
$ rake routes
      profile POST   /profile(.:format)       profiles#create
  new_profile GET    /profile/new(.:format)   profiles#new
 edit_profile GET    /profile/edit(.:format)  profiles#edit
              GET    /profile(.:format)       profiles#show
              PATCH  /profile(.:format)       profiles#update
              PUT    /profile(.:format)       profiles#update
              DELETE /profile(.:format)       profiles#destroy
```

It's assumed that you're in a context where it's meaningful to speak of *the profile*—the one and only—because there's a user to which the profile is scoped. The scoping itself is not automatic; you have to authenticate the user and retrieve the profile from (and/ or save it to) the database explicitly. There's no real magic or mind reading here; it's just an additional routing technique at your disposal if you need it.

3.7   Nested Resources

Let's say you want to perform operations on bids: create, edit, and so forth. You know that every bid is associated with a particular auction. That means that whenever you do anything to a bid, you're really doing something to an auction/bid pair—or, to look at it another way, an auction/bid nest. Bids are at the bottom of a drill-down hierarchical structure that always passes through an auction.

What you're aiming for here is a URL that looks like

```
/auctions/3/bids/5
```

What it does depends on the HTTP verb it comes with, of course. But the semantics of the URL itself is the resource that can be identified as bid 5, belonging to auction 3.

Why not just go for `bids/5` and skip the auction? For a couple of reasons. First, the URL is more informative—longer, it's true, but longer in the service of telling you something about the resource. Second, thanks to the way RESTful routes are engineered in Rails, this kind of URL gives you immediate access to the auction id via `params[:auction_id]`.

To created nested resource routes, put this in `routes.rb`:

```
1 resources :auctions do
2   resources :bids
3 end
```

What that tells the routing mapper is that you want RESTful routes for auction resources—that is, you want `auctions_url`, `edit_auction_url`, and all the rest of it. You also want RESTful routes for bids: `auction_bids_url`, `new_auction_bid_url`, and so forth.

However, the nested resource command also involves you in making a promise. You're promising that whenever you use the bid-named route helpers, you will provide an auction resource in which they can be nested. In your application code, that translates into an argument to the named route method:

```
link_to "See all bids", auction_bids_path(auction)
```

When you make that call, you enable the routing system to add the `/auctions/3` part before the `/bids` part. And on the receiving end—in this case, in the action `bids/index`, which is where that URL points—you'll find the id of `auction` in `params[:auction_id]`. (It's a plural RESTful route, using GET. See Table 3.1 again if you forgot.)

You can nest to any depth. Each level of nesting adds one to the number of arguments you have to supply to the nested routes. This means that for the singular routes (`show`, `edit`, `destroy`), you need at least two arguments:

```
link_to "Delete this bid", auction_bid_path(auction, bid), method: :delete
```

This will enable the routing system to get the information it needs (essentially `auction.id` and `bid.id`) in order to generate the route.

Alternatively, instead of specifying the route to be used in a view helper, such as `link_to`, you can simply pass an object.

```
link_to "Delete this bid", [auction, bid], method: :delete
```

Since the object in this example is an `Array`, Rails infers that the route is nested. And based on the order and class names of the objects in the `Array`, Rails will use the `auction_bid_path` helper behind the scenes.

3.7.1   RESTful Controller Mappings

Something we haven't yet explicitly discussed is how RESTful routes are mapped to a given controller. It was just presented as something that happens automatically, which in fact it does, based on the name of the resource.

Going back to our recurring example, given the nested route

```
1 resources :auctions do
2   resources :bids
3 end
```

there are two controllers that come into play: the `AuctionsController` and the `BidsController`.

3.7.2   Considerations

Is nesting worth it? For single routes, a nested route usually doesn't tell you anything you wouldn't be able to figure out anyway. After all, a bid belongs to an auction.

That means you can access `bid.auction_id` just as easily as you can `params[:auction_id]`, assuming you have a bid object already.

Furthermore, the bid object doesn't depend on the nesting. You'll get `params[:id]` set to 5, and you can dig that record out of the database directly. You don't need to know what auction it belongs to.

```
Bid.find(params[:id])
```

A common rationale for judicious use of nested resources, and the one most often issued by David, is the ease with which you can enforce permissions and context-based constraints. Typically, a nested resource should only be accessible in the context of its parent resource, and it's really easy to enforce that in your code based on the way that you load the nested resource using the parent's Active Record association.

```
auction = Auction.find(params[:auction_id])
bid = auction.bids.find(params[:id]) # prevents auction/bid mismatch
```

If you want to add a bid to an auction, your nested resource URL would be

```
http://localhost:3000/auctions/5/bids/new
```

The auction is identified in the URL rather than having to clutter your new bid form data with hidden fields or resorting to non-RESTful practices.

3.7.3   Deep Nesting?

Jamis Buck is a very influential figure in the Rails community, almost as much as David himself. In February 2007, via his blog,[3] he basically told us that deep nesting was a bad thing and proposed the following rule of thumb: Resources should never be nested more than one level deep.

That advice is based on experience and concerns about practicality. The helper methods for routes nested more than two levels deep become long and unwieldy. It's easy to make mistakes with them and hard to figure out what's wrong when they don't work as expected.

Assume that in our application example, bids have multiple comments. We could nest comments under bids in the routing like this:

```
1 resources :auctions do
2   resources :bids do
3     resources :comments
4   end
5 end
```

Instead, Jamis would have us do the following:

```
1 resources :auctions do
2   resources :bids
3 end
4
5 resources :bids do
```

---

3. http://weblog.jamisbuck.org/2007/2/5/nesting-resources

```
6    resources :comments
7  end
8
9  resources :comments
```

Notice that each resource (except auctions) is defined twice: once in the top-level namespace and one in its context. The rationale? When it comes to parent-child scope, you really only need two levels to work with. The resulting URLs are shorter and the helper methods are easier to work with.

```
auctions_path              # /auctions
auctions_path(1)           # /auctions/1
auction_bids_path(1)       # /auctions/1/bids
bid_path(2)                # /bids/2
bid_comments_path(3)       # /bids/3/comments
comment_path(4)            # /comments/4
```

I personally don't follow Jamis's guideline all the time in my projects, but I have noticed something about limiting the depth of your nested resources: it helps with the maintainability of your codebase in the long run.

Courtenay Says ...

> Many of us disagree with the venerable Jamis. Want to get into fisticuffs at a Rails conference? Ask people whether they believe routes should be nested more than one layer deep.

3.7.4   Shallow Routes

As of Rails 2.3, resource routes accept a `:shallow` option that helps to shorten URLs where possible. The goal is to leave off parent collection URL segments where they are not needed. The end result is that the only nested routes generated are for the `:index`, `:create`, and `:new` actions. The rest are kept in their own *shallow* URL context.

It's easier to illustrate than to explain, so let's define a nested set of resources and set `:shallow` to `true`:

```
1  resources :auctions, shallow: true do
2    resources :bids do
3      resources :comments
4    end
5  end
```

REST

This is alternatively coded as follows (if you're block-happy):

```
1 resources :auctions do
2   shallow do
3     resources :bids do
4       resources :comments
5     end
6   end
7 end
```

The resulting routes are the following:

```
    bid_comments GET      /bids/:bid_id/comments(.:format)
                 POST     /bids/:bid_id/comments(.:format)
 new_bid_comment GET      /bids/:bid_id/comments/new(.:format)
    edit_comment GET      /comments/:id/edit(.:format)
         comment GET      /comments/:id(.:format)
                 PATCH    /comments/:id(.:format)
                 PUT      /comments/:id(.:format)
                 DELETE   /comments/:id(.:format)
    auction_bids GET      /auctions/:auction_id/bids(.:format)
                 POST     /auctions/:auction_id/bids(.:format)
 new_auction_bid GET      /auctions/:auction_id/bids/new(.:format)
        edit_bid GET      /bids/:id/edit(.:format)
             bid GET      /bids/:id(.:format)
                 PATCH    /bids/:id(.:format)
                 PUT      /bids/:id(.:format)
                 DELETE   /bids/:id(.:format)
        auctions GET      /auctions(.:format)
                 POST     /auctions(.:format)
     new_auction GET      /auctions/new(.:format)
    edit_auction GET      /auctions/:id/edit(.:format)
         auction GET      /auctions/:id(.:format)
                 PATCH    /auctions/:id(.:format)
                 PUT      /auctions/:id(.:format)
                 DELETE   /auctions/:id(.:format)
```

If you analyze the routes generated carefully, you'll notice that the nested parts of the URL are only included when they are needed to determine what data to display.

3.8   Routing Concerns

One of the fundamental principles Rails developers follow is "don't repeat yourself" (DRY). Even though this is the case, the `config/routes.rb` file can be prone to having repetition in the form of nested routes that are shared across multiple resources. For example, let's assume in our recurring example that both auctions and bids can have comments associated with them.

```
1 resources :auctions do
2   resources :bids
3   resources :comments
4   resources :image_attachments, only: :index
5 end
6
7 resources :bids do
8   resources :comments
9 end
```

To eliminate some code duplication and to encapsulate shared behavior across routes, Rails 4 introduces the routing method `concern`.

```
1 concern :commentable do
2   resources :comments
3 end
4
5 concern :image_attachable do
6   resources :image_attachments, only: :index
7 end
```

To add a routing concern to a RESTful route, pass the concern to the `:concerns` option.

```
1 resources :auctions, concerns: [:commentable, :image_
        attachable] do
2   resources :bids
3 end
4
5 resources :bids, concerns: :commentable
```

The `:concerns` option can accept one or more routing concerns.

3.9   RESTful Route Customizations

Rails' RESTful routes give you a pretty nice package of named routes, mapped to useful, common, controller actions—the CRUD superset you've already learned about. Sometimes, however, you want to customize things a little more while still taking advantage of the RESTful route naming conventions and the *multiplication table* approach to mixing named routes and HTTP request methods.

The techniques for doing this are useful when, for example, you've got more than one way of viewing a resource that might be described as *showing*. You can't (or shouldn't) use the `show` action itself for more than one such view. Instead, you need to think in terms of different perspectives on a resource and create URLs for each one.

3.9.1   Extra Member Routes

For example, let's say we want to make it possible to retract a bid. The basic nested route for bids looks like this:

```
1 resources :auctions do
2   resources :bids
3 end
```

We'd like to have a `retract` action that shows a form (and perhaps does some screening for retractability). The `retract` isn't the same as `destroy`; it's more like a portal to `destroy`. It's similar to `edit`, which serves as a form portal to `update`. Following the parallel with `edit`/`update`, we want a URL that looks like

```
/auctions/3/bids/5/retract
```

and a helper method called `retract_auction_bid_url`. The way you achieve this is by specifying an extra `member` route for the `bids`, as in Listing 3.1

Listing 3.1   Adding an Extra Member Route
```
1 resources :auctions do
2   resources :bids do
3     member do
4       get :retract
5     end
6   end
7 end
```

Then you can add a retraction link to your view using

```
link_to "Retract", retract_bid_path(auction, bid)
```

and the URL generated will include the `/retract` modifier. That said, you should probably let that link pull up a retraction form (and not trigger the retraction process itself). The reason I say that is because, according to the tenets of HTTP, GET requests should not modify the state of the server; that's what POST requests are for.

So how do you trigger an actual retraction? Is it enough to add a `:method` option to `link_to`?

```
link_to "Retract", retract_bid_path(auction,bid), method: :post
```

Not quite. Remember that in Listing 3.1 we defined the retract route as a `get`, so a POST will not be recognized by the routing system. The solution is to define an extra member route with `post`, like this:

```
1 resources :auctions do
2   resources :bids do
3     member do
4       get :retract
5       post :retract
6     end
7   end
8 end
```

If you're handling more than one HTTP verb with a single action, you should switch to using a single `match` declaration and a `:via` option, like this:

```
1 resources :auctions do
2   resources :bids do
3     member do
4       match :retract, via: [:get, :post]
5     end
6   end
7 end
```

Thanks to the flexibility of the routing system, we can tighten it up further using `match` with an `:on` option, like

```
1 resources :auctions do
2   resources :bids do
3     match :retract, via: [:get, :post], on: :member
4   end
5 end
```

which would result in a route like this (output from `rake routes`):

```
retract_auction_bid GET|POST
/auctions/:auction_id/bids/:id/retract(.:format) bids#retract
```

3.9.2 Extra Collection Routes

You can use the same routing technique to add routes that conceptually apply to an entire collection of resources:

```
1 resources :auctions do
2   collection do
3     match :terminate, via: [:get, :post]
4   end
5 end
```

Here it is in its shorter form:

```
1 resources :auctions do
```

REST

```
2   match :terminate, via: [:get, :post], on: :collection
3 end
```

This example will give you a `terminate_auctions_path` method, which will produce a URL mapping to the `terminate` action of the auctions controller. (A slightly bizarre example, perhaps, but the idea is that it would enable you to end all auctions at once.)

Thus you can fine-tune the routing behavior—even the RESTful routing behavior—of your application, so that you can arrange for special and specialized cases while still thinking in terms of resources.

3.9.3   Custom Action Names

Occasionally, you might want to deviate from the default naming convention for Rails RESTful routes. The `:path_names` option allows you to specify alternate name mappings. The example code shown changes the new and edit actions to Spanish-language equivalents.

```
resources :projects, path_names: { new: 'nuevo', edit: 'cambiar' }
```

The URLs change (but the names of the generated helper methods do not).

```
GET     /projects/nuevo(.:format)         projects#new
GET     /projects/:id/cambiar(.:format) projects#edit
```

3.9.4   Mapping to a Different Controller

You may use the `:controller` option to map a resource to a different controller than the one it would map to by default. This feature is occasionally useful for aliasing resources to a more natural controller name.

```
resources :photos, controller: "images"
```

3.9.5   Routes for New Resources

The routing system has a neat syntax for specifying routes that only apply to new resources—ones that haven't been saved yet. You declare extra routes inside of a nested new block, like this:

```
1 resources :reports do
2   new do
3     post :preview
4   end
5 end
```

This declaration would result in the following route being defined:

```
preview_new_report POST  /reports/new/preview(.:format) reports#preview
```

Refer to your new route within a view form by altering the default `:url`.

```
1 = form_for(report, url: preview_new_report_path) do |f|
2   ...
3   = f.submit "Preview"
```

3.9.6   Considerations for Extra Routes

Referring to extra member and collection actions, David has been quoted as saying, "If you're writing so many additional methods that the repetition is beginning to bug you, you should revisit your intentions. You're probably not being as RESTful as you could be."

The last sentence is key. Adding extra actions corrupts the elegance of your overall RESTful application design, because it leads you away from finding all the resources lurking in your domain.

Keeping in mind that real applications are more complicated than code examples in a reference book, let's see what would happen if we had to model retractions strictly using resources. Rather than tacking a `retract` action onto the `BidsController`, we might feel compelled to introduce a retraction resource, associated with bids, and write a `RetractionController` to handle it.

```
1 resources :bids do
2   resource :retraction
3 end
```

`RetractionController` could now be in charge of everything having to do with retraction activities rather than having that functionality mixed into `BidsController`. And if you think about it, something as weighty as bid retraction would eventually accumulate quite a bit of logic. Some would call breaking it out into its own controller proper separation of concerns or even just good object orientation.

3.10   Controller-Only Resources

The word *resource* has a substantive, noun-like flavor that brings to mind database tables and records. However, a REST resource does not have to map directly to an Active Record model. Resources are high-level abstractions of what's available through your web application. Database operations just happen to be one of the ways that you store and retrieve the data you need to generate representations of resources.

A REST resource doesn't necessarily have to map directly to a controller, either— at least not in theory. You could, if you wanted to, provide REST services whose public identifiers (URIs) did not match the names of your controllers at all.

What all this adds up to is that you might have occasion to create a set of resource routes—and a matching controller—that don't correspond to any model in your application at all. There's nothing wrong with a full resource/controller/model stack where everything matches by name. But you may find cases where the resources you're representing can be encapsulated in a controller but not a model.

An example in the auction application is the sessions controller. Assume a `routes.rb` file containing this line:

```
resource :session
```

It maps the URL `/session` to a `SessionController` as a singleton resource, yet there's no `Session` model. (By the way, it's properly defined as a singleton resource because from the user's perspective there is only one session.)

Why go the RESTful style for authentication? If you think about it, user sessions can be created and destroyed. The creation of a session takes place when a user logs in; when the user logs out, the session is destroyed. The RESTful Rails practice of pairing a new action and view with a `create` action can be followed! The user login form can be the session-creating form, housed in the template file such as `session/new.html.haml`:

```
1 %h1 Log in
2 = form_for :user, url: session_path do |f|
3   %p
4     = f.label :login
5     = f.text_field :login
6   %p
7     = f.label :password
8     = f.password_field :password
9   %p
10    = f.submit "Log in"
```

When the form is submitted, the input is handled by the `create` method of the sessions controller:

```
1 def create
2   if user.try(:authorize, params[:user][:password])
3     flash[:notice] = "Welcome, #{user.first_name}!"
4     redirect_to home_url
```

```
 5    else
 6      flash[:error] = "Login invalid."
 7      redirect_to action: "new"
 8    end
 9  end
10
11  protected
12  def user
13    @user ||= User.find_by(login: params[:user][:login])
14  end
```

Nothing is written to any database table in this action, but it's worthy of the name `create` by virtue of the fact that it creates a session. Furthermore, if you did at some point decide that sessions should be stored in the database, you'd already have a nicely abstracted handling layer.

It pays to remain open-minded, then, about the possibility that CRUD as an action-naming philosophy and CRUD as actual database operations may sometimes occur independently of each other and the possibility that the resource-handling facilities in Rails might usefully be associated with a controller that has no corresponding model. Creating a session on the server isn't a REST-compliant practice, since REST mandates stateless transfers of representations of resources. But it's a good illustration of why and how you might make design decisions involving routes and resources that don't implicate the whole application stack.

Xavier Says …

> Whether sessions are REST-compliant or not depends on the session storage. What REST disallows is not the idea of application state in general but rather the idea of client state stored in the server. REST demands that your requests are complete. For example, putting an `auction_id` in a hidden field of a form or in its action path is fine. There is state in that request the edit action wants to pass to the update action, and you dumped it into the page, so the next request to update a bid carries all what's needed. That's RESTful.
>
> Now using hidden fields and such is not the only way to do this. For example, there is no problem using a `user_id` cookie for authentication. Why? Because a cookie is part of a request. Therefore, I am pretty sure that cookie-based sessions are considered to be RESTful by the same principle. That kind of storage makes your requests self-contained and complete.

Sticking to CRUD-like action names is, in general, a good idea. As long as you're doing lots of creating and destroying anyway, it's easier to think of a user logging in as the creation of a session than to come up with a whole new semantic category for it. Rather than the new concept of *user logs in*, just think of it as a new occurrence of the old concept, *session gets created*.

3.11   Different Representations of Resources

One of the precepts of REST is that the components in a REST-based system exchange representations of resources. The distinction between resources and their representations is vital.

As a client or consumer of REST services, you don't actually retrieve a resource from a server; you retrieve representations of that resource. You also provide representations: A form submission, for example, sends the server a representation of a resource, together with a request—for example, PATCH—that this representation be used as the basis for updating the resource. Representations are the exchange currency of resource management.

3.11.1   The `respond_to` Method

The ability to return different representations in RESTful Rails practice is based on the `respond_to` method in the controller, which, as you've seen in the previous chapter, allows you to return different responses depending on what the client wants. Moreover, when you create resource routes, you automatically get URL recognition for URLs ending with a dot and a `:format` parameter.

For example, assume that you have `resources :auctions` in your routes file and some `respond_to` logic in the `AuctionsController` like the following:

```
1 def index
2   @auctions = Auction.all
3   respond_to do |format|
4     format.html
5     format.xml { render xml: @auctions }
6   end
7 end
```

This will let you to connect to this URL: `/auctions.xml`.

The resource routing will ensure that the `index` action gets executed. It will also recognize the `.xml` at the end of the route and interact with `respond_to` accordingly, returning the XML representation.

There is also a more concise way of handling this now using the `respond_with` method.

```
1 class AuctionsController < ApplicationController
2   respond_to :html, :xml, :json
```

```
3    def index
4      @auctions = Auction.all
5      respond_with(@auctions)
6    end
7  end
```

Here we've told our controller to respond to HTML, XML, and JSON so that each action will automatically return the appropriate content. When the request comes in, the responder would attempt to do the following given a `.json` extension on the URL:

- Attempt to render the associated view with a .json extension
- If no view exists, call `to_json` on the object passed to `responds_with`
- If the object does not respond to `to_json`, call `to_format` on it

For nested and namespaced resources, simply pass all the objects to the `respond _to` method, similar to the way you would generate a route.

```
respond_with(@user, :managed, @client)
```

Of course, all of this is URL recognition. What if you want to generate a URL ending in `.xml`?

3.11.2   Formatted Named Routes

Let's say you want a link to the XML representation of a resource. You can achieve it by passing an extra argument to the RESTful named route:

```
link_to "XML version of this auction", auction_path(@auction, :xml)
```

This will generate the following HTML:

```
<a href="/auctions/1.xml">XML version of this auction</a>
```

When followed, this link will trigger the XML clause of the `respond_to` block in the `show` action of the auctions controller. The resulting XML may not look like much in a browser, but the named route is there if you want it.

The circuit is now complete: You can generate URLs that point to a specific response type, and you can honor requests for different types by using `respond_to`. All told, the routing system and the resource-routing facilities built on top of it give you quite a set of powerful, concise tools for differentiating among requests and, therefore, being able to serve up different representations.

3.12   The RESTful Rails Action Set

Rails REST facilities, ultimately, are about named routes and the controller actions to which they point. The more you use RESTful Rails, the more you get to know each of the seven RESTful actions. How they work across different controllers (and different applications) is of course somewhat different. Still, perhaps because there's a finite number of them and their roles are fairly well delineated, each of the seven tends to have fairly consistent properties and a characteristic *feel* to it.

We're going to take a look at each of the seven actions with examples and comments. You'll encounter all of them again, particularly in Chapter 4, "Working with Controllers," but here you'll get some backstory and start to get a sense of the characteristic usage of them and issues and choices associated with them.

3.12.1   Index

Typically, an index action provides a representation of a plural (or collection) resource. However, to be clear, not all resource collections are mapped to the index action. Your default index representations will usually be generic, although admittedly that has a lot to do with your application-specific needs. But in general, the index action shows the world the most neutral representation possible. A very basic index action looks like the following:

```
1 class AuctionsController < ApplicationController
2   def index
3     @auctions = Auction.all
4   end
5 end
```

The associated view template will display information about each auction, with links to specific information about each one, and will display profiles of the sellers.

You'll certainly encounter situations where you want to display a representation of a collection in a restricted way. In our recurring example, users should be able to see a listing of all their bids, but maybe you don't want users seeing other people's bids.

There are a couple of ways to do this. One way is to test for the presence of a logged-in user and decide what to show based on that. But that's not going to work here. For one thing, the logged-in user might want to see the more public view. For another, the more dependence on server-side state we can eliminate or consolidate, the better.

So let's try looking at the two bid lists, not as public and private versions of the same resource, but as different index resources. The difference can be reflected in the routing like the following:

```
1 resources :auctions do
2   resources :bids do
3     get :manage, on: :collection
4   end
5 end
6 resources :bids
```

We can now organize the bids controller in such a way that access is nicely layered, using action callbacks only where necessary and eliminating conditional branching in the actions themselves:

```
1 class BidsController < ApplicationController
2   before_action :check_authorization, only: :manage
3
4   def index
5     @bids = Bid.all
6   end
7
8   def manage
9     @bids = auction.bids
10  end
11
12  protected
13
14  def auction
15    @auction ||= Auction.find(params[:auction_id])
16  end
17
18  def check_authorization
19    auction.authorized?(current_user)
20  end
21 end
```

There's now a clear distinction between /bids and /auctions/1/bids/manage and the role that they play in your application.

On the named route side, we've now got bids_url and manage_auction _bids_url. We've thus preserved the public, stateless face of the /bids resource and quarantined as much stateful behavior as possible into a discrete member resource, /auctions/1/bids/manage. Don't fret if this mentality doesn't come to you naturally. It's part of the REST learning curve.

Lark Says ...

If they are truly different resources, why not give them each their own controllers? Surely there will be other actions that need to be authorized and scoped to the current user.

3.12.2   Show

The RESTful `show` action is the singular flavor of a resource. That generally translates to a representation of information about one object or one member of a collection. Like `index`, `show` is triggered by a GET request.

A typical—one might say classic—show action looks like this:

```
1 class AuctionController < ApplicationController
2   def show
3     @auction = Auction.find(params[:id])
4   end
5 end
```

You might want to differentiate between publicly available profiles, perhaps based on a different route, and the profile of the current user, which might include modification rights and perhaps different information.

As with index actions, it's good to make your show actions as public as possible and offload the administrative and privileged views onto either a different controller or a different action.

3.12.3   Destroy

Destroy actions are good candidates for administrative safeguarding, though of course it depends on what you're destroying. You might want something like this to protect the `destroy` action:

```
1 class ProductsController < ApplicationController
2   before_action :admin_required, only: :destroy
```

A typical `destroy` action might look like this:

```
1 def destroy
2   product.destroy
3   redirect_to products_url, notice: "Product deleted!"
4 end
```

This approach might be reflected in a simple administrative interface like this:

```
1 %h1 Products
2 - products.each do |product|
3   %p= link_to product.name, product
4   - if current_user.admin?
5     %p= link_to "delete", product, method: :delete
```

That delete link appears depending on whether current user is an admin.

The Rails UJS (unobtrusive JavaScript) API greatly simplifies the HTML emitted for a `destroy` action, using CSS selectors to bind JavaScript to (in this case) the "delete" link. See Chapter 19, "Ajax on Rails," for much more information about how it works.

`DELETE` submissions are dangerous. Rails wants to make them as hard as possible to accidentally trigger—for instance, by a crawler or bot sending requests to your site. So when you specify the `DELETE` method, the JavaScript that submits a form is bound to your "delete" link along with a `rel="nofollow"` attribute on the link. Since bots don't submit forms (and shouldn't follow links marked "nofollow"), this gives a layer of protection to your code.

3.12.4 New and Create

As you've already seen, the `new` and `create` actions go together in RESTful Rails. A "new resource" is really just an entity waiting to be created. Accordingly, the `new` action customarily presents a form, and `create` creates a new record, based on the form input.

Let's say you want a user to be able to create (i.e., start) an auction. You're going to need the following two actions:

1. A `new` action, which will display a form
2. A `create` action, which will create a new `Auction` object based on the form input and proceed to a view (`show` action) of that auction

The `new` action doesn't have to do much. In fact, it has to do nothing. Like any empty action, it can even be left out. Rails will still figure out which view to render. However, your controller will need an auction helper method, like the following:

```
1 protected
2
3 def auction
4   @auction ||= current_user.auctions.build(params[:auction])
5 end
6 helper_method :auction
```

If this technique is alien to you, don't worry. We'll describe it in detail in the section "Decent Exposure" in Chapter 10, "Action View."

A simplistic `new.html.haml` template might look like Listing 3.2.

Listing 3.2 A New Auction Form

```
 1 %h1 Create a new auction
 2 = form_for auction do |f|
 3   = f.label :subject
 4   = f.text_field :subject
 5   %br
 6   = f.label :description
 7   = f.text_field :description
 8   %br
 9   = f.label :reserve
10   = f.text_field :reserve
11   %br
12   = f.label :starting_bid
13   = f.text_field :starting_bid
14   %br
15   = f.label :end_time
16   = f.datetime_select :end_time
17   %br
18   = f.submit "Create"
```

Once the information is filled out by a user, it's time for the main event: the `create` action. Unlike `new`, this action has something to do.

```
1 def create
2   if auction.save
3     redirect_to auction_url(auction), notice: "Auction
         created!"
4   else
5     render :new
6   end
7 end
```

3.12.5 Edit and Update

Like `new` and `create`, the `edit` and `update` actions go together: `edit` provides a form and `update` processes the form input.

The form for editing a record appears similar to the form for creating one. (In fact, you can put much of it in a partial template and use it for both; that's left as an exercise for the reader.)

The `form_for` method is smart enough to check whether the object you pass to it has been persisted or not. If it has, then it recognizes that you are doing an edit and specifies a PATCH method on the form.

3.13 Conclusion

In this chapter, we tackled the tough subject of using REST principles to guide the design of our Rails applications, mainly as they apply to the routing system and controller actions. We learned how the foundation of RESTful Rails is the `resources` method in your routes file and how to use the numerous options available to make sure that you can structure your application exactly how it needs to be structured.

By necessity, we've already introduced many controller-related topics and code examples in our tour of the routing and REST features. In the next chapter, we'll cover controller concepts and the Action Controller API in depth.

REST

## CHAPTER 4

Working with Controllers

Remove all business logic from your controllers and put it in the model. [My] instructions are precise, but following them requires intuition and subtle reasoning.

—Nick Kallen

Like any computer program, your Rails application involves the flow of control from one part of your code to another. The flow of program control gets pretty complex with Rails applications. There are many bits and pieces in the framework, many of which execute each other. And part of the framework's job is to figure out, on the fly, what your application files are called and what's in them, which of course varies from one application to another.

The heart of it all, though, is pretty easy to identify: It's the controller. When someone connects to your application, what they're basically doing is asking the application to execute a controller action. Sure, there are many different flavors of how this can happen and edge cases where it doesn't exactly happen at all. But if you know how controllers fit into the application life cycle, you can anchor everything else around that knowledge. That's why we're covering controllers before the rest of the Rails APIs.

Controllers are the C in MVC. They're the first port of call, after the dispatcher, for the incoming request. They're in charge of the flow of the program: They gather information and make it available to the views.

Controllers are also very closely linked to views, more closely than they're linked to models. It's possible to write the entire model layer of an application before you create a single controller or to have different people working on the controller and model layers who never meet or talk to each other. However, views and controllers are more tightly coupled to one another. They share a lot of information and the names you choose for your variables in the controller will have an effect on what you do in the view.

In this chapter, we're going to look at what happens on the way to a controller action being executed and what happens as a result. In the middle, we'll take a long look at how controller classes themselves are set up, particularly in regard to the many different ways that we can render views. We'll wrap up the chapter with a couple of additional topics related to controllers: action callbacks and streaming.

4.1 Rack

Rack is a modular interface for handling web requests, written in Ruby, with support for many different web servers. It abstracts away the handling of HTTP requests and responses into a single, simple `call` method that can be used by anything from a plain Ruby script all the way to Rails itself.

Listing 2.1   HelloWorld as a Rack Application
```
1 class HelloWorld
2   def call(env)
3     [200, {"Content-Type" => "text/plain"}, ["Hello world!"]]
4   end
5 end
```

An HTTP request invokes the call method and passes in a hash of environment variables, akin to the way that CGI works. The call method should return a three-element array consisting of the status, a hash of response headers, and, finally, the body of the request.

As of Rails 2.3, request handling was moved to Rack and the concept of middleware was introduced. Classes that satisfy Rack's call interface can be chained together as filters. Rack itself includes a number of useful filter classes that do things such as logging and exception handling.

Rails 3 took this one step further and was rearchitected from the ground up to fully leverage Rack filters in a modular and extensible manner. A full explanation of Rails' Rack underpinnings are outside the scope of this book, especially since Rack does not really play a part in day-to-day development of applications. However, it is essential Rails 4 knowledge to understand that much of Action Controller is implemented as Rack middleware modules. Want to see which Rack filters are enabled for your Rails 4 application? There's a rake task for that!

```
$ rake middleware
use Rack::Runtime
use Rack::MethodOverride
```

```
use ActionDispatch::RequestId
use Rails::Rack::Logger
use ActionDispatch::ShowExceptions
use ActionDispatch::DebugExceptions
use ActionDispatch::RemoteIp
use ActionDispatch::Reloader
use ActionDispatch::Callbacks
use ActiveRecord::Migration::CheckPending
use ActiveRecord::ConnectionAdapters::ConnectionManagement
use ActiveRecord::QueryCache
use ActionDispatch::Cookies
use ActionDispatch::Session::CookieStore
use ActionDispatch::Flash
use ActionDispatch::ParamsParser
use Rack::Head
use Rack::ConditionalGet
use Rack::ETag
run Example::Application.routes
```

What's checking for pending Active Record migrations have to do with serving requests anyway?

```
 1 module ActiveRecord
 2   class Migration
 3     class CheckPending
 4       ...
 5
 6       def call(env)
 7         ActiveRecord::Base.logger.silence do
 8           ActiveRecord::Migration.check_pending!
 9         end
10         @app.call(env)
11       end
12     end
13   end
14 end
```

Ah, it's not that pending Active Record migrations has anything specifically to do with serving requests. It's that Rails 4 is designed in such a way that different aspects of its behavior are introduced into the request call chain as individual Rack middleware components or *filters*.

4.1.1   Configuring Your Middleware Stack

Your application object allows you to access and manipulate the Rack middleware stack during initialization via `config.middleware` like the following:

```
 1  # config/application.rb
 2
 3  module Example
 4    class Application < Rails::Application
 5      ...
 6      # Rack::ShowStatus catches all empty responses the app it wraps and
 7      # replaces them with a site explaining the error.
 8      config.middleware.use Rack::ShowStatus
 9    end
10  end
```

Rack Lobster

As I found out trying to experiment with the hilariously named `Rack::Lobster`, your custom Rack middleware classes need to have an explicit `initializer` method, even if they don't require runtime arguments.

The methods of `config.middleware` give you very fine-grained control over the order in which your middleware stack is configured. The `args` parameter is an optional hash of attributes to pass to the `initializer` method of your Rack filter.

4.1.1.1 `config.middleware.insert_after(existing_middleware, new_middleware, args)`
Adds the new middleware after the specified existing middleware in the middleware stack.

4.1.1.2 `config.middleware.insert_before(existing_middleware, new_middleware, args)`
Adds the new middleware before the specified existing middleware in the middleware stack.

4.1.1.3 `config.middleware.delete(middleware)`
Removes a specified middleware from the stack.

4.1.1.4 `config.middleware.swap(existing_middleware, new_middleware, args)`
Swaps a specified middleware from the stack with a new class.

4.1.1.5 `config.middleware.use(new_middleware, args)`
Takes a class reference as its parameter and just adds the desired middleware to the end of the middleware stack.

4.2 Action Dispatch: Where It All Begins

Controller and view code in Rails has always been part of its Action Pack framework. As of Rails 3, dispatching of requests was extracted into its own subcomponent of Action Pack called Action Dispatch. It contains classes that interface the rest of the controller system to Rack.

4.2.1 Request Handling

The entry point to a request is an instance of `ActionDispatch::Routing::RouteSet`, the object on which you can call `draw` at the top of `config/routes.rb`.

The route set chooses the rule that matches and calls its *Rack endpoint*. So a route like

```
get 'foo', to: 'foo#index'
```

has a dispatcher instance associated to it, whose `call` method ends up executing

```
FooController.action(:index).call
```

As covered in the section "Routes as Rack Endpoints" in Chapter 2, "Routing," the route set can call any other type of Rack endpoint, like a Sinatra app, a redirect macro, or a bare lambda. In those cases, no dispatcher is involved.

All of this happens quickly behind the scenes. It's unlikely that you would ever need to dig into the source code of ActionDispatch; it's the sort of thing that you can take for granted to just work. However, to really understand the Rails way, it is important to know what's going on with the dispatcher. In particular, it's important to remember that the various parts of your application are just bits (sometimes long bits) of Ruby code and that they're getting loaded into a running Ruby interpreter.

4.2.2 Getting Intimate with the Dispatcher

Just for the purpose of learning, let's trigger the Rails dispatching mechanism manually. We'll do this little exercise from the ground up, starting with a new Rails application:

```
$ rails new dispatch_me
```

Now create a single controller `demo` with an `index` action (note that Haml is set up as our template language):

```
$ cd dispatch_me/
$ rails generate controller demo index
  create  app/controllers/demo_controller.rb
   route  get "demo/index"
```

```
invoke   haml
create     app/views/demo
create     app/views/demo/index.html.haml
invoke   test_unit
create     test/controllers/demo_controller_test.rb
invoke   helper
create     app/helpers/demo_helper.rb
invoke     test_unit
create       test/helpers/demo_helper_test.rb
invoke   assets
invoke     coffee
create       app/assets/javascripts/demo.js.coffee
invoke     scss
create       app/assets/stylesheets/demo.css.scss
```

If you take a look at app/controllers/demo_controller.rb, you'll see that it has an index action:

```
class DemoController < ApplicationController
  def index
  end
end
```

There's also a view template file, app/views/demo/index.html.haml, with some placeholder language. Just to see things more clearly, let's replace it with something we will definitely recognize when we see it again. Replace the contents of index.html.haml with the following:

```
Hello!
```

Not much of a design accomplishment, but it will do the trick.

Now that we've got a set of dominos lined up, it's just a matter of pushing over the first one: the dispatcher. To do that, start by firing up the Rails console from your Rails application directory.

```
$ rails console
Loading development environment
>>
```

There are some variables from the web server that Rack expects to use for request processing. Since we're going to be invoking the dispatcher manually, we have to set those variables like this in the console (with output lines omitted for brevity):

```
>> env = {}
>> env['REQUEST_METHOD'] = 'GET'
```

```
>> env['PATH_INFO'] = '/demo/index'
>> env['rack.input'] = StringIO.new
```

Now that we've replicated an HTTP environment, we're ready to fool the dispatcher into thinking it's getting a request. Actually, it is getting a request. It's just that it's coming from someone sitting at the console rather than from a proper web server:

```
>> rack_body_proxy = DispatchMe::Application.call(env).last
>> rack_body_proxy.last
=> "<!DOCTYPE html>\n<html>\n<head>\n  <title>DispatchMe</title>\n
<link data-turbolinks-track=\"true\" href=\"/assets/application.css?body=1\"
media=\"all\" rel=\"stylesheet\" />\n<link data-turbolinks-track=\"true\"
href=\"/assets/demo.css?body=1\" media=\"all\" rel=\"stylesheet\" />\n
<script data-turbolinks-track=\"true\"
src=\"/assets/jquery.js?body=1\"></script>\n
<script data-turbolinks-track=\"true\"
src=\"/assets/jquery_ujs.js?body=1\"></script>\n
<script data-turbolinks-track=\"true\"
src=\"/assets/turbolinks.js?body=1\"></script>\n
<script data-turbolinks-track=\"true\"
src=\"/assets/demo.js?body=1\"></script>\n
<script data-turbolinks-track=\"true\"
src=\"/assets/application.js?body=1\"></script>\n
<meta content=\"authenticity_token\" name=\"csrf-param\" />\n
<meta content=\"cmfwNmZzzqRv94sv75OnO5Mon1C0XeWzuG90PUOeqPc=\"
name=\"csrf-token\" />\n</head>\n<body>\n\nHello\n\n\n</body>\n</html>\n"
```

If you want to see everything contained in the `ActionDispatch::Response` object returned from `call`, then try the following code:

```
>> y DispatchMe::Application.call(env)
```

The handy `y` method formats its argument as a YAML string, making it a lot easier to understand. We won't reproduce the output here because it's huge.

So we've executed the `call` method of our Rails application, and as a result, the `index` action got executed, the index template (such as it is) got rendered, and the results of the rendering got wrapped in some HTTP headers and returned.

Just think, if you were a web server rather than a human and you had just done the same thing, you could now return that document, headers, "Hello!," and all, to a client.

You can follow the trail of bread crumbs even further by diving into the Rails source code, but for the purposes of understanding the chain of events in a Rails request and the role of the controller, the peek under the hood we've just done is sufficient.

Controllers

Tim Says …

Note that if you give Rack a path that resolves to a static file, it will be served directly from the web server without involving the Rails stack. As a result, the object returned by the dispatcher for a static file is different than what you might expect.

4.3   Render unto View…

The goal of the typical controller action is to render a view template—that is, to fill out the template and hand the results, usually an HTML document, back to the server for delivery to the client. Oddly—at least it might strike you as a bit odd, though not illogical—you don't actually need to define a controller action, as long as you've got a template that matches the action name.

You can try this out in under-the-hood mode. Go into `app/controller/demo_controller.rb` and delete the `index` action so that the file will look empty, like this:

```
class DemoController < ApplicationController
end
```

Don't delete `app/views/demo/index.html.haml`, and then try the console exercise—`DispatchMe::Application.call(env)` and all that—again. You'll see the same result.

By the way, make sure you reload the console when you make changes—it doesn't react to changes in source code automatically. The easiest way to reload the console is simply to type `reload!`. But be aware that any existing instances of Active Record objects that you're holding on to will also need to be reloaded (using their individual `reload` methods). Sometimes it's simpler to just exit the console and start it up again.

4.3.1   When in Doubt, Render

Rails knows that when it gets a request for the `index` action of the demo controller, what really matters is handing something back to the server. So if there's no `index` action in the controller file, Rails shrugs and says, "Well, let's just assume that if there were an `index` action, it would be empty anyway, and I'd just render `index.html.haml`. So that's what I'll do."

You can learn something from an empty controller action, though. Let's go back to this version of the demo controller:

```
class DemoController < ApplicationController
  def index
  end
end
```

What you learn from seeing the empty action is that, at the end of every controller action, if nothing else is specified, the default behavior is to render the template whose name matches the name of the controller and action, which in this case means `app/views/demo/index.html.haml`.

In other words, every controller action has an implicit `render` command in it. And `render` is a real method. You could write the preceding example like this:

```
def index
  render "demo/index"
end
```

You don't have to, though, because it's assumed that it's what you want, and that is part of what Rails people are talking about when they discuss *convention over configuration*. Don't force the developer to add code to accomplish something that can be assumed to be a certain way.

The `render` command, however, does more than just provide a way of telling Rails to do what it was going to do anyway.

4.3.2   Explicit Rendering

Rendering a template is like putting on a shirt: If you don't like the first one you find in your closet—the default, so to speak—you can reach for another one and put it on instead.

If a controller action doesn't want to render its default template, it can render a different one by calling the `render` method explicitly. Any template file in the `app/views` directory tree is available. (Actually, that's not exactly true. Any template on the whole system is available!) But why would you want your controller action to render a template other than its default? There are several reasons, and by looking at some of them, we can cover all the handy features of the controller's `render` method.

4.3.3   Rendering Another Action's Template

A common reason for rendering an entirely different template is to redisplay a form when it gets submitted with invalid data and needs correction. In such circumstances, the usual web strategy is to redisplay the form with the submitted data and trigger the simultaneous display of some error information so that the user can correct the form and resubmit.

The reason that process involves rendering another template is that the action that processes the form and the action that displays the form may be—and often are—different from each other. Therefore, the action that processes the form needs a way to redisplay the original (form) template instead of treating the form submission as successful and moving on to whatever the next screen might be.

Wow, that was a mouthful of an explanation. Here's a practical example:

```
1 class EventController < ActionController::Base
2   def new
3     # This (empty) action renders the new.html.haml template, which
4     # contains the form for inputting information about the new
5     # event record and is not actually needed.
6   end
7
8   def create
9     # This method processes the form input. The input is available via
10    # the params hash, in the nested hash keyed to :event.
11    @event = Event.new(params[:event])
12    if @event.save
13      # Ignore the next line for now.
14      redirect_to dashboard_path, notice: "Event created!"
15    else
16      render action: 'new' # doesn't execute the new method!
17    end
18  end
19 end
```

On failure—that is, if @event.save does not return true, we render the "new" template. Assuming new.html.haml has been written correctly, this will automatically include the display of error information embedded in the new (but unsaved) Event object.

Note that the template itself doesn't "know" that it has been rendered by the create action rather than the new action. It just does its job: It fills out and expands and interpolates, based on the instructions it contains and the data (in this case, @event) that the controller has passed to it.

4.3.4   Rendering a Different Template Altogether

In a similar fashion, if you are rendering a template for a different action, it is possible to render any template in your application by calling render with a string pointing to the desired template file. The `render` method is very robust in its ability to interpret which template you're trying to refer to.

```
render template: '/products/index.html.haml'
```

A couple of notes: It's not necessary to pass a hash with `:template` because it's the default option. Also, in our testing, all the following permutations worked identically when called from `ProductsController`:

```
render '/products/index.html.haml'
render 'products/index.html.haml'
render 'products/index.html'
render 'products/index'
render 'index'
render :index
```

The `:template` option only works with a path relative to the template root (`app/views`, unless you changed it, which would be extremely unusual).

Tim Says …

Use only enough to disambiguate. The content type defaults to that of the request and if you have two templates that differ only by template language, you're *doing it wrong*.

4.3.5   Rendering a Partial Template

Another option is to render a partial template (usually referred to simply as a *partial*). Usage of partial templates allows you to organize your template code into small files. Partials can also help you to avoid clutter and encourage you to break your template code up into reusable modules.

There are a few ways to trigger partial rendering. The first—and most obvious—is using the `:partial` option to explicitly specify a partial template. Rails has a convention of prefixing partial template filenames with an underscore character, but you never include the underscore when referring to partials.

```
render partial: 'product' # renders app/views/products/_product.html.haml
```

Leaving the underscore off of the partial name applies, even if you're referring to a partial in a different directory than the controller you're currently in!

```
render partial: 'shared/product'
# renders app/views/shared/_product.html.haml
```

Controllers

The second way to trigger partial rendering depends on convention. If you pass render `:partial` an object, Rails will use its class name to find a partial to render. You can even omit the `:partial` option, like in the following example code.

```
render partial: @product
render @product
render 'product'
```

All three lines render the `app/views/products/_product.html.haml` template.

Partial rendering from a controller is mostly used in conjunction with Ajax calls that need to dynamically update segments of an already displayed page. The technique, along with generic use of partials in views, is covered in greater detail in Chapter 10, "Action View."

4.3.6   Rendering Inline Template Code

Occasionally, you need to send the browser the result of translating a snippet of template code too small to merit its own partial. I admit that this practice is contentious, because it is a flagrant violation of proper separation of concerns between the MVC layers.

Rails treats the inline code exactly as if it were a view template. The default type of view template processing is ERb, but passing an additional `:type` option allows you to choose Haml.

```
render inline: "%span.foo #{@foo.name}", type: "haml"
```

Courtenay Says ...

If you were one of my employees, I'd reprimand you for using view code in the controller, even if it is only one line. Keep your view-related code in the views!

4.3.7   Rendering Text

What if you simply need to send plain text back to the browser, particularly when responding to Ajax and certain types of web service requests?

```
render text: 'Submission accepted'
```

Unfortunately, if you don't pass an additional `:content_type` option, Rails will default the response MIME type to text/HTML rather than text/plain. The solution is to be explicit about what you want.

```
render text: 'Submission accepted', content_type: 'text/plain'
```

4.3.8   Rendering Other Types of Structured Data

The `render` command also accepts a series of (convenience) options for returning structured data such as JSON or XML. The content-type of the response will be set appropriately and additional options apply.[1]

4.3.8.1   `:json`

JSON[2] is a small subset of JavaScript selected for its usability as a lightweight data-interchange format. It is mostly used as a way of sending data down to JavaScript code running in a rich web application via Ajax calls. Active Record has built-in support for conversion to JSON, which makes Rails an ideal platform for serving up JSON data, as in the following example:

```
render json: @record
```

As long as the parameter responds to `to_json`, Rails will call it for you, which means you don't have to call it yourself with Active Record objects.

Any additional options passed to `render` `:json` are also included in the invocation of `to_json`.

```
render json: @projects, include: :tasks
```

Additionally, if you're doing JSONP (JSON with padding), you can supply the name of a callback function to be invoked in the browser when it gets your response. Just add a `:callback` option with the name of a valid JavaScript method.

```
render json: @record, callback: 'updateRecordsDisplay'
```

4.3.8.2   `:xml`

Active Record also has built-in support for conversion to XML, as in the following example:

```
render xml: @record
```

As long as the parameter responds to `to_xml`, Rails will call it for you, which means you don't have to call it yourself with Active Record objects.

Any additional options passed to `render` `:xml` are also included in the invocation of `to_xml`.

```
render xml: @projects, include: :tasks
```

---

1. Yehuda has written an excellent description of how to register additional rendering options at `https://blog.engineyard.com/2010/render-options-in-rails-3`

2. For more information on JSON, go to `http://www.json.org/`

Controllers

4.3.9   Rendering Nothing

On rare occasions, you don't want to render anything at all. (To avoid a bug in Safari, rendering nothing actually means sending a single space character back to the browser.)

```
head :unauthorized
```

The `head` method allows you to return a response with no content and a specific status code. You could achieve the same result as the previous code snippet by calling `render nothing: true` and explicitly providing a status.

```
render nothing: true, status: 401
```

The `head` method also accepts an options hash that is interpreted as header names and values to be included with the response. To illustrate, consider the following example that returns an empty response with a status of 201 and also sets the `Location` header:

```
head :created, location: auction_path(@auction)
```

4.3.10   Rendering Options

Most calls to the `render` method accept additional options. Here they are in alphabetical order.

4.3.10.1   `:content_type`

All content flying around the web is associated with a MIME type.[3] For instance, HTML content is labeled with a content-type of `text/html`. However, there are occasions where you want to send the client something other than HTML. Rails doesn't validate the format of the MIME identifier you pass to the `:content_type` option, so make sure it is valid.

4.3.10.2   `:layout`

By default, Rails has conventions regarding the layout template it chooses to wrap your response in, and those conventions are covered in detail in Chapter 10, "Action View." The `:layout` option allows you to specify whether you want a layout template to be rendered if you pass it a boolean value or the name of a layout template, if you want to deviate from the default.

```
render layout: false     # disable layout template
render layout: 'login'   # a template app/views/layouts is assumed
```

---

3. MIME is specified in five RFC documents, so it is much more convenient to point you to a rather good description of MIME provided by Wikipedia at http://en.wikipedia.org/wiki/MIME

4.3.10.3   `:status`

The HTTP protocol includes many standard status codes[4] indicating a variety of conditions in response to a client's request. Rails will automatically use the appropriate status for most common cases, such as `200 OK` for a successful request.

The theory and techniques involved in properly using the full range of HTTP status codes would require a dedicated chapter—or even an entire book. For your convenience, Table 4.1 demonstrates some codes that I've occasionally found useful in my day-to-day Rails programming.

Table 4.1   Example status codes

Status code	Description
200 OK	Everything is fine and here is your content.
201 Created	A new resource has been created and its location can be found in the Location HTTP response header.
307 Temporary Redirect	The requested resource resides temporarily under a different URI.
	Occasionally, you need to temporarily redirect the user to a different action, perhaps while some long-running process is happening or while the account of a particular resource's owner is suspended.

	This particular status code dictates that an HTTP response header named `Location` contain the URI of the resource that the client redirects to. Since the `render` method doesn't take a hash of response header fields, you have to set them manually prior to invoking `render`. Luckily, the `response` hash is in scope within controller methods, as in the following example:
	
	``ruby
	def paid_resource
	  if current_user.account_expired?
	    response.headers['Location'] =
	      account_url(current_user)
	    render text: "Account expired",
	status: 307
	  end
	end
	``

(continued)

---

4. For a full list of HTTP status codes, consult the spec at `http://www.w3.org/Protocols/rfc2616/rfc2616-sec10.html`

Table 4.1   Example status codes (continued)

Status code	Description
401 Unauthorized	Sometimes a user will not provide credentials to view a restricted resource or authentication, and/or authorization will fail. Assuming you're using a Basic or Digest HTTP Authentication scheme, when that happens, you should probably return a `401`.
403 Forbidden The server understood the request but is refusing to fulfill it.	I like to use `403` in conjunction with a short `render :text` message in situations where the client has requested a resource that is not normally available via the web application's interface.
	In other words, the request appears to have happened via artificial means. A human or robot, for reasons innocent or guilty (it doesn't matter), is trying to trick the server into doing something it isn't supposed to do.
	For example, my current Rails application is public-facing and is visited by the GoogleBot daily. Probably due to a bug existing at some point, the URL /favorites was indexed. Unfortunately, /favorites is only supposed to be available to logged-in users. However, once Google knows about a URL, it will keep coming back for it in the future. This is how I told it to stop:

	<pre>def index
	
	    return render nothing: true,
	
	    status: 403 unless logged_in?
	
	    @favorites = current_user.favorites.all
	
	end</pre>

404 Not Found The server cannot find the resource you requested.	You may choose to use `404` when a resource of a specific given id does not exist in your database (whether due to it being an invalid id or due to the resource having been deleted).
	For example, GET /people/2349594934896107 doesn't exist in our database at all, so what do we display? Do we render a show view with a flash message saying no person with that id exists? Not in our RESTful world. A 404 would be better.
	Moreover, if we happen to be using something like `paranoia` and we know that the resource used to exist in the past, we could respond with `410 Gone`.

(continued)

Table 4.1   Example status codes (continued)

Status code	Description
500 Internal Server Error	The server encountered an unexpected condition that prevented it from fulfilling the request. You probably know by now that this is the status code that Rails serves up if you have an error in your code.
503 Service Unavailable The server is temporarily unavailable.	The 503 code comes in handy when taking a site down for maintenance, particularly when upgrading RESTful web services.

4.4   Additional Layout Options

You can specify layout options at the controller class level if you want to reuse layouts for multiple actions.

```
class EventController < ActionController::Base
  layout "events", only: [:index, :new]
  layout "global", except: [:index, :new]
end
```

The `layout` method can accept a String, Symbol, or boolean, with a hash of arguments after.

String Determines the template name to use.

Symbol Call the method with this name, which is expected to return a string with a template name.

true Raises an argument error.

false Do not use a layout.

The optional arguments are either `:only` or `:except` and expect an array of action names that should or should not apply to the layout being specified.

4.5   Redirecting

The life cycle of a Rails application is divided into requests. Rendering a template, whether the default one or an alternate one—or, for that matter, rendering a partial, some text, or anything—is the final step in the handling of a request. Redirecting, however, means terminating the current request and asking the client to initiate a new one.

Look again at the example of the form-handling `create` method:

```
1 def create
2   if @event.save
```

```
3      flash[:notice] = "Event created!"
4      redirect_to :index
5   else
6      render :new
7   end
8 end
```

If the save operation succeeds, we store a message in the flash hash and redirect_
to a completely new action. In this case, it's the index action. The logic here is that
if the new Event record gets saved, the next order of business is to take the user back
to the top-level view.

The main reason to redirect rather than just render a template after creating or
editing a resource (really a POST action) has to do with browser reload behavior. If
you didn't redirect, the user would be prompted to resubmit the form if they hit the
back button or reload.

Sebastian Says ...

Which redirect is the right one? When you use Rails' redirect_to method,
you tell the user agent (i.e., the browser) to perform a new request for a different
URL. That response can mean different things, and it's why modern HTTP has
four different status codes for redirection. The old HTTP 1.0 had two codes:
301, a.k.a. *Moved Permanently*, and 302, a.k.a. *Moved Temporarily*.

A permanent redirect meant that the user agent should forget about the
old URL and use the new one from now on, updating any references it might
have kept (i.e., a bookmark or, in the case of Google, its search databases). A
temporary redirect was a *one-time only* affair. The original URL was still valid,
but for this particular request, the user agent should fetch a new resource from
the redirection URL.

But there was a problem: If the original request had been a POST, what
method should be used for the redirected request? For permanent redirects, it was
safe to assume the new request should be a GET, since that was the case in all
usage scenarios. But temporary redirects were used both for redirecting to a view
of a resource that had just been modified in the original POST request (which
happens to be the most common usage pattern) and for redirecting the entire
original POST request to a new URL that would take care of it.

HTTP 1.1 solved this problem with the introduction of two new status codes: 303, meaning *See Other*, and 307, meaning *Temporary Redirect*. A 303 redirect would tell the user agent to perform a GET request,
regardless of what the original verb was, whereas a 307 would always
use the same method used for the original request. These days, most

browsers handle 302 redirects the same way as 303—with a GET request, which is the argument used by the Rails Core team to keep using 302 in `redirect_to`. A 303 status would be the better alternative, because it leaves no room for interpretation (or confusion), but I guess nobody has found it annoying enough to push for a patch.

If you ever need a 307 redirect—say, to continue processing a POST request in a different action—you can always accomplish your own custom redirect by assigning a path to `response.header["Location"]` and then rendering with `render status: 307`.

4.5.1 The `redirect_to` Method

The `redirect_to` method takes two parameters:

```
redirect_to(target, response_status = {})
```

The `target` parameter takes one of several forms.

Hash The URL will be generated by calling `url_for` with the argument provided.

```
redirect_to action: "show", id: 5
```

Active Record object The URL will be generated by calling `url_for` with the object provided, which should generate a named URL for that record.

```
redirect_to post
```

String starting with protocol like `http://` Used directly as the target URL for redirection.

```
redirect_to "http://www.rubyonrails.org"
redirect_to articles_url
```

String not containing a protocol The current protocol and host is prepended to the argument and used for redirection.

```
redirect_to "/"
redirect_to articles_path
```

`:back` Back to the page that issued the request. Useful for forms that are triggered from multiple places. Shorthand for `redirect_to(request.env["HTTP _REFERRER"])`. When using `redirect_to :back`, if there is no referrer set, a `RedirectBackError` will be raised. You may specify some fallback behavior for this case by rescuing `RedirectBackError`.

Controllers

Redirection happens as a "302 Moved" header unless otherwise specified. The `response_status` parameter takes a hash of arguments. The code can be specified by name or number, as in the following examples:

```
redirect_to post_url(@post), status: :found
redirect_to :atom, status: :moved_permanently
redirect_to post_url(@post), status: 301
redirect_to :atom, status: 302
```

It is also possible to assign a flash message as part of the redirection. There are two special accessors for commonly used flash names `alert` and `notice`, as well as a general purpose `flash` bucket.

```
redirect_to post_url(@post), alert: "Watch it, mister!"
redirect_to post_url(@post), status: :found, notice: "Pay attention to the road."
redirect_to post_url(@post), status: 301, flash: {updated_post_id: @post.id }
redirect_to :atom, alert: "Something serious happened."
```

New to Rails 4 is the ability to register your own flash types by using the new `ActionController::Flash.add_flash_types` macro-style method.

```
class ApplicationController
  ...
  add_flash_types :error
end
```

When a flash type is registered, a special flash accessor similar to `alert` and `notice` becomes available to be used with `redirect_to`.

```
redirect_to post_url(@post), error: "Something went really wrong!"
```

Courtenay Says ...

Remember that redirect and render statements don't magically halt execution of your controller action method. To prevent `DoubleRenderError`, consider explicitly calling `return` after `redirect_to` or `render` like this:

```
1 def show
2   @user = User.find(params[:id])
3   if @user.activated?
4     render :activated and return
5   end
6   ...
7 end
```

4.6 Controller/View Communication

When a view template is rendered, it generally makes use of data that the controller has pulled from the database. In other words, the controller gets what it needs from the model layer and hands it off to the view.

The way Rails implements controller-to-view data handoffs is through instance variables. Typically, a controller action initializes one or more instance variables. Those instance variables can then be used by the view.

There's a bit of irony (and possible confusion for newcomers) in the choice of instance variables to share data between controllers and views. The main reason that instance variables exist is so that objects (whether `Controller` objects, `String` objects, and so on) can hold on to data that they don't share with other objects. When your controller action is executed, everything is happening in the context of a controller object—an instance of, say, `DemoController` or `EventController`. *Context* includes the fact that every instance variable in the code belongs to the controller instance.

When the view template is rendered, the context is that of a different object, an instance of `ActionView::Base`. That instance has its own instance variables and does not have access to those of the controller object.

So instance variables, on the face of it, are about the worst choice for a way for two objects to share data. However, it's possible to make it happen—or make it appear to happen. What Rails does is to loop through the controller object's variables and, for each one, create an instance variable for the view object with the same name and containing the same data.

It's kind of labor intensive for the framework: It's like copying over a grocery list by hand. But the end result is that things are easier for you, the programmer. If you're a Ruby purist, you might wince a little bit at the thought of instance variables serving to connect objects rather than separate them. On the other hand, being a Ruby purist should also include understanding the fact that you can do lots of different things in Ruby—such as copying instance variables in a loop. So there's nothing really un-Ruby-like about it. And it does provide a seamless connection, from the programmer's perspective, between a controller and the template it's rendering.

Stephen Says ...

I'm a cranky old man, and dammit, Rails is wrong, wrong, wrong. Using instance variables to share data with the view sucks. If you want to see how my Decent Exposure library helps you avoid this horrible practice, skip ahead to the section "Decent Exposure" in Chapter 10, "Action View."

4.7   Action Callbacks

Action callbacks enable controllers to run shared pre- and postprocessing code for its actions. These callbacks can be used to do authentication, caching, or auditing before the intended action is performed. Callback declarations are macro-style class methods—that is, they appear at the top of your controller method, inside the class context, before method definitions. We also leave off the parentheses around the method arguments, to emphasize their declarative nature, like this:

```
before_action :require_authentication
```

As with many other macro-style methods in Rails, you can pass as many symbols as you want to the callback method:

```
before_action :security_scan, :audit, :compress
```

Or you can break them out into separate lines, like this:

```
before_action :security_scan
before_action :audit
before_action :compress
```

You should make your action callback methods `protected` or `private`; otherwise, they might be callable as public actions on your controller (via the default route).

Tim Says ...

> In addition to `protected` and `private`, one can declare a method should never be dispatched with the more intention-revealing `hide_action`.

Importantly, action callbacks have access to `request`, `response`, and all the instance variables set by other callbacks in the chain or by the action (in the case of `after` callbacks). Action callbacks can set instance variables to be used by the requested action and often do so.

4.7.1   Action Callback Inheritance

Controller inheritance hierarchies share action callbacks downward. Your average Rails application has an `ApplicationController` from which all other controllers inherit, so if you wanted to add action callbacks that are always run no matter what, that would be the place to do so.

```
class ApplicationController < ActionController::Base
  after_action :compress
```

Subclasses can also add and/or skip already defined action callbacks without affecting the superclass. For example, consider the two related classes in Listing 4.1 and how they interact.

Listing 4.1 A Pair of Cooperating before Callbacks

```
 1 class BankController < ActionController::Base
 2   before_action :audit
 3
 4   protected
 5
 6   def audit
 7     # Record this controller's actions and parameters in an audit log.
 8   end
 9
10 end
11
12 class VaultController < BankController
13   before_action :verify_credentials
14
15   protected
16
17   def verify_credentials
18     # Make sure the user is allowed into the vault.
19   end
20
21 end
```

Any actions performed on `BankController` (or any of its subclasses) will cause the `audit` method to be called before the requested action is executed. On the `Vault Controller`, first the `audit` method is called, followed by `verify_credentials`, because that's the order in which the callbacks were specified. (Callbacks are executed in the class context where they're declared, and the `BankController` has to be loaded before `VaultController`, since it's the parent class.)

If the `audit` method happens to call `render` or `redirect_to` for whatever reason, `verify_credentials` and the requested action are never called. This is called halting the action callback chain.

4.7.2 Action Callback Types

An action callback can take one of three forms: method reference (symbol), external class, or block. The first is by far the most common and works by referencing a protected method somewhere in the inheritance hierarchy of the controller. In the bank example in Listing 4.1, both `BankController` and `VaultController` use this form.

4.7.2.1 Action Callback Classes

Using an external class makes for more easily reused generic callbacks, such as output compression. External callback classes are implemented by having a static callback method on any class and then passing this class to the action callback method, as in Listing 4.2. The name of the class method should match the type of callback desired (e.g., before, after, around).

Listing 4.2 An Output Compression Action Callback

```
1 class OutputCompressionActionCallback
2   def self.after(controller)
3     controller.response.body = compress(controller.response.body)
4   end
5 end
6
7 class NewspaperController < ActionController::Base
8   after_action OutputCompressionActionCallback
9 end
```

The method of the *action callback* class is passed the controller instance it is running in. It gets full access to the controller and can manipulate it as it sees fit. The fact that it gets an instance of the controller to play with also makes it seem like feature envy, and, frankly, I haven't had much use for this technique.

4.7.2.2 Inline Method

The inline method (using a block parameter to the action method) can be used to quickly do something small that doesn't require a lot of explanation or just as a quick test.

```
1 class WeblogController < ActionController::Base
2   before_action do
3     redirect_to new_user_session_path unless authenticated?
4   end
5 end
```

The block is executed in the context of the controller instance, using `instance_eval`. This means that the block has access to both the request and response objects complete with convenience methods for params, session, template, and assigns.

4.7.3 Action Callback Chain Ordering

Using `before_action` and `after_action` appends the specified callbacks to the existing chain. That's usually just fine, but sometimes you care more about the order in which the callbacks are executed. When that's the case, you can use `prepend_before_action` and `prepend_after_action`. Callbacks added by these methods will be put at the beginning of their respective chain and executed before the rest, like the example in Listing 4.3.

Listing 4.3   An Example of Prepending before Action Callbacks

```
1 class ShoppingController < ActionController::Base
2   before_action :verify_open_shop
3
4 class CheckoutController < ShoppingController
5   prepend_before_action :ensure_items_in_cart, :ensure_items_in_stock
```

The action callback chain for the `CheckoutController` is now `:ensure_items_in_cart`, `:ensure_items_in_stock`, `:verify_open_shop`. So if either of the ensure callbacks halts execution, we'll never get around to seeing if the shop is open.

You may pass multiple action callback arguments of each type as well as a block. If a block is given, it is treated as the last argument.

4.7.4   Around Action Callbacks

Around action callbacks wrap an action, executing code both before and after the action that they wrap. They may be declared as method references, blocks, or objects with an `around` class method.

To use a method as an `around_action`, pass a symbol naming the Ruby method. Use `yield` within the method to run the action.

For example, Listing 4.4 has an `around` callback that logs exceptions (not that you need to do anything like this in your application; it's just an example).

Listing 4.4   An `around_action` Callback to Log Exceptions

```
 1 around_action :catch_exceptions
 2
 3 private
 4
 5 def catch_exceptions
 6   yield
 7 rescue => exception
 8   logger.debug "Caught exception! #{exception}"
 9   raise
10 end
```

To use a block as an `around_action`, pass a block taking as `args` both the controller and the action parameters. You can't call `yield` from blocks in Ruby, so explicitly invoke `call` on the action parameter:

```
1 around_action do |controller, action|
2   logger.debug "before #{controller.action_name}"
```

```
3    action.call
4    logger.debug "after #{controller.action_name}"
5  end
```

To use an action callback object with `around_action`, pass an object responding to `:around`. With an action callback method, yield to the block like this:

```
1  around_action BenchmarkingActionCallback
2
3  class BenchmarkingActionCallback
4    def self.around(controller)
5      Benchmark.measure { yield }
6    end
7  end
```

4.7.5 Action Callback Chain Skipping

Declaring an action callback on a base class conveniently applies to its subclasses, but sometimes a subclass should skip some of the action callbacks it inherits from a superclass:

```
1  class ApplicationController < ActionController::Base
2    before_action :authenticate
3    around_action :catch_exceptions
4  end
5
6  class SignupController < ApplicationController
7    skip_before_action :authenticate
8  end
9
10 class HackedTogetherController < ApplicationController
11   skip_action_callback :catch_exceptions
12 end
```

4.7.6 Action Callback Conditions

Action callbacks may be limited to specific actions by declaring the actions to include or exclude, using `:only` or `:except` options. Both options accept single actions (like `only: :index`) or arrays of actions (`except: [:foo, :bar]`).

```
1  class Journal < ActionController::Base
2    before_action :authorize, only: [:edit, :delete]
3
4    around_action except: :index do |controller, action_block|
5      results = Profiler.run(&action_block)
6      controller.response.sub! "</body>", "#{results}</body>"
7    end
8
```

```
 9    private
10
11    def authorize
12      # Redirect to login unless authenticated.
13    end
14 end
```

4.7.7 Action Callback Chain Halting

The `before_action` and `around_action` methods may halt the request before the body of a controller action method is run. This is useful, for example, to deny access to unauthenticated users. As mentioned earlier, all you have to do to halt the before action chain is call `render` or `redirect_to`. After action callbacks will not be executed if the before action chain is halted.

Around action callbacks halt the request unless the action block is called. If an around action callback returns before yielding, it is effectively halting the chain and any after action callbacks will not be run.

4.8 Streaming

Rails has built-in support for streaming binary content back to the requesting client, as opposed to its normal duties rendering view templates.

4.8.1 **ActionController::Live**

Being introduced in Rails 4 is the `ActionController::Live` module, a controller mixin that enables the controller actions to stream on-the-fly generated data to the client.

The `ActionController::Live` mixin adds an I/O-like interface object named `stream` to the `response` object. Using `stream`, one can call `write` to immediately stream data to the client and `close` to explicitly close the stream. The `response` object is equivalent to the what you'd expect in the context of the controller and can be used to control various things in the HTTP response, such as the `Content-Type` header.

The following example demonstrates how one can stream a large amount of on-the-fly generated data to the browser:

```
1 class StreamingController < ApplicationController
2   include ActionController::Live
3
4   # Streams about 180 MB of generated data to the browser.
5   def stream
6     10_000_000.times do |i|
7       response.stream.write "This is line #{i}\n"
8     end
9   ensure
```

Controllers

```
10      response.stream.close
11    end
12 end
```

When using live streaming, there are a couple of things to take into consideration:

- All actions executed from `ActionController::Live` enabled controllers are run in a separate thread. This means the controller action code being executed must be threadsafe.

- A concurrent Ruby web server, such as puma,[5] is required to take advantage of live streaming.

- Headers must be added to the response before anything is written to the client.

- Streams must be closed once finished, otherwise a socket may be left open indefinitely.

For an interesting perspective on why live streaming was added into Rails and how to utilize it to serve server-sent events, make sure to read Aaron Patterson's blog post on the subject.[6]

4.8.2   View Streaming via **render stream: true**

By default, when a view is rendered in Rails, it first renders the template and then the layout of the view. When returning a response to a client, all required Active Record queries are run, and the entire rendered template is returned.

Introduced in version 3.1, Rails added support to stream views to the client. This allows for views to be rendered as they are processed, including only running Active Record scoped queries when they are needed. To achieve this, Rails reverses the ordering that views are rendered. The layout is rendered first to the client, and then each part of the template is processed.

To enable view streaming, pass the option `stream` to the `render` method.

```
1 class EventController < ActionController::Base
2   def index
3     @events = Events.all
4     render stream: true
5   end
6 end
```

---

5. Puma web server, http://puma.io/
6. http://tenderlovemaking.com/2012/07/30/is-it-live.html

This approach can only be used to render templates. To render other types of data, such as JSON, take a look at the section "`ActionController::Live`" in this chapter.

Rails also supports sending buffers and files with two methods in the `Action Controller::Streaming` module: `send_data` and `send_file`.

4.8.3 `send_data(data, options = {})`

The `send_data` method allows you to send textual or binary data in a buffer to the user as a named file. You can set options that affect the content type and apparent filename and alter whether an attempt is made to display the data inline with other content in the browser or the user is prompted to download it as an attachment.

4.8.3.1   Options

The `send_data` method has the following options:

:filename Suggests a filename for the browser to use.

:type Specifies an HTTP content type. Defaults to `'application/octet-stream'`.

:disposition Specifies whether the file will be shown inline or downloaded. Valid values are `inline` and `attachment` (default).

:status Specifies the status code to send with the response. Defaults to `'200 OK'`.

4.8.3.2   Usage Examples

In the following example, we are creating a download of a dynamically generated tarball:

```
send_data my_generate_tarball_method('dir'), filename: 'dir.tgz'
```

In the following example, we are sending a dynamic image to the browser, like for instance a captcha system:

```
1 require 'RMagick'
2
3 class CaptchaController < ApplicationController
4
5   def image
6     # create an RMagic canvas and render difficult to read text on it
7     ...
8
```

```
 9        img = canvas.flatten_images
10        img.format = "JPG"
11
12        # send it to the browser
13        send_data img.to_blob, disposition: 'inline', type: 'image/jpg'
14    end
15 end
```

4.8.4 `send_file(path, options = {})`

The `send_file` method sends an existing file down to the client using `Rack::Sendfile` middleware, which intercepts the response and replaces it with a web server specific `X-Sendfile` header. The web server then becomes responsible for writing the file contents to the client instead of Rails. This can dramatically reduce the amount of work accomplished in Ruby and takes advantage of the web servers optimized file delivery code.[7]

4.8.4.1 Options

Here are the options available for `send_file`:

`:filename` Suggests a filename for the browser to use. Defaults to `File.basename(path)`.

`:type` Specifies an HTTP content type. Defaults to `'application/octet-stream'`.

`:disposition` Specifies whether the file will be shown inline or downloaded. Valid values are `'inline'` and `'attachment'` (default).

`:status` Specifies the status code to send with the response. Defaults to `'200 OK'`.

`:url_based_filename` Should be set to `true` if you want the browser to guess the filename from the URL, which is necessary for I18n filenames on certain browsers (setting `:filename` overrides this option).

There's also a lot more to read about `Content-*` HTTP headers[8] if you'd like to provide the user with additional information that Rails doesn't natively support (such as `Content-Description`).

---

7. For more information, particularly about web server configuration, go to `http://rack.rubyforge.org/doc/Rack/Sendfile.html`

8. See the official spec at `http://www.w3.org/Protocols/rfc2616/rfc2615-sec14.html`

4.8.4.2 Security Considerations

Note that the `send_file` method can be used to read any file accessible to the user running the Rails server process, so be extremely careful to sanitize[9] the `path` parameter if it's in any way coming from untrusted users.

If you want a quick example, try the following controller code:

```
1 class FileController < ActionController::Base
2   def download
3     send_file(params[:path])
4   end
5 end
```

Give it a route:

```
get 'file/download' => 'file#download'
```

Then fire up your server and request any file on your system:

```
$ curl http://localhost:3000/file/download?path=//etc.hosts
##
# Host Database
#
# localhost is used to configure the loopback interface
# when the system is booting.  Do not change this entry.
##
127.0.0.1    localhost
255.255.255.255 broadcasthost
::1              localhost
fe80::1%lo0 localhost
```

Courtenay Says ...

There are few legitimate reasons to serve static files through Rails. Unless you are protecting content, I strongly recommend you cache the file after sending it. There are a few ways to do this. Since a correctly configured web server will serve files in `public/` and bypass `rails`, the easiest is to just copy the newly generated file to the `public` directory after sending it:

```
1 public_dir = File.join(Rails.root, 'public', controller_path)
2 FileUtils.mkdir_p(public_dir)
3 FileUtils.cp(filename, File.join(public_dir, filename))
```

All subsequent views of this resource will be served by the web server.

---

9. Heiko Webers has an old yet still useful write-up about sanitizing filenames at http://www .rorsecurity.info/2007/03/27/working-with-files-in-rails/

4.8.4.3   Usage Examples

Here's the simplest example, just a simple zip file download:

```
send_file '/path/to.zip'
```

Sending a JPG to be displayed inline requires specification of the MIME content-type:

```
send_file '/path/to.jpg',
          type: 'image/jpeg',
          disposition: 'inline'
```

This will show a 404 HTML page in the browser. We append a `charset` declaration to the MIME type information:

```
send_file '/path/to/404.html,
          type: 'text/html; charset=utf-8',
          status: 404
```

How about streaming an FLV file to a browser-based Flash video player?

```
send_file @video_file.path,
          filename: video_file.title + '.flv',
          type: 'video/x-flv',
          disposition: 'inline'
```

Regardless of how you do it, you may wonder why you would need a mechanism to send files to the browser anyway, since it already has one built in that requests files from the `public` directory. Well, many times a web application will front files that need to be protected from public access. (It's a common requirement for membership-based adult websites.)

4.9   Variants

New to Rails 4.1, Action Pack variants add the ability to render different HTML, JSON, and XML templates based on some criteria. To illustrate, assuming we have an application that requires specific templates to be rendered for iPhone devices only, we can set a request variant in a `before_action` callback.

```
1 class ApplicationController < ActionController::Base
2   before_action :set_variant
3
4   protected
5
6   def set_variant
7     request.variant = :mobile if request.user_agent =~ /iPhone/i
8   end
9 end
```

Note

Note that `request.variant` can be set based on any arbitrary condition, such as the existence of certain request headers, the subdomain, the current user, the API version, and so on.

Next, in a controller action, we can explicitly respond to variants like any other format. This includes the ability to execute code specific to the format by supplying a block to the declaration.

```
1  class PostsController < ApplicationController
2    def index
3      ...
4      respond_to do |format|
5        format.html do |html|
6          html.mobile do # renders app/views/posts/index.html+mobile.haml
7            @mobile_only_variable = true
8          end
9        end
10     end
11   end
12 end
```

By default, if no `respond_to` block is declared within your action, Action Pack will automatically render the correct variant template if one exists in your views directory.

Variants are a powerful new feature in Action Pack that can be utilized for more than just rendering views based on a user agent. Since a variant can be set based on any condition, it can be utilized for a variety of use cases, such as rolling out features to a certain group of application users or even A/B testing a template.

4.10   Conclusion

In this chapter, we covered some concepts at the very core of how Rails works: the dispatcher and how controllers render views. Importantly, we covered the use of controller action callbacks, which you will use constantly for all sorts of purposes. The Action Controller API is fundamental knowledge, which you need to understand well along your way to becoming an expert Rails programmer.

Moving on, we'll leave Action Pack and head over to the other major component API of Rails: Active Record.

Controllers

CHAPTER 5

Working with Active Record

An object that wraps a row in a database table or view, encapsulates the database access, and adds domain logic on that data.

—Martin Fowler, *Patterns of Enterprise Architecture*

The Active Record pattern, identified by Martin Fowler in his seminal work, *Patterns of Enterprise Architecture*, maps one domain class to one database table and one instance of that class to each row of that database. It is a simple approach that, while not perfectly applicable in all cases, provides a powerful framework for database access and object persistence in your application.

The Rails Active Record framework includes mechanisms for representing models and their relationships, CRUD (create, read, update, and delete) operations, complex searches, validation, callbacks, and many more features. It relies heavily on *convention over configuration*, so it's easy to use when you're creating a new database schema that can follow those conventions. However, Active Record also provides configuration settings that let you adapt it to work well with legacy database schemas that don't necessarily conform to Rails conventions.

According to Martin Fowler, delivering the keynote address at the inaugural Rails conference in 2006, Ruby on Rails has successfully taken the Active Record pattern much further than anyone imagined it could go. It shows you what you can achieve when you have a single-minded focus on a set of ideals, which in the case of Rails is simplicity.

Active Record

5.1 The Basics

For the sake of completeness, let's briefly review the basics of how Active Record works. In order to create a new model class, the first thing you do is to declare it as a subclass of `ActiveRecord::Base`, using Ruby's class extension syntax:

```
class Client < ActiveRecord::Base
end
```

By convention, an Active Record class named `Client` will be mapped to the `clients` table. Rails understands pluralization, as covered in the section "Pluralization" in Chapter 11, "All about Helpers." Also by convention, Active Record will expect an `id` column to use as the primary key. It should be an integer and incrementing of the key should be managed automatically by the database server when creating new records. Note how the class itself makes no mention of the table name, columns, or their data types.

Each instance of an Active Record class provides access to the data from one row of the backing database table in an object-oriented manner. The columns of that row are represented as attributes of the object, using straightforward-type conversions (Ruby strings for varchars, Ruby dates for dates, etc.) and with no default data validation. Attributes are inferred from the column definition pertaining to the tables with which they're linked. Adding, removing, and changing attributes and their types are done by changing the columns of the table in the database.

When you're running a Rails server in development mode, changes to the database schema are reflected in the Active Record objects immediately via the web browser. However, if you make changes to the schema while you have your Rails console running, the changes will not be reflected automatically, although it is possible to pick up changes manually by typing `reload!` at the console.

Courtenay Says ...

Active Record is a great example of the Rails "Golden Path." If you keep within its limitations, you can go far and fast. Stray from the path, and you might get stuck in the mud. This Golden Path involves many conventions, like naming your tables in the plural form ("users"). It's common for developers who are new to Rails and rival web-framework evangelists to complain about how tables must be named in a particular manner, how there are no constraints in the database layer, that foreign keys are handled all wrong, that enterprise systems must have composite primary keys, and more. Get the complaining out of your system now, because all these defaults are simply defaults and in most cases can be overridden with a single line of code or a plugin.

5.2   Macro-Style Methods

Most of the important classes you write while coding a Rails application are configured using what I call macro-style method invocations (also known in some circles
as a domain-specific language or DSL). Basically, the idea is to have a highly readable block of code at the top of your class that makes it immediately clear how it is
configured.

Macro-style invocations are usually placed at the top of the file, and for good
reason. Those methods declaratively tell Rails how to manage instances, perform
data validation and callbacks, and relate with other models. Many of them do
some amount of metaprogramming, meaning that they participate in adding
behavior to your class at runtime in the form of additional instance variables and
methods.

5.2.1   Relationship Declarations

For example, look at the `Client` class with some relationships declared. We'll talk
about associations extensively in Chapter 7, "Active Record Associations," but all I
want to do right now is to illustrate what I'm talking about when I say "macro-style":

```
1 class Client < ActiveRecord::Base
2   has_many :billing_codes
3   has_many :billable_weeks
4   has_many :timesheets, through: :billable_weeks
5 end
```

As a result of those three `has_many` declarations, the `Client` class gains at least
three new attributes—proxy objects that let you manipulate the associated collections interactively.

I still remember the first time I sat with an experienced Java programmer friend
of mine to teach him some Ruby and Rails. After minutes of profound confusion,
an almost visible light bulb appeared over his head as he proclaimed, "Oh! They're
methods!"

Indeed, they're regular old method calls in the context of the class object. We
leave the parentheses off to emphasize the declarative intention. That's a style issue,
but it just doesn't feel right to me with the parentheses in place, as in the following
code snippet:

```
1 class Client < ActiveRecord::Base
2   has_many(:billing_codes)
3   has_many(:billable_weeks)
4   has_many(:timesheets, through: :billable_weeks)
5 end
```

When the Ruby interpreter loads `client.rb`, it executes those `has_many` methods, which, again, are defined as class methods of Active Record's `Base` class. They are executed in the context of the `Client` class, adding attributes that are subsequently available to `Client` instances. It's a programming model that is potentially strange to newcomers but quickly becomes second nature to the Rails programmer.

5.2.2   Convention over Configuration

Convention over configuration is one of the guiding principles of Ruby on Rails. If we follow Rails conventions, very little explicit configuration is needed, which stands in stark contrast to the reams of configuration that are required to get even a simple application running in other technologies.

It's not that a newly bootstrapped Rails application comes with default configuration in place already, reflecting the conventions that will be used. It's that the conventions are baked into the framework, actually hard-coded into its behavior, and you need to override the default behavior with explicit configuration when applicable.

It's also worth mentioning that most configuration happens in close proximity to what you're configuring. You will see associations, validations, and callback declarations at the top of most Active Record models.

I suspect that the first explicit configuration (over convention) that many of us deal with in Active Record is the mapping between class name and database table, since by default Rails assumes that our database name is simply the pluralized form of our class name.

5.2.3   Setting Names Manually

The `table_name` and `primary_key` setter methods let you use any table and primary names you'd like, but you'll have to specify them explicitly in your model class.

```
1 class Client < ActiveRecord::Base
2   self.table_name = "CLIENT"
3   self.primary_key = "CLIENT_ID"
4 end
```

It's only a couple of extra lines per model, but on a large application it adds unnecessary complexity, so don't do it if you don't absolutely have to.

When you're not at liberty to dictate the naming guidelines for your database schema, such as when a separate DBA group controls all database schemas, then you probably don't have a choice. But if you have flexibility, you should really just follow Rails conventions. They might not be what you're used to, but following them will save you time and unnecessary headaches.

5.2.4   Legacy Naming Schemes

If you are working with legacy schemas, you may be tempted to automatically set `table_name` everywhere, whether you need it or not. Before you get accustomed to doing that, learn the additional options available that might just be more DRY ("don't repeat yourself") and make your life easier.

Let's assume you need to turn off table pluralization altogether; you would set the following attribute to your `config/application.rb`:

```
config.active_record.pluralize_table_names = false
```

There are various other useful attributes of `ActiveRecord::Base`, provided for configuring Rails to work with legacy naming schemes.

5.2.4.1   `primary_key_prefix_type`

Accessor for the prefix type that will be prepended to every primary key column name. If `:table_name` is specified, Active Record will look for `tableid` instead of `id` as the primary column. If `:table_name_with_underscore` is specified, Active Record will look for `table_id` instead of `id`.

5.2.4.2   `table_name_prefix`

Some departments prefix table names with the name of the database. Set this attribute accordingly to avoid having to include the prefix in all your model class names.

5.2.4.3   `table_name_suffix`

Similar to prefix but adds a common ending to all table names.

5.3   Defining Attributes

The list of attributes associated with an Active Record model class is not coded explicitly. At runtime, the Active Record model examines the database schema directly from the server. Adding, removing, and changing attributes and their type is done by manipulating the database itself via Active Record migrations.

The practical implication of the Active Record pattern is that you have to define your database table structure and make sure it exists in the database prior to working with your persistent models. Some people may have issues with that design philosophy, especially if they're coming from a background in top-down design.

The Rails way is undoubtedly to have model classes that map closely to your database schema. On the other hand, remember you can have models that are simple Ruby classes and do not inherit from `ActiveRecord::Base`. Among other things, it is common to use non–Active Record model classes to encapsulate data and logic for the view layer.

5.3.1   Default Attribute Values

Migrations let you define default attribute values by passing a `:default` option to the `column` method, but most of the time you'll want to set default attribute values at the model layer, not the database layer. Default values are part of your domain logic and should be kept together with the rest of the domain logic of your application in the model layer.

A common example is the case when your model should return the string "n/a" instead of a `nil` (or empty) string for an attribute that has not been populated yet. Seems simple enough and it's a good way to learn how attributes exist at runtime.

To begin, let's whip up a quick spec describing the desired behavior:

```
1 describe TimesheetEntry do
2   it "has a category of 'n/a' if not available" do
3     entry = TimesheetEntry.new
4     expect(entry.category).to eq('n/a')
5   end
6 end
```

We run that spec and it fails, as expected. Active Record doesn't provide us with any class-level methods to define default values for models declaratively. So it seems we'll have to create an explicit attribute accessor that provides a default value.

Normally, attribute accessors are handled magically by Active Record's internals, but in this case we're overriding the magic with an explicit getter. All we need to do is define a method with the same name as the attribute and use Ruby's `||` operator, which will short-circuit if `@category` is not nil.

```
1 class TimesheetEntry < ActiveRecord::Base
2   def category
3     @category || 'n/a'
4   end
5 end
```

Now we run the spec and it passes. Great. Are we done? Not quite. We should test a case when the real category value should be returned. I'll insert an example with a not-nil category.

```
1 describe TimesheetEntry do
2   it "returns category when available" do
3     entry = TimesheetEntry.new(category: "TR4W")
4     expect(entry.category).to eq("TR4W")
```

```
5    end
6
7    it "has a category of 'n/a' if not available" do
8      entry = TimesheetEntry.new
9      expect(entry.category).to eq('n/a')
10   end
11 end
```

Uh-oh. The first spec fails. Seems our default "n/a" string is being returned no matter what. That means that @category must not be getting set. Should we even know if it is getting set or not? It is an implementation detail of Active Record, is it not?

The fact that Rails does not use instance variables like @category to store the model attributes is in fact an implementation detail. But model instances have a couple of methods—write_attribute and read_attribute— conveniently provided by Active Record for the purposes of overriding default accessors, which is exactly what we're trying to do. Let's fix our Timesheet Entry class.

```
1 class TimesheetEntry < ActiveRecord::Base
2   def category
3     read_attribute(:category) || 'n/a'
4   end
5 end
```

Now the spec passes. How about a simple example of using write_attribute?

```
1 class SillyFortuneCookie < ActiveRecord::Base
2   def message=(txt)
3     write_attribute(:message, txt + ' in bed')
4   end
5 end
```

Alternatively, both of these examples could have been written with the shorter forms of reading and writing attributes, using square brackets.

```
1 class Specification < ActiveRecord::Base
2   def tolerance
3     self[:tolerance] || 'n/a'
4   end
5 end
6
7 class SillyFortuneCookie < ActiveRecord::Base
8   def message=(txt)
9     self[:message] = txt + ' in bed'
10  end
11 end
```

5.3.2   Serialized Attributes

One of Active Record's coolest features is the ability to mark a column of type `text` as being serialized. Whatever object (more accurately, graph of objects) you assign to that attribute will be stored in the database as YAML, Ruby's native serialization format.

Sebastian Says ...

Text columns usually have a maximum size of 64K, and if your serialized attributes exceed the size constraints, you'll run into a lot of errors. On the other hand, if your serialized attributes are that big, you might want to rethink what you're doing. At least move them into a separate table and use a larger column type if your server allows it.

One of the first things that new Rails developers do when they discover the `se-rialize` declaration is to use it to store a hash of arbitrary objects related to user preferences. Why bother with the complexity of a separate preferences table if you can denormalize that data into the users table instead?

```
1 class User < ActiveRecord::Base
2   serialize :preferences, Hash
3 end
```

The optional second parameter (used in the example) takes a class that limits the type of object that can be stored. The serialized object must be of that class on retrieval, or `SerializationTypeMismatch` will be raised.

The API does not give us an easy way to set a default value. That's unfortunate, because it would be nice to be able to assume that our preferences attribute is already initialized when we want to use it.

```
1 user = User.new
2 # The following line will raise NoMethodError
3 # unless preferences has a default:
4 user.preferences[:inline_help] = false
```

Unless a value has already been set for the attribute, it's going to be `nil`. You might be tempted to set a default YAML string for the serialized attribute at the database level so that it's not `nil` when you're using a newly created object:

```
add_column :users, :preferences, :text, default: "--- {}"
```

However, that approach won't work with MySQL 5.x, which ignores default values for binary and text columns. One possible solution is to overload the attribute's reader method with logic that sets the default value if it's nil.

```
def preferences
  read_attribute(:preferences) || write_attribute(:preferences, {})
end
```

I prefer this method over the alternative, using an `after_initialize` callback, because it incurs a small performance hit only when the preferences attribute is actually used and not at instantiation time of every single `User` object in your system.

5.3.3 `ActiveRecord::Store`

With version 3.2, Rails introduced the `store` declaration, which uses `serialize` behind the scenes to declare a single-column key/value store.

```
class User < ActiveRecord::Base
  store :preferences
end
```

An added benefit of using `store` is that its assigned serialized attribute is set to an empty hash by default, therefore removing the need to set a default by overriding the attribute's reader method or setting one at the database level, as was done in the previous section.

It's possible to add an `:accessors` option to the `store` declaration, which declares read/write accessors in your Active Record model.

```
store :preferences, accessors: [:inline_help]
```

Writing to a store accessor method will create a key/value pair within the serialized hash attribute, as shown in the following example:

```
>> user = User.new
=> #<User id: nil, preferences: {}, ...>
>> user.inline_help = false
=> false
>> user.preferences
=> {"inline_help"=>false}
```

Alternatively, you can use the `store_accessor` declaration to declare read/write accessors for a serialized attribute.

```
store_accessor :inline_help
```

Active Record

5.4 CRUD: Create, Read, Update, and Delete

The four standard operations of a database system combine to form a popular acronym: CRUD. It sounds somewhat negative, because, as a synonym for *garbage* or *unwanted accumulation*, the word *crud* in English has a rather bad connotation. However, in Rails circles, use of the word CRUD is benign. In fact, as in earlier chapters, designing your app to function primarily as RESTful CRUD operations is considered a best practice!

5.4.1 Creating New Active Record Instances

The most straightforward way to create a new instance of an Active Record model is by using a regular Ruby constructor: the class method new. New objects can be instantiated as either empty (by omitting parameters) or preset with attributes but not yet saved. Just pass a hash with key names matching the associated table column names. In both instances, valid attribute keys are determined by the column names of the associated table—hence you can't have attributes that aren't part of the table columns.

You can find out if an Active Record object is saved by looking at the value of its id or, programmatically, by using the methods new_record? and persisted?:

```
>> c = Client.new
=> #<Client id: nil, name: nil, code: nil>
>> c.new_record?
=> true
>> c.persisted?
=> false
```

Active Record constructors take an optional block, which can be used to do additional initialization. The block is executed after any passed-in attributes are set on the instance:

```
>> c = Client.new do |client|
?> client.name = "Nile River Co."
>> client.code = "NRC"
>> end
=> #<Client id: 1, name: "Nile River Co.", code: "NRC">
```

Active Record has a handy-dandy create class method that creates a new instance, persists it to the database, and returns it in one operation:

```
>> c = Client.create(name: "Nile River, Co.", code: "NRC")
=> #<Client id: 1, name: "Nile River, Co.", code: "NRC" ...>
```

The create method takes an optional block, just like new.

5.4.2 Reading Active Record Objects

Finding an existing object by its primary key is very simple and is probably one of the first things we all learn about Rails when we first pick up the framework. Just invoke `find` with the key of the specific instance you want to retrieve. Remember that if an instance is not found, a `RecordNotFound` exception is raised.

```
>> first_project = Project.find(1)
=>   #<Project id: 1 ...>
>> boom_client = Client.find(99)
ActiveRecord::RecordNotFound: Couldn't find Client with ID=99
>> all_clients = Client.all
=> #<ActiveRecord::Relation [#<Client id: 1, name: "Paper Jam Printers",
   code: "PJP" ...>, #<Client id: 2, name: "Goodness Steaks",
   code: "GOOD_STEAKS" ...>]>
>> first_client = Client.first
=> #<Client id: 1, name: "Paper Jam Printers", code: "PJP" ...>
```

By the way, it is entirely common for methods in Ruby to return different types depending on the parameters used, as illustrated in the example. Depending on how `find` is invoked, you will get either a single Active Record object or an array of them.

For convenience, `first`, `last`, and `all` also exist as syntactic sugar wrappers around the find method.

```
>> Product.last
=> #<Product id: 1, name: "leaf", sku: nil,
   created_at: "2010-01-12 03:34:41", updated_at: "2010-01-12 03:34:41">
```

Finally, the `find` method also understands arrays of ids and raises a `RecordNotFound` exception if it can't find all the ids specified:

```
>> Product.find([1, 2])
ActiveRecord::RecordNotFound: Couldn't find all Products with IDs (1,
 2) (found 1 results, but was looking for 2)
```

5.4.3 Reading and Writing Attributes

After you have retrieved a model instance from the database, you can access each of its columns in several ways. The easiest (and clearest to read) is simply with dot notation:

```
>> first_client.name
=> "Paper Jam Printers"
>> first_client.code
=> "PJP"
```

The private `read_attribute` method of Active Record, covered briefly in an earlier section, is useful to know about and comes in handy when you want to override a default attribute accessor. To illustrate, while still in the Rails console, I'll go ahead and reopen the Client class on the fly and override the name accessor to return the value from the database, only reversed:

```
>> class Client < ActiveRecord::Base
>>   def name
>>     read_attribute(:name).reverse
>>   end
>> end
=> nil
>> first_client.name
=> "sretnirP maJ repaP"
```

Hopefully it's not too painfully obvious for me to demonstrate why you need read_ attribute in that scenario. Recursion is a bitch if it's unexpected:

```
>> class Client < ActiveRecord::Base
>>   def name
>>     self.name.reverse
>>   end
>> end
=> nil
>> first_client.name
SystemStackError: stack level too deep
        from (irb):21:in 'name'
        from (irb):21:in 'name'
        from (irb):24
```

As can be expected by the existence of a read_attribute method (and as we covered earlier in the chapter), there is also a write_attribute method that lets you change attribute values. Just as with attribute getter methods, you can override the setter methods and provide your own behavior:

```
1 class Project < ActiveRecord::Base
2   # The description for a project cannot be changed to a blank string.
3   def description=(new_value)
4     write_attribute(:description, new_value) unless new_value.blank?
5   end
6 end
```

The preceding example illustrates a way to do basic validation, since it checks to make sure that a value is not blank before allowing assignment. However, as we'll see in Chapter 8, "Validations," there are better ways to do this.

5.4.3.1   Hash Notation

Yet another way to access attributes is using the `[attribute_name]` operator, which lets you access the attribute as if it were a regular hash.

```
>> first_client['name']
=> "Paper Jam Printers"
>> first_client[:name]
=> "Paper Jam Printers"
```

String versus Symbol

Many Rails methods accept symbol and string parameters interchangeably, and that is potentially very confusing. Which is more correct? The general rule is to use symbols when the string is a name for something and a string when it's a value. You should probably be using symbols when it comes to keys of options, hashes, and the like.

5.4.3.2   The **attributes** Method

There is also an `attributes` method that returns a hash with each attribute and its corresponding value as returned by `read_attribute`. If you use your own custom attribute reader and writer methods, it's important to remember that `attributes` will not use custom attribute readers when accessing its values, but `attributes=` (which lets you do mass assignment) does invoke custom attribute writers.

```
>> first_client.attributes
=> {"name"=>"Paper Jam Printers", "code"=>"PJP", "id"=>1}
```

Being able to grab a hash of all attributes at once is useful when you want to iterate over all of them or pass them in bulk to another function. Note that the hash returned from `attributes` is not a reference to an internal structure of the Active Record object. It is copy, which means that changing its values will have no effect on the object it came from.

```
>> atts = first_client.attributes
=> {"name"=>"Paper Jam Printers", "code"=>"PJP", "id"=>1}
>> atts["name"] = "Def Jam Printers"
=> "Def Jam Printers"
>> first_client.attributes
=> {"name"=>"Paper Jam Printers", "code"=>"PJP", "id"=>1}
```

Active Record

To make changes to an Active Record object's attributes in bulk, it is possible to pass a hash to the `attributes` writer.

5.4.4   Accessing and Manipulating Attributes before They Are Typecast

The Active Record connection adapters—classes that implement behavior specific to databases—fetch results as strings, and Rails takes care of converting them to other data types if necessary based on the type of the database column. For instance, integer types are cast to instances of Ruby's `Fixnum` class, and so on.

Even if you're working with a new instance of an Active Record object and have passed in constructor values as strings, they will be typecast to their proper type when you try to access those values as attributes.

Sometimes you want to be able to read (or manipulate) the raw attribute data without having the column-determined typecast run its course first, and that can be done by using the `attribute_before_type_cast` accessors that are automatically created in your model.

For example, consider the need to deal with currency strings typed in by your end users. Unless you are encapsulating currency values in a currency class (highly recommended, by the way), you need to deal with those pesky dollar signs and commas. Assuming that our `Timesheet` model had a rate attribute defined as a `:decimal` type, the following code would strip out the extraneous characters before typecasting for the save operation:

```
1 class Timesheet < ActiveRecord::Base
2   before_validation :fix_rate
3
4   def fix_rate
5     self[:rate] = rate_before_type_cast.tr('$,','')
6   end
7 end
```

5.4.5   Reloading

The `reload` method does a query to the database and resets the attributes of an Active Record object. The optional options argument is passed to find when reloading so you may do, for example, `record.reload(lock: true)` to reload the same record with an exclusive row lock. (See the section "Database Locking" later in this chapter.)

5.4.6   Cloning

Producing a copy of an Active Record object is done simply by calling `clone`, which produces a shallow copy of that object. It is important to note that no associations will get copied, even though they are stored internally as instance variables.

5.4.7   Custom SQL Queries

The `find_by_sql` class method takes an SQL select query and returns an array of Active Record objects based on the results. Here's a bare-bones example, which you would never actually need to do in a real application:

```
>> Client.find_by_sql("select * from clients")
=> [#<Client id: 1, name: "Paper Jam Printers",
    code: "PJP" ...>, #<Client id: 2, name: "Goodness Steaks",
    code: "GOOD_STEAKS" ...>]
```

I can't stress this enough: You should take care to use `find_by_sql` only when you really need it! For one, it reduces database portability. When you use Active Record's normal find operations, Rails takes care of handling differences between the underlying databases for you.

Note that Active Record already has a ton of built-in functionality abstracting SELECT statements—functionality that it would be very unwise to reinvent. There are lots of cases where, at first glance, it might seem that you might need to use `find_by_sql`, but you actually don't. A common case is when doing a LIKE query:

```
>> Client.find_by_sql("select * from clients where code like 'A%'")
=> [#<Client id: 1, name: "Amazon, Inc" ...>]
```

It turns out that you can easily put that LIKE clause into a conditions option:

```
>> param = "A"
>> Client.where("code like ?", "#{param}%")
=> [#<Client id: 1, name: "Amazon, Inc" ...>]
```

Preventing SQL Injection Attacks

Under the covers, Rails sanitizes[1] your SQL code, provided that you parameterize your query. Active Record executes your SQL using the `connection` `.select_all` method, iterating over the resulting array of hashes and invoking your Active Record's `initialize` method for each row in the result set.
What would this section's example look like unparameterized?

```
>> Client.where("code like '#{params[:code]}%'")
=> [#<Client id: 1, name: "Amazon, Inc" ...>] # NOOOOO!
```

---

1. Sanitization prevents SQL injection attacks. For more information about SQL injection and Rails, see http://guides.rubyonrails.org/security.html#sql-injection

Active Record

Notice the missing question mark as a variable placeholder. Always remember that interpolating user-supplied values into an SQL fragment of any type is very unsafe! Just imagine what would happen to your project if a malicious user called that unsafe find with `params[:code]` set to the following:

```
1 "Amazon'; DELETE FROM users;'
```

This particular example might fail in your own experiments. The outcome is very specific to the type of database/driver that you're using. Some popular databases drivers may even have features that help to prevent SQL injection. I still think it's better to be safe than sorry.

The `count_by_sql` method works in a manner similar to `find_by_sql`.

```
>> Client.count_by_sql("select count(*) from clients")
=> 132
```

Again, you should have a special reason to be using it instead of the more concise alternatives provided by Active Record.

5.4.8   The Query Cache

By default, Rails attempts to optimize performance by turning on a simple query cache. It is a hash stored on the current thread—one for every active database connection. (Most Rails processes will have just one.)

Whenever a `find` (or any other type of select operation) happens and the query cache is active, the corresponding result set is stored in a hash with the SQL that was used to query for them as the key. If the same SQL statement is used again in another operation, the cached result set is used to generate a new set of model objects instead of hitting the database again.

You can enable the query cache manually by wrapping operations in a `cache` block, as in the following example:

```
1 User.cache do
2   puts User.first
3   puts User.first
4   puts User.first
5 end
```

Check your `development.log` and you should see the following entries:

```
User Load (0.1ms)  SELECT "users".* FROM "users" ORDER BY "users"."id"
ASC LIMIT 1
CACHE (0.0ms)  SELECT "users".* FROM "users" ORDER BY "users"."id"
```

```
ASC LIMIT 1 LIMIT 1
CACHE (0.0ms)  SELECT "users".* FROM "users" ORDER BY "users"."id"
ASC LIMIT 1
```

The database was queried only once. Try a similar experiment in your own console without the `cache` block and you'll see that three separate `User Load` events are logged.

Save and delete operations result in the cache being cleared to prevent propagation of instances with invalid states. If you find it necessary to do so for whatever reason, call the `clear_query_cache` class method to clear out the query cache manually.

5.4.8.1   Logging

The log file indicates when data are being read from the query cache instead of the database. Just look for lines starting with CACHE instead of a Model Load.

```
Place Load (0.1ms)  SELECT * FROM places WHERE (places.id = 15749)
CACHE (0.0ms) SELECT * FROM places WHERE (places.id = 15749)
CACHE (0.0ms)  SELECT * FROM places WHERE (places.id = 15749)
```

5.4.8.2   Default Query Caching in Controllers

For performance reasons, Active Record's query cache is turned on by default for the processing of controller actions.

5.4.8.3   Limitations

The Active Record query cache was purposely kept very simple. Since it literally keys cached model instances on the SQL that was used to pull them out of the database, it can't connect multiple `find` invocations that are phrased differently but have the same semantic meaning and results.

For example, "select foo from bar where id = 1" and "select foo from bar where id = 1 limit 1" are considered different queries and will result in two distinct cache entries.

5.4.9   Updating

The simplest way to manipulate attribute values is simply to treat your Active Record object as a plain old Ruby object, meaning via direct assignment using `myprop=(some_value)`.

There are a number of other different ways to update Active Record objects, as illustrated in this section. First, let's look at how to use the `update` class method of `ActiveRecord::Base`:

```
1 class ProjectController < ApplicationController
2   def update
```

```
 3      Project.update(params[:id], params[:project])
 4      redirect_to projects_path
 5    end
 6
 7    def mass_update
 8      Project.update(params[:projects].keys, params[:projects].
          values])
 9      redirect_to projects_path
10    end
11  end
```

The first form of update takes a single numeric id and a hash of attribute values, while the second form takes a list of ids and a list of values and is useful in scenarios where a form submission from a web page with multiple updateable rows is being processed.

The update class method does invoke validation first and will not save a record that fails validation. However, it returns the object whether or not the validation passes. That means that if you want to know whether or not the validation passed, you need to follow up the call to update with a call to valid?.

```
 1  class ProjectController < ApplicationController
 2    def update
 3      project = Project.update(params[:id], params[:project])
 4      if project.valid? # Uh-oh, do we want to run validate again?
 5        redirect_to project
 6      else
 7        render 'edit'
 8      end
 9    end
10  end
```

A problem is that now we are calling valid? twice, since the update call also called it. Perhaps a better option is to use the update instance method once as part of an if statement:

```
 1  class ProjectController < ApplicationController
 2    def update
 3      project = Project.find(params[:id])
 4      if project.update(params[:project])
 5        redirect_to project
 6      else
 7        render 'edit'
 8      end
 9    end
10  end
```

And of course, if you've done some basic Rails programming, you'll recognize that pattern, since it is used in the generated scaffolding code. The `update` method takes a hash of attribute values and returns true or false, depending on whether the save was successful or not, which is dependent on validation passing.

5.4.10   Updating by Condition
Active Record has another class method useful for updating multiple records at once: `update_all`. It maps closely to the way that you would think of using an SQL `update...where` statement. The `update_all` method takes two parameters, the set part of the SQL statement and the conditions, expressed as part of a where clause. The method returns the number of records updated.

I think this is one of those methods that is generally more useful in a scripting context than in a controller method, but you might feel differently. Here is a quick example of how I might go about reassigning all the Rails projects in the system to a new project manager.

```
Project.update_all({manager: 'Ron Campbell'}, technology: 'Rails')
```

The `update_all` method also accepts string parameters, which allows you to leverage the power of SQL!

```
Project.update_all("cost = cost * 3", "lower(technology) LIKE '%microsoft%'")
```

5.4.11   Updating a Particular Instance
The most basic way to update an Active Record object is to manipulate its attributes directly and then call `save`. It's worth noting that `save` will insert a record in the database if necessary or update an existing record with the same primary key.

```
>> project = Project.find(1)
>> project.manager = 'Brett M.'
>> project.save
=> true
```

The `save` method will return true if it was successful or false if it failed for any reason. There is another method—`save!`—that will use exceptions instead. Which one to use depends on whether you plan to deal with errors right away or delegate the problem to another method further up the chain.

It's mostly a matter of style, although the nonbang save and update methods that return a boolean value are often used in controller actions, as the clause for an if condition:

```
 1 class StoryController < ApplicationController
 2   def points
 3     story = Story.find(params[:id])
 4     if story.update_attribute(:points, params[:value])
 5       render text: "#{story.name} updated"
 6     else
 7       render text: "Error updating story points"
 8     end
 9   end
10 end
```

5.4.12   Updating Specific Attributes

The instance methods `update_attribute` and `update` take one key/value pair or hash of attributes, respectively, to be updated on your model and saved to the database in one operation.

The `update_attribute` method updates a single attribute and saves the record, but updates made with this method are not subjected to validation checks! In other words, this method allows you to persist an Active Record model to the database even if the full object isn't valid. Model callbacks are executed, but the `updated_at` is still bumped.

Lark Says ...

I feel dirty whenever I use `update_attribute`.

On the other hand, `update` is subject to validation checks and is often used on update actions and passed the params hash containing updated values.

Active Record also provides an instance method `update_column`, which accepts a single key/value pair. Although similar to `update_attribute`, the `update_column` method not only skips validations checks but also does not run callbacks and skips the bumping of the `updated_at` timestamp.

Being introduced in Rails 4, the `update_columns` method works exactly the same as `update_column`, except that instead of accepting a single key/value pair as a parameter, it accepts a hash of attributes.

Courtenay Says ...

If you have associations on a model, Active Record automatically creates convenience methods for mass assignment. In other words, a `Project` model that `has_many :users` will expose a `user_ids` attribute writer, which gets used by its `update` method. This is an advantage if you're updating associations with check boxes, because you just name the check boxes `project[user_ids][]` and Rails will handle the magic. In some cases, allowing the user to set associations this way would be a security risk.

5.4.13   Convenience Updaters

Rails provides a number of convenience update methods in the form of `increment`, `decrement`, and `toggle`, which do exactly what their names suggest with numeric and boolean attributes. Each has a bang variant (such as `toggle!`) that additionally invokes `update_attribute` after modifying the attribute.

5.4.14   Touching Records

There may be certain cases where updating a time field to indicate a record was viewed is all you require, and Active Record provides a convenience method for doing so in the form of `touch`. This is especially useful for cache autoexpiration, which is covered in Chapter 17, "Caching and Performance."

Using this method on a model with no arguments updates the `updated_at` timestamp field to the current time without firing any callbacks or validation. If a timestamp attribute is provided, it will update that attribute to the current time along with `updated_at`.

```
>> user = User.first
>> user.touch # => sets updated_at to now.
>> user.touch(:viewed_at) # sets viewed_at and updated_at to now.
```

If a `:touch` option is provided to a `belongs_to` relation, it will touch the parent record when the child is touched.

```
class User < ActiveRecord::Base
  belongs_to :client, touch: true
end
```

```
>> user.touch # => also calls user.client.touch
```

5.4.15   **readonly** Attributes

Sometimes you want to designate certain attributes as `readonly`, which prevents them from being updated after the parent object is created. The feature is primarily for use in conjunction with calculated attributes. In fact, Active Record uses this method internally for `counter_cache` attributes, since they are maintained with their own special SQL update statements.

The only time that `readonly` attributes may be set are when the object is not saved yet. The following example code illustrates usage of `attr_readonly`. Note the potential gotcha when trying to update a `readonly` attribute.

```
class Customer < ActiveRecord::Base
  attr_readonly :social_security_number
end
```

```
>> customer = Customer.new(social_security_number: "130803020")
=> #<Customer id: 1, social_security_number: "130803020", ...>
>> customer.social_security_number
=> "130803020"
>> customer.save

>> customer.social_security_number = "000000000"  # Note, no error raised!
>> customer.social_security_number
=> "000000000"

>> customer.save
>> customer.reload
>> customer.social_security_number
=> "130803020"   # the original readonly value is preserved
```

The fact that trying to set a new value for a `readonly` attribute doesn't raise an error bothers my sensibilities, but I understand how it can make using this feature a little bit less code intensive.

You can get a list of all `readonly` attributes via the class method `readonly_attributes`.

```
>> Customer.readonly_attributes
=> #<Set: {"social_security_number"}>
```

5.4.16   Deleting and Destroying

Finally, if you want to remove a record from your database, you have two choices: delete or destroy. If you already have a model instance, you can destroy it:

```
>> bad_timesheet = Timesheet.find(1)

>> bad_timesheet.destroy
=> #<Timesheet id: 1, user_id: "1", submitted: nil,
   created_at: "2006-11-21 05:40:27", updated_at: "2006-11-21 05:40:27">
```

The `delete` method executes a SQL statement to remove the object's data from the database . The `destroy` method will both remove the object from the database and prevent you from modifying it again:

```
>> bad_timesheet.user_id = 2
RuntimeError: can't modify frozen Hash
```

Note that calling `save` on an object that has been destroyed will fail silently. If you need to check whether an object has been destroyed, you can use the `destroyed?` method.

The `destroy` method also has a complimentary bang method, `destroy!`. Calling `destroy!` on an object that cannot be destroyed will result in an `Active Record::RecordNotDestroyed` exception being raised.

You can also call `destroy` and `delete` as class methods, passing the id(s) to delete. Both variants accept a single parameter or array of ids:

```
Timesheet.delete(1)
Timesheet.destroy([2, 3])
```

The naming might seem inconsistent, but it isn't. The `delete` method uses SQL directly and does not load any instances (hence it is faster). The `destroy` method does load the instance of the Active Record object and then calls `destroy` on it as an instance method. The semantic differences are subtle but come into play when you have assigned `before_destroy` callbacks or have dependent associations—child objects that should be deleted automatically along with their parent object.

5.5   Database Locking

Locking is a term for techniques that prevent concurrent users of an application from overwriting each other's work. Active Record doesn't normally use any type of database locking when loading rows of model data from the database. If a given Rails application will only ever have one user updating data at the same time, then you don't have to worry about it.

However, when more than one user may be accessing and updating the exact same data simultaneously, then it is vitally important for you as the developer to think about concurrency. Ask yourself, what types of collisions or race conditions could happen if two users were to try to update a given model at the same time?

There are a number of approaches to dealing with concurrency in database-backed applications, two of which are natively supported by Active Record: optimistic and pessimistic locking. Other approaches exist, such as locking entire database tables. Every approach has strengths and weaknesses, so it is likely that a given application will use a combination of approaches for maximum reliability.

5.5.1   Optimistic Locking

Optimistic locking describes the strategy of detecting and resolving collisions if they occur and is commonly recommended in multiuser situations where collisions should be infrequent. Database records are never actually locked in optimistic locking, making it a bit of a misnomer.

Optimistic locking is a fairly common strategy because so many applications are designed such that a particular user will mostly be updating with data that conceptually belongs to him and not other users, making it rare that two users would compete for updating the same record. The idea behind optimistic locking is that since collisions should occur infrequently, we'll simply deal with them only if they happen.

5.5.1.1   Implementation

If you control your database schema, optimistic locking is really simple to implement. Just add an integer column named lock_version to a given table, with a default value of zero.

```
1 class AddLockVersionToTimesheets < ActiveRecord::Migration
2
3   def change
4     add_column :timesheets, :lock_version, :integer, default: 0
5   end
6
7 end
```

Simply adding that `lock_version` column changes Active Record's behavior. Now if the same record is loaded as two different model instances and saved differently, the first instance will win the update, and the second one will cause an `ActiveRecord::StaleObjectError` to be raised.

We can illustrate optimistic locking behavior with a simple spec:

```
1 describe Timesheet do
2   it "locks optimistically" do
3     t1 = Timesheet.create
4     t2 = Timesheet.find(t1.id)
5
6     t1.rate = 250
7     t2.rate = 175
8
9     expect(t1.save).to be_true
10     expect { t2.save }.to raise_error(ActiveRecord::StaleObjectError)
11   end
12 end
```

The spec passes, because calling `save` on the second instance raises the expected `ActiveRecord::StaleObjectError` exception. Note that the `save` method (without the bang) returns false and does not raise exceptions if the save fails due to validation, but other problems—such as locking in this case—can indeed cause it to raise exceptions.

To use a database column named something other than `lock_version`, change the setting using `locking_column`. To make the change globally, add the following line to your `config/application.rb`:

```
config.active_record.locking_column = :alternate_lock_version
```

Like other Active Record settings, you can also change it on a per-model basis with a declaration in your model class:

```
class Timesheet < ActiveRecord::Base
  self.locking_column = :alternate_lock_version
end
```

5.5.1.2   Handling **StaleObjectError**

Now of course, after adding optimistic locking, you don't want to just leave it at that, or the end user who is on the losing end of the collision would simply see an application error screen. You should try to handle the `StaleObjectError` as gracefully as possible.

Depending on the criticality of the data being updated, you might want to invest time into crafting a user-friendly solution that somehow preserves the changes that the loser was trying to make. At minimum, if the data for the update is easily re-creatable, let the user know why their update failed with controller code that looks something like the following:

```
1 def update
2   timesheet = Timesheet.find(params[:id])
3   timesheet.update(params[:timesheet])
4   # redirect somewhere
5 rescue ActiveRecord::StaleObjectError
6   flash[:error] = "Timesheet was modified while you were editing it."
7   redirect_to [:edit, timesheet]
8 end
```

There are some advantages to optimistic locking. It doesn't require any special feature in the database, and it is fairly easy to implement. As you saw in the example, very little code is required to handle the `StaleObjectError`.

The main disadvantages to optimistic locking are that update operations are a bit slower because the lock version must be checked and that it has the potential for bad user experience, since users don't find out about the failure until after they've potentially lost data.

5.5.2 Pessimistic Locking

Pessimistic locking requires special database support (built into the major databases) and locks down specific database rows during an update operation. It prevents another user from reading data that is about to be updated in order to prevent them from working with stale data.

Pessimistic locking works in conjunction with transactions as in the following example:

```
1 Timesheet.transaction do
2    t = Timesheet.lock.first
3    t.approved = true
4    t.save!
5 end
```

It's also possible to call `lock!` on an existing model instance, which simply calls `reload(lock: true)` under the covers. You wouldn't want to do that on an instance with attribute changes since it would cause them to be discarded by the reload. If you decide you don't want the lock anymore, you can pass `false` to the `lock!` method.

Pessimistic locking takes place at the database level. The SELECT statement generated by Active Record will have a FOR UPDATE (or similar) clause added to it, causing all other connections to be blocked from access to the rows returned by the select statement. The lock is released once the transaction is committed. Theoretically, there are situations (Rails process goes boom midtransaction?!) where the lock would not be released until the connection is terminated or times out.

5.5.3 Considerations

Web applications scale best with optimistic locking, which as we've discussed doesn't really use any database-level locking at all. However, you have to add application logic to handle failure cases. Pessimistic locking is a bit easier to implement but can lead to situations where one Rails process is waiting on another to release a database lock—that is, waiting and not serving any other incoming requests. Remember that Rails processes are typically single threaded.

In my opinion, pessimistic locking should not be super dangerous as it is on other platforms, since in Rails we don't ever persist database transactions across more than a single HTTP request. In fact, it would be impossible to do that in a shared-nothing architecture. (If you're running Rails with JRuby and doing crazy things like storing Active Record object instances in a shared session space, all bets are off.)

A situation to be wary of would be one where you have many users competing for access to a particular record that takes a long time to update. For best results, keep your pessimistic-locking transactions small and make sure that they execute quickly.

5.6   Where Clauses

In mentioning Active Record's `find` method earlier in the chapter, we didn't look at the wealth of options available in addition to finding by primary key and the `first`, `last`, and `all` methods. Each method discussed here returns an `ActiveRecord::Relation`—a chainable object that is lazy evaluated against the database only when the actual records are needed.

5.6.1   `where(*conditions)`

It's very common to need to filter the result set of a find operation (just an SQL SELECT under the covers) by adding conditions (to the WHERE clause). Active Record gives you a number of ways to do just that with the `where` method.

The conditions parameter can be specified as a string or a hash. Parameters are automatically sanitized to prevent SQL-injection attacks.

Passing a hash of conditions will construct a where clause containing a union of all the key/value pairs. If all you need is equality, versus, say, *like* criteria, I advise you to use the hash notation, since it's arguably the most readable of the styles.

```
Product.where(sku: params[:sku])
```

The hash notation is smart enough to create an IN clause if you associate an array of values with a particular key.

```
Product.where(sku: [9400,9500,9900])
```

The simple string form can be used for statements that don't involve data originating outside of your app. It's most useful for doing LIKE comparisons, as well as greater-than/less-than and the use of SQL functions not already built into Active Record. If you do choose to use the string style, additional arguments to the `where` method will be treated as query variables to insert into the where clause.

```
Product.where('description like ? and color = ?', "%#{terms}%", color)
Product.where('sku in (?)', selected_skus)
```

where.not

The Active Record query interface for the most part abstracts SQL from the developer. However, there is a condition that always requires using pure string conditions in a where clause, specifying a NOT condition with <> or !=, depending on the database. Starting in Rails 4, query method not has been added to rectify this.

To use the new query method, it must be chained to a where clause with no arguments:

```
Article.where.not(title: 'Rails 3')
# >> SELECT "articles".* FROM "articles"
#    WHERE ("articles"."title" != 'Rails 3')
```

The not query method can also accept an array to ensure multiple values are not in a field:

```
Article.where.not(title: ['Rails 3', 'Rails 5'])
# >> SELECT "articles".* FROM "articles"
#    WHERE ("articles"."title" NOT IN ('Rails 3', 'Rails 5'))
```

5.6.1.1 Bind Variables

When using multiple parameters in the conditions, it can easily become hard to read exactly what the fourth or fifth question mark is supposed to represent. In those cases, you can resort to named bind variables instead. That's done by replacing the question marks with symbols and supplying a hash with values for the matching symbol keys as a second parameter.

```
Product.where("name = :name AND sku = :sku AND created_at > :date",
              name: "Space Toilet", sku: 80800, date: '2009-01-01')
```

During a quick discussion on IRC about this final form, Robby Russell gave me the following clever snippet:

```
Message.where("subject LIKE :foo OR body LIKE :foo", foo: '%woah%')
```

In other words, when you're using named placeholders (versus question mark characters), you can use the same bind variable more than once. Like, whoa!

Simple hash conditions like this are very common and useful, but they will only generate conditions based on equality with SQL's AND operator.

```
User.where(login: login, password: password).first
```

If you want logic other than AND, you'll have to use one of the other forms available.

5.6.1.2   Boolean Conditions

It's particularly important to take care in specifying conditions that include boolean values. Databases have various different ways of representing boolean values in columns. Some have native boolean data types, and others use a single character, often 1 and 0 or T and F (or even Y and N). Rails will transparently handle the data conversion issues for you if you pass a Ruby boolean object as your parameter:

```
Timesheet.where('submitted = ?', true)
```

5.6.1.3   Nil Conditions

Rails expert Xavier Noria reminds us to take care in specifying conditions that might be nil. Using a question mark doesn't let Rails figure out that a nil supplied as the value of a condition should probably be translated into IS NULL in the resulting SQL query.

Compare the following two find examples and their corresponding SQL queries to understand this common gotcha. The first example does not work as intended, but the second one does work:

```
>> User.where('email = ?', nil)
User Load (151.4ms)   SELECT * FROM users WHERE (email = NULL)

>> User.where(:email => nil)
User Load (15.2ms)   SELECT * FROM users WHERE (users.email IS NULL)
```

5.6.2   `order(*clauses)`

The order method takes one or more symbols (representing column names) or a fragment of SQL, specifying the desired ordering of a result set:

```
Timesheet.order('created_at desc')
```

The SQL spec defaults to ascending order if the ascending/descending option is omitted, which is exactly what happens if you use symbols.

```
Timesheet.order(:created_at)
```

As of Rails 4, order can also accept hash arguments, eliminating the need of writing SQL for descending order clauses.

```
Timesheet.order(created_at: :desc)
```

Wilson Says ...

The SQL spec doesn't prescribe any particular ordering if no "order by" clause is specified in the query. That seems to trip people up, since the common belief is that "ORDER BY id ASC" is the default.

5.6.2.1   Random Ordering

The value of the :order option is not validated by Rails, which means you can pass any code that is understood by the underlying database, not just column/ direction tuples. An example of why that is useful would be if one wanted to fetch a random record:

```
1  # MySQL
2  Timesheet.order('RAND()')
3
4  # Postgres
5  Timesheet.order('RANDOM()')
6
7  # Microsoft SQL Server
8  Timesheet.order('NEWID()')   # uses random uuids to sort
9
10 # Oracle
11 Timesheet.order('dbms_random.value').first
```

Remember that ordering large datasets randomly is known to perform terribly on most databases, particularly MySQL.

Tim Says ...

A clever, performant, and portable way to get a random record is to generate a random offset in Ruby.

```
Timsheet.limit(1).offset(rand(Timesheet.count)).first
```

5.6.3   `limit(number)` and `offset(number)`

The limit method takes an integer value establishing a limit on the number of rows to return from the query. The offset method, which must be chained to limit, specifies the number of rows to skip in the result set and is zero-indexed. (At least it is in MySQL. Other databases may be one-indexed.) Together these options are used for paging results.

For example, a call to find the second page of 10 results in a list of timesheets is the following:

```
Timesheet.limit(10).offset(10)
```

Depending on the particulars of your application's data model, it may make sense to always put some limit on the maximum amount of Active Record objects fetched in any one specific query. Letting the user trigger unbounded queries pulling thousands of Active Record objects into Rails at one time is a recipe for disaster.

5.6.4 `select(*clauses)`

By default, Active Record generates SELECT * FROM queries, but it can be changed if, for example, you want to do a join but not include the joined columns or if you want to add calculated columns to your result set, like this:

```
>> b = BillableWeek.select("mon_hrs + tues_hrs as two_day_total").first
=> #<BillableWeek ...>
>> b.two_day_total
=> 16
```

Now if you actually want to fully use objects with additional attributes that you've added via the `select` method, don't forget the * clause:

```
>> b = BillableWeek.select(:*, "mon_hrs + tues_hrs as two_day_total").first
=> #<BillableWeek id: 1...>
```

Keep in mind that columns not specified in the query, whether by * or explicitly, will not be populated in the resulting objects! So, for instance, continuing the first example, trying to access `created_at` on b has unexpected results:

```
ActiveModel::MissingAttributeError: missing attribute: created_at
```

5.6.5 `from(*tables)`

The `from` method allows you to modify the table name(s) portion of the SQL statements generated by Active Record. You can provide a custom value if you need to include extra tables for joins or to reference a database view.

Here's an example of usage from an application that features tagging:

```
1 def self.find_tagged_with(list)
2   select("#{table_name}.*").
3     from("#{table_name}, tags, taggings").
4     where("#{table_name}.#{primary_key} = taggings.taggable_id
5           and taggings.tag_id = tags.id
```

Active
Record

```
6              and tags.name IN (?)",
7              Tag.parse(list))
8 end
```

(If you're wondering why table_name is used instead of a an explicit value, it's because this code is mixed into a target class using Ruby modules. That subject is covered in Chapter 9, "Advanced Active Record.")

5.6.6 **exists?**

A convenience method for checking the existence of records in the database is included in Active Record as the aptly named exists? method. It takes similar arguments to find and instead of returning records returns a boolean for whether or not the query has results.

```
>> User.create(login: "mack")
=> #<User id: 1, login: "mack">
>> User.exists?(1)
=> true
>> User.exists?(login: "mack")
=> true
>> User.exists?(id: [1, 3, 5])
=> true
>> User.where(login: "mack").exists?
=> true
```

5.6.7 **extending(*modules, &block)**

Specifies one or many modules with methods that will extend the scope with additional methods.

```
1 module Pagination
2   def page(number)
3     # pagination code
4   end
5 end
6
7 scope = Model.all.extending(Pagination)
8 scope.page(params[:page])
```

5.6.8 **group(*args)**

Specifies a GROUP BY SQL clause to add to the query generated by Active Record. Generally you'll want to combine :group with the :select option, since valid SQL requires that all selected columns in a grouped SELECT be either aggregate functions or columns.

```
>> users = Account.select('name, SUM(cash) as money').group('name').to_a
=> [#<User name: "Joe", money: "3500">, #<User name: "Jane", money: "9245">]
```

Keep in mind that those extra columns you bring back might sometimes be strings
if Active Record doesn't try to typecast them. In those cases, you'll have to use `to_i`
and `to_f` to explicitly convert the string to numeric types.

```
>> users.first.money > 1_000_000
ArgumentError: comparison of String with 1000000 failed
  from (irb):8:in '>'
```

5.6.9 `having(*clauses)`

If you need to perform a group query with an SQL HAVING clause, you use the
having method:

```
>> User.group("created_at").having(["created_at > ?", 2.days.ago])
=> [#<User name: "Joe", created_at: "2013-03-05 19:30:11">]
```

5.6.10   `includes(*associations)`

Active Record has the ability to eliminate "N+1" queries by letting you specify which
associations to eager load using the `includes` method or option in your finders. Active
Record will load those relationships with the minimum number of queries possible.

   To eager load first-degree associations, provide `includes` with an array of association names. When accessing these, a database hit to load each one will no longer occur.

```
>> users = User.where(login: "mack").includes(:billable_weeks)
=> [#<User login: "mack">]
>> users.first.billable_weeks.each { |week| puts week }
=> #<Week start_date: "2008-05-01 00:00:00">
```

For second-degree associations, provide a hash with the array as the value for the hash key.

```
>> clients = Client.includes(users: [:avatar])
=> [#<Client id: 1, name: "Hashrocket">]
```

You may add more inclusions following the same pattern.

```
>> Client.includes(
     users: [:avatar, { timesheets: :billable_weeks }]
   )
=> [#<Client id: 1, name: "Hashrocket">]
```

Similarly to `includes`, you may use `eager_load` or `preload` with the same syntax.

```
>> Client.eager_load(
```

```
      users: [:avatar, { timesheets: :billable_weeks }]
   )
=> [#<Client id: 1, name: "Hashrocket">]

>> Client.preload(
      users: [:avatar, { timesheets: :billable_weeks }]
   )
=> [#<Client id: 1, name: "Hashrocket">]
```

5.6.11 `joins`

The `joins` method can be useful when you're grouping and aggregating data from other tables but you don't want to load the associated objects.

```
Buyer.select('buyers.id, count(carts.id) as cart_count').
    joins('left join carts on carts.buyer_id = buyers.id').
    group('buyers.id')
```

However, the most common usage of the `join` method is to allow you to eager fetch additional objects in a single SELECT statement, a technique that is discussed at length in Chapter 7, "Active Record Associations."

5.6.12 `none`

Being introduced in Rails 4 is `ActiveRecord::QueryMethods.none`, a chainable relation that causes a query to return zero records. The query method returns `ActiveRecord::NullRelation`, which is an implementation of the Null Object pattern. It is to be used in instances where you have a method that returns a relation, but there is a condition in which you do not want the database to be queried. All subsequent chained conditions will work without issue, eliminating the need to continuously check if the object you are working with is a relation.

```
 1 def visible
 2   case role
 3   when :reviewer
 4     Post.published
 5   when :bad_user
 6     Post.none
 7   end
 8 end
 9
10 # If chained, the following code will not break for users
11 # with a :bad_user role
12 posts = current_user.visible.where(name: params[:name])
```

5.6.13   `readonly`

Chaining the `readonly` method marks returned objects as `readonly`. You can change their attributes, but you won't be able to save them back to the database.

```
>> c = Comment.readonly.first
=> #<Comment id: 1, body: "Hey beeyotch!">
>> c.body = "Keep it clean!"
=> "Keep it clean!"
>> c.save
ActiveRecord::ReadOnlyRecord: ActiveRecord::ReadOnlyRecord
```

5.6.14   `references`

The query method `references` is used to indicate that an association is referenced by an SQL string and therefore should be joined over being loaded separately. As of Rails 4.1, adding a string condition of an included reference will result in an exception being raised.

Here is an example that selects all Teams that have a member named Tyrion:

```
>> Team.includes(:members).where('members.name = ?', 'Tyrion')
   SQLite3::SQLException: no such column: members.name: SELECT "teams".*
   FROM "teams"  WHERE (members.name = 'Tyrion')
   ActiveRecord::StatementInvalid: SQLite3::SQLException: no such column:
   members.name: SELECT "teams".* FROM "teams"  WHERE (members.name =
   'Tyrion')
   ...
```

To get this example to work in Rails 4.1, we must include query method `references` with the name of the association to join.

```
Team.includes(:members).
  where("members.name = ?", 'Tyrion').references(:members)
```

However, if you were using the hash syntax with association conditions, it would still perform a LEFT OUTER JOIN without any exception being raised:

```
Team.includes(:members).where(members: { name:  'Tyrion' })
```

Note that ordering string SQL snippets on included associations will still work the same way without the need of references:

```
Team.includes(:members).order('members.name')
```

5.6.15   `reorder`

Using `reorder`, you can replace any existing defined order on a given relation.

```
>> Member.order('name DESC').reorder(:id)
Member Load (0.6ms) SELECT "members".* FROM "members" ORDER BY
"members"."id" ASC
```

Any subsequent calls to `order` will be appended to the query.

```
>> Member.order('name DESC').reorder(:id).order(:name)
Member Load (0.6ms) SELECT "members".* FROM "members" ORDER BY
"members".name ASC, "members"."id" ASC
```

5.6.16 `reverse_order`
A convenience method to reverse an existing order clause on a relation.

```
>> Member.order(:name).reverse_order
Member Load (0.4ms)  SELECT "members".* FROM "members" ORDER BY
"members".name DESC
```

5.6.17 `uniq / distinct`
If you need to perform a query with a DISTINCT SQL clause, you can use the `uniq` method.

```
>> User.select(:login).uniq
User Load (0.2ms)  SELECT DISTINCT login FROM "users"
```

5.6.18 `unscope(*args)`
The `unscope` query method is useful when you want to remove an unwanted relation without reconstructing the entire relation chain. For example, to remove an order clause from a relation, add `unscope(:order)`:

```
>> Member.order('name DESC').unscope(:order)
SELECT "members".* FROM "members"
```

Additionally, one can pass a hash as an argument to unscope specific `:where` values. This will cause only the value specified to not be included in the where clause.

```
Member.where(name: "Tyrion", active: true).unscope(where: :name)
```

is equivalent to

```
Member.where(active: true)
```

The following is a listing of the query methods `unscope` accepts:

- `:from`

- `:group`

- `:having`

- `:includes`

- `:joins`

- `:limit`

- `:lock`

- `:offset`

- `:order`

- `:readonly`

- `:select`

- `:where`

5.6.19   `arel_table`

For cases in which you want to generate custom SQL yourself through Arel, you may use the `arel_table` method to gain access to the table for the class.

```
>> users = User.arel_table
>> users.where(users[:login].eq("mack")).to_sql
=> "SELECT `users`.`id`, `users`.`login` FROM `users` WHERE `users`.`login` = 'mack'"
```

You can consult the Arel documentation directly on how to construct custom queries using its DSL.[2]

5.7   Connections to Multiple Databases in Different Models

Connections are created via `ActiveRecord::Base.establish_connection` and retrieved by `ActiveRecord::Base.connection`. All classes inheriting from `ActiveRecord::Base` will use this connection. What if you want some of your models to use a different connection? You can add class-specific connections.

For example, let's say you need to access data residing in a legacy database apart from the database used by the rest of your Rails application. We'll create a new base class that can be used by models that access legacy data. Begin by adding details for the additional database under its own key in `database.yml`. Then call `establish_connection`

---

2. `https://github.com/rails/arel/`

to make `LegacyProjectBase` and all its subclasses use the alternate connection instead.

```
1 class LegacyProjectBase < ActiveRecord::Base
2   establish_connection :legacy_database
3   self.abstract_class = true
4   ...
5 end
```

Incidentally, to make this example work with subclasses, you must specify `self.abstract_class = true` in the class context. Otherwise, Rails considers the subclasses of `LegacyProject` to be using single-table inheritance (STI), which we discuss at length in Chapter 9, "Advanced Active Record."

Xavier Says ...

You can easily point your base class to different databases depending on the Rails environment like this:

```
1 class LegacyProjectBase < ActiveRecord::Base
2   establish_connection "legacy_#{Rails.env}"
3   self.abstract_class = true
4   ...
5 end
```

Then just add multiple entries to `database.yml` to match the resulting connection names—in the case of our example, `legacy_development`, `legacy_test`, and so on.

The `establish_connection` method takes a string (or symbol) key pointing to a configuration already defined in `database.yml`. Alternatively, you can pass it a literal hash of options, although it's messy to put this sort of configuration data right into your model file instead of `database.yml`.

```
class TempProject < ActiveRecord::Base
  establish_connection adapter: 'sqlite3', database: ':memory:'
  ...
end
```

Rails keeps database connections in a connection pool inside the `ActiveRecord::Base` class instance. The connection pool is simply a `Hash` object indexed by Active Record class. During execution, when a connection is needed, the `retrieve_connection` method walks up the class hierarchy until a matching connection is found.

5.8   Using the Database Connection Directly

It is possible to use Active Record's underlying database connections directly, and sometimes it is useful to do so from custom scripts and for one-off or ad hoc testing. Access the connection via the `connection` attribute of any Active Record class. If all your models use the same connection, then use the connection attribute of `ActiveRecord::Base`.

```
ActiveRecord::Base.connection.execute("show tables").values
```

The most basic operation that you can do with a connection is simply to `execute` an SQL statement from the `DatabaseStatements` module. For example, Listing 5.1 shows a method that executes an SQL file statement by statement.

Listing 5.1   Execute an SQL File Line by Line Using Active Record's Connection

```
1 def execute_sql_file(path)
2   File.read(path).split(';').each do |sql|
3     begin
4       ActiveRecord::Base.connection.execute(#{sql}\n") unless sql.blank?
5     rescue ActiveRecord::StatementInvalid
6       $stderr.puts "warning: #{$!}"
7     end
8   end
9 end
```

5.8.1   The `DatabaseStatements` Module

The `ActiveRecord::ConnectionAdapters::DatabaseStatements` module mixes a number of useful methods into the connection object that make it possible to work with the database directly instead of using Active Record models. I've purposely left out some of the methods of this module because they are used internally by Rails to construct SQL statements dynamically, and I don't think they're of much use to application developers.

For the sake of readability in the following `select_` examples, assume that the connection object has been assigned to `conn`, like this:

```
conn = ActiveRecord::Base.connection
```

5.8.1.1   `begin_db_transaction()`

Begins a database transaction manually (and turns off Active Record's default auto-committing behavior).

5.8.1.2 `commit_db_transaction()`

Commits the transaction (and turns on Active Record's default autocommitting behavior again).

5.8.1.3 `delete(sql_statement)`

Executes an SQL DELETE statement provided and returns the number of rows affected.

5.8.1.4 `execute(sql_statement)`

Executes the SQL statement provided in the context of this connection. This method is abstract in the `DatabaseStatements` module and is overridden by specific database adapter implementations. As such, the return type is a result set object corresponding to the adapter in use.

5.8.1.5 `insert(sql_statement)`

Executes an SQL INSERT statement and returns the last autogenerated id from the affected table.

5.8.1.6 `reset_sequence!(table, column, sequence = nil)`

Used in Oracle and Postgres; updates the named sequence to the maximum value of the specified table's column.

5.8.1.7 `rollback_db_transaction()`

Rolls back the currently active transaction (and turns on autocommitting). Called automatically when a transaction block raises an exception or returns false.

5.8.1.8 `select_all(sql_statement)`

Returns an array of record hashes with the column names as keys and column values as values.

```
conn.select_all("select name from businesses limit 5")
=> [{"name"=>"Hopkins Painting"}, {"name"=>"Whelan & Scherr"},
{"name"=>"American Top Security Svc"}, {"name"=>"Life Style Homes"},
{"name"=>"378 Liquor Wine & Beer"}]
```

5.8.1.9 `select_one(sql_statement)`

Works similarly to `select_all` but returns only the first row of the result set as a single hash with the column names as keys and column values as values. Note that this method does not add a limit clause to your SQL statement automatically, so consider adding one to queries on large datasets.

```
>> conn.select_one("select name from businesses")
=> {"name"=>"New York New York Salon"}
```

5.8.1.10 `select_value(sql_statement)`

Works just like `select_one`, except that it returns a single value: the first column value of the first row of the result set.

```
>> conn.select_value("select * from businesses limit 1")
=> "Cimino's Pizza"
```

5.8.1.11 `select_values(sql_statement)`

Works just like `select_value`, except that it returns an array of the values of the first column in all the rows of the result set.

```
>> conn.select_values("select * from businesses limit 5")
=> ["Ottersberg Christine E Dds", "Bally Total Fitness", "Behboodikah,
Mahnaz Md", "Preferred Personnel Solutions", "Thoroughbred Carpets"]
```

5.8.1.12 `update(sql_statement)`

Executes the update statement provided and returns the number of rows affected. Works exactly like `delete`.

5.8.2 Other Connection Methods

The full list of methods available on `connection`, which returns an instance of the underlying database adapter, is fairly long. Most of the Rails adapter implementations define their own custom versions of these methods. That makes sense, since all databases have slight variations in how they handle SQL and very large variations in how they handle extended commands, such as for fetching metadata.

A peek at `abstract_adapter.rb` shows us the default method implementations:

```
1  ...
2
3  # Returns the human-readable name of the adapter.   Use mixed case - one
4  # can always use downcase if needed.
5  def adapter_name
6    'Abstract'
7  end
8
9  # Does this adapter support migrations?   Backend specific, as the
10 # abstract adapter always returns +false+.
11 def supports_migrations?
12   false
13 end
```

Active Record

```
14
15 # Can this adapter determine the primary key for tables not attached
16 # to an Active Record class, such as join tables? Backend specific, as
17 # the abstract adapter always returns +false+.
18 def supports_primary_key?
19   false
20 end
21
22 ...
```

In the following list of method descriptions and code samples, I'm accessing the connection of our sample `time_and_expenses` application in the Rails console, and again I've assigned `connection` to a local variable named `conn`, for convenience.

5.8.2.1 `active?`
Indicates whether the connection is active and ready to perform queries.

5.8.2.2 `adapter_name`
Returns the human-readable name of the adapter, as in the following example:

```
>> conn.adapter_name
=> "SQLite"
```

5.8.2.3 `disconnect!` and `reconnect!`
Closes the active connection or closes and opens a new one in its place, respectively.

5.8.2.4 `raw_connection`
Provides access to the underlying database connection. Useful for when you need to execute a proprietary statement or you're using features of the Ruby database driver that aren't necessarily exposed in Active Record. (In trying to come up with a code sample for this method, I was able to crash the Rails console with ease. There isn't much in the way of error checking for exceptions that you might raise while mucking around with `raw_connection`.)

5.8.2.5 `supports_count_distinct?`
Indicates whether the adapter supports using DISTINCT within COUNT in SQL statements. This is `true` for all adapters except SQLite, which therefore requires a work-around when doing operations such as calculations.

5.8.2.6 `supports_migrations?`
Indicates whether the adapter supports migrations.

5.8.2.7 `tables`

Produces a list of tables in the underlying database schema. It includes tables that aren't usually exposed as Active Record models, such as `schema_info` and `sessions`.

```
>> conn.tables
=> ["schema_migrations", "users", "timesheets", "expense_reports",
"billable_weeks", "clients", "billing_codes", "sessions"]
```

5.8.2.8 `verify!(timeout)`

Lazily verifies this connection, calling `active?` only if it hasn't been called for `timeout` seconds.

5.9   Other Configuration Options

In addition to the configuration options used to instruct Active Record on how to handle naming of tables and primary keys, there are a number of other settings that govern miscellaneous functions. Set them in an initializer.

5.9.0.1 `ActiveRecord::Base.default_timezone`

Tells Rails whether to use `Time.local` (using `:local`) or `Time.utc` (using `:utc`) when pulling dates and times from the database. Defaults to `:local`.172

5.9.0.2 `ActiveRecord::Base.schema_format`

Specifies the format to use when dumping the database schema with certain default rake tasks. Use the `:sql` option to have the schema dumped as potentially database-specific SQL statements. Just beware of incompatibilities if you're trying to use the `:sql` option with different databases for development and testing. The default option is `:ruby`, which dumps the schema as an `ActiveRecord::Schema` file that can be loaded into any database that supports migrations.

5.9.0.3 `ActiveRecord::Base.store_full_sti_class`

Specifies whether Active Record should store the full constant name including namespace when using single-table inheritance (STI), covered in Chapter 9, "Advanced Active Record."

5.10   Conclusion

This chapter covered the fundamentals of Active Record, the framework included with Ruby on Rails for creating database-bound model classes. We've learned how Active Record expresses the convention over configuration philosophy that is such an important part of the Rails way and how to make settings manually, which override the conventions in place.

Active
Record

We've also looked at the methods provided by `ActiveRecord::Base`, the parent class of all persistent models in Rails, which include everything you need to do basic CRUD operations (create, read, update, and delete). Finally, we reviewed how to drill through Active Record to use the database connection whenever you need to do so.

In the following chapter, we continue our coverage of Active Record by learning how migrations help evolve an application's database schema.

CHAPTER 6

Active Record Migrations

Baby step to four o'clock. Baby step to four o'clock.

—Bob Wiley

It's a fact of life that the database schema of your application will evolve over the course of development. Tables are added, names of columns are changed, things are dropped—you get the picture. Without strict conventions and process discipline for the application developers to follow, keeping the database schema in proper lockstep with application code is traditionally a very troublesome job.

Migrations are Rails' way of helping you to evolve the database schema of your application (also known as its DDL) without having to drop and re-create the database each time you make a change. And not having to drop and re-create the database each time a change happens means that you don't lose your development data. That may or may not be that important but is usually very convenient. The only changes made when you execute a migration are those necessary to move the schema from one version to another, whether that move is forward or backward in time.

Of course, being able to evolve your schema without having to re-create your databases and the loading/reloading of data are an order of magnitude more important once you're in production.

6.1 Creating Migrations

Rails provides a generator for creating migrations.

```
$ rails generate migration
Usage:
rails generate migration NAME [field[:type][:index] field[:type][:index]] [options]
```

At minimum, you need to supply a descriptive name for the migration in CamelCase (or underscored_text, since both work), and the generator does the rest. Other generators, such as the model and scaffolding generators, also create migration scripts for you, unless you specify the `--skip-migration` option.

The descriptive part of the migration name is up to you, but most Rails developers that I know try to make it match the schema operation (in simple cases) or at least allude to what's going on inside (in more complex cases).

Note that if you change the classname of your migration to something that doesn't match its filename, you will get an `uninitialized constant` error when that migration gets executed.

6.1.1   Sequencing Migrations

Prior to Rails 2.1, the migrations were sequenced via a simple numbering scheme baked into the name of the migration file and automatically handled by the migration generator. Each migration received a sequential number. There were many inconveniences inherent in that approach, especially in team environments where two developers could check in a migration with the same sequence number. Thankfully those issues have been eliminated by using timestamps to sequence migrations.

Migrations that have already been run are listed in a special database table that Rails maintains. It is named `schema_migrations` and only has one column:

```
mysql> desc schema_migrations;
+---------+--------------+------+-----+---------+-------+
| Field   | Type         | Null | Key | Default | Extra |
+---------+--------------+------+-----+---------+-------+
| version | varchar(255) | NO   | PRI | NULL    |       |
+---------+--------------+------+-----+---------+-------+
1 row in set (0.00 sec)
```

When you pull down new migrations from source control, `rake db:migrate` will check the `schema_migrations` table and execute all migrations that have not yet run (even if they have earlier timestamps than migrations that you've added yourself in the interim).

6.1.2   **change**

Introduced in version 3.1, Rails added the ability to define reversible migrations. In previous versions of Rails, one would have to define two migration instance methods, up and down. The up method included the logic of what to change in the database, while the down method included the logic on how to revert that change. Using the change method, one only needs to specify the up logic for the majority of use cases.

The following migration file 20130313005347_create_clients.rb illustrates creating a new table named clients:

```
1 class CreateClients < ActiveRecord::Migration
2   def change
3     create_table :clients do |t|
4       t.string :name
5       t.string :code
6       t.timestamps
7     end
8   end
9 end
```

As you can see in the example, the migration directive happens within instance method definition change. If we go to the command line in our project folder and type rake db:migrate, the clients table will be created. Rails gives us informative output during the migration process so that we see what is going on:

```
$ rake db:migrate
== CreateClients: migrating ==========================================
-- create_table(:clients)
   -> 0.0448s
== CreateClients: migrated (0.0450s) =================================
```

If you ever need to rollback to an earlier version of the schema, use the migrate task, but pass it a version number to rollback to, as in rake db:migrate VERSION =20130313005347.

6.1.3 reversible

If a migration is very complex, Active Record may not be able to reverse it without a little help. The reversible method acts very similarly to the up and down migration methods that were common in previous versions of Rails. Using reversible, one can specify operations to perform when running a migration and others when reverting it.

In the following example, the reversible method passes logic in a block to methods up and down to enable and disable hstore support in a PostgreSQL database, respectively.

```
1 def change
2   reversible do |dir|
3     dir.up do
4       execute("CREATE EXTENSION hstore")
5     end
6
```

```
 7      dir.down do
 8        execute("DROP EXTENSION hstore")
 9      end
10    end
11
12    add_column :users, :preferences, :hstore
13 end
```

6.1.4   Irreversible Migrations

Some transformations are destructive in a manner that cannot be reversed. Migrations of that kind should raise an `ActiveRecord::IrreversibleMigration` exception in their reversible `down` block. For example, what if someone on your team made a silly mistake and defined the telephone column of your clients table as an integer? You can change the column to a string and the data will migrate cleanly, but going from a string to an integer? Not so much.

```
 1 def change
 2   reversible do |dir|
 3     dir.up do
 4       # Phone number fields are not integers, duh!
 5       change_column :clients, :phone, :string
 6     end
 7
 8     dir.down { raise ActiveRecord::IrreversibleMigration }
 9   end
10 end
```

6.1.5   `create_table(name, options, &block)`

The `create_table` method needs at minimum a name for the table and a block containing column definitions. Why do we specify identifiers with symbols instead of strings? Both will work, but symbols require one less keystroke.

The `create_table` method makes a huge but usually true assumption that we want an autoincrementing, integer-typed, primary key. That is why you don't see it declared in the list of columns. If that assumption happens to be wrong, it's time to pass `create_table` some options in a hash.

For example, how would you define a simple join table consisting of two foreign key columns and not needing its own primary key? Just pass the `create_table` method an `:id` option set to `false`—as a boolean, not a symbol! It will stop the migration from autogenerating a primary key altogether:

```
 1 create_table :ingredients_recipes, id: false do |t|
 2   t.column :ingredient_id, :integer
```

```
3   t.column :recipe_id, :integer
4 end
```

Alternatively, the same functionality can be achieved using the `create_join_table` method, covered later in the chapter.

If all you want to do is change the name of the primary key column from its default of "id," pass the `:id` option a symbol instead. For example, let's say your corporation mandates that primary keys follow the pattern tablename_id. Then the earlier example would look as follows:

```
1 create_table :clients, id: :clients_id do |t|
2   t.column :name, :string
3   t.column :code, :string
4   t.column :created_at, :datetime
5   t.column :updated_at, :datetime
6 end
```

The `force: true` option tells the migration to go ahead and drop the table being defined if it exists. Be careful with this one, since it will produce (possibly unwanted) data loss when run in production. As far as I know, the `:force` option is mostly useful for making sure that the migration puts the database in a known state, but it isn't all that useful daily.

The `:options` option allows you to append custom instructions to the SQL CREATE statement and is useful for adding database-specific commands to your migration. Depending on the database you're using, you might be able to specify things such as character set, collation, comments, min/max sizes, and many other properties using this option.

The `temporary: true` option specifies creation of a temporary table that will only exist during the current connection to the database. In other words, it only exists during the migration. In advanced scenarios, this option might be useful for migrating big sets of data from one table to another, but it is not commonly used.

Sebastian Says ...

A little-known fact is that you can remove old migration files (while still keeping newer ones) to keep the `db/migrate` folder to a manageable size. You can move the older migrations to a `db/archived_migrations` folder or something like that. Once you do trim the size of your migrations folder, use the `rake db:reset` task to (re-)create your database from `db/schema.rb` and load the seeds into your current environment.

Active Record

6.1.6 `change_table(table_name, &block)`

Basically works just like `create_table` and accepts the same kinds of column definitions.

6.1.7 `create_join_table`

In Rails 4, a new migration method `create_join_table` has been added to easily create HABTM join tables. The `create_join_table` accepts at minimum the names of two tables.

```
create_join_table :ingredients, :recipes
```

The preceding code example will create a table named "ingredients_recipes" with no primary key.

The `create_join_table` also accepts an options hash where you can specify the following:

:table_name If you do not agree with the Rails convention of concatenating both tables names with an underscore, the `:table_name` option allows setting an override.

:column_options Add any extra options to append to the foreign key column definitions.

:options, :temporary, and **:force** Accept the same interface as the equivalent options found in `create_table`.

6.1.8   API Reference

The following table details the methods that are available in the context of `create_table` and `change_table` methods within a migration class.

6.1.8.1 `change(column_name, type, options = {})`

Changes the column's definition according to the new options. The options hash optionally contains a hash with arguments that correspond to the options used when adding columns.

```
t.change(:name, :string, limit: 80)
t.change(:description, :text)
```

6.1.8.2 `change_default(column_name, default)`

Sets a new default value for a column.

```
t.change_default(:qualification, 'new')
t.change_default(:authorized, 1)
```

6.1.8.3 `column(column_name, type, options = {})`

Adds a new column to the named table. Uses the same kind of options detailed in the section "Defining Columns" in this chapter.

```
t.column(:name, :string)
```

Note that you can also use the shorthand version by calling it by type. This adds a column (or columns) of the specified type (string, text, integer, float, decimal, datetime, timestamp, time, date, binary, or boolean).

```
t.string(:goat)
t.string(:goat, :sheep)
t.integer(:age, :quantity)
```

6.1.8.4 `index(column_name, options = {})`

Adds a new index to the table. The `column_name` parameter can be one symbol or an array of symbols referring to columns to be indexed. The `name` parameter lets you override the default name that would otherwise be generated.

```
# a simple index
t.index(:name)

# a unique index
t.index([:branch_id, :party_id], unique: true)

# a named index
t.index([:branch_id, :party_id], unique: true, name: 'by_branch_party')
```

Partial Indices

As of Rails 4, the `index` method added support for partial indices via the `:where` option. The main benefit of using a partial index is to reduce the size of an index for commonly used queries within an application.

For example, let's assume a Rails application queries constantly for clients that have a status of "active" within the system. Instead of creating an index on the status column for every client record, we can include only those records that meet the specified criteria:

```
add_index(:clients, :status, where: 'active')
```

Partial indices can only be used with an application using a PostgreSQL database.

6.1.8.5 `belongs_to(args)` and `references(args)`

These two methods are aliases to each other. They add a foreign key column to another model, using Active Record naming conventions. Optionally adds a `_type` column if the `:polymorphic` option is set to true.

```
1 create_table :accounts do
2   t.belongs_to(:person)
3 end
4
5 create_table :comments do
6   t.references(:commentable, polymorphic: true)
7 end
```

A common best practice is to create an index for each foreign key in your database tables. It's so common that Rails 4 has introduced an `:index` option to the `references` and `belongs_to` methods that creates an index for the column immediately after creation. The `index` option accepts a boolean value or the same hash options as the `index` method, covered in the preceding section.

```
create_table :accounts do
  t.belongs_to(:person, index: true)
end
```

6.1.8.6 `remove(*column_names)`

Removes the column(s) specified from the table definition.

```
t.remove(:qualification)
t.remove(:qualification, :experience)
```

6.1.8.7 `remove_index(options = {})`

Removes the given index from the table.

```
# Remove the accounts_branch_id_index from the accounts table.
t.remove_index column: :branch_id

# Remove the accounts_branch_id_party_id_index from the accounts table.
t.remove_index column: [:branch_id, :party_id]

# Remove the index named by_branch_party in the accounts table.
t.remove_index name: :by_branch_party
```

6.1.8.8 `remove_references(*args)` and `remove_belongs_to`

Removes a reference. Optionally removes a `type` column.

```
t.remove_belongs_to(:person)
t.remove_references(:commentable, polymorphic: true)
```

6.1.8.9 `remove_timestamps`
Here's a method that you will never use unless you forgot to add timestamps in the `create_table` block and do it in a later migration. It removes the timestamp columns (`created_at` and `updated_at`) from the table.

6.1.8.10 `rename(column_name, new_column_name)`
Renames a column. The old name comes first—a fact that I usually can't remember.

```
t.rename(:description, :name)
```

6.1.8.11 `revert`
If you have ever wanted to revert a specific migration file explicitly within another migration, now you can. The `revert` method can accept the name of a migration class, which when executed, reverts the given migration.

```
revert CreateProductsMigration
```

The `revert` method can also accept a block of directives to reverse on execution.

6.1.8.12 `timestamps`
Adds Active Record–maintained timestamp (`created_at` and `updated_at`) columns to the table.

```
t.timestamps
```

6.1.9   Defining Columns
Columns can be added to a table using the `column` method, inside the block of a `create_table` statement, or with the `add_column` method. Other than taking the name of the table to add the column to as its first argument, the methods work identically.

```
1 create_table :clients do |t|
2   t.column :name, :string
3 end
4
5 add_column :clients, :code, :string
6 add_column :clients, :created_at, :datetime
```

The first (or second) parameter obviously specifies the name of the column, and the second (or third) obviously specifies its type. The SQL92 standard defines fundamental data types, but each database implementation has its own variation on the standards.

If you're familiar with database column types, when you examine the preceding example, it might strike you as a little weird that there is a database column declared as type `string`, since databases don't have string columns—they have char or varchars types.

6.1.9.1   Column Type Mappings

The reason for declaring a database column as type string is that Rails migrations are meant to be database agnostic. That's why you could (as I've done on occasion) develop using Postgres as your database and deploy in production to Oracle.

A complete discussion of how to go about choosing the right data type for your application needs is outside the scope of this book. However, it is useful to have a reference of how migration's generic types map to database-specific types. The mappings for the databases most commonly used with Rails are in Table 6.1.

Table 6.1   Database types in rails

Migration Type	MySQL	Postgres	SQLite	Oracle	Ruby Class
:binary	blob	bytea	blob	blob	String
:boolean	tinyint(1)	boolean	boolean	number(1)	Boolean
:date	date	date	date	date	Date
:datetime	datetime	timestamp	datetime	date	Time
:decimal	decimal	decimal	decimal	decimal	BigDecimal
:float	float	float	float	number	Float
:integer	int(11)	integer	integer	number(38)	Fixnum
:string	varchar(255)	character varying(255)	varchar(255)	varchar2(255)	String
:text	text	text	text	clob	String
:time	time	time	time	date	Time
:timestamp	datetime	timestamp	datetime	date	Time

Each connection adapter class has a `native_database_types` hash, which establishes the mapping described in Table 6.1. If you need to look up the mappings for a database not listed in Table 6.1, you can pop open the adapter Ruby code and find the `native_database_types` hash, like the following one inside the `PostgreSQLAdapter` class within `postgresql_adapter.rb`:

```
1  NATIVE_DATABASE_TYPES = {
2    primary_key: "serial primary key",
3    string:      { name: "character varying", limit: 255 },
4    text:        { name: "text" },
5    integer:     { name: "integer" },
6    float:       { name: "float" },
7    decimal:     { name: "decimal" },
8    datetime:    { name: "timestamp" },
9    timestamp:   { name: "timestamp" },
10   time:        { name: "time" },
11   date:        { name: "date" },
12   daterange:   { name: "daterange" },
13   numrange:    { name: "numrange" },
14   tsrange:     { name: "tsrange" },
15   tstzrange:   { name: "tstzrange" },
16   int4range:   { name: "int4range" },
17   int8range:   { name: "int8range" },
18   binary:      { name: "bytea" },
19   boolean:     { name: "boolean" },
20   xml:         { name: "xml" },
21   tsvector:    { name: "tsvector" },
22   hstore:      { name: "hstore" },
23   inet:        { name: "inet" },
24   cidr:        { name: "cidr" },
25   macaddr:     { name: "macaddr" },
26   uuid:        { name: "uuid" },
27   json:        { name: "json" },
28   ltree:       { name: "ltree" }
29 }
```

As you may have noticed in the previous code example, the PostgreSQL adapter includes a large amount of column-type mappings that are not available in other databases. Note that using these unique PostgreSQL column types will make a Rails application no longer database agnostic. We cover why you may want to use some of these column types, such as `hstore` and `array`, in Chapter 9, "Advanced Active Record."

6.1.9.2 Column Options

For many column types, just specifying type is not enough information. All column declarations accept the following options:

`default: value`

This sets a default to be used as the initial value of the column for new rows. You don't ever need to explicitly set the default value to `null`. Just leave off this option to get a `null` default value. It's worth noting that MySQL 5.x ignores default values for binary and text columns.

`limit: size`

This adds a size parameter to string, text, binary, or integer columns. Its meaning varies depending on the column type that it is applied to. Generally speaking, limits for string types refer to number of characters, whereas for other types, they refer to the number of bytes used to store the value in the database.

`null: false`

This makes the column required at the database level by adding a `not null` constraint.

6.1.9.3   Decimal Precision

Columns declared as type `:decimal` accept the following options:

`precision: number`

Precision is the total number of digits in a number.

`scale: number`

Scale is the number of digits to the right of the decimal point. For example, the number 123.45 has a precision of 5 and a scale of 2. Logically, the scale cannot be larger than the precision.

Note

Decimal types pose a serious opportunity for data loss during migrations of production data between different kinds of databases. For example, the default precisions between Oracle and SQL Server can cause the migration process to truncate and change the value of your numeric data. It's always a good idea to specify precision details for your data.

6.1.9.4   Column-Type Gotchas

The choice of column type is not necessarily a simple choice and depends on both the database you're using and the requirements of your application.

:binary Depending on your particular usage scenario, storing binary data in the database can cause large performance problems. Active Record doesn't generally exclude any columns when it loads objects from the database, and putting large binary attributes on commonly used models will increase the load on your database server significantly. If you must put binary content in a commonly used class, take advantage of the `:select` method to only bring back the columns you need.

:boolean The way that boolean values are stored varies from database to database. Some use 1 and 0 integer values to represent true and false, respectively. Others use characters such as T and F. Rails handles the mapping between Ruby's `true` and `false` very well, so you don't need to worry about the underlying scheme yourself. Setting attributes directly to database values such as 1 or F may work correctly but is considered an antipattern.

:datetime and **:timestamp** The Ruby class that Rails maps to `datetime` and `timestamp` columns is `Time`. In 32-bit environments, `Time` doesn't work for dates before 1902. Ruby's `DateTime` class does work with year values prior to 1902, and Rails falls back to using it if necessary. It doesn't use `DateTime` to begin for performance reasons. Under the covers, `Time` is implemented in C and is very fast, whereas `DateTime` is written in pure Ruby and is comparatively slow.

:time It's very rare that you want to use a `:time` data type—perhaps if you're modeling an alarm clock. Rails will read the contents of the database as hour, minute, and second values into a Time object with dummy values for the year, month, and day.

:decimal Older versions of Rails (prior to 1.2) did not support the fixed-precision `:decimal` type, and as a result many old Rails applications incorrectly used `:float` data types. Floating-point numbers are by nature imprecise, so it is important to choose `:decimal` instead of `:float` for most business-related applications.

Tim Says ...

If you're using a float to store values that need to be precise, such as money, you're a jackass. Floating point calculations are done in binary rather than decimal, so rounding errors abound in places you wouldn't expect.

```
>> 0.1+0.2 == 0.3
=> false
>> BigDecimal('0.1') + BigDecimal('0.2') == BigDecimal('0.3')
=> true
```

Active Record

:float Don't use floats to store currency values or, more accurately, any type of data that needs fixed precision. Since floating-point numbers are pretty much approximations, any single representation of a number as a float is probably OK. However, once you start doing mathematical operations or comparisons with float values, it is ridiculously easy to introduce difficult-to-diagnose bugs into your application.

:integer and **:string** There aren't many gotchas that I can think of when it comes to integers and strings. They are the basic data building blocks of your application, and many Rails developers leave off the size specification, which results in the default maximum sizes of 11 digits and 255 characters, respectively. You should keep in mind that you won't get an error if you try to store values that exceed the maximum size defined for the database column, which, again, is 255 characters by default. Your string will simply get truncated. Use validations to make sure that user-entered data does not exceed the maximum size allowed.

:text There have been reports of text fields slowing down query performance on some databases—enough to be a consideration for applications that need to scale to high loads. If you must use a text column in a performance-critical application, put it in a separate table.

6.1.9.5 Custom Data Types

If use of database-specific data types (such as `:double` for higher precision than `:float`) is critical to your project, use the `config.active_record.schema _format = :sql` setting in `config/application.rb` to make Rails dump schema information in native SQL DDL format rather than its own cross platform–compatible Ruby code, via the `db/schema.rb` file.

6.1.9.6 "Magic" Timestamp Columns

Rails does magic with datetime columns if they're named a certain way. Active Record will automatically timestamp create operations if the table has columns named `created_at` or `created_on`. The same applies to updates when there are columns named `updated_at` or `updated_on`.

Note that `created_at` and `updated_at` should be defined as `datetime`, but if you use `t.timestamps`, then you don't have to worry about what type of columns they are.

Automatic timestamping can be turned off globally by setting the following variable in an initializer.

```
ActiveRecord::Base.record_timestamps = false
```

The preceding code turns off timestamps for all models, but `record_timestamps` is class-inheritable, so you can also do it on a case-by-case basis by setting `self.record_timestamps` to false at the top of specific model classes.

6.1.10   Command-Line Column Declarations

You can supply name/type pairs on the command line when you invoke the migration generator and it will automatically insert the corresponding `add_column` and `remove_column` methods.

```
$ rails generate migration AddTitleBodyToPosts \
    title:string body:text published:boolean
```

This will create the AddTitleBodyToPosts in db/migrate/20130316164654 _add_title_body_to_posts.rb with this in the `change` migration:

```
1 def change
2   add_column :posts, :title, :string
3   add_column :posts, :body, :text
4   add_column :posts, :published, :boolean
5 end
```

6.2   Data Migration

So far we've only discussed using migration files to modify the schema of your database. Inevitably, you will run into situations where you also need to perform data migrations, whether in conjunction with a schema change or not.

6.2.1   Using SQL

In most cases, you should craft your data migration in raw SQL using the `execute` command that is available inside a migration class.

For example, say you had a `phones` table that kept phone numbers in their component parts, and you later wanted to simplify your model by just having a `number` column instead. You'd write a migration similar to this one:

```
1 class CombineNumberInPhones < ActiveRecord::Migration
2   def change
3     add_column :phones, :number, :string
```

Active Record

```
 4    reversible do |dir|
 5     dir.up{execute("update phones set number=concat(area_code, prefix, suffix)")}
 6       dir.down { ... }
 7     end
 8
 9     remove_column :phones, :area_code
10     remove_column :phones, :prefix
11     remove_column :phones, :suffix
12   end
13 end
```

The naive alternative to using SQL in the previous example would be more lines of code and much slower.

```
1 Phone.find_each do |p|
2   p.number = p.area_code + p.prefix + p.suffix
3   p.save
4 end
```

In this particular case, you could use Active Record's `update_all` method to still do the data migration in one line.

```
Phone.update_all("set number = concat(area_code, prefix, suffix)")
```

However, you might hit problems down the road as your schema evolves; as described in the next section, you'd want to declare an independent `Phone` model in the migration file itself. That's why I advise sticking to raw SQL whenever possible.

6.2.2 Migration Models

If you declare an Active Record model inside of a migration script, it'll be namespaced to that migration class.

```
 1 class HashPasswordsOnUsers < ActiveRecord::Migration
 2   class User < ActiveRecord::Base
 3   end
 4
 5   def change
 6     reversible do |dir|
 7       dir.up do
 8         add_column :users, :hashed_password, :string
 9         User.reset_column_information
10         User.find_each do |user|
11           user.hashed_password = Digest::SHA1.hexdigest(user.password)
12           user.save!
13         end
```

```
14           remove_column :users, :password
15      end
16
17      dir.down { raise ActiveRecord::IrreversibleMigration }
18    end
19  end
20 end
```

Why not use just your application model classes in the migration scripts directly? As your schema evolves, older migrations that use model classes directly can and will break down and become unusable. Properly namespacing migration models prevent you from having to worry about name clashes with your application's model classes or ones that are defined in other migrations.

Durran Says …

Note that Active Record caches column information on the first request to the database, so if you want to perform a data migration immediately after a migration, you may run into a situation where the new columns have not yet been loaded. This is a case where using `reset_column_information` can come in handy. Simply call this class method on your model and everything will be reloaded on the next request.

6.3   `schema.rb`

The file `db/schema.rb` is generated every time you migrate and reflects the latest status of your database schema. You should never edit `db/schema.rb` by hand since this file is autogenerated from the current state of the database. Instead of editing this file, please use the migrations feature of Active Record to incrementally modify your database, and *then* regenerate this schema definition.

Note that this `schema.rb` definition is the authoritative source for your database schema. If you need to create the application database on another system, you should be using `db:schema:load`, not running all the migrations from scratch. The latter is a flawed and unsustainable approach (the more migrations you'll amass, the slower it'll run and the greater likelihood for issues).

It's strongly recommended to check this file into your version control system. First of all, it helps to have one definitive schema definition around for reference. Second, you can run `rake db:schema:load` to create your database schema from scratch without having to run all migrations. That's especially important considering that, as your project evolves, it's likely that it will become impossible to run migrations all the way through from the start due to code incompatibilities, such as renaming of classes named explicitly.

6.4 Database Seeding

The automatically created file db/seeds.rb is a default location for creating seed data for your database. It was introduced in order to stop the practice of inserting seed data in individual migration files if you accept the premise that migrations should never be used for seeding example or base data required by your application. It is executed with the rake db:seed task (or created alongside the database when you run rake db:setup).

At its simplest, the content of seed.rb is simply a series of create! statements that generate baseline data for your application, whether it's default or related to configuration. For example, let's add an admin user and some billing codes to our time and expenses app:

```
1 User.create!(login: 'admin',
2              email: 'admin@example.com',
3              :password: '123', password_confirmation: '123',
4              authorized_approver: true)
5
6 client = Client.create!(name: 'Workbeast', code: 'BEAST')
7 client.billing_codes.create!(name: 'Meetings', code: 'MTG')
8 client.billing_codes.create!(name: 'Development', code: 'DEV')
```

Why use the bang version of the create methods? Because otherwise, you won't find out if you had errors in your seed file. An alternative would be to use first_or_create methods to make seeding idempotent.

```
1 c = Client.where(name: 'Workbeast', code: 'BEAST').first_or_create!
2 c.billing_codes.where(name: 'Meetings', code: 'MTG').first_or_create!
3 c.billing_codes.where(name: 'Development', code: 'DEV').first_or_create!
```

Another common seeding practice worth mentioning is calling delete_all prior to creating new records, so that seeding does not generate duplicate records. This practice avoids the need for idempotent seeding routines and lets you be very secure about exactly what your database will look like after seeding.

```
1 User.delete_all
2 User.create!(login: 'admin', ...
3
4 Client.delete_all
5 client = Client.create!(name: 'Workbeast', ...
```

Carlos Says …

I typically use the `seed.rb` file for data that is essential to *all* environments, including production.

For dummy data that will be only used on development or staging, I prefer to create custom rake tasks under the lib/tasks directory—for example, `lib/tasks/load_dev_data.rake`. This helps keep `seed.rb` clean and free from unnecessary conditionals, like `unless Rails.env.production?`.

6.5 Database-Related Rake Tasks

The following rake tasks are included by default in boilerplate Rails projects.

6.5.0.1 `db:create` and `db:create:all`

Create the database defined in config/database.yml for the current `Rails.env`. If the current environment is development, Rails will create both the local development and test databases (or create all the local databases defined in config/database.yml in the case of `db:create:all`).

6.5.0.2 `db:drop` and `db:drop:all`

Drops the database for the current `RAILS_ENV`. If the current environment is development, Rails will drop both the local development and test databases (or drop all the local databases defined in config/database.yml in the case of `db:drop:all`).

6.5.0.3 `db:forward` and `db:rollback`

The `db:rollback` task moves your database schema back one version. Similarly, the `db:forward` task moves your database schema forward one version and is typically used after rolling back.

6.5.0.4 `db:migrate`

Applies all pending migrations. If a `VERSION` environment variable is provided, then `db:migrate` will apply pending migrations through the migration specified but no further. The `VERSION` is specified as the timestamp portion of the migration filename.

```
# example of migrating up with param
$ rake db:migrate VERSION=20130313005347
==  CreateUsers: migrating ====================================
-- create_table(:users)
   -> 0.0014s
==  CreateUsers: migrated (0.0015s) ===========================
```

Active
Record

If the VERSION provided is older than the current version of the schema, then this task will actually rollback the newer migrations.

```
# example of migrating down with param
$ rake db:migrate VERSION=20130312152614
==  CreateUsers: reverting ==========================================
-- drop_table(:users)
   -> 0.0014s
==  CreateUsers: reverted (0.0015s) ================================
```

6.5.0.5 **db:migrate:down**
Executes the down method of the specified migration only. The VERSION is specified as the timestamp portion of the migration filename.

```
$ rake db:migrate:down VERSION=20130316172801
==  CreateClients: reverting ========================================
-- drop_table(:clients)
   -> 0.0028s
==  CreateClients: reverted (0.0054s) =============================
```

6.5.0.6 **db:migrate:up**
Executes the up method of the specified migration only. The VERSION is specified as the timestamp portion of the migration filename.

```
$ rake db:migrate:down VERSION=20130316172801
==  CreateClients: migrating ========================================
-- create_table(:clients)
   -> 0.0260s
==  CreateClients: migrated (0.0261s) =============================
```

6.5.0.7 **db:migrate:redo**
Executes the down method of the latest migration file immediately followed by its up method. This task is typically used right after correcting a mistake in the up method or to test that a migration is working correctly.

```
$ rake db:migrate:redo
==  AddTimesheetsUpdatedAtToUsers: reverting ========================
-- remove_column(:users, :timesheets_updated_at)
   -> 0.0853s
==  AddTimesheetsUpdatedAtToUsers: reverted (0.0861s) ===============

==  AddTimesheetsUpdatedAtToUsers: migrating ========================
-- add_column(:users, :timesheets_updated_at, :datetime)
   -> 0.3577s
==  AddTimesheetsUpdatedAtToUsers: migrated (0.3579s) ===============
```

6.5.0.8   `db:migrate:reset`

Resets your database for the current environment using your migrations (as opposed to using `schema.rb`).

6.5.1   `db:migrate:status`

Displays the status of all existing migrations in a nicely formatted table. It will show up for migrations that have been applied and down for those that haven't.

This task is useful in situations where you might want to check for recent changes to the schema before actually applying them (right after pulling from the remote repository, for example).

```
$ rake db:migrate:status

database: timesheet_development

 Status   Migration ID    Migration Name
--------------------------------------------------------
   up      20130219005505  Create users
   up      20130219005637  Create timesheets
   up      20130220001021  Add user id to timesheets
  down     20130220022039  Create events
```

6.5.1.1   `db:reset` and `db:setup`

The `db:setup` creates the database for the current environment, loads the schema from `db/schema.rb`, and then loads the seed data. It's used when you're setting up an existing project for the first time on a development workstation. The similar `db:reset` task does the same thing except that it drops and re-creates the database first.

6.5.1.2   `db:schema:dump`

Creates a `db/schema.rb` file that can be portably used against any database supported by Active Record. Note that the creation (or updating) of `schema.rb` happens automatically any time you migrate.

6.5.1.3   `db:schema:load`

Loads `schema.rb` file into the database for the current environment.

6.5.1.4   `db:seed`

Loads the seed data from `db/seeds.rb` as described in this chapter's section, "Database Seeding."

6.5.1.5 `db:structure:dump`

Dumps the database structure to an SQL file containing raw DDL (data description language) code in a format corresponding to the database driver specified in `database .yml` for your current environment.

```
$ rake db:structure:dump

$ cat db/development_structure.sql
CREATE TABLE `avatars` (
  `id` int(11) NOT NULL AUTO_INCREMENT,
  `user_id` int(11) DEFAULT NULL,
  `url` varchar(255) COLLATE utf8_unicode_ci DEFAULT NULL,
  PRIMARY KEY (`id`)
) ENGINE=InnoDB DEFAULT CHARSET=utf8 COLLATE=utf8_unicode_ci;
...
```

I've rarely needed to use this task. It's possible that some Rails teams working in conjunction with DBAs that exercise strict control over their application's database schemas will need this task regularly.

6.5.1.6 `db:test:prepare`

Checks for pending migrations and loads the test schema by doing a `db:schema:dump` followed by a `db:schema:load`.

This task gets used very often during active development whenever you're running specs or tests without using rake. (Standard spec-related rake tasks run `db:test:prepare` automatically for you.)

6.5.1.7 `db:version`

Returns the timestamp of the latest migration file that has been run. It works even if your database has been created from `db/schema.rb`, since it contains the latest version timestamp in it:

```
ActiveRecord::Schema.define(version: 20130316172801)
```

6.6 Conclusion

This chapter covered the fundamentals of Active Record migrations. In the following chapter, we continue our coverage of Active Record by learning about how model objects are related to each other and interact via associations.

CHAPTER 7

Active Record Associations

Any time you can reify something, you can create something that embodies a concept, it gives you leverage to work with it more powerfully. That's exactly what's going on with has_many :through.

—Josh Susser

Active Record associations let you declaratively express relationships between model classes. The power and readability of the Associations API is an important part of what makes working with Rails so special.

This chapter covers the different kinds of Active Record associations available while highlighting use cases and available customizations for each of them. We also take a look at the classes that give us access to relationships themselves.

7.1   The Association Hierarchy

Associations typically appear as methods on Active Record model objects. For example, the method `timesheets` might represent the timesheets associated with a given `user`.

```
user.timesheets
```

However, people might get confused about the type of objects that are returned by association with these methods. This is because they have a way of masquerading as plain old Ruby objects. For instance, in previous versions of Rails, an association collection would seem to return an array of objects, when in fact the return type was actually an association proxy. As of Rails 4, asking any association collection what its return type is will tell you that it is an `ActiveRecord::Associations::CollectionProxy`:

```
>> user.timesheets
=> #<ActiveRecord::Associations::CollectionProxy []>
```

It's actually lying to you, albeit very innocently. Association methods for has_many associations are actually instances of HasManyAssociation.

The CollectionProxy acts like a middleman between the object that owns the association and the actual associated object. Methods that are unknown to the proxy are sent to the target object via method_missing.

Fortunately, it's not the Ruby way to care about the actual class of an object. What messages an object responds to is a lot more significant.

The parent class of all has_many associations is CollectionAssociation and most of the methods that it defines work similarly, regardless of the options declared for the relationship. Before we get much further into the details of the association proxies, let's delve into the most fundamental type of association that is commonly used in Rails applications: the has_many / belongs_to pair, used to define one-to-many relationships.

7.2   One-to-Many Relationships

In our recurring sample application, an example of a one-to-many relationship is the association between the User, Timesheet, and ExpenseReport classes:

```
1 class User < ActiveRecord::Base
2   has_many :timesheets
3   has_many :expense_reports
4 end
```

Timesheets and expense reports should be linked in the opposite direction as well, so that it is possible to reference the user to which a timesheet or expense report belongs.

```
1 class Timesheet < ActiveRecord::Base
2   belongs_to :user
3 end
4
5 class ExpenseReport < ActiveRecord::Base
6   belongs_to :user
7 end
```

When these relationship declarations are executed, Rails uses some metaprogramming magic to dynamically add code to your models. In particular, proxy collection objects are created that let you manipulate the relationship easily. To demonstrate, let's play with these relationships in the console. First, I'll create a user.

```
>> obie = User.create login: 'obie', password: '1234',
password_confirmation: '1234', email: 'obiefernandez@gmail.com'
=> #<User...>
```

Now I'll verify that I have collections for timesheets and expense reports.

```
>> obie.timesheets
Timesheet Load (0.4ms)  SELECT "timesheets".* FROM "timesheets" WHERE
"timesheets"."user_id" = ?  [[nil, 1]]
SQLite3::SQLException: no such column: timesheets.user_id: SELECT
"timesheets".* FROM "timesheets"  WHERE "timesheets"."user_id" = ?
```

As David might say, "Whoops!" I forgot to add the foreign key columns to the `timesheets` and `expense_reports` tables, so in order to go forward I'll generate a migration for the changes:

```
$ rails generate migration add_user_foreign_keys
      invoke   active_record
      create   db/migrate/20130330201532_add_user_foreign_keys.rb
```

Then I'll open `db/migrate/20130330201532_add_user_foreign_keys.rb` and add the missing columns. (Using `change_table` would mean writing many more lines of code, so we'll stick with the traditional `add_column` syntax, which still works fine.)

```
1 class AddUserForeignKeys < ActiveRecord::Migration
2   def change
3     add_column :timesheets, :user_id, :integer
4     add_column :expense_reports, :user_id, :integer
5   end
6 end
```

Running `rake db:migrate` applies the changes:

```
$ rake db:migrate
==  AddUserForeignKeys: migrating=========================================
-- add_column(:timesheets, :user_id, :integer)
   -> 0.0011s
-- add_column(:expense_reports, :user_id, :integer)
   -> 0.0005s
==  AddUserForeignKeys: migrated (0.0018s) ===============================
```

Index Associations for Performance Boost

Premature optimization is the root of all evil. However, most experienced Rails developers don't mind adding indexes for foreign keys at the time that those are created. In the case of our migration example, you'd add the following statements:

```
1 add_index :timesheets, :user_id
2 add_index :expense_reports, :user_id
```

The loading of your associations (which is usually more common than the creation of items) will get a big performance boost.

Now I should be able to add a new blank timesheet to my user and check `timesheets` again to make sure it's there:

```
>> obie = User.find(1)
=> #<User id: 1...>
>> obie.timesheets << Timesheet.new
=> #<ActiveRecord::Associations::CollectionProxy [#<Timesheet id: 1 ...]>
>> obie.timesheets
=> #<ActiveRecord::Associations::CollectionProxy [#<Timesheet id: 1 ...]>
```

Notice that the `Timesheet` object gains an `id` immediately.

7.2.1   Adding Associated Objects to a Collection

As you can deduce from the previous example, appending an object to a `has_many` collection automatically saves that object—that is, unless the parent object (the owner of the collection) is not yet stored in the database. Let's make sure that's the case using Active Record's `reload` method, which refetches the attributes of an object from the database:

```
>> obie.timesheets.reload
=> #<ActiveRecord::Associations::CollectionProxy [#<Timesheet id: 1, user_id: 1 ...]>
```

There it is. The foreign key, `user_id`, was automatically set by the `<<` method. It takes one or more association objects to add to the collection, and since it flattens its argument list and inserts each record, `push` and `concat` behave identically.

In the blank timesheet example, I could have used the `create` method on the association proxy, and it would have worked essentially the same way:

```
>> obie.timesheets.create
=> #<ActiveRecord::Associations::CollectionProxy [#<Timesheet id: 1, user_id: 1 ...]>
```

Even though at first glance `<<` and `create` do the same thing, there are some important differences in how they're implemented that are covered in the following section.

7.2.2   Association Collection Methods

Association collections are basically fancy wrappers around a Ruby array and have
a normal array's methods. Named scopes and all of `ActiveRecord::Base`'s class
methods are also available on association collections, including `find`, `order`,
`where`, and so on.

```
user.timesheets.where(submitted: true).order('updated_at desc')
user.timesheets.late # assuming a scope :late defined on the Timesheet class
```

The following methods of `CollectionProxy` are available to association
collections:

7.2.2.1   `<<(*records)` and `create(attributes = {})`

Both methods will add either a single associated object or many, depending on
whether you pass them an array or not. They both also trigger the `:before_add`
and `:after_add` callbacks (covered in this chapter's section "has_many Options").

   Finally, the return value behavior of both methods varies wildly. The `create`
method returns the new instance created, which is what you'd expect given its counterpart in `ActiveRecord::Base`. The `<<` method returns the association proxy,
which allows chaining and is also natural behavior for a Ruby array.

   However, `<<` will return `false` and not itself if any of the records being added
causes the operation to fail. You shouldn't depend on the return value of `<<` being an
array that you can continue operating on in a chained fashion.

7.2.2.2   `any?` and `many?`

The `any?` method behaves like its `Enumerable` counterpart if you give it a block;
otherwise, it's the opposite of `empty?`. Its companion method `many?`, which is an
Active Support extension to Enumerable, returns true if the size of the collection is
greater than one or if a block is given if two or more elements match the supplied
criteria.

7.2.2.3   `average(column_name, options = {})`

Convenience wrapper for `calculate(:average, ...)`.

7.2.2.4   `build(attributes={}, &block)`

Traditionally, the `build` method has corresponded to the `new` method of Active
Record classes, except that it presets the owner's foreign key and appends it to the
association collection in one operation. However, as of Rails 2.2, the `new` method
has the same behavior and probably should be used instead of `build`.

Active
Record

```
user.timesheets.build(attributes)
user.timesheets.new(attributes) # same as calling build
```

One possible reason to still use `build` is that as a convenience, if the `attributes` parameter is an array of hashes (instead of just one), then `build` executes for each one. However, you would usually accomplish that kind of behavior using `accepts_nested _attributes_for` on the owning class, covered in Chapter 11, "All about Helpers," in section 11.9.3, "Integrating Additional Objects in One Form."

7.2.2.5 `calculate(operation, column_name, options = {})`

Provides aggregate (`:sum`, `:average`, `:minimum`, and `:maximum`) values within the scope of associated records. Covered in detail in Chapter 9, "Advanced Active Record."

7.2.2.6 `clear`

The `clear` method is similar to invoking `delete_all` (covered later in this section); however, instead of returning an array of deleted objects, it is chainable.

7.2.2.7 `count(column_name=nil, options={})`

Counts all associated records in the database. The first parameter, `column_name`, gives you the option of counting on a column instead of generating `COUNT(*)` in the resulting SQL. If the `:counter_sql` option is set for the association, it will be used for the query; otherwise, you can pass a custom value via the options hash of this method.

Assuming that no `:counter_sql` or `:finder_sql` options are set on the association or passed to `count`, the target class's count method is used, scoped to only count associated records.

7.2.2.8 `create(attributes, &block)` and `create!(attributes, &block)`

Instantiates a new record with its foreign key attribute set to the owner's id, adds it to the association collection, and saves it, all in one method call. The bang variant raises `Active::RecordInvalid` if saving fails, while the nonbang variant returns true or false, as you would expect it to based on the behavior of create methods in other places.

The owning record must be saved in order to use create; otherwise, an `Active Record::RecordNotSaved` exception is raised.

```
>> User.new.timesheets.create
ActiveRecord::RecordNotSaved: You cannot call create unless the parent is saved
```

If a block is passed to `create` or `create!`, it will get yielded the newly created instance after the passed-in attributes are assigned but before saving the record to the database.

7.2.2.9 `delete(*records)` and `delete_all`

The `delete` and `delete_all` methods are used to sever specified associations or all of them, respectively. Both methods operate transactionally.

Invoking `delete_all` executes an `SQL UPDATE` that sets foreign keys for all currently associated objects to nil, effectively disassociating them from their parent.

Note

The names of the `delete` and `delete_all` methods can be misleading. By default, they don't delete anything from the database—they only sever associations by clearing the foreign key field of the associated record. This behavior is related to the `:dependent` option, which defaults to `:nullify`. If the association is configured with the `:dependent` option set to `:delete` or `:destroy`, then the associated records will actually be deleted from the database.

7.2.2.10 `destroy(*records)` and `destroy_all`

The `destroy` and `destroy_all` methods are used to remove specified or all associations from the database. Both methods operate transactionally.

The `destroy_all` method takes no parameters; it's an all or nothing affair. When called, it begins a transaction and invokes `destroy` on each object in the association, causing them all to be deleted from the database with individual `DELETE` SQL statements. There are load issues to consider if you plan to use this method with large association collections, since many objects will be loaded into memory at once.

7.2.2.11 `empty?`

Simply calls `size.zero?`.

7.2.2.12 `find(id)`

Finds an associated record by `id`—a really common operation when dealing with nested RESTful resources. Raises `ActiveRecord::RecordNotFound` exception if either the `id` or `foreign_key` of the owner record is not found.

Active Record

7.2.2.13 `first(*args)`

Returns the first associated record. Wondering how Active Record figures out whether to go to the database instead of loading the entire association collection into memory?

```
 1 def fetch_first_or_last_using_find?(args)
 2   if args.first.is_a?(Hash)
 3     true
 4   else
 5     !(loaded? ||
 6       owner.new_record? ||
 7       options[:finder_sql] ||
 8       target.any? {|record| record.new_record? || record.changed? } ||
 9       args.first.kind_of?(Integer))
10   end
11 end
```

Passing `first` an integer argument mimics the semantics of Ruby's `Array` `#first`, returning that number of records.

```
>> c = Client.first
=> #<Client id: 1, name: "Taigan", code: "TAIGAN", created_at: "2010-01-24
03:18:58", updated_at: "2010-01-24 03:18:58">
>> c.billing_codes.first(2)
=> [#<BillingCode id: 1, client_id: 1, code: "MTG", description: "Meetings">,
#<BillingCode id: 2, client_id: 1, code: "DEV", description: "Development">]
```

7.2.2.14 `ids`

Convenience wrapper for `pluck(primary_key)`, covered in detail in Chapter 9, "Advanced Active Record."

7.2.2.15 `include?(record)`

Checks to see if the supplied record exists in the association collection and that it still exists in the underlying database table.

7.2.2.16 `last(*args)`

Returns the last associated record. Refer to description of `first` earlier in this section for more details—it behaves exactly the same except for the obvious.

7.2.2.17 `length`

Returns the size of the collection by loading it and calling `size` on the array.

7.2.2.18 `maximum(column_name, options = {})`

Convenience wrapper for `calculate(:maximum, ...)`, covered in detail in Chapter 9, "Advanced Active Record."

7.2.2.19 `minimum(column_name, options = {})`

Convenience wrapper for `calculate(:minimum, ...)`, covered in detail in Chapter 9, "Advanced Active Record."

7.2.2.20 `new(attributes, &block)`

Instantiates a new record with its foreign key attribute set to the owner's id and adds it to the association collection, in one method call.

7.2.2.21 `pluck(*column_names)`

Returns an array of attribute values, covered in detail in Chapter 9, "Advanced Active Record."

7.2.2.22 `replace(other_array)`

Replaces the collection with `other_array`. Works by deleting objects that exist in the current collection but not in `other_array` and inserting (using `concat`) objects that don't exist in the current collection but do exist in `other_array`.

7.2.2.23 `select(select=nil, &block)`

The `select` method allows the specification one or many attributes to be selected for an association result set.

```
>> user.timesheets.select(:submitted).to_a
=> [#<Timesheet id: nil, submitted: false>,
    #<Timesheet id: nil, submitted: true>]
>> user.timesheets.select([:id,:submitted]).to_a
=> [#<Timesheet id: 1, submitted: false>,
    #<Timesheet id: 2, submitted: true>]
```

Keep in mind that only attributes specified will be populated in the resulting objects! For instance, continuing the first example, trying to access `updated_at` on any of the returned timesheets results in an `ActiveModel::MissingAttribute Error` exception being raised.

```
>> timesheet = user.timesheets.select(:submitted).first
=> #<Timesheet id: nil, submitted: false>
```

Active
Record

```
>> timesheet.updated_at
ActiveModel::MissingAttributeError: missing attribute: updated_at
```

Alternatively, passing a block to the `select` method behaves similarly to `Array#select`. The result set from the database scope is converted into an array of objects and iterated through using `Array#select`, including only objects where the specified block returns true.

7.2.2.24 `size`

If the collection has already been loaded or its owner object has never been saved, the `size` method simply returns the size of the current underlying array of associated objects. Otherwise, assuming default options, a `SELECT COUNT(*)` query is executed to get the size of the associated collection without having to load any objects. The query is bounded to the `:limit` option of the association, if there is any set.

Note that if there is a `counter_cache` option set on the association, then its value is used instead of hitting the database.

When you know that you are starting from an unloaded state and it's likely that there are associated records in the database that you will need to load no matter what, it's more efficient to use `length` instead of `size`.

Some association options, such as `:group` and `:uniq`, come into play when calculating size—basically they will always force all objects to be loaded from the database so that the resulting size of the association array can be returned.

7.2.2.25 `sum(column_name, options = {})`

Convenience wrapper for `calculate(:sum, ...)`, covered in detail in Chapter 9, "Advanced Active Record."

7.2.2.26 `uniq`

Iterates over the target collection and populates an `Array` with the unique values present. Keep in mind that equality of Active Record objects is determined by identity, meaning that the value of the `id` attribute is the same for both objects being compared.

A Warning about Association Names

Don't create associations that have the same name as instance methods of `ActiveRecord::Base`. Since the association adds a method with that name to its model, it will override the inherited method and break things. For instance, `attributes` and `connection` would make really bad choices for association names.

7.3   The `belongs_to` Association

The `belongs_to` class method expresses a relationship from one Active Record object to a single associated object for which it has a foreign key attribute. The trick to remembering whether a class "belongs to" another one is considering which has the foreign key column in its database table.

Assigning an object to a `belongs_to` association will set its foreign key attribute to the owner object's id but will not save the record to the database automatically, as in the following example:

```
>> timesheet = Timesheet.create
=> #<Timesheet id: 1409, user_id: nil...>
>> timesheet.user = obie
=> #<User id: 1, login: "obie"...>
>> timesheet.user.login
=> "obie"
>> timesheet.reload
=> #<Timesheet id: 1409, user_id: nil...>
```

Defining a `belongs_to` relationship on a class creates a method with the same name on its instances. As mentioned earlier, the method is actually a proxy to the related Active Record object and adds capabilities useful for manipulating the relationship.

7.3.1   Reloading the Association

Just invoking the association method will query the database (if necessary) and return an instance of the related object. The method takes a `force_reload` parameter that tells Active Record whether to reload the related object, if it happens to have been cached already by a previous access.

In the following capture from my console, I look up a timesheet and view the `object_id` of its related user object. Notice that the second time I invoke the association via `user`, the `object_id` remains the same. The related object has been cached. However, passing `true` to the accessor reloads the relationship, and I get a new instance.

```
>> ts = Timesheet.first
=> #<Timesheet id: 3, user_id: 1...>
>> ts.user.object_id
=> 70279541443160
>> ts.user.object_id
=> 70279541443160
>> ts.user(true).object_id
=> 70279549419740
```

7.3.2   Building and Creating Related Objects via the Association

During the `belongs_to` method's metaprogramming, it also adds factory methods for creating new instances of the related class and attaching them via the foreign key automatically.

The `build_association` method does not save the new object, but the `create_association` method does. Both methods take an optional hash of attribute parameters with which to initialize the newly instantiated objects. Both are essentially one-line convenience methods, which I don't find particularly useful. It just doesn't usually make sense to create instances in that direction!

To illustrate, I'll simply show the code for building a `User` from a `Timesheet` or creating a `Client` from a `BillingCode`, neither of which would ever happen in real code because it just doesn't make sense to do so:

```
>> ts = Timesheet.first
=> #<Timesheet id: 3, user_id: 1...>

>> ts.build_user
=> #<User id: nil, email: nil...>

>> bc = BillingCode.first
=> #<BillingCode id: 1, code: "TRAVEL"...>

>> bc.create_client
=> #<Client id: 1, name=>nil, code=>nil...>
```

You'll find yourself creating instances of belonging objects from the `has_many` side of the relationship much more often.

7.3.3   `belongs_to` Options

The following options can be passed in a hash to the `belongs_to` method.

7.3.3.1   `autosave: true`

Indicates whether to automatically save the owning record whenever this record is saved. Defaults to `false`.

7.3.3.2   `:class_name`

Assume for a moment that we wanted to establish another `belongs_to` relationship from the `Timesheet` class to `User`, this time modeling the relationship to the approver of the timesheet. You might start by adding an `approver_id` column to the `timesheets` table and an `authorized_approver` column to the `users`

table via a migration. Then you would add a second `belongs_to` declaration to the
`Timesheet` class:

```
1  class Timesheet < ActiveRecord::Base
2    belongs_to :approver
3    belongs_to :user
4    ...
```

Active Record won't be able to figure out what class you're trying to link with, just the
information provided, because you've (legitimately) acted against the Rails convention of naming a relationship according to the related class. It's time for a `:class_
name` parameter.

```
1  class Timesheet < ActiveRecord::Base
2    belongs_to :approver, class_name: 'User'
3    belongs_to :user
4    ...
```

7.3.3.3   `:counter_cache`

Use this option to make Rails automatically update a counter field on the associated
object with the number of belonging objects. The option value can be `true`, in
which case the pluralized name of the belonging class plus `_count` is used, or you
can supply your own column name to be used:

```
counter_cache: true
counter_cache: :number_of_children
```

If a significant percentage of your association collections will be empty at any given
moment, you can optimize performance at the cost of some extra database storage by
using counter caches liberally. The reason is that when the counter cache attribute is
at zero, Rails won't even try to query the database for the associated records!

Note

The value of the counter cache column must be set to zero by default in the
database! Otherwise, the counter caching won't work at all. It's because the
way that Rails implements the counter caching behavior is by adding a simple callback that goes directly to the database with an UPDATE command and
increments the value of the counter. If you're not careful and neglect to set a
default value of zero for the counter cache column on the database or misspell
the column name, the counter cache will still seem to work! There is a magic

method on all classes with `has_many` associations called `collection_count`, just like the counter cache. It will return a correct count value based on the in-memory object, even if you don't have a counter cache option set or the counter cache column value is null!

In the case that a counter cache was altered on the database side, you may tell Active Record to reset a potentially stale value to the correct count via the class method `reset_counters`. It's parameters are the id of the object and a list of association names.

```
Timesheet.reset_counters(5, :weeks)
```

7.3.3.4 `dependent: :destroy` or `:delete`
Specifies a rule that the associated owner record should be destroyed or just deleted from the database, depending on the value of the option. When triggered, `:destroy` will call the dependent's callbacks, whereas `:delete` will not.

Usage of this option *might* make sense in a `has_one` / `belongs_to` pairing. However, it is really unlikely that you want this behavior on `has_many` / `belongs_to` relationship; it just doesn't seem to make sense to code things that way. Additionally, if the owner record has its `:dependent` option set on the corresponding `has_many` association, then destroying one associated record will have the ripple effect of destroying all its siblings.

7.3.3.5 `foreign_key: column_name`
Specifies the name of the foreign key column that should be used to find the associated object. Rails will normally infer this setting from the name of the association by adding `_id` to it. You can override the inferred foreign key name with this option if necessary.

```
# Without the explicit option, Rails would guess administrator_id.

belongs_to :administrator, foreign_key: 'admin_user_id'
```

7.3.3.6 `inverse_of: name_of_has_association`
Explicitly declares the name of the inverse association in a bidirectional relationship. Considered an optimization, use of this option allows Rails to return the same instance of an object no matter which side of the relationship it is accessed from.

This is covered in detail in the section "`inverse_of: name_of_belongs _to_association`" in this chapter.

7.3.3.7   `polymorphic: true`

Use the `:polymorphic` option to specify that an object is related to its association in a polymorphic way, which is the Rails way of saying that the type of the related object is stored in the database along with its foreign key. By making a `belongs_to` relationship polymorphic, you abstract out the association so that any other model in the system can fill it.

Polymorphic associations let you trade some measure of relational integrity for the convenience of implementation in child relationships that are reused across your application. Common examples are models such as photo attachments, comments, notes, line items, and so on.

Let's illustrate by writing a `Comment` class that attaches to its subjects polymorphically. We'll associate it to both expense reports and timesheets. Listing 7.1 has the schema information in migration code, followed by the code for the classes involved. Notice the `:subject_type` column, which stores the class name of the associated class.

Listing 7.1   Comment Class Using Polymorphic Belongs to Relationship

```
1  create_table :comments do |t|
2    t.text :body
3    t.references :subject, polymorphic: true
4
5    # References can be used as a shortcut for following two
         statements.
6    # t.integer :subject_id
7    # t.string  :subject_type
8
9    t.timestamps
10 end
11
12 class Comment < ActiveRecord::Base
13   belongs_to :subject, polymorphic: true
14 end
15
16 class ExpenseReport < ActiveRecord::Base
17   belongs_to :user
18   has_many :comments, as: :subject
19 end
20
21 class Timesheet < ActiveRecord::Base
22   belongs_to :user
23   has_many :comments, as: :subject
24 end
```

As you can see in the `ExpenseReport` and `Timesheet` classes of Listing 7.1, there is a corresponding syntax where you give Active Record a clue that the relationship is polymorphic by specifying `as:` `:subject`. We haven't covered `has_many`'s options yet in this chapter, and polymorphic relationships have their own section in Chapter 9, "Advanced Active Record."

7.3.3.8 `primary_key: column_name`

You should never need to use this option, except perhaps with strange legacy database schemas. It allows you to specify a surrogate column on the owning record to use as the target of the foreign key instead of the usual primary key.

7.3.3.9 `touch: true` or `column_name`

"Touches" the owning record's `updated_at` timestamp or a specific timestamp column specified by `column_name`, if it is supplied. Useful for caching schemes where timestamps are used to invalidate cached view content. The `column_name` option is particularly useful here if you want to do fine-grained fragment caching of the owning record's view.

For example, let's set the foundation for doing just that with the user/timesheet association:

```
$ rails generate migration AddTimesheetsUpdatedAtToUsers
        timesheets_updated_at:datetime
   invoke  active_record
   create    db/migrate/20130413175038_add_timesheets_updated_
        at_to_users.rb

$ rake db:migrate
==  AddTimesheetsUpdatedAtToUsers: migrating ==================
-- add_column(:users, :timesheets_updated_at, :datetime)
   -> 0.0005s
==  AddTimesheetsUpdatedAtToUsers: migrated (0.0005s) ==========

1 class Timesheet < ActiveRecord::Base
2   belongs_to :user, touch: :timesheets_updated_at
3   ...
```

7.3.3.10 `validate: true`

Defaults to `false` on `belongs_to` associations, contrary to its counterpart setting on `has_many`. Tells Active Record to validate the owner record, but only in circumstances where it would normally save the owning record, such as when the record is new and a save is required in order to get a foreign key value.

Tim Says ...

Use `validates_associated` if you want association validation outside of automatic saving.

7.3.4 `belongs_to` Scopes

Sometimes the need arises to have a relationship that must satisfy certain conditions in order for it to be valid. To facilitate this, Rails allows us to supply chain query criteria, or a *scope*, to a relationship definition as an optional second block argument. Active Record scopes are covered in detail in Chapter 9, "Advanced Active Record."

7.3.4.1 `where(*conditions)`

To illustrate supplying a condition to a `belongs_to` relationship, let's assume that the `users` table has a column `approver`:

```
1 class Timesheet < ActiveRecord::Base
2   belongs_to :approver,
3     -> { where(approver: true) },
4     class_name: 'User'
5   ...
6 end
```

Now in order for the assignment of a user to the `approver` field to work, that user must be authorized. I'll go ahead and add a spec that both indicates the intention of my code and shows it in action. I turn my attention to `spec/models/timesheet_spec.rb`.

```
 1 require 'spec_helper'
 2
 3 describe Timesheet do
 4   subject(:timesheet) { Timesheet.create }
 5
 6   describe '#approver' do
 7     it 'may have a user associated as an approver' do
 8       timesheet.approver = User.create(approver: true)
 9       expect(timesheet.approver).to be
10     end
11   end
12 end
```

It's a good start, but I also want to make sure something happens to prevent the system from assigning a nonauthorized user to the `approver` field, so I add another spec:

```
1 it 'cannot be associated with a nonauthorized user' do
2   timesheet.approver = User.create(approver: false)
3   expect(timesheet.approver).to_not be
4 end
```

I have my suspicions about the validity of that spec, though, and as I half expected, it doesn't really work the way I want it to work:

```
1) Timesheet#approver cannot be associated with a nonauthorized user
     Failure/Error: expect(timesheet.approver).to_not be
        expected #<User id: 1, approver: false ...> to evaluate to false
```

The problem is that Active Record (for better or worse—probably worse) allows me to make the invalid assignment. The `scope` option only applies during the query to get the association back from the database. I'll have some more work ahead of me to achieve the desired behavior, but I'll go ahead and prove out Rails' actual behavior by fixing my specs. I'll do so by passing `true` to the `approver` method's optional `force_reload` argument, which tells it to reload its target object:

```
 1 describe Timesheet do
 2   subject(:timesheet) { Timesheet.create }
 3
 4   describe '#approver' do
 5     it 'may have a user associated as an approver' do
 6       timesheet.approver = User.create(approver: true)
 7       timesheet.save
 8       expect(timesheet.approver(true)).to be
 9     end
10
11     it 'cannot be associated with a nonauthorized user' do
12       timesheet.approver = User.create(approver: false)
13       timesheet.save
14       expect(timesheet.approver(true)).to_not be
15     end
16   end
17 end
```

Those two specs do pass, but note that I went ahead and saved the `timesheet`, since just assigning a value to it will not save the record. Then, as mentioned, I took advantage of the `force_reload` parameter to make Rails reload `approver` from the database and not just simply give me the same instance I originally assigned to it.

The lesson to learn is that providing a `scope` on relationships never affects the assignment of associated objects, only how they're read back from the database. To enforce the rule that a timesheet approver must be authorized, you'd need to add a `before_save` callback to the `Timesheet` class itself. Callbacks are covered in detail at the beginning of Chapter 9, "Advanced Active Record."

7.3.4.2 `includes`

In previous versions of Rails, relationship definitions had an `:include` option that would take a list of second-order association names (on the owning record) that should be eager loaded when the current object was loaded. As of Rails 4, the way to do this is supplying an `includes` query method to the scope argument of a relationship.

```
belongs_to :post, -> { includes(:author) }
```

In general, this technique is used to knock N+1 select operations down to N plus the number associations being included. It is rare to use this technique on a `belongs_to` rather than on the `has_many` side.

If necessary, due to conditions or orders referencing tables other than the main one, a SELECT statement with the necessary LEFT OUTER JOINS will be constructed on the fly so that all the data needed to construct a whole object graph is queried in one big database request.

With judicious use of using a relationship scope to include second-order associations and careful benchmarking, you can sometimes improve the performance of your application dramatically, mostly by eliminating N+1 queries. On the other hand, pulling lots of data from the database and instantiating large object trees can be very costly, so using an `includes` scope is no "silver bullet." As they say, your mileage may vary.

7.3.4.3 `select`

Replaces the SQL select clause that is normally generated when loading this association, which usually takes the form `table_name.*`. This is just additional flexibility that it normally never needed.

7.3.4.4 `readonly`

Locks down the reference to the owning record so that you can't modify it. Theoretically, this might make sense in terms of constraining your programming contexts very specifically, but I've never had a use for it. Still, for illustrative purposes, here is an example where I've made the `user` association on `Timesheet` readonly:

```
1 class Timesheet < ActiveRecord::Base
2   belongs_to :user, ~> { readonly }
3   ...
4
5 >> t = Timesheet.first
6 => #<Timesheet id: 1, submitted: nil, user_id: 1...>
7
8 >> t.user
9  => #<User id: 1, login: "admin"...>
10
11 >> t.user.save
12 ActiveRecord::ReadOnlyRecord: ActiveRecord::ReadOnlyRecord
```

7.4   The `has_many` Association

Just like it sounds, the has_many association allows you to define a relationship in which one model has many other models that belong to it. The sheer readability of code constructs such as has_many is a major reason that people fall in love with Rails.

The has_many class method is often used without additional options. If Rails can guess the type of class in the relationship from the name of the association, no additional configuration is necessary. This bit of code should look familiar by now:

```
1 class User < ActiveRecord::Base
2   has_many :timesheets
3   has_many :expense_reports
```

The names of the associations can be singularized and match the names of models in the application, so everything works as expected.

7.4.1   `has_many` Options

Despite the ease of use of has_many, there is a surprising amount of power and customization possible for those who know and understand the options available.

7.4.1.1   `after_add:` callback

Called after a record is added to the collection via the << method. This is not triggered by the collection's `create` method, so careful consideration is needed when relying on association callbacks. A lambda callback will get called directly versus a symbol, which correlates to a method on the owning record that takes the newly added child as a parameter. It's also possible to pass an array of lambda or symbols.

Add callback method options to a has_many by passing one or more symbols corresponding to method names or `Proc` objects. See Listing 7.2 in the :before_ add option for an example.

7.4.1.2 `after_remove: callback`

Called after a record has been removed from the collection with the `delete` method. A lambda callback will get called directly versus a symbol, which correlates to a method on the owning record that takes the newly added child as a parameter. It's also possible to pass an array of lambda or symbols. See Listing 7.2 in the `:before_add` option for an example.

7.4.1.3 `as: association_name`

Specifies the polymorphic `belongs_to` association to use on the related class. (See Chapter 9, "Advanced Active Record," for more about polymorphic relationships.)

7.4.1.4 `autosave: true`

Indicates whether to automatically save *all modified records* in an association collection when the parent is saved. Defaults to `false`, but note that normal Active Record behavior is to save *new* associations records automatically when the parent is saved.

7.4.1.5 `before_add: callback`

Triggered when a record is added to the collection via the `<<` method. (Remember that `concat` and `push` are aliases of `<<`.)

A lambda callback will get called directly versus a symbol, which correlates to a method on the owning record that takes the newly added child as a parameter. It's also possible to pass an array of lambda or symbols.

Raising an exception in the callback will stop the object from getting added to the collection (basically because the callback is triggered right after the type mismatch check and there is no rescue clause to be found inside `<<`).

Listing 7.2   A Simple Example of `:before_add` callback Usage

```
1 has_many :unchangable_posts,
2          class_name: "Post",
3          before_add: :raise_exception
4
5 private
6
7 def raise_exception(object)
8   raise "You can't add a post"
9 end
```

Of course, that would have been a lot shorter code using a `Proc` since it's a one liner. The `owner` parameter is the object with the association. The `record` parameter is the object being added.

```
has_many :unchangable_posts,
  class_name: "Post",
  before_add: ->(owner, record) { raise "Can't do it!" }
```

Here it is one more time with a lambda, which doesn't check the arity of block parameters:

```
has_many :unchangable_posts,
  class_name: "Post",
  before_add: lambda { raise "You can't add a post" }
```

7.4.1.6 `before_remove:` callback

Called before a record is removed from a collection with the `delete` method. See `before_add` for more information. As with `:before_add`, raising an exception stops the remove operation.

```
 1 class User < ActiveRecord::Base
 2   has_many :timesheets,
 3           before_remove: :check_timesheet_destruction,
 4           dependent: :destroy
 5
 6   protected
 7
 8   def check_timesheet_destruction(timesheet)
 9     if timesheet.submitted?
10       raise TimesheetError, "Cannot destroy a submitted
         timesheet."
11     end
12   end
```

Note that this is a somewhat contrived example, because it violates my sense of good object-oriented principles. The `User` class shouldn't really be responsible for knowing when it's OK to delete a timesheet or not. The `check_timesheet_destruction` method would more properly be added as a `before_destroy` callback on the `Timesheet` class.

7.4.1.7 `:class_name`

The `:class_name` option is common to all the associations. It allows you to specify, as a string, the name of the class of the association and is needed when the class name cannot be inferred from the name of the association itself.

```
has_many :draft_timesheets, -> { where(submitted: false) },
class_name: 'Timesheet'
```

7.4.1.8   `dependent: :delete_all`

All associated objects are deleted in fell swoop using a single SQL command. Note: While this option is much faster than `:destroy`, it doesn't trigger any destroy callbacks on the associated objects—you should use this option very carefully. It should only be used on associations that depend solely on the parent object.

7.4.1.9   `dependent: :destroy`

All associated objects are destroyed along with the parent object by iteratively calling their `destroy` methods.

7.4.1.10   `dependent: :nullify`

The default behavior when deleting a record with `has_many` associations is to leave those associated records alone. Their foreign key fields will still point at the record that was deleted. The `:nullify` option tells Active Record to nullify, or clear, the foreign key that joins them to the parent record.

7.4.1.11   `dependent: :restrict_with_exception`

If associated objects are present when the parent object is destroyed, Rails raises an `ActiveRecord::DeleteRestrictionError` exception.

7.4.1.12   `dependent: :restrict_with_error`

An error is added to the parent object if any associated objects are present, rolling back the deletion from the database.

7.4.1.13   `foreign_key: column_name`

Overrides the convention-based foreign key column name that would normally be used in the SQL statement that loads the association. Normally it would be the owning record's class name with `_id` appended to it.

7.4.1.14   `inverse_of: name_of_belongs_to_association`

Explicitly declares the name of the inverse association in a bidirectional relationship. Considered an optimization, use of this option allows Rails to return the same instance of an object no matter which side of the relationship it is accessed from.

Consider the following, using our recurring example *without* the use of `inverse_of`.

```
>> user = User.first
>> timesheet = user.timesheets.first
=> <Timesheet id: 1, user_id: 1...>
```

```
>> timesheet.user.equal? user
=> false
```

If we add :inverse_of to the association objection on User, like

```
has_many :timesheets, inverse_of: :user
```

then timesheet.user.equal? user will be true. Try something similar in one of your apps to see it for yourself.

7.4.1.15 `primary_key: column_name`
Specifies a surrogate key to use instead of the owning record's primary key, whose value should be used when querying to fill the association collection.

7.4.1.16 `:source` and `:source_type`
Used exclusively as additional options to assist in using has_many :through associations with polymorphic belongs_to. Covered in detail later in this chapter.

7.4.1.17 `through: association_name`
Creates an association collection via another association. See the section in this chapter titled "has_many :through" for more information.

7.4.1.18 `validate: false`
In cases where the child records in the association collection would be automatically saved by Active Record, this option (true by default) dictates whether to ensure that they are valid. If you always want to check the validity of associated records when saving the owning record, then use validates_associated :association_name.

7.4.2 `has_many` Scopes
The has_many association provides the ability to customize the query used by the database to retrieve the association collection. This is achieved by passing a scope block to the has_many method definition using any of the standard Active Record query methods, as covered in Chapter 5, "Working with Active Record." In this section, we'll cover the most common scope methods used with has_many associations.

7.4.2.1 `where(*conditions)`
Using the query method where, one could add extra conditions to the Active Record–generated SQL query that brings back the objects in the association.

You can apply extra conditions to an association for a variety of reasons. How about approval of comments?

```
has_many :comments,
```

Plus, there's no rule that you can't have more than one has_many association exposing the same two related tables in different ways. Just remember that you'll probably have to specify the class name too.

```
has_many :pending_comments, -> { where(approved: true) },
  class_name: 'Comment'
```

7.4.2.2   `extending(*extending_modules)`

Specifies one or many modules with methods that will extend the association collection proxy. This is used as an alternative to defining additional methods in a block passed to the has_many method itself. It is discussed in the section "Association Extensions" in this chapter.

7.4.2.3   `group(*args)`

Adds a GROUP BY SQL clause to the queries used to load the contents of the association collection.

7.4.2.4   `having(*clauses)`

Must be used in conjunction with the group query method and adds extra conditions to the resulting SQL query used to load the contents of the association collection.

7.4.2.5   `includes(*associations)`

Takes an array of second-order association names (as an array) that should be eager loaded when this collection is loaded. With judicious use of the includes query method and careful benchmarking, you can sometimes improve the performance of your application dramatically.

To illustrate, let's analyze how includes affects the SQL generated while navigating relationships. We'll use the following simplified versions of Timesheet, BillableWeek, and BillingCode:

```
1 class Timesheet < ActiveRecord::Base
2   has_many :billable_weeks
3 end
4
5 class BillableWeek < ActiveRecord::Base
```

```
 6    belongs_to :timesheet
 7    belongs_to :billing_code
 8  end
 9
10  class BillingCode < ActiveRecord::Base
11    belongs_to :client
12    has_many :billable_weeks
13  end
```

First, I need to set up my test data, so I create a `timesheet` instance and add a couple of billable weeks to it. Then I assign a billable code to each billable week, which results in an object graph (with four objects linked together via associations).

Next I do a fancy one-line `collect`, which gives me an array of the billing codes associated with the timesheet:

```
>> Timesheet.find(3).billable_weeks.collect(&:code)
=> ["TRAVEL", "DEVELOPMENT"]
```

Without the `includes` scope method set on the `billable_weeks` association of `Timesheet`, that operation cost me the following four database hits (copied from `log/development.log` and prettied up a little):

```
Timesheet Load (0.3ms)  SELECT timesheets.* FROM timesheets WHERE
(timesheets.id = 3) LIMIT 1
BillableWeek Load (1.3ms)  SELECT billable_weeks.* FROM billable_weeks WHERE
(billable_weeks.timesheet_id = 3)
BillingCode Load (1.2ms)  SELECT billing_codes.* FROM billing_codes WHERE
(billing_codes.id = 7) LIMIT 1
BillingCode Load (3.2ms)  SELECT billing_codes.* FROM billing_codes WHERE
(billing_codes.id = 8) LIMIT 1
```

This demonstrates the "N+1 select" problem that inadvertently plagues many systems. Any time I need one billable week, it will cost me N select statements to retrieve its associated records. Now let's provide the `billable_weeks` association a scope block using `includes`, after which the `Timesheet` class looks as follows:

```
1  class Timesheet < ActiveRecord::Base
2    has_many :billable_weeks, -> { includes(:billing_code) }
3  end
```

Simple! Rerunning our test statement yields the same results in the console:

```
>> Timesheet.find(3).billable_weeks.collect(&:code)
=> ["TRAVEL", "DEVELOPMENT"]
```

But look at how different the generated SQL is:

```
Timesheet Load (0.4ms) SELECT timesheets.* FROM timesheets WHERE (timesheets.id
= 3) LIMIT 1
BillableWeek Load (0.6ms)  SELECT billable_weeks.* FROM billable_weeks WHERE
(billable_weeks.timesheet_id = 3)
BillingCode Load (2.1ms) SELECT billing_codes.* FROM billing_codes WHERE
(billing_codes.id IN (7,8))
```

Active Record smartly figures out exactly which `BillingCode` records it will need and pulls them in using one query. For large datasets, the performance improvement can be quite dramatic!

It's generally easy to find N+1 select issues just by watching the log scroll by while clicking through the different screens of your application. (Of course, make sure that you're looking at realistic data or the exercise will be pointless.) Screens that might benefit from eager loading will cause a flurry of single-row `SELECT` statements—one for each record in a given association being used.

If you're feeling particularly daring (perhaps masochistic is a better term), you can try including a deep hierarchy of associations by mixing hashes into your `includes` query method, like in this fictional example from a bulletin board:

```
has_many :posts, -> { includes([:author, {comments: {author: :avatar }}]) }
```

That example snippet will grab not only all the comments for a `Post` but all their authors and avatar pictures as well. You can mix and match symbols, arrays, and hashes in any combination to describe the associations you want to load.

The biggest potential problem with "deep" includes is pulling too much data out of the database. You should always start out with the simplest solution that will work and then use benchmarking and analysis to figure out if optimizations such as eager loading help improve your performance.

Wilson Says ...

Let people learn eager loading by crawling across broken glass, like we did. It builds character!

7.4.2.6 `limit(integer)`

Appends a `LIMIT` clause to the SQL generated for loading this association. This option is potentially useful in capping the size of very large association collections. Use in conjunction with the `order` query method to make sure you're grabbing the most relevant records.

7.4.2.7 `offset(integer)`

An integer determining the offset from where the rows should be fetched when loading the association collection. I assume this is here mostly for completeness, since it's hard to envision a valid use case.

7.4.2.8 `order(*clauses)`

Specifies the order in which the associated objects are returned via an "ORDER BY" SQL fragment, such as `"last_name, first_name DESC"`.

7.4.2.9 `readonly`

Sets all records in the association collection to readonly mode, which prevents saving them.

7.4.2.10 `select(expression)`

By default, this is * as in `SELECT * FROM` but can be changed if you, for example, want to add additional calculated columns or "piggyback" additional columns that will be joined with the associated object as it is loaded.

7.4.2.11 `distinct`

Strips duplicate objects from the collection. Sometimes useful in conjunction with `has_many :through`.

7.5 Many-to-Many Relationships

Associating persistent objects via a join table can be one of the trickier aspects of object-relational mapping to implement correctly in a framework. Rails has a couple of techniques that let you represent many-to-many relationships in your model. We'll start with the older and simpler `has_and_belongs_to_many` and then cover the newer `has_many :through`.

7.5.1 `has_and_belongs_to_many`

Before proceeding with this section, I must clear my conscience by stating that `has_and_belongs_to_many` is practically obsolete in the minds of many Rails developers, including the authors of this book. Use `has_many :through` instead and your life should be a lot easier. The section is preserved in this edition almost exactly as it appeared in the previous editions because it contains good techniques that enlighten the reader about nuances of Active Record behavior.

The `has_and_belongs_to_many` method establishes a link between two associated Active Record models via an intermediate join table. Unless the join table is explicitly specified as an option, Rails guesses its name by concatenating the table names of the joined classes in alphabetical order and separated with an underscore.

For example, if I was using has_and_belongs_to_many (or habtm for short) to establish a relationship between Timesheet and BillingCode, the join table would be named billing_codes_timesheets and the relationship would be defined in the models. Both the migration class and models are listed:

```
 1 class CreateBillingCodesTimesheets < ActiveRecord::Migration
 2   def change
 3     create_table :billing_codes_timesheets, id: false do |t|
 4       t.references :billing_code, null: false
 5       t.references :timesheet, null: false
 6     end
 7   end
 8 end
 9
10 class Timesheet < ActiveRecord::Base
11   has_and_belongs_to_many :billing_codes
12 end
13
14 class BillingCode < ActiveRecord::Base
15   has_and_belongs_to_many :timesheets
16 end
```

Note that an id primary key is not needed; hence, the id: false option was passed to the create_table method. Also, since the foreign key columns are both needed, we pass them a null: false option. (In real code, you would also want to make sure both of the foreign key columns were indexed properly.)

Kevin Says ...

A new migration method create_join_table was added to Rails 4 to create a join table using the order of the first two arguments. The migration in the preceding code example is equivalent to the following:

```
 1 class CreateBillingCodesTimesheets < ActiveRecord::Migration
 2   def change
 3     create_join_table :billing_codes, :timesheets
 4   end
 5 end
```

7.5.1.1   Self-Referential Relationship

What about self-referential many-to-many relationships? Linking a model to itself via a habtm relationship is easy—you just have to provide explicit options. In Listing 7.3,

I've created a join table and established a link between related `BillingCode` objects. Again, both the migration and model class are listed:

Listing 7.3 Related Billing Codes

```
 1 class CreateRelatedBillingCodes < ActiveRecord::Migration
 2   def change
 3     create_table :related_billing_codes, id: false do |t|
 4       t.column :first_billing_code_id, :integer, null: false
 5       t.column :second_billing_code_id, :integer, null: false
 6     end
 7   end
 8 end
 9
10 class BillingCode < ActiveRecord::Base
11   has_and_belongs_to_many :related,
12     join_table: 'related_billing_codes',
13     foreign_key: 'first_billing_code_id',
14     association_foreign_key: 'second_billing_code_id',
15     class_name: 'BillingCode'
16 end
```

7.5.1.2 Bidirectional Relationships

It's worth noting that the `related` relationship of the `BillingCode` in Listing 7.3 is not bidirectional. Just because you associate two objects in one direction does not mean they'll be associated in the other direction. But what if you need to automatically establish a bidirectional relationship?

First let's write a spec for the `BillingCode` class to prove our solution. When we add bidirectional, we don't want to break the normal behavior, so at first my spec example establishes that the normal `habtm` relationship works:

```
1 describe BillingCode do
2   let(:travel_code) { BillingCode.create(code: 'TRAVEL') }
3   let(:dev_code) { BillingCode.create(code: 'DEV') }
4
5   it "has a working related habtm association" do
6     travel_code.related << dev_code
7     expect(travel_code.reload.related).to include(dev_code)
8   end
9 end
```

I run the spec and it passes. Now I can modify the example to prove that the bidirectional behavior that we're going to add works. It ends up looking very similar to the first example.

```
1 describe BillingCode do
2   let(:travel_code) { BillingCode.create(code: 'TRAVEL') }
3   let(:dev_code) { BillingCode.create(code: 'DEV') }
4
5   it "has a bidirectional habtm association" do
6     travel_code.related << dev_code
7     expect(travel_code.reload.related).to include(dev_code)
8     expect(dev_code.reload.related).to include(travel_code)
9   end
```

Of course, the new version fails, since we haven't added the new behavior yet. I'll omit the output of running the spec, since it doesn't tell us anything we don't know already.

7.5.1.3   Extra Columns on **has_and_belongs_to_many** Join Tables

Rails won't have a problem with you adding as many extra columns as you want to habtm's join table. The extra attributes will be read in and added onto model objects accessed via the habtm association. However, speaking from experience, the severe annoyances you will deal with in your application code make it really unattractive to go that route.

What kind of annoyances? For one, records returned from join tables with additional attributes will be marked as readonly, because it's not possible to save changes to those additional attributes.

You should also consider that the way that Rails makes those extra columns of the join table available might cause problems in other parts of your codebase. Having extra attributes appear magically on an object is kind of cool, but what happens when you try to access those extra properties on an object that wasn't fetched via the habtm association? Kaboom! Get ready for some potentially bewildering debugging exercises.

Methods of the habtm proxy act just as they would for a has_many relationship. Similarly, habtm shares options with has_many; only its :join_table option is unique. It allows customization of the join table name.

To sum up, habtm is a simple way to establish a many-to-many relationship using a join table. As long as you don't need to capture additional data about the relationship, everything is fine. The problems with habtm begin once you want to add extra columns to the join table, after which you'll want to upgrade the relationship to use has_many :through instead.

7.5.1.4   "Real Join Models" and **habtm**

The Rails documentation advises readers that "it's strongly recommended that you upgrade any [habtm] associations with attributes to a real join model." Use of habtm, which was one of the original innovative features in Rails, fell out of

favor once the ability to create real join models was introduced via the has_many
:through association.

Realistically, habtm is not going to be removed from Rails for a couple of sensible reasons. First of all, plenty of legacy Rails applications need it. Second, habtm
provides a way to join classes without a primary key defined on the join table, which
is occasionally useful. But most of the time you'll find yourself wanting to model
many-to-many relationships with has_many :through.

7.5.2 `has_many :through`

Well-known Rails guy Josh Susser is considered the expert on Active Record
associations—even his blog is called has_many :through. His description of the
:through association, written back when the feature was originally introduced in
Rails 1.1, is so concise and well-written that I couldn't hope to do any better. So here it is:

> The has_many :through association allows you to specify a one-to-many
> relationship indirectly via an intermediate join table. In fact, you can specify
> more than one such relationship via the same table, which effectively makes it
> a replacement for has_and_belongs_to_many. The biggest advantage is
> that the join table contains full-fledged model objects complete with primary
> keys and ancillary data. No more push_with_attributes; join models
> just work the same way all your other Active Record models do.[1]

7.5.2.1 Join Models

To illustrate the has_many :through association, we'll set up a Client model
so that it has many Timesheet objects through a normal has_many association
named billable_weeks.

```
1 class Client < ActiveRecord::Base
2   has_many :billable_weeks
3   has_many :timesheets, through: :billable_weeks
4 end
```

The BillableWeek class was already in our sample application and is ready to be
used as a join model:

```
1 class BillableWeek < ActiveRecord::Base
2   belongs_to :client
3   belongs_to :timesheet
4 end
```

---

1. http://blog.hasmanythrough.com/2006/2/28/association-goodness

We can also set up the inverse relationship, from timesheets to clients, like this:

```
1 class Timesheet < ActiveRecord::Base
2   has_many :billable_weeks
3   has_many :clients, through: :billable_weeks
4 end
```

Notice that has_many :through is always used in conjunction with a normal has_many association. Also, notice that the normal has_many association will often have the same name on both classes that are being joined together, which means the :through option will read the same on both sides.

```
through: :billable_weeks
```

How about the join model; will it always have two belongs_to associations? No.

You can also use has_many :through to easily aggregate has_many or has_one associations on the join model. Forgive me for switching to completely non-realistic domain for a moment—it's only intended to clearly demonstrate what I'm trying to describe:

```
1 class Grandparent < ActiveRecord::Base
2   has_many :parents
3   has_many :grand_children, through: :parents, source: :children
4 end
5
6 class Parent < ActiveRecord::Base
7   belongs_to :grandparent
8   has_many   :children
9 end
```

For the sake of clarity in later chapters, I'll refer to this usage of has_many :through as aggregating.

Courtenay Says ...

We use has_many :through so much! It has pretty much replaced the old has_and_belongs_to_many because it allows your join models to be upgraded to full objects. It's like when you're just dating someone and they start talking about the relationship (or, eventually, marriage). It's an example of an association being promoted to something more important than the individual objects on each side.

7.5.2.2   Usage Considerations and Examples

You can use nonaggregating has_many :through associations in almost the same ways as any other has_many associations. For instance, appending an object to a has_many :through collection will save the object as expected:

```
>> c = Client.create(name: "Trotter's Tomahawks", code "ttom")
=> #<Client id: 5 ...>

>> c.timesheets << Timesheet.new
=> #<ActiveRecord::Associations::CollectionProxy [#<Timesheet id: 2 ...>]>
```

The main benefit of has_many :through is that Active Record takes care of managing the instances of the join model for you. If we call reload on the billable_weeks association, we'll see that there was a billable week object created for us:

```
>> c.billable_weeks.reload.to_a
=> [#<BillableWeek id: 2, tuesday_hours: nil, start_date: nil,
   timesheet_id: 2, billing_code_id: nil, sunday_hours: nil,
   friday_hours: nil, monday_hours: nil, client_id: 2, wednesday_hours: nil,
   saturday_hours: nil, thursday_hours: nil>]
```

The BillableWeek object that was created is properly associated with both the client and the Timesheet. Unfortunately, there are a lot of other attributes (e.g., start_date and the hours columns) that were not populated.

One possible solution is to use create on the billable_weeks association instead and include the new Timesheet object as one of the supplied properties.

```
>> bw = c.billable_weeks.create(start_date: Time.now,
                                timesheet: Timesheet.new)
```

7.5.2.3   Aggregating Associations

When you're using has_many :through to aggregate multiple child associations, there are more significant limitations—essentially, you can query to your hearts content using find and friends, but you can't append or create new records through them.

For example, let's add a billable_weeks association to our sample User class:

```
1 class User < ActiveRecord::Base
2   has_many :timesheets
3   has_many :billable_weeks, through: :timesheets
4   ...
```

The billable_weeks association aggregates all the billable week objects belonging to the user's timesheets.

```
1 class Timesheet < ActiveRecord::Base
2   belongs_to :user
3   has_many :billable_weeks, -> { include(:billing_code) }
4   ...
```

Now let's go into the Rails console and set up some example data so that we can use the new `billable_weeks` collection (on `User`).

```
>> quentin = User.first
=> #<User id: 1, login: "quentin" ...>

>> quentin.timesheets.to_a
=> []

>> ts1 = quentin.timesheets.create
=> #<Timesheet id: 1 ...>

>> ts2 = quentin.timesheets.create
=> #<Timesheet id: 2 ...>

>> ts1.billable_weeks.create(start_date: 1.week.ago)
=> #<BillableWeek id: 1, timesheet_id: 1 ...>

>> ts2.billable_weeks.create(start_date: 2.week.ago)
=> #<BillableWeek id: 2, timesheet_id: 2 ...>

>> quentin.billable_weeks.to_a
=> [#<BillableWeek id: 1, timesheet_id: 1 ...>, #<BillableWeek id: 2,
timesheet_id: 2 ...>]
```

Just for fun, let's see what happens if we try to create a `BillableWeek` with a `User` instance:

```
>> quentin.billable_weeks.create(start_date: 3.weeks.ago)
ActiveRecord::HasManyThroughCantAssociateThroughHasOneOrManyReflection:
Cannot modify association 'User#billable_weeks' because the source
reflection class 'BillableWeek' is associated to 'Timesheet' via :has_many.
```

There you go. Since `BillableWeek` only belongs to a timesheet and not a user, Rails raises a `HasManyThroughCantAssociateThroughHasOneOrMany Reflection` exception.

7.5.2.4   Join Models and Validations

When you append to a nonaggregating `has_many  :through` association with `<<`, Active Record will always create a new join model, even if one already exists for the two records being joined. You can add `validates_uniqueness_of` constraints on the join model to keep duplicate joins from happening.

This is what such a constraint might look like on our `BillableWeek` join model.

```
validates_uniqueness_of :client_id, scope: :timesheet_id
```

That says, in effect, "There should only be one of each client per timesheet."

If your join model has additional attributes with their own validation logic, then there's another important consideration to keep in mind. Adding records directly to a `has_many :through` association causes a new join model to be automatically created with a blank set of attributes. Validations on additional columns of the join model will probably fail. If that happens, you'll need to add new records by creating join model objects and associating them appropriately through their own association proxy.

```
timesheet.billable_weeks.create(start_date: 1.week.ago)
```

7.5.3 `has_many :through` Options

The options for `has_many :through` are the same as the options for `has_many`—remember that `:through` is just an option on `has_many`! However, the use of some of `has_many`'s options change or become more significant when `:through` is used.

First of all, the `:class_name` and `:foreign_key` options are no longer valid since they are implied from the target association on the join model. The following are the rest of the options that have special significance together with `has_many :through`.

7.5.3.1 `source: association_name`

The `:source` option specifies which association to use on the associated class. This option is not mandatory because normally Active Record assumes that the target association is the singular (or plural) version of the `has_many` association name. If your association names don't match up, then you have to set `:source` explicitly.

For example, the following code will use the `BillableWeek`'s sheet association to populate `timesheets`.

```
has_many :timesheets, through: :billable_weeks, source: :sheet
```

7.5.3.2 `source_type: class_name`

The `:source_type` option is needed when you establish a `has_many :through` to a polymorphic `belongs_to` association on the join model. Consider the following example concerning clients and contacts:

```
1 class Client < ActiveRecord::Base
2   has_many :client_contacts
3   has_many :contacts, through: :client_contacts
4 end
5
6 class ClientContact < ActiveRecord::Base
7   belongs_to :client
8   belongs_to :contact, polymorphic: true
9 end
```

In this somewhat contrived example, the most important fact is that a `Client` has many `contacts` through their polymorphic relationship to the join model, `ClientContact`. There isn't a `Contact` class; we just want to be able to refer to contacts in a polymorphic sense, meaning either a `Person` or a `Business`.

```
1 class Person < ActiveRecord::Base
2   has_many :client_contacts, as: :contact
3 end
4
5 class Business < ActiveRecord::Base
6   has_many :client_contacts, as: :contact
7 end
```

Now take a moment to consider the backflips that Active Record would have to perform in order to figure out which tables to query for a client's contacts. Remember that there isn't a contacts table!

```
>> Client.first.contacts
```

Active Record would theoretically need to be aware of every model class that is linked to the other end of the contacts polymorphic association. In fact, it cannot do those kinds of backflips, which is probably a good thing as far as performance is concerned:

```
>> Client.first.contacts
ActiveRecord::HasManyThroughAssociationPolymorphicSourceError: Cannot have a
   has_many :through association 'Client#contacts' on the polymorphic object
   'Contact#contact' without 'source_type'.
```

The only way to make this scenario work (somewhat) is to give Active Record some help by specifying which table it should search when you ask for the `contacts` collection, and you do that with the `source_type` option naming the target class, symbolized like this:

```
1 class Client < ActiveRecord::Base
2   has_many :client_contacts
3   has_many :people, through: :client_contacts,
```

Active Record

```
4              source: :contact, source_type: :person
5
6   has_many :businesses, through: :client_contacts,
7              source: :contact, source_type: :business
8 end
```

After the `:source_type` is specified, the association will work as expected, but sadly we don't get a general purpose `contacts` collection to work with, as it seemed might be possible at first.

```
>> Client.first.people.create!
=> [#<Person id: 1>]
```

If you're upset that you cannot associate `people` and `business` together in a contacts association, you could try writing your own accessor method for a client's contacts:

```
1 class Client < ActiveRecord::Base
2   def contacts
3     people_contacts + business_contacts
4   end
5 end
```

Of course, you should be aware that calling that `contacts` method will result in at least two database requests and will return an `Array`, without the association proxy methods that you might expect it to have.

7.5.4   Unique Association Objects

The `distinct` scope method tells the association to include only unique objects. It is especially useful when using `has_many` `:through`, since two different `Billable Weeks` could reference the same `Timesheet`.

```
>> Client.first.timesheets.reload.to_a
[#<Timesheet id: 1...>, #<Timesheet id: 1...>]
```

It's not extraordinary for two distinct model instances of the same database record to be in memory at the same time—it's just not usually desirable.

```
1 class Client < ActiveRecord::Base
2   has_many :timesheets, -> { distinct }, through:
        :billable_weeks
3 end
```

After adding the `distinct` scope to the `has_many` `:through` association, only one instance per record is returned.

```
>> Client.first.timesheets.reload.to_a
=> [#<Timesheet id: 1...>]
```

7.6 One-to-One Relationships

One of the most basic relationship types is a one-to-one object relationship. In Active Record we declare a one-to-one relationship using the `has_one` and `belongs_to` methods together. As in the case of a `has_many` relationship, you call `belongs_to` on the model whose database table contains the foreign key column linking the two records together.

7.6.1 `has_one`

Conceptually, `has_one` works almost exactly like `has_many` does, except that when the database query is executed to retrieve the related object, a `LIMIT 1` clause is added to the generated SQL so that only one row is returned.

The name of a `has_one` relationship should be singular, which will make it read naturally—for example, `has_one :last_timesheet`, `has_one :primary_account`, `has_one :profile_photo`, and so on. Let's take a look at `has_one` in action by adding avatars for our users.

```
1 class Avatar < ActiveRecord::Base
2   belongs_to :user
3 end
4
5 class User < ActiveRecord::Base
6   has_one :avatar
7   # ... the rest of our User code ...
8 end
```

That's simple enough. Firing this up in `rails console`, we can look at some of the new methods that `has_one` adds to `User`.

```
>> u = User.first
>> u.avatar
=> nil

>> u.build_avatar(url: '/avatars/smiling')
=> #<Avatar id: nil, url: "/avatars/smiling", user_id: 1>

>> u.avatar.save
=> true
```

As you can see, we can use `build_avatar` to build a new avatar object and associate it with the user. While it's great that `has_one` will associate an avatar with the user, it isn't really anything that has_many doesn't already do. So let's take a look at what happens when we assign a new avatar to the user.

```
>> u = User.first
>> u.avatar
=> #<Avatar id: 1, url: "/avatars/smiling", user_id: 1>

>> u.create_avatar(url: '/avatars/frowning')
=> #<Avatar id: 2, url: "/avatars/4567", user_id: 1>

>> Avatar.all.to_a
=> [#<Avatar id: 1, url: "/avatars/smiling", user_id: nil>, #<Avatar id: 2, url:
"/avatars/4567", user_id: 1>]
```

The last line from that console session is the most interesting, because it shows that our initial avatar is now no longer associated with the user. Of course, the previous avatar was not removed from the database, which is something that we want in this scenario. So we'll use the dependent: :destroy option to force avatars to be destroyed when they are no longer associated with a user.

```
1 class User < ActiveRecord::Base
2   has_one :avatar, dependent: :destroy
3 end
```

With some additional fiddling around in the console, we can verify that it works as intended. In doing so, you might notice that Rails only destroys the avatar that was just removed from the user, so bad data that was in your database from before will still remain. Keep this in mind when you decide to add dependent: :destroy to your code and remember to manually clear orphaned data that might otherwise remain.

7.6.1.1 Using **has_one** with **has_many**

As I alluded to earlier, has_one is sometimes used to single out one record of significance alongside an already established has_many relationship. For instance, let's say we want to easily be able to access the last timesheet a user was working on:

```
1 class User < ActiveRecord::Base
2   has_many :timesheets
3
4   has_one  :latest_sheet,
5     -> { order('created_at desc') },
6     class_name: 'Timesheet'
7 end
```

I had to specify a `:class_name` so that Active Record knows what kind of object we're associating. (It can't figure it out based on the name of the association `:latest_sheet`.)

When adding a `has_one` relationship to a model that already has a `has_many` defined to the same related model, it is not necessary to add another `belongs_to` method call to the target object just for the new `has_one`. That might seem a little counterintuitive at first, but if you think about it, the same foreign key value is being used to read the data from the database.

7.6.1.2 **has_one** Options
The options for `has_one` associations are similar to the ones for `has_many`. For your convenience, we briefly cover the most relevant ones here.

7.6.1.3 **:as**
Allows you to set up a polymorphic association, covered in Chapter 9, "Advanced Active Record."

7.6.1.4 **:class_name**
Allows you to specify the class this association uses. When you're doing `has _one :latest_timesheet, class_name: 'Timesheet'`, `class_name: 'Timesheet'` specifies that `latest_timesheet` is actually the last `Timesheet` object in the database that is associated with this user. Normally, this option is inferred by Rails from the name of the association.

7.6.1.5 **:dependent**
The `:dependent` option specifies how Active Record should treat associated objects when the parent object is deleted. (The default is to do nothing with associated objects, which will leave orphaned records in the database.) There are a few different values that you can pass, and they work just like the `:dependent` option of `has_many`. If you pass `:destroy` to it, you tell Rails to destroy the associated object when it is no longer associated with the primary object. Setting the `:dependent` option to `:delete` will destroy the associated object without calling any of Rails' normal hooks. Passing `:restrict_with_exception` causes Rails to throw an exception if there is any associated object present, while `:restrict_with_error` adds an error to the owner object causing validations to fail before saving. Finally, `:nullify` will simply set the foreign key values to `nil` so that the relationship is broken.

7.6.2 `has_one` Scopes

The scopes for has_one associations are similar to the ones for has_many. For your convenience, we briefly cover the most relevant ones here.

7.6.2.1 `where(*conditions)`

Allows you to specify conditions that the object must meet to be included in the association.

```
1 class User < ActiveRecord::Base
2   has_one :manager, -> ( where(type: 'manager')),
3     class_name: 'Person'
```

Here manager is specified as a person object that has type = 'manager'. I almost always use a where scope block in conjunction with has_one. When Active Record loads the association, it's grabbing one of potentially many rows that have the right foreign key. Absent some explicit conditions (or perhaps an order scope), you're leaving it in the hands of the database to pick a row.

7.6.2.2 `order(*clauses)`

Allows you to specify an SQL fragment that will be used to order the results. This is an especially useful option with has_one when trying to associate the latest of something or another.

```
1 class User < ActiveRecord::Base
2   has_one :latest_timesheet,
3           -> { order('created_at desc') },
4           class_name: 'Timesheet'
5 end
```

7.6.2.3 `readonly`

Sets the record in the association to readonly mode, which prevents saving it.

7.7 Working with Unsaved Objects and Associations

You can manipulate objects and associations before they are saved to the database, but there is some special behavior you should be aware of, mostly involving the saving of associated objects. Whether an object is considered unsaved is based on the result of calling new_record?.

7.7.1 One-to-One Associations

Assigning an object to a belongs_to association does not save the parent or the associated object.

Assigning an object to a `has_one` association automatically saves that object and the object being replaced (if there is one) so that their foreign key fields are updated. The exception to this behavior is if the parent object is unsaved, since that would mean that there is no foreign key value to set. If save fails for either of the objects being updated (due to one of them being invalid), the assignment operation returns false and the assignment is cancelled. That behavior makes sense (if you think about it), but it can be the cause of much confusion when you're not aware of it. If you have an association that doesn't seem to work, check the validation rules of the related objects.

7.7.2   Collections

Adding an object to `has_many` and `has_and_belongs_to_many` collections automatically saves it, unless the parent object (the owner of the collection) is not yet stored in the database.

If objects being added to a collection (via << or similar means) fail to save properly, then the addition operation will return `false`. If you want your code to be a little more explicit or you want to add an object to a collection without automatically saving it, then you can use the collection's `build` method. It's exactly like `create` except that it doesn't `save`.

Members of a collection are automatically saved or updated when their parent is saved or updated, unless `autosave: false` is set on the association.

7.7.3   Deletion

Associations that are set with an `autosave: true` option are also afforded the ability to have their records deleted when an inverse record is saved. This is to allow the records from both sides of the association to get persisted within the same transaction and is handled through the `mark_for_destruction` method. Consider our `User` and `Timesheet` models again:

```
1    class User < ActiveRecord::Base
2      has_many :timesheets, autosave: true
3    end
```

If I would like to have a `Timesheet` destroyed when the `User` is saved, mark it for destruction.

```
1 user = User.where(name: "Durran")
2 timesheet = user.timesheets.closed
3 timesheet.mark_for_destruction # => Flags timesheet
4 user.save # => The timesheet gets deleted.
```

Since both are persisted in the same transaction, if the operation were to fail, the database would not be in an inconsistent state. Do note that although the child record did not get deleted in that case, it *still* would be marked for destruction and any later attempts to save the inverse would once again attempt to delete it.

7.8   Association Extensions

The proxy objects that handle access to associations can be extended with your own application code. You can add your own custom finders and factory methods to be used specifically with a particular association.

For example, let's say you wanted a concise way to refer to an account's people by name. You may create an extension on the association like the following:

Listing 7.4   An Association Extension on a People Collection

```
1 class Account < ActiveRecord::Base
2   has_many :people do
3     def named(full_name)
4       first_name, last_name = full_name.split(" ", 2)
5       where(first_name: first_name, last_name: last_name).first_or_create
6     end
7   end
8 end
```

Now we have a `named` method available to use on the `people` collection.

```
1 account = Account.first
2 person = account.people.named("David Heinemeier Hansson")
3 person.first_name # => "David"
4 person.last_name  # => "Heinemeier Hansson"
```

If you need to share the same set of extensions between many associations, you can specify an extension module instead of a block with method definitions. Here is the same feature shown in Listing 7.4, except broken out into its own Ruby module:

```
1 module ByNameExtension
2   def named(full_name)
3     first_name, last_name = full_name.split(" ", 2)
4     where(first_name: first_name, last_name: last_name).
         first_or_create
5   end
6 end
```

Now we can use it to extend many different relationships as long as they're compatible. (Our contract in the example consists of a model with columns `first_name` and `last_name`.)

```
1 class Account < ActiveRecord::Base
2   has_many :people, -> { extending(ByNameExtension) }
3 end
4
5 class Company < ActiveRecord::Base
6   has_many :people, -> { extending(ByNameExtension) }
7 end
```

If you need to use multiple named extension modules, you can pass an array of modules to the `extending` query method instead of a single module, like this:

```
has_many :people, -> { extending(ByNameExtension, ByRecentExtension) }
```

In the case of name conflicts, methods contained in modules added later in the array supersede those earlier in the array.

Consider a Class Method Instead

Unless you have a valid reason to reuse the extension logic with more than one type of model, you're probably better off leveraging the fact that class methods are automatically available on `has_many` associations.

```
1 class Person < ActiveRecord::Base
2   belongs_to :account
3
4   def self.named(full_name)
5     first_name, last_name = full_name.split(" ", 2)
6     where(first_name: first_name, last_name: last_name).first_or_create
7   end
8 end
```

7.9   The `CollectionProxy` Class

`CollectionProxy`, the parent of all association proxies, contributes a handful of useful methods that apply to most kinds of associations and can come into play when you're writing association extensions.

7.9.0.1   Owner, Reflection, and Target

The `owner` method provides a reference to the parent object holding the association.

The `reflection` object is an instance of `ActiveRecord::Reflection::AssociationReflection` and contains all the configuration options for the association. That includes both default settings and those that were passed to the association method when it was declared.

Finally, the `target` is the associated collection of objects (or associated object itself in the case of `belongs_to` and `has_one`).

It might not appear sane to expose these attributes publicly and allow their manipulation. However, without access to them, it would be much more difficult to write advanced association extensions. The `loaded?`, `loaded`, `target`, and `target=` methods are public for similar reasons.

The following code sample demonstrates the use of `owner` within a `published_prior_to` extension method, originally contributed by Wilson Bilkovich:

```
1  class ArticleCategory < ActiveRecord::Base
2    has_ancestry
3
4    has_many :articles do
5      def published_prior_to(date, options = {})
6        if owner.is_root?
7          Article.where('published_at < ? and category_id = ?', date, proxy_owner)
8        else
9          # Self is the "articles" association here, so we inherit its scope.
10         self.all(options)
11       end
12     end
13   end
14 end
```

The `has_ancestry` Active Record extension gem adds the ability to organize Active Record models as a tree structure. The self-referential association is based on a `ancestry` string column. The `owner` reference is used to check if the parent of this association is a "top-level" node in the tree.

7.9.0.2 **reload** and **reset**

The `reset` method puts the association proxy back in its initial state, which is unloaded (cached association objects are cleared). The `reload` method invokes `reset` and then loads associated objects from the database.

7.10 Conclusion

The ability to model associations is what makes Active Record more than just a data-access layer. The ease and elegance with which you can declare those associations are what make Active Record more than your ordinary object-relational mapper.

In this chapter, we covered the basics of how Active Record associations work. We started by taking a look at the class hierarchy of associations classes, starting with `CollectionProxy`. Hopefully, by learning about how associations work under the hood, you've picked up some enhanced understanding about their power and flexibility.

Finally, the options and methods guide for each type of association should be a good reference guide for your day-to-day development activities.

CHAPTER 8

Validations

I have bought this wonderful machine—a computer. Now I am rather an authority on gods, so I identified the machine—it seems to me to be an Old Testament god with a lot of rules and no mercy.

—Joseph Campbell

The Validations API in Active Model, along with its supplementary functionality in Active Record, allows you to declaratively define valid states for your model objects. The validation methods hook into the life cycle of an Active Record model object and are able to inspect the object to determine whether certain attributes are set, have values in a given range, or pass any other logical hurdles that you specify.

In this chapter, we'll describe the validation methods available and how to use them effectively. We'll also explore how those validation methods interact with your model's attributes and how the built-in error-messaging system can be used effectively in your application's user interface to provide descriptive feedback.

Finally, we'll cover how to use Active Model's validation functionality in your own, non–Active Record classes.

8.1 Finding Errors

Validation problems are also known as (drumroll, please…) errors! Every Active Record model object contains a collection of errors, accessible (unsurprisingly) as the `errors` attribute.

When a model object is valid, the `errors` collection is empty. In fact, when you call `valid?` on a model object, it takes the following three steps to find errors (slightly simplified):

241

1. Clears the errors collection

2. Runs validations

3. Returns whether the model's errors collection is now empty or not

If the errors collection ends up empty, the object is valid. In cases where you have to write actual validation logic yourself, you mark an object invalid by adding items to the errors collection using its add methods. Simple as that.

We'll cover the methods of the Errors class in some more detail later on. It makes more sense to look at the validation methods themselves first.

8.2   The Simple Declarative Validations

Whenever possible, you should set validations for your models declaratively by using one or more of the following class methods available to all Active Record classes. Unless otherwise noted, all the validates methods accept a variable number of attributes plus options. There are some options for these validation methods that are common to all of them, and we'll cover them at the end of the section.

8.2.1   `validates_absence_of`

New to Rails 4, the validates_absence_of method ensures specified attributes are blank. It uses the blank? method, defined on Object, which returns true for values that are nil or a blank string " ". It is the polar opposite of the commonly used validates_presence_of validation method, covered later in this section.

```
1 class Account < ActiveRecord::Base
2    validates_absence_of :something_unwanted
3 end
```

When the validates_absence_of validation fails, an error message is stored in the model object reading "attribute must be blank."

8.2.2   `validates_acceptance_of`

Many web applications have screens in which the user is prompted to agree to terms of service or some similar concept, usually involving a check box. No actual database column matching the attribute declared in the validation is required. When you call this method, it will create virtual attributes automatically for each named attribute you specify. I see this validation as a type of syntax sugar since it is so specific to web application programming.

```
1 class Account < ActiveRecord::Base
2   validates_acceptance_of :privacy_policy, :terms_of_service
3 end
```

You can use this validation with or without a boolean columns on the table backing your model. A transient attribute will be created if necessary. Choose to store the value in the database only if you need to keep track of whether the user accepted the term for auditing or other reasons. Mind you, not accepting the term would prevent creation of the record, but it's good to know what is supported.

When the `validates_acceptance_of` validation fails, an error message is stored in the model object reading "attribute must be accepted."

The `:accept` option makes it easy to change the value considered acceptance. The default value is `"1"`, which matches the value supplied by check boxes generated using Rails helper methods.

```
1 class Cancellation < ActiveRecord::Base
2   validates_acceptance_of :account_cancellation, accept: 'YES'
3 end
```

If you use the preceding example in conjunction with a text field connected to the `account_cancellation` attribute, the user would have to type the word *YES* in order for the cancellation object to be valid.

8.2.3   `validates_associated`

Used to ensure that *all* associated objects are valid on save. Works with any kind of association and is specific to Active Record (not Active Model). We emphasize *all* because the default behavior of `has_many` associations is to ensure the validity of their *new* child records on save.

Suggestion

You probably don't need to use this particular validation nowadays since `has_many` associations default to `validate: true`. Additionally, note that one of the implications of that default is that setting `validate: true` carelessly on a `belongs_to` association can cause infinite loop problems.

A `validates_associated` on `belongs_to` will not fail if the association is `nil`. If you want to make sure that the association is populated and valid, you have to use `validates_associated` in conjunction with `validates_presence_of`.

Active
Record

Tim Says ...

It's possible to get similar behavior by using a combination of the `:autosave` and `:validate` options on a `has_many`.

8.2.4 `validates_confirmation_of`

The `validates_confirmation_of` method is another case of syntactic sugar for web applications, since it is so common to include dual-entry text fields to make sure that the user entered critical data such as passwords and email addresses correctly. This validation will create a virtual attribute for the confirmation value and compare the two attributes to make sure they match in order for the model to be valid.

Here's an example, using our fictional `Account` model again:

```
1 class Account < ActiveRecord::Base
2   validates_confirmation_of :password
3 end
```

The user interface used to set values for the `Account` model would need to include extra text fields named with a `_confirmation` suffix, and when submitted, the value of those fields would have to match in order for this validation to pass. A simplified example of matching view code is provided.

```
1 = form_for account do |f|
2   = f.label :login
3   = f.text_field :login
4   = f.label :password
5   = f.password_field :password
6   = f.label :password_confirmation
7   = f.password_field :password_confirmation
8   = f.submit
```

8.2.5 `validates_each`

The `validates_each` method is a little more free form than its companions in the validation family in that it doesn't have a predefined validation function. Instead, you give it an array of attribute names to check and supply a Ruby block to be used in checking each attribute's validity. Notice that parameters for the model instance (`record`), the name of the attribute as a symbol, and the value to check are passed as block parameters. The block function designates the model object as valid or not by merit of adding to its `errors` array or not. The return value of the block is ignored.

There aren't too many situations where this method is necessary, but one plausible example is when interacting with external services for validation. You might wrap the external validation in a façade specific to your application and then call it using a `validates_each` block:

```
1 class Invoice < ActiveRecord::Base
2   validates_each :supplier_id, :purchase_order do |record,
        attr, value|
3     record.errors.add(attr) unless PurchasingSystem.
        validate(attr, value)
4   end
5 end
```

8.2.6 `validates_format_of`

To use `validates_format_of`, you'll have to know how to use Ruby regular expressions.[1] Pass the method one or more attributes to check and a regular expression as the (required) `:with` option. A good example, as shown in the Rails docs, is checking for a valid email address format:

```
1 class Person < ActiveRecord::Base
2   validates_format_of :email,
3     with: /\A([^@\s]+)@((?:[-a-z0-9]+\.)+[a-z]{2,})\z/
4 end
```

By the way, that example is not an RFC-compliant email address format checker.[2]

Courtenay Says ...

Regular expressions are awesome but can get very complex, particularly when validating domain names or email addresses. You can use `#{}` inside regular expressions, so split up your regex into chunks like this:

```
validates_format_of :name, with:
 /\A((localhost)|#{DOMAIN}|#{NUMERIC_IP})#{PORT}\z/
```

That expression is pretty straightforward and easy to understand. The constants themselves are not so easy to understand but easier than if they were all jumbled in together:

---

1. Check out the excellent `http://rubular.com` if you need help composing Ruby regular expressions.

2. If you need to validate email addresses, try the plugin at `https://github.com/spectator/validates_email`

```
1 PORT = /(([:]\d+)?)/
2 DOMAIN = /([a-z0-9\-]+\.?)*([a-z0-9]{2,})\.[a-z]{2,}/
3 NUMERIC_IP = /(?>(?:1?\d?\d|2[0-4]\d|25[0-5])\.){3}
4 (?:1?\d?\d|2[0-4]\d|25[0-5])(?:\/(?:[12]?\d|3[012])|-(?>(?:1?\d?\d|
5 2[0-4]\d|25[0-5])\.){3}(?:1?\d?\d|2[0-4]\d|25[0-5]))?/
```

Lark Says ...

I'll take your readability, Courtenay, and raise you test isolation. Your regular expression should itself be in a constant so you can test it.

8.2.7 `validates_inclusion_of` and `validates_exclusion_of`

These methods take a variable number of attribute names and an `:in` option. When they run, they check to make sure that the value of the attribute is included (or excluded, respectively) in the enumerable object passed as the `:in` option.

The examples in the Rails docs are probably some of the best illustrations of their use, so I'll take inspiration from them:

```
1 class Person < ActiveRecord::Base
2   validates_inclusion_of :gender, in: %w( m f ), message: 'O RLY?'
3   ...
4
5 class Account < ActiveRecord::Base
6   validates_exclusion_of :username,  in: %w( admin superuser ),
7                          message: 'Borat says "Naughty, naughty!"'
8   ...
```

Notice that in the examples, I've introduced usage of the `:message` option, common to all validation methods, to customize the error message constructed and added to the `Errors` collection when the validation fails. We'll cover the default error messages and how to effectively customize them later in the chapter.

8.2.8 `validates_length_of`

The `validates_length_of` method takes a variety of different options to let you concisely specify length constraints for a given attribute of your model.

```
1 class Account < ActiveRecord::Base
2   validates_length_of :login, minimum: 5
3 end
```

8.2.8.1   Constraint Options

The `:minimum` and `:maximum` options work as expected, but don't use them together. To specify a range, use the `:within` option and pass it a Ruby range, as in the following example:

```
1 class Account < ActiveRecord::Base
2   validates_length_of :username, within: 5..20
3 end
```

To specify an exact length of an attribute, use the `:is` option:

```
1 class Account < ActiveRecord::Base
2   validates_length_of :account_number, is: 16
3 end
```

8.2.8.2   Error Message Options

Rails gives you the ability to generate detailed error messages for `validates_length_of` via the `:too_long`, `:too_short`, and `:wrong_length` options. Use `%{count}` in your custom error message as a placeholder for the number corresponding to the constraint.

```
1 class Account < ActiveRecord::Base
2   validates_length_of :account_number, is: 16,
3                       wrong_length: "should be %{count} characters long"
4 end
```

8.2.9   `validates_numericality_of`

The somewhat clumsily named `validates_numericality_of` method is used to ensure that an attribute can only hold a numeric value.

The `:only_integer` option lets you further specify that the value should only be an integer value and defaults to false.

```
1 class Account < ActiveRecord::Base
2   validates_numericality_of :account_number, only_integer: true
3 end
```

The `:even` and `:odd` options do what you would expect and are useful for things like, I don't know, checking electron valences. (Actually, I'm not creative enough to think of what you would use this validation for, but there you go.)

The following comparison options are also available:

Active
Record

- `:equal_to`
- `:greater_than`
- `:greater_than_or_equal_to`
- `:less_than`
- `:less_than_or_equal_to`
- `:other_than`

8.2.9.1   Infinity and Other Special Float Values

Interestingly, Ruby has the concept of infinity built in. If you haven't seen infinity before, try the following in a console:

```
>> (1.0/0.0)
=> Infinity
```

`Infinity` is considered a number by `validates_numericality_of`. Databases (like PostgreSQL) with support for the IEEE 754 standard should allow special float values like `Infinity` to be stored. The other special values are positive infinity (+INF), negative infinity (-INF), and not-a-number (NaN). IEEE 754 also distinguishes between positive zero (+0) and negative zero (–0). NaN is used to represent results of operations that are undefined.

8.2.10   `validates_presence_of`

One of the more common validation methods, `validates_presence_of`, is used to denote mandatory attributes. This method checks whether the attribute is blank using the `blank?` method, defined on `Object`, which returns `true` for values that are `nil` or a blank string (`""`).

```
1 class Account < ActiveRecord::Base
2   validates_presence_of :username, :email, :account_number
3 end
```

A common mistake is to use `validates_presence_of` with a boolean attribute, like the backing field for a check box. If you want to make sure that the attribute is true, use `validates_acceptance_of` instead. The boolean value `false` is considered blank, so if you want to make sure that only `true` or `false` values are set on your model, use the following pattern:

```
validates_inclusion_of :protected, in: [true, false]
```

8.2.10.1   Validating the Presence and/or Existence of Associated Objects

When you're trying to ensure that an association is present, pass `validates _presence_of` its foreign key attribute, not the association variable itself. Note that the validation will fail in cases when both the parent and child object are unsaved (since the foreign key will be blank).

Many developers try to use this validation with the intention of ensuring that associated objects actually exist in the database. Personally, I think that would be a valid use case for an actual foreign-key constraint in the database, but if you want to do the check in your Rails code, then emulate the following example:

```
1 class Timesheet < ActiveRecord::Base
2   belongs_to :user
3   validates_presence_of :user_id
4   validate :user_exists
5
6   protected
7
8   def user_exists
9     errors.add(:user_id, "doesn't exist") unless User.exists?(user_id)
10  end
11 end
```

Without a validation, if your application violates a database foreign key constraint, you will get an Active Record exception.

8.2.11   `validates_uniqueness_of`

The `validates_uniqueness_of` method, also exclusive to Active Record, ensures that the value of an attribute is unique for all models of the same type. This validation does not work by adding a uniqueness constraint at the database level. It does work by constructing and executing a query looking for a matching record in the database. If any record is returned when this method does its query, the validation fails.

```
1 class Account < ActiveRecord::Base
2   validates_uniqueness_of :username
3 end
```

By specifying a `:scope` option, additional attributes can be used to determine uniqueness. You may pass `:scope` one or more attribute names as symbols (putting multiple symbols in an array).

```
1 class Address < ActiveRecord::Base
2   validates_uniqueness_of :line_two, scope: [:line_one, :city, :zip]
3 end
```

Active
Record

It's also possible to specify whether to make the uniqueness constraint case sensitive or not via the :case_sensitive option (ignored for nontextual attributes).

With the addition of support for PostgreSQL array columns in Rails 4, the validates_uniqueness_of method can be used to validate that all items in the array are unique. PostgreSQL array columns are covered in detail in Chapter 9, "Advanced Active Record."

Tim Says ...

This validation is not foolproof, due to a potential race condition between the SELECT query that checks for duplicates and the INSERT or UPDATE that persists the record. An Active Record exception could be generated as a result, so be prepared to handle that failure in your controller. I recommend that you use a unique index constraint in the database if you absolutely must make sure that a column value is unique.

8.2.11.1 Enforcing Uniqueness of Join Models

In the course of using join models (with has_many :through), it seems pretty common to need to make the relationship unique. Consider an application that models students, courses, and registrations with the following code:

```
 1 class Student < ActiveRecord::Base
 2   has_many :registrations
 3   has_many :courses, through: :registrations
 4 end
 5
 6 class Registration < ActiveRecord::Base
 7   belongs_to :student
 8   belongs_to :course
 9 end
10
11 class Course < ActiveRecord::Base
12   has_many :registrations
13   has_many :students, through: :registrations
14 end
```

How do you make sure that a student is not registered more than once for a particular course? The most concise way is to use validates_uniqueness_of with a :scope constraint. The important thing to remember with this technique is to reference the foreign keys, not the names of the associations themselves:

```
1 class Registration < ActiveRecord::Base
2   belongs_to :student
3   belongs_to :course
4
5   validates_uniqueness_of :student_id, scope: :course_id,
6                       message: "can only register once per course"
7 end
```

Notice that since the default error message generated when this validation fails would not make sense, I've provided a custom error message that will result in the expression "Student can only register once per course."

Tim Says ...

Astute readers will notice that the validation was on `student_id` but the error message references "Student." Rails special cases this to do what you mean.

8.2.11.2   Limit Constraint Lookup

As of Rails 4, one can specify criteria that constraints a uniqueness validation against a set of records by setting the `:conditions` option.

To illustrate, let's assume we have an article that requires titles to be unique against all published articles in the database. We can achieve this using `validates_uniqueness_of` by doing the following:

```
1 class Article < ActiveRecord::Base
2   validates_uniqueness_of :title,
3     conditions: -> { where.not(published_at: nil) }
4   ...
5 end
```

When the model is saved, Active Record will query for the title against all articles in the database that are published. If no results are returned, the model is valid.

8.2.12   `validates_with`

All of the validation methods we've covered so far are essentially local to the class in which they are used. If you want to develop a suite of custom, reusable validation classes, then you need a way to apply them to your models, and that is what the `validates_with` method allows you to do.

Active
Record

To implement a custom validator, extend `ActiveRecord::Validator` and implement the `validate` method. The record being validated is available as `record`, and you manipulate its `errors` hash to log validation errors.

The following examples, from Ryan Daigle's excellent post[3] on this feature, demonstrate a reusable email field validator:

```
1 class EmailValidator < ActiveRecord::Validator
2   def validate()
3     record.errors[:email] << "is not valid" unless
4       record.email =~ /\A([^@\s]+)@((?:[-a-z0-9]+\.)+[a-z]
        {2,})\z/
5   end
6 end
7
8 class Account < ActiveRecord::Base
9   validates_with EmailValidator
10 end
```

The example assumes the existence of an email attribute on the record. If you need to make your reusable validator more flexible, you can access validation options at runtime via the `options` hash, like this:

```
1 class EmailValidator < ActiveRecord::Validator
2   def validate()
3     email_field = options[:attr]
4     record.errors[email_field] << "is not valid" unless
5       record.send(email_field) =~ /\A([^@\s]+)@((?:[-a-z0-9]+\.)+[a-z]{2,})\z/
6   end
7 end
8
9 class Account < ActiveRecord::Base
10   validates_with EmailValidator, attr: :email
11 end
```

8.2.13 `RecordInvalid`

Whenever you do so-called bang operations (such as `save!`) and a validation fails, you should be prepared to rescue `ActiveRecord::RecordInvalid`. Validation failures will cause `RecordInvalid` to be raised and its message will contain a description of the failures.

Here's a quick example from one of my applications that has pretty restrictive validations on its `User` model:

---

3. http://ryandaigle.com/articles/2009/8/11/what-s-new-in-edge-rails-independent-model-validators

```
>> u = User.new
=> #<User ...>
>> u.save!
ActiveRecord::RecordInvalid: Validation failed: Name can't be blank,
Password confirmation can't be blank, Password is too short (minimum
is 5 characters), Email can't be blank, Email address format is bad
```

8.3   Common Validation Options

The following options apply to all the validation methods.

8.3.1   `:allow_blank` and `:allow_nil`

In some cases, you only want to trigger a validation if a value is present—in other words, the attribute is optional. There are two options that provide this functionality.

The `:allow_blank` option skips validation if the value is blank according to the `blank?` method. Similarly, the `:allow_nil` option skips the validation if the value of the attribute is nil; it only checks for `nil`, and empty strings `""` are not considered nil—they are considered blank.

8.3.2   `:if` and `:unless`

The `:if` and `:unless` options are covered in the next section, "Conditional Validation."

8.3.3   `:message`

As we've discussed earlier in the chapter, the way that the validation process registers failures is by adding items to the `Errors` collection of the model object being checked. Part of the error item is a specific message describing the validation failure. All the validation methods accept a `:message` option so that you can override the default error message format.

```
1  class Account < ActiveRecord::Base
2    validates_uniqueness_of :username, message: "is already taken"
3  end
```

The default English locale file in ActiveModel defines most of the standard error message templates.

```
inclusion: "is not included in the list"
exclusion: "is reserved"
invalid: "is invalid"
confirmation: "doesn't match %{attribute}"
accepted: "must be accepted"
empty: "can't be empty"
```

Active Record

```
blank: "can't be blank"
present: "must be blank"
too_long: "is too long (maximum is %{count} characters)"
too_short: "is too short (minimum is %{count} characters)"
wrong_length: "is the wrong length (should be %{count} characters)"
not_a_number: "is not a number"
not_an_integer: "must be an integer"
greater_than: "must be greater than %{count}"
greater_than_or_equal_to: "must be greater than or equal to %{count}"
equal_to: "must be equal to %{count}"
less_than: "must be less than %{count}"
less_than_or_equal_to: "must be less than or equal to %{count}"
other_than: "must be other than %{count}"
odd: "must be odd"
even: "must be even"
```

The default messages only use the count variable for interpolation, where appropriate, but model, attribute, and value are always available.

```
validates_uniqueness_of username, message: "%{value} is already registered"
```

8.3.4 :on

By default, validations are run on save (both create and update operations). If you need to do so, you can limit a given validation to just one of those operations by passing the :on option either :create or :update.

Assuming that your application does not support changing emails, one good use for on: :create might be in conjunction with validates_uniqueness_of, since checking uniqueness with a query on large datasets can be time consuming.

```
1 class Account < ActiveRecord::Base
2   validates_uniqueness_of :email, on: :create
3 end
```

8.3.5 :strict

New to Rails 4 is the :strict validation option. Setting :strict to true causes an exception—ActiveModel::StrictValidationFailed—to be raised when a model is invalid.

```
1 class Account < ActiveRecord::Base
2   validates :email, presence: { strict: true }
3 end
```

To override the type of exception raised on error, pass the custom exception to the :strict option.

8.4 Conditional Validation

Since all validation methods are implemented via the Active Model Callback API, they also accept :if and :unless options to determine at runtime (and not during the class definition) whether the validation needs to be run or not. The following three types of arguments can be supplied as :if and :unless options:

Symbol The name of a method to invoke as a symbol. This is probably the most common option and offers the best performance.

String A snippet of Ruby code to eval might be useful when the condition is really short, but keep in mind that evaluating statements is relatively slow.

Proc A block of code to be evaluated with instance_eval, so that self is the current record. Perhaps the most elegant choice for one-line conditionals.

```
validates_presence_of :approver, if: -> { approved? && !legacy? }
```

8.4.1 Usage and Considerations

When does it make sense to use conditional validations? The answer is whenever an object can be validly persisted in more than one state. A very common example involves the User (or Person) model, used for login and authentication.

```
1 validates_presence_of :password, if: :password_required?
2 validates_presence_of :password_confirmation, if: :password_required?
3 validates_length_of :password, within: 4..40, if: :password_required?
4 validates_confirmation_of :password, if: :password_required?
```

This code is not DRY (meaning that it is repetitive). You can refactor it to make it a little dryer using the with_options method that Rails mixes into Object.

```
1 with_options if: :password_required? do |user|
2   user.validates_presence_of :password
3   user.validates_presence_of :password_confirmation
4   user.validates_length_of :password, within: 4..40
5   user.validates_confirmation_of :password
6 end
```

All the example validations check for the two cases when a (plaintext) password field should be required in order for the model to be valid.

```
1 def password_required?
2   encrypted_password.blank? || !password.blank?
3 end
```

The first case is if the `encrypted_password` attribute is blank, because that means we are dealing with a new `User` instance that has not been given a password yet. The other case is when the `password` attribute itself is not blank; perhaps this is happening during an update operation and the user is attempting to reset his or her password.

8.4.2　Validation Contexts

Another way to accomplish conditional validation leverages support for *validation contexts*. Declare a validation and pass the name of an application-specific validation context as the value of the `:on` option. That validation will now only be checked when explicitly invoked using `record.valid?(context_name)`.

Consider the following example involving a report generation app. Saving a report without a name is fine, but publishing one without a name is not.

```
1 class Report < ActiveRecord::Base
2   validates_presence_of :name, on: :publish
3 end
4
5 class ReportsController < ApplicationController
6   expose(:report)
7
8   # POST /reports/1/publish
9   def publish
10     if report.valid? :publish
11       redirect_to report, notice: "Report published"
12     else
13       flash.now.alert = "Can't publish unnamed reports!"
14       render :show
15     end
16   end
17 end
```

8.5　Short-Form Validation

Introduced in Rails 3, the `validates` method identifies an attribute and accepts options that correspond to the validators we've already covered in the chapter. Using `validates` can tighten up your model code nicely.

```
1 validates :username, presence: true,
2   format: { with: /[A-Za-z0-9]+/ },
3   length: { minimum: 3 },
4   uniqueness: true
```

The following options are available for use with the `validates` method.

absence: true Alias for `validates_absence_of`. Supply additional options by replacing `true` with a hash.

```
validates :unwanted, absence: { message: "You shouldn't have set that" }
```

acceptance: true Alias for `validates_acceptance_of`, typically used with check boxes that indicate acceptance of terms. Supply additional options by replacing `true` with a hash.

```
validates :terms, acceptance: { message: 'You must accept terms.' }
```

confirmation: true Alias for `validates_confirmation_of`, typically used to ensure that email and password confirmation fields match up correctly. Supply additional options by replacing `true` with a hash.

```
validates :email, confirmation: { message: 'Try again.' }
```

exclusion: { in: [1,2,3] } Alias for `validates_exclusion_of`. If your only option is the array to exclude against, you can shorten the syntax further by supplying an array as the value.

```
validates :username, exclusion: %w(admin superuser)
```

format: { with: /.*/ } Alias for `validates_format_of`. If your only option is the regular expression, you can shorten the syntax further by making it the value like the following:

```
format: /[A-Za-z0-9]+/
```

inclusion: { in: [1,2,3] } Alias for `validates_inclusion_of`. If your only option is the inclusion array, you can shorten the syntax further by making the array the value.

```
validates :gender, inclusion: %w(male female)
```

length: { minimum: 0, maximum: 1000 } Alias for `validates_length_of`. If your only options are minimum and maximum lengths, you can shorten the syntax further by supplying a Ruby range as the value.

```
validates :username, length: 3..20
```

numericality: true Alias for `validates_numericality_of`. Supply additional options by replacing `true` with a hash.

```
validates :quantity, numericality: { message: 'Supply a number.' }
```

presence: true Alias for `validates_presence_of`. Supply additional options by replacing `true` with a hash.

```
validates :username, presence: { message: 'How do you expect to login?' }
```

uniqueness: true Alias for `validates_uniqueness_of`. Supply additional options by replacing `true` with a hash.

```
validates :quantity, uniqueness: { message: "You're SOL on that login choice, buddy!" }
```

8.6   Custom Validation Techniques

When the existing declarative validation macros are not enough for your application needs, Rails gives you a few custom techniques.

8.6.1   Add Custom Validation Macros to Your Application

Rails has the ability to add custom validation macros (available to all your model classes) by extending `ActiveModel::EachValidator`.

The following example is silly but demonstrates the functionality nicely.

```
1 class ReportLikeValidator < ActiveModel::EachValidator
2   def validate_each(record, attribute, value)
3     unless value["Report"]
4       record.errors.add(attribute, 'does not appear to be a Report')
5     end
6   end
7 end
```

Now that your custom validator exists, it is available to use with the `validates` macro in your model.

```
1 class Report < ActiveRecord::Base
2   validates :name, report_like: true
3 end
```

The key `:report_like` is inferred from the name of the validator class, which in this case was `ReportLikeValidator`.

You can receive options via the `validates` method by adding an `initializer` method to your custom validator class. For example, let's make `ReportLikeValidator` more generic.

```
1 class LikeValidator < ActiveModel::EachValidator
2   def initialize(options)
3     @with = options[:with]
4     super
5   end
6
7   def validate_each(record, attribute, value)
8     unless value[@with]
9       record.errors.add(attribute, "does not appear to be like #{@with}")
10    end
11  end
12 end
```

Our model code would change to the following:

```
1 class Report < ActiveRecord::Base
2   validates :name, like: { with: "Report" }
3 end
```

8.6.2   Create a Custom Validator Class

This technique involves inheriting from `ActiveModel::Validator` and implementing a `validate` method that takes the record to validate.

I'll demonstrate with a really wicked example.

```
1 class RandomlyValidator < ActiveModel::Validator
2   def validate(record)
3     record.errors[:base] << "FAIL #1" unless first_hurdle(record)
4     record.errors[:base] << "FAIL #2" unless second_hurdle(record)
5     record.errors[:base] << "FAIL #3" unless third_hurdle(record)
6   end
7
8   private
9
10  def first_hurdle(record)
11    rand > 0.3
12  end
13
14  def second_hurdle(record)
15    rand > 0.6
16  end
```

```
17
18   def third_hurdle(record)
19     rand > 0.9
20   end
21 end
```

Use your new custom validator in a model with the `validates_with` macro.

```
1 class Report < ActiveRecord::Base
2   validates_with RandomlyValidator
3 end
```

8.6.3   Add a **validate** Method to Your Model

A `validate` instance method might be the way to go if you want to check the state of your object holistically and keep the code for doing so inside of the model class itself. (This is an older technique that I can't fully endorse; it adds complexity to your model class unnecessarily, given how easy it is to create custom validator classes.)

For example, assume that you are dealing with a model object with a set of three integer attributes (`:attr1`, `:attr2`, and `:attr3`) and a precalculated total attribute (`:total`). The total must always equal the sum of the three attributes:

```
1 class CompletelyLameTotalExample < ActiveRecord::Base
2   def validate
3     if total != (attr1 + attr2 + attr3)
4       errors[:total] << "The total doesn't add up!"
5     end
6   end
7 end
```

You can alternatively add an error message to the whole object instead of just a particular attribute using the `:base` key, like this:

```
errors[:base] << "The total doesn't add up!"
```

Remember, the way to mark an object as invalid is to add to its `Errors` object. The return value of a custom validation method is not used.

8.7   Skipping Validations

The methods `update_attribute` and `update_column` don't invoke validations, yet their companion method `update` does. Whoever wrote the API docs believes that this behavior is "especially useful for Boolean flags on existing records."

I don't know if that is entirely true or not, but I do know that it is the source of ongoing contention in the community. Unfortunately, I don't have much more to add other than some simple common sense advice: Be very careful using the `update_attribute` or `update_column` methods. It can easily persist your model objects in invalid states.

8.8   Working with the Errors Hash

Some methods are provided to allow you to add validation errors to the collection manually and alter the state of the `Errors` hash.

8.8.0.1   `errors[:base] = msg`

Adds an error message related to the overall object state itself and not the value of any particular attribute. Make your error messages complete sentences, because Rails does not do any additional processing of them to make them readable.

8.8.0.2   `errors[:attribute] = msg`

Adds an error message related to a particular attribute. The message should be a sentence fragment that reads naturally when prepended with the capitalized name of the attribute.

8.8.0.3   `clear`

As you might expect, the `clear` method clears the `Errors` collection.

8.8.1   Checking for Errors

It's also possible to check the `Errors` object for validation failures on specific attributes by just using square brackets notation. An array is always returned, but it is empty when there aren't any validation errors for the attribute specified.

```
>> user.errors[:login]
=> ["zed is already registered"]
>> user.errors[:password]
=> []
```

Alternatively, one could also access full error messages for a specific attribute using the `full_messages_for` method. Just like accessing validation failures for attributes using bracket notation, an array is always returned.

```
>> user.errors.full_messages_for(:email)
=> ["Email can't be blank"]
```

8.9   Testing Validations with Shoulda

Even though validations are declarative code, if you're doing TDD, then you'll want to specify them before writing them. Luckily, Thoughtbot's Shoulda Matchers library[4] contains a number of matchers designed to easily test validations.

```
1 describe Post do
2     it { should validate_uniqueness_of(:title) }
3     it { should validate_presence_of(:body).with_message(/wtf/) }
4     it { should validate_presence_of(:title) }
5     it { should validate_numericality_of(:user_id) }
6 end
7
8 describe User do
9     it { should_not allow_value("blah").for(:email) }
10    it { should_not allow_value("b lah").for(:email) }
11    it { should allow_value("a@b.com").for(:email) }
12    it { should allow_value("asdf@asdf.com").for(:email) }
13    it { should ensure_length_of(:email).is_at_least(1).is_at_most(100) }
14    it { should ensure_inclusion_of(:age).in_range(1..100) }
15  end
```

8.10   Conclusion

In this (relatively speaking) short chapter, we covered the Active Record Validations API in depth. One of the most appealing aspects of Rails is how we can declaratively specify the criteria for determining the validity of model objects.

---

4. https://github.com/thoughtbot/shoulda-matchers

CHAPTER 9

Advanced Active Record

Respectful debate, honesty, passion, and working systems created an environment that not even the most die-hard enterprise architect could ignore, no matter how buried in Java design patterns. Those who placed technical excellence and pragmaticism above religious attachment and vendor cronyism were easily convinced of the benefits that broadening their definition of acceptable technologies could bring.

—Ryan Tomayko[1]

Active Record is a simple object-relational mapping (ORM) framework compared to other popular ORM frameworks, such as Hibernate in the Java world. Don't let that fool you, though: Under its modest exterior, Active Record has some pretty advanced features. To really get the most effectiveness out of Rails development, you need to have more than a basic understanding of Active Record—things like knowing when to break out of the one-table/one-class pattern or how to leverage Ruby modules to keep your code clean and free of duplication.

In this chapter, we wrap up this book's comprehensive coverage of Active Record by reviewing callbacks, single-table inheritance (STI), and polymorphic models. We also review a little bit of information about metaprogramming and Ruby domain-specific languages (DSLs) as they relate to Active Record.

9.1 Scopes

Scopes (or "named scopes" if you're old school) allow you to define and chain query criteria in a declarative and reusable manner.

---

1. http://lesscode.org/2006/03/12/someone-tell-gosling/

```
1 class Timesheet < ActiveRecord::Base
2   scope :submitted, -> { where(submitted: true) }
3   scope :underutilized, -> { where('total_hours < 40') }
```

To declare a scope, use the `scope` class method, passing it a name as a symbol and a callable object that includes a query criteria within. You can simply use Arel criteria methods such as `where`, `order`, and `limit` to construct the definition as shown in the example. The queries defined in a scope are only evaluated whenever the scope is invoked.

```
1 class User < ActiveRecord::Base
2   scope :delinquent, -> { where('timesheets_updated_at < ?', 1.week.ago) }
```

Invoke scopes as you would class methods.

```
>> User.delinquent
=> [#<User id: 2, timesheets_updated_at: "2013-04-20 20:02:13"...>]
```

Note that instead of using the `scope` macro-style method, you can simply define a class method on an Active Record model that returns a scoped method, such as `where`. To illustrate, the following class method is equivalent to the `delinquent` scope defined in the previous example.

```
1 def self.delinquent
2   where('timesheets_updated_at < ?', 1.week.ago)
3 end
```

9.1.1 Scope Parameters

You can pass arguments to scope invocations by adding parameters to the proc you use to define the scope query.

```
1 class BillableWeek < ActiveRecord::Base
2   scope :newer_than, ->(date) { where('start_date > ?', date) }
```

Then pass the argument to the scope as you would normally.

```
BillableWeek.newer_than(Date.today)
```

9.1.2 Chaining Scopes

One of the benefits of scopes is that you can chain them together to create complex queries from simple ones:

```
>> Timesheet.underutilized.submitted.to_a
=> [#<Timesheet id: 3, submitted: true, total_hours: 37 ...
```

Scopes can be chained together for reuse within scope definitions themselves. For instance, let's say that we always want to constrain the result set of the underuti-lized scope to only submitted timesheets:

```
1  class Timesheet < ActiveRecord::Base
2    scope :submitted, -> { where(submitted: true) }
3    scope :underutilized, -> { submitted.where('total_hours < 40') }
```

9.1.3   Scopes and **has_many**

In addition to being available at the class context, scopes are available automatically on has_many association attributes.

```
>> u = User.find(2)
=> #<User id: 2, username: "obie"...>
>> u.timesheets.size
=> 3
>> u.timesheets.underutilized.size
=> 1
```

9.1.4   Scopes and Joins

You can use Arel's join method to create cross model scopes. For instance, if we gave our recurring example Timesheet a submitted_at date attribute instead of just a boolean, we could add a scope to User allowing us to see who is late on their timesheet submission.

```
1  scope :tardy, -> {
2    joins(:timesheets).
3    where("timesheets.submitted_at <= ?", 7.days.ago).
4    group("users.id")
5  }
```

Arel's to_sql method is useful for debugging scope definitions and usage.

```
>> User.tardy.to_sql
=> "SELECT "users".* FROM "users"
   INNER JOIN "timesheets" ON "timesheets"."user_id" = "users"."id"
   WHERE (timesheets.submitted_at <= '2013-04-13 18:16:15.203293')
   GROUP BY users.id"  # query formatted nicely for the book
```

Note that as demonstrated in the example, it's a good idea to use unambiguous column references (including the table name) in cross model scope definitions so that Arel doesn't get confused.

9.1.5   Scope Combinations

Our example of a cross model scope violates good object-oriented design principles: It contains the logic for determining whether or not a Timesheet is submitted, which is code that properly belongs in the `Timesheet` class. Luckily, we can use Arel's merge method to fix it. First, we put the late logic where it belongs—in `Timesheet`:

```
scope :late, -> { where("timesheet.submitted_at <= ?", 7.days.ago) }
```

Then we use our new `late` scope in `tardy`:

```
scope :tardy, -> {
  joins(:timesheets).group("users.id").merge(Timesheet.late)
}
```

If you have trouble with this technique, make absolutely sure that your scopes' clauses refer to fully qualified column names. (In other words, don't forget to prefix column names with tables.) The console and `to_sql` method is your friend for debugging.

9.1.6   Default Scopes

There may arise use cases where you want certain conditions applied to the finders for your model. Consider that our timesheet application has a default view of open timesheets—we can use a default scope to simplify our general queries.

```
class Timesheet < ActiveRecord::Base
  default_scope { where(status: "open") }
end
```

Now when we query for our `Timesheets`, by default, the open condition will be applied:

```
>> Timesheet.pluck(:status)
=> ["open", "open", "open"]
```

Default scopes also get applied to your models when building or creating them, which can be a great convenience or a nuisance if you are not careful. In our previous example, all new `Timesheets` will be created with a status of "open."

```
>> Timesheet.new
=> #<Timesheet id: nil, status: "open">
>> Timesheet.create
=> #<Timesheet id: 1, status: "open">
```

You can override this behavior by providing your own conditions or scope to override the default setting of the attributes.

```
>> Timesheet.where(status: "new").new
=> #<Timesheet id: nil, status: "new">
>> Timesheet.where(status: "new").create
```

```
=> #<Timesheet id: 1, status: "new">
```

There may be cases where at runtime you want to create a scope and pass it around as a first-class object leveraging your default scope. In this case, Active Record provides the `all` method.

```
>> timesheets = Timesheet.all.order("submitted_at DESC")
=> #<ActiveRecord::Relation [#<Timesheet id: 1, status: "open"]>
>> timesheets.where(name: "Durran Jordan").to_a
=> []
```

There's another approach to scopes that provides a sleeker syntax: `scoping`, which allows the chaining of scopes via nesting within a block.

```
>> Timesheet.order("submitted_at DESC").scoping do
>>    Timesheet.first
>> end
=> #<Timesheet id: 1, status: "open">
```

That's pretty nice, but what if we *don't* want our default scope to be included in our queries? In this case, Active Record takes care of us through the `unscoped` method.

```
>> Timesheet.unscoped.order("submitted_at DESC").to_a
=> [#<Timesheet id: 2, status: "submitted">]
```

Similarly to overriding our default scope with a relation when creating new objects, we can supply `unscoped` as well to remove the default attributes.

```
>> Timesheet.unscoped.new
=> #<Timesheet id: nil, status: nil>
```

9.1.7   Using Scopes for CRUD

You have a wide range of Active Record's CRUD methods available on scopes, which gives you some powerful abilities. For instance, let's give all our underutilized timesheets some extra hours.

```
>> u.timesheets.underutilized.pluck(:total_hours)
=> [37, 38]
```

```
>> u.timesheets.underutilized.update_all("total_hours = total_hours + 2")
=> 2
```

```
>> u.timesheets.underutilized.pluck(:total_hours)
=> [39]
```

Scopes—including a where clause using hashed conditions—will populate attributes of objects built off of them with those attributes as default values. Admittedly, it's a bit difficult to think of a plausible case for this feature, but we'll show it in an example. First, we add the following scope to `Timesheet`:

```
scope :perfect, -> { submitted.where(total_hours: 40) }
```

Now building an object on the `perfect` scope should give us a submitted timesheet with 40 hours.

```
> Timesheet.perfect.build
=> #<Timesheet id: nil, submitted: true, user_id: nil, total_hours: 40 ...>
```

As you've probably realized by now, the Arel underpinnings of Active Record are tremendously powerful and truly elevate the Rails platform.

9.2 Callbacks

This advanced feature of Active Record allows the savvy developer to attach behavior at a variety of different points along a model's life cycle, such as after initialization; before database records are inserted, updated, or removed; and so on.

Callbacks can do a variety of tasks, ranging from simple things such as the logging and massaging of attribute values prior to validation to complex calculations. Callbacks can halt the execution of the life cycle process taking place. Some callbacks can even modify the behavior of the model class on the fly. We'll cover all those scenarios in this section, but first let's get a taste of what a callback looks like. Check out the following silly example:

```
1 class Beethoven < ActiveRecord::Base
2   before_destroy :last_words
3
4   protected
5
6   def last_words
7     logger.info "Friends applaud, the comedy is over"
8   end
9 end
```

So prior to dying (ehrm, being `destroyed`), the last words of the `Beethoven` class will always be logged for posterity. As we'll see soon, there are 14 different opportunities to add behavior to your model in this fashion. Before we get to that list, let's cover the mechanics of registering a callback.

9.2.1 One-Liners

Now if (and only if) your callback routine is really short,[2] you can add it by passing a block to the callback macro. We're talking one-liners!

```
class Napoleon < ActiveRecord::Base
  before_destroy { logger.info "Josephine..." }
  ...
end
```

Since Rails 3, the block passed to a callback is executed via `instance_eval` so that its scope is the record itself (versus needing to act on a passed-in record variable). The following example implements "paranoid" model behavior, covered later in the chapter.

```
1 class Account < ActiveRecord::Base
2   before_destroy { self.update_attribute(:deleted_at, Time.now); false }
3   ...
```

9.2.2 Protected or Private

Except when you're using a block, the access level for callback methods should always be protected or private. It should never be public, since callbacks should never be called from code outside the model.

Believe it or not, there are even more ways to implement callbacks, but we'll cover those techniques later in the chapter. For now, let's look at the lists of callback hooks available.

9.2.3 Matched **before/after** Callbacks

In total, there are 19 types of callbacks you can register on your models! Thirteen of them are matching `before/after` callback pairs, such as `before_validation` and `after_validation`. Four of them are around callbacks, such as `around_save`. (The other two, `after_initialize` and `after_find`, are special, and we'll discuss them later in this section.)

9.2.3.1 List of Callbacks

This is the list of callback hooks available during a `save` operation. (The list varies slightly depending on whether you're saving a new or existing record.)

---

2. If you are browsing old Rails source code, you might come across callback macros receiving a short string of Ruby code to be evaluated in the binding of the model object. That way of adding callbacks was deprecated in Rails 1.2, because you're always better off using a block in those situations.

- `before_validation`
- `after_validation`
- `before_save`
- `around_save`
- `before_create` (for new records) and `before_update` (for existing records)
- `around_create` (for new records) and `around_update` (for existing records)
- `after_create` (for new records) and `after_update` (for existing records)
- `after_save`

Delete operations have their own callbacks:

- `before_destroy`
- `around_destroy`, which executes a `DELETE` database statement on `yield`
- `after_destroy`, which is called after record has been removed from the database and all attributes have been frozen (`readonly`)

Callbacks may be limited to specific Active Record life cycles (`:create`, `:update`, `:destroy`) by explicitly defining which ones can trigger it using the `:on` option. The `:on` option may accept a single lifecycle (like `on: :create`) or an array of life cycles (like `on: [:create, :update]`).

```
# Run only on create.
before_validation :some_callback, on: :create
```

Additionally, transactions have callbacks as well for when you want actions to occur after the database is guaranteed to be in a permanent state. Note that only "after" callbacks exist here due to the nature of transactions—it's a bad idea to be able to interfere with the actual operation itself.

- `after_commit`
- `after_rollback`
- `after_touch`

Skipping Callback Execution

The following Active Record methods, when executed, do not run any callbacks:

- decrement
- decrement_counter
- delete
- delete_all
- increment
- increment_counter
- toggle
- touch
- update_column
- update_columns
- update_all
- update_counters

9.2.4 Halting Execution

If you return a boolean `false` (not `nil`) from a callback method, Active Record halts the execution chain. No further callbacks are executed. The `save` method will return `false`, and `save!` will raise a `RecordNotSaved` error.

Keep in mind that since the last expression of a Ruby method is returned implicitly, it is a pretty common bug to write a callback that halts execution unintentionally. If you have an object with callbacks that mysteriously fails to save, make sure you aren't returning `false` by mistake.

9.2.5 Callback Usages

Of course, the callback you should use for a given situation depends on what you're trying to accomplish. The best I can do is to serve up some examples to inspire you with your own code.

9.2.5.1 Cleaning Up Attribute Formatting with **before_validation** on Create

The most common examples of using `before_validation` callbacks have to do with cleaning up user-entered attributes. For example, the following `CreditCard` class cleans up its `number` attribute so that false negatives don't occur on validation:

```
1 class CreditCard < ActiveRecord::Base
2   before_validation on: :create do
3     # Strip everything in the number except digits.
4     self.number = number.gsub(/[^0-9]/, "")
5   end
6 end
```

9.2.5.2   Geocoding with **before_save**

Assume that you have an application that tracks addresses and has mapping features. Addresses should always be geocoded before saving so that they can be displayed rapidly on a map later.[3]

As is often the case, the wording of the requirement itself points you in the direction of the before_save callback:

```
1 class Address < ActiveRecord::Base
2
3   before_save :geocode
4   validates_presence_of :street, :city, :state, :country
5   ...
6
7   def to_s
8     [street, city, state, country].compact.join(', ')
9   end
10
11   protected
12
13   def geocode
14     result = Geocoder.coordinates(to_s)
15     self.latitude = result.first
16     self.longitude = result.last
17   end
18 end
```

Note

For the sake of this example, we will not be using Geocoder's Active Record extensions.

Before we move on, there are a couple of additional considerations. The preceding code works great if the geocoding succeeds, but what if it doesn't? Do we still want to allow the record to be saved? If not, we should halt the execution chain:

```
1 def geolocate
2   result = Geocoder.coordinates(to_s)
3   return false if result.empty? # halt execution
4
5   self.latitude = result.first
6   self.longitude = result.last
7 end
```

3. I recommend the excellent Geocoder gem available at http://www.rubygeocoder.com

The only problem remaining is that we give the rest of our code (and by extension, the end user) no indication of why the chain was halted. Even though we're not in a validation routine, I think we can put the `errors` collection to good use here:

```
 1 def geolocate
 2   result = Geocoder.coordinates(to_s)
 3   if result.present?
 4     self.latitude = result.first
 5     self.longitude = result.last
 6   else
 7     errors[:base] << "Geocoding failed. Please check address."
 8     false
 9   end
10 end
```

If the geocoding fails, we add a base error message (for the whole object) and halt execution so that the record is not saved.

9.2.5.3 Exercise Your Paranoia with **before_destroy**

What if your application has to handle important kinds of data that, once entered, should never be deleted? Perhaps it would make sense to hook into Active Record's destroy mechanism and somehow mark the record as deleted instead?

The following example depends on the `accounts` table having a `deleted_at` datetime column.

```
1 class Account < ActiveRecord::Base
2   before_destroy do
3     self.update_attribute(:deleted_at, Time.current)
4     false
5   end
6
7   ...
8 end
```

After the `deleted_at` column is populated with the current time, we return `false` in the callback to halt execution. This ensures that the underlying record is not actually deleted from the database.[4]

It's probably worth mentioning that there are ways that Rails allows you to unintentionally circumvent `before_destroy` callbacks:

---

4. Real-life implementation of the example would also need to modify all finders to include conditions where `deleted_at` is null; otherwise, the records marked deleted would continue to show up in the application. That's not a trivial undertaking, and luckily you don't need to do it yourself. There's a Rails plugin named destroyed_at created by Dockyard that does exactly that, and you can find it at https://github.com/dockyard/destroyed_at

- The delete and delete_all class methods of ActiveRecord::Base are almost identical. They remove rows directly from the database without instantiating the corresponding model instances, which means no callbacks will occur.

- Model objects in associations defined with the option dependent: :delete _all will be deleted directly from the database when removed from the collection using the association's clear or delete methods.

9.2.5.4 Cleaning Up Associated Files with **after_destroy**

Model objects that have files associated with them, such as attachment records and uploaded images, can clean up after themselves when deleted using the after _destroy callback. The following method from Thoughtbot's Paperclip[5] gem is a good example:

```
1 # Destroys the file. Called in an after_destroy callback.
2 def destroy_attached_files
3   Paperclip.log("Deleting attachments.")
4   each_attachment do |name, attachment|
5     attachment.send(:flush_deletes)
6   end
7 end
```

9.2.6   Special Callbacks: **after_initialize** and **after_find**

The after_initialize callback is invoked whenever a new Active Record model is instantiated (either from scratch or from the database). Having it available prevents you from having to muck around with overriding the actual initialize method.

The after_find callback is invoked whenever Active Record loads a model object from the database and is actually called before after_initialize if both are implemented. Because after_find and after_initialize are called for each object found and instantiated by finders, performance constraints dictate that they can only be added as methods and not via the callback macros.

What if you want to run some code only the first time a model is ever instantiated and not after each database load? There is no native callback for that scenario, but you can do it using the after_initialize callback. Just add a condition that checks to see if it is a new record:

```
1 after_initialize do
2   if new_record?
```

---

5. Get Paperclip at https://github.com/thoughtbot/paperclip

```
3     ...
4   end
5 end
```

In a number of Rails apps that I've written, I've found it useful to capture user preferences in a serialized hash associated with the User object. The serialize feature of Active Record models makes this possible, since it transparently persists Ruby object graphs to a text column in the database. Unfortunately, you can't pass it a default value, so I have to set one myself:

```
 1 class User < ActiveRecord::Base
 2   serialize :preferences # defaults to nil
 3   ...
 4
 5   protected
 6
 7   def after_initialize
 8     self.preferences ||= Hash.new
 9   end
10 end
```

Using the after_initialize callback, I can automatically populate the preferences attribute of my user model with an empty hash, so that I never have to worry about it being nil when I access it with code such as user.preferences [:show_help_text] = false.

Kevin Says ...

You could change the previous example to not use callbacks by using the Active Record store, a wrapper around serialize that is used exclusively for storing hashes in a database column.

```
 1 class User < ActiveRecord::Base
 2   serialize :preferences # defaults to nil
 3   store :preferences, accessors: [:show_help_text]
 4   ...
 5 end
```

By default, the preferences attribute would be populated with an empty hash. Another added benefit is the ability to explicitly define accessors, removing the need to interact with the underlying hash directly. To illustrate, let's set the show_help_text preference to true:

```
>> user = User.new
=> #<User id: nil, properties: {}, ...>
```

```
>> user.show_help_text = true
=> true
>> user.properties
=> {"show_help_text" => true}
```

Ruby's metaprogramming capabilities combined with the ability to run code whenever a model is loaded using the `after_find` callback are a powerful mix. Since we're not done learning about callbacks yet, we'll come back to uses of `after_find` later on in the chapter in the section "Modifying Active Record Classes at Runtime."

9.2.7   Callback Classes

It is common enough to want to reuse callback code for more than one object that Rails provides a way to write callback classes. All you have to do is pass a given callback queue an object that responds to the name of the callback and takes the model object as a parameter.

Here's our paranoid example from the previous section as a callback class:

```
1 class MarkDeleted
2   def self.before_destroy(model)
3     model.update_attribute(:deleted_at, Time.current)
4     false
5   end
6 end
```

The behavior of `MarkDeleted` is stateless, so I added the callback as a class method. Now you don't have to instantiate `MarkDeleted` objects for no good reason. All you do is pass the class to the callback queue for whichever models you want to have the mark-deleted behavior:

```
1 class Account < ActiveRecord::Base
2   before_destroy MarkDeleted
3   ...
4 end
5
6 class Invoice < ActiveRecord::Base
7   before_destroy MarkDeleted
8   ...
9 end
```

9.2.7.1   Multiple Callback Methods in One Class

There's no rule that says you can't have more than one callback method in a callback class. For example, you might have special audit log requirements to implement:

```
 1 class Auditor
 2   def initialize(audit_log)
 3     @audit_log = audit_log
 4   end
 5
 6   def after_create(model)
 7     @audit_log.created(model.inspect)
 8   end
 9
10   def after_update(model)
11     @audit_log.updated(model.inspect)
12   end
13
14   def after_destroy(model)
15     @audit_log.destroyed(model.inspect)
16   end
17 end
```

To add audit logging to an Active Record class, you would do the following:

```
1 class Account < ActiveRecord::Base
2   after_create Auditor.new(DEFAULT_AUDIT_LOG)
3   after_update Auditor.new(DEFAULT_AUDIT_LOG)
4   after_destroy Auditor.new(DEFAULT_AUDIT_LOG)
5   ...
6 end
```

Wow, that's ugly, having to add three `Auditors` on three lines. We could extract a local variable called `auditor`, but it would still be repetitive. This might be an opportunity to take advantage of Ruby's open classes, allowing you to modify classes that aren't part of your application.

Wouldn't it be better to simply say `acts_as_audited` at the top of the model that needs auditing? We can quickly add it to the `ActiveRecord::Base` class so that it's available for all our models.

On my projects, the file where "quick and dirty" code like the method in Listing 9.1 would reside is `lib/core_ext/active_record_base.rb`, but you can put it anywhere you want. You could even make it a plugin.

Listing 9.1   A Quick-and-Dirty `acts_as_audited` Method

```
1 class ActiveRecord::Base
2   def self.acts_as_audited(audit_log=DEFAULT_AUDIT_LOG)
3     auditor = Auditor.new(audit_log)
4     after_create auditor
5     after_update auditor
6     after_destroy auditor
7   end
8 end
```

Now the top of `Account` is a lot less cluttered:

```
1  class Account < ActiveRecord::Base
2    acts_as_audited
```

9.2.7.2 Testability

When you add callback methods to a model class, you pretty much have to test that they're functioning correctly in conjunction with the model to which they are added. That may or may not be a problem. In contrast, callback classes are easy to test in isolation.

```
1  describe '#after_create' do
2    let(:auditable) { double() }
3    let(:log) { double() }
4    let(:content) { 'foo' }
5
6    it 'audits a model was created' do
7      expect(auditable).to receive(:inspect).and_return(content)
8      expect(log).to receive(:created).and_return(content)
9      Auditor.new(log).after_create(auditable)
10   end
11 end
```

9.3   Calculation Methods

All Active Record classes have a `calculate` method that provides easy access to aggregate function queries in the database. Methods for `count`, `sum`, `average`, `minimum`, and `maximum` have been added as convenient shortcuts.

Calculation methods can be used in combination with Active Record relation methods to customize the query. Since calculation methods do not return an `ActiveRecord::Relation`, they must be the last method in a scope chain.

There are two basic forms of output:

Single Aggregate Value The single value is typecast to `Fixnum` for `COUNT`, `Float` for `AVG`, and the given column's type for everything else.

Grouped Values This returns an ordered hash of the values and groups them by the `:group` option. It takes either a column name or the name of a `belongs_to` association.

The following examples illustrate the usage of various calculation methods.

```
1  Person.calculate(:count, :all) # the same as Person.count
2
3  # SELECT AVG(age) FROM people
4  Person.average(:age)
5
```

```
 6 # Selects the minimum age for everyone with a last name other than "Drake."
 7 Person.where.not(last_name: 'Drake').minimum(:age)
 8
 9 # Selects the minimum age for any family without any minors.
10 Person.having('min(age) > 17').group(:last_name).minimum(:age)
```

9.3.1 `average(column_name, *options)`

Calculates the average value on a given column. The first parameter should be a symbol identifying the column to be averaged.

9.3.2 `count(column_name, *options)`

Count operates using three different approaches. Count without parameters will return a count of all the rows for the model. Count with a `column_name` will return a count of all the rows for the model with the supplied column present.

9.3.3 `ids`

Return all the `ids` for a relation based on its table's primary key.

```
User.ids # SELECT id FROM "users"
```

9.3.4 `maximum(column_name, *options)`

Calculates the maximum value on a given column. The first parameter should be a symbol identifying the column to be calculated.

9.3.5 `minimum(column_name, *options)`

Calculates the minimum value on a given column. The first parameter should be a symbol identifying the column to be calculated.

9.3.6 `pluck(*column_names)`

The `pluck` method queries the database for one or more columns of the underlying table of a model.

```
>> User.pluck(:id, :name)
=> [[1, 'Obie']]
>> User.pluck(:name)
=> ['Obie']
```

It returns an array of values of the specified columns with the corresponding data type.

9.3.7 `sum(column_name, *options)`

Calculates a summed value in the database using SQL. The first parameter should be a symbol identifying the column to be summed.

9.4   Single-Table Inheritance (STI)

A lot of applications start out with a User model of some sort. Over time, as different kinds of users emerge, it might make sense to make a greater distinction between them. Admin and Guest classes are introduced as subclasses of User. Now the shared behavior can reside in User, and the subtype behavior can be pushed down to subclasses. However, all user data can still reside in the users table—all you need to do is introduce a type column that will hold the name of the class to be instantiated for a given row.

To continue explaining single-table inheritance, let's turn back to our example of a recurring Timesheet class. We need to know how many billable_hours are outstanding for a given user. The calculation can be implemented in various ways, but in this case we've chosen to write a pair of class and instance methods on the Timesheet class:

```
 1 class Timesheet < ActiveRecord::Base
 2   ...
 3
 4   def billable_hours_outstanding
 5     if submitted?
 6       billable_weeks.map(&:total_hours).sum
 7     else
 8       0
 9     end
10   end
11
12   def self.billable_hours_outstanding_for(user)
13     user.timesheets.map(&:billable_hours_outstanding).sum
14   end
15
16 end
```

I'm not suggesting that this is good code. It works, but it's inefficient and that if/else condition is a little fishy. Its shortcomings become apparent once requirements emerge about marking a Timesheet as paid. It forces us to modify Timesheet's billable_hours_outstanding method again:

```
1 def billable_hours_outstanding
2   if submitted? && not paid?
3     billable_weeks.map(&:total_hours).sum
4   else
5     0
6   end
7 end
```

That latest change is a clear violation of the open-closed principle,[6] which urges you to write code that is open for extension but closed for modification. We know that we violated the principle, because we were forced to change the `billable_hours_outstanding` method to accommodate the new `Timesheet` status. Though it may not seem like a large problem in our simple example, consider the amount of conditional code that will end up in the `Timesheet` class once we start having to implement functionality such as `paid_hours` and `unsubmitted_hours`.

So what's the answer to this messy question of the constantly changing conditional? Given that you're reading the section of the book about single-table inheritance, it's probably no big surprise that we think one good answer is to use object-oriented inheritance. To do so, let's break our original `Timesheet` class into four classes.

```
1 class Timesheet < ActiveRecord::Base
2   # nonrelevant code ommited
3
4   def self.billable_hours_outstanding_for(user)
5     user.timesheets.map(&:billable_hours_outstanding).sum
6   end
7 end
8
9 class DraftTimesheet < Timesheet
10   def billable_hours_outstanding
11     0
12   end
13 end
14
15 class SubmittedTimesheet < Timesheet
16   def billable_hours_outstanding
17     billable_weeks.map(&:total_hours).sum
18   end
19 end
```

Now when the requirements demand the ability to calculate partially paid timesheets, we need only add some behavior to a `PaidTimesheet` class. No messy conditional statements in sight!

```
1 class PaidTimesheet < Timesheet
2   def billable_hours_outstanding
3     billable_weeks.map(&:total_hours).sum - paid_hours
4   end
5 end
```

---

6. http://en.wikipedia.org/wiki/Open/closed_principle has a good summary.

9.4.1   Mapping Inheritance to the Database

Mapping object inheritance effectively to a relational database is not one of those problems with a definitive solution. We're only going to talk about the one mapping strategy that Rails supports natively, which is single-table inheritance, called STI for short.

In STI, you establish one table in the database to hold all the records for any object in a given inheritance hierarchy. In Active Record STI, that one table is named after the top parent class of the hierarchy. In the example we've been considering, that table would be named `timesheets`.

Hey, that's what it was called before, right? Yes, but to enable STI, we have to add a `type` column to contain a string representing the type of the stored object. The following migration would properly set up the database for our example:

```
1 class AddTypeToTimesheet < ActiveRecord::Migration
2   def change
3     add_column :timesheets, :type, :string
4   end
5 end
```

No default value is needed. Once the type column is added to an Active Record model, Rails will automatically take care of keeping it populated with the right value. Using the console, we can see this behavior in action:

```
>> d = DraftTimesheet.create
>> d.type
=> 'DraftTimesheet'
```

When you try to find an object using the query methods of a base STI class, Rails will automatically instantiate objects using the appropriate subclass. This is especially useful in polymorphic situations, such as the timesheet example we've been describing, where we retrieve all the records for a particular user and then call methods that behave differently depending on the object's class.

```
>> Timesheet.first
=> #<DraftTimesheet:0x2212354...>
```

Note

Rails won't complain about the missing column; it will simply ignore it. Recently, the error message was reworded with a better explanation, but too many developers skim error messages and then spend an hour trying to figure out what's wrong with their models. (A lot of people skim sidebar columns too when reading books, but, hey, at least I am doubling their chances of learning about this problem.)

9.4.2 STI Considerations

Although Rails makes it extremely simple to use single-table inheritance, there are four caveats that you should keep in mind.

First, you cannot have an attribute on two different subclasses with the same name but a different type. Since Rails uses one table to store all subclasses, these attributes with the same name occupy the same column in the table. Frankly, there's not much of a reason that should be a problem unless you've made some pretty bad data-modeling decisions.

Second and more important, you need to have one column per attribute on any subclass, and any attribute that is not shared by all the subclasses must accept `nil` values. In the recurring example, `PaidTimesheet` has a `paid_hours` column that is not used by any of the other subclasses. `DraftTimesheet` and `Submitted Timesheet` will not use the `paid_hours` column and leave it as null in the database. In order to validate data for columns not shared by all subclasses, you must use Active Record validations and not the database.

Third, it is not a good idea to have subclasses with too many unique attributes. If you do, you will have one database table with many null values in it. Normally, a tree of subclasses with a large number of unique attributes suggests that something is wrong with your application design and that you should refactor. If you have an STI table that is getting out of hand, it is time to reconsider your decision to use inheritance to solve your particular problem. Perhaps your base class is too abstract?

Finally, legacy database constraints may require a different name in the database for the `type` column. In this case, you can set the new column name using the class setter method `inheritance_column` in the base class. For the `Timesheet` example, we could do the following:

```
1 class Timesheet < ActiveRecord::Base
2   self.inheritance_column = 'object_type'
3 end
```

Now Rails will automatically populate the `object_type` column with the object's type.

9.4.3 STI and Associations

It seems pretty common for applications, particularly data-management ones, to have models that are very similar in terms of their data payload, mostly varying in their behavior and associations to each other. If you used object-oriented languages prior to Rails, you're probably already accustomed to breaking down problem domains into hierarchical structures.

Take, for instance, a Rails application that deals with the population of states, counties, cities, and neighborhoods. All of these are places, which might lead you to define an STI class named `Place` as shown in Listing 9.2. I've also included the database schema for clarity:[7]

Listing 9.2   The Places Database Schema and the Place Class

```
 1 # == Schema Information
 2 #
 3 # Table name: places
 4 #
 5 #  id  :integer(11)  not null, primary key
 6 #  region_id  :integer(11)
 7 #  type  :string(255)
 8 #  name  :string(255)
 9 #  description  :string(255)
10 #  latitude  :decimal(20, 1)
11 #  longitude  :decimal(20, 1)
12 #  population  :integer(11)
13 #  created_at  :datetime
14 #  updated_at  :datetime
15
16 class Place < ActiveRecord::Base
17 end
```

`Place` is in essence an abstract class. It should not be instantiated, but there is no foolproof way to enforce that in Ruby. (No big deal, this isn't Java!) Now let's go ahead and define concrete subclasses of `Place`:

```
 1 class State < Place
 2   has_many :counties, foreign_key: 'region_id'
 3 end
 4
 5 class County < Place
 6   belongs_to :state, foreign_key: 'region_id'
 7   has_many :cities, foreign_key: 'region_id'
 8 end
 9
10 class City < Place
11   belongs_to :county, foreign_key: 'region_id'
12 end
```

You might be tempted to try adding a `cities` association to `State`, knowing that `has_many :through` works with both `belongs_to` and `has_many` target associations. It would make the `State` class look something like this:

---

7. For autogenerated schema information added to the top of your model classes, try the annotate gem at https://github.com/ctran/annotate_models

```
1 class State < Place
2   has_many :counties, foreign_key: 'region_id'
3   has_many :cities, through: :counties
4 end
```

That would certainly be cool if it worked. Unfortunately, in this particular case, since there's only one underlying table that we're querying, there simply isn't a way to distinguish among the different kinds of objects in the query:

```
Mysql::Error: Not unique table/alias: 'places': SELECT places.* FROM
places INNER JOIN places ON places.region_id = places.id WHERE
((places.region_id = 187912) AND ((places.type = 'County'))) AND
((places.`type` = 'City' ))
```

What would we have to do to make it work? Well, the most realistic would be to use specific foreign keys instead of trying to overload the meaning of region_id for all the subclasses. For starters, the places table would look like the example in Listing 9.3.

Listing 9.3   The Places Database Schema Revised

```
# == Schema Information
#
# Table name: places
#
#  id       :integer(11)  not null, primary key
#  state_id   :integer(11)
#  county_id  :integer(11)
#  type     :string(255)
#  name     :string(255)
#  description  :string(255)
#  latitude   :decimal(20, 1)
#  longitude  :decimal(20, 1)
#  population :integer(11)
#  created_at :datetime
#  updated_at :datetime
```

The subclasses would be simpler without the :foreign_key options on the associations. Plus you could use a regular has_many relationship from State to City instead of the more complicated has_many :through.

```
1 class State < Place
2   has_many :counties
3   has_many :cities
4 end
5
6 class County < Place
7   belongs_to :state
```

```
 8    has_many :cities
 9  end
10
11  class City < Place
12    belongs_to :county
13  end
```

Of course, all those null columns in the places table won't win you any friends with relational database purists. That's nothing, though. Just a little bit later in this chapter, we'll take a second, more in-depth look at polymorphic has_many relationships, that will make the purists positively hate you.

9.5 Abstract Base Model Classes

In contrast to single-table inheritance, it is possible for Active Record models to share common code via inheritance and still be persisted to different database tables. In fact, every Rails developer uses an abstract model in their code whether they realize it or not: ActiveRecord::Base.[8]

The technique involves creating an abstract base model class that persistent subclasses will extend. It's actually one of the simpler techniques that we broach in this chapter. Let's take the Place class from the previous section (refer to Listing 9.3) and revise it to be an abstract base class in Listing 9.4. It's simple really—we just have to add one line of code:

Listing 9.4 The Abstract Place Class

```
1  class Place < ActiveRecord::Base
2    self.abstract_class = true
3  end
```

Marking an Active Record model abstract is essentially the opposite of making it an STI class with a type column. You're telling Rails, "Hey, I don't want you to assume that there is a table named places."

In our running example, it means we would have to establish tables for states, counties, and cities, which might be exactly what we want. Remember, though, that we would no longer be able to query across subtypes with code like Place.all.

Abstract classes is an area of Rails where there aren't too many hard-and-fast rules to guide you—experience and gut feeling will help you out.

In case you haven't noticed yet, both class and instance methods are shared down the inheritance hierarchy of Active Record models. So are constants and other class members brought in through module inclusion. That means we can put all sorts of code inside Place that will be useful to its subclasses.

---

8. http://m.onkey.org/namespaced-models

9.6   Polymorphic `has_many` Relationships

Rails gives you the ability to make one class `belong_to` more than one type of another class, as eloquently stated by blogger Mike Bayer:

> The "polymorphic association," on the other hand, while it bears some resemblance to the regular polymorphic union of a class hierarchy, is not really the same since you're only dealing with a particular association to a single target class from any number of source classes, source classes which don't have anything else to do with each other; i.e. they aren't in any particular inheritance relationship and probably are all persisted in completely different tables. In this way, the polymorphic association has a lot less to do with object inheritance and a lot more to do with aspect-oriented programming (AOP); a particular concept needs to be applied to a divergent set of entities which otherwise are not directly related. Such a concept is referred to as a cross cutting concern, such as, all the entities in your domain need to support a history log of all changes to a common logging table. In the AR example, an Order and a User object are illustrated to both require links to an Address object.[9]

In other words, this is not polymorphism in the typical object-oriented sense of the word; rather, it is something unique to Rails.

9.6.1   In the Case of Models with Comments

In our recurring time and expenses example, let's assume that we want both `BillableWeek` and `Timesheet` to have many comments (a shared `Comment` class). A naive way to solve this problem might be to have the `Comment` class belong to both the `BillableWeek` and `Timesheet` classes and have `billable_week _id` and `timesheet_id` as columns in its database table.

```
1 class Comment < ActiveRecord::Base
2   belongs_to :timesheet
3   belongs_to :expense_report
4 end
```

I call that approach naive because it would be difficult to work with and hard to extend. Among other things, you would need to add code to the application to ensure that a `Comment` never belonged to both a `BillableWeek` and a `Timesheet` at the same time. The code to figure out what a given comment is attached to would be cumbersome

---

9. http://techspot.zzzeek.org/2007/05/29/polymorphic-associations-with-sqlalchemy/

to write. Even worse, every time you want to be able to add comments to another type of class, you'd have to add another nullable foreign key column to the comments table.

Rails solves this problem in an elegant fashion by allowing us to define what it terms polymorphic associations, which we covered when we described the `polymorphic: true` option of the `belongs_to` association in Chapter 7, "Active Record Associations."

9.6.1.1   The Interface

Using a polymorphic association, we need to define only a single `belongs_to` and add a pair of related columns to the underlying database table. From that moment on, any class in our system can have comments attached to it (which would make it commentable) without needing to alter the database schema or the `Comment` model itself.

```
1 class Comment < ActiveRecord::Base
2   belongs_to :commentable, polymorphic: true
3 end
```

There isn't a `Commentable` class (or module) in our application. We named the association `:commentable` because it accurately describes the interface of objects that will be associated in this way. The name `:commentable` will turn up again on the other side of the association:

```
1 class Timesheet < ActiveRecord::Base
2   has_many :comments, as: :commentable
3 end
4
5 class BillableWeek < ActiveRecord::Base
6   has_many :comments, as: :commentable
7 end
```

Here we have the friendly `has_many` association using the `:as` option. The `:as` marks this association as polymorphic and specifies which interface we are using on the other side of the association. While we're on the subject, the other end of a polymorphic `belongs_to` can be either a `has_many` or a `has_one` and work identically.

9.6.1.2   The Database Columns

Here's a migration that will create the `comments` table:

```
1 class CreateComments < ActiveRecord::Migration
2   def change
3     create_table :comments do |t|
4       t.text :body
5       t.integer :commentable
```

```
6       t.string  :commentable_type
7     end
8   end
9 end
```

As you can see, there is a column called `commentable_type`, which stores the class name of associated object. The Migrations API actually gives you a one-line shortcut with the `references` method, which takes a `polymorphic` option:

```
1 create_table :comments do |t|
2   t.text :body
3   t.references :commentable, polymorphic: true
4 end
```

We can see how it comes together using the Rails console (some lines omitted for brevity):

```
>> c = Comment.create(body: 'I could be commenting anything.')
>> t = TimeSheet.create
>> b = BillableWeek.create
>> c.update_attribute(:commentable, t)
=> true
>> "#{c.commentable_type}: #{c.commentable_id}"
=> "Timesheet: 1"
>> c.update_attribute(:commentable, b)
=> true
>> "#{c.commentable_type}: #{c.commentable_id}"
=> "BillableWeek: 1"
```

As you can tell, both the `Timesheet` and the `BillableWeek` that we played with in the console had the same id (1). Thanks to the `commentable_type` attribute, stored as a string, Rails can figure out which is the correct related object.

9.6.1.3   **Has_many :through** and Polymorphics

There are some logical limitations that come into play with polymorphic associations. For instance, since it is impossible for Rails to know the tables necessary to join through a polymorphic association, the following hypothetical code, which tries to find everything that the user has commented on, will not work:

```
1 class Comment < ActiveRecord::Base
2   belongs_to :user # author of the comment
3   belongs_to :commentable, polymorphic: true
4 end
5
6 class User < ActiveRecord::Base
```

Active
Record

```
7    has_many :comments
8    has_many :commentables, through: :comments
9  end
10
11 >> User.first.commentables
12 ActiveRecord::HasManyThroughAssociationPolymorphicSourceError: Cannot
13 have a has_many :through association 'User#commentables' on the polymorphic object
```

If you really need it, has_many :through is possible with polymorphic associations but only by specifying exactly what type of polymorphic associations you want. To do so, you must use the :source_type option. In most cases, you will also need to use the :source option, since the association name will not match the interface name used for the polymorphic association:

```
1 class User < ActiveRecord::Base
2   has_many :comments
3   has_many :commented_timesheets, through: :comments,
4            source: :commentable, source_type: 'Timesheet'
5   has_many :commented_billable_weeks, through: :comments,
6            source: :commentable, source_type: 'BillableWeek'
7 end
```

It's verbose, and the whole scheme loses its elegance if you go this route, but it works:

```
>> User.first.commented_timesheets.to_a
=> [#<Timesheet ...>]
```

9.7 Enums

One of the newest additions to Active Record introduced in Rails 4.1 is the ability to set an attribute as an enumerable. Once an attribute has been set as an enumerable, Active Record will restrict the assignment of the attribute to a collection of predefined values.

To declare an enumerable attribute, use the enum macro-style class method, passing it an attribute name and an array of status values that the attribute can be set to.

```
1 class Post < ActiveRecord::Base
2   enum status: %i(draft published archived)
3   ...
4 end
```

Active Record implicitly maps each predefined value of an enum attribute to an integer; therefore, the column type of the enum attribute must be an integer as well. By default, an enum attribute will be set to nil. To set an initial state, one can set a default value in a migration. It's recommended to set this value to the first declared status, which would map to 0.

```
1 class CreatePosts < ActiveRecord::Migration
2   def change
3     create_table :posts do |t|
4        t.integer :status, default: 0
5     end
6   end
7 end
```

For instance, given our example, the default status of a `Post` model would be "draft":

```
>> Post.new.status
=> "draft"
```

You should never have to work with the underlying integer data type of an `enum` attribute, as Active Record creates both predicate and bang methods for each status value.

```
1 post.draft!
2 post.draft?        # => true
3 post.published?    # => false
4 post.status        # => "draft"
5
6 post.published!
7 post.published?    # => true
8 post.draft?        # => false
9 post.status        # => "published"
10
11 post.status = nil
12 post.status.nil?   # => true
13 post.status        # => nil
```

Active Record also provides scope methods for each status value. Invoking one of these scopes will return all records with that given status.

```
Post.draft
# Post Load (0.1ms)  SELECT "posts".* FROM "posts"
  WHERE   "posts"."status" = 0
```

Note

Active Record creates a class method with a pluralized name of the defined enum on the model that returns a hash with the key and value of each status. In our preceding example, the `Post` model would have a class method named statuses.

```
>> Post.statuses
=> {"draft"=>0, "published"=>1, "archived"=>2}
```

> You should only need to access this class method when you need to know the underlying ordinal value of an enum.

With the addition of the enum attribute, Active Record finally has a simple state machine out of the box. This feature alone should simplify models that had previously depended on multiple boolean fields to manage state. If you require more advanced functionality, such as status transition callbacks and conditional transitions, it's still recommended to use a full-blown state machine like state_machine.[10]

9.8 Foreign-Key Constraints

As we work toward the end of this book's coverage of Active Record, you might have noticed that we haven't really touched on a subject of particular importance to many programmers: foreign-key constraints in the database. That's mainly because use of foreign-key constraints simply isn't the Rails way to tackle the problem of relational integrity. To put it mildly, that opinion is controversial, and some developers have written off Rails (and its authors) for expressing it.

There really isn't anything stopping you from adding foreign-key constraints to your database tables, although you'd do well to wait until after the bulk of development is done. The exception, of course, is those polymorphic associations, which are probably the most extreme manifestation of the Rails opinion against foreign-key constraints. Unless you're armed for battle, you might not want to broach that particular subject with your DBA.

9.9 Modules for Reusing Common Behavior

In this section, we'll talk about one strategy for breaking out functionality that is shared between disparate model classes. Instead of using inheritance, we'll put the shared code into modules.

In the section "Polymorphic has_many Relationships" in this chapter, we described how to add a commenting feature to our recurring sample "Time and Expenses" application. We'll continue fleshing out that example, since it lends itself to factoring out into modules.

The requirements we'll implement are as follows: Both users and approvers should be able to add their comments to a Timesheet or ExpenseReport. Also, since comments are indicators that a timesheet or expense report requires extra scrutiny or processing time, administrators of the application should be able to easily view a

---

10. https://github.com/pluginaweek/state_machine

list of recent comments. Human nature being what it is, administrators occasionally gloss over the comments without actually reading them, so the requirements specify that a mechanism should be provided for marking comments as "OK" first by the approver and then by the administrator.

Again, here is the polymorphic has_many :comments, as: :commentable that we used as the foundation for this functionality:

```
1 class Timesheet < ActiveRecord::Base
2   has_many :comments, as: :commentable
3 end
4
5 class ExpenseReport < ActiveRecord::Base
6   has_many :comments, as: :commentable
7 end
8
9 class Comment < ActiveRecord::Base
10   belongs_to :commentable, polymorphic: true
11 end
```

Next we enable the controller and action for the administrator that list the 10 most recent comments with links to the item to which they are attached.

```
1 class Comment < ActiveRecord::Base
2   scope :recent, -> { order('created_at desc').limit(10) }
3 end
4
5 class CommentsController < ApplicationController
6   before_action :require_admin, only: :recent
7   expose(:recent_comments) { Comment.recent }
8 end
```

Here's some of the simple view template used to display the recent comments:

```
1 %ul.recent.comments
2   - recent_comments.each do |comment|
3     %li.comment
4       %h4= comment.created_at
5       = comment.text
6       .meta
7         Comment on:
8         = link_to comment.commentable.title, comment.commentable
9         # Yes, this would result in N+1 selects.
```

So far, so good. The polymorphic association makes it easy to access all types of comments in one listing. In order to find all the unreviewed comments for an item,

we can use a named scope on the Comment class together with the comments association.

```
1 class Comment < ActiveRecord::Base
2   scope :unreviewed, -> { where(reviewed: false) }
3 end
4
5 >> timesheet.comments.unreviewed
```

Both Timesheet and ExpenseReport currently have identical has_many methods for comments. Essentially, they both share a common interface. They're commentable!

To minimize duplication, we could specify common interfaces that share code in
Ruby by including a module in each of those classes, where the module contains the
code common to all implementations of the common interface. So, mostly for the
sake of example, let's go ahead and define a Commentable module to do just that
and include it in our model classes:

```
 1 module Commentable
 2   has_many :comments, as: :commentable
 3 end
 4
 5 class Timesheet < ActiveRecord::Base
 6   include Commentable
 7 end
 8
 9 class ExpenseReport < ActiveRecord::Base
10   include Commentable
11 end
```

Whoops, this code doesn't work! To fix it, we need to understand an essential aspect
of the way that Ruby interprets our code dealing with open classes.

9.9.1   A Review of Class Scope and Contexts

In many other interpreted, object-oriented programming languages, you have two
phases of execution: one in which the interpreter loads the class definitions and says,
"This is the definition of what I have to work with," and the second in which it executes the code. This makes it difficult (though not necessarily impossible) to add new
methods to a class dynamically during execution.

In contrast, Ruby lets you add methods to a class at any time. In Ruby, when
you type class MyClass, you're doing more than simply telling the interpreter
to define a class; you're telling it to "execute the following code in the scope of
this class."

Let's say you have the following Ruby script:

```
1 class Foo < ActiveRecord::Base
2   has_many :bars
3 end
4 class Foo < ActiveRecord::Base
5   belongs_to :spam
6 end
```

When the interpreter gets to line 1, we are telling it to execute the following code (up to the matching end) in the context of the Foo class object. Because the Foo class object doesn't exist yet, it goes ahead and creates the class. At line 2, we execute the statement has_many :bars in the context of the Foo class object. Whatever the has_many method does, it does right now.

When we again say class Foo at line 4, we are once again telling the interpreter to execute the following code in the context of the Foo class object, but this time, the interpreter already knows about class Foo; it doesn't actually create another class. Therefore, on line 5, we are simply telling the interpreter to execute the belongs_to :spam statement in the context of that same Foo class object.

In order to execute the has_many and belongs_to statements, those methods need to exist in the context in which they are executed. Because these are defined as class methods in ActiveRecord::Base, and we have previously defined class Foo as extending ActiveRecord::Base, the code will execute without a problem.

However, let's say we defined our Commentable module like this:

```
1 module Commentable
2   has_many :comments, as: :commentable
3 end
```

In this case, we get an error when it tries to execute the has_many statement. That's because the has_many method is not defined in the context of the Commentable module object.

Given what we now know about how Ruby is interpreting the code, we now realize that what we really want is for that has_many statement to be executed in the context of the including class.

9.9.2   The **included** Callback

Luckily, Ruby's Module class defines a handy callback that we can use to do just that. If a Module object defines the method included, it gets run whenever that module is included in another module or class. The argument passed to this method is the module/class object into which this module is being included.

We can define an `included` method on our `Commentable` module object so that it executes the `has_many` statement in the context of the including class (`Timesheet`, `ExpenseReport`, etc.):

```
1 module Commentable
2   def self.included(base)
3     base.class_eval do
4       has_many :comments, as: :commentable
5     end
6   end
7 end
```

Now when we include the Commentable module in our model classes, it will execute the `has_many` statement just as if we had typed it into each of those classes' bodies.

The technique is common enough, within Rails and gems, that it was added as a first-class concept in the Active Support API as of Rails 3. The previous example becomes shorter and easier to read as a result:

```
1 # app/models/concerns/commentable.rb
2 module Commentable
3   extend ActiveSupport::Concern
4   included do
5     has_many :comments, as: :commentable
6   end
7 end
```

Whatever is inside of the `included` block will get executed in the class context of the class where the module is included.

As of version 4.0, Rails includes the directory `app/models/concerns` as a place to keep all your application's model *concerns*. Any file found within this directory will automatically be part of the application load path.

Courtenay Says ...

There's a fine balance to strike here. Magic like `include Commentable` certainly saves on typing and makes your model look less complex, but it can also mean that your association code is doing things you don't know about. This can lead to confusion and hours of head scratching while you track down code in a separate module. My personal preference is to leave all associations in the model and extend them with a module. That way you can quickly get a list of all associations just by looking at the code.

9.10   Modifying Active Record Classes at Runtime

The metaprogramming capabilities of Ruby, combined with the `after_find` call-back, open the door to some interesting possibilities, especially if you're willing to blur your perception of the difference between code and data. I'm talking about modifying the behavior of model classes on the fly, as they're loaded into your application.

Listing 9.5 is a drastically simplified example of the technique, which assumes the presence of a `config` column on your model. During the `after_find` call-back, we get a handle to the unique singleton class[11] of the model instance being loaded. Then we execute the contents of the `config` attribute belonging to this particular `Account` instance, using Ruby's `class_eval` method. Since we're doing this using the singleton class for this instance rather than the global `Account` class, other account instances in the system are completely unaffected.

Listing 9.5   Runtime Metaprogramming with `after_find`

```
 1 class Account < ActiveRecord::Base
 2   ...
 3
 4   protected
 5
 6   def after_find
 7     singleton = class << self; self; end
 8     singleton.class_eval(config)
 9   end
10 end
```

I used powerful techniques like this one in a supply chain application that I wrote for a large industrial client. A *lot* is a generic term in the industry used to describe a shipment of product. Depending on the vendor and product involved, the attributes and business logic for a given lot vary quite a bit. Since the set of vendors and products being handled changed on a weekly (sometimes daily) basis, the system needed to be reconfigurable without requiring a production deployment.

Without getting into too much detail, the application allowed the maintenance programmers to easily customize the behavior of the system by manipulating Ruby code stored in the database, associated with whatever product the lot contained.

---

11. I don't expect this to make sense to you unless you are familiar with Ruby's singleton classes and have the ability to evaluate arbitrary strings of Ruby code at runtime. A good place to start is http://yehudakatz.com/2009/11/15/metaprogramming-in-ruby-its-all-about-the-self/

For example, one of the business rules associated with lots of butter being shipped for Acme Dairy Co. might dictate a strictly integral product code, exactly 10 digits in length. The code (stored in the database) associated with the product entry for Acme Dairy's butter product would therefore contain the following two lines:

```
1 validates_numericality_of :product_code, only_integer: true
2 validates_length_of       :product_code, is: 10
```

9.10.1 Considerations

A relatively complete description of everything you can do with Ruby metaprogramming, and how to do it correctly, would fill its own book. For instance, you might realize that doing things like executing arbitrary Ruby code straight out of the database is inherently dangerous. That's why I emphasize again that the examples shown here are very simplified. All I want to do is give you a taste of the possibilities.

If you do decide to begin leveraging these kinds of techniques in real-world applications, you'll have to consider security and approval workflow and a host of other important concerns. Instead of allowing arbitrary Ruby code to be executed, you might feel compelled to limit it to a small subset related to the problem at hand. You might design a compact API or even delve into authoring a domain-specific language (DSL), crafted specifically for expressing the business rules and behaviors that should be loaded dynamically. Proceeding down the rabbit hole, you might write custom parsers for your DSL that could execute it in different contexts—some for error detection and others for reporting. It's one of those areas where the possibilities are quite limitless.

9.10.2 Ruby and Domain-Specific Languages

My former colleague Jay Fields and I pioneered the mix of Ruby metaprogramming, Rails, and internal[12] domain-specific languages while doing Rails application development for clients. I still occasionally speak at conferences and blog about writing DSLs in Ruby.

Jay has also written and delivered talks about his evolution of Ruby DSL techniques, which he calls *business natural languages* (or BNL for short[13]). When developing BNLs, you craft a domain-specific language that is not necessarily valid Ruby

---

12. The qualifier *internal* is used to differentiate a domain-specific language hosted entirely inside of a general-purpose language, such as Ruby, from one that is completely custom and requires its own parser implementation.

13. Googling BNL will give you tons of links to the Toronto-based band Barenaked Ladies, so you're better off going directly to the source at http://blog.jayfields.com/2006/07/business-natural-language-material.html

syntax but is close enough to be transformed easily into Ruby and executed at run-time, as shown in Listing 9.6.

Listing 9.6 Example of Business Natural Language

```
employee John Doe
compensate 500 dollars for each deal closed in the past 30 days
compensate 100 dollars for each active deal that closed more than
365 days ago
compensate 5 percent of gross profits if gross profits are greater than
1,000,000 dollars
compensate 3 percent of gross profits if gross profits are greater than
2,000,000 dollars
compensate 1 percent of gross profits if gross profits are greater than
3,000,000 dollars
```

The ability to leverage advanced techniques such as DSLs is yet another powerful tool in the hands of experienced Rails developers.

Courtenay Says ...

DSLs suck! Except the ones written by Obie, of course. The only people who can read and write most DSLs are their original authors. As a developer taking over a project, it's often quicker to just reimplement instead of learning the quirks and exactly which words you're allowed to use in an existing DSL. In fact, a lot of Ruby metaprogramming sucks too. It's common for people gifted with these new tools to go a bit overboard. I consider metaprogramming, `self.included`, `class_eval`, and friends to be a bit of a code smell on most projects. If you're making a web application, future developers and maintainers of the project will appreciate your using simple, direct, granular, and well-tested methods rather than monkey patching into existing classes or hiding associations in modules. That said, if you can pull it off, your code will become more powerful than you can possibly imagine.

9.11 Using Value Objects

In domain-driven design[14] (DDD), there is a distinction between Entity Objects and Value Objects. All model objects that inherit from `ActiveRecord::Base` could be considered Entity Objects in DDD. An Entity Object cares about identity, since each one is unique. In Active Record, uniqueness is derived from the primary key.

14. http://www.domaindrivendesign.org/

Comparing two different Entity Objects for equality should always return false, even if all its attributes (other than the primary key) are equivalent.

Here is an example comparing two Active Record addresses:

```
>> home = Address.create(city: "Brooklyn", state: "NY")
>> office = Address.create(city: "Brooklyn", state: "NY")
>> home == office
=> false
```

In this case, you are actually creating two new `Address` records and persisting them to the database; therefore, they have different primary key values.

Value Objects, on the other hand, only care that all their attributes are equal. When creating Value Objects for use with Active Record, you do not inherit from `ActiveRecord::Base` but instead simply define a standard Ruby object. This is a form of composition called an *aggregate* in DDD. The attributes of the Value Object are stored in the database together with the parent object, and the standard Ruby object provides a means to interact with those values in a more object-oriented way.

A simple example is of a `Person` with a single `Address`. To model this using composition, first we need a `Person` model with fields for the `Address`. Create it with the following migration:

```
1 class CreatePeople < ActiveRecord::Migration
2   def change
3     create_table :people do |t|
4       t.string :name
5       t.string :address_city
6       t.string :address_state
7     end
8   end
9 end
```

The `Person` model looks like this:

```
1  class Person < ActiveRecord::Base
2    def address
3      @address ||= Address.new(address_city, address_state)
4    end
5
6    def address=(address)
7      self[:address_city] = address.city
8      self[:address_state] = address.state
9
10     @address = address
11   end
12 end
```

We need a corresponding `Address` object, which looks like this:

```
1 class Address
2   attr_reader :city, :state
3
4   def initialize(city, state)
5     @city, @state = city, state
6   end
7
8   def ==(other_address)
9     city == other_address.city && state == other_address.state
10  end
11 end
```

Note that this is just a standard Ruby object that does not inherit from `ActiveRecord::Base`. We have defined reader methods for our attributes and are assigning them upon initialization. We also have to define our own == method for use in comparisons. Wrapping this all up, we get the following usage:

```
>> gary = Person.create(name: "Gary")
>> gary.address_city = "Brooklyn"
>> gary.address_state = "NY"
>> gary.address
=> #<Address:0x007fcbfcce0188 @city="Brooklyn", @state="NY">
```

Alternately you can instantiate the address directly and assign it using the address accessor:

```
>> gary.address = Address.new("Brooklyn", "NY")
>> gary.address
=> #<Address:0x007fcbfa3b2e78 @city="Brooklyn", @state="NY">
```

9.11.1 Immutability

It's also important to treat value objects as immutable. Don't allow them to be changed after creation. Instead, create a new object instance with the new value instead. Active Record will not persist value objects that have been changed through means other than the writer method on the parent object.

9.11.1.1 The Money Gem

A common approach to using Value Objects is in conjunction with the money gem.[15]

```
1 class Expense < ActiveRecord::Base
2   def cost
3     @cost ||= Money.new(cents || 0, currency || Money.default_currency)
4   end
```

---

15. `https://github.com/RubyMoney/money`

```
 5
 6    def cost=(cost)
 7      self[:cents] = cost.cents
 8      self[:currency] = cost.currency.to_s
 9
10      cost
11    end
12 end
```

Remember to add a migration with the two columns—the integer `cents` and the string `currency` that money needs.

```
1 class CreateExpenses < ActiveRecord::Migration
2   def change
3     create_table :expenses do |t|
4       t.integer :cents
5       t.string :currency
6     end
7   end
8 end
```

Now when asking for or setting the cost of an item, we would use a `Money` instance.

```
>> expense = Expense.create(cost: Money.new(1000, "USD"))
>> cost = expense.cost
>> cost.cents
=> 1000
>> expense.currency
=> "USD"
```

9.12   Nonpersisted Models

In Rails 3, if one wanted to use a standard Ruby object with Action View helpers, such as `form_for`, the object had to "act" like an Active Record instance. This involved including/extending various Active Model module mixins and implementing the method `persisted?`. At a minimum, `ActiveModel::Conversion` should be included and `ActiveModel::Naming` extended. These two modules alone provide the object all the methods it needs for Rails to determine partial paths, routes, and naming. Optionally, extending `ActiveModel::Translation` adds internationalization support to your object, while including `ActiveModel::Validations` allows for validations to be defined. All modules are covered in detail in the Active Model API Reference.

To illustrate, let's assume we have a `Contact` class that has attributes for name, email, and message. The following implementation is Action Pack and Action View compatible in both Rails 3 and 4:

```ruby
1  class Contact
2    extend ActiveModel::Naming
3    extend ActiveModel::Translation
4    include ActiveModel::Conversion
5    include ActiveModel::Validations
6
7    attr_accessor :name, :email, :message
8
9    validates :name, presence: true
10   validates :email,
11     format: { with: /\A([^@\s]+)@((?:[-a-z0-9]+\.)+[a-z]
         {2,})\z/ },
12     presence: true
13   validates :message, length: {maximum: 1000}, presence: true
14
15   def initialize(attributes = {})
16     attributes.each do |name, value|
17       send("#{name}=", value)
18     end
19   end
20
21   def persisted?
22     false
23   end
24 end
```

New to Rails 4 is the `ActiveModel::Model`, a module mixin that removes the drudgery of manually having to implement a compatible interface. It takes care of including/extending the modules mentioned earlier, defines an initializer to set all attributes on initialization, and sets `persisted?` to `false` by default. Using `ActiveModel::Model`, the `Contact` class can be implemented as follows:

```ruby
1  class Contact
2    include ActiveModel::Model
3
4    attr_accessor :name, :email, :message
5
6    validates :name, presence: true
7    validates :email,
8      format: { with: /\A([^@\s]+)@((?:[-a-z0-9]+\.)+[a-z]{2,})\z/ },
```

Active Record

```
 9        presence: true
10    validates :message, length: {maximum: 1000}, presence: true
11 end
```

9.13   PostgreSQL Enhancements

Out of all the supported databases available in Active Record, PostgreSQL received the most amount of attention during the development of Rails 4. In this section, we are going to look at the various additions made to the PostgreSQL database adapter.

9.13.1   Schemaless Data with `hstore`

The `hstore` data type from PostgreSQL allows for the storing of key/value pairs or simply a hash within a single column. In other words, if you are using PostgreSQL and Rails 4, you can now have schema-less data within your models.

To get started, first set up your PostgreSQL database to use the hstore extension via the `enable_extension` migration method:

```
1 class AddHstoreExtension < ActiveRecord::Migration
2   def change
3     enable_extension "hstore"
4   end
5 end
```

Next, add the `hstore` column type to a model. For the purpose of our examples, we will be using a `Photo` model with an `hstore` attribute `properties`.

```
1 class AddPropertiesToPhotos < ActiveRecord::Migration
2   change_table :photos do |t|
3     t.hstore :properties
4   end
5 end
```

With the `hstore` column `properties` set up, we are able to write a hash to the database:

```
1 photo = Photo.new
2 photo.properties # nil
3 photo.properties = { aperture: 'f/4.5', shutter_speed: '1/100 secs' }
4 photo.save && photo.reload
5 photo.properties # {:aperture=>"f/4.5", :shutter_speed=>"1/100 secs"}
```

Although this works well enough, Active Record does not keep track of any changes made to the `properties` attribute itself.

```
1 photo.properties[:taken] = Time.current
2 photo.properties
```

```
3 # {:aperture=>"f/4.5", :shutter_speed=>"1/100 secs",
4 # :taken=>Wed, 23 Oct 2013 16:03:35 UTC +00:00}
5
6 photo.save && photo.reload
7 photo.properties # {:aperture=>"f/4.5", :shutter_speed=>"1/100 secs"}
```

As with some other PostgreSQL column types, such as `array` and `json`, you must tell Active Record that a change has taken place via the `<attribute>_will_change!` method. However, a better solution is to use the Active Record `store_accessor` macro-style method to add read/write accessors to hstore values.

```
1 class Photo < ActiveRecord::Base
2   store_accessor :properties, :aperture, :shutter_speed
3 end
```

When we set new values to any of these accessors, Active Record is able to track the changes made to the underlying hash, eliminating the need to call the `<attribute>_will_change!` method. Like any accessor, they can have Active Model validations added to them and also can be used in forms.

```
1 photo = Photo.new
2 photo.aperture = "f/4.5"
3 photo.shutter_speed = "1/100 secs"
4 photo.properties # {"aperture"=>"f/4.5", "shutter_speed"=>"1/100 secs"}
5
6 photo.save && photo.reload
7
8 photo.properties # {"aperture"=>"f/4.5", "shutter_speed"=>"1/100 secs"}
9 photo.aperture = "f/1.4"
10
11 photo.save && photo.reload
12 photo.properties # {"aperture"=>"f/1.4", "shutter_speed"=>"1/100 secs"}
```

Be aware that when an hstore attribute is returned from PostgreSQL, all key/values will be strings.

9.13.1.1   Querying hstore

To query against an hstore value in Active Record, use SQL string conditions with the `where` query method. For the sake of clarity, here are a couple examples of various queries that can be made against an hstore column type:

```
1 # Nonindexed query to find all photos that have a key 'aperture' with a
2 # value of f/1.4
3 Photo.where("properties -> :key = :value", key: 'aperture', value: 'f/1.4')
4
```

```
 5  # Indexed query to find all photos that have a key 'aperture' with a value
 6  # of f/1.4
 7  Photo.where("properties @> 'aperture=>f/1.4'")
 8
 9  # All photos that have a key 'aperture' in properties
10  Photo.where("properties ? :key", key: 'aperture')
11
12  # All photos that do not have a key 'aperture' in properties
13  Photo.where("not properties ? :key", key: 'aperture')
14
15  # All photos that contains all keys 'aperture' and 'shutter_speed'
16  Photo.where("properties ?& ARRAY[:keys]", keys: %w(aperture shutter_speed))
17
18  # All photos that contains any of the keys 'aperture' or 'shutter_speed'
19  Photo.where("properties ?| ARRAY[:keys]", keys: %w(aperture shutter_speed))
```

For more information on how to build hstore queries, you can consult the
PostgreSQL documentation directly.[16]

9.13.1.2 GiST and GIN Indexes

If you are doing any queries on an hstore column type, be sure to add the appropriate
index. When adding an index, you will have to decide to use either GIN or GiST
index types. The distinguishing factor between the two index types is that GIN index
lookups are three times faster than GiST indexes; however, they also take three times
longer to build.

You can define either a GIN or GiST index using Active Record migrations by
setting the index option :using to :gin or :gist, respectively.

```
add_index :photos, :properties, using: :gin
# or
add_index :photos, :properties, using: :gist
```

GIN and GiST indexes support queries with @>, ?, ?&, and ?| operators.

9.13.2 Array Type

Another NoSQL-like column type supported by PostgreSQL and Rails 4 is array.
This allows us to store a collection of a data type, such as strings, within the database
record itself. For instance, assuming we had an Article model, we could store all
the article's tags in an array attribute named tags. Since the tags are not stored in

---

16. http://www.postgresql.org/docs/9.3/static/hstore.html

another table, when Active Record retrieves an article from the database, it does so in a single query.

To declare a column as an array, pass `true` to the `:array` option for a column type such as `string`:

```
1 class AddTagsToArticles < ActiveRecord::Migration
2   def change
3     change_table :articles do |t|
4       t.string :tags, array: true
5     end
6   end
7 end
8 # ALTER TABLE "articles" ADD COLUMN "tags" character varying(255)[]
```

The array column type will also accept the option `:length` to limit the amount of items allowed in the array.

```
t.string :tags, array: true, length: 10
```

To set a default value for an array column, you must use the PostgreSQL array notation (`{value}`). Setting the `default` option to `{}` ensures that every row in the database will default to an empty array.

```
t.string :tags, array: true, default: '{rails,ruby}'
```

The migration in the previous code sample would create an array of strings that defaults every row in the database to have an array containing strings "rails" and "ruby."

```
>> article = Article.create
   (0.1ms)  BEGIN
   SQL (66.2ms)  INSERT INTO "articles" ("created_at", "updated_at") VALUES
   ($1, $2) RETURNING "id"  [["created_at", Wed, 23 Oct 2013 15:03:12

>> article.tags
=> ["rails", "ruby"]
```

Note that Active Record does not track destructive or in-place changes to the `Array` instance.

```
1 article.tags.pop
2 article.tags # ["rails"]
3 article.save && article.reload
4 article.tags # ["rails", "ruby"]
```

To ensure changes are persisted, you must tell Active Record that the attribute has changed by calling `<attribute>_will_change!`.

```
1 article.tags.pop
2 article.tags # ["rails"]
3 article.tags_will_change!
4 article.save && article.reload
5 article.tags # ["rails"]
```

If the `pg_array_parser` gem is included in the application `Gemfile`, Rails will use it when parsing PostgreSQL's array representation. The gem includes a native C extension and JRuby support.

9.13.2.1 Searching in Arrays

If you wish to query against an array column using Active Record, you must use PSQL's methods `ANY` and `ALL`. To demonstrate, given our previous example, using the `ANY` method, we could query for any articles that have the tag "rails":

```
Article.where("'rails' = ANY(tags)")
```

Alternatively, the `ALL` method searches for arrays where all values in the array equal the value specified.

```
Article.where("'rails' = ALL(tags)")
```

As with the hstore column type, if you are doing queries against an `array` column type, the column should be indexed with either GiST or GIN.

```
add_index :articles, :tags, using: 'gin'
```

9.13.3 Network Address Types

PostgreSQL comes with column types exclusively for IPv4, IPv6, and MAC addresses. IPv4 or IPv6 host address are represented with Active Record data types `inet` and `cidr`, where the former accepts values with nonzero bits to the right of the netmask. When Active Record retrieves `inet`/`cidr` data types from the database, it converts the values to `IPAddr` objects. MAC addresses are represented with the `macaddr` data type, which are represented as a string in Ruby.

To set a column as a network address in an Active Record migration, set the data type of the column to `inet`, `cidr`, or `macaddr`:

```
1 class CreateNetworkAddresses < ActiveRecord::Migration
2   def change
3     create_table :network_addresses do |t|
4       t.inet :inet_address
```

```
5         t.cidr :cidr_address
6         t.macaddr :mac_address
7     end
8   end
9 end
```

Setting an `inet` or `cidr` type to an invalid network address will result in an `IP-Addr::InvalidAddressError` exception being raised. If an invalid MAC address is set, an error will occur at the database level resulting in an `Active Record::StatementInvalid:  PG::InvalidTextRepresentation` exception being raised.

```
>> address = NetworkAddress.new
=> #<NetworkAddress id: nil, inet_address: nil, ...>

>> address.inet_address = 'abc'
IPAddr::InvalidAddressError: invalid address

>> address.inet_address = "127.0.0.1"
=> "127.0.0.1"

>> address.inet_address
=> #<IPAddr: IPv4:127.0.0.1/255.255.255.255>

>> address.save && address.reload
=> #<NetworkAddress id: 1,
       inet_address: #<IPAddr: IPv4:127.0.0.1/255.255.255.255>, ...>
```

9.13.4 UUID Type

The `uuid` column type represents a universally unique identifier (UUID), a 128-bit value that is generated by an algorithm that makes it highly unlikely that the same value can be generated twice.

To set a column as a UUID in an Active Record migration, set the type of the column to `uuid`:

```
add_column :table_name, :unique_identifier, :uuid
```

When reading and writing to a UUID attribute, you will always be dealing with a Ruby string:

```
record.unique_identifier = 'a0eebc99-9c0b-4ef8-bb6d-6bb9bd380a11'
```

If an invalid UUID is set, an error will occur at the database level, resulting in an `ActiveRecord::StatementInvalid:  PG::InvalidTextRepresentation` exception being raised.

Active
Record

9.13.5   Range Types

If you have ever needed to store a range of values, Active Record now supports Post-greSQL range types. These ranges can be created with both inclusive and exclusive bounds. The following range types are natively supported:

- `daterange`

- `int4range`

- `int8range`

- `numrange`

- `tsrange`

- `tstzrange`

To illustrate, consider a scheduling application that stores a date range representing the availability of a room.

```
1 class CreateRooms < ActiveRecord::Migration
2   def change
3     create_table :rooms do |t|
4        t.daterange :availability
5     end
6   end
7 end
8
9 room = Room.create(availability: Date.today..Float::INFINITY)
10 room.reload
11 room.availability # Tue, 22 Oct 2013...Infinity
12 room.availability.class # Range
```

Note that the `Range` class does not support exclusive lower bound. For more detailed information about the PostgreSQL range types, consult the official documentation.[17]

9.13.6   JSON Type

Introduced in PostgreSQL 9.2, the `json` column type adds the ability for PostgreSQL to store JSON structured data directly in the database. When an Active Record object has an attribute with the type of `json`, the encoding/decoding of the JSON itself is handled behind the scenes by `ActiveSupport::JSON`. This allows you to set the attribute to a hash or already encoded JSON string. If you attempt to set the JSON attribute to a string that cannot be decoded, a `JSON::ParserError` will be raised.

---

17. `http://www.postgresql.org/docs/9.3/static/rangetypes.html`

To set a column as JSON in an Active Record migration, set the data type of the column to `json`:

```
add_column :users, :preferences, :json
```

To demonstrate, let's play with the `preferences` attribute from the previous example in the console. To begin, I'll create a user with the color preference of blue.

```
>> user = User.create(preferences: { color: "blue"} )
   (0.2ms)  BEGIN
   SQL (1.1ms)  INSERT INTO "users" ("preferences") VALUES ($1) RETURNING
   "id"  [["preferences", {:color=>"blue"}]]
   (0.4ms)  COMMIT
=> #<User id: 1, preferences: {:color=>"blue"}>
```

Next up, let's verify when we retrieve the user from the database that the `preferences` attribute doesn't return a JSON string but a hash representation instead.

```
>> user.reload
   User Load (10.7ms)  SELECT "users".* FROM "users" WHERE "users"."id" = $1
   LIMIT 1  [["id", 1]]
=> #<User id: 1, preferences: {"color"=>"blue"}>

>> user.preferences.class
=> Hash
```

It's important to note that like the `array` data type, Active Record does not track in place changes. This means that updating the existing hash does not persist the changes to the database. To ensure changes are persisted, you must call `<attribute>_will_change!` (`preferences_will_change!` in our previous example) or completely replace the object instance with a new value instead.

9.14 Conclusion

With this chapter we conclude our coverage of Active Record. Among other things, we examined how callbacks let us factor our code in a clean and object-oriented fashion. We also expanded our modeling options by considering single-table inheritance, abstract classes, and Active Record's distinctive polymorphic relationships.

At this point in the book, we've covered two parts of the MVC pattern: the model and the controller. It's now time to delve into the third and final part: the view.

CHAPTER 10

Action View

The very powerful and the very stupid have one thing in common. Instead of altering their views to fit the facts, they alter the facts to fit their views…which can be very uncomfortable if you happen to be one of the facts that needs altering.

—Doctor Who

Controllers are the skeleton and musculature of your Rails application. In which case, models form the heart and mind, and your view templates (based on Action View, the third major component of Rails) are your application's skin—the part that is visible to the outside world.

Action View is the Rails API for putting together the visual component of your application—namely, the HTML and associated content that will be rendered in a web browser whenever someone uses your Rails application. Actually, in this brave new world of REST resources, Action View is involved in generating almost any sort of output you generate.

Action View contains a full-featured templating system based on a Ruby library named ERb. It takes data prepared by the controller layer and interleaves it with view code to create a presentation layer for the end user. It's also one of the first things you learn about Rails and part of the standard Ruby library. I much prefer a templating solution named Haml and have used it all over the book for examples. I think Haml is such a superior choice over ERb that this edition does not cover ERb at all.

In this chapter, we cover the fundamentals of the Action View framework, from effective use of partials to the significant performance boosts possible via caching. If you need to learn Haml, it's covered in detail in Chapter 12, "Haml."

Action View

313

10.1   Layouts and Templates

Rails has easy conventions for template usage related to the location of templates with the Rails project directories.

The app/views directory contains subdirectories corresponding to the name of controllers in your application. Within each controller's view subdirectory, you place a template named to match its corresponding action.

The special app/views/layout directory holds layout templates intended to be reusable containers for your views. Again, naming conventions are used to determine which templates to render, except that this time it is the name of the controller that is used for matching.

10.1.1   Template Filename Conventions

The filename of a template in Rails carries a lot of significance. It's parts, delimited with periods, correspond to the following information:

- Name (usually maps to action)

- Locale (optional)

- Content type

- Templating engine(s)

- Variant (optional, new in Rails 4.1)

10.1.2   Layouts

Action View decides which layout to render based on the inheritance hierarchy of controllers being executed. Most Rails applications have an application.html .haml file in their layout directory. It shares its name with the Application Controller, which is typically extended by all the other controllers in an application; therefore, it is picked up as the default layout for all views.

It is picked up, unless, of course, a more specific layout template is in place, but quite often it makes sense to use just one application-wide template, such as the simple one shown in Listing 10.1.

Listing 10.1   A Simple General-Purpose application.html.haml Layout Template

```
1  !!! 5
2  %html
3    %head
4      %meta{ charset: 'utf-8' }
5      %title TR4W Time and Expenses Sample Application
```

```
6      = csrf_meta_tag
7      = stylesheet_link_tag 'application', media: 'all'
8    %body
9      = yield
```

10.1.3   Yielding Content

The Ruby language's built-in `yield` keyword is put to good use in making layout and action templates collaborate. Notice the use of `yield` at the end of the layout template:

```
1 %body
2   = yield
```

In this case, `yield` by itself is a special message to the rendering system. It marks where to insert the output of the action's rendered output, which is usually the template corresponding to that action.

You can add extra places in your layout where you want to be able to yield content by including additional `yield` invocations—just make sure to pass a unique identifier as the argument. A good example is a layout that has left and right sidebar content (simplified, of course):

```
1 %body
2   .left.sidebar
3     = yield :left
4   .content
5     = yield
6   .right.sidebar
7     = yield :right
```

The `.content` div receives the main template markup generated. But how do you give Rails content for the left and right sidebars? It's easy: just use the `content_for` method anywhere in your template code. I usually stick it at the top of the template so that it's obvious.

```
1 - content_for :left do
2   %h2 Navigation
3   %ul
4     %li ...
5
6 - content_for :right do
7   %h2 Help
8   %p Lorem ipsum dolor sit amet, consectetur adipisicing elit...
9
```

Action
View

```
10 %h1 Page Heading
11 %p ...
```

Besides sidebars and other types of visible content blocks, I suggest you yield for additional content to be added to the HEAD element of your page, as shown in Listing 10.2.

Listing 10.2 Yielding Additional Head Content

```
 1 !!! 5
 2 %html
 3   %head
 4     %meta{ charset: 'utf-8' }
 5     %title TR4W Time and Expenses Sample Application
 6     = csrf_meta_tag
 7     = stylesheet_link_tag 'application', media: 'all'
 8     = yield :head
 9   %body
10     = yield
```

Kevin Says ...

Yielding in the HEAD element is also a great technique to include page-specific meta tags, such as those required for Facebook Open Graph.

10.1.4 Conditional Output

One of the most common idioms you'll use when coding Rails views is to conditionally output content to the view. The most elementary way to control conditional output is to use if statements.

```
1 - if show_subtitle?
2   %h2= article.subtitle
```

A lot of times you can use inline if conditions and shorten your code, since the = outputter doesn't care if you feed it a nil value. Just add a postfix if condition to the statement:

```
%h2= article.subtitle if show_subtitle?
```

Of course, there's a problem with the preceding example. The if statement on a separate line will eliminate the <h2> tags entirely, but the one-liner second example does not.

There are a couple of ways to deal with the problem and keep it a one-liner. First, there's the butt-ugly solution that I've occasionally seen in some Rails applications, which is the only reason I'm mentioning it here!

```
= "<h2>#{h(article.subtitle)}</h2>".html_safe if show_subtitle?
```

A more elegant solution involves Rails' `content_tag` helper method, but admittedly a one-liner is probably not superior to its two-line equivalent in this case.

```
= content_tag('h2', article.subtitle) if show_subtitle?
```

Helper methods, both the ones included in Rails like `content_tag` and the ones that you'll write on your own, are your main tool for building elegant view templates. Helpers are covered extensively in Chapter 11, "All about Helpers."

10.1.5   Decent Exposure

We've seen how layouts and yielding content blocks work, but other than that, how should data get from the controller layer to the view? During preparation of the template, instance variables set during execution of the controller action will be copied over as instance variables of the template context. Even though it's the standard way exposed by Rails documentation, sharing state via instance variables in controllers promotes close coupling with views.

Stephen Caudill's Decent Exposure gem1 provides a declarative manner of exposing an interface to the state that controllers contain, thereby decreasing coupling and improving your testability and overall design.

When invoked, `expose` macro creates a method with the given name, evaluates the provided block, and memoizes the result. This method is then declared as a `helper _method` so that views may have access to it and is made unroutable as an action. When no block is given, `expose` attempts to intuit which resource you want to acquire:

```
# Timesheet.find(params[:timesheet_id] || params[:id])
expose(:timesheet)
```

As the example shows, the symbol passed is used to guess the class name of the object you want to find—useful since almost every controller in a normal Rails uses this kind of code in the show, edit, update, and destroy actions.

In a slightly more complicated scenario, you might need to find an instance of an object that doesn't map cleanly to a simple `find` method.

---

1. http://github.com/voxdolo/decent_exposure

Action View

```
expose(:timesheet) { client.timesheets.find(params[:id]) }
```

In the RESTful controller paradigm, you'll again find yourself using this in show, edit, update, and destroy actions of nested resources.

When the code has become long enough to surpass a single line (but still isn't appropriate to extract into a model method), use a `do...end` style of block, as in the following that uses all three styles:

```
1 expose(:client)
2
3 expose(:timesheet) { client.timesheets.find(params[:id]) }
4
5 expose(:timesheet_approval_presenter) do
6   TimesheetApprovalPresenter.new(timesheet, current_user)
7 end
```

The previous example also demonstrates how `expose` declarations can depend on each other. In fact, proper use of `expose` should eliminate most model-lookup code from your actual controller actions.

At Hashrocket, use of Decent Exposure has proven so beneficial that it has completely replaced direct use of instance variables in controllers and views. The helper methods created by the `expose` macro are just referred to directly in the view.

10.1.6   Standard Instance Variables

More than just instance variables from the controller are copied over to the template. It's not a good idea to depend on some of the following objects directly, and especially not to use them to do data operations. Others are a standard part of most Rails applications.

10.1.6.1   `assigns`

Want to see everything that comes across the controller-view boundary? Throw `= debug(assigns)` into your template and take a look at the output. The `assigns` attribute is essentially internal to Rails, and you should not use it directly in your production code.

10.1.6.2   `base_path`

Local filesystem path pointing to the base directory of your application where templates are kept.

10.1.6.3   `controller`

The current controller instance is made available via `controller`, before it goes out of scope at the end of request processing. You can take advantage of the controller's knowledge of its name (via the `controller_name` attribute) and the action that was just performed (via the `action_name` attribute) in order to structure your CSS more effectively.

```
%body{ class: "#{controller.controller_name} #{controller.action_name}" }
```

That would result in a BODY tag looking something like this, depending on the action executed:

```
<body class="timesheets index">
```

Note

You could also replicate the functionality in the previous example by using the Haml helper method `page_class`.

```
%body{ class: page_class }
```

Hopefully you already know that the C in CSS stands for cascading, which refers to the fact that class names cascade down the tree of elements in your markup code and are available for creation of rules. The trick is to automatically include the controller and action name as classnames of your `body` element so that you can use them to customize look and feel of the page very flexibly later on in the development cycle. For example, here's how you would use the technique to vary the background of header elements depending on the controller path in SCSS:

```
1 body {
2     .timesheets .header {
3         background: image_url(timesheet-bg.png) no-repeat left top;
4     }
5
6     .expense_reports .header {
7         background: image_url(expense-reports-bg.png) no-repeat left top;
8     }
9 }
```

10.1.6.4 `cookies`

The `cookies` variable is a hash containing the user's cookies. There might be situations where it'd be OK to pull values out to affect rendering, but most of the time you'll be using cookies in your controller, not the view.

Action View

10.1.6.5 `flash`

The `flash` has popped up in larger code samples throughout the book so far whenever you want to send the user a message from the controller layer, but only for the
duration of the next request.

```
1 def create
2   if user.try(:authorize, params[:user][:password])
3     flash[:notice] = "Welcome, #{user.first_name}!"
4     redirect_to home_url
5   else
6     flash[:alert] = "Login invalid."
7     redirect_to :new
8   end
9 end
```

A common Rails practice is to use `flash[:notice]` to hold benign notice messages and `flash[:alert]` for communication of a more serious nature.

Note

It's so common to set `flash` notice and `alert` messages on redirects that
Rails allows you to set them in the `redirect_to` method as optional
parameters.

```
1 def create
2   if user.try(:authorize, params[:user][:password])
3     redirect_to home_url, notice: "Welcome, #{user.first_
        name}!"
4   else
5     redirect_to home_url, alert: "Bad login"
6   end
7 end
```

Special accessors for notices and alerts are included as helper methods on the
flash object itself, since their use is so common.

```
1 def create
2   if user.try(:authorize, params[:user][:password])
3     flash.notice = "Welcome, #{user.first_name}!"
4     redirect_to home_url
5   else
6     flash.alert = "Login invalid."
7     redirect_to action: "new"
8   end
9 end
```

10.1.7 Displaying **flash** Messages

Personally, I like to conditionally output both notice and alert messages in div elements, right at the top of my layout, and use CSS to style them, as shown in Listing 10.3:

Listing 10.3 Standardized Flash Notice and Error Placement in application.html.haml

```
1  %html
2    ...
3    %body
4      - if flash.notice
5        .notice= flash.notice
6      - if flash.alert
7        .notice.alert= flash.alert
8
9      = yield
```

The CSS for .notice defines most of the style for the element, and .alert overrides just the aspects that are different for alerts.

10.1.8 **flash.now**

Sometimes you want to give the user a flash message but only for the current request. In fact, a common newbie Rails programming mistake is to set a flash notice and *not* redirect, thereby incorrectly showing a flash message on the following request.

It is possible to make flash cooperate with a render by using the flash.now method.

```
 1  class ReportController < ActionController::Base
 2    def create
 3      if report.save
 4        flash.notice = "#{report.title} has been created."
 5        redirect_to report_path(report)
 6      else
 7        flash.now.alert = "#{@post.title} could not be created."
 8        render :new
 9      end
10    end
11  end
```

The flash.now object also has notice and alert accessors, like its traditional counterpart.

10.1.8.1 **logger**

Do you have something to record for posterity in the logs while you're rendering the view? Use the logger method to get the view's Logger instance—the same as Rails.logger, unless you've changed it.

Action View

10.1.8.2 `params`

This is the same `params` hash that is available in your controller, containing the key/value pairs of your request. I'll occasionally use a value from the `params` hash directly in the view, particularly when I'm dealing with pages that are subject to filtering or row sorting.

```
1 %p
2   Filter by month:
3   = select_tag(:month_filter,
4       options_for_select(@month_options, params[:month_filter]))
```

It's very dangerous from a security perspective to put unfiltered parameter data into the output stream of your template. Chapter 15, "Security," covers that topic in depth.

10.1.8.3 `request` and `response`

The HTTP `request` and `response` objects are exposed to the view, but other than for debugging purposes, I can't think of any reason you would want to use them directly from your template.

10.1.8.4 `session`

The `session` variable is the user's session hash. There might be situations where it'd be OK to pull values out to affect rendering, but I shudder to think that you might try to set values in the session from the view layer. Use with care and primarily for debugging, just like `request` and `response`.

10.2 Partials

A partial is a fragment of template code. The Rails way is to use partials to factor view code into modular chunks that can be assembled in layouts with as little repetition as possible. In older versions of Rails, the syntax for including a partial within a template started with `render  :partial`, but now passing a string to `render` within your view will get interpreted to mean you want to render a partial. Partial template names must begin with an underscore, which serves to set them apart visually within a given view template directory. However, you leave the underscore out when you refer to them.

```
1 %h1 Details
2 = render 'details'
```

10.2.1 Simple Use Cases

The simplest partial use case is simply to extract a portion of template code. Some developers divide their templates into logical parts by using partial extraction.

Sometimes it is easier to understand the structure of a screen if the significant parts are factored out of it. For instance, Listing 10.4 is a simple user registration screen that has its parts factored out into partials.

Listing 10.4 Simple User Registration Form with Partials

```
 1  %h1 User Registration
 2  = error_messages_for :user
 3  = form_for :user, url: users_path do
 4    .registration
 5      .details.demographics
 6        = render 'details'
 7        = render 'demographics'
 8      .location
 9        = render 'location'
10      .opt_in
11        = render 'opt_in'
12      .terms
13        = render 'terms'
14    %p= submit_tag 'Register'
```

While we're at it, let me pop open one of those partials. To conserve space, we'll take a look at one of the smaller ones, the partial containing the opt-in check boxes of this particular app. The source is in Listing 10.5; notice that its name begins with an underscore.

Listing 10.5 The Opt-In Partial in the File `app/views/users/_opt_in.html.haml`

```
1  %fieldset#opt_in
2    %legend Spam Opt In
3    %p
4      = check_box :user, :send_event_updates
5      Send me updates about events!
6      %br
7      = check_box :user, :send_site_updates
8      Notify me about new services
```

Personally, I like partials to be entirely contained inside a semantically significant markup container. In the case of the opt-in partial in Listing 10.5, both check box controls are contained inside a single `fieldset` element, which I've given an `id` attribute. Following that rule, more as a loose guideline than anything else, helps me mentally identify how the contents of this partial are going to fit inside the parent template. If we were dealing with other markup, perhaps outside of a form, I might choose to wrap the partial markup inside a well-identified `div` container instead of a `fieldset`.

Action
View

Why not include the `td` markup inside the partial templates? It's a matter of style—I like to be able to see the complete markup skeleton in one piece. In this case, the skeleton is the table structure that you see in Listing 10.4. If portions of that table were inside the partial templates, it would obfuscate the layout of the page. I do admit that this is one of those areas where personal style and preference should take precedence, and I can only advise you as to what has worked for me, personally.

10.2.2 Reuse of Partials

Since the registration form is neatly factored out into its component parts, it is easy to create a simple edit form using some of its partials, as in Listing 10.6.

Listing 10.6   Simple User Edit Form Reusing Some of the Same Partials

```
1 %h1 Edit User
2 = form_for :user, url: user_path(@user), method: :put do
3   .settings
4     .details
5       = render 'details'
6     .demographics
7       = render 'demographics'
8   .opt_in
9     = render 'opt_in'
10  %p= submit_tag 'Save Settings'
```

If you compare Listings 10.4 and 10.6, you'll notice that the structure of the table changed a little bit in the edit form, and it has less content than the registration form. Perhaps the location is handled in greater detail on another screen, and certainly you don't want to require agreement of terms every time the user changes her settings.

10.2.3 Shared Partials

Until now we've been considering the use of partials that reside in the same directory as their parent template. However, you can easily refer to partials that are in other directories just by prefixing the directory name. You still leave off the underscore, which has always felt a little weird.

Let's add a `captcha` partial to the bottom of the registration form from Listing 10.4 to help prevent spammers from invading our web application:

```
1   ...
2     .terms
3       = render 'terms'
4     .captcha
5       = render 'shared/captcha'
6   %p= submit_tag 'Register'
```

Since the `captcha` partial is used in various different parts of the application, it makes sense to let it reside in a shared folder rather than any particular view folder. However, you do have to be a little bit careful when you move existing template code into a shared partial. It's quite possible to inadvertently craft a partial that depends implicitly on where it's rendered.

For example, take the case of the Rails-talk mailing list member with a troublesome partial defined in `login/_login.html.haml`:

```
1  = form_tag do
2    %fieldset
3      %label
4        Username:
5        = text_field_tag :username, params[:username]
6      %br
7      %label
8        Password:
9        = password_field_tag :password, params[:password]
10     %br
11     = submit_tag "Login"
```

The login form submission worked when he rendered this partial as part of the login controller's `login` action ("the login page") but not when it was included as part of the view for any other section of her website. The problem is that `form_tag` (covered in the next chapter) normally takes an optional action parameter telling it where to post its information. If you leave out the action, the form will post back to its current URL, which will vary for shared partials, depending on where they're being used from.

10.2.4 Passing Variables to Partials

Partials inherit the method exposed to their parent templates implicitly. That's why the form helpers used in the partials of Listings 10.4 and 10.6 work: They rely implicitly on a `user` method to be in scope. I feel it's fine to use this implicit sharing in some cases, particularly when the partials are tightly bound to their parent templates. It would be especially true in cases where the only reason you broke out a partial in the first place was to reduce the size and complexity of a particularly large template.

However, once you get into the practice of breaking out partial templates for reuse, depending on implicit context gets a lot more dicey. That's why Rails supports the passing of locally scoped variables to partial templates, as in the following snippet:

```
= render 'shared/address', form: form
```

The values of the optional hash are converted into locally scoped variables (no @ sign) in the partial. Listing 10.7 is a variation on the registration template. This time we're using the version of `form_for` that yields a block parameter representing the form to its form helper methods. We'll pass that form parameter on, too.

Listing 10.7   Simple User Registration Template Passing Form as Local Variable
```
1 %h1 User Registration
2 = form_for :user, url: users_path do |form|
3   .registration
4     .details.address.demographics
5       = render 'details', form: form
6       = render 'shared/address', form: form
7   %p= form.submit 'Register'
```

And finally, in Listing 10.8 we have the shared address form.

Listing 10.8   A Simple Shared Address Partial Using Local Variable
```
 1 %fieldset.address
 2   %legend Address
 3   %p
 4     %label Street
 5     %br
 6     = form.text_area :street, rows: 2, cols: 40
 7   %p
 8     %label City
 9     %br
10     = form.text_field :city
11   %p
12     %label State
13     %br
14     = form.text_field :state, size: 2
15   %p
16     %label Zip
17     %br
18     = form.text_field :zip, size: 15
```

The form helper methods, which we'll cover in Chapter 11, "All about Helpers," have a variation in which they are called on the `form` variable yielded by the `form_for` method. That is exactly what we passed on to these partials

10.2.4.1   The `local_assigns` Hash
If you need to check for the presence of a certain local variable in a partial, you need to do it by checking the `local_assigns` hash that is part of every

template. Using `defined?` variable won't work due to limitations of the rendering system.

```
1  - if local_assigns.has_key? :special
2    = special
```

10.2.5   Rendering an Object

The `render` method also provides a shorthand syntax to render an object into a partial, which strictly depends on Rails naming conventions.

```
= render entry
```

The partial corresponding to the last code snippet is named `_entry.html.haml` and gets a local variable named `entry`. This is equivalent to the following:

```
= render partial: 'entry', object: entry
```

To set a different local variable name other than the name of the partial, one could use the `locals` hash as seen earlier in the chapter or specify the desired name through the `:as` option.

```
= render partial: 'entry', object: some_entry, as: :item
```

10.2.6   Rendering Collections

One of the best uses of partials is to render collections. Once you get into the habit of rendering collections with partials, you won't want to go back to the relative ugliness of cluttering your templates with `for` and `each` loops. When the `render` method gets an `Enumerable` as its first argument, it assumes that you want to render a collection of partials.

```
render entries
```

It is simple and precise yet very dependent on a naming conventions. The objects being rendered are exposed to the partial template as a local variable named the same as the partial template itself. In turn the template should be named according to the class of the objects being rendered.

   The partial corresponding to the last code snippet is named `_entry.html.haml` and gets a local variable named `entry`.

```
1 = div_for(entry) do
2    = entry.description
3    #{distance_of_time_in_words_to_now entry.created_at} ago
```

Kevin Says ...

If the collection passed into the render method is empty, nil is returned. Using this knowledge, you can write code such as the following to provide fallback content:

```
= render(entries) || "No entries exist"
```

Since the partial template used is based on the class of each item, you can easily render a heterogeneous collection of objects. This technique is particularly useful in conjunction with collections of STI subclasses.

If you want to override that behavior, then revert to the older partial syntax and specify the :partial and :collection options explicitly, as follows:

```
partial: 'entry', collection: @entries
```

10.2.6.1 The `partial_counter` Variable

There's another variable set for collection-rendered partials that doesn't get much attention. It's a zero-indexed counter variable that tracks the number of times a partial has been rendered. It's useful for rendering numbered lists of things. The name of the variable is the name of the partial, plus _counter.

```
1  = div_for(entry) do
2    "#{entry_counter}:#{entry.description}
3    #{distance_of_time_in_words_to_now entry.created_at} ago"
```

10.2.6.2 Sharing Collection Partials

If you wanted to use the same partial that you use with a collection, except with a single entry object, you'd have to pass it that single instance via the locals hash described in the preceding section, like this:

```
render 'entry', entry: some_entry
```

10.2.7 Logging

If you take a look at your development log, you'll notice that it shows which partials have been rendered and how long they took.

```
Rendering template within layouts/application
Rendering listings/index
Rendered listings/_listing 0.6ms)
Rendered listings/_listing 0.3ms)
Rendered listings/_listing 0.2ms)
Rendered listings/_listing 0.2ms)
```

```
Rendered listings/_listing 0.2ms)
Rendered layouts/_login 2.4ms)
Rendered layouts/_header 3.3ms)
Rendered layouts/_footer 0.1ms)
```

10.3   Conclusion

In this chapter, we've covered the Action View framework with a detailed explanation of templating and how the Rails rendering system works. We've also covered the use of partials in depth, since their use is essential for effective Rails programming.

Now it's time to cover the mechanism whereby you can inject a whole bunch of smarts into your view layer without cluttering up your templates: helpers.

CHAPTER 11

All about Helpers

Thank you for helping Helpers Helping the Helpless. Your help was very…helpful!

—Mrs. Duong in the movie *The Weekenders*

Throughout the book so far, we've already covered some of the helper methods provided by Rails to help you assemble the user interface of your web application. This chapter lists and explains all the helper modules and their methods, followed by instructions on effectively creating your own helpers.

Note

This chapter is essentially reference material. Although every effort has been made to make it readable straight through, you will notice that coverage of Action View's helper modules is arranged alphabetically, starting with `ActiveModelHelper` and ending with `UrlHelper`. Within each module's section, the methods are broken up into logical groups whenever appropriate.

This chapter is published under the Creative Commons Attribution-ShareAlike 4.0 license, `http://creativecommons.org/licenses/by-sa/4.0/`.

11.1 `ActiveModelHelper`

The `ActiveModelHelper` module contains helper methods for quickly creating forms from objects that follow Active Model conventions, starting with Active Record models. The `form` method is able to create an entire form for all the basic content types of a given record. However, it does not know how to assemble user-interface components for manipulating associations. Most Rails developers assemble

Helpers

331

their own forms from scratch using methods from `FormHelper` instead of using this module. However, this module does contain some useful helpers for reporting validation errors in your forms that you will use regularly.

Note that since Rails 3, you must add the following gem to your `Gemfile` in order to use this module.

```
gem 'dynamic_form'
```

11.1.1   Reporting Validation Errors

The `error_message_on` and `error_messages_for` methods help you add formatted validation error information to your templates in a consistent fashion.

11.1.1.1   `error_message_on(object, method, *options)`

Returns a `div` tag containing the error message attached to the specified method on the object, if one exists. It's useful for showing validation errors inline next to the corresponding form field. The `object` argument of the method can be an actual object reference or a symbol corresponding to the name of an instance variable. The `method` should be a symbol corresponding to the name of the attribute on the object for which to render an error message.

The contents can be specialized with options for pre- and post-text and custom CSS class.

prepend_text: string Fragment to prepend to error messages generated.

append_text: string Fragment to append to error messages generated.

css_class: class_name CSS class name for `div` generated wrapping the error message. Defaults to `formError`.

Use of this method is common when the user-interface requirements specify individual validation messages per input field of a form, as in the following real-life example:

```
1  .form_field
2    .field_label
3      %span.required *
4      %label First Name
5    .textual
6      = form.text_field :first_name
7      = form.error_message_on :first_name
```

As in the example, the `error_message_on` helper is most commonly accessed via the `form` block variable of `form_for` and its variants. When used via the `form` variable, you leave off the first argument (specifying the object) since it's implied.

11.1.1.2 `error_messages_for(*params)`

Returns a `div` tag containing all the error messages for all the objects held in instance variables identified as parameters.

```
1 = form_for @person do |form|
2   = form.error_messages
3   .text-field
4     = form.label :name, "Name"
5     = form.text_field :name
```

As in the example, the `error_message_for` helper is most commonly accessed via the `form` block variable of `form_for` and its variants. When used via the `form` variable, it is called `error_messages` and you leave off the first argument (specifying the object) since it's implied.

This method was used by Rails scaffolding before version 3 but rarely in real production applications. The Rails API documentation advises you to use this method's implementation as inspiration to meet your own requirements:

> This is a prepackaged presentation of the errors with embedded strings and a certain HTML structure. If what you need is significantly different from the default presentation, it makes plenty of sense to access the object.errors instance yourself and set it up. View the source of this method to see how easy it is.

We'll go ahead and reproduce the source of the method here with the warning that you should not try to use it as inspiration unless you have a good grasp of Ruby! On the other hand, if you have time to study the way that this method is implemented, it will definitely teach you a lot about the way that Rails is implemented, which is its own distinctive flavor of Ruby.

```
1 def error_messages_for(*params)
2   options = params.extract_options!.symbolize_keys
3
4   objects = Array.wrap(options.delete(:object) || params).map do |object|
5     object = instance_variable_get("@#{object}") unless object.
6       respond_to?(:to_model)
7     object = convert_to_model(object)
8
9     if object.class.respond_to?(:model_name)
10      options[:object_name] ||= object.class.model_name.human.downcase
```

Helpers

```
11      end
12
13      object
14    end
15
16    objects.compact!
17    count = objects.inject(0) { |sum, object| sum + object.errors.count }
18
19    unless count.zero?
20      html = {}
21      [:id, :class].each do |key|
22        if options.include?(key)
23          value = options[key]
24          html[key] = value unless value.blank?
25        else
26          html[key] = 'error_explanation'
27        end
28      end
29      options[:object_name] ||= params.first
30
31      I18n.with_options locale: options[:locale],
32        scope: [:activerecord, :errors, :template] do |locale|
33        header_message = if options.include?(:header_message)
34          options[:header_message]
35        else
36          locale.t :header, count: count,
37            model: options[:object_name].to_s.gsub('_', ' ')
38        end
39
40        message =options.include?(:message) ? options[:message] :locale.t(:body)
41
42        error_messages = objects.sum do |object|
43          object.errors.full_messages.map do |msg|
44            content_tag(:li, msg)
45          end
46        end.join.html_safe
47
48        contents = ''
49        contents << content_tag(options[:header_tag] ||
50          :h2, header_message) unless header_message.blank?
51        contents << content_tag(:p, message) unless message.blank?
52        contents << content_tag(:ul, error_messages)
53
54        content_tag(:div, contents.html_safe, html)
55      end
56    else
57      ''
58    end
59  end
```

Later on in the chapter we'll talk extensively about writing your own helper methods.

11.1.2 Automatic Form Creation

The next couple of methods are used for automatic field creation. You can try using them too, but I suspect that their usefulness is somewhat limited in real applications.

11.1.2.1 `form(name, options)`

Returns an entire form with input tags and everything for a named model object. Here are the code examples given in the dynamic form API documentation, using a hypothetical `Post` object from a bulletin board application as an example:

```
 1 form("post")
 2 # => <form action='/posts/create' method='post'>
 3 #       <p>
 4 #         <label for="post_title">Title</label><br />
 5 #         <input id="post_title" name="post[title]" size="30"
         type="text"
 6 #           value="Hello World" />
 7 #       </p>
 8 #       <p>
 9 #         <label for="post_body">Body</label><br />
10 #         <textarea cols="40" id="post_body" name="post[body]"
11 #           rows="20"></textarea>
12 #       </p>
13 #       <input name="commit" type="submit" value="Create" />
14 #     </form>
```

Internally, the method calls `record.persisted?` to infer whether the action for the form should be `create` or `update`. It is possible to explicitly specify the action of the form (and the value of the submit button along with it) by using the `:action` option.

If you need the form to have its `enctype` set to `multipart`, useful for file uploads, set the `options[:multipart]` to `true`.

You can also pass in an `:input_block` option, using Ruby's `Proc.new` idiom to create a new anonymous code block. The block you supply will be invoked for each content column of your model, and its return value will be inserted into the form.

```
 1 form("entry", action: "sign",
 2     input_block: Proc.new { |record, column|
 3       "#{column.human_name}: #{input(record, column.name)}<br />"
 4 })
 5 # => <form action="/entries/sign" method="post">
 6 #       Message:
 7 #         <input id="entry_message" name="entry[message]" size="30"
```

```
 8 #          type="text" /><br />
 9 #      <input name="commit" type="submit" value="Sign" />
10 #   </form>
```

That example's builder block, as it is referred to in the dynamic_form API docs, uses the input helper method, which is also part of this module and is covered in the next section of this chapter.

Finally, it's also possible to add additional content to the form by giving the call to form a block, as in the following snippet:

```
1 form("entry", action: "sign") do |form|
2   form << content_tag("b", "Department")
3   form << collection_select("department", "id", @departments, "id", "name")
4 end
```

The block is yielded a string accumulator (named form in the example), to which you append any additional content that you want to appear between the main input fields and the submit tag.

11.1.2.2 `input(name, method, options)`

The appropriately named input method takes some identifying information and automatically generates an HTML input tag based on an attribute of an Active Record model. Going back to the Post example used in the explanation of form, here is the code snippet given in the Rails API docs:

```
1 input("post", "title")
2 # => <input id="post_title" name="post[title]" size="30"
3 #       type="text" value="Hello World" />
```

To quickly show you the types of input fields generated by this method, I'll simply reproduce a portion of the code from the module itself:

```
 1 def to_tag(options = {})
 2   case column_type
 3   when :string
 4     field_type = @method_name.include?("password") ?
       "password" : "text"
 5     to_input_field_tag(field_type, options)
 6   when :text
 7     to_text_area_tag(options)
 8   when :integer, :float, :decimal
 9     to_input_field_tag("text", options)
10   when :date
11     to_date_select_tag(options)
```

```
12      when :datetime, :timestamp
13        to_datetime_select_tag(options)
14      when :time
15        to_time_select_tag(options)
16      when :boolean
17        to_boolean_select_tag(options).html_safe
18    end
19 end
```

11.1.3   Customizing the Way Validation Errors Are Highlighted

By default, when Rails marks a field in your form that failed a validation check, it does so by wrapping that field in a `div` element with the class name `field _with_errors`. This behavior is customizable, since it is accomplished via a `Proc` object stored as a configuration property of the `ActionView::Base` class:

```
1 module ActionView
2   class Base
3     cattr_accessor :field_error_proc
4     @@field_error_proc = Proc.new{ |html_tag, instance|
5       "<div class=\"field_with_errors\">#{html_tag}</div>".
         html_safe
6     }
7   end
8
9   ...
```

Armed with this knowledge, changing the validation error behavior is as simple as overriding Action View's `field_error_proc` attribute with your own custom `Proc`. I would suggest doing so in an initializer file.

In Listing 11.1, I changed the setting so that the input fields with validation errors are prefixed with a red ERROR message.

Listing 11.1 Custom Validation Error Display

```
1 ActionView::Base.field_error_proc =
2   Proc.new do |html_tag,instance|
3     %(<div style="color:red">ERROR</div>) + html_tag
4   end
```

It has been suggested by many people that it would have been a much better default solution to simply add a `field_with_errors` CSS class to the input tag itself instead of wrapping it with an extra `div` tag. Indeed, that would have made many of our lives easier, since an extra `div` often breaks pixel-perfect layouts. However,

Helpers

since `html_tag` is already constructed at the time when the `field_error_proc` is invoked, it is not trivial to modify its contents.

11.2 `AssetTagHelper`

According to the Rails API docs, this module

> provides methods for generating HTML that links views to assets such as images, javascripts, stylesheets, and feeds. These methods do not verify the assets exist before linking to them.

The `AssetTagHelper` module includes some methods that you will use daily during active Rails development, particularly `image_tag`.

11.2.1 Head Helpers

Some of the helper methods in this module help you add content to the `head` element of your HTML document.

11.2.1.1 `auto_discovery_link_tag(type = :rss,`
`url_options = {}, tag_options = {})`

Returns a link tag that browsers and news readers can use to autodetect an RSS or ATOM feed. The type can either be `:rss` (default) or `:atom`. Control the link options in `url_for` format using the `url_options`.

You can modify the `link` tag itself using the `tag_options` parameter:

`:rel` The relation of this link. Defaults to `"alternate"`.

`:type` Override MIME type (such as `"application/atom+xml"`) that Rails would otherwise generate automatically for you.

`:title` The title of the link. Defaults to a capitalized type.

Here are examples of usages of `auto_discovery_link_tag` as shown in the Rails API docs:

```
1  auto_discovery_link_tag
2  # => <link rel="alternate" type="application/rss+xml" title="RSS"
3  #          href="http://www.currenthost.com/controller/action" />
4
5  auto_discovery_link_tag(:atom)
6  # => <link rel="alternate" type="application/atom+xml" title="ATOM"
```

```
 7 #          href="http://www.currenthost.com/controller/action" />
 8
 9 auto_discovery_link_tag(:rss, {action: "feed"})
10 # => <link rel="alternate" type="application/rss+xml" title="RSS"
11 #          href="http://www.currenthost.com/controller/feed" />
12
13 auto_discovery_link_tag(:rss, {action: "feed"}, {title: "My RSS"})
14 # => <link rel="alternate" type="application/rss+xml" title="My RSS"
15 #          href="http://www.currenthost.com/controller/feed" />
```

11.2.1.2 `favicon_link_tag(source='favicon.ico', options={})`

Returns a link loading a favicon file. By default, Rails will set the icon to `favicon
.ico`. You may specify a different file in the first argument.

The `favicon_link_tag` helper accepts an optional options hash that accepts
the following:

:rel Specify the relation of this link. Defaults to shortcut icon.

:type Override the autogenerated MIME type. Defaults to image/vnd.microsoft.icon.

```
1 favicon_link_tag '/myicon.ico'
2 # => <link href="/assets/favicon.ico" rel="shortcut icon"
3 #        type="image/vnd.microsoft.icon" />
```

11.2.1.3 `javascript_include_tag(*sources)`

Returns a `script` tag for each of the sources provided. You can pass in the filename
(the `.js` extension is optional) of JavaScript files that exist in your `app/assets/
javascripts` directory for inclusion into the current page, or you can pass their
full path relative to your document root.

```
1 javascript_include_tag "xmlhr"
2 # => <script src="/assets/xmlhr.js?1284139606"></script>
3
4 javascript_include_tag "common", "/elsewhere/cools"
5 # => <script src="/assets/common.js?1284139606"></script>
6 #      <script src="/elsewhere/cools.js?1423139606"></script>
```

When the Asset Pipeline is enabled, passing the name of the manifest file as a
source will include all JavaScript or CoffeeScript files that are specified within
the manifest.

```
javascript_include_tag "application"
```

Note

By default, not including the `.js` extension to a JavaScript source will result in `.js` being suffixed to the filename. However, this does not play well with JavaScript templating languages, as they have extensions of their own. To rectify this, as of Rails 4.1, setting the option `:extname` to `false` will result in the `javascript_include_tag` helper to not append `.js` to the supplied source.

```
javascript_include_tag 'templates.jst', extname: false
# => <script src="/javascripts/templates.jst"></script>
```

11.2.1.4 `javascript_path(source, options = {})`

Computes the path to a JavaScript asset in the `app/assets/javascripts` directory. If the source parameter is provided without an extension, Rails will append `.js` at the end. A full path (from the document root) will also be appended and used internally by the `javascript_include_tag` to build the script path output to your markup.

11.2.1.5 `stylesheet_link_tag(*sources)`

Returns a stylesheet `link` tag for the sources specified as arguments. If you don't specify an extension, `.css` will be appended automatically. Just like other helper methods that take a variable number of arguments plus options, you can pass a hash of options as the last argument and they will be added as attributes to the tag.

```
 1 stylesheet_link_tag "style"
 2 # => <link href="/stylesheets/style.css" media="screen"
 3 #       rel="Stylesheet" type="text/css" />
 4
 5 stylesheet_link_tag "style", media: "all"
 6 # => <link href="/stylesheets/style.css" media="all"
 7 #       rel="Stylesheet" type="text/css" />
 8
 9 stylesheet_link_tag "random.styles", "/css/stylish"
10 # => <link href="/stylesheets/random.styles" media="screen"
11 #       rel="Stylesheet" type="text/css" />
12 #     <link href="/css/stylish.css" media="screen"
13 #       rel="Stylesheet" type="text/css" />
```

11.2.1.6 `stylesheet_path(source)`

Computes the path to a stylesheet asset in the `app/assets/stylesheets` directory. If the source filename has no extension, `.css` will be appended. Full paths from the document root will be passed through. Used internally by `stylesheet_link_tag` to build the stylesheet path.

11.2.2   Asset Helpers

This module also contains a series of helper methods that generate asset-related markup. It's important to generate asset tags dynamically, because often assets are either packaged together or served up from a different server source than your regular content. Asset helper methods also timestamp your asset source URLs to prevent browser caching problems.

11.2.2.1 `audio_path(source)`

Computes the path to an audio asset in the `public/audios` directory, which you would have to add yourself to your Rails project since it's not generated by default. Full paths from the document root will be passed through. Used internally by `audio_tag` to build the audio path.

11.2.2.2 `audio_tag(source, options = {})`

Returns an HTML5 audio tag based on the `source` argument.

```
1 audio_tag("sound")
2 # => <audio src="/audios/sound" />
3
4 audio_tag("sound.wav")
5 # => <audio src="/audios/sound.wav" />
6
7 audio_tag("sound.wav", autoplay: true, controls: true)
8 # => <audio autoplay="autoplay" controls="controls" src="/audios/sound.wav" />
```

11.2.2.3 `font_path(source, options = {})`

Computes the path to a font asset in the `app/assets/fonts` directory, which you would have to add yourself to your Rails project since it's not generated by default. Full paths from the document root (beginning with a "/") will be passed through.

```
1 font_path("font.ttf") # => /assets/font.ttf
2 font_path("dir/font.ttf") # => /assets/dir/font.ttf
3 font_path("/dir/font.ttf") # => /dir/font.ttf
```

11.2.2.4 `image_path(source)`

Computes the path to an image asset in the `app/assets/images` directory. Full paths from the document root (beginning with a "/") will be passed through. This method is used internally by `image_tag` to build the image path.

```
1 image_path("edit.png")   # => /assets/edit.png
2 image_path("icons/edit.png")   # => /images/icons/edit.png
3 image_path("/icons/edit.png")   # => /icons/edit.png
```

Helpers

Courtenay Says ...

The `image_tag` method makes use of the `image_path` method that we cover later in the chapter. This helpful method determines the path to use in the tag. You can call a controller "image" and have it work as a resource, despite the seemingly conflicting name, because for its internal use, ActionView aliases the method to `path_to_image`.

11.2.2.5 `image_tag(source, options = {})`

Returns an `img` tag for use in a template. The `source` parameter can be a full path or a file that exists in your images directory. You can add additional arbitrary attributes to the `img` tag using the options parameter. The following two options are treated specially:

:alt If no alternate text is given, the filename part of the source is used after being capitalized and stripping off the extension.

:size Supplied as `widthxheight` so `"30x45"` becomes the attributes `width="30"` and `height="45"`. The `:size` option will fail silently if the value is not in the correct format.

```
1 image_tag("icon.png")
2 # => <img src="/assets/icon.png" alt="Icon" />
3
4 image_tag("icon.png", size: "16x10", alt: "Edit Entry")
5 # => <img src="/assets/icon.png" width="16" height="10" alt="Edit Entry" />
6
7 image_tag("/photos/dog.jpg", class: 'icon')
8 # => <img src="/photos/icon.gif" alt="Dog" class="icon"/>
```

11.2.2.6 `video_path`

Computes the path to a video asset in the `public/videos` directory, which you would have to add yourself to your Rails project since it's not generated by default. Full paths from the document root will be passed through. Used internally by `video_tag` to build the video's `src` attribute.

11.2.2.7 `video_tag(sources, options = {})`

Returns an HTML5 `video` tag for the `sources`. If `sources` is a string, a single video tag will be returned. If `sources` is an array, a `video` tag with nested `source` tags for each source will be returned. The sources can be full paths or files that exists in your public videos directory.

You can add normal HTML video element attributes using the options hash. The options supports two additional keys for convenience and conformance:

:poster Set an image (like a screenshot) to be shown before the video loads. The path is calculated using image_path.

:size Supplied as widthxheight in the same manner as image_tag. The :size option can also accept a stringified number, which sets both width and height to the supplied value.

```
1  video_tag("trailer")
2  # => <video src="/videos/trailer" />
3
4  video_tag("trailer.ogg")
5  # => <video src="/videos/trailer.ogg" />
6
7  video_tag("trail.ogg", controls: true, autobuffer: true)
8  # => <video autobuffer="autobuffer" controls="controls"
9  #         src="/videos/trail.ogg" />
10
11 video_tag("trail.m4v", size: "16x10", poster: "screenshot.png")
12 # => <video src="/videos/trailer.m4v" width="16" height="10"
13 #         poster="/images/screenshot.png" />
14
15 video_tag(["trailer.ogg", "trailer.flv"])
16 # => <video>
17 #         <source src="trailer.ogg"/>
18 #         <source src="trailer.flv"/>
19 #     </video>
```

11.2.3   Using Asset Hosts

By default, Rails links to assets on the current host in the public folder, but you can direct Rails to link to assets from a dedicated asset server by setting Action Controller::Base.asset_host in a configuration file, typically in config/environments/production.rb so that it doesn't affect your development environment. For example, you'd define assets.example.com to be your asset host this way:

```
config.action_controller.asset_host = "assets.example.com"
```

The helpers we've covered take that into account when generating their markup:

```
1 image_tag("rails.png")
2 # => <img alt="Rails"
3 #          src="http://assets.example.com/images/rails.png?1230601161" />
4
5 stylesheet_link_tag("application")
6 # => <link
7 #      href="http://assets.example.com/stylesheets/application.css?1232285206"
8 #        media="screen" rel="stylesheet" type="text/css" />
```

Browsers typically open at most two simultaneous connections to a single host. In the worst case scenario, with many asset files, only two files at a time will be downloaded. You can alleviate this bottleneck by using a %d wildcard in your asset_host setting. For example, "assets%d.example.com." If that wildcard is present, Rails distributes asset requests among the corresponding four hosts: "assets0 .example.com," "assets1.example.com," and so on. With this trick, browsers will open eight simultaneous connections rather than two.

```
1 image_tag("rails.png")
2 # => <img alt="Rails"
3 #          src="http://assets0.example.com/images/rails.png?1230601161" />
4
5 stylesheet_link_tag("application")
6 # => <link
7 #      href="http://assets2.example.com/stylesheets/application.css?1232285206"
8 #        media="screen" rel="stylesheet" type="text/css" />
```

To get this technique working in a production deployment, you can either set up four actual hosts with the same asset content or use wildcard DNS to CNAME the wildcard to a single asset host. You can read more about setting up your DNS CNAME records from your hosting provider. Note that this technique is purely a browser performance optimization and is unrelated to server load balancing.[1]

Alternatively, you can exert more control over the asset host by setting asset _host to a proc like the following:

```
config.action_controller.asset_host = Proc.new { |source|
  "http://assets#{rand(2) + 1}.example.com"
}
```

The example generates http://assets1.example.com and http://assets2 .example.com randomly. This option is useful, for example, if you need fewer/more

---

1. See http://www.die.net/musings/page_load_time/ for background information.

than four hosts, custom host names, and so on. As you see, the proc takes a `source` parameter. That's a string with the absolute path of the asset with any extensions and timestamps in place—for example, `/images/rails.png?1230601161`.

```
1  config.action_controller.asset_host = Proc.new { |source|
2    if source.starts_with?('/images')
3      "http://images.example.com"
4    else
5      "http://assets.example.com"
6    end
7  }
8
9  image_tag("rails.png")
10 # => <img alt="Rails"
11       src="http://images.example.com/images/rails.png?1230601161" />
12
13 stylesheet_link_tag("application")
14 # => <link href="http://assets.example.com/stylesheets/application.css?1232285206"
15       media="screen" rel="stylesheet" type="text/css" />
```

Alternatively you may ask for a second parameter `request`, which is particularly useful for serving assets from an SSL-protected page. The following example disables asset hosting for HTTPS connections while still sending assets for plain HTTP requests from asset hosts. If you don't have SSL certificates for each of the asset hosts, this technique allows you to avoid warnings in the client about mixed media.

```
1  ActionController::Base.asset_host = Proc.new { |source, request|
2    if request.ssl?
3      "#{request.protocol}#{request.host_with_port}"
4    else
5      "#{request.protocol}assets.example.com"
6    end
7  }
```

For easier testing and reuse, you can also implement a custom asset host object that responds to `call` and takes either one or two parameters just like the proc.

```
config.action_controller.asset_host = AssetHostingWithMinimumSsl.new(
  "http://asset%d.example.com", "https://asset1.example.com"
)
```

11.2.4 For Plugins Only

A handful of class methods in `AssetTagHelper` relate to configuration and are intended for use in plugins.

Helpers

- `register_javascript_expansion`

- `register_stylesheet_expansion`

11.3 **AtomFeedHelper**

Provides an `atom_feed` helper to aid in generating ATOM feeds in builder templates.

```
1  atom_feed do |feed|
2    feed.title("My great blog!")
3    feed.updated(@posts.first.created_at)
4
5    @posts.each do |post|
6      feed.entry(post) do |entry|
7        entry.title(post.title)
8        entry.content(post.body, type: 'html')
9
10       entry.author do |author|
11         author.name("DHH")
12       end
13     end
14   end
15 end
```

The options for `atom_feed` are the following:

:language Defaults to `"en-US"`.

:root_url The HTML alternative that this feed is doubling for. Defaults to `"/"` on the current host.

:url The URL for this feed. Defaults to the current URL.

:id The id for this feed. Defaults to `tag:#{request.host},#{options}:#{request.fullpath.split(".")}`.

:schema_date The date at which the tag scheme for the feed was first used. A good default is the year you created the feed. See `http://feedvalidator.org/docs/error/InvalidTAG.html` for more information. If not specified, 2005 is used (as an "I don't care" value).

:instruct Hash of XML processing instructions in the form of {target => {attribute => value, ...}} or {target => [{attribute => value, ...},]}.

Other namespaces can be added to the root element:

```
1  atom_feed(
2    'xmlns:app' => 'http://www.w3.org/2007/app',
3    'xmlns:openSearch' => 'http://a9.com/-/spec/opensearch/1.1/'
4  ) do |feed|
5    feed.title("My great blog!")
6    feed.updated((@posts.first.created_at))
7    feed.tag!(openSearch:totalResults, 10)
8
9    @posts.each do |post|
10     feed.entry(post) do |entry|
11       entry.title(post.title)
12       entry.content(post.body, type: 'html')
13       entry.tag!('app:edited', Time.now)
14
15       entry.author do |author|
16         author.name("DHH")
17       end
18     end
19   end
20 end
```

The ATOM spec defines five elements that may directly contain XHTML content if
`type: 'xhtml'` is specified as an attribute:

- content

- rights

- title

- subtitle

- summary

If any of these elements contain XHTML content, this helper will take care of the
needed enclosing div and an XHTML namespace declaration.

```
1  entry.summary type: 'xhtml' do |xhtml|
2    xhtml.p pluralize(order.line_items.count, "line item")
3    xhtml.p "Shipped to #{order.address}"
4    xhtml.p "Paid by #{order.pay_type}"
5  end
```

The `atom_feed` method yields an `AtomFeedBuilder` instance. Nested elements
also yield `AtomBuilder` instances.

Helpers

11.4 `CacheHelper`

This module contains helper methods related to caching fragments of a view. Fragment caching is useful when certain elements of an action change frequently or depend on complicated state, while other parts rarely change or can be shared among multiple parties. The boundaries of a fragment to be cached are defined within a view template using the `cache` helper method. This topic is covered in detail in the caching section of Chapter 17, "Caching and Performance."

11.5 `CaptureHelper`

One of the great features of Rails views is that you are not limited to rendering a single *flow* of content. Along the way, you can define blocks of template code that should be inserted into other parts of the page during rendering using `yield`. The technique is accomplished via a pair of methods from the `CaptureHelper` module.

11.5.0.1 `capture(&block)`

The `capture` method lets you capture part of a template's output (inside a block) and assign it to an instance variable. The value of that variable can subsequently be used anywhere else on the template.

```
1  - message_html = capture do
2    %div
3      This is a message
```

I don't think the `capture` method is that useful on its own in a template. It's a lot more useful when you use it in your own custom helper methods. It gives you the ability to write your own helpers that grab template content wrapped using a block. We cover that technique later on in this chapter in the section "Writing Your Own View Helpers."

11.5.0.2 `content_for(name, &block)`

We mentioned the `content_for` method in Chapter 10, "Action View," in the section "Yielding Content." It allows you to designate a part of your template as content for another part of the page. It works similarly to its sister method `capture` (in fact, it uses `capture` itself). Instead of returning the contents of the block provided to it, it stores the content to be retrieved using `yield` elsewhere in the template (or, most commonly, in the surrounding layout).

A common example is to insert *sidebar* content into a layout. In the following example, the link will not appear in the *flow* of the view template. It will appear elsewhere in the template, wherever `yield :navigation_sidebar` appears.

```
1 - content_for :navigation_sidebar do
2   = link_to 'Detail Page', item_detail_path(item)
```

11.5.0.3 **content_for?(name)**

Using this method, you can check whether the template will ultimately yield any content under a particular name using the content_for helper method so that you can make layout decisions earlier in the template. The following example clearly illustrates usage of this method by altering the CSS class of the body element dynamically:

```
1 %body{class: content_for?(:right_col) ? 'one-column' : 'two-column'}
2   = yield
3   = yield :right_col
```

11.5.0.4 **provide(name, content = nil, &block)**

The provide helper method works the same way as content_for, except for when used with streaming. When streaming, provide flushes the current buffer straight back to the layout and stops looking for more contents.

If you want to concatenate multiple times to the same buffer when rendering a given template, you should use content_for instead.

11.6 **CsrfHelper**

The CsrfHelper module only contains one method, named csrf_meta_tags. Including it in the <head> section of your template will output meta tags "csrf-param" and "csrf-token" with the name of the cross-site request forgery protection parameter and token, respectively.

```
1 %head
2   = csrf_meta_tags
```

The meta tags "csrf-param" and "csrf-token" are used by Rails to generate dynamic forms that implement nonremote links with :method.

11.7 **DateHelper**

The DateHelper module is used primarily to create HTML select tags for different kinds of calendar data. It also features one of the longest-named helper methods, a beast peculiar to Rails, called distance_of_time_in_words_to_now.

Lark Says …

I guess that helper method name was too much of a mouthful, since at some point it was aliased to time_ago_in_words.

Helpers

11.7.1 The Date and Time Selection Helpers

The following methods help you create form field input tags dealing with date and time data. All of them are prepared for multiparameter assignment to an Active Record object. That's a fancy way of saying that even though they appear in the HTML form as separate input fields, when they are posted back to the server, it is understood that they refer to a single attribute of the model. That's some Rails magic for you!

11.7.1.1 `date_select(object_name, method, options = {}, html_options = {})`

Returns a matched set of three `select` tags (one each for year, month, and day) preselected for accessing a specified date-based attribute (identified by the `method` parameter) on an object assigned to the template (identified by `object_name`).

It's possible to tailor the selects through the options hash, which accepts all the keys that each of the individual select builders do (like `:use_month_numbers` for `select_month`).

The `date_select` method also takes `:discard_year`, `:discard_month`, and `:discard_day` options, which drop the corresponding `select` tag from the set of three. Common sense dictates that discarding the month select will also automatically discard the day select. If the day is omitted but not the month, Rails will assume that the day should be the first of the month.

It's also possible to explicitly set the order of the tags using the `:order` option with an array of symbols `:year`, `:month`, and `:day` in the desired order. Symbols may be omitted and the respective `select` tag is not included.

Passing `disabled: true` as part of the options will make elements inaccessible for change (see Listing 11.2).

Listing 11.2 Examples of `date_select`

```
1 date_select("post", "written_on")
2
3 date_select("post", "written_on", start_year: 1995,
4                                   use_month_numbers: true,
5                                   discard_day: true,
6                                   include_blank: true)
7
8 date_select("post", "written_on", order: [:day, :month, :year])
9
10 date_select("user", "birthday",  order: [:month, :day])
```

If anything is passed in the `html_options` hash, it will be applied to every select tag in the set.

11.7.1.2 `datetime_select(object_name, method, options = {}, html_options = {})`

Works exactly like `date_select` except for the addition of hour and minute `select` tags. Seconds may be added with the option `:include_seconds`. Along with the addition of time information come additional discarding options: `:discard_hour`, `:discard_minute`, and `:discard_seconds`.

Setting the `ampm` option to `true` returns hours in the AM/PM format.

```
1 datetime_select("post", "written_on")
2
3 datetime_select("post", "written_on", ampm: true)
```

11.7.1.3 `time_select(object_name, method, options = {}, html_options = {})`

Returns a set of `select` tags (one for hour, minute, and optionally second) preselected for accessing a specified time-based attribute (identified by `method`) on an object assigned to the template (identified by `object_name`). You can include the seconds by setting the `:include_seconds` option to `true`.

As with `datetime_select`, setting `ampm: true` will result in hours displayed in the AM/PM format.

```
1 time_select("post", "sunrise")
2
3 time_select("post", "written_on", include_seconds: true)
4
5 time_select("game", "written_on", ampm: true)
```

11.7.2   The Individual Date and Time Select Helpers

Sometimes you need just a particular element of a date or time, and Rails obliges you with a comprehensive set of individual date and time select helpers. In contrast to the date and time helpers that we just looked at, the following helpers are not bound to an instance variable on the page. Instead, they all take a date or time Ruby object as their first parameter. (All of these methods have a set of common options, covered in the following subsection.)

11.7.2.1 `select_date(date = Date.current, options = {}, html_options = {})`

Returns a set of `select` tags (one each for year, month, and day) preselected with the date provided (or the current date). It's possible to explicitly set the order of the tags using the `:order` option with an array of symbols `:year`, `:month`, and `:day` in the desired order.

Helpers

```
select_date(started_at, order: [:year, :month, :day])
```

11.7.2.2 `select_datetime(datetime = Time.current, options = {}, html_options = {})`

Returns a set of `select` tags (one each for year, month, day, hour, and minute), preselected with the datetime. Optionally, setting the `include_seconds: true` option adds a seconds field. It's also possible to explicitly set the order of the tags using the `:order` option with an array of symbols `:year`, `:month`, `:day`, `:hour`, `:minute`, and `:seconds` in the desired order. You can also add character values for the `:date_separator` and `:time_separator` options to control visual display of the elements (they default to `"/"` and `":"`).

11.7.2.3 `select_day(date, options = {}, html_options = {})`

Returns a `select` tag with options for each of the days 1 through 31 with the current day selected. The date can also be substituted for a day value ranging from 1 to 31. If displaying days with a leading zero is your preference, setting the option `use_two_digit_numbers` to true will accomplish this.

```
1  select_day(started_at)
2
3  select_day(10)
4
5  select_day(5, use_two_digit_numbers: true)
```

By default, the field name defaults to `day` but can be overridden using the `:field_name` option.

11.7.2.4 `select_hour(datetime, options = {}, html_options = {})`

Returns a `select` tag with options for each of the hours 0 through 23, with the current hour selected. The `datetime` parameter can be substituted with an hour number from 0 to 23. Setting the `ampm` option to true will result in hours displayed in the AM/PM format. By default, the field name defaults to `hour` but can be overridden using the `:field_name` option.

11.7.2.5 `select_minute(datetime, options = {}, html_options = {})`

Returns a `select` tag with options for each of the minutes 0 through 59 with the current minute selected. Also can return a `select` tag with options by `minute_step` from 0 through 59 with the 00 minute selected. The `datetime` parameter can be substituted by a seconds value of 0 to 59. By default, the field name defaults to `minute` but can be overridden using the `:field_name` option.

11.7.2.6 `select_month(date, options = {}, html_options = {})`

Returns a `select` tag with options for each of the months January through December with the current month selected. By default, the month names are presented as user options in the drop-down selection and the month numbers (1 through 12) are used as values submitted to the server.

It's also possible to use month numbers for the presentation instead of names by setting `use_month_numbers:  true`. To display month numbers with a leading zero, set option `:use_two_digit_numbers` to true. If you happen to want both numbers and names, set `add_month_numbers:  true`. If you would prefer to show month names as abbreviations, set the `:use_short_month` option to true. Finally, if you want to use your own month names, set the value of the `:use_month_names` key in your options to an array of 12 month names.

```
1  # Will use keys like "January," "March"
2  select_month(Date.today)
3
4  # Will use keys like "1," "3"
5  select_month(Date.today, use_month_numbers: true)
6
7  # Will use keys like "1 - January," "3 - March"
8  select_month(Date.today, add_month_numbers: true)
9
10 # Will use keys like "Jan," "Mar"
11 select_month(Date.today, use_short_month: true)
12
13 # Will use keys like "Januar" "Marts"
14 select_month(Date.today, use_month_names: %w(Januar Februar
15 Marts ...))
```

By default, the field name defaults to `month` but can be overridden using the `:field_name` option.

11.7.2.7 `select_second(datetime, options = {}, html _options = {})`

Returns a `select` tag with options for each of the seconds 0 through 59 with the current second selected. The `datetime` parameter can either be a `DateTime` object or a second given as a number. By default, the field name defaults to second but can be overridden using the :field_name option.

11.7.2.8 `select_time(datetime = Time.current, options = {}, html_options = {})`

Returns a set of HTML select tags (one for hour and minute). You can set the :time_separator option to format the output. It's possible to take an input for sections by setting option :include_seconds to true.

```
select_time(some_time, time_separator: ':', include_seconds: true)
```

11.7.2.9 `select_year(date, options = {}, html_options = {})`

Returns a select tag with options for each of the five years on each side of the current year, which is selected. The five-year radius can be changed using the :start_year and :end_year options. Both ascending and descending year lists are supported by making :start_year less than or greater than :end_year. The date parameter can either be a Date object or a year given as a number.

```
1 # ascending year values
2 select_year(Date.today, start_year: 1992, end_year: 2007)
3
4 # descending year values
5 select_year(Date.today, start_year: 2005, end_year: 1900)
```

By default, the field name defaults to year but can be overridden using the :field_name option.

11.7.3 Common Options for Date Selection Helpers

All the select-type methods share a number of common options that are as follows:

:discard_type Set to true if you want to discard the type part of the select name. If set to true, the select_month method would use simply date (which can be overwritten using :prefix) instead of date[month].

:field_name Allows you to override the natural name of a select tag (from day, minute, and so on).

:include_blank Set to true if it should be possible to set an empty date.

:prefix Overwrites the default prefix of date used for the names of the select tags. Specifying birthday would result in a name of birthday[month] instead of date[month] when passed to the select_month method.

:use_hidden Set to `true` to embed the value of the datetime into the page as an HTML hidden input instead of a `select` tag.

:disabled Set to true if you want show the select fields as disabled.

:prompt Set to true (for a generic prompt), a prompt string or a hash of prompt strings for :year, :month, :day, :hour, :minute, and :second.

11.7.4 **distance_in_time** Methods with Complex Descriptive Names

Some `distance_in_time` methods have really long, complex descriptive names that nobody can ever remember without looking them up—well, at least for the first dozen times or so.

I find the following methods to be a perfect example of the Rails way when it comes to API design. Instead of going with a shorter and necessarily more cryptic alternative, the framework author decided to keep the name long and descriptive. It's one of those cases where a nonprogrammer can look at your code and understand what it's doing. Well, probably.

I also find these methods remarkable in that they are part of why people sometimes consider Rails part of the Web 2.0 phenomenon. What other web framework would include ways to humanize the display of timestamps?

11.7.4.1 **distance_of_time_in_words(from_time, to_time = 0, include_seconds_or_options = {}, options = {}))**

Reports the approximate distance in time between two `Time`, `DateTime`, or `Date` objects or integers as seconds. Set the `include_seconds` parameter to `true` if you want more detailed approximations when the distance is less than one minute. The easiest way to show what this method does is via examples:

```
>> from_time = Time.current

>> helper.distance_of_time_in_words(from_time, from_time + 50.minutes)
=> about 1 hour

>> helper.distance_of_time_in_words(from_time, from_time + 15.seconds)
=> less than a minute

>> helper.distance_of_time_in_words(from_time, from_time + 15.seconds,
      include_seconds: true)
=> less than 20 seconds

>> helper.distance_of_time_in_words(from_time, 3.years.from_now)
=> about 3 years
```

Helpers

The Rails API docs ask you to note that Rails calculates 1 year as 365.25 days.

11.7.4.2 `distance_of_time_in_words_to_now(from_` `time, include_seconds_or_options = {})`

Works exactly like `distance_of_time_in_words` except that the `to_time` is hard-coded to the current time. Usually invoked on `created_at` or `updated_at` attributes of your model, followed by the string `ago` in your template, as in the following example:

```
1 %strong= comment.user.name
2 %br
3 %small= "#{distance_of_time_in_words_to_now(review.created_at)} ago"
```

Note, this method is aliased to `time_ago_in_words` for those who prefer shorter method names.

11.7.5 `time_tag(date_or_time, *args, &block)`

Introduced in Rails 3.1, the `time_tag` returns an HTML5 time element for a given date or time. Using the semantic `time_tag` helper ensures that your date or time within your markup is in a machine-readable format. Setting the option `pubdate` to true will add the attribute to the tag, indicating that the date or time is a publishing date. The following examples show the output one can expect when using it:

```
 1 time_tag(Date.current)
 2 # => <time datetime="2013-08-13">August 13, 2013</time>
 3
 4 time_tag(Time.current)
 5 # => <time datetime="2013-08-13T14:58:29Z">August 13, 2013 14:58</time>
 6
 7 time_tag(Time.current, pubdate: true)
 8 # => <time datetime="2013-08-13T15:02:56Z" pubdate="pubdate">August
         13, 2013 15:02</time>
 9
10 = time_tag(Date.current) do
11   %strong Once upon a time
12 # => <time datetime="2013-08-13"><strong>Once upon a time</strong></time>
```

11.8 `DebugHelper`

The `DebugHelper` module only contains one method, named `debug`. Output it in your template, passing it an object that you want dumped to YAML and displayed in the browser inside PRE tags. Useful for debugging during development but not much else.

11.9 `FormHelper`

The `FormHelper` module provides a set of methods for working with HTML forms, especially as they relate to Active Record model objects assigned to the template. Its methods correspond to each type of HTML input fields (such as text, password, select, etc.) available. When the form is submitted, the value of the input fields are bundled into the `params` that is passed to the controller.

There are two types of form helper methods. The types found in this module are meant to work specifically with Active Record model attributes, and the similarly named versions in the `FormTagHelper` module are not.

Note

The form helper methods in this section can also be used with non–Active Record models, as long as the model passes the Active Model Lint tests found in module `ActiveModel::Lint::Tests`. The easiest way to do this is to include the module mixin `ActiveModel::Model` to your class.

11.9.1 Creating Forms for Models

The core method of this helper is called `form_for`, and we covered it to some extent in Chapter 3, "REST, Resources, and Rails." The helper method yields a `form` object, on which you can invoke input helper methods, omitting their first argument. Usage of `form_for` leads to succinct form code:

```
1 = form_for offer do |f|
2   = f.label :version, 'Version'
3   = f.text_field :version
4   %br
5   = f.label :author, 'Author'
6   = f.text_field :author
```

The `form_for` block argument is a form builder object that carries the model. Thus the idea is that

```
= f.text_field :first_name
```

gets expanded to

```
= text_field :person, :first_name
```

Helpers

If you want the resulting params hash posted to your controller to be named based on something other than the class name of the object you pass to `form_for`, you can pass an arbitrary symbol to the `:as` option:

```
= form_for person, as: :client do |f|
```

In that case, the call to `text_field`

```
= f.text_field :first_name
```

would get expanded to

```
= text_field :client, :first_name, object: person
```

11.9.1.1 `form_for` Options

In any of its variants, the rightmost argument to `form_for` is an optional hash of options:

:url The URL the form is submitted to. It takes the same fields you pass to `url_for` or `link_to`. In particular you may pass here a named route directly as well. Defaults to the current action.

:namespace A namespace that will be prefixed with an underscore on the generated HTML id of the form.

:html Optional HTML attributes for the `form` tag.

:builder Optional form builder class (instead of `ActionView::Helpers::FormBuilder`).

11.9.1.2 Resource-Oriented Style

The preferred way to use `form_for` is to rely on automated resource identification, which will use the conventions and named routes of that approach instead of manually configuring the `:url` option.

For example, if `post` is an existing record to be edited, then the resource-oriented style

```
= form_for post do |f|
```

is equivalent to

```
= form_for post, as: :post, url: post_path(post),
    method: :patch, html: { class: "edit_post",
    id: "edit_post_45" } do |f|
```

The `form_for` method also recognizes new records by calling `new?` on the object you pass to it.

```
= form_for(Post.new) do |f|
```

expands to

```
= form_for post, as: :post, url: posts_path, html: {class: "new_post",
    id: "new_post" } do |f|
```

The individual conventions can be overridden by supplying an object argument plus `:url`, `:method` and/or `:html` options.

```
= form_for(post, url: super_post_path(post)) do |f|
```

You can create forms with namespaced routes by passing an array as the first argument, as in the following example, which would map to a `admin_post_url`:

```
= form_for([:admin, post]) do |f|
```

The following example is the equivalent (old-school) version of `form_tag`, which doesn't use a yielded form object and explicitly names the object being used in the input fields:

```
1 = form_tag people_path do
2   .field
3     = label :person, :first_name
4     = text_field :person, :first_name
5   .field
6     = label :person, :last_name
7     = text_field :person, :last_name
8   .buttons
9     = submit_tag 'Create'
```

The first version has slightly less repetition (remember your DRY principle) and is almost always going to be more convenient as long as you're rendering Active Record objects.

11.9.1.3   Variables Are Optional

If you explicitly specify the object name parameter for input fields rather than letting them be supplied by the form, keep in mind that it doesn't have to match a *live* object instance in scope for the template. Rails won't complain if the object is not there. It will simply put blank values in the resulting form.

Helpers

11.9.1.4   Rails-Generated Form Conventions

The HTML generated by the `form_for` invocations in the preceding example is characteristic of Rails forms and follows specific naming conventions.

In case you're wondering, the `authenticity_token` hidden field with gibberish up near the top of the form has to do with protection against malicious cross-site request forgery (CSRF) attacks.

```
1  <form accept-charset="UTF-8" action="/people" method="post">
2    <div style="margin:0;padding:0;display:inline">
3      <input name="utf8" type="hidden" value="&#x2713;" />
4      <input name="authenticity_token" type="hidden"
5             value="afl+6u3J/2meoHtve69q+tD9gPc3/QUsHCqPh85Z4WU=" /></div>
6      <div class='field'>
7        <label for="person_first_name">First name</label>
8        <input id="person_first_name" name="person[first_name]" type="text" />
9      </div>
10     <div class='field'>
11       <label for="person_last_name">Last name</label>
12       <input id="person_last_name" name="person[last_name]" type="text" />
13     </div>
14     <div class='buttons'>
15       <input name="commit" type="submit" value="Create" />
16     </div>
17   </form>
```

When this form is submitted, the `params` hash will look like the following example (using the format reflected in your development log for every request):

```
Parameters: {"utf8"=>"✓",
"authenticity_token"=>"afl+6u3J/2meoHtve69q+tD9gPc3/
        QUsHCqPh85Z4WU=",
"person"=>{"first_name"=>"William", "last_name"=>"Smith"},
"commit"=>"Create"}
```

As you can see, the `params` hash has a nested `"person"` value, which is accessed using `params[:person]` in the controller. That's pretty fundamental Rails knowledge, and I'd be surprised if you didn't know it already. I promise we won't rehash much more basic knowledge after the following section.

11.9.1.5   Displaying Existing Values

If you were editing an existing instance of `Person`, that object's attribute values would have been filled into the form. That's also pretty fundamental Rails knowledge. What about if you want to edit a new model object instance, prepopulated with certain values? Do you have to pass the values as options to the input helper methods? No. Since the form helpers display the values of the model's attributes, it would simply be a matter of initializing the object with the desired values in the controller, as follows:

```
1  # Using the gem decent exposure
2  expose(:person) do
3    if person_id = (params[:person_id] || params[:id])
4      Person.find(person_id)
5    else
6      # Set default values that you want to appear in the form
7      Person.new(first_name: 'First', last_name: 'Last')
8    end
9  end
```

Since you're only using `new`, no record is persisted to the database, and your default values magically appear in the input fields.

11.9.2   How Form Helpers Get Their Values

A rather important lesson to learn about Rails form helper methods is that the value they display comes directly from the database prior to *meddling* by the developer. Unless you know what you're doing, you may get some unexpected results if you try to override the values to be displayed in a form.

Let's illustrate with a simple `LineItem` model, which has a decimal `rate` attribute (by merits of a `rate` column in its database table). We'll override its implicit rate accessor with one of our own:

```
1  class LineItem < ActiveRecord::Base
2    def rate
3      "A RATE"
4    end
5  end
```

In normal situations, the overridden accessor is hiding access to the real rate attribute, as we can illustrate using the console.

```
>> li = LineItem.new
=> #<LineItem ...>
>> li.rate
=> "A RATE"
```

However, suppose you were to compose a form to edit line items using form helpers:

```
1  = form_for line_item do |f|
2    = f.text_field :rate
```

You would find that it works normally, as if that overridden `rate` accessor doesn't exist. The fact is that Rails form helpers use special methods named `attribute_before_type_cast` (which are covered in Chapter 5, "Working with Active Record"). The preceding example would use the method `rate_before_type_cast` and bypass the overriding method we defined.

11.9.3 Integrating Additional Objects in One Form

The `fields_for` helper method creates a scope around a specific model object like `form_for` but doesn't create the form tags themselves. Neither does it have an actual HTML representation as a `div` or `fieldset`. The `fields_for` method is suitable for specifying additional model objects in the same form, particularly associations of the main object being represented in the form.

11.9.3.1 Generic Examples

The following simple example represents a person and its associated permissions.

```
1  = form_for person do |f| %>
2    First name:
3    = f.text_field :first_name
4    Last name:
5    = f.text_field :last_name
6    .permissions
7      = fields_for person.permission do |permission_fields|
8        Admin?:
9        = permission_fields.check_box :admin
```

11.9.3.2 Nested Attributes Examples

When the object belonging to the current scope has a nested attribute writer for a certain attribute, `fields_for` will yield a new scope for that attribute. This allows you to create forms that set or change the attributes of a parent object and its associations in one go.

Nested attribute writers are normal setter methods named after an association. The most common way of defining these writers is either by declaring `accepts_nested_attributes_for` in a model definition or by defining a method with the proper name. For example, the attribute writer for the association `:address` is called `address_attributes=`.

Whether a one-to-one or one-to-many style form builder will be yielded depends on whether the normal reader method returns a single object or an `array` of objects. Consider a simple Ruby `Person` class that returns a single `Address` from its `address` reader method and responds to the `address_attributes=` writer method:

```
1 class Person
2   def address
3     @address
4   end
5
6   def address_attributes=(attributes)
7     # Process the attributes hash
8   end
9 end
```

This model can now be used with a nested `fields_for`, like the following:

```
1 = form_for person do |f|
2   = f.fields_for :address do |address_fields|
3     Street:
4     = address_fields.text_field :street
5     Zip code:
6     = address_fields.text_field :zip_code
```

When `address` is already an association on a `Person`, you can use `accepts_nested_attributes_for` to define the writer method for you, like the following:

```
1 class Person < ActiveRecord::Base
2   has_one :address
3   accepts_nested_attributes_for :address
4 end
```

If you want to destroy the associated model through the form, you have to enable it first using the `:allow_destroy` option for `accepts_nested_attributes_for`, like the following:

```
1 class Person < ActiveRecord::Base
2   has_one :address
3   accepts_nested_attributes_for :address, allow_destroy: true
4 end
```

Now when you use a check box form element specially named `_destroy` with a value that evaluates to `true`, the logic generated by `accepts_nested_attribute_for` will destroy the associated model. (This is a super useful technique for list screens that allow deletion of multiple records at once using check boxes.)

```
1 = form_for person do |f|
2   = f.fields_for :address do |address_fields|
```

```
3    Delete this address:
4    = address_fields.check_box :_destroy
```

11.9.3.3 `fields_for` with One-to-Many Associations

Consider a `Person` class that returns an array of `Project` instances from the `projects` reader method and responds to the `projects_attributes=` writer method:

```
1 class Person < ActiveRecord::Base
2   def projects
3     [@project1, @project2]
4   end
5
6   def projects_attributes=(attributes)
7     # Process the attributes hash.
8   end
9 end
```

This model can now be used with a nested `fields_for` helper method in a form. The block given to the nested `fields_for` call will be repeated for each instance in the collection automatically:

```
1 = form_for person do |f|
2   = f.fields_for :projects do |project_fields|
3     .project
4       Name:
5       = project_fields.text_field :name
```

It's also possible to specify the instance to be used by doing the iteration yourself. The symbol passed to `fields_for` refers to the reader method of the parent object of the form, but the second argument contains the actual object to be used for fields:

```
1 = form_for person do |f|
2   - person.projects.select(&:active?).each do |project|
3     = f.fields_for :projects, project do |project_fields|
4       .project
5         Name:
6         = project_fields.text_field :name
```

Since `fields_for` also understands a collection as its second argument in that situation, you can shrink that last example to the following code. Just inline the projects collection:

```
1 = form_for person do |f|
2   = f.fields_for :projects, projects.select(&:active?) do |project_fields|
```

```
3        .project
4          Name:
5            = project_fields.text_field :name
```

If in our example `Person` was an Active Record model and `projects` was one of its `has_many` associations, then you could use `accepts_nested_attributes_for` to define the writer method for you:

```
1 class Person < ActiveRecord::Base
2   has_many :projects
3   accepts_nested_attributes_for :projects
4 end
```

As with using `accepts_nested_attributes_for` with a `belongs_to` association, if you want to destroy any of the associated models through the form, you have to enable it first using the `:allow_destroy` option:

```
1 class Person < ActiveRecord::Base
2   has_many :projects
3   accepts_nested_attributes_for :projects, allow_destroy: true
4 end
```

This will allow you to specify which models to destroy in the attributes hash by adding a boolean form element named `_destroy`.

```
1 = form_for person do |form|
2   = form.fields_for :projects do |project_fields|
3     Delete this project
4       = project_fields.check_box :_destroy
```

11.9.3.4 Saving Nested Attributes

Nested records are updated on save, even when the intermediate parent record is unchanged. For example, consider the following model code:

```
 1 class Project < ActiveRecord::Base
 2   has_many :tasks
 3   accepts_nested_attributes_for :tasks
 4 end
 5
 6 class Task < ActiveRecord::Base
 7   belongs_to :project
 8   has_many :assignments
 9   accepts_nested_attributes_for :assignments
10 end
11
12 class Assignment < ActiveRecord::Base
```

Helpers

```
13    belongs_to :task
14 end
```

The following spec snippet illustrates nested saving:

```
 1 # Setup project, task, and assignment objects...
 2 project.update(name: project.name,
 3                tasks_attributes: [{
 4                                    id: task.id,
 5                                    name: task.name,
 6                                    assignments_attributes: [
 7                                      {
 8                                        id: assignment.id,
 9                                        name: 'Paul'
10                                      }]
11                }]
12
13 assignment.reload
14 expect(assignment.name).to eq('Paul')
```

11.9.4   Customized Form Builders

Under the covers, the `form_for` method uses a class named `ActionView::`
`Helpers::FormBuilder`. An instance of it is yielded to the form block. Conveniently, you can subclass it in your application to override existing or define additional form helpers.

For example, let's say you made a builder class to automatically add labels to form
inputs when `text_field` is called. You'd enable it with the `:builder` option like
the following:

```
= form_for person, builder: LabelingFormBuilder do |f|
```

Instructions on making custom form builder classes would fill its own chapter, but
one could view the source of some popular Rails form builders such as SimpleForm2
and formtasic3 to learn more.

11.9.5   Form Inputs

For each if these methods, there is a similarly named form builder method that omits
the `object_name` parameter.

---

2. https://github.com/plataformatec/simple_form
3. https://github.com/justinfrench/formtastic

11.9.5.1 `check_box(object_name, method, options = {}, checked_value = "1", unchecked_value = "0")`

This helper gives you an extra hidden input field to ensure that a false value is passed even if the check box is unchecked.

```
check_box('timesheet', 'approved')
# => <input name="timesheet[approved]" type="hidden" value="0"/>
#    <input checked="checked" type="checkbox" id="timesheet_approved"
#       name="timesheet[approved]" value="1" />
```

11.9.5.2 `color_field(object_name, method, options = {})`

Creates a color input field that allows the setting of a color via hex values. The default value of a `color_field` is set to #000000.

```
color_field(:car, :paint_color)
# => <input id="car_paint_color" name="car[paint_color]" type="color"
#       value="#000000" />"
```

This method is otherwise identical to `text_field`.

11.9.5.3 `date_field(object_name, method, options = {})`

Creates a date input field. If an object is provided to the helper, it calls `to_date` on it to attempt setting the default value.

```
date_field(:person, :birthday)
# => <input id="person_birthday" name="person[birthday]" type="date" />
```

To override the default value, pass a string in the format YYYY-MM-DD to the option `:value`. This method is otherwise identical to `text_field`.

11.9.5.4 `datetime_field(object_name, method, options = {})`

Creates an input field of type "datetype," which accepts time in UTC. If a `DateTime` or `ActiveSupport::TimeWithZone` instance is provided to the helper, it calls `strftime` with "%Y-%m-%dT%T.%L%z" on the object's value to attempt setting a default value.

Helpers

```
datetime_field(:post, :publish_at)
# => <input id="post_publish_at" name="post[publish_at]" type="-
        datetime" />
```

The `datetime_field` accepts options `:min`, `:max`, which allow setting the minimum and maximum acceptable values, respectively.

```
datetime_field(:invoice, :invoiced_on,
  min: Time.current.beginning_of_year,
  max: Time.current.end_of_year)
# => <input id="invoice_invoiced_on" max="2013-12-31T23:59:59.999+0000"
#       min="2013-01-01T00:00:00.000+0000" name="invoice[invoiced_on]"
#       type="datetime" />
```

To override the default value, pass a string in the format "%Y-%m-%dT%T.%L%z" to the option `:value`. This method is otherwise identical to `text_field`.

11.9.5.5 `datetime_local_field(object_name, method, options = {})`

Creates an input field of type "datetime-local." This method is otherwise identical to `datetime_field`, except that the value used is local over UTC. If a `DateTime` or `ActiveSupport::TimeWithZone` instance is provided to the helper, it calls `strftime` with "%Y-%m-%dT%T" on the object's value to attempt setting a default value.

11.9.5.6 `email_field(object_name, method, options = {})`

Creates an email input field. This method is otherwise identical to `text_field`.

11.9.5.7 `file_field(object_name, method, options = {})`

Creates a file upload field and automatically adds `multipart: true` to the enclosing form. See `file_field_tag` for details.

11.9.5.8 `hidden_field(object_name, method, options = {})`

Creates a hidden field, with parameters similar to `text_field`.

11.9.5.9 `label(object_name, method, content_or _options = nil, options = nil, &block)`

Creates a label tag with the `for` attribute pointed at the specified input field.

```
label('timesheet', 'approved')
# => <label for="timesheet_approved">Approved</label>
```

```
label('timesheet', 'approved', 'Approved?')
# => <label for="timesheet_approved">Approved?</label>
```

Many of us like to link labels to input fields by nesting. (Many would say that's the correct usage of labels.) As of Rails 3, the `label` helper accepts a block so that nesting is possible and works as would be expected. As a result, instead of having to do

```
= f.label :terms, "<span>Accept #{link_to 'Terms', terms_path}</span>"
```

you can do the much more elegant and maintainable

```
= f.label :terms do
    %span Accept #{link_to "Terms", terms_path}
```

11.9.5.10 `month_field(object_name, method, options = {})`

Creates an input field of type "month" without any time zone information. A month is represented by four digits for the year, followed by a hyphen and ending with two digits representing the month (e.g., 2013-08).

If a `DateTime` or `ActiveSupport::TimeWithZone` instance is provided to the helper, it calls `strftime` with "%Y-%m" on the object's value to attempt setting a default value.

```
month_field(:user, :born_on)
# => <input id="user_born_on" name="user[born_on]" type="month" />
```

To override the default value, pass a string in the format "%Y-%m" to the option `:value`. This method is otherwise identical to `datetime_field`.

11.9.5.11 `number_field(object_name, method, options = {})`

Creates a number input field. This method is otherwise identical to `text_field` with the following additional options:

:min The minimum acceptable value.

:max The maximum acceptable value.

:in A range specifying the :min and :max values.

:step The acceptable value granularity.

11.9.5.12 `password_field(object_name, method, options = {})`

Creates a password input field. This method is otherwise identical to `text_field` but renders with a nil value by default for security reasons. If you want to prepopulate the user's password, you can do something like the following:

```
password_field(:user, :password, value: user.password)
```

11.9.5.13 `radio_button(object_name, method, tag_value, options = {})`

Creates a radio button input field. Make sure to give all your radio button options user the same `name` so that the browser will consider them linked.

```
= radio_button(:post, :category, :rails)
= radio_button(:post, :category, :ruby)
```

11.9.5.14 `range_field(object_name, method, options = {})`

Creates a range input field. This method is otherwise identical to `number_field`.

11.9.5.15 `search_field(object_name, method, options = {})`

Creates a search input field. This method is otherwise identical to `text_field`.

11.9.5.16 `telephone_field(object_name, method, options = {})`

Creates a telephone input field. This method is otherwise identical to `text_field` and is aliased as `phone_field`.

11.9.5.17 `submit(value = nil, options = {})`

Creates a submit button with the text value as the caption. The option `:disable_with` can be used to provide a name for disabled versions of the submit button.

11.9.5.18 `text_area(object_name, method, options = {})`

Creates a multiline text input field (the `textarea` tag). The `:size` option lets you easily specify the dimensions of the text area instead of having to resort to explicit `:rows` and `:cols` options.

```
text_area(:comment, :body, size: "25x10")
# => <textarea name="comment[body]" id="comment_body" cols="25" rows="10">
#    </textarea>
```

11.9.5.19 `text_field(object_name, method, options = {})`
Creates a standard text input field.

11.9.5.20 `time_field(object_name, method, options = {})`
Creates an input field of type "time." If a `DateTime` or `ActiveSupport::Time
WithZone` instance is provided to the helper, it calls `strftime` with "%T.%L" on
the object's value to attempt setting a default value.

```
time_field(:task, :started_at)
# => <input id="task_started_at" name="task[started_at]" type="time" />
```

To override the default value, pass a string in the format "%T.%L" to the option
`:value`. This method is otherwise identical to `datetime_field`.

11.9.5.21 `url_field(object_name, method, options = {})`
Creates an input field of type "url." This method is otherwise identical to `text_field`.

11.9.5.22 `week_field(object_name, method, options = {})`
Creates an input field of type "week." If a `DateTime` or `ActiveSupport
::TimeWithZone` instance is provided to the helper, it calls `strftime` with
"%Y-W%W" on the object's value to attempt setting a default value.

```
week_field(:task, :started_at)
# => <input id="task_started_at" name="task[started_at]" type="week" />
```

To override the default value, pass a string in the format "%Y-W%W" to the option
`:value`. This method is otherwise identical to `datetime_field`.

11.10 `FormOptionsHelper`
The methods in the `FormOptionsHelper` module are all about helping you work
with HTML `select` elements by giving you ways to turn collections of objects into
`option` tags.

11.10.1   Select Helpers
The following methods help you to create `select` tags based on a pair of `object`
and `attribute` identifiers.

Helpers

11.10.1.1 `collection_select(object, method, collection, value_method, text_method, options = {}, html_options = {})`

Returns both `select` and `option` tags for the given `object` and `method` using `options_from_collection_for_select` (also in this module) to generate the list of `option` tags from the `collection` parameter.

11.10.1.2 `grouped_collection_select(object, method, collection, group_method, group_label_ method, option_key_method, option_value_ method, options = {}, html_options = {})`

Returns `select`, `optgroup`, and `option` tags for the given `object` and `method` using `option_groups_from_collection_for_select` (covered later in this chapter).

11.10.1.3 `select(object, method, collection, value_ method, text_method, options = {}, html_ options = {})`

Creates a `select` tag and a series of contained `option` tags for the provided `object` and attribute. The value of the attribute currently held by the object (if any) will be selected, provided that the object is available (not nil). See `options_for_select` section for the required format of the choices parameter.

Here's a small example where the value of `@post.person_id` is 1:

```
1 = select(:post, :person_id,
2     Person.all.collect { |p| [ p.name, p.id ] },
3     { include_blank: true })
```

Executing that helper code would generate the following HTML output:

```
1 <select id="post_person_id" name="post[person_id]">
2   <option value=""></option>
3   <option value="1" selected="selected">David</option>
4   <option value="2">Sam</option>
5   <option value="3">Tobias</option>
6 </select>
```

If necessary, specify `selected: value` to explicitly set the selection or `selected: nil` to leave all options unselected. The `include_blank: true` option inserts a blank `option` tag at the beginning of the list so that there is no preselected value. Also, one can disable specific values by setting a single value or an array of values to the `:disabled` option.

11.10.1.4 `time_zone_select(object, method, priority_zones = nil, options = {}, html_options = {})`

Returns `select` and `option` tags for the given object and method, using `time_zone_options_for_select` to generate the list of `option` tags.

In addition to the `:include_blank` option documented in the preceding section, this method also supports a `:model` option, which defaults to `ActiveSupport::TimeZone`. This may be used to specify a different time zone model object.

Additionally, setting the `priority_zones` parameter with an array of `ActiveSupport::TimeZone` objects will list any specified priority time zones above any other.

```
1  time_zone_select(:user, :time_zone, [
2    ActiveSupport::TimeZone['Eastern Time (US & Canada)'],
3    ActiveSupport::TimeZone['Pacific Time (US & Canada)']
4  ])
5  # => <select id="user_time_zone" name="user[time_zone]">
6  #        <option value="Eastern Time (US & Canada)">
7  #          (GMT-05:00) Eastern Time (US & Canada)
8  #        </option>
9  #        <option value="Pacific Time (US & Canada)">
10 #          (GMT-08:00) Pacific Time (US & Canada)
11 #        </option>
12 #        <option disabled="disabled" value="">-------------</option>
13 #        <option value="American Samoa">(GMT-11:00) American Samoa</option>
14 #        ...
```

Finally, setting the option `:default` to an instance of `ActiveSupport::TimeZone` sets the default selected value if none was set.

11.10.2 Check Box/Radio Helpers

The following methods create `input` tags of type "checkbox" or "radio" based on a collection.

11.10.2.1 `collection_check_boxes(object, method, collection, value_method, text_method, options = {}, html_options = {}, &block)`

The form helper `collection_check_boxes` creates a collection of check boxes and associated labels based on a collection.

To illustrate, assuming we have a `Post` model that has multiple categories, using the `collection_check_boxes` helper, we can add the ability to set the `category_ids` of the post:

```
1 collection_check_boxes(:post, :category_ids, Category.all, :id, :name)
2 # => <input id="post_category_ids_1" name="post[category_ids][]"
3 #      type="checkbox" value="1" />
4 #    <label for="post_category_ids_1">Ruby on Rails</label>
5 #    <input id="post_category_ids_2" name="post[category_ids][]"
6 #      type="checkbox" value="2" />
7 #    <label for="post_category_ids_2">Ruby</label>
8 #    ...
```

If one wanted to change the way the labels and check boxes are rendered, passing a block will yield a builder:

```
1 collection_check_boxes(:post, :category_ids, Category.all,
2   :id, :name) do |item|
3   item.label(class: 'check-box') { item.check_box(class:
        'check-box') }
4 end
```

The builder also has access to methods `object`, `text`, and `value` of the current item being rendered.

11.10.2.2 `collection_radio_buttons(object, method, collection, value_method, text_method, options = {}, html_options = {}, &block)`

The form helper `collection_radio_buttons` creates a collection of radio buttons and associated labels based on a collection. It is predominately used to set an individual value, such as a `belongs_to` relationship on a model.

Kevin Says ...

Use `collection_radio_buttons` with a collection that only has a handful of items unless you want your page to be polluted with radio buttons. Fallback to a `collection_select` for a large collection.

```
1 collection_radio_buttons(:post, :author_id, Author.all, :id, :name)
2 # => <input id="post_author_1" name="post[author_id][]"
3 #      type="radio" value="1" />
4 #    <label for="post_author_1">Obie</label>
5 #    <input id="post_author_2" name="post[author_id][]"
6 #      type="radio" value="2" />
7 #    <label for="post_author_2">Kevin</label>
8 #    ...
```

Similar to the `collection_check_boxes` helper, if one wanted to change the way the labels and radio buttons are rendered, passing a block will yield a builder:

```
1 collection_radio_buttons(:post, :author_id,
2   Author.all, :id, :name) do |item|
3   item.label(class: 'radio-button') {
4     item.radio_button(class: 'radio-button')
5   }
6 end
```

The builder also has access to methods `object`, `text`, and `value` of the current item being rendered.

11.10.3   Option Helpers

For all the following methods, only `option` tags are returned, so you have to invoke them from within a select helper or otherwise wrap them in a `select` tag.

11.10.3.1   `grouped_options_for_select(grouped_options, selected_key = nil, options = {})`

Returns a string of `option` tags, like `options_for_select`, but surrounds them with `optgroup` tags.

11.10.3.2   `option_groups_from_collection_for_ select(collection, group_method, group_ label_method, option_key_method, option_ value_method, selected_key = nil)`

Returns a string of `option` tags, like `options_from_collection_for_ select`, but surrounds them with `optgroup` tags. The `collection` should return a subarray of items when calling `group_method` on it. Each group in the collection should return its own name when calling `group_label_method`. The `option_key_method` and `option_value_method` parameters are used to calculate `option` tag attributes.

It's probably much easier to show in an example than to explain in words.

```
option_groups_from_collection_for_select(@continents, :countries,
  :continent_name, :country_id, :country_name, @selected_country.id)
```

This example could output the following HTML:

```
1 <optgroup label="Africa">
2   <option value="1">Egypt</option>
3   <option value="4">Rwanda</option>
4   ...
5 </optgroup>
6 <optgroup label="Asia">
```

```
7    <option value="3" selected="selected">China</option>
8    <option value="12">India</option>
9    <option value="5">Japan</option>
10   ...
11  </optgroup>
```

For the sake of clarity, here are the model classes reflected in the example:

```
1  class Continent
2    def initialize(name, countries)
3      @continent_name = name; @countries = countries
4    end
5
6    def continent_name
7      @continent_name
8    end
9
10   def countries
11     @countries
12   end
13 end
14
15 class Country
16   def initialize(id, name)
17     @id, @name = id, name
18   end
19
20   def country_id
21     @id
22   end
23
24   def country_name
25     @name
26   end
27 end
```

11.10.3.3 `options_for_select(container, selected = nil)`

Accepts a container (hash, array, or anything else enumerable) and returns a string of option tags. Given a container where the elements respond to first and last (such as a two-element array), the "lasts" serve as option values and the "firsts" as option text. It's not too hard to put together an expression that constructs a two-element array using the map and collect iterators.

For example, assume you have a collection of businesses to display and you're using a select field to allow the user to filter based on the category of the businesses. The category is not a simple string; in this example, it's a proper model related to the business via a belongs_to association:

```
 1  class Business < ActiveRecord::Base
 2    belongs_to :category
 3  end
 4
 5  class Category < ActiveRecord::Base
 6    has_many :businesses
 7
 8    def <=>(other)
 9      ...
10    end
11  end
```

A simplified version of the template code for displaying that collection of businesses
might look like the following:

```
- opts = businesses.map(&:category).collect { |c| [c.name, c.id] }
= select_tag(:filter, options_for_select(opts, params[:filter]))
```

The first line puts together the container expected by options_for_select by
first aggregating the category attributes of the businesses collection using map
and the nifty &:method syntax. The second line generates the select tag using those
options (covered later in the chapter). Realistically, you want to massage that category
list a little more so that it is ordered correctly and does not contain duplicates:

```
... businesses.map(&:category).uniq.sort.collect {...
```

Particularly with smaller sets of data, it's perfectly acceptable to do this level of data
manipulation in Ruby code. And of course, you probably don't want to ever shove
hundreds or especially thousands of rows in a select tag, making this technique
quite useful. Remember to implement the spaceship method in your model if you
need it to be sortable by the sort method.

Also, it's worthwhile to experiment with eager loading in these cases so you don't
end up with an individual database query for each of the objects represented in the
select tag. In the case of our example, the controller would populate the businesses
collection using code like this:

```
expose(:businesses) do
  Business.where(...).includes(:category)
end
```

Hashes are turned into a form acceptable to options_for_select automatically—
the keys become *firsts* and values become *lasts*.

If selected parameter is specified (with either a value or an array of values for
multiple selections), the matching *last* or element will get the selected attribute:

```
1  options_for_select([["Dollar", "$"], ["Kroner", "DKK"]])
2  # => <option value="$">Dollar</option>
3  #    <option value="DKK">Kroner</option>
4
5  options_for_select([ "VISA", "MasterCard" ], "MasterCard")
6  # => <option>VISA</option>
7  #    <option selected="selected">MasterCard</option>
8
9  options_for_select({ "Basic" => "$20", "Plus" => "$40" }, "$40")
10 # => <option value="$20">Basic</option>
11 #    <option value="$40" selected="selected">Plus</option>
12
13 >> options_for_select([ "VISA", "MasterCard", "Discover" ],
14                       ["VISA", "Discover"])
15 # => <option selected="selected">VISA</option>
16 #    <option>MasterCard</option>
17 #    <option selected="selected">Discover</option>
```

A lot of people have trouble getting this method to correctly display their selected item. Make sure that the value you pass to `selected` matches the type contained in the object collection of the `select`; otherwise, it won't work. In the following example, assuming `price` is a numeric value, without the `to_s`, selection would be broken, since the values passed as options are all strings:

```
1  options_for_select({ "Basic" => "20", "Plus" => "40" }, price.to_s)
2  # => <option value="20">Basic</option>
3  #    <option value="40" selected="selected">Plus</option>
```

11.10.3.4 `options_from_collection_for_select` `(collection, value_method, text_method, selected=nil)`

Returns a string of `option` tags that have been compiled by iterating over the collection and assigning the result of a call to the `value_method` as the option value and the `text_method` as the option text. If selected is specified, the element returning a match on `value_method` will get preselected.

```
1  options_from_collection_for_select(Person.all, :id, :name)
2  # => <option value="1">David</option>
3       <option value="2">Sam</option>
4       ...
```

11.10.3.5 `time_zone_options_for_select` `(selected = nil, priority_zones = nil, model = ::ActiveSupport::TimeZone)`

Returns a string of `option` tags for pretty much any time zone in the world. Supply a `ActiveSupport::TimeZone` name as selected to have it preselected. You can also supply an array of `ActiveSupport::TimeZone` objects as `priority _zones` so that they will be listed above the rest of the (long) list. `TimeZone .us_zones` is a convenience method that gives you a list of the US time zones only.

The `selected` parameter must be either `nil` or a string that names an `Active Support::TimeZone` (covered in Appendix B).

11.11 FormTagHelper

The following helper methods generate HTML form and input tags based on explicit naming and values, contrary to the similar methods present in `FormHelper`, which require association to an Active Record model instance. All of these helper methods take an `options` hash, which may contain special options or simply additional attribute values that should be added to the HTML tag being generated.

11.11.0.1 button_tag(content_or_options = nil, options = nil, &block)

Creates a button element that can be used to define a submit, reset, or generic button to be used with JavaScript.

```
1 button_tag('Submit')
2 # => <button name="button" type="submit">Submit</button>
3
4 button_tag('Some call to action',type: 'button')
5 # => <button name="button" type="button">Some call to action</button>
```

11.11.0.2 check_box_tag(name, value = "1", checked = false, options = {})

Creates a check box input field. Unlike its fancier cousin, `check_box` in `Form-Helper`, this helper does not give you an extra hidden input field to ensure that a false value is passed even if the check box is unchecked.

```
1 check_box_tag('remember_me')
2 # => <input id="remember_me" name="remember_me" type="checkbox" value="1"/>
3
4 check_box_tag('remember_me', 1, true)
5 # => <input checked="checked" id="remember_me" name="remember_me"
6 #       type="checkbox" value="1" />
```

11.11.0.3 color_field_tag(name, value = nil, options = {})

Creates a color input field that allows the setting of a color via hex values. This method is otherwise identical to `text_field_tag`.

11.11.0.4 `date_field_tag(name, value = nil, options = {})`

Creates a date input field. This method is otherwise identical to `text_field_tag`.

11.11.0.5 `datetime_field_tag(name, value = nil, options = {})`

Creates a datetime input field, which accepts time in UTC. This method is otherwise identical to `text_field_tag` with the following additional options:

`:min` The minimum acceptable value.

`:max` The maximum acceptable value.

`:step` The acceptable value granularity.

11.11.0.6 `datetime_local_field_tag(name, value = nil, options = {})`

Creates an input field of type "datetime-local." This method is otherwise identical to `datetime_field_tag`, except that the value is not in UTC.

11.11.0.7 `email_field_tag(name, value = nil, options = {})`

Creates an email input field. This method is otherwise identical to `text_field_tag`.

11.11.0.8 `field_set_tag(legend = nil, options = nil, &block)`

Wraps the contents of the given block in a `fieldset` tag and optionally gives it a `legend` tag.

11.11.0.9 `file_field_tag(name, options = {})`

Creates a file upload field. Remember to set your HTML form to multipart or file uploads will mysteriously not work:

```
1 = form_tag '/upload', multipart: true do
2   = label_tag :file, 'File to Upload'
3   = file_field_tag :file
4   = submit_tag
```

The controller action will receive a `File` object pointing to the uploaded file as it exists in a tempfile on your system. The processing of an uploaded file is beyond the scope of this book. If you're smart, you'll use Jonas Nicklas's excellent CarrierWave gem instead of reinventing the wheel.4

11.11.0.10 `form_tag(url_for_options = {}, options = {}, &block)`

Starts a `form` tag, with its action attribute set to the URL passed as the `url_for_options` parameter.

The `:method` option defaults to POST. Browsers handle HTTP GET and POST natively; if you specify "patch" or "delete" or if any other HTTP verb is used, a hidden input field will be inserted with the name `_method` and a value corresponding to the `method` supplied. The Rails request dispatcher understands the `_method` parameter, which is the basis for the RESTful techniques you learned in Chapter 3, "REST, Resources, and Rails."

The `:multipart` option allows you to specify that you will be including file-upload fields in the form submission and the server should be ready to handle those files accordingly.

The `:authenticity_token` option is used only if you need to pass a custom authenticity token string or want to disable it by setting the option to `false`.

Setting the option `:remote` to true will allow the unobtrusive JavaScript drivers to take control of the submit behavior (covered in Chapter 19, "Ajax on Rails").

```
1 form_tag('/posts')
2 # => <form action="/posts" method="post">
3
4 >> form_tag('/posts/1', method: :patch)
5 # => <form action="/posts/1" method="post">
6 #        <input name="_method" type="hidden" value="patch" />
7 #        ...
8
9 form_tag('/upload', multipart: true)
10 # => <form action="/upload" method="post" enctype="multipart/form-data">
```

You might note that all parameters to `form_tag` are optional. If you leave them off, you'll get a form that posts back to the URL that it came from—a quick and dirty solution that I use quite often when prototyping or experimenting. To quickly set up a controller action that handles postbacks, just include an `if/else` condition that checks the request method—something like the following:

```
1 def add
2   if request.post?
```

4. https://github.com/carrierwaveuploader/carrierwave

```
3     # handle the posted params
4     redirect_to :back
5   end
6 end
```

Notice that if the request is a post, I handle the form params and then redirect back to the original URL (using redirect_to :back). Otherwise, execution simply falls through and would render whatever template is associated with the action.

11.11.0.11 hidden_field_tag(name, value = nil, options = {})

Creates a hidden field with parameters similar to text_field_tag.

11.11.0.12 image_submit_tag(source, options = {})

Displays an image that, when clicked, will submit the form. The interface for this method is the same as its cousin image_tag in the AssetTagHelper module.

Image input tags are popular replacements for standard submit tags because they make an application look fancier. They are also used to detect the location of the mouse cursor on click—the params hash will include x and y data.

11.11.0.13 label_tag(name = nil, content_or_options = nil, options = nil, &block)

Creates a label tag with the for attribute set to name.

11.11.0.14 month_field_tag(name, value = nil, options = {})

Creates an input field of type "month." This method is otherwise identical to text_field_tag with the following additional options:

:min The minimum acceptable value.

:max The maximum acceptable value.

:step The acceptable value granularity.

11.11.0.15 number_field_tag(name, value = nil, options = {})

Creates a number input field. This method is otherwise identical to text_field_tag with the following additional options:

:min The minimum acceptable value.

:max The maximum acceptable value.

:in A range specifying the :min and :max values.

:step The acceptable value granularity.

11.11.0.16 `password_field_tag(name = "password", value = nil, options = {})`

Creates a password input field. This method is otherwise identical to `text_field_tag`.

11.11.0.17 `radio_button_tag(name, value, checked = false, options = {})`

Creates a radio button input field. Make sure to give all your radio button options the same name so the browser will consider them linked.

11.11.0.18 `range_field_tag(name, value = nil, options = {})`

Creates a range input field. This method is otherwise identical to `number _field_tag`.

11.11.0.19 `search_field_tag(name, value = nil, options = {})`

Creates a search input field. This method is otherwise identical to `text_field_tag`.

11.11.0.20 `select_tag(name, option_tags = nil, options = {})`

Creates a drop-down selection box or, if the :multiple option is set to true, a multiple-choice selection box. The option_tags parameter is an actual string of option tags to put inside the select tag. You should not have to generate that string explicitly yourself. Instead, use the helpers in FormOptions (covered in the previous section of this chapter), which can be used to create common select boxes such as countries, time zones, or associated records.

11.11.0.21 `submit_tag(value = "Save changes", options = {})`

Creates a submit button with the text value as the caption. In conjunction with the unobtrusive JavaScript driver, one can set a :data attribute named :disable_ with that can be used to provide a name for disabled versions of the submit button.

```
submit_tag('Save article', data: { disable_with: 'Please wait...' })
# => <input data-disable-with="Please wait..."
#      name="commit" type="submit" value="Save article" />
```

11.11.0.22 `telephone_field_tag(name, value = nil, options = {})`

Creates a telephone input field. This method is otherwise identical to `text_field_tag` and is aliased as `phone_field_tag`.

11.11.0.23 `text_area_tag(name, content = nil, options = {})`

Creates a multiline text input field (the `textarea` tag). The `:size` option lets you easily specify the dimensions of the text area instead of having to resort to explicit `:rows` and `:cols` options.

```
text_area_tag(:body, nil, size: "25x10")
# => <textarea name="body" id="body" cols="25" rows="10"></textarea>
```

11.11.0.24 `text_field_tag(name, value = nil, options = {})`

Creates a standard text input field.

11.11.0.25 `time_field_tag(name, value = nil, options = {})`

Creates an input field of type "time." This method is otherwise identical to `text_field_tag` with the following additional options:

:min The minimum acceptable value.

:max The maximum acceptable value.

:step The acceptable value granularity.

11.11.0.26 `url_field_tag(name, value = nil, options = {})`

Creates an input field of type "url." This method is otherwise identical to `text_field_tag`.

11.11.0.27 `utf8_enforcer_tag()`

Creates the hidden UTF-8 enforcer tag.

```
utf8_enforcer_tag
# => <input name="utf8" type="hidden" value="&#x2713;" />
```

11.11.0.28 **week_field_tag(name, value = nil, options = {})**

Creates an input field of type "week." This method is otherwise identical to `text_field_tag` with the following additional options:

:min The minimum acceptable value.

:max The maximum acceptable value.

:step The acceptable value granularity.

11.12 **JavaScriptHelper**

Provides helper methods to facilitate inclusion of JavaScript code in your templates.

11.12.0.1 **escape_javascript(javascript)**

Escapes line breaks; single and double quotes are used for JavaScript segments. It's also aliased as `j`.

11.12.0.2 **javascript_tag(content_or_options_with_ block = nil, html_options = {}, &block)**

Outputs a `script` tag with the content inside. The `html_options` are added as tag attributes.

11.13 **NumberHelper**

This module provides assistance in converting numeric data to formatted strings suitable for displaying in your view. Methods are provided for phone numbers, currency, percentages, precision, positional notation, and file size.

11.13.0.1 **number_to_currency(number, options = {})**

Formats a number into a currency string. You can customize the format in the options hash.

:locale Sets the locale to be used for formatting. Defaults to current locale.

:precision Sets the level of precision. Defaults to 2.

:unit Sets the denomination of the currency. Defaults to "$".

:separator Sets the separator between the units. Defaults to "`.`".

:delimiter Sets the thousands delimiter. Defaults to "`,`".

:format Sets the format for nonnegative numbers. Defaults to "`%u%n`".

:negative_format Sets the format for negative numbers. Defaults to prepending a hyphen to the formatted number.

:raise Setting to `true` raises `InvalidNumberError` when the number is invalid.

```
 1  number_to_currency(1234567890.50)
 2  # => $1,234,567,890.50
 3
 4  number_to_currency(1234567890.506)
 5  # => $1,234,567,890.51
 6
 7  number_to_currency(1234567890.506, precision: 3)
 8  # => $1,234,567,890.506
 9
10  number_to_currency(1234567890.50, unit: "&pound;", separator: ",",
11    delimiter: "")
12  # => &pound;1234567890,50
```

11.13.0.2 `number_to_human_size(number, options = {})`

Formats a number that is more readable to humans. Useful for numbers that are extremely large. You can customize the format in the options hash.

:locale Sets the locale to be used for formatting. Defaults to current locale.

:precision Sets the level of precision. Defaults to 3.

:significant If true, precision will be the number of significant_digits; otherwise, the number of fractional digits are used. Defaults to true.

:separator Sets the separator between fractional and integer digits. Defaults to "`.`".

:delimiter Sets the thousands delimiter. Defaults to "`"`".

:strip_insignificant_zeros Setting to true removes insignificant zeros after the decimal separator. Defaults to true.

:units A hash of unit quantifier names or a string containing an I18n scope indicating where to find this hash. It might have the following keys:

integers: :unit, :ten, *:hundred, :thousand, :million, *:billion,
  :trillion, *:quadrillion

fractionals: :deci, :centi, *:milli, :micro, :nano, *:pico, :femto

:format Sets the format for nonnegative numbers. Defaults to `"%n  %u"`. The
field types are the following:

```
%u: The quantifier
%n: The number
```

```
1  number_to_human(123)                        # => "123"
2  number_to_human(1234)                       # => "1.23 Thousand"
3  number_to_human(1234567)                    # => "1.23 Million"
4  number_to_human(489939, precision: 4)       # => "489.9 Thousand"
```

Kevin Says ...

Rails provides the ability to set your own custom unit qualifier by setting the
:units option.

```
1  number_to_human(10000, units: {unit: "m", thousand: "km"})  # => "10 km"
```

11.13.0.3   `number_to_human_size(number, options = {})`
Formats the bytes in size into a more understandable representation. Useful for
reporting file sizes to users. You can customize the format in the options hash.

:locale Sets the locale to be used for formatting. Defaults to current locale.

:precision Sets the level of precision. Defaults to 3.

:significant If true, precision will be the number of `significant_digits`;
otherwise, the number of fractional digits are used. Defaults to true.

:separator Sets the separator between fractional and integer digits. Defaults to `"."`.

:delimiter Sets the thousands delimiter. Defaults to `""`.

:strip_insignificant_zeros Setting to true removes insignificant zeros after
the decimal separator. Defaults to true.

:format Sets the format for nonnegative numbers. Defaults to `"%u%n"`.

:prefix Setting to :si formats the number using the SI prefix. Defaults to
:binary.

:raise Setting to true raises InvalidNumberError when the number is invalid.

```
1  number_to_human_size(123)                    => 123 Bytes
2  number_to_human_size(1234)                   => 1.21 KB
3  number_to_human_size(12345)                  => 12.1 KB
4  number_to_human_size(1234567)                => 1.18 MB
5  number_to_human_size(1234567890)             => 1.15 GB
6  number_to_human_size(1234567890123)          => 1.12 TB
7  number_to_human_size(1234567, precision: 2)  => 1.2 MB
```

11.13.0.4 `number_to_percentage(number, options = {})`
Formats a number as a percentage string. You can customize the format in the
options hash.

:locale Sets the locale to be used for formatting. Defaults to current locale.

:precision Sets the level of precision. Defaults to 3.

:significant If true, precision will be the number of significant_digits; otherwise, the number of fractional digits are used. Defaults to false.

:separator Sets the separator between the units. Defaults to ".".

:delimiter Sets the thousands delimiter. Defaults to "".

:strip_insignificant_zeros Setting to true removes insignificant zeros after the decimal separator. Defaults to false.

:format Sets the format of the percentage string. Defaults to "%n%".

:raise Setting to true raises InvalidNumberError when the number is
invalid.

```
1  number_to_percentage(100)                    => 100.000%
2  number_to_percentage(100, precision: 0)      => 100%
3  number_to_percentage(302.0574, precision: 2) => 302.06%
```

11.13.0.5 `number_to_phone(number, options = {})`
Formats a number as a US phone number. You can customize the format in the
options hash.

:area_code Adds parentheses around the area code.

:delimiter Specifies the delimiter to use. Defaults to `"-"`.

:extension Specifies an extension to add to the end of the generated number.

:country_code Sets the country code for the phone number.

:raise Setting to `true` raises `InvalidNumberError` when the number is invalid.

```
1 number_to_phone(1235551234)                  # => "123-555-1234"
2 number_to_phone(1235551234, area_code: true)  # => "(123) 555-1234"
3 number_to_phone(1235551234, delimiter: " ")    # => "123 555 1234"
```

11.13.0.6 `number_with_delimiter(number, options = {})`

Formats a number with grouped thousands using a delimiter. You can customize the format in the options hash.

:locale Sets the locale to be used for formatting. Defaults to current locale.

:delimiter Sets the thousands delimiter. Defaults to `","`.

:separator Sets the separator between the units. Defaults to `"."`.

:raise Setting to `true` raises `InvalidNumberError` when the number is invalid.

```
1 number_with_delimiter(12345678)                # => "12,345,678"
2 number_with_delimiter(12345678.05)             # => "12,345,678.05"
3 number_with_delimiter(12345678, delimiter: ".") # => "12.345.678"
```

11.13.0.7 `number_with_precision(number, options = {})`

Formats a number with the specified level of precision. You can customize the format in the options hash.

:locale Sets the locale to be used for formatting. Defaults to current locale.

:precision Sets the level of precision. Defaults to 3.

Helpers

:significant If true, precision will be the number of significant_digits; otherwise, the number of fractional digits are used. Defaults to false.

:separator Sets the separator between the units. Defaults to " . "

:delimiter Sets the thousands delimiter. Defaults to " ".

:strip_insignificant_zeros Setting to true removes insignificant zeros after the decimal separator. Defaults to false.

:raise Setting to true raises InvalidNumberError when the number is invalid.

```
1 number_with_precision(111.2345)                # => "111.235"
2 number_with_precision(111.2345, precision: 2) # => "111.23"
```

11.14 OutputSafetyHelper
This is an extremely simple helper module, barely worth mentioning.

11.14.0.1 raw(stringish)
Bypasses HTML sanitization by calling to_s and then html_safe on the argument passed to it.

11.14.0.2 safe_join(array, sep=$,)
Returns an HTML safe string by first escaping all array items and joining them by calling Array#join using the supplied separator. The returned string is also called with html_safe for good measure.

```
safe_join(["<p>foo</p>".html_safe, "<p>bar</p>"], "<br />")
# => "<p>foo</p><br /><p>bar</p>"
```

11.15 RecordTagHelper
This module assists in creation of HTML markup code that follows good, clean naming conventions.

11.15.0.1 content_tag_for(tag_name, single_or_ multiple_records, prefix = nil, options = nil, &block)
This helper method creates an HTML element with id and class parameters that relate to the specified Active Record object. For instance, assuming @person is an instance of a Person class with an id value of 123, the template code

```
= content_tag_for(:tr, @person) do
  %td= @person.first_name
  %td= @person.last_name
```

will produce the following HTML:

```
<tr id="person_123" class="person">
  ...
</tr>
```

If you require the HTML id attribute to have a prefix, you can specify it as a third argument:

```
content_tag_for(:tr, @person, :foo) do ...
# => "<tr id="foo_person_123" class="person">..."
```

The content_tag_for helper also accepts a hash of options, which will be converted to additional HTML attributes on the tag. If you specify a :class value, it will be combined with the default class name for your object instead of replacing it (since replacing it would defeat the purpose of the method!).

```
content_tag_for(:tr, @person, :foo, class: 'highlight') do ...
# => "<tr id="foo_person_123" class="person highlight">..."
```

11.15.0.2 `div_for(record, *args, &block)`
Produces a wrapper div element with id and class parameters that relate to the specified Active Record object. This method is exactly like content_tag_for except that it's hard-coded to output div elements.

11.16 **RenderingHelper**
This module contains helper methods related to rendering from a view context to be used with an ActionView::Renderer object. Development of an Action View renderer is outside the scope of this book, but for those who are interested, investigating the source code for ActionView::TemplateRenderer and Action View::PartialRenderer would be a good starting point.[5]

11.17 **SanitizeHelper**
The SanitizeHelper module provides a set of methods for scrubbing text of undesired HTML elements. Rails sanitizes and escapes HTML content by default,

---

5. https://github.com/rails/rails/tree/4-0-stable/actionpack/lib/action_view/renderer

so this helper is really intended to assist with the inclusion of dynamic content into your views.

11.17.0.1 `sanitize(html, options = {})`

Encodes all tags and strip all attributes (not specifically allowed) from the `html` string passed to it. Also strips `href` and `src` tags with invalid protocols, particularly in an effort to prevent abuse of `javascript` attribute values.

```
= sanitize @article.body
```

With its default settings, the `sanitize` method does its best to counter known hacker tricks such as using Unicode/ASCII/hex values to get past the JavaScript filters.

You can customize the behavior of `sanitize` by adding or removing allowable tags and attributes using the `:attributes` or `:tags` options.

```
= sanitize @article.body, tags: %w(table tr td),
    attributes: %w(id class style)
```

It's possible to add tags to the default allowed tags in your application by altering the value of `config.action_view.sanitized_allowed_tags` in an initializer. For instance, the following code adds support for basic HTML tables.

```
1 class Application < Rails::Application
2   config.action_view.sanitized_allowed_tags = 'table', 'tr', 'td'
3 end
```

You can also remove some of the tags that are allowed by default.

```
1 class Application < Rails::Application
2   config.after_initialize do
3     ActionView::Base.sanitized_allowed_tags.delete 'div'
4   end
5 end
```

Or you can change them altogether.

```
1 class Application < Rails::Application
2   config.action_view.sanitized_allowed_attributes = 'id', 'class', 'style'
3 end
```

Sanitizing user-provided text does not guarantee that the resulting markup will be valid (conforming to a document type) or even well-formed. The output may still contain unescaped <, >, and & characters that confuse browsers and adversely affect rendering.

11.17.0.2 `sanitize_css(style)`

Sanitizes a block of CSS code. Used by `sanitize` when it comes across a style attribute in HTML being sanitized.

11.17.0.3 `strip_links(html)`

Strips all link tags from text leaving just the link text.

```
1 strip_links('<a href="http://www.rubyonrails.org">Ruby on Rails</a>')
2 # => Ruby on Rails
3
4 strip_links('Please email me at <a href="mailto:me@email.com">me@email.com</a>.')
5 # => Please email me at me@email.com.
6
7 strip_links('Blog: <a href="http://www.myblog.com/" class="nav">Visit</a>.')
8 # => Blog: Visit
```

11.17.0.4 `strip_tags(html)`

Strips all tags from the supplied HTML string, including comments. Its HTML parsing ability is limited by that of the HTML scanner tokenizer built into Rails.[6]

```
1 strip_tags("Strip <i>these</i> tags!")
2 # => Strip these tags!
3
4 strip_tags("<b>Bold</b> no more!  <a href='more.html'>See more here</a>...")
5 # => Bold no more!  See more here...
6
7 strip_tags("<div id='top-bar'>Welcome to my website!</div>")
8 # => Welcome to my website!
```

11.18   TagHelper

This module provides helper methods for generating HTML tags programmatically.

11.18.0.1 `cdata_section(content)`

Returns a CDATA section wrapping the given `content`. CDATA sections are used to escape blocks of text containing characters that would otherwise be recognized as markup. CDATA sections begin with the string `<![CDATA[` and end with (and may not contain) the string `]]>`.

---

6. You can examine the source code of the html scanner yourself by opening up `https://github.com/rails/rails/blob/4-0-stable/actionpack/lib/action_view/vendor/html-scanner/html/sanitizer.rb`

11.18.0.2 `content_tag(name, content_or_options_with_block = nil, options = nil, escape = true, &block)`

Returns an HTML block tag of type name surrounding the content. Add HTML attributes by passing an attributes hash as options. Instead of passing the content as an argument, you can also use a block to hold additional markup (and/or additional calls to content_tag), in which case you pass your options as the second parameter. Set escape to false to disable attribute value escaping.

Here are some simple examples of using content_tag without a block:

```
1 content_tag(:p, "Hello world!")
2 # => <p>Hello world!</p>
3
4 content_tag(:div, content_tag(:p, "Hello!"), class: "message")
5 # => <div class="message"><p>Hello!</p></div>
6
7 content_tag("select", options, multiple: true)
8 # => <select multiple="multiple">...options...</select>
```

Here it is with content in a block (shown as template code rather than in the console):

```
= content_tag :div, class: "strong" do
  Hello world!
```

The preceding code produces the following HTML:

```
<div class="strong">Hello world!</div>
```

11.18.0.3 `escape_once(html)`

Returns an escaped version of HTML without affecting existing escaped entities.

```
1 escape_once("1 > 2 & 3")
2 # => "1 &lt; 2 & 3"
3
4 escape_once("&lt;&lt; Accept & Checkout")
5 # => "&lt;&lt; Accept & Checkout"
```

11.18.0.4 `tag(name, options = nil, open = false, escape = true)`

Returns an empty HTML tag of type name, which by default is XHTML compliant. Setting open to true will create an open tag compatible with HTML 4.0 and below. Add HTML attributes by passing an attributes hash to options. Set escape to false to disable attribute value escaping.

The options hash is used with attributes with no value (e.g., `disabled` and `readonly`), which you can give a value of `true` in the options hash. You can use symbols or strings for the attribute names.

```
1 tag("br")
2 # => <br />
3
4 tag("br", nil, true)
5 # => <br>
6
7 tag("input", type: 'text', disabled: true)
8 # => <input type="text" disabled="disabled" />
9
10 tag("img", src: "open.png")
11 # => <img src="open.png" />
```

11.19   **TextHelper**

The methods in this module provide filtering, formatting, and string transformation capabilities.

11.19.0.1   `concat(string)`

The preferred method of outputting text in your views is to use the `=` expression in Haml syntax or the `<%= expression %>` in eRuby syntax. The regular puts and print methods do not operate as expected in an eRuby code block—that is, if you expected them to output to the browser. If you absolutely must output text within a nonoutput code block like `- expression` in Haml or `<% expression %>` in eRuby, you can use the `concat` method. I've found that this method can be especially useful when combined with `capture` in your own custom helper method implementations.

The following example code defines a helper method that wraps its block content in a div with a particular CSS class.

```
1 def wrap(&block)
2   concat(content_tag(:div, capture(&block), class: "wrapped_content"))
3 end
```

You would use it in your template as follows:

```
1 - wrap do
2   My wrapped content
```

11.19.0.2 `current_cycle(name = "default")`

Returns the current cycle string after a cycle has been started. Useful for complex table highlighting or any other design need that requires the current cycle string in more than one place.

```
1  - # Alternate background colors with coordinating text color.
2  - [1,2,3,4].each do |item|
3    %div(style="background-color:#{cycle('red', 'green', 'blue')}")
4      %span(style="color:dark#{current_cycle}")= item
```

11.19.0.3 `cycle(first_value, *values)`

Creates a `Cycle` object whose `to_s` method cycles through elements of the array of values passed to it every time it is called. This can be used, for example, to alternate classes for table rows. Here's an example that alternates CSS classes for even and odd numbers, assuming that the `@items` variable holds an array with 1 through 4:

```
1  %table
2    - @items.each do |item|
3      %tr{ class: cycle('even', 'odd') }
4        %td= item
```

As you can tell from the example, you don't have to store the reference to the cycle in a local variable or anything like that; you just call the `cycle` method repeatedly. That's convenient, but it means that nested cycles need an identifier. The solution is to pass cycle a `name: cycle_name` option as its last parameter. Also, you can manually reset a cycle by calling `reset_cycle` and passing it the name of the cycle to reset. For example, here is some data to iterate over:

```
1  # Cycle CSS classes for rows and text colors for values within each row.
2  @items = [{first: 'Robert', middle: 'Daniel', last: 'James'},
3           {first: 'Emily', last: 'Hicks'},
4           {first: 'June', middle: 'Dae', last: 'Jones'}]
```

And here is the template code. Since the number of cells rendered varies, we want to make sure to reset the colors cycle before looping:

```
1  - @items.each do |item|
2    %tr{ class: cycle('even', 'odd', name: 'row_class') }
3      - item.values.each do |value|
4        %td{ class: cycle('red', 'green', name: 'colors') }
5          = value
6        - reset_cycle 'colors'
```

11.19.0.4 `excerpt(text, phrase, options = {})`

Extracts an excerpt from text that matches the first instance of `phrase`. The `:radius` option expands the excerpt on each side of the first occurrence of `phrase` by the number of characters defined in `:radius` (which defaults to 100). If the excerpt radius overflows the beginning or end of the text, the `:omission` option will be prepended/appended accordingly. Use the `:separator` option to set the delimitation. If the phrase isn't found, nil is returned.

```
1  excerpt('This is an example', 'an', radius: 5)
2  # => "...s is an examp..."
3
4  excerpt('This is an example', 'is', radius: 5)
5  # => "This is an..."
6
7  excerpt('This is an example', 'is')
8  # => "This is an example"
9
10 excerpt('This next thing is an example', 'ex', radius: 2)
11 # => "...next..."
12
13 excerpt('This is also an example', 'an', radius: 8, omission: '<chop> ')
14 # => "<chop> is also an example"
```

11.19.0.5 `highlight(text, phrases, options = {})`

Highlights one or more phrases everywhere in text by inserting into a highlighter template. The highlighter can be specialized by passing the option `:highlighter` as a single-quoted string with `\1` where the phrase is to be inserted.

```
1  highlight('You searched for: rails', 'rails')
2  # => You searched for: <mark>rails</mark>
3
4  highlight('You searched for: ruby, rails, dhh', 'actionpack')
5  # => You searched for: ruby, rails, dhh
6
7  highlight('You searched for: rails', ['for', 'rails'],
8    highlighter: '<em>\1</em>')
9  # => You searched <em>for</em>: <em>rails</em>
10
11 highlight('You searched for: rails', 'rails',
12   highlighter: '<a href="search?q=\1">\1</a>')
13 # => You searched for: <a href="search?q=rails">rails</a>
```

Note that as of Rails 4, the `highlight` helper now uses the HTML5 `mark` tag by default.

Helpers

11.19.0.6 **pluralize(count, singular, plural = nil)**

Attempts to pluralize the singular word unless count is 1. If the plural is supplied, it will use that when count is > 1. If the ActiveSupport Inflector is loaded, it will use the Inflector to determine the plural form; otherwise, it will just add an "s" to the singular word.

```
 1  pluralize(1, 'person')
 2  # => 1 person
 3
 4  pluralize(2, 'person')
 5  # => 2 people
 6
 7  pluralize(3, 'person', 'users')
 8  # => 3 users
 9
10  pluralize(0, 'person')
11  # => 0 people
```

11.19.0.7 **reset_cycle(name = "default")**

Resets a cycle (see the cycle method in this section) so that it starts cycling from its first element the next time it is called. Pass in a name to reset a named cycle.

11.19.0.8 **simple_format(text, html_options = {}, options = {})**

Returns text transformed into HTML using simple formatting rules. Two or more consecutive newlines (\n\n) are considered to denote a paragraph and thus are wrapped in p tags. One newline (\n) is considered to be a line break and a br tag is appended. This method does not remove the newlines from the text.

Any attributes set in html_options will be added to all outputted paragraphs. The following options are also available:

:sanitize Setting this option to false will not sanitize any text.

:wrapper_tag A string representing the wrapper tag. Defaults to "p".

11.19.0.9 **truncate(text, options = {}, &block)**

If text is longer than the :length option (defaults to 30), text will be truncated to the length specified and the last three characters will be replaced with the :omission (defaults to "..."). The :separator option allows defining the delimitation. Finally, to not escape the output, set :escape to false.

```
1 truncate("Once upon a time in a world far far away", length: 7)
2 => "Once..."
3
4 truncate("Once upon a time in a world far far away")
5 # => "Once upon a time in a world..."
6
7 truncate("And they found that many people were sleeping better.",
8   length: 25, omission: '... (continued)')
9 # => "And they f... (continued)"
```

11.19.0.10 `word_wrap(text, options = {})`

Wraps the text into lines no longer than the `:line_width` option. This method breaks on the first whitespace character that does not exceed `:line_width` (which is 80 by default).

```
1 word_wrap('Once upon a time')
2 # => Once upon a time
3
4 word_wrap('Once upon a time', line_width: 8)
5 # => Once\nupon a\ntime
6
7 word_wrap('Once upon a time', line_width: 1)
8 # => Once\nupon\na\ntime
```

11.20 **TranslationHelper** and the I18n API

I18n stands for *internationalization* and the I18n gem that ships with Rails makes it easy to support multiple languages other than English in your Rails applications. When you internationalize your app, you do a sweep of all the textual content in your models and views that needs to be translated, as well as demarking data like currency and dates, which should be subject to localization.[7]

Rails provides an easy-to-use and extensible framework for translating your application to a single custom language other than English or for providing multilanguage support in your application.

The process of *internationalization* in Rails involves the abstraction of strings and other locale-specific parts of your application (such as dates and currency formats) out of the codebase and into a locale file.

---

7. This section is an authorized remix of the complete guide to using I18n in Rails by Sven Fuchs and Karel Minarik, available at `http://guides.rubyonrails.org/i18n.html`

The process of *localization* means to provide translations and localized formats for the abstractions created during internationalization. In the process of *localizing* your application, you'll probably want to do following three things:

- Replace or add to Rails' default locale.

- Add abstract strings used in your application to keyed dictionaries—for example, flash messages, static text in your views, and so on.

- Store the resulting dictionaries somewhere.

Internationalization is a complex problem. Natural languages differ in so many ways (e.g., in pluralization rules) that it is hard to provide tools for solving all problems at once. For that reason, the Rails I18n API focuses on the following:

- Providing support for English and similar languages by default

- Making it easy to customize and extend everything for other languages

As part of this solution, every static string in the Rails framework—for example, Active Record validation messages, time and date formats, and so on—has been internationalized, so *localization* of a Rails application means *overriding* Rails defaults.

11.20.1   Localized Views

Before diving into the more complicated localization techniques, let's briefly cover a simple way to translate views that is useful for content-heavy pages. Assume you have a `BooksController` in your application. Your `index` action renders content in `app/views/books/index.html.haml` template. When you put a *localized variant* of that template such as `index.es.html.haml` in the same directory, Rails will recognize it as the appropriate template to use when the locale is set to `:es`. If the locale is set to the default, the generic `index.html.haml` view will be used normally.

You can make use of this feature when working with a large amount of static content that would be clumsy to maintain inside locale dictionaries. Just bear in mind that any changes to a template must be kept in sync with all its translations.

11.20.2   TranslationHelper Methods

The following two methods are provided for use in your views and assume that I18n support is set up in your application.

11.20.2.1 `localize(*args)` Aliased to `l`

Delegates to Active Support's `I18n#translate` method with no additional functionality. Normally, you would want to use `translate` instead.

11.20.2.2 `translate(key, options = {})` Aliased to `t`

Delegates to Active Support's `I18n#translate` method while performing three additional functions. First, it'll catch `MissingTranslationData` exceptions and turn them into inline spans that contain the missing key so that you can see them within your views when keys are missing.

Second, it'll automatically scope the key provided by the current partial if the key starts with a period. So if you call `translate(".foo")` from the `people/index.html.haml` template, you'll be calling `I18n.translate("people.index.foo")`. This makes it less repetitive to translate many keys within the same partials and gives you a simple framework for scoping them consistently. If you don't prepend the key with a period, nothing is converted.

Third, it'll mark the translation as safe HTML if the key has the suffix "_html" or the last element of the key is the word "html." For example, calling translate ("header.html") will return a safe HTML string that won't be escaped.

11.20.3 I18n Setup

There are just a few simple steps to get up and running with I18n support for your application.

Following the *convention over configuration* philosophy, Rails will set up your application with reasonable defaults. If you need different settings, you can overwrite them easily.

Rails adds all `.rb` and `.yml` files from the `config/locales` directory to your translations load path automatically.[8] The default `en.yml` locale in this directory contains a sample pair of translation strings:

```
1 en:
2   hello: "Hello world"
```

This means that in the `:en` locale, the key `hello` will map to the "Hello world" string.[9]

---

8. The translations load path is just an array of paths to your translation files that will be loaded automatically and available in your application. You can pick whatever directory and translation file naming scheme makes sense for you.

9. Every string inside Rails is internationalized in this way; see, for instance, Active Record validation messages in the file or time and date formats in the file.

Helpers

You can use YAML or standard Ruby hashes to store translations in the default (`Simple`) backend.

Unless you change it, the I18n library will use English (`:en`) as its default locale for looking up translations. Change the default in using code similar to the following:

```
config.i18n.default_locale = :de
```

Note

The I18n library takes a *pragmatic approach* to locale keys after some discussion,[10] including only the *locale* ("language") part, like `:en`, `:pl`, not the *region* part, like `:en-US` or `:en-UK`, which are traditionally used for separating "languages" and "regional setting" or "dialects." Many international applications use only the "language" element of a locale such as `:cz`, `:th`, or `:es` (for Czech, Thai, and Spanish). However, there are also regional differences within different language groups that may be important. For instance, in the `:en-US` locale, you would have $ as a currency symbol, while in `:en-UK`, you would have £. Nothing stops you from separating regional and other settings in this way: you just have to provide full "English–United Kingdom" locale in a `:en-UK` dictionary. Rails I18n plugins such as Globalize3[11] may help you implement it.

11.20.4   Setting and Passing the Locale

If you want to translate your Rails application to a single language other than English, you can just set `default_locale` to your locale in `application.rb` as shown earlier, and it will persist through the requests. However, you probably want to provide support for more locales in your application, depending on the user's preference. In such case, you need to set and pass the locale between requests.

Warning

You may be tempted to store the chosen locale in a *session* or a *cookie. Do not do so.* The locale should be transparent and a part of the URL. This way, you don't break people's basic assumptions about the web itself: If you send a URL of some page to a friend, she should see the same page and the same content.

---

10. https://groups.google.com/forum/?hl=en#!topic/rails-i18n/FN7eLH2-1HA
11. https://github.com/svenfuchs/globalize3

You can set the locale in a `before_action` in your `ApplicationController` like the following:

```
1 before_action :set_locale
2
3 def set_locale
4   # If params[:locale] is nil, then I18n.default_locale will be used.
5   I18n.locale = params[:locale]
6 end
```

This approach requires you to pass the locale as a URL query parameter, as in `http://example.com/books?locale=pt`. (This is, for example, Google's approach.)

Getting the locale from `params` and setting it accordingly is not the hard part of this technique. Including the locale parameter in every URL generated by your application *is* the hard part. To include an explicit option in every URL, as illustrated by

```
= link_to books_url(locale: I18n.locale)
```

would be tedious at best and impossible to maintain at worst.

A `default_url_options` method in `ApplicationController` is useful precisely in this scenario. It enables us to set defaults for `url_for` and helper methods dependent on it.

```
1 def default_url_options(options={})
2   logger.debug "default_url_options is passed options: #{options.inspect}\n"
3   { locale: I18n.locale }
4 end
```

Every helper method dependent on `url_for` (e.g., helpers for named routes like `root_path` or `root_url`, resource routes like `books_path` or `books_url`, etc.) will now automatically include the locale in the query string, like this:

```
http://localhost:3000/?locale=ja
```

Having the locale hang at the end of every path in your application can negatively impact readability of your URLs. Moreover, from an architectural standpoint, locales are a concept that live above other parts of your application domain, and your URLs should probably reflect that.

You might want your URLs to look more like `www.example.com/en/books` (which loads the English locale) and `www.example.com/nl/books` (which loads the Netherlands locale). This is achievable with the same `default_url_options` strategy we just reviewed. You just have to set up your routes with a `scope` option in this way:

```
1  # config/routes.rb
2  scope "/:locale" do
3    resources :books
4  end
```

Even with this approach, you still need to take special care of the root URL of your application. A URL like `http://localhost:3000/nl` will not work automatically, because the `root "books#index"` declaration in your `routes.rb` doesn't take locale into account. After all, there should only be one "root" of your website.

A possible solution is to map a URL like this:

```
# config/routes.rb
get '/:locale' => "dashboard#index"
```

Do take special care about the order of your routes, so this route declaration does not break other ones. It would be most wise to add it directly before the `root` declaration at the end of your routes file.

Warning

This solution has currently one rather big **downside**. Due to the `default_url_options` implementation, you have to pass the `:id` option explicitly, like `link_to 'Show', book_url(id: book)`, and not depend on Rails' magic in code like `link_to 'Show', book`. If this should be a problem, have a look at Sven Fuchs's routing_filter[12] plugin, which simplifies work with routes in this way.

11.20.4.1 Setting the Locale from the Domain Name

Another option you have is to set the locale from the domain name where your application runs. For example, we want `www.example.com` to load the English (or default) locale and `www.example.es` to load the Spanish locale. Thus the *top-level domain name* is used for locale setting. This has several advantages:

- The locale is a very *obvious* part of the URL.
- People intuitively grasp in which language the content will be displayed.
- It is very trivial to implement in Rails.
- Search engines seem to like that content in different languages lives at different, interlinked domains.

---

12. `https://github.com/svenfuchs/routing-filter`

You can implement it like this in your `ApplicationController`:

```
1 before_action :set_locale
2
3 def set_locale
4   I18n.locale = extract_locale_from_uri
5 end
6
7 # Get locale from top-level domain or return nil.
8 def extract_locale_from_tld
9   parsed_locale = request.host.split('.').last
10  (available_locales.include? parsed_locale) ? parsed_locale  : nil
11 end
```

Try adding localhost aliases to your file to test this technique.

```
127.0.0.1 application.com

127.0.0.1 application.it

127.0.0.1 application.pl
```

11.20.4.2   Setting the Locale from the Host Name

We can also set the locale from the subdomain in a very similar way inside of `ApplicationController`.

```
1 before_action :set_locale
2
3 def set_locale
4   I18n.locale = extract_locale_from_uri
5 end
6
7 def extract_locale_from_subdomain
8   parsed_locale = request.subdomains.first
9   (available_locales.include? parsed_locale) ? parsed_locale  : nil
10 end
```

11.20.5   Setting Locale from Client-Supplied Information

In specific cases, it would make sense to set the locale from client-supplied information—that is, not from the URL. This information may come from the users' preferred language (set in their browser), it can be based on the users' geographical location inferred from their IP, or users can provide it simply by choosing the locale in your application interface, saving it to their profile. This approach is more suitable for web-based applications or services, not for websites.

Helpers

11.20.5.1   Using **Accept-Language**

One source of client-supplied information would be an `Accept-Language` HTTP header. People may set this in their browser[13] or other clients (such as `curl`).

A trivial implementation of setting locale based on the `Accept-Language` header in `ApplicationController` might be the following:

```
 1 before_action :set_locale
 2
 3 def set_locale
 4   I18n.locale = extract_locale_from_accept_language_header
 5   logger.debug "* Locale set to '#{I18n.locale}'"
 6 end
 7
 8 private
 9
10 def extract_locale_from_accept_language_header
11   request.env['HTTP_ACCEPT_LANGUAGE'].scan(/^[a-z]{2}/).first
12 end
```

In real production environments, you should use much more robust code than the previous example. Try plugins such as Iain Hecker's http_accept_language14 or even Rack middleware such as locale.[15]

11.20.5.2   Using GeoIP (or Similar) Database

Yet another way of choosing the locale from client information would be to use a database for mapping the client IP to the region, such as GeoIP Lite Country.[16] The mechanics of the code would be very similar to the previous code—you would need to query the database for the user's IP and look up your preferred locale for the country/region/city returned.

11.20.5.3   User Profile

You can also provide users of your application with means to set (and possibly override) the locale in your application interface. Again, mechanics for this approach would be very similar to the previous code—you'd probably let users choose a locale from a drop-down list and save it to their profile in the database. Then you'd set the locale to this value using a `before_action` in `ApplicationController`.

---

13. http://www.w3.org/International/questions/qa-lang-priorities
14. https://github.com/iain/http_accept_language
15. https://github.com/rack/rack-contrib/blob/master/lib/rack/contrib/locale.rb
16. http://dev.maxmind.com/geoip/legacy/geolite/

11.20.6 Internationalizing Your Application

After you've set up I18n support for your Ruby on Rails application and told it which locale to use and how to preserve it between requests, you're ready for the really interesting part of the process: actually internationalizing your application.

11.20.6.1 The Public I18n API

First of all, you should be acquainted with the I18n API. The two most important methods of the I18n API are the following:

```
translate # Look up text translations.
localize  # Localize Date and Time objects to local formats.
```

These have the aliases #t and #l so you can use them like the following:

```
I18n.t 'store.title'
I18n.l Time.now
```

11.20.6.2 The Process

Take the following basic pieces of a simple Rails application as an example for describing the process.

```
 1 # config/routes.rb
 2 Rails.application.routes.draw do
 3   root "home#index"
 4 end
 5
 6 # app/controllers/home_controller.rb
 7 class HomeController < ApplicationController
 8   def index
 9     flash[:notice] = "Welcome"
10   end
11 end
12
13 # app/views/home/index.html.haml
14 %h1 Hello world!
15 %p.notice= flash[:notice]
```

The example has two strings that are currently hard-coded in English. To internationalize this code, we must replace those strings with calls to Rails' #t helper with a key that makes sense for the translation.

```
 1 # app/controllers/home_controller.rb
 2 class HomeController < ApplicationController
 3   def index
 4     flash[:notice] = t(:welcome_flash)
```

```
 5   end
 6 end
 7
 8 # app/views/home/index.html.haml
 9 %h1= t(:hello_world)
10 %p.notice= flash[:notice]
```

Now when you render this view, it will show an error message that tells you that the translations for the keys :hello_world and :welcome_flash are missing.

Rails adds a t (translate) helper method to your views so that you do not need to spell out I18n.t all the time. Additionally, this helper will catch missing translations and wrap the resulting error message into a <span class="translation_missing">.

To make the example work, you would add the missing translations into the dictionary files (thereby doing the localization part of the work):

```
1 # config/locale/en.yml
2 en:
3   hello_world: Hello World
4   welcome_flash: Welcome
5
6 # config/locale/pirate.yml
7 pirate:
8   hello_world: Ahoy World
9   welcome_flash: All aboard!
```

Note

You need to restart the server when you add or edit locale files.

You may use YAML (.yml) or plain Ruby (.rb) files for storing your translations. YAML is the preferred option among Rails developers. However, it has one big disadvantage. YAML is very sensitive to whitespace and special characters, so the application may not load your dictionary properly. Ruby files will crash your application on first request, so you can easily find what's wrong. (If you encounter any "weird issues" with YAML dictionaries, try putting the relevant portion of your dictionary into a Ruby file.)

11.20.6.3 Adding Date/Time Formats

Okay! Now let's add a timestamp to the view so we can demo the date/time localization feature as well. To localize the time format, you pass the time object to I18n.l or use Rails' #l helper method in your views.

```
1 # app/views/home/index.html.haml
```

```
2 %h1= t(:hello_world)
3 %p.notice= flash[:notice]
4 %p= l(Time.now, format: :short)
```

And in our pirate translations file, let's add a time format (it's already there in Rails' defaults for English):

```
1 # config/locale/pirate.yml
2 pirate:
3   time:
4     formats:
5       short: "arrrround %H'ish"
```

The `rails-i18n` *repository*

There's a great chance that somebody has already done much of the hard work of translating Rails' defaults for your locale. See the Rails-I18n repository at GitHub[17] for an archive of various locale files. When you put such file(s) in `config/locale/` directory, they will automatically be ready for use.

11.20.7   Organization of Locale Files

Putting translations for all parts of your application in one file per locale could be hard to manage. You can store these files in a hierarchy that makes sense to you.

For example, your `config/locale` directory could look like this:

```
|-defaults
|---es.rb
|---en.rb
|-models
|---book
|-----es.rb
|-----en.rb
|-views
|---defaults
|-----es.rb
|-----en.rb
|---books
|-----es.rb
|-----en.rb
|---users
|-----es.rb
|-----en.rb
```

---

17. https://github.com/svenfuchs/rails-i18n

```
|---navigation
|-----es.rb
|-----en.rb
```

This way, you can separate model and model attribute names from text inside views and all of those values from the "defaults" (e.g., date and time formats). Other stores for the I18n library could provide different means of such separation.

Note

The default locale loading mechanism in Rails does not load locale files in nested dictionaries, like we have here. So for this to work, we must explicitly tell Rails to look further through settings in the following:

```
1    # config/application.rb
2    config.i18n.load_path += Dir[File.join(Rails.root, 'config',
3      'locales', '**', '*.{rb,yml}')]
```

11.20.8 Looking Up Translations

11.20.8.1 Basic Lookup, Scopes, and Nested Keys

Translations are looked up by keys that can be both symbols or strings, so these calls are equivalent:

```
I18n.t :message
I18n.t 'message'
```

The `translate` method also takes a `:scope` option that can contain one or more additional keys that will be used to specify a "namespace" or scope for a translation key:

```
I18n.t :invalid, scope: [:activerecord, :errors, :messages]
```

This looks up the `:invalid` message in the Active Record error messages.

Additionally, both the key and scopes can be specified as dot-separated keys as in the following:

```
I18n.translate :"activerecord.errors.messages.invalid"
```

Thus the following four calls are equivalent:

```
I18n.t 'activerecord.errors.messages.invalid'
I18n.t 'errors.messages.invalid', scope: :activerecord
I18n.t :invalid, scope: 'activerecord.errors.messages'
```

```
I18n.t :invalid, scope: [:activerecord, :errors, :messages]
```

11.20.8.2   Default Values

When a :default option is given, its value will be returned if the translation is missing:

```
I18n.t :missing, default: 'Not here'
# => 'Not here'
```

If the :default value is a symbol, it will be used as a key and translated. One can provide multiple values as default. The first one that results in a value will be returned.

For example, the following are first tries to translate the key :missing and then the key :also_missing. As both do not yield a result, the string "Not here" will be returned:

```
I18n.t :missing, default: [:also_missing, 'Not here']
# => 'Not here'
```

11.20.8.3   Bulk and Namespace Lookup

To look up multiple translations at once, an array of keys can be passed:

```
I18n.t [:odd, :even], scope: 'activerecord.errors.messages'
# => ["must be odd", "must be even"]
```

Also, a key can translate to a (potentially nested) hash of grouped translations. For instance, one can receive *all* Active Record error messages as a hash with the following:

```
I18n.t 'activerecord.errors.messages'
# => { inclusion: "is not included in the list", exclusion: ... }
```

11.20.8.4   View Scoped Keys

Rails implements a convenient way to reference keys inside of views. Assume you have the following local file:

```
1 es:
2   books:
3     index:
4       title: "Título"
```

You can reference the value of books.index.title inside of the app/views/books/index.html.haml template by prefixing the key name with a dot. Rails will automatically fill in the scope based on the identity of the view.

```
= t '.title'
```

11.20.8.5   Interpolation

In many cases you want to abstract your translations in such a way that variables can be interpolated into the translation. For this reason, the I18n API provides an interpolation feature.

All options besides :default and :scope that are passed to translate will be interpolated to the translation:

```
I18n.backend.store_translations :en, thanks: 'Thanks, %{name}!'
I18n.translate :thanks, name: 'Jeremy'
# => 'Thanks, Jeremy!'
```

If a translation uses :default or :scope as an interpolation variable, an I18n::ReservedInterpolationKey exception is raised. If a translation expects an interpolation variable but this has not been passed to translate, an I18n::MissingInterpolationArgument exception is raised.

11.20.8.6   Pluralization

In English there are only one singular and one plural form for a given string—for example, "1 message" and "2 messages"—but other languages have different grammars with additional or fewer plural forms.[18] Thus the I18n API provides a flexible pluralization feature.

The :count interpolation variable has a special role in that it both is interpolated to the translation and used to pick a pluralization from the translations according to the pluralization rules defined by Unicode:

```
1  I18n.backend.store_translations :en, inbox: {
2    one: '1 message',
3    other: '%{count} messages'
4  }
5
6  I18n.translate :inbox, count: 2
7  # => '2 messages'
8
9  I18n.translate :inbox, count: 1
10 # => 'one message'
```

The algorithm for pluralizations in :en is as simple as the following:

```
1 entry[count == 1 ? 0 : 1]
```

The translation denoted as :one is regarded as singular versus any other value regarded as plural (including the count being zero).

---

18. http://www.unicode.org/cldr/charts/supplemental/language_plural_rules.html

If the lookup for the key does not return a hash suitable for pluralization, an `I18n::InvalidPluralizationData` exception is raised.

11.20.9 How to Store Your Custom Translations

The `Simple` backend shipped with Active Support allows you to store translations in both plain Ruby and YAML format. A Ruby hash locale file would look like this:

```
1 {
2   pt: {
3     foo: {
4       bar: "baz"
5     }
6   }
7 }
```

The equivalent YAML file would look like this:

```
1 pt:
2   foo:
3     bar: baz
```

In both cases, the top-level key is the locale. `:foo` is a namespace key and `:bar` is the key for the translation "baz."

Here is a real example from the Active Support `en.yml` translations YAML file:

```
1 en:
2   date:
3     formats:
4       default: "%Y-%m-%d"
5       short: "%b %d"
6       long: "%B %d, %Y"
```

So all the following equivalent lookups will return the `:short` date format `"%B %d"`:

```
1 I18n.t 'date.formats.short'
2 I18n.t 'formats.short', scope: :date
3 I18n.t :short, scope: 'date.formats'
4 I18n.t :short, scope: [:date, :formats]
```

Generally, we recommend using YAML as a format for storing translations.

11.20.9.1 Translations for Active Record Models

You can use the methods `Model.human_name` and `Model.human_attribute_name(attribute)` to transparently look up translations for your model and attribute names.

For example, when you add the following translations

```
1 en:
2   activerecord:
3     models:
4       user: Dude
5     attributes:
6       user:
7         login: "Handle"
8         # will translate User attribute "login" as "Handle"
```

`User.human_name` will return "Dude" and `User.human_attribute_name`
(`:login`) will return "Handle."

11.20.9.2 Error Message Scopes

Active Record validation error messages can also be translated easily. Active
Record gives you a couple of namespaces where you can place your message
translations in order to provide different messages and translation for certain
models, attributes, and/or validations. It also transparently takes single table
inheritance into account.

This gives you powerful means to flexibly adjust your messages to your application's needs.

Consider a `User` model with a `validates_presence_of` validation for the
name attribute like this:

```
1 class User < ActiveRecord::Base
2   validates_presence_of :name
3 end
```

The key for the error message in this case is `:blank`. Active Record will look up this
key in the namespaces:

```
1 activerecord.errors.models.[model_name].attributes.[attribute_name]
2 activerecord.errors.models.[model_name]
3 activerecord.errors.messages
```

Thus in our example it will try the following keys in this order and return the first result:

```
1 activerecord.errors.models.user.attributes.name.blank
2 activerecord.errors.models.user.blank
3 activerecord.errors.messages.blank
```

When your models are additionally using inheritance, then the messages are looked
up in the inheritance chain.

For example, you might have an `Admin` model inheriting from `User`:

```
1  class Admin < User
2    validates_presence_of :name
3  end
```

Then Active Record will look for messages in this order:

```
1  activerecord.errors.models.admin.attributes.title.blank
2  activerecord.errors.models.admin.blank
3  activerecord.errors.models.user.attributes.title.blank
4  activerecord.errors.models.user.blank
5  activerecord.errors.messages.blank
```

This way, you can provide special translations for various error messages at different points in your models' inheritance chain and in the attributes, models, or default scopes.

11.20.9.3 Error Message Interpolation

The translated model name, translated attribute name, and value are always available for interpolation.

So, for example, instead of the default error message `"cannot be blank"`, you could use the attribute name like `"Please fill in your %{attribute}"`.

Table 11.1 Error message interpolation

Validation interpolation	Option	Message	Interpolation
validates_confirmation_of	–	:confirmation	–
validates_acceptance_of	–	:accepted	–
validates_presence_of	–	:blank	–
validates_length_of	:within, :in	:too_short	count
validates_length_of	:within, :in	:too_long	count
validates_length_of	:is	:wrong_length	count
validates_length_of	:minimum	:too_short	count
validates_length_of	:maximum	:too_long	count
validates_format_of	–	:taken	–
validates_uniqueness_of	–	:invalid	–
validates_inclusion_of	–	:inclusion	–
validates_exclusion_of	–	:exclusion	–
validates_associated	–	:invalid	–

Helpers

(continued)

Table 11.1   Error message interpolation (continued)

Validation interpolation	Option	Message	Interpolation
validates_numericality _of	–	:not_a_number	–
validates_numericality _of	:greater_ than	:greater_than	count
validates_numericality _of	:greater _than_or _equal_to	:greater_than _or_equal_to	count
validates_numericality _of	:equal_to	:equal_to	count
validates_numericality _of	:less _than_or _equal_to	::less_than _or_equal_to	count
validates_numericality _of	:odd	:odd	–
validates_numericality _of	:even	:even	–

11.20.10   Overview of Other Built-In Methods That Provide I18n Support

Rails uses fixed strings and other localizations, such as format strings and other format information in a couple of helpers. Here's a brief overview.

11.20.10.1   Action View Helper Methods

- `distance_of_time_in_words` translates and pluralizes its result and interpolates the number of seconds, minutes, hours, and so on. See `datetime .distance_in_words`[19] translations.

- `datetime_select` and `select_month` use translated month names for populating the resulting select tag. See `date.month_names`[20] for translations. `datetime_select` also looks up the order option from `date.order`[21] (unless you pass the option explicitly). All date selection helpers translate the

---

19.   https://github.com/rails/rails/blob/4-0-stable/actionpack/lib/action_view/locale/ en.yml#L4

20.   https://github.com/rails/rails/blob/4-0-stable/activesupport/lib/active_support/ locale/en.yml#L155

21.   https://github.com/rails/rails/blob/4-0-stable/activesupport/lib/active_support/ locale/en.yml#L18

prompt using the translations in the datetime.prompts[22] scope if applicable. Note the number_to_currency, number_with_precision, number_to _percentage, number_with_delimiter, and number_to_human _size helpers use the number format settings located in the number[23] scope.

11.20.10.2   Active Record Methods

- human_name and human_attribute_name use translations for model names and attribute names if available in the activerecord.models[24] scope. They also support translations for inherited class names (e.g., for use with STI) as explained in "Error message scopes."

- ActiveRecord::Errors#generate_message (which is used by Active Record validations but may also be used manually) uses human_name and human_attribute_name. It also translates the error message and supports translations for inherited class names as explained in "Error message scopes."

- ActiveRecord::Errors#full_messages prepends the attribute name to the error message using a separator that will be looked up from activerecord .errors.format (and that defaults to "%{attribute} %{message}").

11.20.10.3   Active Support Methods

Array#to_sentence uses format settings as given in the support.array scope.

11.20.11   Exception Handling

In some contexts you might want to extend I18n's default exception handling behavior. For instance, the default exception handling does not allow to catch missing translations during automated tests easily. For this purpose, a different exception handler can be specified. The specified exception handler must be a method on the I18n module. You would add code similar to the following to your file or other kind of initializer.

```
1 module I18n
2   def just_raise_that_exception(*args)
```

22. https://github.com/rails/rails/blob/4-0-stable/actionpack/lib/action_view/locale/
en.yml#L39

23. https://github.com/rails/rails/blob/4-0-stable/activesupport/lib/active_support/
locale/en.yml#L37

24. https://github.com/rails/rails/blob/4-0-stable/activerecord/lib/active_record/
locale/en.yml#L37

Helpers

```
3       raise args.first
4    end
5 end
6
7 I18n.exception_handler = :just_raise_that_exception
```

This would reraise all caught exceptions, including `MissingTranslationData`.

11.21 `UrlHelper`

This module provides a set of methods for making links and getting URLs that depend on the routing subsystem, covered extensively in Chapter 2, "Routing," and Chapter 3, "REST, Resources, and Rails."

11.21.0.1 `button_to(name = nil, options = nil, html_options = nil, &block)`

Generates a form containing a single button that submits to the URL created by the set of options. This is the safest method to ensure that links that cause changes to your data are not triggered by search bots or accelerators. If the HTML button does not work with your layout, you can also consider using the `link_to` method (also in this module) with the `:method` modifier.

The options hash accepts the same options as the `url_for` method.

The generated form element has a class name of `button-to` to allow styling of the form itself and its children. This class name can be overridden by setting `:form_class` in `:html_options`. The `:method` option works just like the `link_to` helper. If no `:method` modifier is given, it defaults to performing a POST operation.

```
 1 button_to("New", action: "new")
 2 # => "<form method="post" action="/controller/new" class="button-to">
 3 #         <div><input value="New" type="submit" /></div>
 4 #      </form>"
 5
 6 button_to "Delete Image", { action: "delete", id: @image.id },
 7    method: :delete, data: { confirm: "Are you sure?" }
 8 # => "<form method="post" action="/images/delete/1" class="button_to">
 9 #         <div>
10 #           <input type="hidden" name="_method" value="delete" />
11 #           <input data-confirm='Are you sure?'
12 #             value="Delete Image" type="submit" />
13 #           <input name="authenticity_token" type="hidden"
14 #             value="10f2163b45388899..."/>
15 #         </div>
16 #      </form>"
```

11.21.0.2   `current_page?(options)`

Returns `true` if the current request URI was generated by the given options. For example, let's assume that we're currently rendering the `/shop/checkout` action:

```
1  current_page?(action: 'process')
2  # => false
3
4  current_page?(action: 'checkout') # controller is implied
5  # => true
6
7  current_page?(controller: 'shop', action: 'checkout')
8  # => true
```

11.21.0.3   `link_to(name = nil, options = nil,`
`html_options = nil, &block)`

One of the fundamental helper methods. Creates a link tag of the given name using a URL created by the set of options. The valid options are covered in the description of this module's `url_for` method. It's also possible to pass a string instead of an options hash to get a link tag that uses the value of the string as the href for the link. If `nil` is passed as a name, the link itself will become the name.

:data Adds custom data attributes.

method: symbol Specify an alternative HTTP verb for this request (other than GET). This modifier will dynamically create an HTML form and immediately submit the form for processing using the HTTP verb specified (`:post`, `:patch`, or `:delete`).

remote: true Allows the unobtrusive JavaScript driver to make an Ajax request to the URL instead of following the link.

The following data attributes work alongside the unobtrusive JavaScript driver:

confirm: 'question?' The unobtrusive JavaScript driver will display a JavaScript confirmation prompt with the question specified. If the user accepts, the link is processed normally; otherwise, no action is taken.

:disable_with Used by the unobtrusive JavaScript driver to provide a name for disabled versions.

Generally speaking, GET requests should be idempotent—that is, they do not modify the state of any resource on the server and can be called one or many times without a problem. Requests that modify server-side resources or trigger dangerous actions like

Helpers

deleting a record should not usually be linked with a normal hyperlink, since search bots and so-called browser accelerators can follow those links while spidering your site, leaving a trail of chaos.

If the user has JavaScript disabled, the request will always fall back to using GET, no matter what :method you have specified. This is accomplished by including a valid href attribute. If you are relying on the POST behavior, your controller code should check for it using the post?, delete?, or patch? methods of request.

As usual, the html_options will accept a hash of HTML attributes for the link tag.

```
1  = link_to "Help", help_widgets_path
2
3  = link_to "Rails", "http://rubyonrails.org/",
4      data: { confirm: "Are you sure?" }
5
6  = link_to "Delete", widget_path(@widget), method: :delete,
7      data: { confirm: "Are you sure?" }
8
9  [Renders in the browser as...]
10
11 <a href="/widgets/help">Help</a>
12
13 <a href="http://rubyonrails.org/" data-confirm="Are you sure?">Rails</a>
14
15 <a href="/widgets/42" rel="nofollow" data-method="delete"
16    data-confirm="Are you sure?">View</a>
```

11.21.0.4 `link_to_if(condition, name, options = {}, html_options = {}, &block)`

Creates a link tag using the same options as link_to if the condition is true; otherwise, only the name is output (or block is evaluated for an alternative value, if one is supplied).

11.21.0.5 `link_to_unless(condition, name, options = {}, html_options = {}, &block)`

Creates a link tag using the same options as link_to unless the condition is true, in which case only the name is output (or block is evaluated for an alternative value, if one is supplied).

11.21.0.6 `link_to_unless_current(name, options = {}, html_options = {}, &block)`

Creates a link tag using the same options as link_to unless the condition is true, in which case only the name is output (or block is evaluated for an alternative value, if one is supplied).

This method is pretty useful sometimes. Remember that the block given to `link_to_unless_current` is evaluated if the current action is the action given. So if we had a comments page and wanted to render a "Go Back" link instead of a link to the comments page, we could do something like the following:

```
1 link_to_unless_current("Comment", { controller: 'comments', action: 'new}) do
2   link_to("Go back", posts_path)
3 end
```

11.21.0.7 `mail_to(email_address, name = nil, html_options = {}, &block)`

Creates a `mailto` link tag to the specified `email_address`, which is also used as the name of the link unless `name` is specified. Additional HTML attributes for the link can be passed in `html_options`.

The `mail_to` helper has several methods for customizing the email address itself by passing special keys to `html_options`:

:subject The subject line of the email.

:body The body of the email.

:cc Add cc recipients to the email.

:bcc Add bcc recipients to the email.

Here are some examples of usages:

```
 1 mail_to "me@domain.com"
 2 # => <a href="mailto:me@domain.com">me@domain.com</a>
 3
 4 mail_to "me@domain.com", "My email"
 5 # => <a href="mailto:me@domain.com">My email</a>
 6
 7 mail_to "me@domain.com", "My email", cc: "ccaddress@domain.com",
 8   subject: "This is an email"
 9 # => <a href="mailto:me@domain.com?cc=ccaddress@domain.com&
10     subject=This%20is%20an%20email">My email</a>
```

Note

In previous versions of Rails, the `mail_to` helper provided options for encoding the email address to hinder email harvesters. If your application is still dependent on these options, add the `actionview-encoded_mail_to` gem to your `Gemfile`.

Helpers

11.21.0.8   Redirecting Back

If you pass the magic symbol `:back` to any method that uses `url_for` under the covers (`redirect_to`, etc.), the contents of the `HTTP_REFERRER` request header will be returned. (If a referrer is not set for the current request, it will return `javascript:history.back()` to try to make the browser go back one page.)

```
url_for(:back)
# => "javascript:history.back()"
```

11.22   Writing Your Own View Helpers

As you develop an application in Rails, you should be on the lookout for opportunities to refactor duplicated view code into your own helper methods. As you think of these helpers, you add them to one of the helper modules defined in the `app/helpers` folder of your application.

There is an art to effectively writing helper methods, similar in nature to what it takes to write effective APIs. Helper methods are basically a custom, application-level API for your view code. It is difficult to teach API design in a book form. It's the sort of knowledge that you gain by apprenticing with more experienced programmers and lots of trial and error. Nevertheless, in this section, we'll review some varied use cases and implementation styles that we hope will inspire you in your application design.

11.22.1   Small Optimizations: The Title Helper

Here is a simple helper method that has been of use to me on many projects now. It's called `page_title`, and it combines two simple functions essential to a good HTML document:

- Setting the `title` of the page in the document's `head`

- Setting the content of the page's `h1` element

This helper assumes that you want the `title` and `h1` elements of the page to be the same and has a dependency on your application template. The code for the helper is in Listing 11.3 and would be added to `app/helpers/application_helper.rb`, since it is applicable to all views.

Listing 11.3 The `page_title` Helper
```
1 def page_title(name)
2   content_for(:title) { name }
3   content_tag("h1", name)
4 end
```

First it sets content to be yielded in the layout as `:title` and then it outputs an h1 element containing the same text. I could have used string interpolation on the second line, such as `"<h1>#{name}</h1>"`, but it would have been sloppier than using the built-in Rails helper method `content_tag`.

My application template is now written to `yield :title` so that it gets the page title.

```
1  %html
2    %head
3      %title= yield :title
```

As should be obvious, you call the `page_title` method in your view template where you want to have an h1 element:

```
1  - page_title "New User"
2  = form_for(user) do |f|
3    ...
```

11.22.2 Encapsulating View Logic: The `photo_for` Helper

Here's another relatively simple helper. This time, instead of simply outputting data, we are encapsulating some view logic that decides whether to display a user's profile photo or a placeholder image. It's logic that you would otherwise have to repeat over and over again throughout your application.

The dependency (or contract) for this particular helper is that the user object being passed in has a `profile_photo` associated to it, which is an attachment model based on Rick Olson's old attachment_fu Rails plugin. The code in Listing 11.4 should be easy enough to understand without delving into the details of `attachment_fu`. Since this is an example, I broke out the logic for setting `src` into an `if/else` structure; otherwise, this would be a perfect place to use Ruby's ternary operator.

Listing 11.4 The `photo_for` Helper Encapsulating Common View Logic

```
1  def photo_for(user, size=:thumb)
2    if user.profile_photo
3      src = user.profile_photo.public_filename(size)
4    else
5      src = 'user_placeholder.png'
6    end
7    link_to(image_tag(src), user_path(user))
8  end
```

Tim Says ...

Luckily, the latest generation of attachment plugins such as Paperclip and
CarrierWave use a NullObject pattern to alleviate the need for you to do this
sort of thing.

11.22.3 Smart View: The **breadcrumbs** Helper

Lots of web applications feature user-interface concepts called breadcrumbs. They
are made by creating a list of links, positioned near the top of the page, that display
how far the user has navigated into a hierarchically organized application. I think
it makes sense to extract breadcrumb logic into its own helper method instead of
leaving it in a layout template.

The trick to our example implementation (shown in Listing 11.5) is to use the
presence of helper methods exposed by the controller, on a convention specific to your
application, to determine whether to add elements to an array of breadcrumb links.

Listing 11.5 breadcrumbs Helper Method for a Corporate Directory Application

```
 1 def breadcrumbs
 2   return if controller.controller_name == 'home'
 3
 4   html = [link_to('Home', root_path)]
 5
 6   # first level
 7   html << link_to(company.name, company) if respond_to? :company
 8
 9   # second level
10   html << link_to(department.name, department) if respond_to? :department
11
12   # third and final level
13   html << link_to(employee.name, employee) if respond_to? :employee
14
15   html.join(' > ').html_safe
16 end
```

Here's the line-by-line explanation of the code, noting where certain application-
design assumptions are made:

On line 2, we abort execution if we're in the context of the application's homep-
age controller, since its pages don't ever need breadcrumbs. A simple return with no
value implicitly returns nil, which is fine for our purposes. Nothing will be output
to the layout template.

On line 4, we are starting to build an array of HTML links, held in the html
local variable, which will ultimately hold the contents of our breadcrumb trail. The

first link of the breadcrumb trail always points to the home page of the application, which of course will vary, but since it's always there, we use it to initialize the array. In this example, it uses a named route called `root_path`.

After the `html` array is initialized, all we have to do is check for the presence of the methods returning objects that make up the hierarchy (lines 7 to 13). It is assumed that if a department is being displayed, its parent company will also be in scope. If an employee is being displayed, both department and company will be in scope as well. This is not just an arbitrary design choice. It is a common pattern in Rails applications that are modeled on REST principles and use nested resource routes.

Finally, on line 15, the array of HTML links is joined with the > character to give the entire string the traditional breadcrumb appearance. The call to `html_safe` tells the rendering system that this is HTML code and we're cool with that—don't sanitize it!

11.23   Wrapping and Generalizing Partials

I don't think that partials (by themselves) lead to particularly elegant or concise template code. Whenever there's a shared partial template that gets used over and over again in my application, I will take the time to wrap it up in a custom helper method that conveys its purpose and formalizes its parameters. If appropriate, I might even generalize its implementation to make it more of a lightweight, reusable component. (Gasp!)

11.23.1   A `tiles` Helper

Let's trace the steps to writing a helper method that wraps what I consider to be a general-purpose partial. Listing 11.6 contains code for a partial for a piece of a user interface that is common to many applications and generally referred to as a tile. It pairs a small thumbnail photo of something on the left side of the widget with a linked name and description on the right.

Tiles can also represent other models in your application, such as users and files. As I mentioned, tiles are a very common construct in modern user interfaces and operating systems. So let's take the cities tiles partial and transform it into something that can be used to display other types of data.

Note

I realize that it has become passé to use HTML tables, and I happen to agree that `div`-based layouts plus CSS are a lot more fun and flexible to work with. However, for the sake of simplicity in this example, and since the UI structure we're describing is tabular, I've decided to structure it using a table.

Listing 11.6   A Tiles Partial Prior to Wrapping and Generalization

```
1  %table.cities.tiles
2    - cities.in_groups_of(columns) do |row|
3      %tr
4        - row.each do |city|
5          %td[city]
6            .left
7              = image_tag(city.photo.url(:thumb))
8            .right
9              .title
10               = city.name
11             .description
12               = city.description
```

11.23.1.1   Explanation of the Tiles Partial Code

Since we're going to transform this city-specific partial into a generalized UI component, I want to make sure that the code we start with makes absolute sense to you first. Before proceeding, I'm going through the implementation line by line and explaining what everything in Listing 11.6 does.

Line 1 opens up the partial with a table element and gives it semantically significant CSS classes so that the table and its contents can be properly styled.

Line 2 leverages a useful `Array` extension method provided by Active Support called `in_groups_of`. It uses both of the local variables: `cities` and `columns`. Both will need to be passed into this partial using the `:locals` option of the `render :partial` method. The `cities` variable will hold the list of cities to be displayed, and `columns` is an integer representing how many city tiles each row should contain. A loop iterates over the number of rows that will be displayed in this table.

Line 3 begins a table row using the `tr` element.

Line 4 begins a loop over the tiles for each row to be displayed, yielding a `city` for each.

Line 5 opens a `td` element and uses Haml's *object reference* notation to autogenerate a `dom_id` attribute for the table cell in the style of `city_98`, `city_99`, and so on.

Line 6 opens a `div` element for the left side of the tile and has the CSS class name needed so that it can be styled properly.

Line 7 calls the `image_tag` helper to insert a thumbnail photo of the city.

Skipping along, lines 9–10 insert the content for the `.title div` element—in this case, the name and state of the city.

Line 12 directly invokes the `description` method.

11.23.1.2   Calling the Tiles Partial Code

In order to use this partial, we have to call `render :partial` with the two required parameters specified in the `:locals` hash:

```
1 = render "cities/tiles", cities: @user.cities, columns: 3
```

I'm guessing that most experienced Rails developers have written some partial code similar to this and tried to figure out a way to include default values for some of the parameters. In this case, it would be really nice to not have to specify `:columns` all the time, since in most cases we want there to be three.

The problem is that since the parameters are passed via the `:locals` hash and become local variables, there isn't an easy way to insert a default value in the partial itself. If you left off the `columns: n` part of your partial call, Rails would bomb with an exception about `columns` not being a local variable or method. It's not the same as an instance variable, which defaults to `nil` and can be used willy-nilly.

Experienced Rubyists probably know that you can use the `defined?` method to figure out whether a local variable is in scope or not, but the resulting code would be very ugly. The following code might be considered elegant, but it doesn't work![25]

```
columns = 3 unless defined? columns
```

Instead of teaching you how to jump through annoying Ruby idiom hoops, I'll show you how to tackle this challenge the Rails way, and that is where we can start discussing the helper wrapping technique.

Tim Says ...

Obie might not want to make you jump through Ruby idiom hoops, but I don't mind.

11.23.1.3   Write the Helper Method

First, I'll add a new helper method to the `CitiesHelper` module of my application, like in Listing 11.7. It's going to be fairly simple at first. In thinking about the name of the method, it occurs to me that I like the way that `tiled(cities)` will read instead of `tiles(cities)`, so I name it that way.

---

25. If you want to know why it doesn't work, you'll have to buy the first book in this series: *The Ruby Way* (ISBN: 0-6723288-4-4).

Helpers

Listing 11.7 The `CitiesHelper` Tiled Method
```
1 module CitiesHelper
2   def tiled(cities, columns=3)
3     render "cities/tiles", cities: cities, columns: columns
4   end
5 end
```

Right from the start, I can take care of that default `columns` parameter by giving the helper method parameter for columns a default value. That's just a normal feature of Ruby. Now instead of specifying the `render :partial` call in my view template, I can simply write `= tiled(cities)`, which is considerably more elegant and terse. It also serves to decouple the implementation of the tiled city table from the view. If I need to change the way that the tiled table is rendered in the future, I just have to do it in one place: the helper method.

11.23.2   Generalizing Partials

Now that we've set the stage, the fun can begin. The first thing we'll do is move the helper method to the `ApplicationHelper` module so that it's available to all view templates. We'll also move the partial template file to `app/views/shared/_tiled_table.html.haml` to denote that it isn't associated with a particular kind of view and to more accurately convey its use. As a matter of good code style, I also do a sweep through the implementation and generalize the identifiers appropriately. The reference to `cities` on line 2 becomes `collection`. The block variable `city` on line 4 becomes `item`. Listing 11.8 has the new partial code.

Listing 11.8 Tiles Partial Code with Revised Naming
```
 1 %table.tiles
 2   - collection.in_groups_of(columns) do |row|
 3     %tr
 4       - row.each do |item|
 5         %td[item]
 6           .left
 7             = image_tag(item.photo.public_filename(:thumb))
 8           .right
 9             .title
10               = item.name
11             .description
12               = item.description
```

There's still the matter of a contract between this partial code and the objects that it is rendering. Namely, they must respond to the following messages:

photo, name, and description. A survey of other models in my application reveals that I need more flexibility. Some things have names, but others have titles. Sometimes I want the description to appear under the name of the object represented, but other times I want to be able to insert additional data about the object plus some links.

11.23.2.1 Lambda: The Ultimate Flexibility

Ruby allows you to store references to anonymous methods (also known as *procs* or *lambdas*) and call them whenever you want.[26] Knowing this capability is there, what becomes possible? For starters, we can use lambdas to pass in blocks of code that will fill in parts of our partial dynamically.

For example, the current code for showing the thumbnail is a big problem. Since the code varies greatly depending on the object being handled, I want to be able to pass in instructions for how to get a thumbnail image without having to resort to big if/else statements or putting view logic in my model classes. Please take a moment to understand the problem I'm describing, and then take a look at how we solve it in Listing 11.9. Hint: The thumbnail, link, title, and description variables hold lambdas!

Listing 11.9 Tiles Partial Code Refactored to Use Lambdas

```
1  .left
2    = link_to thumbnail.call(item), link.call(item)
3  .right
4    .title
5      = link_to title.call(item), link.call(item)
6    .description
7      = description.call(item)
```

Notice that in Listing 11.9, the contents of the left and right div elements come from variables containing lambdas. On line 2, we make a call to link_to, and both of its arguments are dynamic. A similar construct on line 5 takes care of generating the title link. In both cases, the first lambda should return the output of a call to image_tag and the second should return a URL. In all of these lambda usages, the item currently being rendered is passed to the lambdas as a block variable.

---

26. If you're familiar with Ruby already, you might know that Proc.new is an alternate way to create anonymous blocks of code. I prefer lambda, at least in Ruby 1.9, because of subtle behavior differences. Lambda blocks check the arity of the argument list passed to them when call is invoked, and explicitly calling return in a lambda block works correctly.

Helpers

Wilson Says …

Things like `link.call(item)` could potentially look even sassier as `link[item]`, except that you'll shoot your eye out doing it. (`Proc#[]` is an alias for `Proc#call`.)

11.23.2.2   The New Tiled Helper Method

If you now direct your attention to Listing 11.10, you'll notice that the `tiled` method is changed considerably. In order to keep my positional argument list down to a manageable size, I've switched over to taking a hash of options as the last parameter to the `tiled` method. This approach is useful, and it mimics the way that almost all helper methods take options in Rails.

Default values are provided for all parameters, and they are all passed along to the partial via the `:locals` hash given to `render`.

Listing 11.10   The Tiled Collection Helper Method with Lambda Parameters

```
 1 module ApplicationHelper
 2
 3   def tiled(collection, opts={})
 4     opts[:columns] ||= 3
 5
 6     opts[:thumbnail] ||= lambda do |item|
 7       image_tag(item.photo.url(:thumb))
 8     end
 9
10     opts[:title] ||= lambda { |item| item.to_s }
11
12     opts[:description] ||= lambda { |item| item.description }
13
14     opts[:link] ||= lambda { |item| item }
15
16     render "shared/tiled_table",
17       collection: collection,
18       columns: opts[:columns],
19       link: opts[:link],
20       thumbnail: opts[:thumbnail],
21       title: opts[:title],
22       description: opts[:description]
23   end
24 end
```

Finally, to wrap up this example, here's a snippet showing how to invoke our new `tiled` helper method from a template, overriding the default behavior for links:

```
1 tiled(cities, link: lambda { |city| showcase_city_path(city) })
```

The `showcase_city_path` method is available to the lambda block since it is a closure, meaning that it inherits the execution context in which it is created.

11.24 Conclusion

This very long chapter served as a thorough reference of helper methods, both those provided by Rails and ideas for ones that you will write yourself. Effective use of helper methods leads to more elegant and maintainable view templates. At this point you should also have a good overview about how I18n support in Ruby on Rails works, and you should be ready to start translating your project.

Before we fully conclude our coverage of Action View, we'll jump into the world of Ajax and JavaScript. Arguably, one of the main reasons for Rails' continued popularity is its support for those two crucial technologies of Web 2.0.

This chapter is published under the Creative Commons Attribution-ShareAlike 4.0 license, `http://creativecommons.org/licenses/by-sa/4.0/`.

CHAPTER 12

Haml

HAML gave us a great take on how views can also be done. It looks a little cryptic at first, but don't let that shake you off. Once you internalize the meaning of %, #, and . it should be all good (and you already know most just from CSS)....Additionally, I can't help but have respect for a Canadian who manages to swear more than I did during my vendoritis rant and drink beer at the same time. A perfect example of the diversity in the Rails community. Very much part of what makes us special.

—David talking about Haml and Hampton Catlin[1]

Haml[2] is a "whitespace-sensitive" HTML templating engine that uses indentation to determine the hierarchy of an HTML document. Haml was created because its creator, Hampton Catlin, was tired of having to type markup and wanted all his output code to be beautifully formatted. What he invented was a new templating engine that removed a lot of noisy boilerplate, such as angle brackets (from ERb), and did away with the need to close blocks and HTML tags.

We love Haml because it's truly minimal, allowing a developer to focus simply on the structure of the page and not on the content. Today it's common to keep view logic out of your templates, but that directive has been a guiding principle of Haml since its beginning. According to the 2012 Ruby Survey,[3] 36.96 percent of Rubyists prefer Haml over ERb, and 15.84 percent demand it in their projects. Haml is also the standard templating engine at various professional Ruby agencies, such as Hashrocket, Envy Labs, Remarkable Labs, and Astrails.

---

1. http://david.heinemeierhansson.com/arc/2006_09.html
2. http://haml.info
3. http://survey.hamptoncatlin.com/survey/stats

In this chapter, we'll cover the fundamentals of Haml, from creating HTML elements to using filters to create other kinds of textual content embedded in your document.

12.1 Getting Started

To start using the Haml template language over ERb in your project, first add the `haml-rails` gem to your `Gemfile` and run `bundle install`.

```
# Gemfile
gem 'haml-rails'
```

The benefit of using `haml-rails` over simply the `haml` gem is it adds support for Rails-specific features. For instance, when you use a controller or scaffold generator, `haml-rails` will generate Haml views instead of using the Rails default of ERb. The `haml-rails` gem also configures Haml templates to work with Rails 4 cache digests out of the box.

12.2 The Basics

In this section, we'll cover how to create HTML elements and attributes using Haml.

12.2.1 Creating an Element

To create an HTML element in Haml, one simply needs to prefix the percent character (`%`) to an element name. The element name can be any string, allowing you to use newly added HTML5 elements, such as `header`.

Haml

```
%header content
```

HTML

```
<header>content</header>
```

Haml will automatically handle generating opening and closing tags for the element on compilation. Not only does this make templates more concise and clean, it also eliminates common errors such forgetting to not close an HTML tags.

12.2.2 Attributes

Attributes in Haml are defined using two styles. The first style involves defining attributes between curly braces (`{}`). These attribute "brackets" are really just Ruby hashes and are evaluated as such. Because of this, local variables and Ruby logic can be used when defining attributes.

```
%a{ title: @article.title, href: article_path(@article) } Title
```

The second style follows the more traditional way of defining HTML attributes using brackets. Note that attributes are separated by white space, not commas.

```
%a(title=@article.title href=article_path(@article)) Title
```

Multiline Attributes

Attribute hashes can be separated on multiple lines for readability. All new lines must be placed right after the comma:

```
1  %a{ title: @article.title,
2      href: article_path(@article) } Title
```

12.2.2.1 Data Attributes

Introduced with HTML5, data attributes allow custom data to be embedded in any HTML element by prefixing an attribute with `data-`. Instead of littering the attribute hash with multiple attribute keys prefixed with `data-`, one can define all their data attributes in a nested hash associated with the key `:data`, like this:

Haml

```
%article{ data: { author_id: 1 } } Lorem Ipsum...
```

HTML

```
<article data-author-id='123'>Lorem Ipsum...</article>
```

Note that underscores are automatically replaced with a hyphen. Not that you'd want to, but you can change this behavior by setting the Haml configuration option `hyphenate_data_attrs` to `false`. (Haml configuration options are covered in detail later in this chapter.)

It's also possible to nest data hashes more than one level to reduce verbosity when attributes share common roots.

Haml

```
%article{ data: { author: {id: 1, name: "Kevin Wu" } } } Lorem Ipsum...
```

HTML

```
<article data-author-id='123' data-author-name='Kevin Wu'>Lorem Ipsum...</article>
```

12.2.2.2 Boolean Attributes

In HTML, there exists certain attributes that do not have a value associated with them, such as `required`.

```
<input type="text" required>
```

These are referred to as *boolean* attributes in Haml, since their value does not matter—only that they're present. To represent these attributes in using the hash-style attribute syntax, set the value of the attribute to `true`.

```
%input{ type: 'text', required: true }
```

Otherwise, if you're using the HTML attribute style syntax, a boolean value doesn't have to be set at all.

```
%input(type="text" required)
```

XHTML

If the format of Haml is set to `:xhtml`, boolean attributes will be set to their name. To illustrate, given the previous example, Haml would render the following HTML:

```
<input type="text" required="required" />
```

12.2.3 Classes and IDs

Haml was designed to promote the DRY principle (not repeating code unnecessarily). As such, it provides a shorthand syntax for adding id and class attributes to an element. The syntax is borrowed from CSS, where ids are represented by a pound (#) and classes by a period (.). Both of these signs must be placed immediately after the element and before an attributes hash.

Haml

```
1 #content
2   .entry.featured
3     %h3.title Haml
4     %p.body Lorem Ipsum...
```

HTML

```
1 <div id='content'>
2   <div class='entry featured'>
3     <h3 class='title'>Haml</h3>
4     <p class='body'>Lorem Ipsum...</p>
5   </div>
6 </div>
```

As the previous example shows, multiple class names can be specified similarly to CSS by chaining the class names together with periods. In a slightly more complicated scenario, the shortcut CSS style class and id syntax can be combined with longhand attributes. Both values are merged together when compiled down to HTML.

Haml

```
%article.featured{ class: @article.visibility }
```

HTML

```
<article class='feature visible'>...</article>
```

Haml has some serious tricks up its sleeves for dealing with complex id and class attributes. For instance, an array of class names will automatically be joined with a space.

Haml

```
%article{ class: [@article.visibility, @article.category] }
```

HTML

```
<article class='visible breakingnews'>...</article>
```

Arrays of id values will be joined with an underscore.

Haml

```
%article{ id: [@article.category, :article, @article.id] }
```

HTML

```
<article id='sports_article_1234'>...</article>
```

Haml

Note that the array is flattened and any elements that evaluate to false or nil will be dropped automatically. This lets you do some pretty clever tricks at the possible expense of readability and maintainability.

```
1 %article{ class: [@article.visibility,
2   @article.published_at < 4.hours.ago && 'breakingnews'] }
```

In the example, if the article was published less than four hours ago, then `breakingnews` will be added a one of the CSS classes of the element. While we're on the subject, remember that it is advisable to migrate this kind of logic into your Ruby classes. In this particular example, we might give the `Article` class (or one of its presenters or decorator classes) a `breakingnews?` method and use it instead of inlining the business logic.

```
1 def breaking?
2   published_at < 4.hours.ago
3 end
```

```
%article{ class: [@article.visibility, @article.breaking? &&
'breakingnews'] }
```

If `breaking?` returns false, then the Ruby expression short-circuits to false, and Haml ignores that particular class name.

12.2.4 Implicit Divs
The default elements of Haml are divs. Since they are used so often in markup, one can simply define a div with a class or id using `.` or `#` respectively.

Haml

```
1 #container
2   .content Lorem Ipsum...
```

HTML

```
1 <div id="container">
2   <div class="content">
3     Lorem Ipsum...
4   </div>
5 </div>
```

Implicit Div Creation

Not having to specify div tags explicitly helps your markup be more semantic from the start, placing focus on the intention of the div instead of treating it as just another markup container. It's also one of the main reasons that we recommend Haml over ERb. We believe that Haml templates lessen mental burden by communicating the structure of your DOM in way that maps cleanly to the CSS that will be applied to the document.

12.2.5 Empty Tags

In HTML, there are certain elements that don't require a closing tag, such as `br`.[4] By default, Haml will not add a closing tag for the following tags:

- `area`
- `base`
- `br`
- `col`
- `hr`
- `img`
- `input`
- `link`
- `meta`
- `param`

To illustrate, consider the following example:

```
%hr
```

would render HTML

```
<hr>
```

or XHTML

```
<hr />
```

Adding a forward slash character (`/`) at the end of a tag definition causes Haml to treat it as being an empty element. The list of empty tags Haml uses can be overridden using the `autoclose` configuration setting. Haml configuration options are covered in detail later in this chapter.

---

4. For a definitive explanation of why some HTML elements like `<br/>` close themselves, while others like `<script>` need a closing tag, read `http://www.colorglare.com/2014/02/03/to-close-or-not-to-close.html`

12.3   Doctype

A doctype must be the first item in any HTML document. By including the characters ! ! ! at the beginning of a template, Haml will automatically generate a doctype based on the configuration option :format, set to :html5 by default. Adding ! ! ! to a template would result in the following HTML:

```
<!DOCTYPE html>
```

Haml also allows the specifying of a specific doctype after ! ! !. A complete listing of supported doctypes can be found on Haml's reference website.[5]

12.4   Comments

There are two types of comments in Haml: those that appear in rendered HTML and those that don't.

12.4.1   HTML Comments

To leave a comment that will be rendered by Haml, place a forward slash (/) at the beginning of the line you want commented. Anything nested under that line will also be commented out.

```
/ Some comment
```

```
<!-- Some comment -->
```

You can use this feature to produce Internet Explorer conditional comments by suffixing the condition in square brackets like this:

```
/[if lt IE 9]
```

12.4.2   Haml Comments

Besides conditional comments for targeting Internet Explorer, comments left in your markup are meant to communicate a message to other developers working with the template. These messages should not be rendered to the browser, as they are specific to your team. In Haml, starting a line with -# ensures any text following the pound sign isn't rendered at all.

Haml

```
-# Some important comment...
%h1 The Rails 4 Way
```

---

5. http://haml.info/docs/yardoc/file.REFERENCE.html#doctype_

HTML

```
<h1>The Rails 4 Way</h1>
```

If any text is nested beneath this kind of *silent comment*, it will also be omitted from the resulting output.

12.5 Evaluating Ruby Code

Somewhat similar to ERb, using the equals character (=) results in Haml evaluating Ruby code following the character and outputting the result into the document.

Haml

```
%p= %w(foo bar).join(' ')
```

HTML

```
<p>foo bar</p>
```

Alternatively, using the hyphen character (-) evaluates Ruby code but doesn't insert its output into the resulting document. This is commonly used in combination with if/else statements and loops.

```
- if flash.notice
  .notice= flash.notice
```

Note that Ruby blocks don't need to be explicitly closed in Haml. As seen in the previous example, any indentation beneath a Ruby evaluation command indicates a block.

Kevin Says ...

> Do not use - to set variables. If you find yourself doing so, this is an indication that you need to create some form of view object, such as a presenter or decorator.

Lines of Ruby code can be broken up over multiple lines as long as each line except the last ends with a comma.

```
= image_tag post.mage_url,
    class: 'featured-image'
```

Haml

12.5.1   Interpolation

Ruby code can be interpolated in two ways in Haml: inline with plain text using #{ }
or using string interpolation in combination with =. To illustrate, the following two
lines of Haml code samples are equivalent:

```
%p By: #{post.author_name}
%p= "By: #{post.author_name}"
```

12.5.2   Escaping/Unescaping HTML

To match the default Rails XSS protection scheme, Haml will sanitize any HTML-
sensitive characters from the output of =. This results in any = call to behave like &=.

Haml

```
&= "Cookies & Cream"
```

HTML

```
Cookies &amp; Cream
```

Alternatively, to unescape HTML with Haml, simply use != instead of =. If the
Haml configuration option escape_html is set to false, then any call to = will
behave like !=. (You probably will never want to do that.)

Haml

```
!= "Remember the awful <blink> tag?"
```

HTML

```
Remember the awful <blink> tag?
```

12.5.3   Escaping the First Character of a Line

On rare occasion, you might want to start a line of your template with a character
such as = that would normally be interpreted. You may escape the first character of
a line using a backslash.

Haml

```
%p
  \= equality for all =
```

HTML

```
<p>
  = equality for all =
</p>
```

12.5.4   Multiline Declarations

Haml is meant to be used for layout and design. Although one can technically write multiline declarations within a template, the creators of Haml made this intentionally awkward to discourage people from doing so.

If you for some reason do need declarations that span multiple lines in a template, you can do so by adding multiline operator (|) to the end of each line.

```
1  #content
2    %p= h( |
3      "While possible to write" +            |
4      "multiline Ruby code, " +              |
5      "it is not the Haml way," +            |
6      "as you should eliminate as much Ruby" +  |
7      "in your views as possible.")          |
```

We highly recommend extracting multiline Ruby code into helpers, decorators, or presenters.

12.6   Helpers

Haml provides a variety of helpers that are useful for day-to-day development, such as creating list items for each item in a collection and setting CSS ids and classes based on a model or controller.

12.6.1   Object Reference **[ ]**

Given an object, such as an Active Record instance, Haml can output an HTML element with the id and class attributes set by that object via the [ ] operator. For instance, assuming @post is an instance of a Post class with an id value of 1, then the template code

```
1  %li[@post]
2    %h4= @post.title
3    = @post.excerpt
```

renders

```
<li class='post' id='post_1'>...</li>
```

Haml

This is similar to using Rails helpers `div_for` and `content_tag_for`, covered in Chapter 11, "All about Helpers."

12.6.2 `page_class`

Returns the name of the current controller and action to be used with the `class` attribute of an HTML element. This is commonly used with the `body` element to allow for easy style targeting based on a particular controller or action. To illustrate, assuming the current controller is `PostsController` and action `index`,

```
%body{ class: page_class }
```

renders

```
<body class='posts index'>
```

12.6.3 `list_of(enum, opts = {}) { |item| ... }`

Given an `Enumerable` object and a block, the `list_of` method will iterate and yield the results of the block into sequential `<li>` elements.

Haml

```
1 %ul
2   = list_of [1, 2, 3] do |item|
3     Number #{item}
```

HTML

```
1 <ul>
2     <li>Number 1</li>
3     <li>Number 2</li>
4     <li>Number 3</li>
5 </ul>
```

12.7 Filters

Haml ships with a collection of filters that allows you to pass arbitrary blocks of text content as input to another processor, with the resulting output inserted into the document. The syntax for using a filter is a colon followed by the name of the filter. For example, to use the markdown filter,

```
1 :markdown
2   # The Rails 4 Way
3
4   Some awesome **Rails**-related content.
```

renders

```
1 <h1>The Rails 4 Way</h1>
2
3 <p>Some awesome <strong>Rails</strong>-related content.</p>
```

Here is a table of all the filters that Haml supports by default:

Table 12.1   Default Haml filters

`:cdata`	Surrounds the filtered text with CDATA tags.
`:coffee`	Compiles filtered text into JavaScript using CoffeeScript.
`:css`	Surrounds the filtered text with `style` tags.
`:ERb`	Parses the filtered text with ERb. All Embedded Ruby code is evaluated in the same context as the Haml template.
`:escaped`	Escapes filtered text.
`:javascript`	Surrounds the filtered text with `script` tag.
`:less`	Compiles filtered text into CSS using Less.
`:markdown`	Parses the filtered text with Markdown.
`:plain`	Does not parse filtered text. Can be used to insert chunks of HTML that will be inserted as is without going through Haml.
`:preserve`	Inserts filtered text with whitespace preserved.
`:ruby`	Parses the filtered text with the Ruby interpreter. Ruby code is evaluated in the same context as the Haml template.
`:sass`	Compiles filtered text into CSS using Sass.
`:scss`	Same as the `:sass` filter, except it uses the SCSS syntax to produce the CSS output.

Some filters require external gems to be added to your `Gemfile` in order to work. For instance, the `:markdown` filter requires a markdown gem, such as `redcarpet`.

12.8   Haml and Content

In Chris Eppstein's blog post "Haml Sucks for Content,"[6] he stated his opinions on why one shouldn't use Haml to build content:

---

6. `http://chriseppstein.github.io/blog/2010/02/08/haml-sucks-for-content`

Haml

Haml's use of CSS syntax for IDs and class names should make it very clear: The markup you write in Haml is intended to be styled by your stylesheets. Conversely, content does not usually have specific styling—it is styled by tags.

Essentially, what Chris was trying to convey is to not use native Haml syntax for creating anything other than skeletal (or structural) HTML markup. Use of filters to inline reader content, such as in this example using the `:markdown` filter,

```
1 %p
2    Do
3    %strong not
4    use
5    %a{ href: "http://haml.info" } Haml
6    for content.
```

is equivalent to the following markdown within a filter:

```
1 :markdown
2    Do **not* use [Haml](http://haml.info) for content.
```

We like this idea but admit that your mileage may vary. It really depends on the type of project you're working on and the capabilities of the person that will be maintaining the Haml template source files.

12.9 Configuration Options

Haml provides various configuration options to control exactly how markup is rendered. Options can be set by setting the `Haml::Template.options` hash in a Rails initializer.

```
# config/initializers/haml.rb
Haml::Template.options[:format] = :html5
```

12.9.1 `autoclose`

The `autoclose` option accepts an array of all tags that Haml should self-close if no content is present. Defaults to `['meta', 'img', 'link', 'br', 'hr', 'input', 'area', 'param', 'col', 'base']`.

12.9.2 `cdata`

Determines if Haml will include CDATA sections around JavaScript and CSS blocks when using the `:javascript` and `:css` filters, respectively.

When `format` is set to `html`, it defaults to false. If the `format` is `xhtml`, `cdata` will always be set to true and cannot be overridden.

This option also affects the filters * :sass, * :scss, * :less, and * :coffeescript.

12.9.3 `compiler_class`
The compiler class to use when compiling Haml to HTML. Defaults to Haml::Compiler.

12.9.4 `Encoding`
The default encoding for HTML output is Encoding.default_internal. If that is not set, the default is the encoding of the Haml template.

The encoding option can be set to either a string or an Encoding object.

12.9.5 `escape_attrs`
If set to true (default), will escape all HTML-sensitive characters in attributes.

12.9.6 `escape_html`
When Haml is used with a Rails project, the escape_html option is automatically set to true to match Rails' XSS protection scheme. This causes = to behave like &= in Haml templates.

12.9.7 `format`
Specifies the output format of a Haml template. By default, it's set to :html5.

Other options include the following:

- :html4
- :xhtml. Will cause Haml to automatically generate self-closing tags and wrap the output of JavaScript and CSS filters inside CDATA.

12.9.8 `hyphenate_data_attrs`
Haml converts all underscores in all data attributes to hyphens by default. To disable this functionality, set hyphenate_data_attrs to false.

12.9.9 `mime_type`
The MIME type that rendered Haml templates are servered with. If this is set to text/xml, then the format will be overridden to :xhtml, even if it has been set to :html4 or :html5.

12.9.10 `parser_class`
The parser class to use. Defaults to Haml::Parser.

Haml

12.9.11 `preserve`

The `preserve` option accepts that an array of all tags should have their newlines preserved using the `preserve` helper. Defaults to `['textarea', 'pre']`.

12.9.12 `remove_whitespace`

Setting to `true` causes all tags to be treated as if whitespace removal Haml operators are present. Defaults to `false`.

12.9.13 `ugly`

Haml does not attempt to format or indent the output HTML of a rendered template. By default, `ugly` is set to `false` in every Rails environment except `production`. This enables you to view the rendered HTML in a pleasing format when you're in development but yields higher performance in production.

12.10   Conclusion

In this chapter, we learned how Haml helps developers create clear, well-indented markup in your Rails applications. In the following chapter, we will cover how to manage sessions with Active Record, Memcached, and cookies.

CHAPTER 13

Session Management

I'd hate to wake up some morning and find out that you weren't you!

— Dr. Miles J. Binnell in *Invasion of the Body Snatchers*

HTTP is a stateless protocol. Without the concept of a session (a concept not unique to Rails), there'd be no way to know that any HTTP request was related to another one. You'd never have an easy way to know who is accessing your application! Identification of your user (and, presumably, authentication) would have to happen on each and every request handled by the server.[1]

Luckily, whenever a new user accesses our Rails application, a new session is automatically created. Using the session, we can maintain just enough server-side state to make our lives as web programmers significantly easier.

We use the word *session* to refer both to the time that a user is actively using the application as well as to the persistent hash data structure that we keep around for that user. That data structure takes the form of a hash, identified by a unique session id, a 32-character string of random hex numbers. When a new session is created, Rails automatically sends a cookie to the browser containing the session id for future reference. From that point on, each request from the browser sends the session id back to the server, and continuity can be maintained.

The Rails way to design web applications dictates minimal use of the session for storage of stateful data. In keeping with the *share nothing* philosophy embraced by Rails, the proper place for persistent storage of data is the database, period. The

1. If you are really new to web programming and want a very thorough explanation of how web-based session management works, you may want to read the information available at http://www.technicalinfo.net/papers/WebBasedSessionManagement.html

Session

bottom line is that the longer you keep objects in the user's session hash, the more problems you create for yourself in trying to keep those objects from becoming stale (in other words, out of date in relation to the database).

This chapter deals with matters related to session use, starting with the question of what to put in the session.

13.1   What to Store in the Session

Deciding what to store in the session hash does not have to be difficult if you simply commit to storing as little as possible in it. Generally speaking, integers (for key values) and short-string messages are OK. Objects are not.

13.1.1   The Current User

There is one important integer that most Rails applications store in the session, and that is the `current_user_id`—not the current user object but its id. Even if you roll your own login and authentication code (which you shouldn't do), don't store the entire `User` (or `Person`) in the session while the user is logged in. (See Chapter 14, "Authentication and Authorization," for more information about keeping track of the current user.) The authentication system should take care of loading the user instance from the database prior to each request and making it available in a consistent fashion via a method on your `ApplicationController`. In particular, following this advice will ensure that you are able to disable access to given users without having to wait for their session to expire.

13.1.2   Session Use Guidelines

Here are some more general guidelines on storing objects in the session:

- They must be serializable by Ruby's Marshal API, which excludes certain types of objects such as a database connection and other types of I/O objects.

- Large object graphs may exceed the size available for session storage. Whether this limitation is in effect for you depends on the session store chosen and is covered later in the chapter.

- Critical data should not be stored in the session, since it can be suddenly lost by the user ending her session (by closing the browser or clearing her cookies).

- Objects with attributes that change often should not be kept in the session.

- Modifying the structure of an object and keeping old versions of it stored in the session is a recipe for disaster. Deployment scripts should clear old sessions to prevent this sort of problem from occurring, but with certain types of session stores, such as the cookie store, this problem is hard to mitigate. The simple answer (again) is to just not keep anything except for the occasional id in the session.

13.2   Session Options

You used to be able to turn off the session, but since Rails 2.3, applications that don't need sessions don't have to worry about them. Sessions are lazy loaded, which means unless you access the session in a controller action, there is no performance implication.

13.3   Storage Mechanisms

The mechanism via which sessions are persisted can vary. Rails' default behavior is to store session data as cookies in the browser, which is fine for almost all applications. If you need to exceed the 4KB storage limit inherent in using cookies, then you can opt for an alternative session store. But, of course, you shouldn't be exceeding that limit, because you shouldn't be keeping much other than an id or two in the session.

There are also some potential security concerns around session-replay attacks involving cookies, which might push you in the direction of using an alternative session storage.

13.3.1   Active Record Session Store

In previous version of Rails, the ability to switch over to storing sessions in the database was built into the framework itself. However, as of version 4.0, the Active Record session store has been extracted into its own gem.

To get started using the Active Record session store, add the `activerecord -session_store` gem to your `Gemfile` and run `bundle`:

```
# Gemfile
gem 'activerecord-session_store'
```

The next step is to create the necessary migration using a generator provided by the gem for that very purpose and run the migration to create the new table:

```
$ rails generate active_record:session_migration
    create  db/migrate/20130821195235_add_sessions_table.rb
$ rake db:migrate
==  AddSessionsTable: migrating =============================================
-- create_table(:sessions)
   -> 0.0095s
-- add_index(:sessions, :session_id)
   -> 0.0004s
-- add_index(:sessions, :updated_at)
   -> 0.0004s
==  AddSessionsTable: migrated (0.0104s)=====================================
```

Session

The final step is to tell Rails to use the new sessions table to store sessions via a setting in `config/initializers/session_store.rb`:

```
Rails.application.config.session_store :active_record_store
```

That's all there is to it.

Kevin Says ...

The biggest problem with using the Active Record session store is that it adds an unnecessary load on your database. Each time a user reads or writes from the session, the database will be hit.

13.3.2 Memcached Session Storage

If you are running an extremely high-traffic Rails deployment, you're probably already leveraging Memcached in some way or another. The `memcached` server daemon is a remote-process memory cache that helps power some of the most highly trafficked sites on the Internet.

The Memcached session storage option lets you use your `memcached` server as the repository for session data and is blazing fast. It's also nice because it has built-in expiration, meaning you don't have to expire old sessions yourself.

To use Memcached, the first step is to add the `dalli` gem to your `Gemfile` and run `bundle`:

```
# Gemfile
gem 'dalli'
```

Next, set up your Rails environment to use Memcached as its cache store. At a minimum, one can set the configuration setting `cache_store` to `:mem_cache_store`:

```
# config/environments/production.rb
config.cache_store = :mem_cache_store
```

Note

In Rails 4, when defining a `cache_store` using option `:mem_cache_store`, the `dalli`[2] gem is used behind the scenes instead of the `memcache-client` gem. Besides being threadsafe, which Rails 4 is by default, here are some of the reasons why Dalli is the new default Memcached client:

---

2. `https://github.com/mperham/dalli`

- It is approximately 20 percent faster than the `memcache-client` gem.
- Dalli has the ability to handle failover with recovery and adjustable timeouts.
- Dalli uses the newer Memcached binary protocol.

For more details, see the section "Cache Storage" in Chapter 17, "Caching and Performance."

Next, modify Rails' default session store setting in `config/initializers/session_store.rb`. At minimum, replace the contents of the file with the following:

```
Rails.application.config.
  session_store ActionDispatch::Session::CacheStore
```

This will tell Rails to use the `cache_store` of the application as the underlying session store as well. Additionally, one could explicitly set the amount of seconds a session is available for by setting the `:expire_after` option.

```
Rails.application.config.
  session_store ActionDispatch::Session::CacheStore,
    expires_after: 20.minutes
```

13.3.3   The Controversial CookieStore

In February 2007, core team member Jeremy Kemper made a pretty bold commit to Rails. He changed the default session storage mechanism from the venerable `PStore` to a new system based on a `CookieStore`. His commit message summed it up well:

> Introduce a cookie-based session store as the Rails default. Sessions typically contain at most a user_id and flash message; both fit within the 4K cookie size limit. A secure hash is included with the cookie to ensure data integrity (a user cannot alter his user_id without knowing the secret key included in the hash). If you have more than 4K of session data or don't want your data to be visible to the user, pick another session store. Cookie-based sessions are dramatically faster than the alternatives.

I describe the `CookieStore` as controversial because of the fallout over making it the default session storage mechanism. For one, it imposes a very strict size limit—only 4KB. A significant size constraint like that is fine if you're following the Rails way and not storing anything other than integers and short strings in the session. If you're bucking the guidelines, well, you might have an issue with it.

Session

13.3.3.1   Encrypted Cookies

Lots of people have complained about the inherent insecurity of storing session information, including the current user information on the user's browser. In Rails 3, cookies were only digitally signed, which verified that they were generated by the user's application and were difficult to alter. However, the contents of the cookie could still be easily read by the user. As of Rails 4, all cookies are encrypted by default, making them not only hard to alter but hard to read too.

13.3.3.2   Replay Attacks

Another problem with cookie-based session storage is its vulnerability to replay attacks, which generated an enormous message thread on the Rails core mailing list. S. Robert James kicked off the thread[3] by describing a replay attack example:

1. User receives credits, stored in her session.

2. User buys something.

3. User gets her new, lower credits stored in her session.

4. Evil hacker takes her saved cookie from step 1 and pastes it back in her browser's cookie jar. Now she's gotten her credits back.

- This is normally solved using something called nonce. Each signing includes a once-only code, and the signer keeps track of all the codes and rejects any message with the code repeated. But that's very hard to do here, since there may be several app servers serving up the same application.

- Of course, we could store the nonce in the database, but that defeats the entire purpose!

The short answer is, do not store sensitive data in the session. Ever. The longer answer is that coordination of nonces across multiple servers would require remote process interaction on a per-request basis, which negates the benefits of using the cookie session storage to begin with.

The cookie session storage also has potential issues with replay attacks that let malicious users on shared computers use stolen cookies to log in to an application that the user thought he had logged out of. The bottom line is that if you decide to

---

3. If you want to read the whole thread (all 83 messages of it), simply search Google for "Replay attacks with cookie session." The results should include a link to the topic on the Ruby on Rails: Core Google Group.

use the cookie session storage on an application with security concerns, please consider the implications of doing so carefully.

13.3.4 Cleaning Up Old Sessions

If you're using the `activerecord-session_store` gem, you can write your own little utilities for keeping the size of your session store under control. Listing 13.1 is a class that you can add to your `/lib` folder and invoke from the production console or a script whenever you need to do so.

Listing 13.1 `SessionMaintenance` Class for Cleaning Up Old Sessions

```
1 class SessionMaintenance
2   def self.cleanup(period = 24.hours.ago)
3     session_store = ActiveRecord::SessionStore::Session
4     session_store.where('updated_at < ?', period).delete_all
5   end
6 end
```

13.4 Cookies

This section is about using cookies, not the cookie session store. The cookie container, as it's known, looks like a hash and is available via the `cookies` method in the scope of controllers. Lots of Rails developers use cookies to store user preferences and other small nonsensitive bits of data. Be careful not to store sensitive data in cookies, since they can be read by users. The `cookies` container is also available by default in view templates and helpers.

13.4.1 Reading and Writing Cookies

The cookie container is filled with cookies received along with the request and sends out any cookies that you write to it with the response. Note that cookies are read by value, so you won't get the cookie object itself back, just the value it holds as a string (or as an array of strings if it holds multiple values).

To create or update cookies, you simply assign values using the brackets operator. You may assign either a single string value or a hash containing options, such as `:expires`, which takes a number of seconds before which the cookie should be deleted by the browser. Remember that Rails convenience methods for time are useful here:

```
1 # writing a simple session cookie
2 cookies[:list_mode] = "false"
3
```

```
4 # specifying options; curly brackets are needed to avoid syntax error
5 cookies[:recheck] = { value: "false",  expires: 5.minutes.from_now }
```

I find the :path options useful in allowing you to set options specific to particular sections or even particular records of your application. The :path option is set to '1', the root of your application, by default.

The :domain option allows you to specify a domain, which is most often used when you are serving up your application from a particular host but want to set cookies for the whole domain.

```
1 cookies[:login] = {
2   value: @user.security_token,
3   domain: '.domain.com',
4   expires: Time.now.next_year
5 }
```

Cookies can also be written using the :secure option, and Rails will only ever transmit them over a secure HTTPS connection:

```
# writing a simple session cookie
cookies[:account_number] = { value: @account.number, secure: true }
```

The :httponly option tells Rails whether cookies can be accessible via scripting or only HTTP. It defaults to false.

Finally, you can delete cookies using the delete method:

```
cookies.delete :list_mode
```

13.4.1.1 Permanent Cookies
Writing cookies to the response via the cookies.permanent hash automatically gives them an expiration date 20 years in the future.

```
1 cookies.permanent[:remember_me] = current_user.id
```

13.4.1.2 Signed Cookies
Writing cookies to the response via the cookies.signed hash generates signed representations of cookies to prevent tampering of those cookies' values by the end user. If a signed cookie was tampered with, an ActiveSupport::Message Verifier::InvalidSignature exception will be raised when that cookie is read in a subsequent request.

```
cookies.signed[:remember_me] = current_user.id
```

13.5   Conclusion

Deciding how to use the session is one of the more challenging tasks that faces a web application developer. That's why we put a couple of sections about it right in the beginning of this chapter. We also covered the various options available for configuring sessions, including storage mechanisms and methods for timing out sessions and the session lifecycle. We also covered use of a closely related topic: browser cookies.

Session

CHAPTER 14

Authentication and Authorization

Thanks goodness [*sic*], there's only about a billion of these because DHH doesn't think auth/auth [*sic*] belongs in the core.

—George Hotelling

If you're building a web application, more often than not you will likely need some form of user security. User security can be broken up into two categories: authentication, which verifies the identity of a user, and authorization, which verifies what they can do.

In version 3.1, Rails introduced `has_secure_password`, which adds methods to set and authenticate against a BCrypt password. Although this functionality now exists in the framework, it is only a small part of a robust authentication solution. We still need to write our own authentication code or have to look outside of Rails core for a suitable solution.

In this chapter, we'll cover authentication library Devise, writing your own authentication code with `has_secure_password`, and the authorization library pundit.

14.1 Devise

Devise[1] is a highly modular Rack-based authentication framework that sits on top of Warden. It has a robust feature set and leverages the use of Rails generators, and you only need to use what is suitable for your application.

---

1. https://github.com/plataformatec/devise

14.1.1   Getting Started

Add the `devise` gem to your project's `Gemfile` and `bundle install`. Then you can generate the Devise configuration by running the following:

```
1 $ rails generate devise:install
```

This will create the initializer for Devise and an English-version I18n YAML for Devise's messages. Devise will also alert you at this step to remember to do some mandatory Rails configuration if you have not done so already. This includes setting your default host for Action Mailer, setting up your root route and making sure your flash messages will render in the application's default layout.

14.1.2   Modules

Adding authentication functionality to your models using Devise is based on the concept of adding different modules to your class based on only what you need. The available modules for you to use are the following:

database-authenticatable Handles authentication of a user as well as password encryption.

confirmable Adds the ability to require email confirmation of user accounts.

lockable Can lock an account after *n* number of failed login attempts.

recoverable Provides password reset functionality.

registerable Alters user sign-up to be handled in a registration process, along with account management.

rememberable Provides *remember me* functionality.

timeoutable Allows sessions to be expired in a configurable time frame.

trackable: Stores login counts, timestamps, and IP addresses.

validatable Adds customizable validations to email and password.

omniauthable Adds Omniauth[2] support.

---

2. `https://github.com/intridea/omniauth`

Knowing which modules you wish to include in your model is important for setting up your models, migrations, and configuration options later on.

14.1.3   Models

To set up authentication in a model, run the Devise generator for that model and then edit it. For the purpose of our examples, we will use the ever-so-exciting `User` model.

```
$ rails generate devise User
```

This will create your model, a database migration, and route for your shiny new model. Devise will have given some default modules to use, which you will need to alter in your migration and model if you want to use different modules. In our example, we only use a subset of what is offered.

Our resulting database migration looks like this:

```
1  class DeviseCreateUsers < ActiveRecord::Migration
2    def change
3      create_table(:users) do |t|
4        ## Database authenticatable
5        t.string :email,              null: false, default: ""
6        t.string :encrypted_password, null: false, default: ""
7
8        ## Recoverable
9        t.string   :reset_password_token
10       t.datetime :reset_password_sent_at
11
12       ## Rememberable
13       t.datetime :remember_created_at
14
15       ## Trackable
16       t.integer  :sign_in_count, default: 0
17       t.datetime :current_sign_in_at
18       t.datetime :last_sign_in_at
19       t.string   :current_sign_in_ip
20       t.string   :last_sign_in_ip
21
22       ## Confirmable
23       # t.string   :confirmation_token
24       # t.datetime :confirmed_at
25       # t.datetime :confirmation_sent_at
26       # t.string   :unconfirmed_email # Only if using reconfirmable
27
28       ## Lockable
29       # t.integer  :failed_attempts, default: 0 # Only if lock strategy
30       #   is :failed_attempts
```

Auth

```
31        # t.string   :unlock_token # Only if unlock strategy is :email or :both
32        # t.datetime :locked_at
33
34        t.timestamps
35      end
36
37      add_index :users, :email,                  unique: true
38      add_index :users, :reset_password_token, unique: true
39      # add_index :users, :confirmation_token,   unique: true
40      # add_index :users, :unlock_token,         unique: true
41    end
42 end
```

We then modify our `User` model to mirror the modules we included in our migration.

```
1 class User < ActiveRecord::Base
2    # Include default devise modules. Others available are the following:
3    # :confirmable, :lockable, :timeoutable, and :omniauthable
4    devise :database_authenticatable, :registerable,
5           :recoverable, :rememberable, :trackable, :validatable
6 end
```

Now we're ready to `rake db:migrate` and let the magic happen.

14.1.4 Controllers

Devise provides some handy helper methods that can be used in your controllers to authenticate your model or get access to the currently signed-in person. For example, if you want to restrict access in a controller, you may use one of the helpers as a `before_action`.

```
1 class MeatProcessorController < ApplicationController
2    before_action :authenticate_user!
3 end
```

You can also access the currently signed-in user via the `current_user` helper method or the current session via the `user_session` method. Use `user_signed_in?` if you want to check if the user had logged in without using the `before_action`.

Thais Says …

The helper methods are generated dynamically, so in the case where your authenticated models are named differently, use the model name instead of user in the examples. An instance of this could be with an `Admin` model—your helpers would be `current_admin`, `admin_signed_in?`, and `admin_session`.

14.1.5 Views

Devise is built as a Rails engine and comes with views for all your included modules. All you need to do is write some CSS and you're off to the races. However, there may be some situations where you want to customize them, and Devise provides a nifty script to copy all the internal views into your application.

```
rails generate devise_views
```

If you are authenticating more than one model and don't want to use the same views for both, just set the following option in your `config/initializers/devise.rb`:

```
config.scoped_views = true
```

ERb to Haml

The views extracted from the Devise Rails Engine are ERb templates. If your preference is to use Haml for templates, one can convert the Devise ERb templates via the `html2haml` gem.

After the gem is installed, run the following command from the root of your Rails project:

```
$ for file in app/views/devise/**/*.erb; do html2haml -e $file
    ${file%erb}haml && rm $file; done
```

14.1.6 Configuration

When you first set up Devise using `rails generate devise:install`, a `devise.rb` was tossed into your `config/initializers` directory. This initializer is where all the configuration for Devise is set, and it is already packed full of commented-out goodies for all configuration options with excellent descriptions for each option.

Durran Says …

Using MongoDB as your main database? Under the general configuration section in the initializer, switch the require of `active---record` to `mongoid` for pure awesomeness.

Devise comes with internationalization support out of the box and ships with English message definitions located in `config/locales/devise.en.yml`. (You'll see this was created after you ran the install generator at setup.) This file can be used as the template for Devise's messages in any other language by staying with the same naming convention for each file. Create a Chilean Spanish translation in `config/locales/devise.cl.yml`, weon.

14.1.7 Strong Parameters

With the addition of Strong Parameters to Rails 4, Devise has followed suit and moved the concern of mass assignment to the controller. In Devise, mass-assignment parameter sanitation occurs in the following three actions:

sign_in Corresponding to controller action `Devise::SessionsController`#new, only authentication keys, such as `email`, are permitted.

sign_up Corresponding to controller action `Devise::Registrations Controller#create`, permits authentication keys, `password`, and `password _confirmation`.

account_update Corresponding to controller action `Devise::Registrations Controller#update`, permits authentication keys, `password`, `password _confirmation`, and `current_password`.

If you require additional parameters to be permitted by Devise, the simplest way to do so is through a `before_action` callback in `ApplicationController`.

```
1 class ApplicationController < ActionController::Base
2   before_action :devise_permitted_parameters, if: :devise_controller?
3
4   protected
5
6   def devise_permitted_parameters
7     devise_parameter_sanitizer.for(:sign_up) << :phone_number
8   end
9 end
```

Additionally, passing a block to `devise_parameter_sanitizer`, one can completely change the Devise defaults.

```
1 class ApplicationController < ActionController::Base
2   before_action :devise_permitted_parameters, if: :devise_controller?
3
4   protected
5
6   def devise_permitted_parameters
7     devise_parameter_sanitizer.
8       for(:sign_in) { |user| user.permit(:email, :password, :remember_me,
```

```
 9            :username) }
10    end
11 end
```

For more details on strong parameters, see Chapter 15, "Security."

14.1.8   Extensions

There are plenty of third-party extensions out there for Devise that come in handy if you are authenticating using different methods.

cas_authenticatable Allows for single sign-on using CAS.

ldap_authenticatable Authenticate users using LDAP.

rpx_connectable Adds support for using RPX authentication.

A complete list of extensions can be found at `https://github.com/plata formatec/devise/wiki/Extensions`.

14.1.9   Testing with Devise

To enable Devise test helpers in controller specs, create the spec support file `devise.rb` in the `spec/support` folder.

```
1 # spec/support/devise.rb
2 RSpec.configure do |config|
3   config.include Devise::TestHelpers, type: :controller
4 end
```

This will add helper methods `sign_in` and `sign_out`, which allow creating and destroying a session for a controller spec, respectively. Both methods accept an instance of a `Devise` model.

```
 1 require 'spec_helper'
 2
 3 describe AuthenticatedController do
 4   let(:user) { FactoryGirl.create(:user) }
 5
 6   before do
 7     sign_in user
 8   end
 9
10   ...
11 end
```

Auth

14.1.10   Summary
Devise is an excellent solution if you want a large number of standard features out of the box while writing almost no code at all. It has a clean and easy-to-understand API and can be used with little to no ramp-up time on any application.

14.2 `has_secure_password`
Prior to version 3.1, Rails did not include any sort of standard authentication mechanism. That changed with the introduction of `has_secure_password`, an ActiveModel mechanism that adds methods to set and authenticate against a BCrypt password.[3] However, `has_secure_password` is only a small piece to a complete authentication solution. Unlike other solutions like Devise, one still needs to implement a few extra items in order to get `has_secure_password` running properly.

14.2.1   Getting Started
To use Active Model's `has_secure_password`, add the required gem dependency `bcrypt-ruby` to your `Gemfile` and run `bundle install`.

```
gem 'bcrypt-ruby', '~> 3.0.0'
```

14.2.2   Creating the Models
To add authentication to a model, it must have an attribute named `password _digest`. For the purpose of our example, let's generate a new `User` model that will authenticate with an email and password.

```
$ rails generate model User email:string password_digest:string
```

Edit the `CreateUsers` migration to add the columns your application needs to satisfy its authentication requirements.

```
1 class CreateUsers < ActiveRecord::Migration
2   def change
3     create_table :users do |t|
4       t.string :email
5       t.string :password_digest
6       t.timestamps
7
8       t.index(:email, unique: true)
```

---

3. A BCrypt password is based on the Blowfish cipher, which incorporates a salt and is resistant to brute-force attacks. For more information, see the Wikipedia article on the subject: http://en.wikipedia .org/wiki/Bcrypt

```
 9     end
10   end
11 end
```

Next, set up your `User` model by adding the macro-style method `has_secure _password`. We've added a uniqueness validation for `email` to ensure we can only have one email per user.

```
1 class User < ActiveRecord::Base
2   has_secure_password
3
4   validates :email, presence: true, uniqueness: { case_sensitive: false }
5 end
```

A virtual attribute `password` is added to the model, which when set, automatically copies its encrypted value to `password_digest`. Validations on `create` for the presence and confirmation of `password` are also added.

To illustrate, let's create and authenticate a user in the console:

```
>> user = User.create(email: 'user@example.com')
=> #<User id: nil, email: "user@example.com", password_digest: nil,
   created_at: nil, updated_at: nil>
>> user.valid?
=> false
>> user.errors.full_messages
=> ["Password can't be blank"]
>> user = User.create(email: 'user@example.com', password: 'therails4way',
     password_confirmation: 'therails4way')
=> #<User id: 1, email: "user@example.com", password_digest:
   "$2a$10$RZfWUZiGze9Bk13PFOYB5eWKZuJUMAnqU/90rpcywGja...",
   created_at: "2013-10-01 15:26:55", updated_at: "2013-10-01 15:26:55">
>> user.authenticate('abcdefgh')
=> false
>> user.authenticate('therails4way')
=> #<User id: 1, email: "user@example.com", password_digest:
   "$2a$10$RZfWUZiGze9Bk13PFOYB5eWKZuJUMAnqU/90rpcywGja...",
   created_at: "2013-10-01 15:26:55", updated_at: "2013-10-01 15:26:55">
```

14.2.3 Setting Up the Controllers

Once the `User` model has been set up, we need to create a sessions controller to manage the session for your authenticated model. A resourceful controller for "users" is also required, but its implementation will depend on your application's requirements.

To create the controllers, run the following in the terminal:

```
$ rails generate controller sessions
$ rails generate controller users
```

In your `ApplicationController`, you will need to provide access to the current user so that all your controllers can access this information easily.

```
1 class ApplicationController < ActionController::Base
2   protect_from_forgery with: :exception
3
4   helper_method :current_user
5
6   protected
7
8   def current_user
9     @current_user ||= User.find(session[:user_id]) if session[:user_id]
10  end
11 end
```

The `SessionsController` should respond to `new`, `create`, and `destroy` in order to leverage all basic sign-in/out functionality.

```
1 class SessionsController < ApplicationController
2   def new
3   end
4
5   def create
6     user = User.where(email: params[:email]).first
7
8     if user && user.authenticate(params[:password])
9       session[:user_id] = user.id
10      redirect_to root_url, notice: 'Signed in successfully.'
11    else
12      flash.now.alert = 'Invalid email or password.'
13      render :new
14    end
15  end
16
17  def destroy
18    session[:user_id] = nil
19    redirect_to root_url, notice: 'Signed out successfully.'
20  end
21 end
```

Make sure you've added the routes for the new controllers.

```
1 Rails.application.routes.draw do
2   resource :session, only: [:new, :create, :destroy]
3   resources :users
4   ...
5 end
```

Finally, create a view app/views/sessions/new.html.haml containing a sign-in form to allow users to create a session within your application:

```
1 %h1 Sign in
2
3 - if flash.alert
4   .alert= flash.alert
5
6 = form_tag session_path do
7   .field
8     = label_tag :email
9     = email_field_tag :email, params[:email],
10        placeholder: 'Enter your email address', required: true
11
12  .field
13    = label_tag :password
14    = password_field_tag :password, params[:password],
15        placeholder: 'Enter your password', required: true
16
17    = submit_tag 'Sign in'
```

14.2.4   Controller, Limiting Access to Actions

Now that you are authenticating, you will want to control access to specific controller actions. A common pattern for handling this is through the use of action callbacks in your controllers, where the authentication checks reside in your ApplicationController.

```
1 class ApplicationController < ActionController::Base
2   ...
3
4   protected
5
6   def authenticate
7     unless current_user
8       redirect_to new_session_url,
9         alert: 'You need to sign in or sign up before continuing.'
10    end
11  end
12 end
13
14 class DashboardController < ApplicationController
15   before_action :authenticate
16 end
```

14.2.5   Summary

We've only scratched the surface of implementing a full-blown authentication solution using has_secure_password. Although the implementation is simple, it leaves a bit to be desired. Some things to consider when creating your authentication framework from scratch include "remember me" functionality, the ability for a user to reset a password, token authentication, and so on.

14.3   Pundit

Authorization is the function of specifying access rights to resources[4] such as models. Once a user has been authenticated within an application, using authorization, one can limit a user from performing certain actions—for instance, updating a record. Besides actions, one could even limit what is visible to a user based on their role. For example, if we created a blog application, a normal user should only be able to view published posts, while an administrator should be able to view all posts within the application.

Pundit[5] is a minimal authorization library created by the folks at Elabs that is focused around a notion of policy classes. A policy is a class that has the same name as a model class, suffixed with the word "Policy." It accepts both a user and model instance that are used to determine if the provided user has permissions to perform certain actions.

Kevin Says ...

The second argument to a Pundit policy can by any object, not necessarily just an Active Record instance.

14.3.1   Getting Started

Add the `pundit` gem to your project's `Gemfile` and `bundle install`. Then you can install Pundit by running the `pundit:install` generator:

```
$ rails generate pundit:install
```

This will create an application policy in `app/policies` for Pundit. Although optional, inheriting from `ApplicationPolicy` for each of your policy files is recommended, as it ensures by default no resourceful action is authorized.

```
1  # app/policies/application_policy.rb
2  class ApplicationPolicy
3    attr_reader :user, :record
4
5    def initialize(user, record)
6      @user = user
7      @record = record
```

---

4. http://en.wikipedia.org/wiki/Authorization
5. https://github.com/elabs/pundit

```
 8      end
 9
10      def index?
11         false
12      end
13
14      def show?
15         scope.where(id: record.id).exists?
16      end
17
18      def create?
19         false
20      end
21
22      def new?
23         create?
24      end
25
26      def update?
27         false
28      end
29
30      def edit?
31         update?
32      end
33
34      def destroy?
35         false
36      end
37
38      def scope
39         Pundit.policy_scope!(user, record.class)
40      end
41 end
```

Next, to include the Pundit methods within a controller, include Pundit in your
ApplicationController:

```
1 class ApplicationController < ActionController::Base
2    include Pundit
3 end
```

14.3.2 Creating a Policy

To create a policy for a model, run the Pundit generator for that model and then edit
it. To illustrate, we will use the Post model from the preceding example of a blog
application.

```
$ rails generate pundit:policy post
```

The generator creates the following `PostPolicy` in the `app/policies` folder:

```
1 class PostPolicy < ApplicationPolicy
2   class Scope < Struct.new(:user, :scope)
3     def resolve
4       scope
5     end
6   end
7 end
```

In the case of our example, let's guard against nonadministrator users from creating a blog post by implementing the `create?` predicate method.

```
1 class PostPolicy < ApplicationPolicy
2   def create?
3     user.admin?
4   end
5   ...
6 end
```

Besides checking against a role, one can add permission conditions based on the record itself. For example, in this blogging application, an administrator can only delete a post if it hasn't been published.

```
1 class PostPolicy < ApplicationPolicy
2   def destroy?
3     user.admin? && !record.published?
4   end
5   ...
6 end
```

14.3.3   Controller Integration

Pundit provides various helper methods to be used in controllers to authorize a user to perform an action against a record. For example, the `authorize` method will automatically infer the policy file based on the passed-in record instance. To illustrate, let's check if the current user can create a post within the `PostsController`:

```
1 class PostsController < ApplicationController
2   expose(:post)
3
4   def create
5     authorize post
6     post.save
7     respond_with(post)
```

```
8    end
9
10   ...
11 end
```

The call to `authorize` is equivalent to `PostPolicy.new(current_user,`
`@post).create?`. If the user is not authorized, Pundit will raise a `Not`
`AuthorizedError` exception.

Note

The `authorize` method will gain access to the currently logged-in user by
calling the `current_user` method. This can be overridden by implementing a method called `pundit_user` in your controller.

If you want to ensure authorization is always executed within your controllers,
Pundit also provides a method `verify_authorized` that raises an exception if
`authorize` hasn't been called. This method should be run within an `after_`
`action` callback.

```
1 class ApplicationController < ActionController::Base
2   after_filter :verify_authorized, except: :index
3 end
```

14.3.4 Policy Scopes

Using Pundit, we can define a scope within a policy to limit what records are returned
based on a user role. For example, in our recurring blogging application example, an
administrator should be able to view all posts, whereas a user should only be able to
view posts that have been published. This is achieved by implementing a nested class
named `Scope` under the policy class. The instances of the scope must respond to the
method `resolve`, which should return an `ActiveRecord::Relation`.

```
1 class PostPolicy < ApplicationPolicy
2   class Scope < Struct.new(:user, :scope)
3     def resolve
4       if user.admin?
5         scope
6       else
7         scope.where(published: true)
8       end
9     end
10  end
11  ...
12 end
```

Pundit provides a helper method `policy_scope` that infers the policy file based on the class passed into it and returns the scope specific to the current user's permissions.

```
1 def index
2   @posts = policy_scope(Post)
3 end
```

This is equivalent to the following:

```
1 def index
2   @posts = PostPolicy::Scope.new(current_user, Post).resolve
3 end
```

To ensure policy scopes are always called for specific controller actions, run `verify_policy_scoped` in an `after_action` callback. If `policy_scope` is not called, an exception will be raised.

```
1 class ApplicationController < ActionController::Base
2   after_filter :verify_policy_scoped, only: :index
3 end
```

14.3.5 Strong Parameters

Pundit also makes it possible to explicitly set which attributes are allowed to be mass-assigned with strong parameters based on a user role.

```
 1 # app/policies/assignment_policy
 2 class AssignmentPolicy < ApplicationPolicy
 3   def permitted_attributes
 4     if user.admin?
 5       [:title, :question, :answer, :status]
 6     else
 7       [:answer]
 8     end
 9   end
10 end
11
12 # app/controllers/assignments_controller.rb
13 class AssignmentsController < ApplicationController
14   expose(:assignment, attributes: :assignment_params)
15
16   def update
17     assignment.save
18     respond_with(assignment)
19   end
20
```

```
21    private
22
23    def assignment_params
24      params.require(:assignment).
25        permit(policy(assignment).permitted_attributes)
26    end
27 end
```

14.3.6 Testing Policies

Although Pundit comes with its own RSpec matchers for testing, our preference is to use an RSpec matcher created by the team at Thunderbolt Labs[6], as it provides better readability.

To get started, add the following into a file under `spec/support`:

```
1 # spec/support/matchers/permit_matcher.rb
2 RSpec::Matchers.define :permit do |action|
3   match do |policy|
4     policy.public_send("#{action}?")
5   end
6
7   failure_message do |policy|
8     "#{policy.class} does not permit #{action} on #{policy.record} for
9       #{policy.user.inspect}."
10  end
11
12  failure_message_when_negated do |policy|
13    "#{policy.class} does not forbid #{action} on #{policy.record} for
14      #{policy.user.inspect}."
15  end
16 end
```

Using this RSpec matcher, one can test policies that look like the following:

```
1 # spec/policies/post_policy.rb
2 require 'spec_helper'
3
4 describe PostPolicy do
5   subject(:policy) { PostPolicy.new(user, post) }
6
7   let(:post) { FactoryGirl.build_stubbed(:post) }
8
9   context "for a visitor" do
10    let(:user) { nil }
11
12    it { is_expected.to permit(:show) }
```

---

6. http://thunderboltlabs.com/blog/2013/03/27/testing-pundit-policies-with-rspec

```
13    it { is_expected.to_not permit(:create) }
14    it { is_expected.to_not permit(:new) }
15    it { is_expected.to_not permit(:update) }
16    it { is_expected.to_not permit(:edit) }
17    it { is_expected.to_not permit(:destroy) }
18  end
19
20  context "for an administrator" do
21    let(:user) { FactoryGirl.create(:administrator) }
22
23    it { is_expected.to permit(:show)   }
24    it { is_expected.to permit(:create) }
25    it { is_expected.to permit(:new) }
26    it { is_expected.to permit(:update) }
27    it { is_expected.to permit(:edit) }
28    it { is_expected.to permit(:destroy) }
29  end
30 end
```

14.4 Conclusion

We've covered the most popular authentication and authorization frameworks for
Rails at the moment, but there are plenty more out there to examine if these are not
suited for your application. Also, we covered how easy it is to roll your own simple
authentication solution using has_secure_password.

CHAPTER 15

Security

Ruby on Rails security sucks lolz amirite? No. Well, no to the nuance. Software security does, in general, suck. Virtually every production system has security bugs in it. When you bring pen testers in to audit your app, to a first approximation, your app will lose. While Ruby on Rails cherishes its Cool-Kid-Not-Lame-Enterprise-Consultingware image, software which is absolutely Big Freaking Enterprise consultingware, like say the J2EE framework or Spring, have seen similar vulnerabilities in the past.

—Patrick McKenzie[1]

Security is a very wide topic—one that we can't possibly cover in a single book chapter. Still there are things that every competent web developer using Rails should know.

Unlike many other software engineering topics, security is not something that you can solve by investing more hours to fix bugs or inefficient algorithms. Nor is it something you can do by trial and error. You have to know most common attack vectors and how to avoid vulnerabilities.

We will look into common web application security problems and the ways that Rails deals with them, as well as general security guidelines and practices. Along the way, we will discuss management of passwords and other private information, log masking, mass-assignment attributes protection, SQL injection, cross-site scripting (XSS), cross-site request forgery (XSRF), and more.

15.1 Password Management

One can say leaking your customer's plain text passwords is probably one of the most embarrassing security problems to have. Especially as the "do not store plain

---

1. http://www.kalzumeus.com/2013/01/31/what-the-rails-security-issue-means-for-your
-startup/

text passwords" mantra is widely known and doing the right thing is really not that hard. It's quite easy, actually. It usually boils down to using one of the many libraries available. It's also not something that you need to pay constant attention to. You do it once, and you are done.

The biggest problem with storing plain text passwords is that many people use the same password on multiple sites, and so in an event of a leak, you not only expose users' accounts in your application but also potentially put a lot of other accounts at risk.

The solution is simple and well known: securely hash all passwords. Secure hashing is not the same as encryption, as encryption assumes ability to decrypt and secure hash is a one-way function. Once you pass the password through it, there is no way to get it back in the original form.

Popular hash functions include MD5 and SHA1. MD5 is considered insecure and is no longer used for password security,[2] but you'll occasionally see it used to hash values that are not under attack.

"How do you check a hashed password?" you might ask. It's simple, actually: when we need to test a password given to a login form, we just pass it through the same one-way hash function and compare the results.

The actual low-level details are a bit more complicated, as we also want to protect against what is known as dictionary rainbow table attack. An attacker might get access to a database of hashed user passwords and compare the hashes to a table of hashes of dictionary words. Statistically, if you have enough users, a significant amount of them will use dictionary words for their passwords. This will allow an attacker to find out their password from the rainbow table and, using other information you have stored (like user email), try to gain access to those users' accounts on other services.

The solution for this problem is using a *salt*, or a random string that is generated for every user during account creation and that is used together with the user's password when calculating hashed password that we store in the database.

Since the salt is random for every user, there is no way to prepare a dictionary table of every dictionary word with every possible salt. So the attacker is left with the brute force attack: actually trying to pick passwords one by one by trying every possible password combination with the user's salt.

To make it even harder on the attacker, most "serious" password storage libraries use a secure hashing algorithms that was intentionally made very "expensive" to compute, usually by doing a lot of rounds of hash function computation in a sequence.

---

2. CarnegieMellon's Software Engineering Institute says that MD5 "should be considered cryptographically broken and unsuitable for further use": http://www.kb.cert.org/vuls/id/836068

We've delved into the gory details, and you might wonder if it involves a lot of work to implement this stuff in Rails. Actually, all the popular authentication libraries like Authlogic and Devise implement this functionality out of the box. If you don't want to use a third-party gem, Rails itself has straightforward support for secure password storage with the help of the popular BCrypt library.

To add secure hashed passwords to an ActiveModel class, you just need to call the has_secure_password class method.

The usage is very simple:

```
1 class User
2   has_secure_password
3 end
```

According to the Rails documentation,

> This mechanism requires you to have a password_digest attribute.
>
> Validations for presence of password on create, confirmation of password (using a password_confirmation attribute) are automatically added. If you wish to turn off validations, pass validations: false as an argument. You can add more validations by hand if need be.
>
> If you don't need the confirmation validation, just don't set any value to the password_confirmation attribute and the validation will not be triggered.
>
> You need to add bcrypt-ruby (~> 3.0.0) to Gemfile to use #has_secure_ password:
>
> ```
> gem '"bcrypt-ruby'", '"~> 3.0.0'"
> ```

To actually validate the password during authentication, you can use the authenticate method, which will be made available on your objects:

```
User.find_by(email: "john@doe.com").try(:authenticate, params[:-
password])
```

The method will return the object itself if the password matches or returns with nil.

15.2 Log Masking

Great, we are no longer storing the passwords in the database. We are not done, though. We might still be leaking the passwords and other sensitive information into the application logs. For every request, Rails logs the request parameters into the log file unless the parameter name includes one of the "filtered" strings. For a "filtered" parameter, Rails will replace the value by [FILTERED] before the logging:

```
Started POST
  "/users?name=john&password=[FILTERED]&password_confirmation=[FILTERED]"
  for 127.0.0.1 at 2013-02-24 22:29:59 +0000
Processing by UsersController#create as */*
  Parameters: {"name"=>"john", "password"=>"[FILTERED]",
  "password_confirmation"=>"[FILTERED]"}
```

Rails protects any parameter that includes password in its name by default, so both password and password_confirmation are already covered. If your password is using a differently named parameter, or if you want to protect other information (for example, credit card numbers), you should add those parameter names to the special Rails configuration variable filter_parameters.

A Rails 4 project generated with the standard Rails generator will generate config/initializers/filter_parameter_logging.rb with the following line:

```
Rails.application.config.filter_parameters += [:password]
```

To protect another parameter, simply add it to the array—for example,

```
Rails.application.config.filter_parameters += [:password, :cc, :ccv]
```

15.3   SSL (Secure Sockets Layer)

So now our apps are secure, right? We properly encrypted our passwords in the database, and we filtered sensitive data from being recorded in our logs. Well, we're not quite finished with security yet. The password and other sensitive information is still vulnerable to eavesdropping while in transit from the user's browser to your web server.

To completely secure the information, you need to use SSL (Secure Sockets Layer). Configuring and managing SSL for your web server is out of the scope of this book, but there are things to be done on the Rails side, which we will cover now.

First, set config.force_ssl = true in your configuration file to force all access to the application over SSL. Then specify use of Strict Transport Security HTTP header[3] and secure cookies.

The force_ssl setting works by redirecting to an HTTPS URL with the same parameters if you try to access the application via plain HTTP.

---

3. http://tools.ietf.org/html/draft-hodges-strict-transport-sec-02

Trying to access a non-GET HTTP action with HTTP might not actually work as you cannot redirect to a POST request. The way to go is to use force_ssl on the GET request that renders the form, in which case standard form helpers will keep the HTTPS format for the form submit action.

If you want a fine-grained control over the forcing of SSL connections, you can supply parameters to a controller's force_ssl class method. It accepts the same kind of options as a before_action as well as :host and :port options in case you need to specify a domain.

```
class UsersController < ApplicationController
    force_ssl only: [:new, :edit], host: "www.foobar.com"
```

If class-level options are not suitable for your application, you can always roll your own logic inside an action method. The ssl? method of a request option returns true if the request was received over an HTTPS connection.

15.4   Model Mass-Assignment Attributes Protection

Since its origins, Rails has featured a convenient mass-assignment feature allowing assignment of multiple model attributes by passing a hash of values. As such, it's common to create a model using User.create(params[:user]) and to update it later using User.update(params[:user]).

Without protection, direct mass-assignment access to all model attributes would be easy to exploit. For example, if you happen to define an is_admin boolean field in the "users" table, an attacker could give themselves admin privileges by sneaking along is_admin=true on an otherwise innocent registration form.

In the previous Rails versions, mass-assignment protection was implemented on the model level using attr_accessible and attr_protected class-level methods.

In a nutshell, you could call attr_accessible with a list of model attributes to indicate that those attributes are safe to mass-update. attr_protected would do the opposite, disabling access to passed attributes. This is referred to as whitelisting and blacklisting, respectively.

There were several practical problems with the former approach:

- It was too cumbersome to use, as it restricted mass-assignment globally, including tests and access from other models. In those cases, you usually know very well which attributes you are assigning and having to jump through hoops to do so. The result wasn't very pleasant.

- Simple whitelisting and blacklisting didn't allow for special cases where access to attributes depend on other attributes or other records—for example, user roles and permissions.

- Models don't feel like the right place to define these kinds of restrictions, since most of the time we only need restrictions on mass-assignment when passing unfiltered parameters to models inside a controller action method.

Rails 4 introduces a new and improved way of controlling mass-assignment attributes. The functionality was made available and proven in earlier Rails versions with the `strong_parameters` gem. The new approach forbids mass-assignment of a model attribute from a controller unless that attribute was whitelisted.

The big difference is that whitelisting is configured using two simple methods (`permit` and `require`) that are exposed on a controller's `params` hash. Calls to those methods can be chained to validate nested `params` hashes.

Calling `require` will validate that the parameter is actually present and throw an `ActionController::ParameterMissing` exception if it is not. It will also return the "extracted" value of the parameter.

```
params.require(:user)
```

An `ActionController::ParameterMissing` exception, unless unhandled, will bubble up to the Rails dispatcher and result in HTTP 400 Bad Request response.

Calling `permit` with a list of attributes will allow those attributes to "pass through" to the model during mass-assignment, but only if the value is one of the supported "scalar" types: `String`, `Symbol`, `NilClass`, `Numeric`, `TrueClass`, `FalseClass`, `Date`, `Time`, `DateTime`, `StringIO`, `IO`, `ActionDispatch::Http::UploadedFile`, or `Rack::Test::UploadedFile`. This restriction disables evil injection of arrays, hashes, or any other objects.

```
params.require(:user).permit(
  :name, :email, :password, :password_confirmation)
```

Another option is to pass a hash. This will allow you to declare that one of the attributes can contain an array of scalar values:

```
params.permit(ids: [])
```

To whitelist all the attributes in a given hash, call `permit!` method on it:

```
params.require(:log_entry).permit!
```

Using a combination of `permit` and `require`, it's relatively easy to implement different parameter filtering options for creating new records and updating existing records or any other "complicated" logic required:

Listing 15.1 A Typical `UsersController` with Param Filtering

```
 1 class UsersController < ApplicationController
 2
 3   def create
 4     user = User.create!(create_params)
 5     redirect_to user
 6   end
 7
 8   def update
 9     user = User.find(params[:id])
10     user.update!(update_params)
11     redirect_to user
12   end
13
14 private
15
16   def create_params
17     params.require(:user).permit(:name, :email, :password,
18       :password_confirmation)
19   end
20
21   def update_params
22     params.require(:user).permit(name: true, email: true,
         tags: [])
23   end
24 end
```

15.5 SQL Injection

SQL injection attacks were very popular when people wrote SQL code for their applications by hand. Even today, if you're not careful, you can introduce code that is susceptible to this kind of attack.

15.5.1 What Is an SQL Injection?

SQL injection is a catch-all description for attacks on SQL database-driven application. The attacker includes malicious fragments of SQL code in otherwise legitimate input provided to the application in the hopes that the application "messes up" and sends those fragments along to the database to be executed.

Let's see how this can happen. Suppose that we implemented product search functionality in our application using the following piece of code:

```
1 class ProductsController < ApplicationController
2   def search
3     @products = Product.where("name LIKE '"%#{params[:search_terms]}%'"")
4   end
5 end
```

For a search string "test," this code will execute the following SQL query:

```
SELECT * FROM products WHERE name LIKE '"%test%'";
```

This is OK so far. But what if the user submits `search_terms` with a value of `'";DELETE FROM users;`?

In this case, the resulting SQL code sent to the database is the following:

```
SELECT * FROM products WHERE name LIKE '"%'";DELETE FROM users;%'";
```

That second statement will wipe out the entire "users" table in the database.

Using variations on the same theme, an attacker could modify the users table to reset an administrator's password or retrieve data that he shouldn't have access to.

To protect from this attack, we could start escaping all the user input ourselves, but fortunately we don't have to do that, as Active Record already does it for us; we just need to know how to use it correctly.

The first rule to remember is to never directly inject users' input into any string that will be used as a part of an SQL query. Instead, we should use variable substitution facility provided by Active Record (and other object-mapping software—they all have it):

```
@products = Product.where('"name LIKE ?'", "%#{params[:query]}%")
```

The "?" character in the query fragment serves as a variable placeholder. You can have more than one in any given query; just make sure to pass the right number of variables to interpolate.

You can read more about it this behavior in Chapter 5, "Working with Active Record."

15.6   Cross-Site Scripting (XSS)

Cross-site scripting (XSS) is one of the most common security vulnerabilities, but that doesn't make it any less severe. When successfully exploited, it can give an attacker a bypass around application authorization and authentication mechanisms and leak personal information.

The attack works by injecting a client-side executable code into the application pages. An example of such a code can be a JavaScript that "leaks" cookies to a remote server, which would allow the attacker to "clone" any affected session. So if the attacker is able to lay his hands on the administrator session, he would be able to impersonate an administrator without actually passing the required authentication procedures, just by using an already authenticated session.

There are several ways an attack code can "leak" the information. One of the simplest ones is to insert an image tag into the DOM with an image reference to the attacker's server and an image path and image path including the leaked information. The attacker's server access logs will capture the information where it can be retrieved later.

All recent versions of Rails make it relatively easy to avoid this kind of attack. In this section, we will discuss the key elements provided by Rails to defend against XSS attacks and point out things to watch out for.

The most common mistake leading to an XSS vulnerability is failing to escape user input when rendering HTML. There are several possible vectors of attack for exploiting this mistake.

Attack code can be first saved into the database (like, for example, injecting it into a post title or comment body), in which case such a database record becomes infected. Anyone visiting a page with infected data will run the malicious JavaScript code embedded in the record, allowing the attacker to access the visiting user's session and do whatever they're allowed to do.

Another vector involves passing attack code as a URL parameter that is directly rendered into the page, causing the victim to visit an "infected" URL.

In both cases, the victim's browser is exposed to the attack code, which will execute in the browser's context. The solution is to always "escape" or "sanitize" unsafe HTML content.

In this context, "escaping" means replacing some of the string characters with an HTML escape sequence that will remove the special meaning from the text and cause it to render as a regular text. Sanitizing, on the other hand, means validating the HTML content to ensure only "good" HTML tags and attributes are used.

Note that sanitizing is inherently less secure than escaping and should only be used where rendered content must contain HTML markup. An example would be a WYSIWYG HTML editor on a textarea that manages code that is later rendered on a page.

15.6.1   HTML Escaping

In previous versions of Rails, you had to think hard about escaping and utilize the h view helper method to escape potentially unsafe content. Rails core fielded a lot of criticism for making our code "unsafe by default." Having to think about escaping turns out to be very error prone, and many developers forgot to do it properly. Recent versions of Rails (starting with 3.0) do a much better job. Every string is tagged as either safe or unsafe. All unsafe strings are automatically escaped by default. You only need to think about explicitly managing the "safeness" of strings when you're writing helpers that output HTML into your template.

For obvious reasons, all Rails HTML helpers will output "safe" strings that can be directly rendered on a page. Otherwise, you would have to call `html_safe` on the output of a helper.

For example, let's look at the following view fragment:

```
%li= link_to @user.name, user_path(@user), class: user_class(@user)
```

The user's name will be escaped and so will the return value of the `user_class` view helper method (assuming it wasn't tagged as safe). The result of `user_path(@user)` is an unsafe string, so it will be escaped as well.

The net result of those changes in later versions of Rails is that it becomes easy to ensure proper HTML escaping. The "right thing" will be done in most cases, and Rails will play it safe by default. Occasionally, Rails feels like it escapes "too much" when you forget to use `html_safe` on the return value of a custom view helper method. But the error is usually easy to spot.

Even though Rails is safe by default, you should still be very careful when you call `html_safe`. Calling it on an unsafe input without validation will absolutely create an XSS vulnerability in your application.

The most common source of confusion about needing `html_safe` in view helper methods happens when manipulating literal strings.

```
1 def paragraphize(text)
2   text.split("\r\n\r\n").map do |paragraph|
3     content_tag(:p, paragraph)
4   end.join.html_safe
5 end
```

The call to `content_tag` on line 3 will properly escape its input, so we don't have to manually escape `paragraph`. It is itself a view helper method, so it will tag its return value as `html_safe`. However, `join` will join the safe strings from `content_tag` with an unsafe `" "`, which is used as the default join string. You'll scratch your head and wonder what's going on before adding the final `html_safe` in a state of confusion.

15.6.2   HTML Sanitization

In contrast to escaping, sanitization leaves some HTML intact. The idea is to only leave "safe" HTML tags that we want and to remove all the rest. As usual with filtering problems, there are two approaches: blacklisting and whitelisting.

Blacklisting involves trying to detect and remove "bad" HTML fragments, like JavaScript tags or script content in links.

Whitelisting only allows HTML elements that are explicitly allowed and escapes anything else.

Blacklisting is not a secure solution, since new hacks are being devised all the time and there's no way we'd be able to be 100 percent sure that our blacklist is complete at all times. Therefore, we *must* use the whitelisting approach.

Rails has a `SanitizeHelper` module "for scrubbing text of undesired HTML elements." It includes several methods for our disposal that we already covered in Chapter 11, "All about Helpers," so we won't repeat them here.

15.6.3   Input versus Output Escaping

One more thing to discuss about HTML escaping is timing. When should we do it—on input of user data or during rendering (output)?

The rule of thumb is to escape on output. The rationale being that we might want to render the content in different formats, and each has its own escaping requirements. For example, escaping HTML on input will not help us if the output format is JSON, which requires escaping of quote characters and not HTML tags.

Sanitization also mostly makes sense on output, as it will allow us to change the rules without reapplying them on all the data already stored.

Especially cautious application developers might decide to escape and sanitize on both input and output, but we find that it usually isn't necessary.

15.7   XSRF (Cross-Site Request Forgery)

Cross-site request forgery (usually abbreviated as CSRF or XSRF) is a type of web application vulnerability that allows an attacker to modify application state on behalf of a user that is logged into the application by luring the user to click on a carefully crafted link, visit a page, or even just open an email with malicious embedded images.

Assume that an intern named Frank at a banking institution implemented account fund transfer functionality as an HTTP GET method, like so:

```
1 GET /transfers?from_account_id=123&to_account_id=456&amount=1000
```

Note: You would *never* do something like this in real life; this example is for illustrative purposes only. In fact, if you're following proper RESTful practices, a GET would not make any modifications to server state. We're about to see why.

Of course, everyone, even interns, knows you should authenticate banking transfers. So Frank does some research on Rails security and properly authenticates and authorizes the request.

You see the problem yet? No? Assume an end user logs into her online banking, leaves it logged in, and flips over to check her email in another browser tab. Even a relatively unsophisticated attacker could send him an HTML email with the following image:

```
<img src="http://banking-domain/transfers?from_account_id=<users_account_id>
&to_account_id=<attacker_account_id>&amount=1000">
```

It's a long shot, but if this image is opened by the victim's browser while it is authenticated and authorized, the transfer will get executed because the session cookie from the bank is still valid.

Fortunately for the bank, Frank's code was reviewed, and the reviewer pointed out the problem. So Frank *fixed* the problem by modifying the transfer action to use a POST instead of GET.

Are the bank's customers safe yet? Not quite. An attacker can still "lure" victims to an innocent-looking site that hosts JavaScript that will post to the fund transfer URL from within victim's browser.

So how do we protect ourselves against this chicanery?

15.7.1   Restricting HTTP Method for Actions with Side Effects

We must only allow side effects on non-GET requests (e.g., POST, DELETE, PATCH). This is actually specified by HTTP protocol guidelines, and there are two ways to accomplish the restriction in Rails.

We can restrict the request methods at the routing level:

```
1 post '"transfers'" => '"transfers#create'"
2
3 resources :users do
4   post :activate, on: :member
5 end
```

Rails' standard `resources` routing helper exhibits the correct behavior by default. It will require POST to access `create`, PATCH to access `update`, and DELETE to access `destroy`. You need to be careful when you define your own nonresource routes, especially if you use `:action` segment routes.

The truly paranoid among us can use a controller class method called `verify` to make sure that proper methods are used for controller actions with side effects:

```
1 class UsersController < ApplicationController
2   verify method: [:post, :put, :delete], only: [:activate, :create,
3     :update], redirect_to: '"/"'
```

15.7.2   Require Security Token for Protected Requests

Using proper HTTP request methods is not enough. We need to ensure that the requests originate from our application. You could check the referrer of HTTP requests, but the proper way to do it is to include a security token as a parameter or header on protected requests and validate the token on the server side.

Rails has built-in facilities to handle exactly this kind of security check. The boilerplate implementation of `ApplicationController` generated for new apps includes the following code:

```
1 class ApplicationController
2   # Prevent CSRF attacks by raising an exception.
3   # For APIs, you may want to use :null_session instead.
4   protect_from_forgery with: :exception
5 end
```

This code adds a `verify_authenticity_token` before action callback to all requests in your application. The `protect_from_forgery` method takes `:if` / `:except` parameters just like a normal `before_action` declaration.

Additionally, the `with` parameter accepts one of the supported protection strategies: `:exception`, `:null_session`, or `:reset_session`.

:exception Raises `ActionController::InvalidAuthenticityToken` exception.

:reset_session Resets the user's session.

:null_session Executes the request as if no session exists. Used by default if no `with` parameter is supplied.

The difference between `:reset_session` and `:null_session` is that `:null_session` doesn't actually change the session; it only substitutes an empty one for the current requests, while `:reset_session` will leave it empty for subsequent requests as well.

Security

15.7.3   Client-Side Security Token Handling

Now that we are requiring a security token on the server side, we need to pass it from the client side. Standard Rails form helpers (e.g., `form_for`) will include the token as a hidden parameter.

The same goes for the Rails link helpers that generate non-GET Ajax requests (e.g., `link_to` with `method:` `:post`). Note that the actual handling of security tokens is done in the UJS JavaScript library (e.g., `'"jquery-rails'"`). You can check out the implementation of the `handleMethod` function in `jquery_ujs` `.js` if you're curious about it.

To function properly, the browser needs access to the security token from the server. It is provided with a call to `csrf_meta_tags` in your application layout header section:

```
%head
  ....
  = csrf_meta_tags
```

This will render two meta tags:

```
<meta content="authenticity_token" name="csrf-param" />
<meta content="...." name="csrf-token" />
```

The actual token is stored in the session. It is generated for the first time when it is needed and preserved for the duration of the session. The call to `csrf_meta_tags` is included in the boilerplate application template of a fresh Rails app.

15.8   Session Fixation Attacks

A session fixation attack is something to be aware of if you implement your own session management. The Rails cookies session store is immune from these types of attacks.

Many session security implementations depend on the session id being a secret. If the attacker is successfully able to force a user to use their session id and log into the system, the attacker can get access to the authenticated session by using that id.

Session fixation attacks are only possible when hackers are able to force the setting of a third session `id` in the user's browser through a URL or other means. For example, in some configurations of PHP, you can allow a session id to be passed as a URL parameter called `_my_app_session_id`. The attacker can send victims to the malicious link, which then redirects back to the target system, including a session id that they generated.

Defending against this hack is pretty simple. Whenever you elevate a user's privileges, call the `reset_session` helper, which ensures that their session id is changed. Attackers are left with an old unauthenticated session.

Any decent Rails authentication system, like Devise, already protects you from session fixation attacks. So you don't usually need to worry about it unless you are doing something unusual.

15.9   Keeping Secrets

As a general rule, you should not store secret things in your source code. This includes passwords, security tokens, API keys, and so on. Assume that a determined attacker will gain access to your source code and use it to their advantage if they can.

So where do you store secret parts of your application's configuration, including API keys and tokens for external services? The recommended way is to get those from your shell environment.

For example, let's say you need to configure a Pubnub service. The following code will allow you to configure Pubnub using five environment variables. (Put it in `config/initializers/pubnub.rb`.)

```
1 PUBNUB = Pubnub.new(
2     ENV["PUBNUB_PUBLISH_KEY"],
3     ENV["PUBNUB_SUBSCRIBE_KEY"],
4     ENV["PUBNUB_SECRET_KEY"],
5     ENV["PUBNUB_CYPHER"] || "",
6     ENV["PUBNUB_SSL"] == "true")
```

If you deploy to Heroku, you can easily configure environment variables using `heroku` command line tool:

```
$ heroku config:add PUBNUB_PUBLISH_KEY=.... PUBNUB_SUBSCRIBE_KEY=... ...
```

Other deployment options should allow you to define environment variables easily since it's a common need.

Even if you have no easy way to control environment directly, you almost always have a way to add extra files to the deployment directory. You can load such a file into your environment like this (adding this code to the top of your `config/application.rb`):

```
1 # Change this path according to your needs.
2 ENV_PATH = File.expand_path('../env.rb'", __FILE__)
3 require ENV_PATH if File.exists?(ENV_PATH)
```

The `env.rb` file can assign environment variables as needed:

```
ENV["PUBNUB_PUBLISH_KEY"] = "..."
```

Important

Rails by default stores a very important secret in the source code. Take a look at `config/secrets.yml`:

```
Rails.application.secrets.secret_key_base = '...'"
```

Change this to the following:

```
1  # config/secrets.yml
2
3  ...
4
5  production:
6    secret_key_base: <%= ENV["SECRET_KEY_BASE"] %>
```

This token is used to sign the session cookie, and it allows anyone that has it to modify session to their liking, bypassing most security measures.

15.10   Conclusion

Security is a topic that should never be taken lightly, especially when developing business-critical applications. Since exploits are always being discovered, it's very important to keep up to date on new developments. We recommend that you check out `http://guides.rubyonrails.org/security.html` and `http://railssecurity.com/` for the latest information available.

Finally, you should consider using Code Climate[4] to automatically analyze and audit your Rails code after every Git push. Tell Bryan and Noah that *The Rails™ 4 Way* crew sent you.

---

4. `http://codeclimate.com`

CHAPTER 16

Action Mailer

It's a cool way to send emails without tons of code.

—Jake Scruggs

Integration with email is a crucial part of most modern web application projects. Whether it's sign-up confirmations, password recovery, or account control via email, you'll be happy to hear that Rails offers great support for both sending and receiving email, thanks to its Action Mailer framework.

In this chapter, we'll cover what's needed to set up your deployment to be able to send and receive mail with the Action Mailer framework and what's needed to write mailer models, which are the entities in Rails that encapsulate code having to do with email handling.

16.1 Setup

By default, Rails will try to send email via SMTP (port 25) of localhost. If you are running Rails on a host that has an SMTP daemon running and it accepts SMTP email locally, you don't have to do anything else in order to send mail. If you don't have SMTP available on localhost, you have to decide how your system will send email.

When not using SMTP directly, the main options are to use sendmail or to give Rails information on how to connect to an external mail server. Most organizations have SMTP servers available for this type of use, although it's worth noting that, due to abuse, many hosting providers have stopped offering shared SMTP service.

Most serious production deployments use third-party SMTP services that specialize in delivering automated email, avoiding user spam filters and blacklists.

16.2   Mailer Models

Assuming the mail system is configured, let's go ahead and create a mailer model that
will contain code pertaining to sending and receiving a class of email. Rails provides
a generator to get us started rapidly. Our mailer will send out a notice to any user of
our sample application who is late entering their time.

```
$ rails generate mailer LateNotice
  create  app/mailers/late_notice.rb
  invoke  haml
  create    app/views/late_notice
  invoke  rspec
  create    spec/mailers/late_notice_spec.rb
```

A view folder for the mailer is created at `app/views/late_notice`, and the
mailer itself is stubbed out at `app/mailers/late_notice.rb`:

```
1 class LateNotice < ActionMailer::Base
2   default from: "from@example.com"
3 end
```

Kind of like a default Active Record subclass, there's not much there at the start.

16.2.1   Preparing Outbound Email Messages

You work with Action Mailer classes by defining public mailer methods that correspond to types of emails that you want to send. Inside the public method, you assign
any variables that will be needed by the email message template and then call the
mail method, which is conceptually similar to the render method used in controllers.

Continuing with our example, let's write a `late_timesheet` mailer method
that takes `user` and `week_of` parameters. Notice that it sets the basic information
needed to send our notice email (see Listing 16.1).

Listing 16.1   Adding a Mailer Method
```
 1 class LateNotice < ActionMailer::Base
 2    default from: "system@timeandexpenses.com"
 3
 4    def late_timesheet(user, week_of)
 5      @recipient = user.name
 6      @week = week_of
 7      attachments["image.png"] = File.read("/images/image.
       png")
 8      mail(
 9        to: user.email,
10        subject: "[Time and Expenses] Timesheet notice"
11      )
```

```
12      end
13    end
```

Inside the method we've created, we have access to a few methods to set up the message for delivery, including the `mail` method shown earlier:

attachments Allows you to add normal and inline file attachments to your message.

```
1 attachments["myfile.zip"] = File.read("/myfile.zip")
2 attachments.inline["logo.png"] = File.read("/logo.png")
```

headers Allows you to supply a hash of custom email headers.

```
1 headers("X-Author" => "Obie Fernandez")
```

mail Sets up the email that will get sent. It accepts a hash of headers that a `Mail::Message` will accept and allows an optional block. If no block is specified, views will be used to construct the email with the same name as the method in the mailer. If a block is specified, these can be customized.

Note also the change of the default from address to one set up for our application. Here is a sample list of the headers that you can include in the hash passed to the mail method or in the default macro. In addition to these, you may pass any email header that is needed when sending—that is, `{ "X-Spam" => value }`.

subject The subject line for the message.

to The recipient addresses for the message, either as a string (for a single address) or an array (for multiple addresses). Remember that this method expects actual address strings, not your application's user objects.

```
users.map(&:email)
```

from Specifies the from address for the message as a string (required).

cc Specifies carbon copy recipient (cc:) addresses for the message, either as a string (for a single address) or an array for multiple addresses.

bcc Specifies blind recipient (bcc:) addresses for the message, either as a string (for a single address) or an array for multiple addresses.

reply_to Sets the email for the reply-to header.

Mail

date An optional explicit sent on date for the message, usually passed `Time.now`. Will be automatically set by the delivery mechanism if you don't supply a value and cannot be set using the default macro.

The `mail` method can either take a block or not if you want to do custom formats similar to Rails routes.

```
1 mail(to: "user@example.com") do |format|
2   format.text
3   format.html
4 end
```

The body of the email is created by using an Action View template (regular Haml or ERb) that has the instance variables in the mailer available as instance variables in the template. So the corresponding body template for the mailer method in Listing 16.1 could look like the following:

```
1 Dear #{@recipient},
2
3 Your timesheet for the week of #{@week} is late.
```

And if the recipient was Aslak, the email generated would look like this:

```
Date: Sun, 12 Dec 2004 00:00:00 +0100
From: system@timeandexpenses.com
To: aslak.hellesoy@gmail.com
Subject: [Time and Expenses] Late timesheet notice

Dear Aslak Hellesoy,

Your timesheet for the week of Aug 15th is late.
```

16.2.2   HTML Email Messages

To send mail as HTML, make sure your view template generates HTML and that the corresponding template name corresponds to the email method name. For our `late_timesheet` method, this would be in `app/views/late_notice/late_timesheet.html.haml` (or `.erb`). You can also override this template name in the `mail` block.

```
1 mail(to: "user@example.com") do |format|
2   format.text
3   format.html { render "another_template" }
4 end
```

16.2.3 Multipart Messages

If a plain text and HTML template are present for a specific mailer action, the text template and the HTML template will both get sent by default as a multipart message. The HTML part will be flagged as alternative content for those email clients that support it.

16.2.3.1 Implicit Multipart Messages

As mentioned earlier in the chapter, multipart messages can also be used implicitly without invoking the `part` method, because Action Mailer will automatically detect and use multipart templates, where each template is named after the name of the action followed by the content type. Each such detected template will be added as a separate part to the message.

For example, if the following templates existed, each would be rendered and added as a separate part to the message with the corresponding content type. The same body hash is passed to each template.

- `signup_notification.text.haml`

- `signup_notification.text.html.haml`

- `signup_notification.text.xml.builder`

- `signup_notification.text.yaml.erb`

16.2.4 Attachments

Including attachments in emails is relatively simple; just use the method in your class.

```
1 class LateNotice < ActionMailer::Base
2   def late_timesheet(user, week_of)
3     @recipient = user.name
4     attachments["image.png"] = File.read("/images/image.png")
5     mail(
6       to: user.email,
7       from: "test@myapp.com",
8       subject: "[Time and Expenses] Timesheet notice"
9     )
10   end
11 end
```

If you wanted to attach the image inline, use `attachments.inline`.

```
attachments.inline["image.png"] = File.read("/images/image.png")
```

You can access this attachment in the template if need be via the `attachments` hash and then calling `url` on that object for the image's relative content id (cid:) path.

```
1 Dear #{@recipient},
2
3 Your timesheet is late. Here's a photo depicting our sadness:
4
5 = image_tag attachments['image.png'].url, alt: "Invoicing"
```

16.2.5 Generating URLs

Generating application URLs is handled through named routes or using the `url_for` helper. Since mail does not have request context like controllers do, the host configuration option needs to be set. The best practice for this is to define them in the corresponding environment configuration, although it can be defined on a per mailer basis.

```
# config/environments/production.rb
config.action_mailer.default_url_options = { host: 'accounting.com' }
```

In your mailer, you can now generate your URL. It is important to note that you cannot use the _path variation for your named routes since they must be rendered as absolute URLs.

```
 1 class LateNotice < ActionMailer::Base
 2   def late_timesheet(user, week_of)
 3     @recipient = user.name
 4     @link = user_url(user)
 5     mail(
 6       to: user.email,
 7       from: "test@myapp.com",
 8       subject: "[Time and Expenses] Timesheet notice"
 9     )
10   end
11 end
```

When generating URLs through `url_for`, the controller and action also need to be specified. If you have provided a default host, then the `:only_path` option must be provided to tell the helper to generate an absolute path.

```
= url_for(controller: "users", action: "update", only_path: false)
```

16.2.6 Mailer Layouts

Mailer layouts behave just like controller layouts. To be automatically recognized, they need to have the same name as the mailer itself. In our previous case, they would automatically be used for our HTML emails. You can also add custom layouts if your heart desires, either at the class level or as a render option.

```
1 class LateNotice < ActionMailer::Base
2   layout "alternative"
3
4   def late_timesheet(user, week_of)
5     mail(to: user.email) do |format|
6       format.html { render layout: "another" }
7     end
8   end
9 end
```

We've now talked extensively about preparing email messages for sending, but what about actually sending them to the recipients?

16.2.7   Sending an Email

Sending emails only involves getting an object from your mailer and delivering it.

```
1 aslak = User.find_by(name: "Aslak Hellesoy")
2 message = LateNotice.late_timesheet(aslak, 1.week.ago)
3 message.deliver
```

16.2.8   Callbacks

As of Rails 4, the ability to define action callbacks for a mailer was added. Like their Action Controller counterparts, one could specify `before_action`, `after_action`, and `around_action` callbacks to run shared pre- and postprocessing code within a mailer.

Callbacks can accept one or more symbols, representing a matching method in the mailer class:

```
before_action :set_headers
```

Or you can pass the callback a block to execute, like this:

```
before_action { logger.info "Sending out an email!" }
```

A common example of why you would use a callback in a mailer is to set inline attachments, such as images that are used within the email template.

```
1 class LateNotice < ActionMailer::Base
2   before_action :set_inline_attachments
3
4   def late_timesheet(user, week_of)
5     @recipient = user.name
```

```
 6    mail(
 7      to: user.email,
 8      from: "test@myapp.com",
 9      subject: "[Time and Expenses] Timesheet notice"
10    )
11  end
12
13  protected
14
15  def set_inline_attachments
16    attachments["logo.png"] = File.read("/images/logo.png")
17  end
18 end
```

Action callbacks are covered in detail in Chapter 4, "Working with Controllers," in the "Action Callbacks" section.

16.3   Receiving Emails

To receive emails, you need to write a public method named `receive` on one of your application's `ActionMailer::Base` subclasses. It will take a `Mail::Message`[1] object instance as its single parameter. When there is incoming email to handle, you call an instance method named `receive` on your Mailer class. The raw email string is converted into a `Mail::Message` object automatically, and your `receive` method is invoked for further processing. You don't have to implement the `receive` class method yourself; it is inherited from `ActionMailer::Base`.[2]

That's all pretty confusing to explain but simple in practice. Listing 16.2 shows an example.

Listing 16.2   The Simple `MessageArchiver` Mailer Class with a Receive Method

```
1 class MessageArchiver < ActionMailer::Base
2
3   def receive(email)
4     person = Person.where(email: email.to.first).first!
5     person.emails.create(
6       subject: email.subject,
7       body: email.body
8     )
```

---

1. `http://github.com/mikel/mail`

2. If you are using a third-party email service, such as SendGrid, be sure to check out the Griddler gem by Thoughtbot. It's a Rails engine that hands off preprocessed email objects to a class solely responsible for processing the incoming email: `http://github.com/thoughtbot/griddler`

```
 9     end
10   end
```

The `receive` class method can be the target for a Postfix recipe or any other mail-handler process that can pipe the contents of the email to another process. The `rails runner` command makes it easy to handle incoming mail:

```
$ rails runner 'MessageArchiver.receive(STDIN.read)'
```

That way, when a message is received, the `receive` class method would be fed the raw string content of the incoming email via `STDIN`.

16.3.1   Handling Incoming Attachments

Processing files attached to incoming email messages is just a matter of using the `attachments` attribute of `Mail::Message`, as in Listing 16.3. This example assumes that you have a `Person` class with a `has_many` association `photos` that contains a Carrierwave attachment.[3]

```
 1 class PhotoByEmail < ActionMailer::Base
 2
 3   def receive(email)
 4     from = email.from.first
 5     person = Person.where(email: from).first
 6     logger.warn("Person not found [#{from}]") and return unless person
 7
 8     if email.has_attachments?
 9       email.attachments.each do |file|
10         person.photos.create(asset: file)
11       end
12     end
13   end
14 end
```

There's not much more to it than that, except of course wrestling with the configuration of your mail processor (outside of Rails), since they are notoriously difficult to configure.[4] After you have your mail processor calling the `rails runner` command correctly, add a `crontab` so that incoming mail is handled about every five minutes or so, depending on the needs of your application.

---

3. Carrierwave, created by Jonas Nicklas, can be found at http://github.com/jnicklas/carrierwave
4. Rob Orsini, author of O'Reilly's *Rails Cookbook* recommends getmail, which you can get from http://pyropus.ca/software/getmail

16.4   Server Configuration

Most of the time, you don't have to configure anything specifically to get mail sending to work, because your production server will have `sendmail` installed and Action Mailer will happily use it to send emails.

If you don't have sendmail installed on your server, you can try setting up Rails to send email directly via SMTP. The `ActionMailer::Base` class has a hash named `smtp_settings` that holds configuration information. The settings here will vary depending on the SMTP server that you use.

The sample (as shown in Listing 16.3) demonstrates the SMTP server settings that are available (and their default values). You'll want to add similar code to your `config/environment.rb` file:

Listing 16.3   SMTP Settings for `ActionMailer`
```
1  ActionMailer::Base.smtp_settings = {
2      address: 'smtp.yourserver.com', # default: localhost
3      port: 25,  # default: 25
4      domain: 'yourserver.com', # default: localhost.localdomain
5      user_name: 'user', # no default
6      password: 'password', # no default
7      authentication: :plain  # :plain, :login or :cram_md5
8  }
```

16.5   Testing Email Content

Ben Mabey's `email_spec`[5] gem provides a nice way to test your mailers using RSpec. Add it to your Gemfile and first make the following additions to your `spec/spec_helper.rb`.

```
1  RSpec.configure do |config|
2    config.include(EmailSpec::Helpers)
3    config.include(EmailSpec::Matchers)
4  end
```

Mailer specs reside in `spec/mailers`, and `email_spec` provides convenience matchers for asserting that the mailer contains the right attributes.

reply_to Checks the reply-to value.

deliver_to Verifies the recipient.

deliver_from Assertion for the sender.

---

5. http://github.com/bmabey/email-spec

bcc_to Verifies the Bcc.

cc_to Verifies the Cc.

have_subject Performs matching of the subject text.

include_email_with_subject Performs matching of the subject text in multiple emails.

have_body_text Matches for text in the body.

have_header Checks for a matching email header.

These matchers can then be used to assert that the generated email has the correct content included in it.

```
 1 require "spec_helper"
 2
 3 describe InvoiceMailer do
 4   let(:invoice) { Invoice.new(name: "Acme", email: "joe@example.com") }
 5
 6   describe "#create_late" do
 7     subject(:email) { InvoiceMailer.create_late(invoice) }
 8
 9     it "delivers to the invoice email" do
10       expect(email).to deliver_to("joe@example.com")
11     end
12
13     it "contains the invoice name" do
14       expect(email).to have_body_text(/Acme/)
15     end
16
17     it "has a late invoice subject" do
18       expect(email).to have_subject(/Late Invoice/)
19     end
20   end
21 end
```

If you're attempting to test whether or not the mailer gets called and sends the email, it is recommended to simply check via a mock that the deliver method got executed.

16.6 Previews

By default in Rails, all email messages sent in development via Action Mailer are delivered in test mode. This means that if you send an email from your application, the output of that message would display in your development log. While this can show you if the output is correct, it does not indicate if the email message is rendered correctly. A way around this would be to connect your development environment to an actual SMTP server. Even though this would allow you to view the email in your mail client of choice, it's also a very bad idea, as you could potentially email real people.

New to Action Mailer as of Rails 4.1 is previews, which provides a means of rendering plain text and HTML mail templates in your browser without having to deliver them.

To create a preview, define a class that inherits from `ActionMailer::Preview`. Methods defined within the class must return a `Mail::Message` object, which can be created by calling a mailer method.

```
1 class LateNoticePreview < ActionMailer::Preview
2   def late_timesheet
3     user = FactoryGirl.create(:user)
4     LateNotice.late_timesheet(user, 1.week.ago)
5   end
6 end
```

By default, all previews are located in the `test/mailers/previews` directory; however, this directory path can be overridden using the `preview_path` configuration option.

```
1 # For those using RSpec
2 config.action_mailer.preview_path = "#{Rails.root}/spec/mailers/previews"
```

To obtain a listing of all Action Mailer previews available within your application, navigate to `http://localhost:3000/rails/mailers/` while running a local development server instance.

16.7   Conclusion

In this chapter, we learned how Rails makes sending and receiving email easy. With relatively little code, you can set up your application to send out email, even HTML email with inline graphics attachments. Receiving email is even easier, except perhaps for setting up mail-processing scripts and cron jobs. We also briefly covered the configuration settings that go in your application's environment-specific configuration related to mail.

CHAPTER 17

Caching and Performance

Watch me lean and watch me rock.

—Soulja Boy

Historically, Rails has suffered from an unfair barrage of criticisms over perceived weaknesses in scalability. Luckily, the continued success of Rails in high-traffic usage at companies such as Groupon has made liars of the critics. Nowadays, you can make your Rails application very responsive and scalable with ease. The mechanisms used to squeeze maximum performance out of your Rails apps are the subject of this chapter.

View caching lets you specify that anything from entire pages down to fragments of the page should be captured to disk as HTML files and sent along by your web server on future requests with minimal involvement from Rails itself. ETag support means that in best-case scenarios, it's not even necessary to send any content at all back to the browser beyond a couple of HTTP headers.

17.1 View Caching

ActiveView's templating system is both flexible and powerful. However, it is decidedly not very fast, even in the best-case scenarios. Therefore, once you get the basic functionality of your app coded, it's worth doing a review of your views and figuring out how to cache their content to achieve maximum performance. Sometimes, just rendering a page can consume 80 percent of the average request processing time.[1]

---

1. http://www.appneta.com/blog/russian-doll-caching/

Historically, there have been three types of view caching in Rails. As of Rails 4, two of those types—action and page caching—were extracted into officially supported but separate gems. Even though a consensus is emerging that "Russian doll" caching using fragment caching is enough, we briefly cover the other two methods here for the sake of completeness:

Page Caching The output of an entire controller action is cached to disk, with no further involvement by the Rails dispatcher.

Action Caching The output of an entire controller action is cached, but the Rails dispatcher is still involved in subsequent requests and controller filters are executed.

Fragment Caching Arbitrary reusable bits and pieces of your page's output are cached to prevent having to render them again in the future.

Knowing that your application will eventually require caching should influence your design decisions. Projects with optional authentication often have controller actions that are impossible to page or action cache, because they handle both login states internally.

Most of the time, you won't have too many pages with completely static content that can be cached using `caches_page` or `caches_action`, and that's where fragment caching comes into play. It's also the main reason that these two pieces of functionality were extracted out of core Rails.

For scalability reasons, you might be tempted to page cache skeleton markup or content that is common to all users and then use Ajax to subsequently modify the page. It works, but I can tell you from experience that it's difficult to develop and maintain and probably not worth the effort for most applications.

17.1.1 Page Caching

The simplest form of caching is page caching, triggered by use of the `caches_page` macro-style method in a controller. It tells Rails to capture the entire output of the request to disk so that it is served up directly by the web server on subsequent requests without the involvement of the dispatcher. On subsequent requests, nothing will be logged to the Rails log, nor will controller filters be triggered—absolutely nothing to do with Rails will happen, just like the static HTML that happens with files served from your project's `public` directory.

```
1 class HomepageController < ApplicationController
2   caches_page :index
```

```
3
4   def index
5     ...
```

In Rails 4, if you want to use page caching you need to add a gem to your `Gemfile`:

```
gem 'actionpack-page_caching'
```

Next, include the module and specify the folder in which to store cached pages in `ApplicationController`:

```
1 class ApplicationController < ActionController::Base
2   include ActionController::Caching::Pages
3   self.page_cache_directory = "#{Rails.root.to_s}/public/cache/
        pages"
4 end
```

For classic Rails behavior, you may set the `page_cache_directory` to the public root, but if you don't, then ensure that your web server knows where to find cached versions.[2]

17.1.1.1   Sample Nginx/Puma Configuration File with Page Caching Enabled

```
1 upstream puma_server_domain_tld {
2   server unix:/path/to/the/puma/socket;
3 }
4 server {
5   listen 80;
6   server_name domain.tld;
7   root /path/to/the/app;
8   location / {
9     proxy_set_header X-Forwarded-For $proxy_add_x_forwarded_for;
10    proxy_set_header Host $http_host;
11    proxy_redirect off;
12    # Try the $uri, then the uri inside the cache folder, then the puma socket.
13    try_files $uri /page_cache/$uri /page_cache/$uri.html @puma;
14  }
15  location @puma{
16    proxy_pass http://puma_server_domain_tld;
17    break;
18  }
19 }
```

---

2. http://www.rubytutorial.io/page-caching-with-rails-4

Caching

17.1.2   Action Caching

By definition, if there's anything that has to change on every request or specific to
an end user's view of that page, page caching is not an option. On the other hand, if
all we need to do is run some filters that check conditions before displaying the page
requested, the `caches_action` method will work. It's almost like page caching,
except that controller filters are executed prior to serving the cached HTML file.
That gives you the option to do some extra processing, redirect, or even blow away
the existing action cache and rerender if necessary.

As with page caching, this functionality has been extracted from Rails 4, so you
need to add the official action caching gem to your Gemfile in order to use it:

```
gem 'actionpack-action_caching'
```

Action caching is implemented with fragment caching (covered later in this chapter)
and an `around_action` controller callback. The output of the cached action is
keyed based on the current host and the path, which means that it will still work even
with Rails applications serving multiple subdomains using a DNS wildcard. Also,
different representations of the same resource, such as HTML and XML, are treated
like separate requests and cached separately.

Listing 17.1 (like most of the listings in this chapter) is taken from a dead-simple
blog application with public and private entries. On default requests, we run a filter
that figures out whether the visitor is logged in and redirects them to the `public`
action if not.

Listing 17.1   A Controller That Uses Page and Action Caching

```
 1 class EntriesController < ApplicationController
 2   before_action :check_logged_in, only: [:index]
 3
 4   caches_page :public
 5   caches_action :index
 6
 7   def public
 8     @entries = Entry.where(private: false).limit(10)
 9     render :index
10   end
11
12   def index
13     @entries = Entry.limit(10)
14   end
15
16   private
17
```

```
18   def check_logged_in
19     redirect_to action: 'public' unless logged_in?
20   end
21
22 end
```

The `public` action displays only the public entries and is visible to anyone, which is what makes it a candidate for page caching. However, since it doesn't require its own template, we just call `render :index` explicitly at the end of the `public` action.

Caching in Development Mode

I wanted to mention up front that caching is disabled in development mode. If you want to play with caching during development, you'll need to edit the following setting in the `config/environments/development.rb` file:

```
config.action_controller.perform_caching = false
```

Of course, remember to change it back before checking it into your project repository or you might face some very confusing errors down the road. In his great screencast on the subject, Geoffrey Grosenbach suggests adding another environment mode to your project named `development_with_caching`, with caching turned on just for experimentation; `http://peepcode.com/products/page-action-and-fragment-caching`.

17.1.3 Fragment Caching

Users are accustomed to all sorts of dynamic content on the page, and your application layout will be filled with things like welcome messages and notification counts. Fragment caching allows us to capture parts of the rendered page and serve them up on subsequent requests without needing to render their content again. The performance improvement is not quite as dramatic as with page or action caching, since the Rails dispatcher is still involved in serving the request, and often the database is still hit with requests. However, automatic key expiration means that "sweeping" old cached content is significantly easier than with page or action caching. And actually, the best way to use fragment caching is on top of a cache store like Memcached that'll automatically kick out old entries—meaning there's little to no sweeping required.[3]

---

3. It's also possible to do the same with Redis. See `http://antirez.com/post/redis-as-LRU-cache.html`

17.1.3.1   The `cache` Method

Fragment caching is by its very nature something that you specify in your view template rather than at the controller level. You do so using the `cache` view helper method of the `ActionView::Helpers::CacheHelper` module. In addition to its optional parameters, the method takes a block, which allows you to easily wrap content that should be cached.

Once we log in to the sample application reflected in Listing 17.1, the header section should probably display information about the user, so action caching the index page is out of the question. We'll remove the `caches_action` directive from the `EntriesController` but leave `cache_page` in place for the `public` action. Then we'll go into the `entries/index.html.haml` template and add fragment caching, as shown in Listing 17.2:

Listing 17.2   The Index Template with Cache Directive

```
1 %h1 #{@user.name}'s Journal
2 %ul.entries
3   - cache do
4     = render partial: 'entry', collection: @entries
```

Just like that, the HTML that renders the collection of entries is stored as a cached fragment associated with the entries page. Future requests will not need to rerender the entries. Here's what it looks like when Rails checks to see whether the content is already in the cache:

```
"get" "views/localhost:3000/entries/d57823a936b2ee781687c74c44e056a0"
```

The cache was not *warm* on the first request, so Rails renders the content and sets it into the cache for future use:

```
"setex" "views/localhost:3000/entries/d57823a936b2ee781687c74c44e056a0"
"5400" "\x04\bo: ActiveSupport::Cache::Entry\b:\x0b@valueI\"\x02\xbbf
<li class="entry">...
```

If you analyze the structure of the keys being sent to the cache (in this case Redis), you'll notice that they are composed of several distinct parts.

views/ Indicates that we are doing some view caching.

hostname/ The host and port serving up the content. Note that this doesn't break with virtual hostnames since the name of the server itself is used.

type/ In the case of our example, it's `entries`, but that spot in the key would contain some indicator of the type of data being rendered. If you do not provide a specific key name, it will be set to the name of the controller serving up the content.

`digest/` The remaining hexadecimal string is an MD5 hash of the template content, so that changing the content of the template *busts* the cache. This is new functionality in Rails 4 that eliminates the need for home-brewed template versioning schemes. Most template dependencies can be derived from calls to render in the template itself.[4]

Warning

Despite the nifty cache-busting behavior of adding template digests to your cache keys automatically, there are some situations where changes to the way you're generating markup will not bust the cache correctly. The primary case is when you have markup generated in a helper method and you change the body of that helper method. The digest hash generated for templates that use that helper method will not change; they have no way of knowing to do so. There is no super elegant solution to this problem. Rails core suggests adding a comment to the template where the helper is used and modifying it whenever the behavior of the helper changes.[5]

17.1.3.2 Fragment Cache Keys

The cache method takes an optional name parameter that we left blank in Listing 17.2. That's an acceptable solution when there is only one cached fragment on a page. Usually there'll be more than one. Therefore, it's a good practice to identify the fragment in a way that will prevent collisions with other fragments, whether they are on the same page or not. Listing 17.3 is an enhanced version of the entries page. Since this blog handles content for multiple users, we're keying the list of entries off the user object itself.

Listing 17.3 Enhanced Version of the Entries Page

```
1 %h1 #{@user.name}'s Journal
2
3 - cache @user do
4   %ul.entries
5     = render partial: 'entry', collection: @entries
6
7 - content_for :sidebar do
```

---

4. https://github.com/rails/cache_digests#implicit-dependencies
5. https://github.com/rails/cache_digests#explicit-dependencies

```
8    - cache [@user, :recent_comments] do
9      = render partial: 'comment', collection: @recent_comments
```

Notice that we've also added recent comments in the sidebar and named those fragment cache accordingly to show how to namespace cache keys. Also note the use of an array in place of a name or single object for those declarations to create a *compound key*.

After the code in Listing 17.3 is rendered, there will be at least two fragments in the cache, keyed as follows:

```
views/users/1-20131126171127/1e4adb3067d5a7598ea1d0fd0f7b7ff1
views/users/1-20131126171127/recent_comments/1f440155af81f1358d8f97a099395802
```

Note that the recent comments are correctly identified with a suffix. We'll also add a suffix to the cache of entries to make sure that we don't have future conflicts.

```
1    - cache [@user, :entries] do
2      %ul.entries
3        = render partial: 'entry', collection: @entries
4      ...
```

17.1.3.3   Accounting for URL Parameters

Earlier versions of Rails transparently used elements of the page's URL to key fragments in the cache. It was an elegant solution to a somewhat difficult problem of caching pages that take parameters. Consider, for instance, what would happen if you added pagination, filtering, or sorting to your list of blog entries in our sample app: the cache directive would ignore the parameters because it's keying strictly on the identity of the user object. Therefore, we need to add any other relevant parameters to a compound key for that page content.

For example, let's expand our compound key for user entries by adding the page number requested:

```
1    - cache [@user, :entries, page: params[:page]] do
2      %ul.entries
3        = render partial: 'entry', collection: @entries
```

The key mechanism understands hashes as part of the compound key and adds their content using a slash delimiter.

```
views/users/1-20131126171127/entries/page/1/1e4adb3067d5a7598ea1d0fd0f7b7ff1
views/users/1-20131126171127/entries/page/2/1e4adb3067d5a7598ea1d0fd0f7b7ff1
views/users/1-20131126171127/entries/page/3/1e4adb3067d5a7598ea1d0fd0f7b7ff1
etc...
```

If your site is localized, you probably want to include the user's locale in the compound key so that you don't serve up the wrong languages to visitors from different places.

```
1 - cache [@user, :entries, locale: @user.locale, page: params[:page]] do
2   %ul.entries
3     = render partial: 'entry', collection: @entries
```

As you can tell, construction of cache keys can get complicated, and that's a lot of logic to be carrying around in our view templates. DRY up your code if necessary by extracting into a view helper and/or overriding the key object's `cache_key` method.

```
1 class User
2   def cache_key
3     [super, locale].join '-'
4   end
```

Object Keys

As you've seen in our examples so far, the `cache` method accepts objects, whether by themselves or in an array as its name parameter. When you do that, it'll call cache_key or `to_param` on the object provided to get a name for the fragment. By default, Active Record and Mongoid objects respond to cache_key with a dashed combination of their id and updated_at timestamp (if available).

17.1.3.4   Global Fragments

Sometimes, you'll want to fragment cache content that is not specific to single part of your application. To add globally keyed fragments to the cache, simply use the name parameter of the `cache` helper method, but give it a string identifier instead of an object or array.

In Listing 17.4, we cache the site stats partial for every user, using simply `:site_stats` as the key.

Listing 17.4   Caching the Stats Partial across the Site

```
1 %h1 #{@user.name}'s Journal
2
3 - cache [@user, :entries, page: params[:page]] do
4   %ul.entries
5     = render partial: 'entry', collection: @entries
6
7 - content_for :sidebar do
8   - cache(:site_stats) do
9     = render partial: 'site_stats'
10   ...
```

Caching

Now requesting the page results in the following key being added to the cache:

```
views/site_stats/1e4adb3067d5a7598ea1d0fd0f7b7ff1
```

17.1.4   Russian Doll Caching

If you nest calls to the `cache` method and provide objects as key names, you get a strategy referred to as "Russian doll" caching by David[6] and others.[7]

To take advantage of this strategy, let's update our example code, assuming that a user has many entries (and remembering that this is a simple blog application).

Listing 17.5   Russian Doll Nesting

```
 1 %h1 #{@user.name}'s Journal
 2
 3 - cache [@user, :entries, page: params[:page]] do
 4   %ul.entries
 5     = render partial: 'entry', collection: @entries
 6
 7 - content_for :sidebar do
 8   - cache(:site_stats) do
 9     = render partial: 'site_stats'
10
11 # entries/_entry.html.haml
12
13 - cache entry do
14   %li[entry]
15     %p.content= entry.content
16     ...
```

Now we retain fast performance even if the top-level cache is busted. For instance, adding a new entry would update the timestamp of the `@user`, but only the new entry has to be rendered. The rest of the content already exists as smaller fragments that are not invalid and can get reused.

Listing 17.6   Example of Using Touch to Invalidate a Parent Record's Cache Key

```
1 class User < ActiveRecord::Base
2   has_many :entries
3 end
4
5 class Entry < ActiveRecord::Base
```

---

6. http://signalvnoise.com/posts/3113-how-key-based-cache-expiration-works

7. http://blog.remarkablelabs.com/2012/12/russian-doll-caching-cache-digests-rails-4
-countdown-to-2013

```
6    belongs_to: user, touch: true
7 end
```

For this to work correctly, there has to be a way for the parent object (@user in the case of the example) to be updated automatically when one of its dependent objects changes. That's where the touch functionality of Active Record and other object mapper libraries comes in, as demonstrated in Listing 17.6.

Outside of the Rails world, the Russian doll strategy is also known as *generational caching*.

I have found that using this strategy can dramatically improve application performance and lessen database load considerably. It can save tons of expensive table scans from happening in the database. By sparing the database of these requests, other queries that do hit the database can be completed more quickly.

In order to maintain cache consistency, this strategy is conservative in nature; this results in keys being expired that don't necessarily need to be expired. For example if you update a post in a particular category, this strategy will expire all the keys for all the categories. While this may seem somewhat inefficient and ripe for optimization, I've often found that most applications are so read-heavy that these types of optimization don't make a noticeable overall performance difference. Plus, the code to implement those optimizations then become application or model specific, and more difficult to maintain.

…[I]n this strategy nothing is ever explicitly deleted from the cache. This has some implications with respect to the caching tool and eviction policy that you use. This strategy was designed to be used with caches that employ a Least Recently Used (LRU) eviction policy (like Memcached). An LRU policy will result in keys the with old generations being evicted first, which is precisely what you want. Other eviction policies can be used (e.g., FIFO) although they may not be as effective.

—Jonathan Kupferman, discussing web
application caching strategies[8]

Later in the chapter, we discuss how to configure Memcached as your application's cache.

---

8. http://www.regexprn.com/2011/06/web-application-caching-strategies_05.html

Caching

> David details an extreme form of Russian doll caching in his seminal blog post "How Basecamp Next Got to Be So Damn Fast without Using Much Client-Side UI."[9] The level of detail he goes into is too much for this book, but we recommend his strategy of aggressively cached reuse of identical bits of markup in many different contexts of his app. CSS modifies the display of the underlying markup to fit its context properly.

17.1.5   Conditional Caching

Rails provides `cache_if` and `cache_unless` convenience helpers that wrap the `cache` method and add a boolean parameter.

```
- cache_unless current_user.admin?, @expensive_stats_to_calculate do
  ...
```

17.1.6   Expiration of Cached Content

Whenever you use caching, you need to consider any and all situations that will cause the cache to become stale and out of date. As we've seen, so-called *generational caching* attempts to solve cache expiry by tying the keys to information about the versions of the underlying objects. But if you don't use generational caching, then you need to write code that manually sweeps away old cached content or makes it time out so that new content to be cached in its place.

17.1.6.1   Time-Based Expiry

The simplest strategy for cache invalidation is simply time based—that is, tell the cache to automatically invalidate content after a set time period. All the Rails cache providers (Memcached, Redis, etc.) accept an option for time-based expiry. Just add `:expires_in` to your fragment cache directive:

```
- cache @entry, expire_in: 2.hours do
  = render @post
```

We can tell you from experience that this kind of cache invalidation is only good for a narrow set of circumstances. Most of the time, you only want to invalidate when underlying data changes state.

17.1.6.2   Expiring Pages and Actions

The `expire_page` and `expire_action` controller methods let you explicitly delete content from the cache in your action so that it is regenerated on the next

---

9. `http://signalvnoise.com/posts/3112-how-basecamp-next-got-to-be-so-damn-fast`
`-without-using-much-client-side-ui`

request. There are various ways to identify the content to expire, but one of them is by passing a hash with `url_for` conventions used elsewhere in Rails. Since this topic is now esoteric in Rails 4, we leave it as a research exercise for the motivated reader.

17.1.6.3 Expiring Fragments

The sample blogging app we've been playing with has globally cached content to clear out, for which we'll be using the `expire_fragment` method.

```
1 def create
2   @entry = @user.entries.build(params[:entry])
3   if @entry.save
4     expire_fragment(:site_stats)
5     redirect_to entries_path(@entry)
6   else
7     render action: 'new'
8   end
9 end
```

This isn't the greatest or most current Rails code in the world. All it's doing is showing you basic use of `expire_fragment`. Remember that the key you provide to `expire_fragment` needs to match the key you used to set the cache in the first place. The difficulty in maintaining this kind of code is the reason that key invalidation is considered one of the hardest problems in computer science!

Occasionally, you might want to blow away any cached content that references a particular bit of data. Luckily, the `expire_fragment` method also understands regular expressions. In the following example, we invalidate anything related to a particular user:

```
expire_fragment(%r{@user.cache_key})
```

> The big gotcha with regular expressions and `expire_fragment` is that it is not supported with the most common caching service used on Rails production systems: Memcached.

17.1.7 Automatic Cache Expiry with Sweepers

Since caching is a unique concern, it tends to feel like something that should be applied in an aspect-oriented fashion instead of procedurally.

A `Sweeper` class is kind of like an `ActiveRecord Observer` object, except that it's specialized for use in expiring cached content. When you write a sweeper, you tell it which of your models to observe for changes, just as you would with callback classes and observers.

Caching

Remember that observers are no longer included in Rails 4 by default, so if you need sweepers, you'll have to add the official observers gem to your Gemfile.

```
gem 'rails-observers'
```

Listing 17.7 Moving Expiry Logic Out of Controller into a Sweeper Class
```
 1 class EntrySweeper < ActionController::Caching::Sweeper
 2   observe Entry
 3
 4   def expire_cached_content(entry)
 5     expire_page controller: 'entries', action: 'public'
 6     expire_fragment(:site_stats)
 7   end
 8
 9   alias_method :after_commit, :expire_cached_content
10   alias_method :after_destroy, :expire_cached_content
11
12 end
```

Once you have a `Sweeper` class written, you still have to tell your controller to use that sweeper in conjunction with its actions. Here's the top of the revised entries controller:

```
1 class EntriesController < ApplicationController
2   caches_page :public
3   cache_sweeper :entry_sweeper, only: [:create, :update,
        :destroy]
4   ...
```

Like many other controller macros, the `cache_sweeper` method takes `:only` and `:except` options. There's no need to bother the sweeper for actions that can't modify the state of the application, so we do indeed include the `:only` option in our example.

17.1.8 Avoiding Extra Database Activity

Once you have fragments of your view cached, you might think to yourself that it no longer makes sense to do the database queries that supply those fragments with their data. After all, the results of those database queries will not be used again until the cached fragments are expired. The `fragment_exist?` method lets you check for the existence of cached content and takes the same parameters that you used with the associated `cache` method.

Here's how we would modify the index action accordingly:

```
1 def index
2   unless fragment_exist? [@user, :entries, page: params[:page]]
3     @entries = Entry.all.limit(10)
4   end
5 end
```

Now the finder method will only get executed if the cache needs to be refreshed. However, as Tim pointed out in previous editions of this book, the whole issue is moot if you use Decent Exposure[10] to make data available to your views via methods, not instance variables. Because decent exposure method invocations are inside the templates instead of your controllers, inside the blocks passed to the `cache` method, the problem solves itself.

We actually disputed whether to even include this section in the current edition. Since view rendering is so much slower than database access, avoidance of database calls represents a minor additional optimization on top of the usual fragment caching, meaning you should only have to worry about this if you're trying to squeeze every last bit of performance out of your application—and even then, we advise you to really think about it.

17.1.9   Cache Logging

If you've turned on caching during development, you can actually monitor the Rails console or development log for messages about caching and expiration.

```
Write fragment views/pages/52781671756e6bd2fa060000-20131110153647/
stats/1f440155af81f1358d8f97a099395802 (1.4ms)
Cache digest for pages/_page.html: 1f440155af81f1358d8f97a099395802
Read fragment views/pages/52781604756e6bd2fa050000-20131104214748/
stats/1f440155af81f1358d8f97a099395802 (0.3ms)
```

17.1.10   Cache Storage

You can set up your application's default cache store by calling `config.cache_store=` in the `Application` definition inside your `config/application.rb` `file` or in an environment specific configuration file. The first argument will be the cache store to use and the rest of the argument will be passed as arguments to the cache store constructor.

By default, Rails gives you three different options for storage of action and fragment cache data. Other options require installation of third-party gems.[11]

---

10. https://github.com/voxdolo/decent_exposure
11. See http://edgeguides.rubyonrails.org/caching_with_rails.html#cache-stores for a full list of support cache providers, including Terracotta's Ehcache.

Caching

`ActiveSupport::Cache::FileStore` Keeps the fragments on disk in the `cache_path`, which works well for all types of environments (except Heroku) and shares the fragments for all the web server processes running off the same application directory.

`ActiveSupport::Cache::MemoryStore` Keeps fragments in process memory in a threadsafe fashion. This store can potentially consume an unacceptable amount of memory if you do not limit it and implement a good expiration strategy. The cache store has a bounded size specified by the `:size` options to the initializer (default is `32.megabytes`). When the cache exceeds the allotted size, a cleanup will occur and the least recently used entries will be removed. Note that only small Rails applications that are deployed on a single process will ever benefit from this configuration.

`ActiveSupport::Cache::MemCacheStore` Keeps the fragments in a separate process using a proven cache server named `memcached`.

17.1.10.1   Configuration Examples

The `:memory_store` option is enabled by default. Unlike session data, which is limited in size, fragment-cached data can grow to be quite large, which means you almost certainly don't want to use this default option in production.

```
config.cache_store = :memory_store, expire_in: 1.minute, compress: true
config.cache_store = :file_store, "/path/to/cache/directory"
```

All cache stores take the following hash options as their last parameter:

`expires_in` Supplies a time for items to be expired from the cache.

`compress` Specifies to use compression or not.

`compress_threshold` Specifies the threshold at which to compress, with the default being 16k.

`namespace` If your application shares a cache with others, this option can be used to create a namespace for it.

`race_condition_ttl` This option is used in conjunction with the `:expires_in` option on content that is accessed and updated heavily. It prevents multiple processes from trying to simultaneously repopulate the same key. The value of the option sets the number of seconds that an expired entry can be reused (be *stale*) while a new value is being regenerated.

17.1.10.2   Limitations of File-Based Storage

As long as you're hosting your Rails application on a single server, setting up caching is fairly straightforward and easy to implement (but, of course, coding it is a different story).

If you think about the implications of running a cached application on a cluster of distinct physical servers, you might realize that cache invalidation is going to be painful. Unless you set up the file storage to point at a shared filesystem such as NFS or GFS, it won't work.

17.2   Data Caching

Each of the caching mechanisms described in the previous section is actually using an implementation of an `ActiveSupport::Cache::Store`, covered in detail in Appendix B.

Rails actually always exposes its default cache store via the `Rails.cache` method, and you can use it anywhere in your application or from the console:

```
1 >> Rails.cache.write(:color, :red)
2 => true
3 >> Rails.cache.read :color
4 => :red
```

17.2.1   Eliminating Extra Database Lookups

One of the most common patterns of simple cache usage is to eliminate database lookups for commonly accessed data, using the cache's `fetch` method. For the following example, assume that your application's user objects are queried very often by id. The `fetch` method takes a block that is executed and used to populate the cache when the lookup *misses*—that is, a value is not already present.

Listing 17.8 Cache management with an Active Record model

```
1 class User < ActiveRecord::Base
2   def self.fetch(id)
3     Rails.cache.fetch("user_#{id}") { User.find(id) }
4   end
5
6   def after_commit
7     Rails.cache.write("user_#{id}", self)
8   end
9
```

```
10   def after_destroy
11     Rails.cache.delete("city_#{id}")
12   end
13 end
```

With relatively little effort, you could convert the code in Listing 17.8 into a
`Concern` and include it wherever needed.

17.2.2   Initializing New Caches

We can also initialize a new cache directly or through `ActiveSupport::Cache`
`.lookup_store` if we want to use different caches for different reasons (not that we recommend doing that). Either one of these methods of creating a new cache takes the same
expiration and compression options mentioned previously, and the same three stores exist
as for fragment caching: `FileStore`, `MemoryStore`, and `MemCacheStore`.

```
1 ActiveSupport::Cache::MemCacheStore.new(
2   expire_in: 5.seconds
3 )
4 ActiveSupport::Cache.lookup_store(
5   :mem_cache_store, compress: true
6 )
```

Once you have your cache object, you can read and write to it via its very simple API,
and any Ruby object that can be serialized can be cached, including nils.

```
1 cache = ActiveSupport::Cache::MemoryStore.new
2 cache.write(:name, "John Doe")
3 cache.fetch(:name) # => "John Doe"
```

17.2.3   **fetch** Options

There are several now-familiar options that can be passed to `fetch` in order to
provide different types of behavior for each of the different stores. Additional options than those listed here are available based on the individual cache
implementations.

:compress Uses compression for this request.

:expire_in Tells an individual key in the cache to expire in n seconds.

:force If set to true, forces the cache to delete the supplied key.

:race_condition_ttl Supplies seconds as an integer and a block. When an
   item in the cache is expired for less than the number of seconds, its time gets
   updated and its value is set to the result of the block.

There are other available functions on caches, and additional options can be passed depending on the specific cache store implementation.

delete(name, options) Deletes a value for the key.

exist?(name, options) Returns true if a value exists for the provided key.

read(name, options) Gets a value for the supplied key or returns nil if none found.

read_multi(*names) Returns the values for the supplied keys as a hash of key/value pairs.

write(name, value, options) Writes a value to the cache.

17.3 Control of Web Caching

Action Controller offers a pair of methods for easily setting HTTP 1.1 Cache-Control headers. Their default behavior is to issue a *private* instruction so that intermediate caches (web proxies) must not cache the response. In this context, *private* only controls where the response may be cached and not the privacy of the message content.

The `public` setting indicates that the response may be cached by any cache or proxy and should never be used in conjunction with data served up for *a particular end user.*

Using `curl --head`, we can examine the way that these methods affect HTTP responses. For reference, let's examine the output of a normal index action.

```
 1 $ curl --head localhost:3000/reports
 2 HTTP/1.1 200 OK
 3 Etag: "070a386229cd857a15b2f5cb2089b987"
 4 Connection: Keep-Alive
 5 Content-Type: text/html; charset=utf-8
 6 Date: Wed, 15 Sep 2010 04:01:30 GMT
 7 Server: WEBrick/1.3.1 (Ruby/1.8.7/2009-06-12)
 8 X-Runtime: 0.032448
 9 Content-Length: 0
10 Cache-Control: max-age=0, private, must-revalidate
11 Set-Cookie: ...124cc92; path=/; HttpOnly
```

Don't get confused by the content length being zero. That's only because `curl --head` issues a HEAD request. If you're experimenting with your own Rails app, try `curl -v localhost:3000` to see all the HTTP headers plus the body content.

17.3.1 `expires_in(seconds, options = )`

This method will overwrite an existing `Cache-Control` header.

Examples include the following:

```
expires_in 20.minutes
expires_in 3.hours, public: true
expires in 3.hours, 'max-stale' => 5.hours, public: true
```

Setting expiration to 20 minutes alters our reference output as follows:

```
Cache-Control: max-age=1200, private
```

17.3.2 `expires_now`

Sets a HTTP 1.1 Cache-Control header of the response to `no-cache`, informing web proxies and browsers that they should not cache the response for subsequent requests.

17.4 ETags

The bulk of this chapter deals with caching content so that the server does less work than it would have to do otherwise but still incurs the cost of transporting page data to the browser. The *ETags* scheme, where *E* stands for *entity*, allows you to avoid sending any content to the browser at all if nothing has changed on the server since the last time a particular resource was requested. A properly implemented ETags scheme is one of the most significant performance improvements that can be implemented on a high-traffic website.[12]

Rendering automatically inserts the `Etag` header on *200 OK* responses, calculated as an MD5 hash of the response body. If a subsequent request comes in that has a matching `Etag`,[13] the response will be changed to a *304 Not Modified* and the response body will be set to an empty string.

The key to performance gains is to short-circuit the controller action and prevent rendering if you know that the resulting `Etag` is going to be the same as the one associated with the current request. I believe you're actually being a good Internet citizen by paying attention to proper use of ETags in your application. According to RFC 2616,[14] "the preferred behavior for an HTTP/1.1 origin server is to send both a strong entity tag and a Last-Modified value."

Rails does not set a `Last-Modified` response header by default, so it's up to you to do so using one of the following methods.

---

12. Tim Bray wrote a now classic blog post on the topic at http://www.tbray.org/ongoing/When/200x/2008/08/14/Rails-ETags

13. http://www.w3.org/Protocols/rfc2616/rfc2616-sec14.html#sec14.19

14. http://www.w3.org/Protocols/rfc2616/rfc2616-sec13.html#sec13.3.4

17.4.1   `fresh_when(options)`

Sets `ETag` and/or `Last-Modified` headers and renders a `304 Not Modified` response if the request is already *fresh*. Freshness is calculated using the `cache_key` method of the object (or array of objects) passed as the `:etag` option.

For example, the following controller action shows a public article:

```
1 expose(:article)
2
3 def show
4   fresh_when(etag: article,
5             last_modified: article.created_at.utc,
6             public: true)
7 end
```

This code will only render the show template when necessary. As you can tell, this is superior even to view caching because there is no need to check the server's cache, and data payload delivered to the browser is almost completely eliminated.

17.4.2   `stale?(options)`

Sets the `ETag` and/or `Last-Modified` headers on the response and checks them against the client request (using `fresh_when`). If the request doesn't match the options provided, the request is considered stale and should be generated from scratch.

You want to use this method instead of `fresh_when` if there is additional logic needed at the controller level in order to render your view.

```
1 expose(:article)
2
3 expose(:statistics) do
4   article.really_expensive_operation_to_calculate_stats
5 end
6
7 def show
8   if stale?(etag: article,
9             last_modified: article.created_at.utc,
10            public: true)
11    # decent_exposure memoizes the result, later used by the
       view.
12    statistics()
13
14    respond_to do |format|
15      ...
16    end
17  end
18 end
```

The normal rendering workflow is only triggered inside of the `stale?` conditional, if needed.

17.5 Conclusion

We've just covered a fairly complicated subject: caching. Knowing how to use caching will really save your bacon when you work on Rails applications that need to scale. Indeed, developers of high-traffic Rails websites tend to see Rails as a fancy HTML generation platform with which to create content ripe for caching.

CHAPTER 18

Background Processing

People count up the faults of those who keep them waiting.

—French proverb

Users of modern websites have lofty expectations when it comes to application responsiveness—most likely they will expect behavior and speed similar to that of desktop applications. Proper user experience guidelines would dictate that no HTTP request/response cycle should take more than a second to execute; however, there will be actions that arise that simply cannot achieve this time constraint.

Tasks of this nature can range from simple, long-running tasks due to network latency to more complex tasks that require heavy processing on the server. Examples of these actions could be sending an email or processing video, respectively. In these situations, it is best to have the actions execute asynchronously, so that the responsiveness of the application remains swift while the procedures run.

In this chapter, these types of tasks are referred to as background jobs. They include any execution that is handled in a separate process from the Rails application. Rails and Ruby have several libraries and techniques for performing this work—most notably the following:

- Delayed Job
- Sidekiq
- Resque
- Rails Runner

This chapter will cover each of these tools, discussing the strengths and weaknesses of each one so that you may determine what is appropriate for your application.

18.1 Delayed Job

Delayed Job[1] is a robust background processing library that is essentially a highly configurable priority queue. It provides various approaches to handling asynchronous actions, including the following:

- Custom background jobs
- Permanently marked background methods
- Background execution of methods at runtime

Delayed Job requires a persistence store to save all queue related operations. Along with the delayed_job gem, a backend gem is required to get up and running. Supported options are the following:

- Active Record with the delayed_job_active_record gem
- Mongoid (for use with MongoDB) with the delayed_job_mongoid gem

18.1.1 Getting Started

Add the delayed_job and delayed_job_active_record gems to your application's Gemfile, and then run the generator to create your execution and migration scripts.

```
$ rails generate delayed_job:active_record
```

This will create the database migration that will need to be run to set up the delayed_jobs table in the database as well as a command to run Delayed Job.

To change the default settings for Delayed Job, first add a delayed_job.rb in your config/initializers directory. Options then can be configured by calling various methods on Delayed::Worker, which include settings for changing the behavior of the queue with respect to tries, timeouts, maximum run times, sleep delays, and other options.

```
1 Delayed::Worker.destroy_failed_jobs = false
2 Delayed::Worker.sleep_delay = 30
3 Delayed::Worker.max_attempts = 5
4 Delayed::Worker.max_run_time = 1.hour
5 Delayed::Worker.max_priority = 10
```

---

1. https://github.com/collectiveidea/delayed_job

18.1.2   Creating Jobs

Delayed Job can create background jobs using three different techniques, and which one you use depends on your personal style.

The first option is to chain any method that you wish to execute asynchronously after a call to `Object#delay`. This is good for cases where some common functionality needs to execute in the background in certain situations but is acceptable to run synchronously in others.

```
1 # Execute normally
2 mailer.send_email(user)
3
4 # Execute asynchronously
5 mailer.delay.send_email(user)
```

The second technique is to tell Delayed Job to execute every call to a method in the background via the `Object.handle_asynchronously` macro.

```
1 class Mailer
2   def send_email(user)
3     UserMailer.activation(user).deliver
4   end
5
6   handle_asynchronously :send_email
7 end
```

Durran Says …

When using `handle_asynchronously`, make sure the declaration is after the method definition, since Delayed Job uses `alias_method_chain` internally to set up the behavior.

Lastly, you may create a custom job by creating a separate Ruby object that only needs to respond to `perform`. That job can then be run at any point by telling Delayed Job to enqueue the action.

```
 1 class EmailJob &lessthan; Struct.new(:user_id)
 2   def perform
 3     user = User.find(user_id)
 4     UserMailer.activation(user).deliver
 5   end
 6 end
 7
 8 # Enqueue a job with default settings
 9 Delayed::Job.enqueue EmailJob.new(user.id)
10
```

Background

```
11 # Enqueue a job with priority of 1
12 Delayed::Job.enqueue EmailJob.new(user.id), priority: 1
13
14 # Enqueue a job with priority of 0, starting tomorrow
15 Delayed::Job.enqueue EmailJob.new(user.id),priority: 0,
       run_at: 1.day.from_now
```

18.1.3   Running

To start up Delayed Job workers, use the `delayed_job` command created by the generator. This allows for starting a single worker or multiple workers on their own processes and also provides the ability to stop all workers.

```
1 # Start a single worker.
2 RAILS_ENV=staging bin/delayed_job start
3
4 # Start multiple workers, each in a separate process.
5 RAILS_ENV=production bin/delayed_job -n 4 start
6
7 # Stop all workers.
8 RAILS_ENV=staging bin/delayed_job stop
```

Durran Says ...

Delayed Job workers generally have a lifecycle that is equivalent to an application deployment. Because of this, their memory consumption grows over time and may eventually have high swap usage, causing workers to become unresponsive. A good practice is to have a monitoring tool like God or monit watching jobs and restart them when their memory usage hits a certain point.

18.1.4   Summary

Delayed Job is an excellent choice when you want the ease of setup, need to schedule jobs for later dates, or want to add priorities to jobs in your queue. It works well in situations where the total number of jobs is low and the tasks they execute are not long running or consume large amounts of memory.

Do note that if you are using Delayed Job with a relational database backend and have a large number of jobs, performance issues may arise due to the table locking the framework employs. Since jobs may have a long lifecycle, be wary of resource consumption due to workers not releasing memory once jobs are finished executing. Also, where job execution can take a long period of time, higher priority jobs will still wait for the other jobs to complete before being processed. In these cases, using a nonrelational backend such as MongoDB or potentially another library such as Sidekiq may be advisable.

18.2 Sidekiq

Sidekiq[2] is a full-featured background processing library with support for multiple weighted queues, scheduled jobs, and sending asynchronous Action Mailer emails. Like Resque (covered later in this chapter), Sidekiq uses Redis for its storage engine, minimizing the overhead of job processing.

Sidekiq is currently the best-performing and most memory-efficient background processing library in the Ruby ecosystem. It is multithreaded, which allows Sidekiq to process jobs in parallel without the overhead of having to run multiple processes. This also means Sidekiq can process jobs with a much smaller memory footprint compared to other background processing libraries, such as Delayed Job or Resque. According to the official documentation,[3] one Sidekiq process can process a magnitude more than its competitors:

> You'll find that you might need 50 200MB resque processes to peg your CPU, whereas one 300MB Sidekiq process will peg the same CPU and perform the same amount of work.

Since it's multithreaded, all code executed by Sidekiq should be threadsafe.

18.2.1 Getting Started

To integrate Sidekiq into your Rails application, add the `sidekiq` gem in your `Gemfile` and run `bundle install`.

```
# Gemfile
gem 'sidekiq'
```

By default, Sidekiq will assume that Redis can be found at `localhost:6379`. To override the location of the Redis server used by Sidekiq (for production deployments, you will probably need to point Sidekiq to an external Redis server), create a Rails initializer that configures `redis` in both `Sidekiq.configure_server` and `Sidekiq.configure_client` code blocks.

```
1  # config/initializers/sidekiq.rb
2
3  Sidekiq.configure_server do |config|
4    config.redis = {
5      url: 'redis://redis.example.com:6379/10',
6      namespace: 'tr4w'
```

---

2. http://sidekiq.org

3. https://github.com/mperham/sidekiq/blob/master/README.md

```
 7   }
 8 end
 9
10 Sidekiq.configure_client do |config|
11   config.redis = {
12     url: 'redis://redis.example.com:6379/10',
13     namespace: 'tr4w'
14   }
15 end
```

Note that setting the :namespace option is completely optional but highly recommended if Sidekiq is sharing access to a Redis database.

Juanito Says ...

Sidekiq requires Redis 2.4 or greater.

18.2.2 Workers

To create a worker in Sidekiq, one must create a class in the app/workers folder that includes the module Sidekiq::Worker and responds to perform.

```
1 class EmailWorker
2   include Sidekiq::Worker
3
4   def perform(user_id)
5     user = User.find(@user_id)
6     UserMailer.activation(user).deliver
7   end
8 end
```

To enqueue a job on the worker, simply call the perform_async class method passing any arguments required by the perform method of the worker.

```
1 EmailWorker.perform_async(1)
```

Be aware that all worker jobs are stored in the Redis database as JSON objects, meaning you must ensure the arguments provided to your worker can be serialized to JSON. For the sake of clarity, in the previous example, instead of passing an instance of User, we provided the worker with an identifier for the record. The worker would then be responsible for querying the User record from the database.

Sidekiq workers can be configured via the `sidekiq_options` macro-style method. The following are available options:

:backtrace Specifies whether or not to save error backtraces to the retry payload, defaulting to `false`. The error backtrace is used for display purposes in the Sidekiq web UI. Alternatively, you can specify the number of lines to save (i.e., backtrace: 15).

:queue The name of queue for the worker, defaulting to "default."

:retry By default, a worker is able to retry jobs until it's successfully completed. Setting the `:retry` option to `false` will instruct Sidekiq to run a job only once. Alternatively, you can specify the maximum number of times a job is retried (i.e., `retry: 5`).

```
1 class SomeWorker
2   include Sidekiq::Worker
3   sidekiq_options queue: :high_priority, retry: 5, backtrace:
        true
4
5   def perform
6     ...
7   end
8 end
```

18.2.3   Scheduled Jobs

Out of the box, Sidekiq has the ability to schedule when jobs will be executed. To delay the execution of a job for a specific interval, enqueue the job by calling `perform_in`.

```
EmailWorker.perform_in(1.hour, 1)
```

A job can also be scheduled for a specific time using the enqueue method `perform_at`.

```
EmailWorker.perform_at(2.days.from_now, 1)
```

18.2.4   Delayed Action Mailer

When Sidekiq is included in a Rails application, it adds three methods to Action Mailer that allow for email deliveries to be executed asynchronous.

Background

Note

The following methods are also available on Active Record classes to execute class methods asynchronously. It's strongly not recommended to call these methods on Active Record instances.

```
1 User.delay(1.hour).some_background_operation
```

18.2.4.1 `delay`
Calling `delay` from a mailer will result in the email being added to the `Delayed-Mailer` worker for processing.

```
UserMailer.delay.activation(user.id)
```

18.2.4.2 `delay_for(interval)`
Using `delay_for`, an email can be scheduled for delivery at a specific time interval.

```
UserMailer.delay_for(10.minutes).status_report(user.id)
```

18.2.4.3 `delay_until(timestamp)`
The last Action Mailer method added by Sidekiq is `delay_until`. Sidekiq will wait until the specified time to attempt delivery of the email.

```
1 UserMailer.delay_for(1.day).status_report(user.id)
2 UserMailer.delay_until(1.day.from_now).status_report(user.id)
```

18.2.5   Running
To start up Sidekiq workers, run the `sidekiq` command from the root of your Rails application.

```
$ bundle exec sidekiq
```

This allows for starting a Sidekiq process that begins processing against the "default" queue. To use multiple queues, you can pass the name of a queue and optional weight to the `sidekiq` command.

```
$ bundle exec sidekiq -q default -q critical,2
```

Queues have a weight of 1 by default. If a queue has a higher weight, it will be checked that many more times than a queue with a weight of 1. For instance, in the previous example, the *critical* queue is checked twice as often as *default*.

Stopping jobs involves sending signals to the `sidekiq` process, which then takes the appropriate action on all processors:

TERM Signals that Sidekiq should shut down within the `-t` timeout option. Any jobs that are not completed within the timeout period are pushed back into Redis. These jobs are executed again once Sidekiq restarts. By default, the timeout period is eight seconds.

USR1 Continues working on current jobs but stops accepting any new ones.

18.2.5.1   Concurrency

By default, Sidekiq starts up 25 concurrent processors. To explicitly set the amount of processors for Sidekiq to use, pass the `-c` option to the `sidekiq` command.

```
1 $ bundle exec sidekiq -c 100
```

Active Record Database Connections

When using Sidekiq alongside Active Record, ensure that the Active Record connection pool setting `pool` is close or equal to the number of Sidekiq processors.

```
1 production:
2   adapter: postgresql
3   database: example_production
4   pool: 25
```

18.2.5.2   `sidekiq.yml`

If you find yourself having to specify different options to the `sidekiq` command for multiple environments, you configure Sidekiq using a YAML file.

```
 1 # config/sidekiq.yml
 2 ---
 3 :concurrency: 10
 4 :queues:
 5   - [default, 1]
 6   - [critical, 5]
 7 staging:
 8   :concurrency: 25
 9 production:
10   :concurrency: 100
```

Now when starting the `sidekiq` command, pass the path of `sidekiq.yml` to the
`-C` option.

```
1 $ bundle exec sidekiq -e $RAILS_ENV -C config/sidekiq.yml
```

18.2.6   Error Handling

Sidekiq ships with support to notify the following exception notification services if
an error occurs within a worker during processing:

- Airbrake

- Exceptional

- ExceptionNotifier

- Honeybadger

Other services, such as Sentry and New Relic, implement their own Sidekiq middleware that handles the reporting of errors. Installation usually involves adding a single
`require` statement to a Rails initializer.

```
# config/initializers/sentry.rb
require 'raven/sidekiq'
```

18.2.7   Monitoring

When Resque was released, it set a precedent for Ruby background processing libraries by shipping with a web interface to monitor your queues and jobs. Sidekiq follows suit and also comes with a Sinatra application that can be run standalone or be
mounted with your Rails application.

To run the web interface standalone, create a `config.ru` file and boot it with
any Rack server:

```
1 require 'sidekiq'
2
3 Sidekiq.configure_client do |config|
4   config.redis = { size: 1 }
5 end
6
7 require 'sidekiq/web'
8 run Sidekiq::Web
```

If you prefer to access the web interface within your Rails application, explicitly
mount `Sidekiq::Web` to a path in your `config/routes.rb` file.

```
1 require 'sidekiq/web'
```

```
2
3 Rails.application.routes.draw do
4   mount Sidekiq::Web =&greaterthan; '/sidekiq'
5   ...
6 end
```

Since the web interface is a Sinatra application, you will need to add the `sinatra` gem to your `Gemfile`.

```
# Gemfile
gem 'sinatra', '&greaterthan;= 1.3.0', require: nil
```

18.2.8 Summary

Sidekiq is highly recommended for any Rails application that has a large number of jobs. It's the fastest and most efficient background processing library available, due to the fact that it is multithreaded.

With a Redis backend, Sidekiq does not suffer from the potential database locking issues that can arise when using Delayed Job and has significantly better performance with respect to queue management over both Delayed Job and Resque.

Note that Redis stores all its data in memory, so if you are expecting a large amount of jobs but do not have a significant amount of RAM to spare, you may need to look at a different framework.

18.3 Resque

Resque[4] is a background processing framework that supports multiple queues and, like Sidekiq, uses Redis for its persistent storage. Resque also comes with a Sinatra web application to monitor the queues and jobs.

Resque workers are Ruby objects or modules that respond to a class method. Jobs are stored in the database as JSON objects, and because of this, only primitives can be passed as arguments to the actions. Resque also provides hooks into the worker and job lifecycles, as well as the ability to configure custom failure mechanisms.

Due to Resque's use of Redis as its storage engine, the overhead of job processing is unnoticeable. Resque uses a parent/child forking architecture, which makes its resource consumption predictable and easily managed.

18.3.1 Getting Started

First, in your `Gemfile` add the `resque` gem and then configure Resque by creating a Rails initializer and a `resque.yml` to store the configuration options. The YAML

---

4. https://github.com/resque/resque

should be key/value pairs of environment name with the Redis host and port, and the initializer should load the YAML and set up the Redis options.

Configuring failure backends can also be done in the same manner—Resque supports persistence to Redis or Airbrake notifications out of the box, but custom backends can be easily created by inheriting from `Resque::Failure::Base`. In `config/resque.yml`, it will look like the following:

```
1 development: localhost:6379
2 staging:     localhost:6379
3 production:  localhost:6379
```

The `config/initializers/resque.rb` looks like the following:

```
 1 require 'resque/failure/multiple'
 2 require 'resque/failure/airbrake'
 3 require 'resque/failure/redis'
 4
 5 rails_env = ENV['RAILS_ENV'] || 'development'
 6 config = YAML.load_file(Rails.root.join 'config','resque.yml')
 7 Resque.redis = config[rails_env]
 8
 9 Resque::Failure::Airbrake.configure do |config|
10   config.api_key = 'abcdefg'
11   config.secure = true
12 end
13 Resque::Failure::Multiple.classes = [Resque::Failure::Redis,
14   Resque::Failure::Airbrake]
15 Resque::Failure.backend = Resque::Failure::Multiple
```

18.3.2 Creating Jobs

Jobs in Resque are plain old Ruby objects that respond to a `perform` class method and define which queue they should be processed in. The simplest way to define the queue is to set an instance variable on the job itself.

```
 1 class EmailJob
 2   @queue = :communications
 3
 4   def self.perform(user_id)
 5     user = User.find(user_id)
 6     UserMailer.activation(user).deliver
 7   end
 8 end
 9
10 # Enqueue the job.
11 Resque.enqueue(EmailJob, user.id)
```

18.3.3   Hooks

Resque provides lifecycle hooks that can be used to add additional behavior—for example, adding an automatic retry for a failed job. There are two categories of hooks: worker hooks and job hooks.

The available worker hooks are `before_first_fork`, `before_fork`, and `after_fork`. Before hooks are executed in the parent process where the after hook executes in the child process. This is important to note since changes in the parent process will be permanent for the life of the worker, whereas changes in the child process will be lost when the job completes.

```
1  # Before the worker's first fork
2  Resque.before_first_fork do
3    puts "Creating worker"
4  end
5
6  # Before every worker fork
7  Resque.before_fork do |job|
8    puts "Forking worker"
9  end
10
11  # After every worker fork
12  Resque.after_fork do |job|
13    puts "Child forked"
14  end
```

Job hooks differ slightly from worker hooks in that they are defined on the action classes themselves and are defined as class methods with the hook name as the prefix. The available hooks for jobs are `before_perform`, `after_perform`, `around_perform`, and `on_failure`.

An example job that needs to retry itself automatically on failure and log some information before it starts processing would look like this:

```
1  class EmailJob
2    class << self
3      def perform(user_id)
4        user = User.find(user_id)
5        UserMailer.activation(user).deliver
6      end
7
8      def before_perform_log(*args)
9        Logger.info "Starting Email
           Job"
10      end
11
```

```
12     def on_failure_retry(error, *args)
13       Resque.enqueue self, *args
14     end
15   end
16 end
```

18.3.4 Plugins

Resque has a very good plugin ecosystem to provide it with additional useful features. Most plugins are modules that are included in your job classes only to be used on specific jobs that need the extra functionality. Plugins of note are listed in the following text and a complete list can be found at `https://github.com/resque/resque/wiki/plugins`.

resque-scheduler A job scheduler built on top of Resque.

resque-throttle Restricts the frequency that jobs are run.

resque-retry Adds configurable retry and exponential backoff behavior for failed jobs.

resque_mailer Adds ability to send Action Mailer emails asynchronously.

18.3.5 Running

Resque comes with two rake tasks that can be used to run workers: one to run a single worker for one or more queues and the second to run multiple workers. Configuration options are supplied as environment variables when running the tasks and allow for defining the queue for the workers to monitor, logging verbosity, and the number or workers to start.

```
# Start 1 worker for the communications queue.
$ QUEUE=communications rake environment resque:work

# Start 6 workers for the communications queue.
$ QUEUE=communications COUNT=6 rake resque:workers

# Start 2 workers for all queues.
$ QUEUE=* COUNT=2 rake resque:workers
```

Stopping jobs involves sending signals to the parent Resque workers, which then take the appropriate action on the child and themselves:

QUIT Waits for the forked child to finish processing and then exists.

TERM/INT Immediately kills the child process and exits.

USR1 Immediately kills the child process but leaves the parent worker running.

USR2 Finishes processing the child action and then waits for CONT before spawn-
ing another.

CONT Continues to start jobs again if it was halted by a USR2.

18.3.6   Monitoring

One of the really nice features of Resque is the web interface that it ships with for
monitoring your queues and jobs. It can run standalone or be mounted with your
Rails application.

To run standalone, simply run `resque-web` from the command line. If you
prefer to access the web interface within your Rails application, explicitly mount an
instance of `Resque::Server.new` to a path in your `config/routes.rb` file.

```
1  require &doublestraightquo;resque/server&doublestraightquo;
2
3  Rails.application.routes.draw do
4    mount Resque::Server.new =&greaterthan; '/resque'
5    ...
6  end
```

18.3.7   Summary

Resque is recommended where a large number of jobs are in play and your code
is not threadsafe. It does not support priority queuing but does support multiple
queues, which is advantageous when jobs can be categorized together and given pools
of workers to run them.

Since it uses a Redis backend, Resque does not suffer from the potential database
locking issues that can arise when using Delayed Job. However, being single-threaded
means that Resque requires a process for every worker you want to run in parallel.

18.4   Rails Runner

Rails comes with a built-in tool for running tasks independent of the web cycle. The
`rails runner` command simply loads the default Rails environment and then
executes some specified Ruby code. Popular uses include the following:

- Importing "batch" external data
- Executing any (class) method in your models

- Running intensive calculations, delivering emails in batches, or executing scheduled tasks

Usages involving `rails runner` that you should avoid at all costs are the following:

- Processing incoming email
- Tasks that take longer to run as your database grows

18.4.1   Getting Started

For example, let us suppose that you have a model called "Report." The `Report` model has a class method called `generate_rankings`, which you can call from the command line using the following:

```
$ rails runner 'Report.generate_rankings'
```

Since we have access to all Rails, we can even use the Active Record finder methods to extract data from our application.[5]

```
$ rails runner 'User.pluck(:email).each { |e| puts e }'
charles.quinn@highgroove.com
me@seebq.com
bill.gates@microsoft.com
obie@obiefernandez.com
```

This example demonstrates that we have access to the `User` model and are able to execute arbitrary Rails code. In this case, we've collected some email addresses that we can now spam to our heart's content. (Just kidding!)

18.4.2   Usage Notes

There are some things to remember when using `rails runner`. You must specify the production environment using the `-e` option; otherwise, it defaults to development. The `rails runner` help option tells us the following:

```
$ rails runner -h

Usage: rails runner [options] ('Some.ruby(code)' or a filename)
    -e, --environment=name  Specifies the environment for the
        runner
                            to operate under (test/development/
        production).
                            Default: development
```

---

5. Be careful to escape any characters that have specific meaning to your shell.

Using `rails runner`, we can easily script any batch operations that need to run using `cron` or another system scheduler. For example, you might calculate the most popular or highest-ranking product in your e-commerce application every few minutes or nightly rather than make an expensive query on every request:

```
$ rails runner -e production 'Product.calculate_top_ranking'
```

A sample `crontab` to run that script might look like this:

```
0 */5 * * *   root   /usr/local/bin/ruby \
/apps/exampledotcom/current/script/rails runner -e production \
'Product.calculate_top_ranking'
```

The script will run every five hours to update the `Product` model's top rankings.

18.4.3   Considerations

On the positive side: It doesn't get any easier and there are no additional libraries to install. That's about it.

As for negatives, the `rails runner` process loads the entire Rails environment. For some tasks, particularly short-lived ones, that can be quite wasteful of resources. Also, nothing prevents multiple copies of the same script from running simultaneously, which can be catastrophically bad, depending on the contents of the script.

Wilson Says ...

Do not process incoming email with `rails runner`. It's a Denial of Service attack waiting to happen.

18.4.4   Summary

The Rails Runner is useful for short tasks that need to run infrequently, but jobs that require more heavy lifting, reporting, and robust failover mechanisms are best handled by other libraries.

18.5   Conclusion

Most web applications today will need to incorporate some form of asynchronous behavior, and we've covered some of the important libraries available when needing to implement background processing. There are many other frameworks and techniques available for handling this, so choose the solution that is right for your needs—just remember to never make your users wait.

Background

CHAPTER 19

Ajax on Rails

Ajax isn't a technology. It's really several technologies, each flourishing in its own right, coming together in powerful new ways

—Jesse J. Garrett, who coined the name Ajax

Ajax is an acronym that stands for asynchronous JavaScript and XML. It encompasses techniques that allow us to liven up web pages with behaviors that happen outside the normal HTTP request life cycle (without a page refresh).

Some example use cases for Ajax techniques are the following:

- "Type ahead" input suggestion, as in Google search
- Asynchronous form data delivery
- Seamless navigation of web-presented maps, as in Google Maps
- Dynamically updated lists and tables, as in Gmail and other web-based email services
- Web-based spreadsheets
- Forms that allow in-place editing
- Live preview of formatted writing alongside a text input

Ajax is made possible by the `XMLHttpRequestObject` (or XHR for short), an API that is available in all modern browsers. It allows JavaScript code on the browser to exchange data with the server and use it to change the user interface of your application on the fly without needing a page refresh. Working directly with XHR in a cross browser–compatible way is difficult, to say the least; however, we are lucky as the open-source ecosystem flourishes with Ajax JavaScript libraries.

Incidentally, Ajax, especially in Rails, has very little to do with XML, despite its presence there at the end of the acronym. In fact, by default Rails 4 does not include XML parsing (however, this can be reenabled). The payload of those asynchronous requests going back and forth to the server can be anything. Often it's just a matter of form parameters posted to the server and receiving snippets of HTML back for dynamic insertion into the page's DOM. Many times it even makes sense for the server to send back data encoded in a simple kind of JavaScript called JavaScript object notation (JSON).

It's outside the scope of this book to teach you the fundamentals of JavaScript and/or Ajax. It's also outside of our scope to dive into the design considerations of adding Ajax to your application, elements of which are lengthy and occasionally controversial. Proper coverage of those subjects would require a whole book and there are many such books to choose from in the marketplace. Therefore, the rest of the chapter will assume that you understand what Ajax is and why you would use it in your applications. It also assumes that you have a basic understanding of JavaScript programming.

19.0.1   Firebug

Firebug[1] is an extremely powerful extension for Firefox and a must-have tool for doing Ajax work. It lets you inspect Ajax requests and probe the DOM of the page extensively, even letting you change elements and CSS styles on the fly and see the results on your browser screen. It also has a very powerful JavaScript debugger that you can use to set watch expressions and breakpoints.

Firebug also has an interactive console that allows you to experiment with JavaScript in the browser just as you would use `irb` in Ruby. In some cases, the code samples in this chapter are copied from the Firebug console, which has a >>> prompt.

As I've jokingly told many of my Ruby on Rails students when covering Ajax on Rails, "Even if you don't listen to anything else I say, use Firebug! The productivity gains you experience, which will make up for my fee very quickly."

Kevin Says ...

Alternatively, if you use Chrome or Safari, both browsers have similar built-in tools. My personal preference is the Chrome DevTools,[2] which is continuously improved with each new release of Chrome.

---

1. The first step to getting the Firebug plugin for Firefox is to visit `http://www.getfirebug.com`
2. `http://developers.google.com/chrome-developer-tools/`

19.1   Unobtrusive JavaScript

The unobtrusive JavaScript (UJS) features in Rails provide a library-independent API for specifying Ajax actions. The Rails team has provided UJS implementations for both jQuery and Prototype, available under `https://github.com/rails/jquery-ujs` and `https://github.com/rails/prototype-rails`, respectively. By default, newly generated Rails applications use jQuery as its JavaScript library of choice.

To integrate jQuery into your Rails application, simply include the `jquery-rails` gem in your `Gemfile` and run `bundle install`. Next, ensure that the right directives are present in your JavaScript manifest file (as seen in the following text).

```
1 # Gemfile
2 gem 'jquery-rails'
```

```
1 // app/assets/javascripts/application.js
2 //= require jquery
3 //= require jquery_ujs
```

By including those require statements in your JavaScript manifest file, both the jQuery and `jquery_ujs` libraries will automatically be bundled up along with the rest of your assets and served to the browser efficiently. Use of manifest files is covered in detail in Chapter 20, "Asset Pipeline."

19.1.1   UJS Usage

Prior to version 3.0, Rails was not unobtrusive, resulting in generated markup being coupled to your JavaScript library of choice. For example, one of the most dramatic changes caused by the move to UJS was the way that delete links were generated.

```
1 = link_to 'Delete', user_path(1), method: :delete,
2     data: { confirm: "Are you sure?" }
```

Prior to the use of UJS techniques, the resulting HTML would look something like the following:

```
1 <a href="/users/1" onclick="if (confirm('Sure?')) { var f =
2   document.createElement('form'); f.style.display = 'none';
3   this.parentNode.appendChild(f); f.method = 'POST'; f.action =
4   this.href;var m = document.createElement('input'); m.setAttribute('type',
5   'hidden'); m.setAttribute('name', '_method'); m.setAttribute('value',
6   'delete'); f.appendChild(m);f.submit(); };return false;">Delete</a>
```

Now taking advantage of UJS, it will look like this:

Ajax

```
1  <a data-confirm="Are you sure?" data-method="delete" href="/users/1"
2    rel="nofollow">Delete</a>
```

Note that Rails uses the standard HTML5 `data-` attributes method as a means to attach custom events to DOM elements.

Also required for Rails UJS support is the `csrf_meta_tag`, which must be placed in the head of the document and adds the `csrf-param` and `csrf-token` meta tags used in dynamic form generation.

```
1  %head
2    = csrf_meta_tag
```

CSRF stands for cross-site request forgery and the `csrf_meta_tag` is one method of helping to prevent the attack from happening. CSRF is covered in detail in Chapter 15, "Security."

19.1.2   Helpers

As covered in Chapter 11, "All about Helpers," Rails ships with view helper methods to generate markup for common HTML elements. The following is a listing of Action View helpers that have hooks to enable Ajax behavior via the unobtrusive JavaScript driver.

19.1.2.1   `button_to`

The `button_to` helper generates a form containing a single button that submits to the URL created by the set of options. Setting the `:remote` option to `true` allows the unobtrusive JavaScript driver to make an Ajax request in the background to the URL.

To illustrate, the markup

```
= button_to("New User", new_user_path, remote: true)
```

generates

```
1  <form action="/users/new" class="button_to" data-remote="true"
2    method="post">
3    <div>
4      <input type="submit" value="New User">
5      <input name="authenticity_token" type="hidden"
6        value="HDVQ/5AHK+f5ChqN8qaah8Pd0gZzkoa21vqbvbayHBY=">
7    </div>
8  </form>
```

To display a JavaScript confirmation prompt with a question specified, supply data attribute :confirm with a question. If accepted, the button will be submitted normally; otherwise, no action is taken.

```
= button_to("Deactivate", user, data: { confirm: 'Are you sure?' })
```

The unobtrusive JavaScript driver also allows for the disabling of the button when clicked via the :disable_with data attribute. This prevents duplicate requests from hitting the server from subsequent button clicks by a user. If used in combination with remote: true, once the request is complete, the unobtrusive JavaScript driver will re-enable the button and reset the text to its original value.

```
1 = button_to("Deactivate", user, data: { disable_with: 'Deactivating...' })
```

19.1.2.2 `form_for`

The form_for helper is used to create forms with an Active Model instance. To enable the submission of a form via Ajax, set the :remote option to true. For instance, assuming we had a form to create a new user,

```
1 = form_for(user, remote: true) do |f|
2   ...
```

would generate

```
1 <form accept-charset="UTF-8" action="/users" class="new_user"
2   data-remote="true" id="new_user" method="post">
3   ...
4 </form>
```

19.1.2.3 `form_tag`

Like form_for, the form_tag accepts the :remote option to allow for Ajax form submission. For detailed information on form_tag, see Chapter 11, "All about Helpers."

19.1.2.4 `link_to`

The link_to helper creates a link tag of the given name using a URL created by the set of options. Setting the option :remote to true allows the unobtrusive JavaScript driver to make an Ajax request to the URL instead of following the link.

```
= link_to "User", user, remote: true
```

By default, all links will always perform an HTTP GET request. To specify an alternative HTTP verb, such as DELETE, one can set the :method option with the desired HTTP verb (:post, :patch, or :delete).

Ajax

```
= link_to "Delete User", user, method: :delete
```

If the user has JavaScript disabled, the request will always fall back to using GET, no matter what :method you have specified.

The link_to helper also accepts data attributes :confirm and :disable _with, covered earlier in the "button_to" section in this chapter.

19.1.3   jQuery UJS Custom Events

When a form, link, or button is marked with the data-remote attribute, the jQuery UJS driver fires the custom events depicted in Table 19.1.

Table 19.1   jQuery UJS driver custom events

Event name	Parameters	Occurrence
ajax:before	event	Ajax event is started; aborts if stopped
ajax:beforeSend	event, xhr, settings	Before request is sent, aborts if stopped
ajax:send	event, xhr	Request is sent
ajax:success	event, data, status, xhr	Request completed and HTTP response was a success
ajax:error	event, xhr, status, error	Request completed and HTTP response returned an error
ajax:complete	event, xhr, status	After request completed, regardless of outcome
ajax:aborted: required	event, elements	When there exists blank required field in a form, continues with submission if stopped
ajax:aborted:file	event, elements	When there exists a populated file field in the form, aborts if stopped

This allows you, for instance, to handle the success/failure of Ajax submissions. To illustrate, let's bind to both the ajax:success and ajax:error events in the following CoffeeScript:

```
1  $(document).ready ->
2    $("#new_user")
3      .on "ajax:success", (event, data, status, xhr) ->
4        $(@).append xhr.responseText
5      .on "ajax:error", (event, xhr, status, error) ->
6        $(@).append "Something bad happened"
```

19.2   Turbolinks

Rails 4 introduces a new, controversial feature called Turbolinks. Turbolinks is JavaScript library that, when enabled, attaches a click handler to all links of a HTML page. When a link is clicked, Turbolinks will execute an Ajax request and replace the contents of the current page with the response's `<body>` tag.

Using Turbolinks also changes the address of the current page, allowing users to bookmark a specific page and use the back button as they normally would. Turbolinks uses the HTML5 history API to achieve this.

The biggest advantage of Turbolinks is that it enables the user's browser to only fetch the required stylesheets, JavaScripts, and even images once to render the page. Turbolinks effectively makes your site appear faster and more responsive.

To integrate Turbolinks into your existing Rails application, simply include the `turbolinks` gem in your `Gemfile` and run `bundle install`. Next, add "require `turbolinks`" in your JavaScript manifest file.

```
1 # Gemfile
2 gem 'turbolinks'
```

```
1 // app/assets/javascripts/application.js
2 //= require jquery
3 //= require jquery_ujs
4 //= require turbolinks
```

19.2.1   Turbolinks Usage

In Rails 4, Turbolinks is enabled by default but can be disabled if you prefer not to use it. To disable the use of Turbolinks for a specific link on a page, simply use the `data-no-turbolink` tag like so:

```
= link_to 'User', user_path(1), 'data-no-turbolink' => true
```

It does not depend on any particular framework, such as jQuery or ZeptoJS, and is intended on being as unobtrusive as possible.

One caveat to Turbolinks is it only will work with GET requests. You can, however, send POST requests to a Turbolink-enabled link, as long as it sends a redirect instead of an immediate render. This is because the method must return the user's browser to a location that can be rendered on a GET request. (pushState does not record the HTTP method, only the path per request.)

19.2.2   Turbolinks Events

When using Turbolinks, the DOM's `ready` event will only be fired on the initial page request, as it overrides the normal page-loading process. This means you cannot

Ajax

rely on `DOMContentLoaded` or `jQuery.ready()` to trigger code evaluation. To trigger code that is dependent on the loading of a page in Turbolinks, one must attach to the custom Turbolinks `page:change` event.

```
1  $(document).on "page:change", ->
2      alert "loaded!"
```

When Turbolinks requests a fresh version of a page from the server, the following events are fired on `document`:

page:before-change A link that is Turbolinks-enabled has been clicked. Returning `false` will cancel the Turbolinks process.

page:fetch Turbolinks has started fetching a new target page.

page:receive The new target page has been fetched from the server.

page:change The page has been parsed and changed to the new version.

page:update If jQuery is included, triggered on jQuery's `ajaxSuccess` event.

page:load End of page-loading process.

By default, Turbolinks caches 10-page loads to reduce requests to the server. In this case, the `page:restore` event is fired at the end of the restore process.

`jquery.turbolinks`

If you have an existing Rails application that extensively binds to the `jQuery.ready` event, you may want to look at using the `jquery.turbolinks` library.[3] When Turbolinks triggers the `page:load` event on a document, `jquery.turbolinks` will automatically `jQuery.ready` events as well.

19.2.3 Controversy

Turbolinks undoubtedly speeds up many sites by avoiding the reprocessing of the `<head>` tag. It was mature enough for the Rails core team to bundle it as an official part of Rails. Yet it has plenty of critics. Some raise objections about the headaches of making sure that all the Ajax functions of a large application actually work correctly with Turbolinks enabled. Others point out how it breaks apps in older browsers such as IE8. And others point out that it is inefficient, because most

---

3. https://github.com/kossnocorp/jquery.turbolinks

applications could get away with refreshing sections of the page smaller than the entire <body> element.

We think it's worth giving Turbolinks a try in your application, especially if you're starting from scratch and can take its challenges into account from the beginning of a project. However, we also admit that we've disabled it in a lot of our projects. Your mileage may vary.

Here are some of the issues that you may need to address with your use of Turbolinks:[4]

Memory Leaks Turbolinks does not clear or reload your JavaScript when the page changes. You could potentially see the effects of memory leaks in your applications, especially if you use a lot of JavaScript.

Event Bindings You have to take older browsers into consideration. Make sure you listen for page:* events, as well as DOMContentLoaded.

Client-Side Frameworks Turbolinks may not play nicely with other client-side frameworks like Backbone, Angular, Knockout, Ember, and so on.

19.3 Ajax and JSON

JavaScript object notation (JSON) is a simple way to encode JavaScript objects. It is also considered a language-independent data format, making it a compact, human-readable, and versatile interchange format. This is the preferred method of interchanging data between the web application code running on the server and any code running in the browser, particularly for Ajax requests.

Rails provides a `to_json` on every object, using a sensible mechanism to do so for every type. For example, `BigDecimal` objects, although numbers, are serialized to JSON as strings, since that is the best way to represent a `BigDecimal` in a language-independent manner. You can always customize the `to_json` method of any of your classes if you wish, but it should not be necessary to do so.

19.3.1 Ajax link_to

To illustrate an Ajax request, let's enable our Client controller to respond to JSON and provide a method to supply the number of draft timesheets outstanding for each client:

```
1 respond_to :html, :xml, :json
2 ...
3 # GET /clients/counts
```

---

4. http://net.tutsplus.com/tutorials/ruby/digging-into-rails-4

```
4  # GET /clients/counts.json
5  def counts
6    respond_with(Client.all_with_counts) do |format|
7      format.html { redirect_to clients_path }
8    end
9  end
```

This uses the Client class method `all_with_counts`, which returns an array of hashmaps:

```
1  def self.all_with_counts
2    all.map do |client|
3      { id: client.id, draft_timesheets_count: client.timesheets.
         draft.count }
4    end
5  end
```

When GET `/clients/counts` is requested and the content type is JSON, the response is the following:

```
1  [{"draft_timesheets_count":0, "id":20},
2   {"draft_timesheets_count":1, "id":21}]
```

You will note in the code example that HTML and XML are also supported content types for the response, so it's up to the client to decide which format works best for them. We'll look at formats other than JSON in the next few sections.

In this case, our Client index view requests a response in JSON format:

```
1  - content_for :head do
2    = javascript_include_tag 'clients.js'
3  ...
4  %table#clients_list
5  ...
6    - @clients.each do |client|
7      %tr[client]
8        %td= client.name
9        %td= client.code
10       %td.draft_timesheets_count= client.timesheets.draft.count
11 ...
12 = link_to 'Update draft timesheets count', counts_clients_path,
13     remote: true, data: { type: :json }, id: 'update_draft_timesheets'
```

To complete the asynchronous part of this Ajax-enabled feature, we also need to add an event handler to the UJS `ajax:success` event, fired when the Ajax call on the `update_draft_timesheets` element completes successfully. Here, jQuery is used to bind a JavaScript function to the event once the page has loaded. This is defined in `clients.js`:

```
1  $(function() {
2    $("#update_draft_timesheets").on("ajax:success", function(event, data) {
3      $(data).each(function() {
4        var td = $('#client_' + this.id + ' .draft_timesheets_count')
5        td.html(this.draft_timesheets_count);
6      });
7    });
8  });
```

In each row of the `clients` listing, the respective `td` with a class of `draft_timesheets_count` is updated in place with the values from the JSON response. There is no need for a page refresh, and user experience is improved.

As an architectural constraint, this does require this snippet of JavaScript to have intimate knowledge of the target page's HTML structure and how to transform the JSON into changes on the DOM. This is a major reason JSON is the best format for decoupling the presentation layer of your application or, more important, when the page is requesting JSON from another application altogether.

Sometimes, however, it may be desirable for the server to respond with a snippet of HTML, used to replace a region of the target page.

19.4 Ajax and HTML

The Ruby classes in your Rails application will normally contain the bulk of that application's logic and state. Ajax-heavy applications can leverage that logic and state by transferring HTML—rather than JSON—to manipulate the DOM.

A web application may respond to an Ajax request with an HTML fragment, used to insert or replace an existing part of the page. This is usually done when the transformation relies on complex business rules and perhaps complex state that would be inefficient to duplicate in JavaScript.

Let's say your application needs to display clients in some sort of priority order, and that order is highly variable and dependent on the current context. There could be a swag of rules dictating what order they are shown in. Perhaps it's that whenever a client has more than a number of draft timesheets, we want to flag that in the page.

```
1  %td.draft_timesheets_count
2    - if client.timesheets.draft.count > 3
3      %span.drafts-overlimit WARNING!
4      %br
5    = client.timesheets.draft.count
```

Along with that, let's say on a Friday or Saturday, we need to group clients by their *hottest spending day* so we can make ourselves an action plan for the beginning of the following week.

These are just two business rules that, when combined, are a bit of a handful to implement in both Rails and JavaScript. Applications tend to have many more than just two combined rules, and it quickly becomes prohibitive to implement those rules in JavaScript to transform JSON into DOM changes. That's particularly true when the page making the Ajax call is external and not one we've written.

We can opt to transfer HTML in the Ajax call and, using JavaScript, to update a section of the page with that HTML. Under one context, the snippet of HTML returned could look like the following:

```
 1 <tr id="client_22" class="client"></tr>
 2 <tr>
 3   <td></td><td>Aardworkers</td><td>AARD</td><td>$4321</td>
 4   <td class="draft_timesheets_count">0</td>
 5 </tr>
 6 <tr id="client_23" class="client"></tr>
 7 <tr>
 8   <td></td><td>Zorganization</td><td>ZORG</td><td>$9999</td>
 9   <td class="draft_timesheets_count">1</td>
10 </tr>
```

Whereas, in another context, it could look like this:

```
 1 <tr>
 2   <td>Friday</td>
 3 </tr>
 4 <tr>
 5   <td>Saturday</td>
 6 </tr>
 7 <tr id="client_24" class="client"></tr>
 8 <tr>
 9   <td></td><td>Hashrocket</td><td>HR</td><td>$12000</td>
10   <td class="draft_timesheets_count">
11     <span class="drafts-overlimit">WARNING!</span>
12     5
13   </td>
14 </tr>
15 <tr id="client_22" class="client"></tr>
16 <tr>
17   <td></td><td>Aardworkers</td><td>AARD</td><td>$4321</td>
18   <td class="draft_timesheets_count">0</td>
19 </tr>
```

The JavaScript event handler for the Ajax response then just needs to update the
innerHTML of a particular HTML element to alter the page without having to
know anything about the business rules used to determine what the resulting HTML
should be.

19.5   Ajax and JavaScript

The primary reason you want to work with a JavaScript response to an Ajax request
is when it is for JSONP (JSON with padding). JSONP *pads*, or wraps, JSON data in
a call to a JavaScript function that exists on your page. You specify the name of that
function in a callback query string parameter. Note that some public APIs may
use something other than callback, but it has become the convention in Rails and
most JSONP applications.

Xavier Says …

> Although the Wikipedia entry[5] for Ajax does not specifically mention JSONP,
> and the request is not XHR by Rails' definition, we'd like to think of it as Ajax
> anyway—it is, after all, asynchronous JavaScript.

JSONP is one technique for obtaining cross domain data, avoiding the browser's
same-origin policy. This introduces a pile of safety and security issues that are beyond
the scope of this book. However, if you need to use JSONP, the Rails stack provides
an easy way to handle JSONP requests (with Rack::JSONP) or make JSONP requests (with UJS and jQuery).

To respond to JSONP requests, activate the Rack JSONP module from the
rack-contrib RubyGem in your environment.rb file:

```
1 class Application < Rails::Application
2   require 'rack/contrib'
3   config.middleware.use 'Rack::JSONP'
4   ...
```

Then just use UJS to tell jQuery it's a JSONP call by altering the data-type to
jsonp:

```
1 = link_to 'Update draft timesheets count', counts_clients_path,
2     remote: true, data: { type: :jsonp }, id: 'update_draft_timesheets'
```

jQuery automatically adds the ?callback= and random function name to the

---

5. http://en.wikipedia.org/wiki/Ajax_(programming)

query string of the request URI. In addition to this, it also adds the necessary `script` tags to our document to bypass the same-origin policy. Our existing event handler is bound to `ajax:success`, so it is called with the data just like before. Now, though, it can receive that data from another web application.

jQuery also makes the request as if it is for JavaScript, so our Rails controller needs to `respond_to :js`. Unfortunately, the Rails automatic rendering for JavaScript responses isn't there yet, so we add a special handler for JavaScript in our controller:

```
1 respond_to :html, :js
2 ...
3
4 def counts
5   respond_with(Client.all_with_counts) do |format|
6     format.html { redirect_to clients_path }
7     format.js { render json: Client.all_with_counts.to_json }
8   end
9 end
```

We still convert our data to JSON. The `Rack::JSONP` module then *pads* that JSON data in a call to the JavaScript function specified in the query string of the request. The response looks like this:

```
jsonp123456789([{"id":1,"draft_timesheets_count":0},
{"id":2,"draft_timesheets_count":1}])
```

When the Ajax response is complete, your Ajax event handler is called and the JSON data are passed to it as a parameter.

19.6   Conclusion

The success of Rails is often correlated to the rise of Web 2.0, and one of the factors linking Rails into that phenomenon is its baked-in support for Ajax. There are a ton of books about Ajax programming, as it's a big subject, but it is an important enough part of Rails that we felt the need to include a quick introduction to it as part of this book.

CHAPTER 20

Asset Pipeline

It's not enough to solve the problem; we have to have the pleasure.

—DHH, RailsConf 2011 keynote

The Asset Pipeline is one of those Rails *magic* features that makes developers' lives so easy that once you master it, you will never want to go back. It also significantly improves perceived performance of your application and reduces burdens on your application server. It's a huge win for Rails overall that nonetheless might make you want to tear your hair out and switch to (shudder) Django until you understand how it works. Persevere! We promise it's worth the learning curve. According to David, the Asset Pipeline was by far his favorite element of the Rails 3.1 release.

"Wait," you might ask, "what is an asset?"

It's simple: By "assets," we mean images, JavaScript, CSS, and other static files that we need in order to properly render our pages.

Web applications built with early versions of Rails shared common problems with managing static assets. Before the Asset Pipeline, you just dumped all your JavaScript files into the `public/javascripts` directory, all your CSS files into `public/stylesheets`, and your image files into `public/images` without any structure. Afterward, you could load all your JavaScript files within your templates using the helper `<%= javascript_include_tag :all %>`. It completely ignored files in subdirectories of `public/javascripts`, so that if you wanted to organize your assets into subdirectories, you had to manually load them into your layout. What a mess!

There were other inconveniences as well. For instance, if you wanted to load the files in a certain order, you had to replace the `:all` directive with a manually maintained list of "includes" in the exact order that you needed. When you wanted to use a library that came with JavaScript and CSS files (e.g., Twitter Bootstrap), you had to copy those files into your public directory and keep it under source control so that they will be available for the running application. Worse, you had to read the readme files carefully to figure out just what files exactly do you needed to copy and in which exact order you had to load them. Not fun.

20.1   Asset Pipeline

The major goal of the Asset Pipeline is to make management of static assets easy— even trivial. In this chapter, we discuss the organization of assets and how they can be packaged into neat external gem dependencies, available asset preprocessors and compressors, helpers that assist us with the Asset Pipeline, and more.

Incidentally, automated asset management is not a new concept. It has existed since before the Rails era, and plugins to add this critical functionality to Rails began appearing many years ago. The most successful one is Sprockets, written primarily by Sam Stephenson of 37Signals and Rails core team fame. Sprockets was eventually incorporated into Rails itself and is at the core of the Rails Asset Pipeline implementation.

In Rails 4, the whole Asset Pipeline was extracted into a separate gem "sprockets-rails" and can be removed from your application Gemfile to disable it.

20.2   Wish List

Which features of asset management solutions would be most useful to us in building a Rails application?

For starters, we could *organize* the asset files into a sensible directory tree instead of "junk drawer" directories filled haphazardly.

We might also want to *compress* all our assets so that they can be served faster to web browsers and eat up less bandwidth.

We could also *consolidate* multiple source files of the same kind (JavaScript or CSS) into single files, reducing the number of HTTP requests made by the browser and significantly improving page load times.

On the other hand, compressing and consolidating all those source files could make *debugging* during development a nightmare, so our wish list would also include the ability to turn those features off except for production environments.

What else? To speed up page loading times even more, we might "preshrink" our asset files with the *maximum compression level*, so that our web server doesn't waste CPU cycles zipping up the same files repeatedly on each request.

We would also want to include *cache-busting* features, giving us the ability to force expiration of stale assets from all cache layers (HTTP proxies, browsers, etc.) when their content changes.

Furthermore, we might want the ability to transparently *compile* languages such as CoffeeScript for JavaScript assets and Sass and Less for CSS stylesheets.

All the highlighted features in our wish list and more are part of the Asset Pipeline, making this aspect of Rails programming a lot more enjoyable than in earlier versions.

20.3   The Big Picture

We could try to describe how the entire Asset Pipeline works at the high level now, but it would require too many forward references to stuff we haven't yet explained. Therefore, we are going to build out our understanding from the bottom up. Keep in mind the overall goal: concatenating and serving asset files and "bundles" composed of multiple files, which can possibly be pre- and postprocessed or compiled from different formats.

Now let's dive in.

20.4   Organization: Where Does Everything Go?

Asset Pipeline continues with the Rails tradition of separate directories for images, stylesheets, and scripts but adds an additional dimension of organization. There are now three locations where you store assets in your project directory. Those are `app/assets`, `lib/assets`, and `vendor/assets`.

This small change already gives us a much better way to organize the project files. Files specific to the current project go into `app/assets`, external libraries go into `vendor/assets`, and assets for your own libraries can go into `lib/assets`.

You can still put files into the `public` directory and Rails will serve them same as before with no processing.

You no longer need to copy the static assets bundled with your gems into your project directory. The Asset Pipeline will find them automatically and make them available for your application (more on this later).

20.5   Manifest Files

The organizational structure doesn't just involve new directories. If you look into the `app/assets` directory of a freshly generated Rails 4 application, you'll notice a couple of files with include directives in them: `app/assets/javascripts/application.js` and `app/assets/stylesheets/application.css`. Those are called asset manifest files, and they specify instructions on where the pipeline processor can find other assets and in which order to load them. The loaded files are concatenated into a single "bundle" file named after the manifest.

Let's take a look at `application.js`:

```
1  // This is a manifest file that'll be compiled into application.js,
2  // which will include all the following files.
3  //
4  // Any JavaScript/Coffee file within this directory, lib/assets/javascripts,
5  // vendor/assets/javascripts, or vendor/assets/javascripts of plugins,
6  // if any, can be referenced here using a relative path.
7  //
8  // It's not advisable to add code directly here, but if you do, it'll
9  // appear at the bottom of the compiled file.
10 //
11 // WARNING: THE FIRST BLANK LINE MARKS THE END OF WHAT'S TO BE PROCESSED;
12 // ANY BLANK LINE SHOULD GO AFTER THE REQUIRES BELOW.
13 //
14 //= require jquery
15 //= require jquery_ujs
16 //= require turbolinks
17 //= require_tree .
```

Here is the `application.css`:

```
1  /*
2   * This is a manifest file that'll be compiled into application.css,
3   * which will include all the files listed below.
4   *
5   * Any CSS and SCSS files within this directory, lib/assets/stylesheets,
6   * vendor/assets/stylesheets, or vendor/assets/stylesheets of plugins,
7   * if any, can be referenced here using a relative path.
8   *
9   * You're free to add application-wide styles to this file and they'll
10  * appear at the top of the compiled file, but it's generally better
11  * to create a new file per style scope.
12  *
13  *= require_self
14  *= require_tree .
15  */
```

A manifest is just a JavaScript or CSS file with a commented block at the beginning of the file that includes special directives in it that specify other files of the same format to concatenate in the exact order. Several comment formats are supported:

```
1  // This is a single-line comment (JavaScript, SCSS):
2  //= require foo
```

```
1 /* This is a multiline comment (CSS, SCSS, JavaScript):
2  *= require foo
3  */
```

```
1 # This is a single-line comment, too (CoffeeScript):
2 #= require foo
```

Note the equal signs at the beginning of the lines. If you skip those, the directives won't work.

Make as many manifest files as you need. For example, the admin.css and admin.js manifest could contain the JS and CSS files that are used for the admin section of an application.

20.5.1   Manifest Directives

There are several manifest directives available:

require The most basic one, it concatenates the content of the referenced file you specify into the final packaged asset "bundle." It will only do it once, even if the same filename appears multiple times in the manifest, either directly or as a part of require_tree (discussed later in this list).

include Just like require except it inserts the file again if it appears in the manifest more than once.

require_self Inserts the content of the file itself (after the directives). This is often useful when you want to make sure that JavaScript code from a manifest comes before any other code that is loaded with require_tree. We see an example of that in the default application.css.

require_directory Loads all the files of the same format in the specified directory in an alphabetical order. It skips files that were already loaded.

require_tree Just like require_directory except it also recursively loads all the files in subdirectories as well. It skips files that were already loaded as well.

depend_on Declares a dependency on a file without actually loading it into the "bundle." It can be useful to force Rails to recompile cached asset bundle in response to the change in this file, even if it is not concatenated into the bundle directly.

Directives are processed in the order they are read in the file, but when you use require_tree, there is no guarantee of the order in which the files will be included.

Pipeline

If for dependency reasons you need to make sure of a certain order, just require those files explicitly.

20.5.2   Search Path

When you require an asset from a manifest file, Rails searches for it in all directories in its search path. You do not need to specify file extensions. The processor assumes you are looking for files that match the type of the manifest file itself.

The search path can be accessed through the Rails configuration variable `config` `.assets.paths`, which is just an array of directory names that serve as the search path. By modifying it you can add your own paths to the list.

```
1  config.assets.paths << Rails.root.join("app", "flash", "assets")
```

The search path includes all the directories that are *directly* under the default assets locations `app/assets`, `lib/assets`, and `vendor/assets` by default, meaning you can easily add other directories for new asset types to the list by creating them under any of the standard asset locations—for example, `app/assets/fonts`.

Files in subdirectories can be accessed by using a relative path:

```
1  // This will load the app/assets/javascripts/library/foo.js.
2  //= require 'library/foo'
```

The directories are traversed in the order that they appear in the search path. The first file with the required name "wins."

Note that all the directories in the search path are "equal" and can store files of any format. It means you can put your JavaScript files in `app/assets/stylesheets` and CSS files in `app/assets/javascripts` and Rails will work just the same. But your fellow developers will probably stop talking to you.

20.5.3   Gemified Assets

As mentioned before, gems can contain assets, and there are gems that exist with the sole purpose of packaging asset files for Asset Pipeline.

To make gem assets available to an application, the gem has to define an "engine"—that is, a class that inherits from `Rails::Engine`. Once "required" it will add `app/assets`, `lib/assets`, and `vendor/assets` directories from the gem to the search path.

Let's see the example from jquery-rails. You can find its engine in the `lib/jquery/ui/rails/engine.rb` file of the gem's source code:

```
1 module Jquery
2   module Ui
3     module Rails
4       class Engine < ::Rails::Engine
5       end
6     end
7   end
8 end
```

This Ruby file is loaded when you include this gem in your application; as a result, all the subdirectories of the gem's `vendor/assets` directory are added to the search path.

20.5.4   Index Files

Index files make inclusion of "bundles" of files easy. If, for example, your Foobar library has a directory `lib/assets/foobar` with `index.js` file inside, Rails will recognize this file as a manifest and let you include the whole "bundle" with a single directive:

```
//= require 'foobar'
```

As with your Rails project, manifest files can encapsulate all the gem asset files and ensure proper load order without any additional effort on your part.

20.5.5   Format Handlers

Asset Pipeline is not called a pipeline for nothing. Source files go into one end, get processed and compiled (if necessary), concatenated and compressed, and then come out of the other end of the pipeline as bundles. There are multiple stages that the source files go through while traversing the pipeline.

There are many format handlers available with Rails, with more available as third-party gems. Some of them are compilers, like CoffeeScript, that compile one format into another. Others are more simple preprocessors like "Interpolated Strings" engine, which performs Ruby substitution—for example, #{...}—regardless of the underlying format of the file, so that it can process a CoffeeScript file before it will be compiled into JavaScript.

Before we continue with individual handlers, we should discuss the file-naming scheme, because the file extensions used on an asset determine which handlers are invoked. Asset files that are intended for compilation/preprocessing can have more than one extension concatenated one after the other.

When asked to serve `products` in a manifest, either explicitly or as part of a compound require directive, the Asset Pipeline constructs the output by iteratively processing the file from one format into the next. It starts with the processing corresponding to the rightmost file extension and continues until the requested leftmost extension format is obtained.

For example, let's dissect the processing of an asset source file named `products.css.sass.erb.str`.

The pipeline will first pass this file through an Interpolated Strings engine and then the ERb template engine, after which the result is treated as a Sass file. Sass files get compiled into normal CSS, which is in turn served to the browser as the final result.[1]

In case it wasn't obvious, the order in which you specify the file extensions is important. If you were to name a file `foo.css.erb.sass`, the first processor to get the file would be the Sass compiler, and it would blow up when it encountered ERb tags.

Naturally, for this entire scheme to work, preprocessors and/or compilers should be available for all the relevant formats. A wide swath of preprocessing power is provided to Rails by a gem named Tilt, a generic interface to multiple Ruby template engines.[2]

Table 20.1   Template engines supported by Tilt

Engine	File extensions	Required libraries
Asciidoctor	`.ad, .adoc, .asciidoc`	`asciidoctor (>= 0.1.0)`
ERb	`.erb, .rhtml`	`none (included ruby stdlib)`
Interpolated String	`.str`	`none (included ruby core)`
Erubis	`.erb, .rhtml, .erubis erubis`	
Haml	`.haml`	`haml`
Sass	`.sass`	`haml (< 3.1) or sass (>= 3.1)`
Scss	`.scss`	`haml (< 3.1) or sass (>= 3.1)`
Less CSS	`.less`	`less`
Builder	`.builder`	`builder`
Liquid	`.liquid`	`liquid`
RDiscount	`.markdown, .mkd, .md`	`rdiscount`
Redcarpet	`.markdown, .mkd, .md`	`redcarpet`

(continued)

---

1. We are ignoring postprocessing for a moment.
2. For an up-to-date list of supported formats, please refer to Tilt's readme file: `https://github.com/rtomayko/tilt`

Table 20.1   Template engines supported by Tilt (continued)

Engine	File extensions	Required libraries
BlueCloth	`.markdown, .mkd, .md`	`bluecloth`
Kramdown	`.markdown, .mkd, .md`	`kramdown`
Maruku	`.markdown, .mkd, .md`	`maruku`
RedCloth	`.textile`	`redcloth`
RDoc	`.rdoc`	`rdoc`
Radius	`.radius`	`radius`
Markaby	`.mab`	`markaby`
Nokogiri	`.nokogiri`	`nokogiri`
CoffeeScript	`.coffee`	`coffee-script (+ javascript)`
Creole (wiki markup)	`.wiki, .creole`	`creole`
WikiCloth (wiki markup)	`.wiki, .mediawiki, .mw`	`wikicloth`
Yajl	`.yajl`	`yajl-ruby`
CSV	`.rcsv`	`none (Ruby >= 1.9), fastercsv (Ruby < 1.9)`

Note

Quite a few of the extensions recognized by Tilt have dependencies on gems that don't automatically come with Rails.

20.6   Custom Format Handlers

Even though Tilt provides quite a few formats, you might need to implement your own. Template handler classes have a simple interface. They define a class attribute named `default_handler` containing the desired MIME type of the content and a class method with the signature `call(template)` that receives the template content and returns the processed result.

For example, here is the handler class from the Rabl[3] gem, used to generate JSON using templates.

```
1 module ActionView
2   module Template::Handlers
3     class Rabl
4       class_attribute :default_format
```

---

3. https://github.com/nesquena/rabl

Pipeline

```
5          self.default_format = Mime::JSON
6
7      def self.call(template)
8          # omitted for clarity...
9      end
10    end
11   end
12 end
```

Note that by convention, template handlers are defined in the `ActionView::Template::Handlers` module. Once your custom code is available to your application in the `lib` folder or as a gem, register it using the `register_template_handler` method, providing the extension to match and the handler class:

```
1 ActionView::Template.register_template_handler :rabl,
      ActionView::Template::Handlers::Rabl
```

20.7 Postprocessing

In addition to preprocessing various formats into JavaScripts and stylesheets, the Asset Pipeline can also postprocess the results. By default postprocessing compressors are available for both stylesheets and JavaScripts.

20.7.1 Stylesheets

By default stylesheets are compressed using the YUI Compressor,[4] which is the only stylesheets compressor available out of the box with Rails.

You can control it by changing the `config.assets.css_compressor` configuration option, which is set to `yui` by default.

When using Sass in a Rails project, one could set the CSS compressor to use Sass's standard compressor with the `config.assets.css_compressor = :sass` option.

20.7.2 JavaScripts

There are several JavaScript compression options available: `:closure`, `:uglifier`, and `:yui`, provided by `closure-compiler`, `uglifier`, or `yui-compressor` gems, respectively.

The `:uglifier` option is the default, but you can control it by changing the `config.assets.js_compressor` configuration option.

---

4. `http://yui.github.io/yuicompressor/css.html`

20.7.3   Custom Compressor

You can use a custom postprocessor by defining a class with a `compress` method that accepts a string and assigning an instance of it to one of the previous configuration options, like this:

```
1 class MyProcessor
2   def compress(string)
3     # do something
4   end
5 end
6
7 config.assets.css_compressor = MyProcessor.new
```

20.8   Helpers

To link assets into your Rails templates, you use the same old helpers as always: `javascript_include_tag` and `stylesheet_link_tag`. Call these helpers in the <head> of your layout template, passing them the name of your manifest files.

```
1 <%= stylesheet_link_tag "application" %>
2 <%= javascript_include_tag "application" %>
```

One of the common frustrations of the Asset Pipeline learning curve is figuring out that you don't need to explicitly link to every asset file in your layout template anymore. Unless you break off large portions of assets for different parts of your app (most commonly, for admin sections), you'll just need one each for the `application` `.js` and `application.css` files. If you try to explicitly include or link to assets that are bundled up, your app will work in development mode where it's possible to serve up assets dynamically. However, it will break in production where assets must be precompiled. The bundled-up assets will simply not exist.

You'll know that you're running into this problem when you get the following error:

```
ActionView::Template::Error (foo.js isn't precompiled)
```

To fix this problem, make sure that `foo.js` is required in one of your manifest files, and get rid of the call to javascript_include_tag "foo."

By default, Rails only seeks to precompile assets named "application." If you have a good reason to break off additional bundles of assets, like for the admin section of your app, tell the pipeline to precompile those bundles by adding the names of the manifest files to the `config.assets.precompile` array in `config/application.rb`.

```
config.assets.precompile += %w(admin.js optional.js}
```

Note that the most maddening incarnation of this problem happens with older Rails plugin gems that were written before the advent of the Asset Pipeline and that contain explicit requires to their asset dependencies. Luckily, as gems are updated, this problem is becoming less common than it was in the days of Rails 3.x.

20.8.1 Images

The venerable `image_tag` helper has been updated so that it knows to search `asset/ images` and not just the public folder. It will also search through the paths specified in the `config.assets.paths` setting and any additional paths added by gems. If you're passing user-supplied data to the `image_tag` helper, note that a blank or non-existent path will raise a server exception during processing of the template.

20.8.2 Getting the URL of an Asset File

The `asset_path` and `asset_url` helpers can be used if you need to generate the URL of an asset. But you'd need to make sure to include the `.erb` file extension at the rightmost position. For example, consider the following snippet of JavaScript taken from a file named `transitions.js.erb`:

```
this.loadImage('<%= asset_path "noise.jpg" %>');
```

The Asset Pipeline runs the source through ERb processing first and interpolates in the correct path to the desired JPG file.

20.8.3 Built-In SASS Asset Path Helpers

Similarly, in a SASS stylesheet named `layout.css.scss.erb`, you might have the following code, but you wouldn't for reasons that we'll explain momentarily:

```
1 header {
2     background-image: url("<%= asset_path "header-photo-vert.jpg" %>");
3 }
```

Because this is such a common construct, Rails' SASS processing has built-in helpers, useful for referencing image, font, video, audio, and other stylesheet assets.

```
1 header {
2     background-image: image-url("header-photo-vert.jpg");
3 }
```

Reusing a familiar pattern, `image-url("rails.png")` becomes `url(/assets/ rails.png)` and `image-path("rails.png")` becomes `"/assets/rails.png"`. The more generic form can also be used, but the asset path and class must both be specified: `asset-url("rails.png", image)` becomes `url(/assets/rails.png)` and `asset-path("rails.png", image)` becomes `"/assets/rails.png"`.

20.8.4   Data URIs

You can easily embed the source of an image directly into a CSS file using the Data URL scheme[5] with the `asset_data_uri` method, like this:

```
1  icon {
2      background: url(<%= asset_data_uri 'icon.png' %>)
3  }
```

Many different kinds of content can be inlined using data URLs, although a full explanation of each is outside the scope of this book. Generally speaking, you want to keep the size of inlined data small to avoid blowing up the size of your CSS file.

20.9   Fingerprinting

In the past, Rails encoded and appended an asset's file timestamp to all asset paths like this:

```
<link href="/assets/foo.css?1385926153" media="screen" rel="stylesheet" />
```

This simple scheme allowed you to set a cache expiration date for the asset far into the future but still instantly invalidate it by updating the file. The updated timestamp changed the resulting URL, which busted the cache.

Note that in order for this scheme to work correctly, all your application servers had to return the same timestamps. In other words, they needed to have their clocks synchronized. If one of them drifted out of sync, you would see different timestamps at random, and the caching wouldn't work properly.

Another problem with the old approach was that it appended the timestamps as a query parameter. Not all cache implementations treat query parameters as parts of their cache key, leading to stale cache hits or no caching at all.

Yet another problem was that with many deployment methods, file timestamps would change on each deployment. This led to unnecessary cache invalidations after each production deploy.

The new Asset Pipeline drops the timestamping scheme and uses content fingerprinting instead. Fingerprinting makes the filename dependent on the files' content, so that the filename only ever changes when the actual file content is changed.

---

5. http://tools.ietf.org/html/rfc2397

It's worth knowing that these two lines

```
1 <%= javascript_include_tag "application" %>
2 <%= stylesheet_link_tag "application" %>
```

will look like this in production:

```
1 <script src="/assets/application-908e25f4bf641868d8683022a5b62f54.js">
2 </script>
3 <link
4   href="/assets/application-4dd5b109ee3439da54f5bdfd78a80473.css"
5   media="screen" rel="stylesheet"></link>
```

20.10   Serving the Files

To take full advantage of asset fingerprinting provided by the Asset Pipeline, you should configure your web server to set headers on your precompiled assets to a far-future expiration date. With cache headers in place, a client will only request an asset once until either the filename changes or the cache has expired.

Here's an example for Apache:

```
1 # The Expires* directives require the Apache module `mod_expires` to be enabled.
2 <Location /assets/>
3   # Use of ETag is discouraged when Last-Modified is present.
4   Header unset ETag
5   FileETag None
6   # RFC says only cache for one year.
7   ExpiresActive On
8   ExpiresDefault "access plus 1 year"
9 </Location>
```

And here's one for Nginx:

```
1 location ~ ^/assets/ {
2   expires 1y;
3   add_header Cache-Control public;
4   add_header  Last-Modified "";
5   add_header ETag "";
6   break;
7 }
```

The fingerprinting feature is controller by the `config.assets.digest` Rails setting. By default it is only set in "production" environment.

Note that the Asset Pipeline always makes copies of nonfingerprinted asset files available in the same /assets directory.

While you're thinking about how your asset files are being served, it's worth investigating the possibility of seriously improving app performance by having your web server serve asset files directly instead of involving the Rails stack. Apache and Nginx support this option out of the box, and you enable it by turning on the right option in `production.rb`:

```
1  # config.action_dispatch.x_sendfile_header = "X-Sendfile" # for apache
2  # config.action_dispatch.x_sendfile_header = 'X-Accel-Redirect' # for nginx
```

20.10.1   GZip Compression

When the Asset Pipeline precompiles a file, it generates a full-compression gzipped version as well. Thus, alongside /assets/application.css, there is also /assets/application.css.gz. The benefit of doing it during the precompilation process and not on the fly (which is supported by default by my most sane server configurations) is that it only happens once, allowing the use of the maximum compression level to minimize file size.

Some configuration is needed on the web server side to serve those precompressed files.

For Nginx you only need to add `gzip_static on;` to the configuration:

```
1  location ~ ^/assets/ {
2    expires       1y;
3    add_header   Cache-Control public;
4    add_header   Last-Modified "";
5    add_header   ETag "";
6    gzip_static on;
7    break;
8  }
```

20.11   Rake Tasks

When in production mode, Rails expects all manifests and asset files to be precompiled on disk and available to be served up by your web server out of the location specified in `config.assets.prefix` setting, which defaults to `public/assets`. Compiled asset files should not be versioned in source control, and the default `.gitignore` file for Rails includes a line for `public/assets/*`.

As part of deploying your application to production, you'll call the following rake task to create compiled versions of your assets directly on the server:

```
$  RAILS_ENV=production bundle exec rake assets:precompile
```

Note that Heroku automatically does this step for you in such a way that is compatible with its otherwise readonly filesystem. However, Heroku also prevents your Rails application from being initialized as part of asset precompilation, and certain references to objects or methods will not be available, causing the compile process to fail. To catch these errors, precompile assets on your development machine, noting any errors that arise.

Also note that local precompilation will result in a bunch of unwanted files in your /public/assets directory that will be served up instead of the originals. You'll be scratching your head wondering why changes to your JS and CSS files are not being reflected in your browser. If that happens, you need to delete the compiled assets. Use the rake assets:clobber task to get rid of them.

The official Asset Pipeline guide[6] goes into great detail about using precompiled assets with development mode or even setting up Rails to compile assets on the fly. It's rare that you would want or need to do either.

20.12   Conclusion

The Asset Pipeline was one of the great additions to Rails 3 and a big part of what makes Ruby on Rails a cutting-edge and industry-leading framework. In this chapter, we've covered the major aspects of working with the Asset Pipeline.

---

6. http://guides.rubyonrails.org/asset_pipeline.html#local-precompilation

CHAPTER 21

RSpec

I do not think there is any thrill that can go through the human heart like that felt by the inventor as he sees some creation of the brain unfolding to success.

—Nikola Tesla

RSpec is a Ruby domain-specific language for specifying the desired behavior of Ruby code. Its strongest appeal is that RSpec scripts (or simply *specs*) can achieve a remarkable degree of readability, letting the authors express their intention with greater readability and fluidity than is achievable using `ActiveSupport::TestCase` style methods and assertions.

`RSpec::Rails`, a drop-in replacement for the Rails testing subsystem, supplies verification, mocking, and stubbing features customized for use with Rails models, controllers, and views. Since switching to RSpec, I have never needed to touch `ActiveSupport::TestCase` for anything significant again. RSpec is simply that good.

21.1 Introduction

Since RSpec scripts are so readable, I can't really think of a better way of introducing you to the framework than to dive into an actual spec. Listing 21.1 is part of a real-world RSpec script defining the behavior of a `Payment` in a Hashrocket client project named Workbeast.com. As you're reading the spec, let the descriptions attached to the blocks of code come together to form sentences that describe the desired behavior.

Listing 21.1 Excerpt of Workbeast.com's Timesheet Spec

```
1 require 'spec_helper'
2
3 describe Timesheet do
```

```
 4    subject(:timesheet) { FactoryGirl.build(:timesheet) }
 5
 6    describe "validation of hours worked" do
 7      it "fails without a number" do
 8        timesheet.hours_worked = 'abc'
 9        expect(timesheet.error_on(:hours_worked).size).to eq(1)
10      end
11
12      it "passes with a number" do
13        timesheet.hours_worked = '123'
14        expect(timesheet.error_on(:hours_worked)).to be_empty
15      end
16
17    end
18
19    context "when submitted" do
20      it "sends an email notification to the manager" do
21        expect(Notifier).to receive(:send_later).
22          with(:deliver_timesheet_submitted, timesheet)
23        timesheet.submit
24      end
25
26      it "notifies its opening" do
27        expect(timesheet.opening).to_not be_nil
28        expect(timesheet.opening).to receive(:fill)
29        timesheet.submit
30      end
31    end
32 end
```

In the example, the fragment

```
1 describe Timesheet do
2   subject(:timesheet) { FactoryGirl.build(:timesheet) }
3
4   describe "validation of hours worked" do
5     it "fails without a number" do
6       timesheet.hours_worked = 'abc'
7       expect(timesheet.error_on(:hours_worked).size).to eq(1)
8     end
```

should be understood to mean "Timesheet validation of hours worked fails without a number."

RSpec scripts are collections of behaviors, which in turn have collections of examples. The `describe` method creates a `Behavior` object under the covers. The behavior sets the context for a set of specification examples defined with the it method, and you should pass a sentence fragment that accurately describes the context you're about to specify.

You can use RSpec to specify and test model and controller classes—as well as view templates—as individual units in isolation, like we did in Listing 21.1. RSpec can also be used to create integration tests that exercise the entire Rails stack from top to bottom.

```
 1  feature "Search Colleagues" do
 2    let(:user) { FactoryGirl.create(:user, name: 'Joe') }
 3
 4    let(:public_user) do
 5      FactoryGirl.create(:user, name: 'Pete', privacy_level: 'Public')
 6    end
 7
 8    let(:private_user) do
 9      FactoryGirl.create(:user, name: 'Nancy', privacy_level: 'Private')
10    end
11
12    background { login_as user }
13
14    scenario "takes you to the search results page" do
15      email_search_for(user, public_user.email)
16      expect(current_path).to eq(search_colleagues_path)
17    end
18
19    scenario "doesn't return the current user" do
20      email_search_for(user, user.email)
21      expect(page).to_not have_content(user.name)
22    end
23
24    scenario "doesn't return private users" do
25      email_search_for(user, private_user.email)
26      expect(page).to_not have_content(private_user.name)
27    end
28
29    context "when the user is not their colleague" do
30      scenario "shows the 'Add colleague' button" do
31        email_search_for(user, FactoryGirl.create(:user).email)
32        expect(page).to have_button('#add-colleague',
33          text: 'Add as Colleague')
34      end
35    end
36
37    def email_search_for(current_user, email)
38      visit colleagues_path
39      fill_in 'Search', with: email
40      click_button 'Search'
```

Rspec

```
41    end
42 end
```

Use of methods such as `visit` and `fill_in` and checking the contents of objects such as `page` hint at what this spec is doing: running your entire Rails application.

Capybara

Note that the "feature" DSL provided by RSpec demonstrated in the previous example is dependent on the Capybara[1] gem version 2.0 or later.

21.2   Basic Syntax and API

Let's run through some of the basic syntactical features of RSpec, which we've just encountered in the code listings. RSpec is essentially a domain-specific language for creating specifications. The following API methods form the vocabulary of the language.

21.2.1   `describe` and `context`

The `describe` and `context` methods are used to group together related examples of behavior. They are aliases, both taking a string description as their first argument and a block to define the context of their scope.

When writing model specs or anything that smacks of a unit test, you can pass a Ruby class as the first argument to `describe`. Doing so also creates an implicit subject for the examples, which we'll hold off on explaining for the moment. (If you're impatient, you can jump ahead in this section to "Implicit Subject.")

```
1 describe Timesheet do
2    let(:timesheet) { FactoryGirl.create(:timesheet) }
```

21.2.2   `let(:name) { expression }`

The `let` method simplifies the creation of memoized attributes for use in your spec. *Memoized* means that the code block associated with the `let` is executed once and stored for future invocations, increasing performance. Use of `let` also allows you to lessen your dependence on instance variables by creating a proper interface to the attributes needed in the spec.

So why use the `let` method? Let's step through a typical spec-coding session to understand the motivation. Imagine that you're writing a spec, and it all starts simply enough with a local `blog_post` variable.

---

1. https://github.com/jnicklas/capybara

```
1 describe BlogPost do
2   it "does something" do
3     blog_post = BlogPost.new title: 'Hello'
4     expect(blog_post).to ...
5   end
6 end
```

You continue on, writing another similar example, and you start to see some duplication. The `blog_post` creation is being done twice.

```
1 describe BlogPost do
2   it "does something" do
3     blog_post = BlogPost.new title: 'Hello'
4     expect(blog_post).to ....
5   end
6
7   it "does something else" do
8     blog_post = BlogPost.new title: 'Hello'
9     expect(blog_post).to ...
10   end
11 end
```

So you refactor the instance creation into a before block and start using an instance variable in the examples.

```
1 describe BlogPost do
2   before do
3     @blog_post = BlogPost.new title: 'Hello'
4   end
5
6   it "does something" do
7     expect(@blog_post).to ...
8   end
9
10   it "does something else" do
11     expect(@blog_post).to ...
12   end
13 end
```

And here comes the punchline: You replace the instance variables with a *variable* described by a let expression.

```
1 describe BlogPost do
2   let(:blog_post) { BlogPost.new title: 'Hello' }
3
4   it "does something" do
5     expect(blog_post).to ...
6   end
```

Rspec

```
 7
 8   it "does something else" do
 9     expect(@blog_post).to ...
10   end
11 end
```

The advantages of using `let` are mostly in the realm of readability. One, it gets rid of all those instance variables and at signs (@) blotting your code. Two, it gets rid of the `before` block, which arguably has no business setting up a bunch variables in the first place. And three, it shows you *who the players are*. A set of `let` blocks at the top of an example group reads like a cast of characters in a playbill. You can always refer to it when you're deep in the code of an example.

21.2.3 `let!(:name) { expression }`

There are instances where the lazy evaluation of `let` will not suffice and you need the value memoized immediately. This is found often in cases of integration testing and is where `let!` comes into play.

```
 1 describe BlogPost do
 2   let(:blog_post) { BlogPost.create title: 'Hello' }
 3   let!(:comment) { blog_post.comments.create text: 'first post' }
 4
 5   describe "#comment" do
 6     before do
 7       blog_post.comment("finally got a first post")
 8     end
 9
10     it "adds the comment" do
11       expect(blog_post.comments.count).to eq(2)
12     end
13   end
14 end
```

Since the comment block would never have been executed for the first assertion if you used a `let` definition, only one comment would have been added in this spec, even though the implementation may be working. By using `let!` we ensure the initial comment gets created and the spec will now pass.

21.2.4 `before` and `after`

The `before` and `after` (before's reclusive cousin) methods are akin to the `setup` and `teardown` methods of xUnit frameworks like `MiniTest`. They are used to set up the state as it should be prior to running an example and, if necessary, to clean up the state after the example has run. None of the example behaviors we've seen so far required an `after` block because, frankly, it's rare to need `after` in Rails programming.

Before and after code can be inserted in any `describe` or `context` blocks, and by default they execute for each `it` block that shares their scope.

21.2.5 `it`

The `it` method also takes a description plus a block, similar to `describe`. As mentioned, the idea is to complete the thought that was started in the `describe` method so that it forms a complete sentence. Your assertions (a.k.a. expectations) will always happen within the context of an `it` block, and you should try to limit yourself to one expectation per `it` block.

```
1    context "when there are no search results" do
2      before do
3        email_search_for(user, '123')
4      end
5
6      it "shows the search form" do
7        expect(current_url).to eq(colleagues_url)
8      end
9
10     it "renders an error message" do
11       expect(page).to have_selector('.error',
12         text: 'No matching email addresses found.')
13     end
14   end
```

21.2.6 `specify`

The `specify` method is simply an alias of the `it` method. However, it's mainly used in a different construct to improve readability. Consider the following old-school RSpec example:

```
1 describe BlogPost do
2   let(:blog_post) { BlogPost.new title: 'foo' }
3
4   it "to not be published" do
5     expect(blog_post).to_not be_published
6   end
7 end
```

Note how the example says "to not be published" in plain English, and the Ruby code within says essentially the same thing: `expect(blog_post).to_not be_published`. This is a situation where `specify` comes in handy. Examine the alternative example implementation:

```
1 describe BlogPost do
2   let(:blog_post) { BlogPost.new title: 'foo' }
3   specify { expect(blog_post).to_not be_published }
4 end
```

The English phrase has been removed, and the Ruby code has been moved into a block passed to the `specify` method. Since the Ruby block already reads like English, there's no need to repeat yourself. Especially since RSpec automatically (which is pretty cool) generates English output by inspection. Here's what the RSpec documentation formatter (`--format documentation`) output looks like:

```
BlogPost
  should not be published
```

21.2.7 `pending`
When you leave the block off of an example, RSpec treats it as pending.

```
1 describe GeneralController do
2   describe "GET to index" do
3     it "will be implemented eventually"
4   end
5 end
```

RSpec prints out pending examples at the end of its run output, which makes it potentially useful for tracking work in progress.

```
Pending:
  GeneralController on GET to index will be implemented eventually
    # Not yet implemented
    # ./spec/controllers/general_controller_spec.rb:6

Finished in 0.00024 seconds
1 example, 0 failures, 1 pending

Randomized with seed 31820
```

A quick and easy way to mark existing examples as pending is to prepend the `it` method with an x, like so:

```
1 describe GeneralController do
2   describe "on GET to index" do
3     xit "should be successful" do
4       get :index
5       expect(response).to be_successful
6     end
7   end
8 end
```

This is especially useful for debugging and refactoring.

You can also explicitly create pending examples by inserting a call to the `pending` method anywhere inside of an example.

```
1  describe GeneralController do
2    describe "on GET to index" do
3      it "is successful" do
4        pending("not implemented yet")
5      end
6    end
7  end
```

Interestingly, you can use `pending` with a block to keep broken code from failing your spec. However, if at some point in the future the broken code does execute without an error, the pending block will cause a failure.

```
1  describe BlogPost do
2    it "defaults to rating of 3.0" do
3      pending "implementation of new rating algorithm" do
4        expect(BlogPost.new.rating).to eq(3.0)
5      end
6    end
7  end
```

Note that you can make all examples in a group pending simply by calling `pending` once in the group's `before` block.

```
1  describe 'Veg-O-Matic' do
2    before { pending }
3
4    it 'slices' do
5      # will not run, instead displays "slices (PENDING: TODO)"
6    end
7
8    it 'dices' do
9      # will also be pending
10   end
11
12   it 'juliennes' do
13     # will also be pending
14   end
15 end
```

21.2.8 `expect(...).to` / `expect(...).not_to`

As of RSpec 3.0, the preferred way to define positive and negative expectations is to use the new expect syntax. Instead of using `should` and `should_not` to set expectations, one uses `expect(...).to` and `expect(...).to_not`, respectively. Note that the should syntax is still available in RSpec for backward compatibility, but the team encourages moving over to the expect syntax for new projects.

Although the syntax is different from the older should syntax, the new expect syntax works exactly the same. First, you must pass the value/block you want to execute an expectation against to the expect method. Next, chain a method call to or to_not methods to specify if the expectation is to be positive or negative, respectively. Finally, you must pass a matcher to the to/to_not method, which will fail the example if it does not match.

```
1 expect(page).to have_selector('.error',
2   text: 'No matching email addresses found.')
3
4 # equivalent to
5
6 page.should have_selector('.error',
7   text: 'No matching email addresses found.')
```

There are several ways to generate expectation matchers and pass them to expect(...).to (and expect(...).to_not):

```
1 expect(receiver).to eq(expected) # any value
2 # Passes if (receiver == expected)
3
4 expect(receiver).to eql(expected)
5 # Passes if (receiver.eql?(expected))
6
7 expect(receiver).to match(regexp)
8 # Passes if (receiver =~ regexp)
```

The process of learning to write expectations is probably one of the meatier parts of the RSpec learning curve. One of the most common idioms is expect(...).to eq(...), akin to MiniTest's assert_equal assertion.

21.2.8.1 **change** and **raise_error**

When you expect the execution of a block of code to change a value of an object or throw an exception, then expect with its block syntax is your answer. Here's an example:

```
1 expect {
2   BlogPost.create title: 'Hello'
3 }.to change(BlogPost, :count).by(1)
```

This is just a more readable DSL-style version of the RSpec's older lambda-based syntax:

```
1 lambda {
2   BlogPost.create title: 'Hello'
3 }.should change { BlogPost.count }.by(1)
```

Simply put, `expect`, using a block as input, is an alias of the `lambda` keyword, and the `to` method is an alias of the `should` method.

Then comes the `change` matcher. This is where you inspect the attribute or value that you're interested in. In our example, we're making sure that the record was saved to the database, thus increasing the record count by 1.

There are a few different variations on the `change` syntax. Here's one more example, where we're more explicit about before and after values by further chaining `from` and `to` methods:

```
1 describe "#publish!" do
2   let(:blog_post) { BlogPost.create title: 'Hello' }
3
4   it "updates published_on date" do
5     expect {
6       blog_post.publish!
7     }.to change { blog_post.published_on }.from(nil).to(Date.today)
8   end
9 end
```

Here the `published_on` attribute is examined both before and after invocation of the `expect` block. This style of change assertion comes in handy when you want to ensure a precondition of the value. Asserting `from` guarantees a known starting point.

Besides expecting changes, the other common expectation has to do with code that should generate exceptions:

```
 1 describe "#unpublish!" do
 2   context "when brand new" do
 3     let(:blog_post) { BlogPost.create title: 'Hello' }
 4
 5     it "raises an exception" do
 6       expect {
 7         blog_post.unpublish!
 8       }.to raise_error(NotPublishedError, /not yet published/)
 9     end
10   end
11 end
```

In this example, we attempt to "unpublish" a brand new blog post that hasn't been published yet. Therefore, we expect an exception to be raised.

Rspec

21.2.9   Implicit Subject

Whether you know it or not, every RSpec example group has a *subject*. Think of it as *the thing being described*. Let's start with an easy example:

```
1 describe BlogPost do
2   it { is_expected.to be_invalid }
3 end
```

By convention, the implicit subject here is a `BlogPost.new` instance. The `is_expected` call may look like it is being called *off of nothing*, but actually the call is delegated by the example to the implicit subject. It's just as if you'd written the following expression:

```
expect(BlogPost.new).to be_invalid
```

21.2.10   Explicit Subject

If the implicit subject of the example group doesn't quite do the job for you, you can specify a subject explicitly. For example, maybe we need to tweak a couple of the blog post's attributes on instantiation:

```
1 describe BlogPost do
2   subject { BlogPost.new title: 'foo', body: 'bar' }
3   it { is_expected.to be_valid }
4 end
```

Here we have the same delegation story as with implicit subject. The `is_expected` `.to be_valid` call is delegated to the subject.

You can also talk to the subject directly. For example, you may need to invoke a method off the subject to change object state:

```
1 describe BlogPost do
2   subject { BlogPost.new title: 'foo', body: 'bar' }
3
4   it "sets published timestamp" do
5     subject.publish!
6     expect(subject).to be_published
7   end
8 end
```

Here we call the `publish!` method off the subject. Mentioning `subject` directly is the way we get ahold of that `BlogPost` instance we set up. Finally, we assert that `published?` boolean is true.

Kevin Says ...

Although you can explicitly call `subject` within your specs, it's not very intention revealing. Instead, use "named subjects," which allow for a subject to be assigned an intention-revealing name. To demonstrate, here is the preceding example using a "named subject":

```
1 describe BlogPost do
2   subject(:blog_post) { BlogPost.new title: 'foo', body: 'bar' }
3
4   it "sets published timestamp" do
5     blog_post.publish!
6     expect(blog_post).to be_published
7   end
8 end
```

21.3   Matchers

Thanks to `method_missing`, RSpec can support arbitrary predicates; that is, it understands that if you invoke something that begins with `be_`, then it should use the rest of the method name as an indicator of which predicate-style method to invoke the target object. (By convention, a predicate method in Ruby ends with a ? and should return the equivalent of `true` or `false`.) The simplest hard-coded predicate-style matchers are the following:

```
1 expect(target).to be
2 expect(target).to be_true
3 expect(target).to be_truthy # not nil or false
4 expect(target).to be_false
5 expect(target).to be_falsy  # nil or false
6 expect(target).to be_nil
7 expect(target).to_not be_nil
```

Arbitrary predicate matchers can assert against any target and even support parameters!

```
1 expect(thing).to be                      # passes if thing is not nil or false
2 expect(collection).to be_empty           # passes if target.empty?
3 expect(target).to_not be_empty           # passes unless target.empty?
4 expect(target).to_not be_under_age(16)   # passes unless target.under_age?(16)
```

As an alternative to prefixing arbitrary predicate matchers with `be_`, you may choose from the indefinite article versions `be_a_` and `be_an_`, making your specs read much more naturally:

```
1 expect("a string").to be_an_instance_of(String)
2 expect(3).to be_a_kind_of(Fixnum)
3 expect(3).to be_a_kind_of(Numeric)
4 expect(3).to be_an_instance_of(Fixnum)
5 expect(3).to_not be_instance_of(Numeric) #fails
```

The cleverness (madness?) doesn't stop there. RSpec will even understand `have_` prefixes as referring to predicates like `has_key?`:

```
1 expect({foo: "foo"}).to have_key(:foo)
2 expect({bar: "bar"}).to_not have_key(:foo)
```

RSpec has a number of expectation matchers for working with classes that implement module `Enumerable`. You can specify whether an array should include a particular element or if a string contains a substring. This one always weirds me out when I see it in code because my brain wants to think that `include` is some sort of language keyword meant for mixing modules into classes. It's just a method, so it can be overridden easily.

```
1 expect([1, 2, 3]).to include(1)
2 expect([1, 2, 3]).to_not include(4)
3 expect("foobar").to include("bar")
4 expect("foobar").to_not include("baz")
```

RSpec also includes a range matcher that can be used to see if a value is covered within a given range.

```
expect(1..10).to cover(3)
```

21.4   Custom Expectation Matchers

When you find that none of the stock expectation matchers provide a natural-feeling expectation, you can very easily write your own. All you need to do is write a Ruby class that implements the following two methods:

- `matches?(actual)`
- `failure_message`

The following methods are optional for your custom matcher class:

- `does_not_match?(actual)`
- `failure_message_when_negated`
- `description`

The example given in the RSpec API documentation is a game in which players can be in various zones on a virtual board. To specify that a player bob should be in zone 4, you could write a spec like the following:

```
expect(bob.current_zone).to eq(Zone.new("4"))
```

However, it's more expressive to say one of the following, using the custom matcher in Listing 21.2:

Listing 21.2 BeInZone Custom Expectation Matcher Class

```
 1  # expect(bob) to be_in_zone(4) and expect(bob).to_not be_in_zone(3)
 2  class BeInZone
 3    def initialize(expected)
 4      @expected = expected
 5    end
 6
 7    def matches?(actual)
 8      @actual = actual
 9      @actual.current_zone.eql?(Zone.new(@expected))
10    end
11
12    def failure_message
13      "expected #{@actual.inspect} to be in Zone #{@expected}"
14    end
15
16    def failure_message_when_negated
17      "expected #{@actual.inspect} not to be in Zone #{@expected}"
18    end
19  end
```

In addition to the matcher class, you would need to write the following method so that it'd be in scope for your spec.

```
1  def be_in_zone(expected)
2    BeInZone.new(expected)
3  end
```

This is normally done by including the method and the class in a module, which is then included in your spec.

```
1  describe "Player behavior" do
2    include CustomGameMatchers
3    ...
4  end
```

Or you can include helpers globally in a `spec_helper.rb` file required from your spec file(s):

```
1 RSpec.configure do |config|
2   config.include CustomGameMatchers
3 end
```

21.4.1   Custom Matcher DSL

RSpec includes a DSL for easier definition of custom matchers. The DSL's directives match the methods you implement on custom matcher classes. Just add code similar to the following example in a file within the `spec/support` directory.

```
1 require 'nokogiri'
2
3 RSpec::Matchers.define :contain_text do |expected|
4   match do |response_body|
5     squished(response_body).include?(expected.to_s)
6   end
7
8   failure_message do |actual|
9     "expected the following element's content to include
10     #{expected.inspect}:\n\n#{response_text(actual)}"
11   end
12
13   failure_message_when_negated  do |actual|
14     "expected the following element's content to not
15     include #{expected.inspect}:\n\n#{squished(actual)}"
16   end
17
18   def squished(response_body)
19     Nokogiri::XML(response_body).text.squish
20   end
21 end
```

21.4.2   *Fluent* Chaining

You can create matchers that obey a fluent interface using the chain method:

```
1 RSpec::Matchers.define(:tip) do |expected_tip|
2   chain(:on) do |bill|
3     @bill = bill
4   end
5
6   match do |person|
7     person.tip_for(@bill) == expected_tip
8   end
9 end
```

This matcher can be used as follows:

```
1 describe Customer do
2   it { is_expected.to tip(10).on(50) }
3 end
```

In this way, you can begin to create your own fluent domain-specific languages for testing your complex business logic in a very readable way.

21.5   Shared Behaviors

Often you'll want to specify similar behavior in multiple specs. It would be silly to type out the same code over and over. Fortunately, RSpec has shared behaviors that aren't run individually but rather are included into other behaviors; they are defined using shared_examples.

```
 1 shared_examples "a phone field" do
 2   it "has 10 digits" do
 3     business = Business.new(phone_field: '8004567890')
 4     expect(business.errors_on(:phone_field)).to be_empty
 5   end
 6 end
 7
 8 shared_examples "an optional phone field" do
 9   it "handles nil" do
10     business = Business.new phone_field: nil
11     expect(business.attributes[phone_field]).to be_nil
12   end
13 end
```

You can invoke a shared example using the it_behaves_like method in place of an it.

```
 1 describe "phone" do
 2   let(:phone_field) { :phone }
 3   it_behaves_like "a phone field"
 4 end
 5
 6 describe "fax" do
 7   let(:phone_field) { :fax }
 8   it_behaves_like "a phone field"
 9   it_behaves_like "an optional phone field"
10 end
```

You can put the code for shared examples almost anywhere, but the default convention is to create a file named spec/support/shared_examples.rb to hold them.

Rspec

21.6   Shared Context

When used in combination, `shared_context` and `include_context` allow you to share `before/after` hooks, `subject` declarations, `let` declarations, and method definitions across example groups. This is useful in cases when several examples share some state. To define a shared context, supply a name and block of code to the `shared_context` macro-style method.

```
1  shared_context 'authenticated user' do
2    let(:current_user) { FactoryGirl.create(:user) }
3
4    before do
5      sign_in current_user
6    end
7  end
```

To include a shared context in your examples, use the `include_context` macro-style method.

```
1  context "user is authenticated" do
2    include_context 'authenticated user'
3    ...
4  end
```

The recommended location to place `shared_context` definitions is in the `spec/support` directory.

21.7   RSpec's Mocks and Stubs

It's possible to use a number of mocking frameworks, including Mocha, Flexmock, RR, and more. In our examples, however, we'll use RSpec's own mocking and stubbing facilities, which are almost the same and equally powerful—mostly the method names vary.[2]

21.7.1   Test Doubles

A test double is an object that stands in for another in your system during a code example. To create a test double object, you simply call the `double` method anywhere in a spec and give it a name as an optional parameter. It's a good idea to give test double objects a name if you will be using more than one of them in your spec. If you use multiple anonymous test doubles, you'll probably have a hard time telling them apart if one fails.

---

2. Confused about the difference between mocks and stubs? Read Martin Fowler's explanation at http://www.martinfowler.com/articles/mocksArentStubs.html.

```
echo = double('echo')
```

With a test double, you can set expectations about what messages are sent to your test double during the course of your spec (commonly known as a mock). Test doubles with message expectations will cause a spec to fail if those expectations are not met. To set an expectation on a test double, we invoke `receive`.

```
expect(echo).to receive(:sound)
```

The chained method `with` is used to define expected parameters. If we care about the return value, we chain `and_return` at the end of the expectation or use a block.

```
1 expect(echo).to receive(:sound).with("hey").and_return("hey")
2 expect(echo).to receive(:sound).with("hey") { "hey" }
```

Note

In older versions of RSpec, you would define mock and stub objects via the `mock` and `stub` methods, respectively. Although these methods are still available in RSpec 3.0, they are available only for backward compatibility and may be removed in a future version.

21.7.2   Null Objects

Occasionally, you just want an object for testing purposes that accepts any message passed to it—a pattern known as null object. It's possible to make one using the `as_null_object` method with a test double object.

```
null_object = double('null').as_null_object
```

21.7.3   Method Stubs

You can easily create a stub object in RSpec via the `double` factory method. You pass stub a name and default attributes as a hash.

```
yodeler = double('yodeler', yodels?: true)
```

By the way, there's no rule that the name parameter of a mock or stub needs to be a string. It's pretty typical to pass `double` a class reference corresponding to the real type of object.

```
yodeler = double(Yodeler, yodels?: true)
```

Rspec

21.7.4   Partial Mocking and Stubbing

You can install or replace methods on any object, not just doubles, with a technique called partial mocking and stubbing. RSpec supports the following two formats for declaring method stubs on existing objects:

```
1  allow(invoice).to receive(:hourly_total) { 123.45 }
2  allow(invoice).to receive(:billed_expenses).and_return(543.21)
```

Even though RSpec's authors warn us about partial stubbing in their docs, the ability to do it is really useful in practice.

21.7.5   `receive_message_chain`

It's really common to find yourself writing some gnarly code when you rely on `double` to spec behavior of nested method calls.[3] But sometimes you need to stub methods *down a dot chain*, where one method is invoked on another method, which is itself invoked on another method, and so on. For example, you may need to stub out a set of recent, unpublished blog posts in chronological order, like `BlogPost` `.recent.unpublished.chronological`.

Try to figure out what's going on in the following example. I bet it takes you more than a few seconds!

```
1  allow(BlogPost).to receive(:recent).
2    and_return(double(unpublished: double(chronological: [double,
3      double, double])))
```

That example code can be factored to be more verbose, which makes it a little easier to understand but is still pretty bad.

```
1  chronological = [double, double, double]
2  unpublished = double(chronological: chronological)
3  recent = double(unpublished: unpublished)
4  allow(BlogPost).to receive(recent).and_return(recent)
```

Luckily, RSpec gives you the `receive_method_chain` method, which understands exactly what you're trying to do here and dramatically simplifies the code needed:

```
allow(BlogPost).to receive_method_chain(:recent, :unpublished, :chronological).
  and_return([double, double, double])
```

However, just because it's so easy to stub the chain doesn't mean it's the right thing to do. The question to ask yourself is, "Why am I testing something related to methods

---

3. Active Record scopes are notoriously prone to causing this problem.

so deep down a chain? Could I move my tests down to that lower level?" Demeter would be proud.

21.8 Running Specs

Specs are executable documents. Each example block is executed inside its own object instance to make sure that the integrity of each is preserved (with regard to instance variables, etc.).

If I run one of the Workbeast specs using the `rspec` command that should have been installed on my system by the RSpec gem, I'll get output similar to that of `Test::Unit`—familiar, comfortable, and passing, just not too informative.

```
$ rspec spec/models/colleague_import_spec.rb
.........

Finished in 0.330223 seconds
9 examples, 0 failures
```

RSpec is capable of outputting results of a spec run in many formats. The traditional dots output that looks just like `Test::Unit` is called progress and, as we saw a moment ago, is the default. However, if we add the `-fd` command-line parameter to `rspec`, we can cause it to output the results of its run in a very different and much more interesting format: the documentation format.

```
$ rspec -fd spec/models/billing_code_spec.rb
BillingCode
  has a bidirectional habtm association
  removes bidirectional association on deletion

Finished in 0.066201 seconds
2 examples, 0 failures
```

Nice, huh? If this is the first time you're seeing this kind of output, I wouldn't be surprised if you drifted off in speculation about whether RSpec could help you deal with sadistic PHB-imposed[4] documentation requirements.

Having these sorts of self-documenting abilities is one of the biggest wins you get in choosing RSpec. It compels many people to work toward better spec coverage of their project. I also know from experience that development managers tend to really appreciate RSpec's output, even to the extent of incorporating it into their project deliverables.

Besides the different formatting, there are all sorts of other command-line options available. Just type `rspec --help` to see them all.

---

4. Pointy-haired boss, as per *Dilbert* comic strips.

Rspec

That does it for our introduction to RSpec. Now we'll take a look at using RSpec with Ruby on Rails.

21.9   RSpec Rails Gem

The RSpec Rails gem provides four different contexts for specs corresponding to the four major kinds of objects you write in Rails. Along with the API support you need to write Rails specs, it also provides code generators and a bundle of rake tasks.

21.9.1   Installation

Assuming you have the `rspec-rails` gem bundled already, you should run the `rspec:install` generator provided to set up your project for use with RSpec.

```
$ rails generate rspec:install
      create  .rspec
      create  spec
      create  spec/spec_helper.rb
```

The generator will add the files and directories necessary to use RSpec with your Rails project.

21.9.1.1   RSpec and Rake

The `rspec.rake` script sets the default rake task to run all specs in your `/spec` directory tree. It also creates specific `rake spec` tasks for each of the usual spec directories.

```
$ rake -T spec
rake spec                 # Run all specs in spec directory (excluding plugin specs)
rake spec:controllers     # Run the code examples in spec/controllers
rake spec:helpers         # Run the code examples in spec/helpers
rake spec:lib             # Run the code examples in spec/lib
rake spec:mailers         # Run the code examples in spec/mailers
rake spec:models          # Run the code examples in spec/models
rake spec:requests        # Run the code examples in spec/requests
rake spec:routing         # Run the code examples in spec/routing
rake spec:views           # Run the code examples in spec/views
```

21.9.1.2   RSpec and Generators

RSpec ensures that other generators in your project are aware of it as your chosen test library. Subsequently, it will be used for a command-line generation of models, controllers, and so on.

```
$ rails generate model Invoice
      invoke     active_record
      create     db/migrate/20100304010121_create_invoices.rb
```

```
create      app/models/invoice.rb
invoke      rspec
create      spec/models/invoice_spec.rb
```

21.9.1.3   RSpec Options

The `.rspec` file contains a list of default command-line options. The generated file looks like this:

```
--color
--format progress
```

You can change it to suit your preference. I like my spec output in color but usually prefer the more verbose output of `--format documentation`.

Tim Says ...

I go back and forth between preferring the dots of the `progress` format and the verbose output of the `documentation` format. With the more verbose output and long spec suites, it's easy to miss if something failed if you look away from your screen, especially on terminals with short buffers.

Here are some additional options that you might want to set in your `.rspec`:

```
--fail-fast        Tells RSpec to stop running the test suite on the
                   first failed test

-b, --backtrace    Enable full backtrace

-p, --profile      Enable profiling of examples w/output of top
                   10 slowest examples
```

21.9.1.4   The RSpec Helper Script

As opposed to command-line options, major settings and configuration of your spec suite are kept in `spec/spec_helper.rb`, which is always required at the top of an RSpec spec.

A boilerplate copy is generated by default when you install RSpec into your project. Let's go through it section by section and cover what it does.

First of all, we ensure that the Rails environment is set to `test`. Remember that RSpec replaces the standard `MiniTest`-based suite that is generated by default for Rails apps.

```
ENV["RAILS_ENV"] ||= 'test'
```

Rspec

Next the Rails environment and RSpec Rails are loaded up.

```
1 require File.expand_path("../../config/environment", __FILE__)
2 require 'rspec/rails'
```

RSpec has the notion of supporting files containing custom matchers and any other code that helps set up additional functionality for your spec suite, so it scans the spec/support directory to find those files, akin to Rails initializers.

```
1 # Requires supporting files with custom matchers and macros and so on,
2 # in ./support/ and its subdirectories.
3 Dir[Rails.root.join("spec/support/**/*.rb")].each { |f| require f }
```

If Active Record is being utilized in the project, RSpec will check to see if there are any pending migrations before the tests are run.

```
1 # Checks for pending migrations before tests are run.
2 # If you are not using ActiveRecord, you can remove this line.
3 ActiveRecord::Migration.check_pending! if defined?(ActiveRecord::Migration)
```

Finally, there is a block of configuration for your spec suite where you can set fixture paths, transaction options, and mocking frameworks.

```
 1 RSpec.configure do |config|
 2   # ## Mock Framework
 3   #
 4   # If you prefer to use mocha, flexmock, or RR, uncomment the appropriate line:
 5   #
 6   # config.mock_with :mocha
 7   # config.mock_with :flexmock
 8   # config.mock_with :rr
 9
10   # Remove this line if you're not using ActiveRecord or ActiveRecord
11   # fixtures.
12   config.fixture_path = "#{::Rails.root}/spec/fixtures"
13
14   # If you're not using ActiveRecord, or you'd prefer not to run each of
15   # your examples within a transaction, remove the following line or assign
16   # false instead of true.
17   config.use_transactional_fixtures = true
18
19   # Run specs in random order to surface order dependencies. If you find an
20   # order dependency and want to debug it, you can fix the order by
21   # providing the seed, which is printed after each run.
22   #     --seed 1234
23   config.order = "random"
24 end
```

Tim Says ...

Traditionally, a lot of extra helper methods were put into the `spec_helper` file, hence its name. However, nowadays it's generally easier to organize your additions in `spec/support` files for the same reasons `config/initializers` can be easier to manage than sticking everything in `config/environment.rb`.

While we're on the subject, keep in mind that any methods defined at the top level of a support file will become global methods available from all objects, which almost certainly is not what you want. Instead, create a module and mix it in, just like you'd do in any other part of your application.

```
1 module AuthenticationHelpers
2   def sign_in_as(user)
3     # ...
4   end
5 end
6
7 Rspec.configure do |config|
8   config.include AuthenticationHelpers
9 end
```

21.9.2 Model Specs

Model specs help you design and verify the domain model of your Rails application, both Active Record and your own classes. RSpec Rails doesn't provide too much special functionality for model specs because there's not really much needed beyond what's provided by the base library. Let's generate a `Schedule` model and examine the default spec that is created along with it.

```
1 $ rails generate model Schedule name:string
2     invoke  active_record
3     create    db/migrate/20131202160457_create_schedules.rb
4     create    app/models/schedule.rb
5     invoke    rspec
6     create      spec/models/schedule_spec.rb
```

The boilerplate `spec/models/schedule_spec.rb` looks like this:

```
1 require 'spec_helper'
2
3 describe Schedule do
4   pending "add some examples to (or delete) #{__FILE__}"
5 end
```

Assume, for example, that our Schedule class has a collection of day objects.

```
1 class Schedule < ActiveRecord::Base
2   has_many :days
3 end
```

Let's specify that we should be able to get a roll-up total of hours from schedule objects. Instead of fixtures, we'll mock out the days dependency.

```
1 require 'spec_helper'
2
3 describe Schedule do
4   let(:schedule) { Schedule.new }
5
6   it "should calculate total hours" do
7     days = double('days')
8     expect(days).to receive(:sum).with(:hours).and_return(40)
9     allow(schedule).to receive(:days).and_return(days)
10    expect(schedule.total_hours).to eq(40)
11  end
12 end
```

Here we've taken advantage of the fact that association proxies in Rails are rich objects. Active Record gives us several methods for running database aggregate functions. We set up an expectation that days should receive the sum method with one argument—:hours—and return 40. We can satisfy this specification with a very simple implementation:

```
1 class Schedule
2   has_many :days
3
4   def total_hours
5     days.sum :hours
6   end
7 end
```

A potential benefit of mocking the days proxy is that we no longer rely on the database[5] in order to write our specifications and implement the total_hours method, which will make this particular spec execute lightning fast.

On the other hand, a valid criticism of this approach is that it makes our code harder to refactor. Our spec would fail if we changed the implementation of

---

5. Well that's not quite true. Active Record still connects to the database to get the column information for Schedule. However, you could stub that information out as well to remove your dependency on the database completely.

`total_hours` to use `Enumerable#inject`, even though the external behavior doesn't change. Specifications are describing not only the visible behavior of objects but also the interactions between an object and its associated objects as well. Mocking the association proxy in this case lets us clearly specify how a `Schedule` should interact with its `Days`.

Leading mock objects advocates see mock objects as a temporary design tool. You may have noticed that we haven't defined the `Day` class yet. So another benefit of using mock objects is that they allow us to specify behavior in true isolation and during design time. There's no need to break our design rhythm by stopping to create the `Day` class and database table. This may not seem like a big deal for such a simple example, but for more involved specifications, it is really helpful to just focus on the design task at hand. After the database and real object models exist, you can go back and replace the mock `days` with calls to the real deal. This is a subtle yet very powerful message about mocks that is usually missed.

21.9.3 Controller Specs

RSpec gives you the ability to specify your controllers either in isolation from their associated views or together with them, as in regular Rails tests. According to the API docs,

> Controller Specs support running specs for Controllers in two modes, which represent the tension between the more granular testing common in TDD and the more high-level testing built into rails. BDD sits somewhere in between: we want to achieve a balance between specs that are close enough to the code to enable quick fault isolation and far enough away from the code to enable refactoring with minimal changes to the existing specs.

The controller class is passed to the `describe` method like this:

```
describe MessagesController do
```

An optional second parameter can be provided to include additional information.

I typically group my controller examples by action and HTTP method. This example requires a logged-in user, so I stub my application controller's `current_user` accessor to return a user record via FactoryGirl.

```
before(:each) do
  allow(controller).to receive(:current_user) { FactoryGirl.create(user) }
```

Rspec

Next, I create a stubbed factory for `Message` object using the `build_stubbed` FactoryGirl method. I want this stubbed message to be returned whenever `Message.all` is called during the spec.

```
@message = double(Message)
allow(Message).to receive(:all) { [@message] }
```

Now I can start specifying the behavior of actions (in this case, the `index` action). The most basic expectation is that the response should be successful—HTTP's 200 OK response code.

```
1 it "is successful" do
2   get :index
3   expect(response.status).to eq(200)
4 end
```

Additional expectations that should be done for most controller actions include the template to be rendered and variable assignment.

```
1 it "renders the index template " do
2   get :index
3   expect(response).to render_template(:index)
4 end
5
6 it "assigns the found messages for the view" do
7   get :index
8   expect(assigns(:messages)).to include(@message)
9 end
```

Previously we saw how to stub out a model's association proxy. Instead of stubbing the controller's `current_user` method to return an actual user from the database, we can have it return a double.

```
@user = double(User, name: "Quentin")
allow(controller).to receive(:current_user) { @user }
```

21.9.3.1   Isolation and Integration Modes

By default, RSpec on Rails controller specs run in isolation mode, meaning that view templates are not involved. The benefit of this mode is that you can spec the controller in complete isolation of the view, hence the name. Maybe you can sucker someone else into maintaining the view specs?

That *sucker* comment is of course facetious. Having separate view specs is not as difficult as it's made out to be sometimes. It also provides much better *fault isolation*, which is a fancy way of saying that you'll have an easier time figuring out what's wrong when something fails.

If you prefer to exercise your views in conjunction with your controller logic inside the same controller specs, just as traditional Rails functional tests do, then you can tell RSpec on Rails to run in integration mode using the render _views macro. It's not an all-or-nothing decision. You can specify modes on a per-behavior basis.

```
describe "Requesting /messages using GET" do
  render_views
```

When you invoke render_views, the controller specs will be executed once with view rendering turned on.

21.9.3.2   Specifying Errors

Ordinarily, Rails rescues exceptions that occur during action processing so that it can respond with a 501 error code and give you that great error page with the stack trace, the request variables, and so on. In order to directly specify that an action should raise an error, you bypass Rails' default handling of errors and those specified with rescue_from with RSpec method bypass_rescue.

To illustrate, assume the ApplicationController invokes rescue_from for the exception AccessDenied and redirects to 401.html:

```
1 class ApplicationController < ActionController::Base
2   rescue_from AccessDenied, with: :access_denied
3
4   private
5
6   def access_denied
7     redirect_to "/401.html"
8   end
9 end
```

Then we could test an error was raised for a controller action using bypass_rescue.

```
1 it "raises an error" do
2   bypass_rescue
3   expect { get :index }.to raise_error(AccessDenied)
4 end
```

If bypass_rescue was not included in the preceding example, the spec would have failed due to Rails rescuing the exception and redirecting to the page 401 .html.

Rspec

21.9.3.3   Specifying Routes

One of Rails' central components is routing. The routing mechanism is the way Rails takes an incoming request URL and maps it to the correct controller and action. Given its importance, it is a good idea to specify the routes in your application. You can do this by providing specs in the spec/routes directory and with two matchers to use: route_to and be_routable.

```
1  context "Messages routing" do
2    it "routes /messages/ to messages#show" do
3      expect(get:  "/messages").to route_to(
4        controller: "articles",
5        action: "index"
6      )
7    end
8
9    it "does not route an update action" do
10     expect(post: "/messages").to_not be_routable
11   end
12 end
```

21.9.4   View Specs

Controller specs let us integrate the view to make sure there are no errors with the view, but we can do one better by specifying the views themselves. RSpec will let us write a specification for a view, completely isolated from the underlying controller. We can specify that certain tags exist and that the right data are outputted.

Let's say we want to write a page that displays a private message sent between members of an Internet forum. RSpec creates the spec/views/messages directory when we use the controller generator. The first thing we would do is create a file in that directory for the show view, naming it show.html.haml_spec.rb. Next we would set up the information to be displayed on the page.

```
1  describe "messages/show.html.haml" do
2    before(:each) do
3      @message = FactoryGirl.build_stubbed(:message, subject: "RSpec rocks!")
4
5      sender = FactoryGirl.build_stubbed(:person, name: "Obie Fernandez")
6      expect(@message).to receive(:sender).and_return(sender)
7
8      recipient = FactoryGirl.build_stubbed(:person, name: "Pat Maddox")
9      expect(@message).to receive(:recipient).and_return(recipient)
```

If you want to be a little more concise at the cost of one really long line of code that you'll have to break up into multiple lines, you can create the mocks inline like this:

```
1 describe "messages/show.html.haml " do
2   before(:each) do
3     @message = FactoryGirl.build_stubbed(:message,
4       subject: "RSpec rocks!",
5       sender: FactoryGirl.build_stubbed(:person, name: "Obie Fernandez"),
6       recipient: FactoryGirl.build_stubbed(:person, name: "Pat Maddox"))
```

Either way, this is standard mock usage similar to what we've seen before. Again, mocking the objects used in the view allows us to completely isolate the specification.

21.9.4.1   Assigning Instance Variables

We now need to assign the message to the view. The `rspec_rails` gem gives us a method named `assign` method to do just that.

```
assign(:message, @message)
```

Fantastic! Now we are ready to begin specifying the view page. We'd like to specify that the message subject is displayed and wrapped in an <h1> tag. The Capybara expectation `have _selector` takes two arguments—the tag selector and a hash of options such as `:text`.

```
1 it "displays the message subject" do
2   render "messages/show"
3   expect(rendered).to have_selector('h1', text: 'RSpec rocks!')
4 end
```

HTML tags often have an id associated with them. We would like our page to create a <div> with the id `message_info` for displaying the sender and recipient's names. We can pass the id to `have_selector` as well.

```
1 it "displays a div with id message_info" do
2   render "messages/show"
3   expect(rendered).to have_selector('div#message_info')
4 end
```

21.9.5   Helper Specs

It's really easy to write specs for your custom helper modules. Just pass `describe` to your helper module and it will be mixed into a special `helper` object in the spec class so that its methods are available to your example code.

```
1 describe ProfileHelper do
2   it "profile_photo should return nil if user's photos is empty" do
3     user = mock_model(User, photos: [])
4     expect(helper.profile_photo(user)).to be_nil
5   end
6 end
```

Rspec

21.9.6   Feature Specs

A well-written acceptance test suite is an essential ingredient in the success of any complex software project, particularly those run on Agile principles and methodologies, such as extreme programming. One of the best definitions for an *acceptance test* is from the Extreme Programming official website:

> The customer specifies scenarios to test when a user story has been correctly implemented. A story can have one or many acceptance tests, whatever it takes to ensure the functionality works.[6]

Stated simply, acceptance tests let us know that we are done implementing a given feature, or user story in XP lingo. Incidentally, RSpec ships with a DSL that allows defining examples using the same XP lingo we are used to. Instead of using the describe method to group together related examples of behavior, we use feature. To specify a scenario for a given feature, we use the scenario method with a description instead of it. Although these methods are simply aliases for existing RSpec methods, they add a level of readability and provide a visual differentiator from isolated RSpec examples.

```
1 require 'spec_helper'
2
3 feature "Some Awesome Feature" do
4   background do
5     # Set up some common state for all scenarios
6     # same as `before(:each)`
7   end
8
9   scenario "A feature scenario" do
10     ...
11   end
12 end
```

All feature specs should be located in the spec/features directory.

21.9.6.1   Getting Started

To use RSpec's feature DSL for acceptance tests, you must first add the capybara gem to your application's Gemfile under the test group and run bundle.

```
1 # Gemfile
2
3 group :test do
4   gem 'capybara', '~> 2.2.0'
```

---

6. http://www.extremeprogramming.org/rules/functionaltests.html

```
5   ...
6 end
```

To enable Capybara in RSpec, in your `spec/spec_helper.rb` file, require `capybara/rspec`:

```
require 'capybara/rspec'
```

21.9.6.2 Using Capybara

Capybara provides a DSL that allows you to interact with your application as you would via a web browser.

```
 1 require 'spec_helper'
 2
 3 feature 'Authentication' do
 4   let(:email) { 'bruce@wayneenterprises.com' }
 5   let(:password) { 'batman' }
 6
 7   scenario "signs in with correct credentials" do
 8     FactoryGirl.create :user, email: email, password: password
 9     visit(new_user_session_path)
10     fill_in 'Email', with: email
11     fill_in 'Password', with: password
12     click_on 'Sign in'
13     expect(current_path).to eq(dashboard_path)
14     expect(page).to have_content('Signed in successfully')
15   end
16
17   ...
18 end
```

Navigating to a web page using Capybara is done via the `visit` method. The method will perform a GET request on the supplied path.

```
visit('/dashboard')
visit(new_user_session_path)
```

To interact with a web page, Capybara provides action methods that allow the clicking of buttons or links and the ability to fill in forms. The following are a listing of action methods you can expect to find in a Capybara feature spec:

```
attach_file('Image', '/path/to/image.jpg')
check('A Checkbox')
choose('A Radio Button')
click_link('Link Text')
click_button('Save')
```

Rspec

```
click_on('Link Text') # a link or a button
fill_in('Name', with: 'Bruce')
select('Option', from: 'Select Box')
uncheck('A Checkbox')
```

For a full reference of each action method, see the Capybara official documentation.[7]

Finally, Capybara provides various matchers to assert that a page contains a CSS selector, an XPath, or content.

```
expect(page).to have_selector('header h1')
expect(page).to have_css('header h1')

expect(page).to have_selector(:xpath, '//header/h1')
expect(page).to have_xpath('//header/h1')

expect(page).to have_content('TR4W')
```

21.9.6.3 Capybara Drivers

By default, Capybara uses `Rack::Test` as a headless driver to interact with your web application. It is best suited for acceptance tests that don't require any outside interaction or JavaScript testing. You can also override the driver Capybara uses through the `default_driver` configuration setting.

```
Capybara.default_driver = :selenium
```

If only some scenarios test JavaScript, you can keep `:rack_test` as the default driver and explicitly set a driver for JavaScript.

```
Capybara.javascript_driver = :poltergeist
```

For any scenarios that require the JavaScript driver, add `js: true` following the scenario description.

```
scenario "JavaScript dependent scenario", js: true do
...
end
```

These driver settings should be set in `spec/spec_helper.rb`.

Database Cleaner

When Capybara runs, it takes care of starting and stopping the HTTP server that will be used for testing the application. However, some drivers require

---

7. http://rubydoc.info/github/jnicklas/capybara/master/Capybara/Node/Actions

an actual HTTP server, such as Selenium and Poltergeist. Those drivers are started in another thread as a result.

Since the drivers are in another thread, applications that are dependent on an SQL database cannot use the default RSpec strategy of running every test in a transaction. This is because transactions are not shared across threads. If you were to run a Capybara driver like `:poltergeist` in a transaction, any data you set in RSpec for the scenario would not be available to Capybara.

Using the gem `database_cleaner`, we can configure RSpec to use a truncation strategy instead for JavaScript-dependent scenarios. Using truncation, the entire database is emptied out after each test instead of running in a transaction.

```
 1 RSpec.configure do |config|
 2   config.before(:suite) do
 3     DatabaseCleaner.clean_with(:truncation)
 4   end
 5
 6   config.before(:each) do
 7     DatabaseCleaner.strategy = :transaction
 8   end
 9
10   config.before(:each, js: true) do
11     DatabaseCleaner.strategy = :truncation
12   end
13
14   config.before(:each) do
15     DatabaseCleaner.start
16   end
17
18   config.after(:each) do
19     DatabaseCleaner.clean
20   end
21
22 end
```

21.10   RSpec Tools

There are several open-source projects that enhance RSpec's functionality and your productivity or can be used in conjunction with RSpec and other testing libraries.

21.10.1   Guard-RSpec

Guard-RSpec[8] is an automated testing framework that runs your spec suite when files are modified.

---

8. `https://github.com/guard/guard-rspec`

21.10.2   Spring

As your application grows, an automated test suite can start to slow down your workflow when writing specs at a frequent rate. This is due to the nature of Rails needing to load the environment for each spec run. Spring[9] alleviates this by loading the Rails environment only once and having the remaining specs use the preloaded environment. Spring is included by default in Rails 4.1.

21.10.3   Specjour

Specjour[10] is a tool aimed at lowering the run times of your entire spec suite. It distributes your specs over a LAN via Bonjour, running the specs in parallel on the number of workers it finds.

21.10.4   SimpleCov

SimpleCov is a code coverage tool for Ruby.[11] You can run it on your specs to see how much of your production code is covered. It provides HTML output to easily tell what code is covered by specs and what isn't. The results are outputted into a directory named `coverage` and contain a set of HTML files that you can browse by opening `index.html`.

21.11   Conclusion

You've gotten a taste of the different testing experience that RSpec delivers. At first it may seem like the same thing as `MiniTest` with some words substituted and shifted around. One of the key points of TDD is that it's about design rather than testing. This is a lesson that every good TDDer learns through lots of experience. RSpec uses a different vocabulary and style to emphasize that point. It comes with the lesson baked in so that you can attain the greatest benefits of TDD right away.

---

9. `https://github.com/rails/spring`

10. `https://github.com/sandro/specjour`

11. `https://github.com/colszowka/simplecov`

CHAPTER 22

XML

Structure is nothing if it is all you got. Skeletons spook people if they try to walk around on their own. I really wonder why XML does not.

—Erik Naggum

XML doesn't get much respect from the Rails community. It's *enterprisey*. In the Ruby world, that other markup language, YAML (YAML ain't markup language), and data interchange format, JSON (JavaScript object notation), get a heck of a lot more attention. However, use of XML is a fact of life for many projects, especially when it comes to interoperability with legacy systems. Luckily, Ruby on Rails gives us some pretty good functionality related to XML.

This chapter examines how to both generate and parse XML in your Rails applications, starting with a thorough examination of the `to_xml` method that most objects have in Rails.

22.1 The `to_xml` Method

Sometimes you just want an XML representation of an object, and Active Record models provide easy, automatic XML generation via the `to_xml` method. Let's play with this method in the console and see what it can do.

I'll fire up the console for my book-authoring sample application and find an Active Record object to manipulate.

```
>> User.find_by(login: 'obie')
 => #<User id: 8, login: "obie", email: "obie@example.com",
    crypted_password: "4a6046804fc4dc3183ad9012fbfee91c85723d8c",
    salt: "399754af1b01cf3d4b87da5478d82674b0438eb8",
    created_at: "2010-05-18 19:31:40", updated_at: "2010-05-18 19:31:40",
```

```
remember_token: nil, remember_token_expires_at: nil,
authorized_approver: true, client_id: nil, timesheets_updated_at: nil>
```

There we go—a `User` instance. Let's see that instance as its generic XML representation.

```
>> User.find_by(login: 'obie').to_xml
=> "<?xml version=\"1.0\" encoding=\"UTF-8\"?>\n<user>\n
   <authorized-approver type=\"boolean\">true</authorized-approver>\n
   <salt>399754af1b01cf3d4b87da5478d82674b0438eb8</salt>\n
   <created-at type=\"datetime\">2010-05-18T19:31:40Z</created-at>\n
   <crypted-password>4a6046804fc4dc3183ad9012fbfee91c85723d8c
   </crypted-password>\n  <remember-token-expires-at type=\"datetime\"
   nil=\"true\"></remember-token-expires-at>\n
   <updated-at type=\"datetime\">2010-05-18T19:31:40Z</updated-at>\n
   <id type=\"integer\">8</id>\n  <client-id type=\"integer\"
   nil=\"true\"></client-id>\n  <remember-token nil=\"true\">
   </remember-token>\n <login>obie</login>\n
   <email>obie@example.com</email>\n  <timesheets-updated-at
   type=\"datetime\" nil=\"true\"></timesheets-updated-at>\n</user>\n"
```

Ugh, that's ugly. Ruby's `print` function might help us out here.

```
>> print User.find_by(login: 'obie').to_xml

1  <?xml version="1.0" encoding="UTF-8"?>
2  <user>
3    <authorized-approver type="boolean">true</authorized-approver>
4    <salt>399754af1b01cf3d4b87da5478d82674b0438eb8</salt>
5    <created-at type="datetime">2010-05-18T19:31:40Z</created-at>
6
7    <crypted-password>4a6046804fc4dc3183ad9012fbfee91c85723d8c
8    </crypted-password>
9    <remember-token-expires-at type="datetime" nil="true">
10   </remember-token-expires-at>
11   <updated-at type="datetime">2010-05-18T19:31:40Z</updated-at>
12   <id type="integer">8</id>
13   <client-id type="integer" nil="true"></client-id>
14   <remember-token nil="true"></remember-token>
15   <login>obie</login>
16   <email>obie@example.com</email>
17   <timesheets-updated-at type="datetime" nil="true"></timesheets-updated-at>
18 </user>
```

Much better! So what do we have here? Looks like a fairly straightforward serialized representation of our `User` instance in XML.

22.1.1   Customizing `to_xml` Output

The standard processing instruction is at the top followed by an element name corresponding to the class name of the object. The properties are represented as subelements, with nonstring data fields including a `type` attribute. Mind you, this is the default behavior, and we can customize it with some additional parameters to the `to_xml` method.

We'll strip down that XML representation of a user to just an email and login using the `only` parameter. It's provided in a familiar options hash with the value of the `:only` parameter as an array:

```
>> print User.find_by(login: 'obie').to_xml(only: [:email, :login])
```

```
1 <?xml version="1.0" encoding="UTF-8"?>
2 <user>
3   <login>obie</login>
4   <email>obie@example.com</email>
5 </user>
```

Following the familiar Rails convention, the `only` parameter is complemented by its inverse, `except`, which will exclude the specified properties. What if I want my user's email and login as a snippet of XML that will be included in another document? Then let's get rid of that pesky instruction, too, using the `skip_instruct` parameter.

```
>> print User.find_by(login: 'obie').to_xml(only: [:email, :login], skip_instruct: true)
```

```
1 <user>
2   <login>obie</login>
3   <email>obie@example.com</email>
4 </user>
```

We can change the root element in our XML representation of `User` and the indenting from two to four spaces by using the `root` and `indent` parameters, respectively.

```
>> print User.find_by(login: 'obie').to_xml(root: 'employee', indent: 4)
```

```
1 <?xml version="1.0" encoding="UTF-8"?>
2 <employee>
3   <authorized-approver type="boolean">true</authorized-approver>
4   <salt>399754af1b01cf3d4b87da5478d82674b0438eb8</salt>
5   <created-at type="datetime">2010-05-18T19:31:40Z</created-at>
6   <crypted-password>4a6046804fc4dc3183ad9012fbfee91c85723d8c</crypted-password>
7   <remember-token-expires-at type="datetime" nil="true"></remember-token-expires-at>
8   <updated-at type="datetime">2010-05-18T19:31:40Z</updated-at>
9   <id type="integer">8</id>
```

```
10    <client-id type="integer" nil="true"></client-id>
11    <remember-token nil="true"></remember-token>
12    <login>obie</login>
13    <email>obie@example.com</email>
14    <timesheets-updated-at type="datetime" nil="true"></timesheets-updated-at>
15  </employee>
```

By default Rails converts CamelCase and underscore attribute names to dashes as in
created-at and client-id. You can force underscore attribute names by setting
the dasherize parameter to false.

```
>> print User.find_by(login: 'obie').to_xml(dasherize: false,
     only: [:created_at, :client_id])

1  <?xml version="1.0" encoding="UTF-8"?>
2  <user>
3    <created_at type="datetime">2010-05-18T19:31:40Z</created_at>
4    <client_id type="integer" nil="true"></client_id>
5  </user>
```

In the preceding output, the attribute type is included. This too can be configured
using the skip_types parameter.

```
>> print User.find_by(login: 'obie').to_xml(skip_types: true,
     only: [:created_at, :client_id])

1  <?xml version="1.0" encoding="UTF-8"?>
2  <user>
3    <created-at>2010-05-18T19:31:40Z</created-at>
4    <client-id nil="true"></client-id>
5  </user>
```

22.1.2   Associations and `to_xml`

So far we've only worked with a base Active Record and not with any of its associations. What if we wanted an XML representation of not just a book but also its associated chapters? Rails provides the :include parameter for just this purpose. The
:include parameter will also take an array or associations to represent in XML.

```
>> print User.find_by(login: 'obie').to_xml(include: :timesheets)

1  <?xml version="1.0" encoding="UTF-8"?>
2  <user>
3    <authorized-approver type="boolean">true</authorized-approver>
4    <salt>399754af1b01cf3d4b87da5478d82674b0438eb8</salt>
5    <created-at type="datetime">2010-05-18T19:31:40Z</created-at>
6    <crypted-password>
7      4a6046804fc4dc3183ad9012fbfee91c85723d8c
```

```
 8    </crypted-password>
 9    <remember-token-expires-at type="datetime"
10    nil="true"></remember-token-expires-at>
11    <updated-at type="datetime">2010-05-18T19:31:40Z</updated-at>
12    <id type="integer">8</id>
13    <client-id type="integer" nil="true"></client-id>
14    <remember-token nil="true"></remember-token>
15    <login>obie</login>
16    <email>obie@example.com</email>
17    <timesheets-updated-at type="datetime" nil="true"></timesheets-updated-at>
18    <timesheets type="array">
19      <timesheet>
20        <created-at type="datetime">2010-05-04T19:31:40Z</created-at>
21        <updated-at type="datetime">2010-05-18T19:31:40Z</updated-at>
22        <lock-version type="integer">0</lock-version>
23        <id type="integer">8</id>
24        <user-id type="integer">8</user-id>
25        <submitted type="boolean">true</submitted>
26        <approver-id type="integer">7</approver-id>
27      </timesheet>
28      <timesheet>
29        <created-at type="datetime">2010-05-18T19:31:40Z</created-at>
30        <updated-at type="datetime">2010-05-18T19:31:40Z</updated-at>
31        <lock-version type="integer">0</lock-version>
32        <id type="integer">9</id>
33        <user-id type="integer">8</user-id>
34        <submitted type="boolean">false</submitted>
35        <approver-id type="integer" nil="true"></approver-id>
36      </timesheet>
37      <timesheet>
38        <created-at type="datetime">2010-05-11T19:31:40Z</created-at>
39        <updated-at type="datetime">2010-05-18T19:31:40Z</updated-at>
40        <lock-version type="integer">0</lock-version>
41        <id type="integer">10</id>
42        <user-id type="integer">8</user-id>
43        <submitted type="boolean">false</submitted>
44        <approver-id type="integer" nil="true"></approver-id>
45      </timesheet>
46    </timesheets>
47  </user>
```

Rails has a much more useful to_xml method on core classes. For example, arrays are easily serializable to XML, with element names inferred from the name of the Ruby type:

```
>> print ['cat', 'dog', 'ferret'].to_xml

1 <?xml version="1.0" encoding="UTF-8"?>
2 <strings type="array">
```

```
3    <string>cat</string>
4    <string>dog</string>
5    <string>ferret</string>
6  </strings>
```

If you have mixed types in the array, this is also reflected in the XML output:

```
>> print [3, 'cat', 'dog', :ferret].to_xml

1  <?xml version="1.0" encoding="UTF-8"?>
2  <objects type="array">
3    <object type="integer">3</object>
4    <object>cat</object>
5    <object>dog</object>
6    <object type="symbol">ferret</object>
7  </objects>
```

To construct a more semantic structure, the root option on to_xml triggers more expressive element names:

```
>> print ['cat', 'dog', 'ferret'].to_xml(root: 'pets')

1  <?xml version="1.0" encoding="UTF-8"?>
2  <pets type="array">
3    <pet>cat</pet>
4    <pet>dog</pet>
5    <pet>ferret</pet>
6  </pets>
```

Ruby hashes are naturally representable in XML, with keys corresponding to element names and their values corresponding to element contents. Rails automatically calls to_s on the values to get string values for them:

```
>> print({owners: ['Chad', 'Trixie'], pets: ['cat', 'dog', 'ferret'],
     id: 123}.to_xml(root: 'registry'))

 1  <?xml version="1.0" encoding="UTF-8"?>
 2  <registry>
 3    <pets type="array">
 4      <pet>cat</pet>
 5      <pet>dog</pet>
 6      <pet>ferret</pet>
 7    </pets>
 8    <owners type="array">
 9      <owner>Chad</owner>
10      <owner>Trixie</owner>
11    </owners>
12    <id type="integer">123</id>
13  </registry>
```

Josh G. Says …

This simplistic serialization may not be appropriate for certain interoperability contexts, especially if the output must pass XML Schema (XSD) validation when the order of elements is often important. In Ruby 1.9.x and 2.0, the Hash class uses insertion order. This may not be adequate for producing output that matches an XSD. The section "The XML Builder" in this chapter will discuss `Builder::XmlMarkup` to address this situation.

The `:include` option of `to_xml` is not used on `Array` and `Hash` objects.

22.1.3   Advanced **to_xml** Usage

By default, Active Record's `to_xml` method only serializes persistent attributes into XML. However, there are times when transient, derived, or calculated values need to be serialized out into XML form as well. For example, our `User` model has a method that returns only draft timesheets:

```
1 class User < ActiveRecord::Base
2   ...
3   def draft_timesheets
4     timesheets.draft
5   end
6   ...
7 end
```

To include the result of this method when we serialize the XML, we use the `:methods` parameter:

```
>> print User.find_by(login: 'obie').to_xml(methods: :draft_timesheets)

 1 <?xml version="1.0" encoding="UTF-8"?>
 2 <user>
 3   <id type="integer">8</id>
 4   ...
 5   <draft-timesheets type="array">
 6     <draft-timesheet>
 7       <created-at type="datetime">2010-05-18T19:31:40Z</created-at>
 8       <updated-at type="datetime">2010-05-18T19:31:40Z</updated-at>
 9       <lock-version type="integer">0</lock-version>
10       <id type="integer">9</id>
11       <user-id type="integer">8</user-id>
12       <submitted type="boolean">false</submitted>
13       <approver-id type="integer" nil="true"></approver-id>
14     </draft-timesheet>
15     <draft-timesheet>
16       <created-at type="datetime">2010-05-11T19:31:40Z</created-at>
```

```
17        <updated-at type="datetime">2010-05-18T19:31:40Z</updated-at>
18        <lock-version type="integer">0</lock-version>
19        <id type="integer">10</id>
20        <user-id type="integer">8</user-id>
21        <submitted type="boolean">false</submitted>
22        <approver-id type="integer" nil="true"></approver-id>
23      </draft-timesheet>
24    </draft-timesheets>
25  </user>
```

We could also set the `methods` parameter to an array of method names to be called.

22.1.4   Dynamic Runtime Attributes

In cases where we want to include extra elements unrelated to the object being serialized, we can pass `to_xml` a block or use the `:procs` option.

    If we are using the same logic applied to different `to_xml` calls, we can construct
lambdas ahead of time and use one or more of them in the `:procs` option. They will
be called with `to_xml`'s option hash, through which we access the underlying `Xml`
`Builder`. (`XmlBuilder` provides the principal means of XML generation in Rails.)

```
>> current_user = User.find_by(login: 'admin')
>> generated_at = lambda { |opts| opts[:builder].tag!('generated-at',
      Time.now.utc.iso8601) }
>> generated_by = lambda { |opts| opts[:builder].tag!('generated-by',
      current_user.email) }

>> print(User.find_by(login: 'obie').to_xml(procs: [generated_at,
      generated_by]))

 1  <?xml version="1.0" encoding="UTF-8"?>
 2  <user>
 3    ...
 4    <id type="integer">8</id>
 5    <client-id type="integer" nil="true"></client-id>
 6    <remember-token nil="true"></remember-token>
 7    <login>obie</login>
 8    <email>obie@example.com</email>
 9    <timesheets-updated-at type="datetime" nil="true"></timesheets-updated-at>
10    <generated-at>2010-05-18T19:33:49Z</generated-at>
11    <generated-by>admin@example.com</generated-by>
12  </user>

>> print Timesheet.all.to_xml(procs: [generated_at, generated_by])

 1  <?xml version="1.0" encoding="UTF-8"?>
 2  <timesheets type="array">
 3    <timesheet>
```

```
 4      ...
 5      <id type="integer">8</id>
 6      <user-id type="integer">8</user-id>
 7      <submitted type="boolean">true</submitted>
 8      <approver-id type="integer">7</approver-id>
 9      <generated-at>2010-05-18T20:18:30Z</generated-at>
10      <generated-by>admin@example.com</generated-by>
11    </timesheet>
12    <timesheet>
13      ...
14      <id type="integer">9</id>
15      <user-id type="integer">8</user-id>
16      <submitted type="boolean">false</submitted>
17      <approver-id type="integer" nil="true"></approver-id>
18      <generated-at>2010-05-18T20:18:30Z</generated-at>
19      <generated-by>admin@example.com</generated-by>
20    </timesheet>
21    <timesheet>
22      ...
23      <id type="integer">10</id>
24      <user-id type="integer">8</user-id>
25      <submitted type="boolean">false</submitted>
26      <approver-id type="integer" nil="true"></approver-id>
27      <generated-at>2010-05-18T20:18:30Z</generated-at>
28      <generated-by>admin@example.com</generated-by>
29    </timesheet>
30  </timesheets>
```

Note that the :procs are applied to each top-level resource in the collection (or the single resource if the top level is not a collection). Use the sample application to compare the output with the output from the following:

```
>> print User.all.to_xml(include: :timesheets, procs: [generated_at,
   generated_by])
```

To add custom elements only to the root node, to_xml will yield an Xml Builder instance when given a block:

```
>> print(User.all.to_xml { |xml| xml.tag! 'generated-by', current_user.email })
```

```
1  <?xml version="1.0" encoding="UTF-8"?>
2  <users type="array">
3    <user>...</user>
4    <user>...</user>
5    <generated-by>admin@example.com</generated-by>
6  </users>
```

Unfortunately, both :procs and the optional block are hobbled by a puzzling limitation: The record being serialized is not exposed to the procs being passed in as arguments, so only data external to the object may be added in this fashion.

To gain complete control over the XML serialization of Rails objects, you need to override the to_xml method and implement it yourself.

22.1.5 Overriding `to_xml`

Sometimes you need to do something out of the ordinary when trying to represent data in XML form. In those situations, you can create the XML by hand.

```
1 class User < ActiveRecord::Base
2   ...
3   def to_xml(options = {}, &block)
4     xml = options[:builder] || ::Builder::XmlMarkup.new(options)
5     xml.instruct! unless options[:skip_instruct]
6     xml.user do
7       xml.tag!(:email, email)
8     end
9   end
10   ...
11 end
```

This would give the following result:

```
>> print User.first.to_xml
```

```
1 <?xml version="1.0" encoding="UTF-8"?><user><email>admin@example.com</email></user>
```

Of course, you could just go ahead and use good object-oriented design and use a class responsible for translating between your model and an external representation.

22.2 The XML Builder

`Builder::XmlMarkup` is the class used internally by Rails when it needs to generate XML. When to_xml is not enough and you need to generate custom XML, you will use Builder instances directly. Fortunately, the Builder API is one of the most powerful Ruby libraries available and is very easy to use, once you get the hang of it.

The API documentation says, "All (well, almost all) methods sent to an Xml Markup object will be translated to the equivalent XML markup. Any method with a block will be treated as an XML markup tag with nested markup in the block."

That is a very concise way of describing how Builder works, but it is easier to understand with some examples, again taken from Builder's API documentation. The xml variable is a Builder::XmlMarkup instance:

```
 1 xm.em("emphasized")               # => <em>emphasized</em>
 2 xm.em { xm.b("emp & bold") }      # => <em><b>emph &amp; bold</b></em>
 3
 4 xm.a("foo", "href"=>"http://foo.org")
 5                                    # => <a href="http://foo.org">foo</a>
 6
 7 xm.div { br }                     # => <div><br/></div>
 8
 9 xm.target("name"=>"foo", "option"=>"bar")
10                                    # => <target name="foo" option="bar"/>
11
12 xm.instruct!                       # <?xml version="1.0" encoding="UTF-8"?>
13
14 xm.html {                         # <html>
15   xm.head {                       #   <head>
16     xm.title("History")           #     <title>History</title>
17   }                               #   </head>
18   xm.body {                       #   <body>
19     xm.comment! "HI"              #     <!-- HI -->
20     xm.h1("Header")               #     <h1>Header</h1>
21     xm.p("paragraph")             #     <p>paragraph</p>
22   }                               #   </body>
23 }                                 # </html>
```

A common use for `Builder::XmlBuilder` is to render XML in response to a request. Previously, we talked about overriding `to_xml` on Active Record to generate our custom XML. Another way, though not as recommended, is to use an XML template.

We could alter our `UsersController#show` method to use an XML template by changing it from

```
 1 def UsersController < ApplicationController
 2   ...
 3   def show
 4     @user = User.find(params[:id])
 5     respond_to do |format|
 6       format.html
 7       format.xml { render xml: @user.to_xml }
 8     end
 9   end
10   ...
11 end
```

to

```
 1 def UsersController < ApplicationController
 2   ...
```

```
 3    def show
 4      @user = User.find(params[:id])
 5      respond_to do |format|
 6        format.html
 7        format.xml
 8      end
 9    end
10    ...
11  end
```

Now Rails will look for a file called show.xml.builder in the app/views/
users directory. That file contains Builder::XmlMarkup code like the following:

```
 1  xml.user {                                    # <user>
 2    xml.email @user.email                       #   <email>...</email>
 3    xml.timesheets {                            #   <timesheets>
 4      @user.timesheets.each { |timesheet|       #
 5        xml.timesheet {                          #     <timesheet>
 6          xml.draft timesheet.submitted?         #       <draft>true</draft>
 7        }                                         #     </timesheet>
 8      }                                           #
 9    }                                             #   </timesheets>
10  }                                              # </user>
```

In this view the variable xml is an instance of Builder::XmlMarkup. Just as in
views, we have access to the instance variables we set in our controller, in this case
@user. Using the Builder in a view can provide a convenient way to generate
XML.

22.3   Parsing XML

Ruby has a full-featured XML library named Nokogiri, and covering it in any level of
detail is outside the scope of this book. If you have basic parsing needs, such as parsing
responses from web services, you can use the simple XML parsing capability built into
Rails.

22.3.1   Turning XML into Hashes

Rails lets you turn arbitrary snippets of XML markup into Ruby hashes with the
from_xml method that it adds to the Hash class.

To demonstrate, we'll throw together a string of simplistic XML and turn it into a hash:

```
>> xml = <<-XML
<pets>
  <cat>Franzi</cat>
  <dog>Susie</dog>
  <horse>Red</horse>
```

```
</pets>
XML
```

```
1 >> Hash.from_xml(xml)
2 => {"pets"=>{"cat"=>"Franzi", "dog"=>"Susie", "horse"=>"Red"}}
```

There are no options for `from_xml`. You can also pass it an `IO` object:

```
>> Hash.from_xml(File.new('pets.xml'))
=> {"pets"=>{"cat"=>"Franzi", "dog"=>"Susie", "horse"=>"Red"}}
```

22.3.2 Typecasting

Typecasting is done by using a `type` attribute in the XML elements. For example, here's the autogenerated XML for a `User` object.

```
>> print User.first.to_xml
```

```
 1 <?xml version="1.0" encoding="UTF-8"?>
 2 <user>
 3   <authorized-approver type="boolean">true</authorized-approver>
 4   <salt>034fbec79d0ca2cd7d892f205d56ea95174ff557</salt>
 5   <created-at type="datetime">2010-05-18T19:31:40Z</created-at>
 6   <crypted-password>98dfc463d9122a1af0a5dc817601de437c69f365
 7   </crypted-password>
 8   <remember-token-expires-at type="datetime" nil="true" />
 9   <updated-at type="datetime">2010-05-18T19:31:40Z</updated-at>
10   <id type="integer">7</id>
11   <client-id type="integer" nil="true" />
12   <remember-token nil="true" />
13   <login>admin</login>
14   <email>admin@example.com</email>
15   <timesheets-updated-at type="datetime" nil="true" />
16 </user>
```

As part of the `to_xml` method, Rails sets attributes called `type` that identify the class of the value being serialized. If we take this XML and feed it to the `from_xml` method, Rails will typecast the strings to their corresponding Ruby objects:

```
>> Hash.from_xml(User.first.to_xml)
=> {"user"=>{"salt"=>"034fbec79d0ca2cd7d892f205d56ea95174ff557",
   "authorized_approver"=>true,
   "created_at"=>Tue May 18 19:31:40 UTC 2010, "remember_token_expires_at"=>nil,
   "crypted_password"=>"98dfc463d9122a1af0a5dc817601de437c69f365",
   "updated_at"=>Tue May 18 19:31:40 UTC 2010, "id"=>7, "client_id"=>nil,
   "remember_token"=>nil, "login"=>"admin",
       "timesheets_updated_at"=>nil,
   "email"=>"admin@example.com"}}
```

22.4   Conclusion

In practice, the `to_xml` and `from_xml` methods meet the XML handling needs for most situations that the average Rails developer will ever encounter. Their simplicity masks a great degree of flexibility and power, and in this chapter, we attempted to explain them in sufficient detail to inspire your own exploration of XML handling in the Ruby world.

Active Model API Reference

Active Model is a Rails library containing various modules used in developing frameworks that need to interact with the Rails Action Pack and Action View libraries. This came about by extracting common functionality that was not persistence specific out of Active Record, so that third-party libraries did not have to copy code from Rails or monkey patch helpers in order to conform to the API.

Out of this extraction came extremely useful reusable functionality to developers of Rails compatible libraries, such as dirty attributes, validations, and serialization into JSON or XML. And simply by using these modules, developers could be DRY and not need to rewrite what has already been done before.

Section headings reflect the name of the class or module where the API method is located and are organized in alphabetical order for easy lookup. Subsections appear according to the name of the Ruby file in which they exist within Active Model's `lib` directory. Finally, the sub-subsections are the API methods themselves.

A.1 `AttributeMethods`

Adds the ability for your class to have custom prefixes and suffixes on your methods. It's used by adding the definitions for the prefixes and suffixes, defining which methods on the object will use them and then implementing the common behavior for when those methods are called. An example implementation is as follows:

```
1 class Record
2    include ActiveModel::AttributeMethods
3
4    attribute_method_prefix 'reset_'
5    attribute_method_suffix '_highest?'
6    define_attribute_methods :score
```

```
 7
 8    attr_accessor :score
 9    attr_accessor :previous_score
10
11    private
12
13    def reset_attribute(attribute)
14      send("#{attribute}=", nil)
15    end
16
17    def attribute_highest?(attribute)
18      attribute > 1000 ? true : false
19    end
20 end
```

A.1.1 `active_model/attribute_methods.rb`

`alias_attribute(new_name, old_name)`

This useful method allows you to easily make aliases for attributes, including their reader and writer methods.

```
 1 class Person
 2    include ActiveModel::AttributeMethods
 3    attr_accessor :name
 4    alias_attribute :full_name, :name
 5 end
 6
 7
 8 person = Person.new
 9 person.name = "John Smith"
10 person.name        # => "John Smith"
11 person.full_name # => "John Smith"
```

`attribute_method_affix(*affixes)`

Defines a prefix and suffix that, when used in conjunction with `define_attribute_methods`, creates a instance method with the prefix and suffix wrapping the previous method name.

`attribute_method_prefix(*prefixes)`

Defines a prefix that, when used in conjunction with `define_attribute_methods`, creates an instance method with the prefix and the previous method name.

attribute_method_suffix(*suffixes)

Defines a suffix that, when used in conjunction with define_attribute_methods, creates an instance method with the suffix and the previous method name.

define_attribute_method(attr_name)

Declares an attribute that will get prefixed and suffixed. The define_attribute_method should be defined *after* any prefix, suffix, or affix definitions or they will not hook in.

```
1  class Record
2    include ActiveModel::AttributeMethods
3
4    attribute_method_prefix 'reset_'
5    define_attribute_methods :score
6
7    attr_accessor :score
8
9    private
10
11   def reset_attribute(attribute)
12     send("#{attribute}=", nil)
13   end
14 end
15
16 record = Record.new
17 record.score = 1
18 record.reset_score # => nil
```

define_attribute_methods(*attr_names)

Declares the attributes that will get prefixed and suffixed. Note that define_attribute_methods should be defined *after* any prefix, suffix, or affix definitions.

generated_attribute_methods

Returns whether or not the dynamic attribute methods have been generated.

undefine_attribute_methods

Removes all the attribute method definitions previously defined.

A.2 Callbacks

Gives any class Active Record style callbacks. It is used by defining the callbacks that the model will use and then in your model running the callbacks at the appropriate time. Once defined you have access to before, after, and around custom methods.

```
 1 class Record
 2   extend ActiveModel::Callbacks
 3
 4   define_model_callbacks :create
 5   define_model_callbacks :update, only: :before
 6
 7   before_update :my_callback
 8
 9   def create
10     run_callbacks :create do
11       # Your create code here
12     end
13   end
14
15   def update
16     run_callbacks :update do
17       # Your update code here
18     end
19   end
20
21   private
22
23   def my_callback
24     # Your callback code here
25   end
26 end
```

A.2.1 `active_model/callbacks.rb`

`define_model_callbacks(*callbacks)`

Defines the callback hooks that can be used in the model, which will dynamically provide you with a `before`, `after`, and `around` hook for each name passed. Optionally, one can supply an `:only` option to specify which callbacks you want created.

```
 1 define_model_callbacks :create, only: :after
```

Defined callbacks can accept a callback class by passing the given callback an object that responds to the name of the callback and takes the model object as a parameter.

```
 1 class Record
 2   extend ActiveModel::Callbacks
 3   define_model_callbacks :create
 4
 5   before_create SomeCallbackClass
 6 end
 7
```

```
 8 class SomeCallbackClass
 9   def self.before_create(obj)
10     # Obj is the Record instance the callback is being called on.
11   end
12 end
```

A.3   Conversion

A simple module that, when included, gives the standard Rails conversion methods to your model. The only requirement for including this class is that your model contains a `persisted?` method and an `id` method.

A.3.1   `active_model/conversion.rb`

to_model

Returns `self`. If your model is not Active Model compliant, then override this method.

to_key

Returns an enumerable of primary key attributes or `nil` if the object is not persisted.

to_param

Return a URL-friendly version of the object's primary key or `nil` if the object is not persisted.

to_partial_path

Returns a string identifying the path associated with the object.

```
record = Record.new
record.to_partial_path # => "records/record"
```

Used by Action View to find a suitable partial to represent the object.

A.4   Dirty

A powerful module that allows for tracking in your object what changes have been made to it since it was last initialized. It creates a handful of dynamic methods based on which attributes you define as attribute methods on your class and requires that you also tell the attribute setters that they are being tracked for changes. (You can optionally also store previous changes each time your object is persisted as well.)

```
1 class User
2   include ActiveModel::Dirty
3
```

```
 4    define_attribute_methods :email
 5
 6    def email
 7      @email
 8    end
 9
10    def email=(value)
11      email_will_change! unless value == @email
12      @email = value
13    end
14
15    def save
16      @previously_changed = changes
17      @changed_attributes.clear
18    end
19 end
```

In the previous example, the following dynamic methods would then be available for checking the dirty state of the flagged field. (Assume user is an instance of the User class.)

```
 1 # Returns an array of the old and new values.
 2 user.email_change
 3
 4 # Returns true if the value has changed.
 5 user.email_changed?
 6
 7 # Resets the attribute back to the original value.
 8 user.reset_email!
 9
10 # Returns the old value of a changed field.
11 user.email_was
12
13 # Flags an attribute that will be changed.
14 user.email_will_change!
```

A.4.1 `active_model/dirty.rb`

changed
Returns an array of fields whose values have changed on the object.

changed?
Returns whether or not the object's attributes have changed.

As of Rails 4.1, one can determine if an attribute has changed from one value to another by supplying hash options :from and :to.

```
user.name_changed?(from: 'Prince', to: 'Symbol')
```

changed_attributes
Returns a hash of the fields that have changed with their original values.

changes
Returns a hash of changes with the attribute names as the keys and the values being an array of the old and new value for that field.

previous_changes
Returns a hash of previous changes before the object was persisted with the attribute names as the keys and the values being an array of the old and new value for that field.

A.5   Errors
A module that provides a common interface for handling application error messages.

Note that in order for your object to be compatible with the Errors API with I18n and validations support, it needs to extend ActiveModel::Naming and ActiveModel::Translation and include ActiveModel::Validations.

```
1 class User
2   extend ActiveModel::Naming
3   extend ActiveModel::Translation
4   include ActiveModel::Validations
5
6   attr_reader :errors
7   attr_accessor :name
8
9   def initialize
10     @errors = ActiveModel::Errors.new(self)
11   end
12 end
```

A.5.1   active_model/errors.rb

[](attribute)
Returns the errors for the supplied attribute as an array.

```
1 user.errors[:name] # => ["is invalid"]
```

[]=(attribute, error)

Adds the provided error message to the `attribute` errors.

```
1 user.errors[:name] = 'must be implemented'
```

add(attribute, message = nil, options = {})

Adds an error message for the supplied attribute. If no message is provided, `:invalid` is assumed. Options allowed are the following:

:strict If set to `true`, will raise `ActiveModel::StrictValidation Failed` over adding an error.

```
>> user.errors.add(:name)
=> ["is invalid"]
>> user.errors.add(:name, 'must be implemented')
=> ["is invalid", "must be implemented"]
```

add_on_blank(attributes, options = {})

Adds a "blank" error message for each specified attribute that is blank.

```
user.errors.add_on_blank(:name)
user.errors[:name] # => ["can't be blank"]
```

add_on_empty(attributes, options = {})

Adds an error message for each specified attribute that is empty.

```
user.errors.add_on_empty(:name)
user.errors[:name] # => ["can't be empty"]
```

added?(attribute, message = nil, options = {})

Returns `true` if an error on the attribute with the given message is present.

```
user.errors.add :name, :blank
user.errors.added? :name, :blank # => true
```

as_json(options=nil)

Returns a hash that can be used as the JSON representation for this object. Available options are the following:

:full_messages If set to `true`, returns full errors messages for each attribute.

```
>> user.errors.as_json
=> {:name=>["can't be blank"]}
```

```
>> user.errors.as_json(full_messages: true)
=> {:name=>["Name can't be blank"]}
```

blank? / empty?
Returns `true` if there are no errors on the object and `false` otherwise.

count
Returns the total number of error messages.

delete(key)
Deletes all messages for specified `key`.

```
1 user.errors[:name] # => ["can't be blank"]
2 user.errors.delete(:name)
3 user.errors[:name] # => []
```

each
Iterates through the error keys, yielding the attribute and the errors for each. If an attribute has more than one error message, it will yield for each one.

```
1 user.errors.each do |attribute, error|
2   ...
3 end
```

full_message(attribute, message)
Returns a full message for a given attribute.

full_messages
Returns all the error messages as an array.

full_messages_for(attribute)
Returns an array of all the full error messages for a given attribute.

```
1 user.errors.full_messages_for(:name)
```

generate_message(attr, message = :invalid, options = {})
Generates a translated error message under the scope `activemodel.errors` `.messages` for the supplied attribute. Messages are looked up via the following pattern: `models.MODEL.attributes.ATTRIBUTE.MESSAGE`. If a translation is not found, Active Model will then look in `models.MODEL.MESSAGE`. If that

yields no translations, it will return a default message (`activemodel.errors`
`.messages.MESSAGE`).

The following are available options:

`:strict` If set to `true`, will raise `ActiveModel::StrictValidation`
`Failed` over adding an error.

If inheritance is being used in your models and no error messages are found for the model, messages will be looked up on the parent model.

get(key)
Returns an array of error messages for the given `key`.

```
1 user.errors.get(:name)
```

has_key?(attribute) / include?(attribute)
Returns `true` if the error messages include an error for the given `attribute`.

```
user.errors.include?(:name) # => true
```

keys
Returns all message keys.

set(key, value)
Sets the messages for a key.

```
user.errors.set(:name, ['must be implemented'])
```

size
Returns the total number of error messages.

to_a
Returns an array of all the error messages with the attribute name included in each.

to_hash(full_messages = false)
Returns a hash of all the error messages with the attribute name set as the key and messages as values. If `full_messages` is set to `true`, it will contain full messages.

to_xml

Returns the errors hash as XML.

values

Returns all message values.

A.6   **ForbiddenAttributesError**

Defines the `ForbiddenAttributesError` exception, which is raised when forbidden attributes are used for mass assignment.

```
1 params = ActionController::Parameters.new(name: 'Bob')
2 User.new(params) # => ActiveModel::ForbiddenAttributesError
3 params.permit!
4 User.new(params) # =>  #<User:0x007fefd4389020 ...>
```

A.7   **Lint::Tests**

You can check whether an object is compatible with the Active Model API by including `ActiveModel::Lint::Tests`. It contains assertions that tell you whether your object is fully compliant.

The tests only check compatibility. They don't attempt to determine the correctness of the returned values. For instance, you could implement `valid?` to always return `true` and the tests would still pass. It's up to you to ensure that the values are correct.

Objects you pass in are expected to return a compliant object from a call to `to_model`. Generally speaking, `to_model` just returns `self`.

A.8   **Model**

`Model` is a module mixin that includes the required interface for a Ruby object to work with Action Pack and Action View. Classes that include `Model` get several other Active Model features out of the box, such as the following:

- Model name introspection
- Conversions
- Translations
- Validations

Like Active Record objects, `Model` objects can also be initialized with a hash of attributes.

```
1 class Contact
2   include ActiveModel::Model
```

Active
Model

```
3
4   attr_accessor :name, :email, :message
5
6   validates :name, presence: true
7   validates :email, presence: true
8   validates :message, presence: true, length: { maximum: 300 }
9 end
```

The implementation of `Model` is only 24 lines of code, reproduced here for reference purposes:

```
1 module ActiveModel
2   module Model
3     def self.included(base)
4       base.class_eval do
5         extend  ActiveModel::Naming
6         extend  ActiveModel::Translation
7         include ActiveModel::Validations
8         include ActiveModel::Conversion
9       end
10    end
11
12    def initialize(params={})
13      params.each do |attr, value|
14        self.public_send("#{attr}=", value)
15      end if params
16
17      super()
18    end
19
20    def persisted?
21      false
22    end
23  end
24 end
```

A.9 Name

Name extends `String` and wraps a bunch of logic around your object's name information so that it can be used with Rails.

How much name information could there be? Take a look at Name's constructor.

```
1 def initialize(klass, namespace = nil, name = nil)
2   @name = name || klass.name
3
4   raise ArgumentError, "Class name cannot be blank. You need to supply a
5     name argument when anonymous class given" if @name.blank?
```

```
 6
 7  @unnamespaced = @name.sub(/^#{namespace.name}::/, '') if namespace
 8  @klass        = klass
 9  @singular     = _singularize(@name)
10  @plural       = ActiveSupport::Inflector.pluralize(@singular)
11  @element      = ActiveSupport::Inflector.
12    underscore(ActiveSupport::Inflector.demodulize(@name))
13  @human        = ActiveSupport::Inflector.humanize(@element)
14  @collection   = ActiveSupport::Inflector.tableize(@name)
15  @param_key    = (namespace ? _singularize(@unnamespaced) : @singular)
16  @i18n_key     = @name.underscore.to_sym
17
18  @route_key            = (namespace ? ActiveSupport::Inflector.
19    pluralize(@param_key) : @plural.dup)
20  @singular_route_key = ActiveSupport::Inflector.singularize(@route_key)
21  @route_key << "_index" if @plural == @singular
22 end
```

All this information is calculated and stored at initialization time, presumably since
it's used all over Rails.

A.9.1   `active_model/naming.rb`

`cache_key` / `collection`
Returns an underscored plural version of the model name.

`element`
Returns an underscored version of the model name.

`human`
Returns a translated human-readable version of the model name using I18n. The
basic recipe is to capitalize the first word of the name.

```
1 BlogPost.model_name.human # => "Blog post"
```

`i18n_key`
Returns a symbol of the model name to be used as an I18n key.

`param_key`
Returns a version of the model name to be used for params names.

`plural`
Returns a pluralized version of the model name.

route_key

Returns a version of the model name to use while generating route names.

singular

Returns a singularized version of the model name.

singular_route_key

Returns a singularized version of the model name to use while generating route names.

A.10 Naming

Naming is the module that you extend in your class to get name type information for your model.

A.10.1 active_model/naming.rb

model_name

Returns an ActiveModel::Name instance for the object. Used by Action Pack and Action View for naming-related functionality, such as routing.

A.11 SecurePassword

Including the SecurePassword module adds a single macro-style method has_secure_password to your class, which adds the ability to set and authenticate against a BCrypt password.

A full explanation of how to use has_secure_password is provided in the Chapter 14, "Authentication and Authorization," in the section "has_secure_password."

A.12 Serialization

Serialization is a module to include in your models when you want to represent your model as a serializable hash. You only need to define an attributes method, and the rest is handled for you.

```
1 class User
2   include ActiveModel::Serialization
3   attr_accessor :first_name, :last_name
4
5   def attributes
6     { 'first_name' => @first_name, 'last_name' => @last_name }
7   end
8 end
```

A.12.1 `active_model/serialization.rb`

`serializable_hash(options = nil)`

Returns the serializable hash representation of your model. Options provided can be one of the following:

`:except` Do not include these attributes.

`:methods` Include the supplied methods. The method name will be set as the key and its output the value.

`:only` Only include the supplied attributes.

A.13 **Serializers::JSON**

`Serializers::JSON` is a module to include in your models when you want to provide a JSON representation of your object. It automatically includes the module and depends on the `attributes` and `attributes=` methods to be present.

```
1 class User
2   include ActiveModel::Serializers::JSON
3   attr_accessor :first_name, :last_name
4
5   def attributes
6     { 'first_name' => @first_name, 'last_name' => @last_name }
7   end
8
9   def attributes=(attrs)
10    @first_name = attrs['first_name']
11    @last_name = attrs['last_name']
12  end
13 end
```

A.13.1 `active_model/serializers/json.rb`

`as_json(options = nil)`

Returns a hash that can be used as the JSON representation for this object.

`from_json(json)`

Decodes the supplied JSON, sets the attributes on the model, and returns `self`.

A.14 **Serializers::Xml**

`Serializers::Xml` is a module to include in your models when you want to provide an XML representation of your object. It automatically includes the module and depends on the `attributes` and `attributes=` methods to be present.

```
 1 class Pet
 2   include ActiveModel::Serializers::XML
 3   attr_accessor :name
 4
 5   def attributes
 6     { 'name' => @name }
 7   end
 8
 9   def attributes=(attrs)
10     @name = attrs['name']
11   end
12 end
```

A.14.1 `active_model/serializers/xml.rb`

`from_xml(xml)`

Decodes the supplied XML, sets the attributes on the model, and returns `self`.

`to_xml(options = {}, &block)`

Returns an XML representation of the object. Available options are the following:

:builder Supply a custom builder to generate the markup.

:except Do not include supplied attributes in the XML.

:indent Number of spaces to indent the XML.

:methods Include the supplied methods. The method name will be set as the key and its output the value.

:namespace Sets the XMLNS.

:only Only include the supplied attributes.

:skip_instruct Skip processing instructions.

:skip_types Skip typing.

:type Add a type to the XML tags.

A.15 Translation

`Translation` provides the ability to add internationalization support to your model.

```
1 class User
2   extend ActiveModel::Translation
3 end
```

A.15.1 `active_model/translation.rb`

`human_attribute_name(attribute, options = {})`

Transforms attribute names into a human-readable format with options. Available options are the following:

`:default` The default text for the attribute name.

`i18n_scope`

Returns the `i18n_scope` for the class (`:activemodel`). Can be overridden if you want a custom lookup namespace.

`lookup_ancestors`

Gets all ancestors of this class that support I18n.

A.16 Validations

`Validations` adds a fully featured validations framework to your model. This includes the means to validate the following types of scenarios plus the ability to create custom validators.

- Absence of a field

- Acceptance of a field

- Confirmation of a field

- Exclusion of a field from a set of values

- Format of a field against a regular expression

- Inclusion of a field in a set of values

- Length of a field

- Numericality of a field

- Presence of a field

- Size of a field

```
1 class User
2   include ActiveModel::Validations
3
```

```
4    attr_accessor :name
5
6    validates_each :name do |record, attribute, value|
7      record.errors.add(attribute, 'should be present') if value.nil?
8    end
9  end
```

A.16.1 `active_model/validations`

Note that available base options for validation macros that use options are as follows. If the specific validation has additional options, they will be explained there. All options are supplied as a hash and are the last element of the first set of arguments to the macros.

:allow_nil Specify whether to validate `nil` attributes.

:if Only run if the supplied method or proc returns `true`.

:on Define when the validation will run.

:strict If set to `true`, will raise `ActiveModel::StrictValidationFailed` over adding an error. It can also be set to any other exception.

:unless Only run if the supplied method or proc returns `false`.

`Validations.attribute_method?(attribute)`

Returns `true` if a method is defined for the supplied attribute.

```
1  class User
2    include ActiveModel::Validations
3
4    attr_accessor :name
5  end
6
7  User.attribute_method?(:name) # => true
```

`Validations.clear_validators!`

Clears all the validators and validations.

`errors`

Get all the errors for the model.

`invalid?(context = nil)`

Checks if the object is invalid given the optional context.

valid?(context = nil)

Checks if the object is valid given the optional context.

Validations.validate(*args, &block)

Adds a single validation to the model. Can be a method name as a symbol or a block with options. An additional option is the following:

:allow_blank Specify whether to validate blank attributes.

Validations.validates_each(*attrs, &block)

Validates each of the attribute names against the supplied block. Options are passed in as a hash as the last element in the `attrs` argument. An additional option is the following:

:allow_blank Specify whether to validate blank attributes.

A.16.2 `active_model/validations/absence`

validates_absence_of(*args)

Validates that an attribute is blank.

```
1 validates_absence_of :name
```

An additional option is the following:

:message An optional custom error message. Defaults to "must be blank."

A.16.3 `active_model/validations/acceptance`

validates_acceptance_of(*args)

Validates that an attribute was accepted.

```
validates_acceptance_of :terms, on: :create
```

The following are additional options:

:accept Specify the value that is considered accepted.

:message An optional custom error message. Defaults to "must be accepted."

A.16.4 `active_model/validations/callbacks`

The `ActiveModel::Validations::Callbacks` module callbacks `before _validation` and `after_validation` to your model.

```
1 class Record
2   include ActiveModel::Validations::Callbacks
3
4   before_validation :some_before_validation_logic
5   after_validation  :some_after_validation_logic
6 end
```

The interface is the same as `ActiveModel::Callbacks` covered earlier in this appendix.

A.16.5 `active_model/validations/confirmation`

`validates_confirmation_of(*args)`

Validates that an attribute was confirmed. Adds a virtual `*_confirmation` attribute that exists for validating the confirmation of the attribute. For example, validating the confirmation of a `password` attribute would result in the validator adding an accessor for `password_confirmation`.

```
validates_confirmation_of :password, message: "Please try again."
```

The following is an additional option:

:message An optional custom error message. Defaults to "doesn't match confirmation."

A.16.6 `active_model/validations/exclusion`

`validates_exclusion_of(*args)`

Validates that an attribute does not have a value supplied in the list.

```
validates_exclusion_of :age, in: 18..55
```

The following are additional options:

:allow_blank Specify whether to validate blank attributes.

:in An enumerable or range to check the value against. Can also be supplied as a proc, lambda, or symbol that returns an enumerable.

:message An optional custom error message. Defaults to "is reserved."

A.16.7 `active_model/validations/format`

`validates_format_of(*args)`

Validates that an attribute conforms to the supplied format.

```
validates_format_of :phone, with: /\A[\d\-\(\)\sx]+\z/
```

The following are additional options:

:allow_blank Specify whether to validate blank attributes.

:message An optional custom error message. Defaults to "is invalid."

:multiline Set to `true` if the regular expression contains anchors that match the beginning or end of lines as opposed to the beginning or end of the string.

:with The regular expression to check if the format matches.

:without The regular expression to check that the format does not match.

A.16.8 `active_model/validations/inclusion`

`validates_inclusion_of(*args)`

Validates that an attribute is a value supplied in the list.

```
validates_inclusion_of :state, in: [ "CA", "NY" ]
```

The following are additional options:

:allow_blank Specify whether to validate blank attributes.

:in An enumerable or range to check the value against. Can also be supplied as a proc, lambda, or symbol that returns an enumerable.

:message An optional custom error message. Defaults to "is not included in the list."

A.16.9 `active_model/validations/length`

`validates_length_of(*args)`

Validates that an attribute adheres to the supplied length limitations.

```
validates_length_of :name, maximum: 48
```

The following are additional options:

:allow_blank Specify whether to validate blank attributes.

:in Specify the range the length of the attribute can fall within.

:is Specify the exact length of the attribute.

:maximum Specify the maximum length of the attribute.

:message The error message to use for a :minimum, :maximum or :is violation.

:minimum Specify the minimum length of the attribute.

:tokenizer A block to define how the string should be broken up. Defaults to ->(value) { value.split(//) }.

:too_long Define a custom message if the attribute is too long. Defaults to "is too long (maximum is %{count} characters)."

:too_short Define a custom message if the attribute is too short. Defaults to "is too short (min is %{count} characters)."

:within Specify the range the length of the attribute can fall within.

* **:wrong_length** Define a custom message for an incorrect length. Defaults to "is the wrong length (should be %{count} characters)."

A.16.10 `active_model/validations/numericality`

`validates_numericality_of(*args)`

Validates that an attribute is numeric and optionally in a specified value range.

```
validates_numericality_of :score, only_integer: true
```

The following are additional options:

:equal_to Specify a value the attribute must be exactly.

:even Specify that the value must be even.

:greater_than Specify a value the attribute must be greater than.

:greater_than_or_equal_to Specify a value the attribute must be greater than or equal to.

:less_than Specify a value the attribute must be less than.

:less_than_or_equal_to Specify a value the attribute must be less than or equal to.

:message An optional custom error message, defaulting to "is not a number."

:odd Specify that the value must be odd.

:only_integer Specify whether the value has to be an integer.

:other_than Specify a value the attribute must be other than.

The following can also be supplied with a proc or a symbol that corresponds to a method:

- `:equal_to`
- `:greater_than`
- `:greater_than_or_equal_to`
- `:less_than`
- `:less_than_or_equal_to`

```
validates_numericality_of :width, less_than: ->(person) {person.height }
```

A.16.11 `active_model/validations/presence`

`validates_presence_of(*args)`
Validates that an attribute is not blank.

```
validates_presence_of :foo
```

The following is an additional option:

:message An optional custom error message. Defaults to "can't be blank."

A.16.12 `active_model/validations/validates`

`validates(*attributes)`
A method that allows setting all default validators and any custom validator classes ending in "Validator." To illustrate, with a single declaration to `validates`, we can set an attribute to validate presence and uniqueness.

```
validates :username, presence: true, uniqueness: true
```

The hash supplied to `validates` can also handle arrays, ranges, regular expressions, and strings in shortcut form.

```
1 validates :email, format: /@/
2 validates :gender, inclusion: %w(male female)
3 validates :password, length: 6..20
```

`validates!(*attributes)`

The `validates!` method allows setting all default validators and any custom validator
classes ending in "Validator." The difference between `validates` and `validates!` is
that in the latter all errors are considered exception. Essentially, it's the same as defining
`validates` with the `:strict` option set to `true`.

A.16.13 `active_model/validations/with`

`validates_with(*args, &block)`

Validates the model with a supplied custom validator. The validator class must
respond to and handle the options and error message addition internally.

```
1 class NameValidator < ActiveModel::Validator
2   def validate(object)
3     # Some validation logic here
4   end
5 end
6
7 class User
8   include ActiveModel::Validations
9   validates_with NameValidator, on: :update
10 end
```

`validators`

Get all the validators being used by the class.

`validators_on(*attributes)`

Get all the validators for the supplied attributes.

```
User.validators_on(:name)
```

A.17 **Validator**

`Validator` provides a class that custom validators can extend to seamlessly integrate into the `ActiveModel::Validations` API. It only requires that the new
class defines a `validate` method.

A full explanation of how to use `Validator` and `EachValidator` is provided
in the Chapter 8, "Validations," in the section "Custom Validation Techniques."

```
1 class ScoreValidator < ActiveModel::Validator
2   include ActiveModel::Validations
3
4   def validate(object)
5     # Perform validations and add errors here.
6   end
7 end
```

A.17.1 `active_model/validator.rb`

`kind`

Returns the type of the validator, which is a symbol of the underscored class name without "Validator" included.

`validate(record)`

This method must be overwritten in the validator in order to actually handle the validation itself.

Active
Model

APPENDIX B

Active Support API Reference

Active Support is a Rails library containing utility classes and extensions to Ruby's built-in libraries. It usually doesn't get much attention on its own—you might even call its modules the supporting cast members of the Rails ensemble.

However, Active Support's low profile doesn't diminish its importance in day-to-day Rails programming. To ensure that this book is useful as an offline programming companion, here is a complete, enhanced version of the Rails Active Support API reference, supplemented in most cases with realistic example usages and commentary. As you are reviewing the material in this appendix, note that many of the methods featured here are used primarily by other Rails libraries and are not particularly useful to application developers.

Section headings reflect the name of the class or module where the API method is located and are organized in alphabetical order for easy lookup. Subsections appear according to the name of the Ruby file in which they exist within Active Support's `lib` directory. Finally, the sub-subsections are the API methods themselves.

B.1 **Array**

The following methods provide additional functionality for accessing array elements.

B.1.1 **active_support/core_ext/array/access**

from(position)

Returns the tail of the array starting from the `position` specified. Note that the position is zero-indexed.

```
>> %w(foo bar baz quux).from(2)
=> ["baz", "quux"]
```

`to(position)`

Returns the beginning elements of the array up to `position` specified. Note that the position is zero-indexed.

```
>> %w(foo bar baz quux).to(2)
=> ["foo", "bar", "baz"]
```

`second`

Equivalent to calling `self[1]`.

```
>> %w(foo bar baz quux).second
=> "bar"
```

`third`

Equivalent to `self[2]`.

`fourth`

Equivalent to `self[3]`.

`fifth`

Equivalent to `self[4]`.

`forty_two`

Equivalent to calling `self[41]`—a humorous addition to the API by David.

B.1.2 `active_support/core_ext/array/conversions`

The following methods are used for converting Ruby arrays into other formats.

`to_formatted_s(format = :default)`

Two formats are supported: `:default` and `:db`. The `:default` format delegates to the normal `to_s` method for an array, which just creates a string representation of the array.

```
>> %w(foo bar baz quux).to_s
=> "[\"foo\", \"bar\", \"baz\", \"quux\"]"
```

The much more interesting `:db` option returns `"null"` if the array is empty or concatenates the `id` fields of its member elements into a comma-delimited string with code like this:

```
collect { |element| element.id }.join(",")
```

In other words, the :db formatting is meant to work with Active Record objects (or other types of objects that properly respond to id). If the contents of the array do not respond to id, a NoMethodError exception is raised.

```
>> %w(foo bar baz quux).to_s(:db)
NoMethodError: undefined method 'id' for "foo":String
```

to_s
The to_s method of Array is aliased to to_formatted_s.

to_default_s
The to_default_s method of Array is aliased to to_s.

to_sentence(options = {})
Converts the array to a comma-separated sentence in which the last element is joined by a connector word.

```
>> %w(alcohol tobacco firearms).to_sentence
=> "alcohol, tobacco, and firearms"
```

The following options are available for to_sentence:

:words_connector The sign or word used to join the elements in arrays with two or more elements (default: ", ").

:two_words_connector The sign or word used to join the elements in arrays with two elements (default: " and").

:last_word_connector The sign or word used to join the last element in arrays with three or more elements (default: ", and").

:locale If I18n is available, you can set a locale and use the connector options defined on the "support.array" namespace.

to_xml(options = {}) |xml| ...
As covered in Chapter 22, "XML," the to_xml method on Array can be used to create an XML collection by iteratively calling to_xml on its members and wrapping the entire thing in an enclosing element. If the array element does not respond to to_xml, an XML representation of the object will be returned.

```
>> ["riding","high"].to_xml
=> "<?xml version=\"1.0\" encoding=\"UTF-8\"?>\n<strings type=\"array\">\n
```

```
<string>riding</string>\n  <string>high</string>\n</strings>\n"
```

The following example yields the `Builder` object to an optional block so that arbitrary markup can be inserted at the bottom of the generated XML as the last child of the enclosing element.

```
1 {foo: "foo", bar: 42}.to_xml do |xml|
2    xml.did_it "again"
3 end
```

This outputs the following XML:

```
1 <?xml version="1.0" encoding="UTF-8"?>
2 <hash>
3    <bar type="integer">42</bar>
4    <foo>foo</foo>
5    <did_it>again</did_it>
6 </hash>
```

The options for `to_xml` are the following:

:builder Defaults to a new instance of `Builder::XmlMarkup`. Specify explicitly if you're calling `to_xml` on this array as part of a larger XML construction routine.

:children Sets the name to use for element tags explicitly. Defaults to singularized version of the `:root` name by default.

:dasherize Determines whether or not to turn underscores to dashes in tag names (defaults to `true`).

:indent Indent level to use for generated XML (defaults to two spaces).

:root The tag name to use for the enclosing element. If no `:root` is supplied and all members of the array are of the same class, the dashed, pluralized form of the first element's class name is used as a default. Otherwise, the default `:root` is `objects`.

:skip_instruct Determines whether or not to generate an XML instruction tag by calling `instruct!` on `Builder`.

:skip_types Determines whether or not to include a `type="array"` attribute on the enclosing element.

B.1.3 `active_support/core_ext/array/extract_options`

Active Support provides a method for extracting Rails-style options from a variable-length set of argument parameters.

extract_options!

Extracts options from a variable set of arguments. It's a bang method because it removes and returns the last element in the array if it's a hash; otherwise, it returns a blank hash and the source array is unmodified.

```
1 def options(*args)
2   args.extract_options!
3 end
4
5 >> options(1, 2)
6 => {}
7
8 >> options(1, 2, a: :b)
9 => {:a=>:b}
```

B.1.4 `active_support/core_ext/array/grouping`

Methods used for splitting array elements into logical groupings.

in_groups(number, fill_with = nil) { |group| ... }

The `in_groups` method splits an array into a `number` of equally sized groups. If a `fill_with` parameter is provided, its value is used to pad the groups into equal sizes.

```
1 %w(1 2 3 4 5 6 7 8 9 10).in_groups(3) { |group| p group }
2 ["1", "2", "3", "4"]
3 ["5", "6", "7", nil]
4 ["8", "9", "10", nil]
5
6 %w(1 2 3 4 5 6 7).in_groups(3, ' ') { |group| p group }
7 ["1", "2", "3"]
8 ["4", "5", " "]
9 ["6", "7", " "]
```

In the special case that you don't want equally sized groups (in other words, no padding), then pass `false` as the value of `fill_with`.

```
1 %w(1 2 3 4 5 6 7).in_groups(3, false) { |group| p group }
2 ["1", "2", "3"]
3 ["4", "5"]
4 ["6", "7"]
```

`in_groups_of(number, fill_with = nil) { |group| ... }`

Related to its sibling `in_groups`, the `in_groups_of` method splits an array into groups of the specified `number` size, padding any remaining slots. The `fill_with` parameter is used for padding and defaults to `nil`. If a block is provided, it is called with each group; otherwise, a two-dimensional array is returned.

```
>> %w(1 2 3 4 5 6 7).in_groups_of(3)
=> [[1, 2, 3], [4, 5, 6], [7, nil, nil]

>> %w(1 2 3).in_groups_of(2, ' ') { |group| puts group.to_s }
=> ["1", "2"]
   ["3", " "]
   nil
```

Passing `false` to the `fill_with` parameter inhibits the fill behavior.

```
>> %w(1 2 3).in_groups_of(2, false) { |group| puts group.to_s }
=> ["1", "2"]
   ["3"]
   nil
```

The `in_groups_of` method is particularly useful for batch processing model objects and generating table rows in view templates.

`split(value = nil, &block)`

Divides an array into one or more subarrays based on either a delimiting value

```
>> [1, 2, 3, 4, 5].split(3)
=> [[1, 2], [4, 5]]
```

or the result of an optional block

```
>> (1..8).to_a.split { |i| i % 3 == 0 }
=> [[1, 2], [4, 5], [7, 8]]
```

B.1.5 `active_support/core_ext/array/prepend_and_append`

Adds two aliases that are more similar to the human way of thinking about adding items to a list.

`append`

The `append` method of `Array` is aliased to `<<`.

prepend

The prepend method of Array is aliased to unshift.

B.1.6 `active_support/core_ext/array/wrap`

A convenience method added to the Array class.

Array.wrap(object)

Wraps the object in an Array unless it's an Array. If nil is supplied, an empty list is returned. Otherwise, the wrap method will convert the supplied object to an Array using to_ary if it implements that. It differs with Array() in that it does not call to_a on the argument:

```
1 Array(foo: :bar)          # => [[:foo, :bar]]
2 Array.wrap(foo: :bar)     # => [{:foo => :bar}]
3
4 Array("foo\nbar")         # => ["foo\nbar"]
5 Array.wrap("foo\nbar")    # => ["foo\nbar"]
6
7 Array(nil)                # => []
8 Array.wrap(nil)           # => []
```

B.1.7 `active_support/core_ext/object/blank`

blank?

Alias for empty?

B.1.8 `active_support/core_ext/object/to_param`

to_param

Calls to_param on all its elements and joins the result with slashes. This is used by the url_for method in Action Pack.

```
>> ["riding","high","and","I","want","to","make"].to_param
=> "riding/high/and/I/want/to/make"
```

B.2 ActiveSupport::BacktraceCleaner

B.2.1 `active_support/backtrace_cleaner`

Many backtraces include too much information that's not relevant for the context. This makes it hard to find the signal in the backtrace and adds debugging time. With a custom BacktraceCleaner, you can set up filters and silencers for your particular context so only the relevant lines are included.

If you want to change the setting of Rails' built-in `BacktraceCleaner` to show as much as possible, you can call `BacktraceCleaner.remove_silencers!` in your console, specs, or an application initializer. Also, if you need to reconfigure an existing `BacktraceCleaner` so that it does not filter or modify the paths of any lines of the backtrace, you can call `BacktraceCleaner#remove _filters!`. These two methods will give you a completely untouched backtrace.

```
1 bc = ActiveSupport::BacktraceCleaner.new
2 bc.add_filter   { |line| line.gsub(Rails.root, '') }
3 bc.add_silencer { |line| line =~ /mongrel|rubygems/ }
4
5 # will strip the Rails.root prefix and skip any lines from mongrel or rubygems
6 bc.clean(exception.backtrace)
```

This is inspired by the Quiet Backtrace gem by Thoughtbot.

B.3 Benchmark
The following method provides additional functionality for returning in benchmark results in a human-readable format.

B.3.1 ms
Benchmark real time in milliseconds.

```
>> Benchmark.realtime { User.all }
=> 8.0e-05


>> Benchmark.ms { User.all }
=> 0.074
```

B.4 ActiveSupport::Benchmarkable
`Benchmarkable` allows you to measure the execution time of a block in a template and records the result to the log.

B.4.1 active_support/benchmarkable

benchmark(message = "Benchmarking", options = {})
Wrap this block around expensive operations or possible bottlenecks to get a time reading for the operation. For example, let's say you thought your file-processing method was taking too long. You could wrap it in a benchmark block.

```
1 benchmark "Process data files" do
2   expensive_files_operation
3 end
```

That would add an entry like "Process data files (345.2ms)" to the log, which can then be used to compare timings when optimizing your code.

You may give an optional logger level as the `:level` option. Valid options are `:debug`, `:info`, `:warn`, and `:error`. The default level is `:info`.

```
1 benchmark "Low-level files", level: :debug do
2   lowlevel_files_operation
3 end
```

Finally, you can pass true as the third argument to silence all log activity inside the block. This is great for boiling down a noisy block to just a single statement:

```
1 benchmark "Process data files", level: :info, silence: true do
2   expensive_and_chatty_files_operation
3 end
```

B.5   BigDecimal

B.5.1   active_support/core_ext/big_decimal/ conversions

to_formatted_s(*args)

Emits a string representation of the number without any scientific notation and without losing precision.

```
>> bd = BigDecimal.new("843948787497834987498347349987.839723497347")
=> #<BigDecimal:269fabc,'0.8439487874 9783498749 8347349878 3972349734 7E29',44(48)>
>> bd.to_s
=> "843948787497834987498347349987.839723497347"
```

to_s

The `to_s` method of `BigDecimal` is aliased to `to_formatted_s`.

B.5.2   active_support/json/encoding

A BigDecimal would be naturally represented as a JSON number. Most libraries, however, parse noninteger JSON numbers directly as floats. Clients using those libraries would get in general a wrong number and will have no way to recover the lost precision other than manually inspecting the string with the JSON code itself.

That's why a JSON string is returned. The JSON literal is not numeric, but if the other end knows by contract that the data are supposed to be a BigDecimal, it still has the chance to postprocess the string and get the real value.

`as_json`

Returns `self.to_s`.

B.6 `ActiveSupport::Cache::Store`

An abstract cache store class. There are multiple cache store implementations, each having its own additional features. `MemCacheStore` is currently the most popular cache store for large production websites.

Some implementations may not support all methods beyond the basic cache methods of `fetch`, `read`, `write`, `exist?`, and `delete`.

`ActiveSupport::Cache::Store` can store any serializable Ruby object.

```
>> cache = ActiveSupport::Cache::MemoryStore.new
=> <#ActiveSupport::Cache::MemoryStore entries=0, size=0, options={}>
>> cache.read("city")
=> nil
>> cache.write("city", "Duckburgh")
=> true
>> cache.read("city")
=> "Duckburgh"
```

Keys are always translated into strings and are case sensitive.

```
>> cache.read("city") == cache.read(:city)
=> true
```

When an object is specified as a key, its `cache_key` method will be called *if it is defined*. Otherwise, the `to_param` method will be called.

```
>> r = Report.first
=> #<Report id: 1, name: "Special", created_at: ...>
>> r.cache_key
=> "reports/1-20131001152655016228000"
>> r.to_param
=> "1"
```

Hashes and arrays can also be used as keys. The elements will be delimited by slashes, and hash elements will be sorted by key so they are consistent.

```
>> cache.write ["USA","FL","Jacksonville"], "Obie"
=> true
>> cache.read "USA/FL/Jacksonville"
=> "Obie"
```

Nil values can be cached.

If your cache is on a shared infrastructure, you can define a namespace for your cache entries. If a namespace is defined, it will be prefixed on every key. To set a global namespace, set the :namespace to the constructor of the cache store. The default value will include the application name and Rails environment.

```
cache = ActiveSupport::Cache::MemoryStore.new(namespace: 'tr4w')
```

All caches support autoexpiring content after a specified number of seconds. To set the cache entry time to live, you can specify :expires_in as an option either to the constructor to have it affect all entries or to the fetch or write methods for just one entry.

```
1 cache = ActiveSupport::Cache::MemoryStore.new(expire_in: 5.minutes)
2 cache.write(key, value, expires_in: 1.minute) # Set a lower value for one entry.
```

It's a recommended practice to set the :race_condition_ttl option in conjunction with :expires_in. When a cache entry is used frequently and the system is under a heavy load, a dog pile effect can occur during expiration. During this scenario, since the cache has expired, multiple processes will try to read the data natively and attempt to regenerate the same cache entry simultaneously. Using :race_condition_ttl, one can set the number of seconds an expired entry can be reused while a new value is being regenerated. The first process to encounter the stale cache will attempt to write a new value, while other processes will continue to use slightly state data for the period defined in :race_condition_ttl. Like the :expires_in option, :race_condition_ttl can be set globally or in the fetch or write methods for a single entry.

Caches can also store values in a compressed format to save space and reduce time spent sending data. Since there is some overhead, values must be large enough to warrant compression. To turn on compression pass compress: true in the initializer or to fetch or write. To specify the threshold at which to compress values, set :compress_threshold. The default threshold is 16K.

cleanup(options = nil)
Cleanup the cache by removing expired entries. Not all cache implementations may support this method. Options are passed to the underlying cache implementation.

clear(options = nil)
Clear the entire cache. Not all cache implementations may support this method. You should be careful with this method since it could affect other processes if you are using a shared cache. Options are passed to the underlying cache implementation.

decrement(name, amount = 1, options = nil)

Decrement an integer value in the cache. Options are passed to the underlying cache implementation.

delete(name, options = nil)

Delete an entry in the cache. Returns true if there was an entry to delete. Options are passed to the underlying cache implementation.

delete_matched(matcher, options = nil)

Delete all entries whose keys match a pattern. Options are passed to the underlying cache implementation.

```
>> Rails.cache.write :color, :red
=> true
>> Rails.cache.read :color
=> :red
>> Rails.cache.delete_matched "c"
=> ["city", "color", "USA/FL/Jacksonville"]
>> Rails.cache.read :color
=> nil
```

exist?(name, options = nil)

Return true if the cache contains an entry with this name. Options are passed to the underlying cache implementation.

fetch(name, options = nil)

Fetches data from the cache using the given key. If there is data in the cache with the given key, then that data are returned.

If there is no such data in the cache (a cache miss occurred), then nil will be returned. However, if a block has been passed, then that block will be run in the event of a cache miss. The return value of the block will be written to the cache under the given cache key, and that return value will be returned.

```
1 cache.write("today", "Monday")
2 cache.fetch("today")   # => "Monday"
3
4 cache.fetch("city")    # => nil
5 cache.fetch("city") do
6   "Duckburgh"
7 end
8 cache.fetch("city")    # => "Duckburgh"
```

You may also specify additional options via the options argument. Setting :force => true will force a cache miss:

```
1 cache.write("today", "Monday")
2 cache.fetch("today", force: true)  # => nil
```

Setting :compress will store a large cache entry set by the call in a compressed format.

Setting :expires_in will set an expiration time on the cache entry if it is set by call.

Setting :race_condition_ttl will invoke logic on entries set with an :expires_in option. If an entry is found in the cache that is expired and it has been expired for less than the number of seconds specified by this option and a block was passed to the method call, then the expiration future time of the entry in the cache will be updated to the amount of seconds in specified in race_condition_ttl. The block will then be evaluated and written to the cache.

This is very useful in situations where a cache entry is used very frequently under a heavy load. The first process to find an expired cache entry will then become responsible for regenerating that entry while other processes continue to use the slightly out-of-date entry. This can prevent race conditions where too many processes are trying to regenerate the entry all at once. If the process regenerating the entry errors out, the entry will be regenerated after the specified number of seconds.

```
1 # Set all values to expire after one minute.
2 cache = ActiveSupport::Cache::MemoryStore.new(expires_in: 1.minute)
3
4 cache.write("foo", "original value")
5 val_1 = nil
6 val_2 = nil
7 sleep 60
8
9 Thread.new do
10   val_1 = cache.fetch("foo", race_condition_ttl: 10) do
11     sleep 1
12     "new value 1"
13   end
14 end
15
16 Thread.new do
17   val_2 = cache.fetch("foo", race_condition_ttl: 10) do
18     "new value 2"
19   end
20 end
```

Active Support

```
21
22 # val_1 => "new value 1"
23 # val_2 => "original value"
24 # sleep 10 # First thread extends the life of cache by another 10 seconds
25 # cache.fetch("foo") => "new value 1"
```

Other options will be handled by the specific cache store implementation. Internally, fetch calls `read_entry` and calls `write_entry` on a cache miss. Options will be passed to the read and write calls.

For example, MemCacheStore's write method supports the `:raw` option, which tells the Memcached server to store all values as strings. We can use this option with `fetch` too:

```
1 cache = ActiveSupport::Cache::MemCacheStore.new
2 cache.fetch("foo", force: true, raw: true) do
3   :bar
4 end
5 cache.fetch("foo")  # => "bar"
```

increment(name, amount = 1, options = nil)
Increments an integer value in the cache. Options are passed to the underlying cache implementation.

mute
Silences the logger within a block.

options
Gets the default options set when the cache was created.

read(name, options = nil)
Fetches data from the cache, using the given key. If there are data in the cache with the given key, then those data are returned. Otherwise, `nil` is returned. Options are passed to the underlying cache implementation.

read_multi(*names)
Read multiple values at once from the cache. Options can be passed in the last argument. Some cache implementation may optimize this method.

Returns a hash mapping the names provided to the values found.

```
>> cache.write :color, :red
=> true
>> cache.write :smell, :roses
```

```
=> true
>> cache.read_multi :color, :smell
=> {:color=>:red, :smell=>:roses}
```

silence!
Silences the logger.

write(name, value, options = nil)
Writes the given value to the cache with the given key.

You may also specify additional options via the `options` argument. The specific cache store implementation will decide what to do with options.

B.7 ActiveSupport::CachingKeyGenerator
`CachingKeyGenerator` is a wrapper around `KeyGenerator`, which avoids re-executing the key generation process when it's called using the same `salt` and `key_size`.

B.7.1 active_support/key_generator

initialize(key_generator)
Creates a new instance of `CachingKeyGenerator`.

generate_key(salt, key_size=64)
Returns a derived key suitable for use. The default key_size is chosen to be compatible with the default settings of `ActiveSupport::MessageVerifier`, such as `OpenSSL::Digest::SHA1#block_length`. Subsequent calls to `generate_key` will return a cached key if the supplied `salt` and `key_size` are the same.

B.8 ActiveSupport::Callbacks
Callbacks are hooks into the lifecycle of an object that allow you to trigger logic before or after an alteration of the object state. Mixing in this module allows you to define callbacks in your class.

For instance, assume you have the following code in your application:

```
1 class Storage
2   include ActiveSupport::Callbacks
3
4   define_callbacks :save
5 end
6
7 class ConfigStorage < Storage
```

```
 8    set_callback :save, :before, :saving_message
 9
10    def saving_message
11      puts "saving..."
12    end
13
14    set_callback :save, :after do |object|
15      puts "saved"
16    end
17
18    def save
19      run_callbacks :save do
20        puts "- running save callbacks"
21      end
22    end
23  end
```

Running the preceding code using

```
1 config = ConfigStorage.new
2 config.save
```

would output

```
saving...
- running save callbacks
saved
```

Note that callback defined on parent classes are inherited.

B.8.1 `active_support/callbacks`

The following methods are used to configure custom callbacks on your class-es and are what Rails itself uses to create callbacks such as `before_action` in Action Pack and `before_save` in Active Record. Note that this is rather advanced functionality that you typically won't need in your day-to-day Rails programming.

`define_callbacks(*callbacks)`

Define callbacks types for your custom class.

```
1 module MyOwnORM
2   class Base
3     define_callbacks :validate
4   end
5 end
```

The following options determine the operation of the callback:

:terminator Indicates when a `before` callback is considered to be halted.

```
1 define_callbacks :validate, terminator: "result == false"
```

In the previous example, if any before validate callbacks return `false`, other callbacks are not executed. Defaults to `false`.

:skip_after_callbacks_if_terminated Determines if `after` callbacks should be terminated by the `:terminator` option. By default, `after` callbacks are executed no matter if callback chain was terminated or not.

:scope Specify which methods should be executed when a class is given as callback.

```
 1 class Audit
 2   def before(caller)
 3     puts 'before is called'
 4   end
 5
 6   def before_save(caller)
 7     puts 'before_save is called'
 8   end
 9 end
10
11 class Account
12   include ActiveSupport::Callbacks
13
14   define_callbacks :save
15   set_callback :save, :before, Audit.new
16
17   def save
18     run_callbacks :save do
19       puts 'saving...'
20     end
21   end
22 end
```

Calling `save` in the previous example will execute `Audit#before`. If the callback is defined with a `[:kind, :name]` scope

```
1 define_callbacks :save, scope: [:kind, :name]
```

the method named `"#{kind}_#{name}"` would be invoked in the given class. In this case, `Audit#before_save` would be invoked.

The `:scope` option defaults to `:kind`.

Active
Support

reset_callbacks(symbol)

Remove all set callbacks for the given event.

set_callback(name, *filter_list, &block)

Set callbacks for a given event.

```
1 set_callback :save, :before, :before_method
2 set_callback :save, :after,  :after_method, if: :condition
3 set_callback :save, :around,
4   ->(r, &block) { stuff; result = block.call; stuff }
```

The second argument indicates whether the callback :before, :after, or
:around is to be run. By default, if nothing is set, :before is assumed. The first
example can also be expressed as the following:

```
set_callback :save, :before_method
```

The callback that the callback invokes can be specified as a symbol that references
the name of an instance method or as a proc, lambda, or block. If a proc, lambda, or
block is supplied, its body is evaluated in the context of the current object. A current
object can optionally be set.

skip_callback(name, *filter_list, &block)

Skip a previously defined callback for a given type. The options :if or :unless
may be passed in order to control when the callback is skipped.

B.9 Class

Rails extends Ruby's Class object with a number class methods that then become
available on all other classes in the runtime, regardless of type.

B.9.1 active_support/core_ext/class/attribute

The following method allows for the creation of attributes on Ruby classes.

class_attribute(*attrs)

Declare one or more class-level attributes whose value is inheritable and overwritable
by subclasses and instances, like so:

```
1 class Base
2   class_attribute :setting
3 end
```

```
 4
 5 class Subclass < Base
 6 end
 7
 8 >> Base.setting = "foo"
 9 => "foo"
10
11 >> Subclass.setting
12 => "foo"
13
14 >> Subclass.setting = "bar"
15 => "bar"
16
17 >> Subclass.setting
18 => "bar"
19
20 >> Base.setting
21 => "foo"
```

This behavior matches normal Ruby method inheritance: Think of writing an attribute on a subclass as overriding the parent's reader method. Instances may overwrite
the class value in the same way. (Note that the following code samples create anonymous classes to illustrate usage in a more concise fashion.)

```
 1 klass = Class.new { class_attribute :setting }
 2 object = klass.new
 3
 4 >> klass.setting = "foo
 5 => "foo"
 6
 7 >> object.setting = "bar"
 8 => "bar"
 9
10 >> klass.setting
11 => "foo"
```

To opt out of the instance writer method, pass `instance_writer: false`.

```
 1 klass = Class.new { class_attribute :setting, instance_writer: false }
 2
 3 >> klass.new.setting
 4 NoMethodError: undefined method `setting='
```

The `class_attribute` method also works with singleton classes, as can be seen
in the following example.

```
1 klass = Class.new { class_attribute :setting }
2
3 >> klass.singleton_class.setting = "foo"
4 => "foo"
```

Alternatively, setting `instance_reader: false` causes `class_attribute` to not define a reader method.

For convenience, a predicate method is defined as well, which allows you to see if an attribute has been set on a particular class instance.

```
 1 klass = Class.new { class_attribute :setting }
 2
 3 >> klass.setting?
 4 => false
 5
 6 >> klass.setting = "foo"
 7 => "foo"
 8
 9 >> klass.setting?
10 => true
```

To opt out of defining a predicate method, set `instance_predicate` to `false`.

```
1 klass = Class.new { class_attribute :setting, instance_predicate: false }
2
3 >> klass.setting?
4 NoMethodError: undefined method `setting?'
```

B.9.2 `active_support/core_ext/class/attribute _accessors`

Extends the class object with class and instance accessors for class attributes, just like the native `attr*` accessors for instance attributes.

`cattr_accessor(*syms)`

Creates both reader and writer methods for supplied method names `syms`.

```
1 class Person
2   cattr_accessor :hair_colors
3 end
4
5 >> Person.hair_colors = [:brown, :black, :blonde, :red]
6
7 >> Person.new.hair_colors
8 => [:brown, :black, :blonde, :red]
```

cattr_reader(*syms)

Creates class and instance reader methods for supplied method names syms.

cattr_writer(*syms)

Creates class and instance writer methods for supplied method names syms.

B.9.3 active_support/core_ext/class/attribute _accessors

Extends the class object with class and instance accessors for class attributes, just like the native attr* accessors for instance attributes.

B.9.4 active_support/core_ext/class/delegating _attributes

Primarily for internal use by Rails.

superclass_delegating_accessors(name, options = {})

Generates class methods name, name=, and name?. These methods dispatch to the private _name and _name= methods, making them overridable by subclasses.

If an instances should be able to access the attribute, then pass instance _reader: true in the options to generate a name method accessible to instances.

B.9.5 active_support/core_ext/class/subclasses

Provides methods that introspect the inheritance hierarchy of a class. Used extensively in Active Record.

subclasses

Returns an array with the names of the subclasses of self as strings.

```
1 Integer.subclasses # => ["Bignum", "Fixnum"]
```

descendants

Returns an array of all class objects found that are subclasses of self.

B.10 ActiveSupport::Concern

B.10.1 active_support/concern

The Concern module is only 26 lines of Ruby code. Using it, you can make your code more modular and have less dependency problems than ever before.

You use `Concern` to define common behavior that you want to mix into other application classes or into Rails itself in the case of plugins.

A `Concern` module has two elements: the `included` block and the `Class Methods` module.

```
1  require 'active_support/concern'
2
3  module Foo
4    extend ActiveSupport::Concern
5
6    included do
7      self.send(:do_something_in_mixin_class)
8    end
9
10   module ClassMethods
11     def bar
12       ...
13     end
14   end
15
16   def baz
17     ...
18   end
19 end
```

To use your custom `Concern` module, just mix it into a class.

```
1  class Widget
2    include Foo
3  end
```

The `included` block will be triggered at inclusion time. Methods in `Class Methods` will get added to `Widget` as class methods. All other methods will get added to `Widget` as instance methods.

See `ActiveSupport::Configurable` for a good example of how `Concern` is used internally by Rails.

B.11 `ActiveSupport::Concurrency`

B.11.1 `ActiveSupport::Concurrency::Latch`

The `Latch` class is used internally by Rails to test streaming controllers. It is being included here for completeness. The initializer of `Latch` accepts a single argument, representing the number of threads in the test.

await

Creates lock object for blocks with mutual exclusion and waits until the latch count is greater than zero.

release

Creates lock object for blocks with mutual exclusion. It decreases the latch count if its greater than zero and wakes up all threads waiting for this lock if the count reaches zero.

B.12   `ActiveSupport::Configurable`

This `Configurable` module is used internally by Rails to add configuration settings to `AbstractController::Base`. You can use it yourself to add configuration to your classes.

B.12.1   `active_support/configurable`

The implementation of `Configurable` is done as a `Concern` that is mixed into other classes.

config

Return the configuration of the object instance.

config_accessor(*names)

Creates configuration properties accessible via class and instance contexts. The names parameter expects one or more symbols corresponding to property names.

```
1 module ActionController
2   class Base < Metal
3     config_accessor :assets_dir, :javascripts_dir, :stylesheets_dir
4   end
5 end
```

configure

Yields `config`.

B.13   Date

Active Support provides a wide array of extensions to Ruby's built-in `date` and `time` classes to simplify conversion and calculation tasks in simple-to-understand language.

B.13.1   `active_support/core_ext/date/acts_like`

Duck types a `date`-like class. See `Object#acts_like?` for more explanation.

```
1 class Date
2   def acts_like_date?
3     true
4   end
5 end
```

B.13.2 `active_support/core_ext/date/calculations`

The following methods enable the use of calculations with `Date` objects.

+(other) / -(other)

Rails extends the existing + and - operator so that a `since` calculation is performed when the `other` argument is an instance of `ActiveSupport::Duration` (the type of object returned by methods such as `10.minutes` and `9.months`).

```
>> Date.today + 1.day == Date.today.tomorrow
=> true
```

advance(options)

Provides precise `Date` calculations for years, months, and days. The `options` parameter takes a hash with any of these keys: `:years`, `:months`, `:weeks`, and `:days`.

```
>> Date.new(2006, 2, 28) == Date.new(2005, 2, 28).advance(years: 1)
=> true
```

ago(seconds)

Converts `Date` to a `Time` (or `DateTime` if necessary) with the time portion set to the beginning of the day (0:00) and then subtracts the specified number of seconds.

```
>> Time.utc(2005, 2, 20, 23, 59, 15) == Date.new(2005, 2, 21).ago(45)
=> true
```

at_beginning_of_day / at_midnight / beginning_of_day / midnight

Converts `Date` to a `Time` (or `DateTime` if necessary), with the time portion set to the beginning of the day (0:00).

```
>> Time.utc(2005,2,21,0,0,0) == Date.new(2005,2,21).beginning_of_day
=> true
```

at_beginning_of_month / beginning_of_month

Returns a new `Date` object representing the start of the month (first of the month). Objects will have their time set to 0:00.

```
>> Date.new(2005, 2, 1) == Date.new(2005,2,21).beginning_of_month
=> true
```

at_beginning_of_quarter / beginning_of_quarter
Returns a new `Date` object representing the start of the calendar-based quarter (first of January, April, July, and October).

```
>> Date.new(2005, 4, 1) == Date.new(2005, 6, 30).beginning_of_quarter
=> true
```

at_beginning_of_week
Alias for `beginning_of_week`.

at_beginning_of_year / beginning_of_year
Returns a new `Date` object representing the start of the calendar year (first of January).

```
>> Date.new(2005, 1, 1) == Date.new(2005, 2, 22).beginning_of_year
=> true
```

at_end_of_day / end_of_day
Converts `Date` to a `Time` (or `DateTime` if necessary), with the time portion set to the end of the day (23:59:59).

at_end_of_month / end_of_month
Returns a new `Date` object representing the last day of the calendar month.

```
>> Date.new(2005, 3, 31) == Date.new(2005,3,20).end_of_month
=> true
```

at_end_of_quarter / end_of_quarter
Returns a new `Date` object representing the end of the calendar-based quarter (March 31, June 30, September 30).

at_end_of_week
Alias for `end_of_week`.

at_end_of_year / end_of_year
Returns a new `Date` object representing the end of the year.

```
>> Date.new(2013, 12, 31) == Date.new(2013, 10, 1).end_of_year
=> true
```

Active
Support

beginning_of_week

Returns a new Date object representing the beginning of the week. By default, based on Date.beginning_of_week.

```
>> Date.new(2005, 1, 31) == Date.new(2005, 2, 4).beginning_of_week
=> true
```

Date.beginning_of_week

Returns the week start for the current request/thread.

```
>> Date.beginning_of_week
=> :monday
```

Can be set Date.beginning_of_week or configuration option beginning_of_week in your Rails application configuration.

Date.beginning_of_week=(week_start)

Sets Date.beginning_of_week to a week start for current request/thread.
The method accepts the following symbols:

- :monday

- :tuesday

- :wednesday

- :thursday

- :friday

- :saturday

- :sunday

change(options)

Returns a new Date where one or more of the elements have been changed according to the options parameter.
The valid options are :year, :month, and :day.

```
>> Date.new(2007, 5, 12).change(day: 1) == Date.new(2007, 5, 1)
=> true

>> Date.new(2007, 5, 12).change(year: 2005, month: 1) == Date.
      new(2005, 1, 12)
=> true
```

Date.current

The preferred way to get the current date when your Rails application is time zone aware. Returns `Time.zone.today` when `config.time_zone` is set; otherwise, just returns `Date.today`.

days_ago(days)

Returns a new `Date` object minus the specified number of days.

```
>> Date.new(2013, 10, 1).days_ago(5)
=> Thu, 26 Sep 2013
```

days_since(days)

Returns a new `Date` object representing the time a number of specified days into the future.

```
>> Date.new(2013, 10, 5) == Date.new(2013, 10, 1).days_since(4)
=> true
```

days_to_week_start(start_day = Date.beginning_of_week)

Returns the number of days to the start of the week.

```
>> Date.new(2013, 10, 10).days_to_week_start
=> 3
```

end_of_week(start_day = Date.beginning_of_week)

Returns a new `Date` object representing the end of the week.

```
>> Date.new(2013, 10, 13) == Date.new(2013, 10, 10).end_of_week
=> true
```

Date.find_beginning_of_week!(week_start)

Returns the week start day symbol or raises an ArgumentError if an invalid symbol is set.

```
>> Date.find_beginning_of_week!(:saturday)
=> :saturday
>> Date.find_beginning_of_week!(:foobar)
ArgumentError: Invalid beginning of week: foobar
```

future?

Returns `true` if the `Date` instance is in the future.

```
>> (Date.current + 1.day).future?
=> true
```

last_month / prev_month
Convenience method for `months_ago(1)`.

last_quarter / prev_quarter
Convenience method for `months_ago(3)`.

last_week(start_day = Date.beginning_of_week) / prev_week
Returns a new `Date` object representing the given day in the previous week.

last_year / prev_year
Convenience method for `years_ago(1)`.

middle_of_day / noon
Returns a new `Date` object representing the middle of the day.

monday
Convenience method for `beginning_of_week(:monday)`.

months_ago(months)
Returns a new `Date` object representing the time a number of specified months ago.

```
>> Date.new(2005, 1, 1) == Date.new(2005, 3, 1).months_ago(2)
=> true
```

months_since(months)
Returns a new `Date` object representing the time a number of specified months into the past or the future. Supply a negative number of months to go back to the past.

```
>> Date.today.months_ago(1) == Date.today.months_since(-1)
=> true
```

next_month
Convenience method for `months_since(1)`.

next_quarter
Convenience method for `months_since(3)`.

next_week(given_day_in_next_week =
Date.beginning_of_week))
Returns a new Date object representing the start of the given day in the following
calendar week.

```
>> Date.new(2005, 3, 4) == Date.new(2005, 2, 22).next_
        week(:friday)
=> true
```

next_year
Convenience method for years_since(1).

past?
Returns true if Date is in the past.

```
>> (Date.current - 1.day).past?
=> true
```

since(seconds) / in(seconds)
Converts Date to a Time (or DateTime if necessary) with the time portion set to
the beginning of the day (0:00) and then adds the specified number of seconds.

```
>> Time.local(2005, 2, 21, 0, 0, 45) == Date.new(2005, 2, 21).
        since(45)
=> true
```

sunday
Convenience method for end_of_week(:monday).

today?
Returns true if the Date instance is today.

```
>> Date.current.today?
=> true
```

Date.tomorrow
Convenience method that returns a new Date (or DateTime) representing the time
one day in the future.

```
>> Date.tomorrow
=> Thu, 10 Oct 2013
```

tomorrow

Returns a new Date object advanced by one day.

```
>> Date.new(2007, 3, 1) == Date.new(2007, 2, 28).tomorrow
=> true
```

weeks_ago(weeks)

Returns a new Date object representing the time a number of specified weeks ago.

```
>> Date.new(2013, 10, 1) == Date.new(2013, 10, 8).weeks_ago(1)
=> true
```

weeks_since(weeks)

Returns a new Date object representing the time a number of specified weeks into the future.

```
>> Date.new(2013, 10, 8) == Date.new(2013, 10, 1).weeks_since(1)
=> true
```

years_ago(years)

Returns a new Date object representing the time a number of specified years ago.

```
>> Date.new(2000, 6, 5) == Date.new(2007, 6, 5).years_ago(7)
=> true
```

years_since(years)

Returns a new Date object representing the time a number of specified years into the future.

```
>> Date.new(2007, 6, 5) == Date.new(2006, 6, 5).years_since(1)
=> true
```

Date.yesterday

Convenience method that returns a new Date object representing the time one day in the past.

```
>> Date.yesterday
=> Tue, 08 Oct 2013
```

yesterday

Returns a new Date object subtracted by one day.

```
>> Date.new(2007, 2, 21) == Date.new(2007, 2, 22).yesterday
=> true
```

B.13.3 `active_support/core_ext/date/conversions`

The following methods facilitate the conversion of date data into various formats.

`readable_inspect`

Overrides the default inspect method with a human-readable one.

```
>> Date.current
=> Wed, 02 Jun 2010
```

`to_formatted_s(format = :default)`

Converts a `Date` object into its string representation, according to the predefined formats in the `DATE_FORMATS` constant. (Aliased as `to_s`. Original `to_s` is aliased as `to_default_s`.)

The following hash of formats dictates the behavior of the `to_s` method.

```
 1 DATE_FORMATS = {
 2   :short        => '%e %b',
 3   :long         => '%B %e, %Y',
 4   :db           => '%Y-%m-%d',
 5   :number       => '%Y%m%d',
 6   :long_ordinal => lambda { |date|
 7     day_format = ActiveSupport::Inflector.ordinalize(date.day)
 8     date.strftime("%B #{day_format}, %Y") # => "April 25th, 2007"
 9   },
10   :rfc822       => '%e %b %Y'
11 }
```

`to_time(timezone = :local)`

Converts a `Date` object into a Ruby `Time` object; time is set to beginning of day. The time zone can be `:local` or `:utc`.

```
>> Time.local(2005, 2, 21) == Date.new(2005, 2, 21).to_time
=> true
```

Note that Active Support explicitly removes the `Date#to_time` method in Ruby 2.0, as it converts local time only.

`xmlschema`

Returns a string that represents the time as defined by XML Schema within the current time zone (also known as iso8601):

```
CCYY-MM-DDThh:mm:ssTZD
```

Active
Support

Note that Active Support explicitly removes the `Date#xmlschema` method in Ruby 2.0, as it converts a date to a string *without* the time component.

B.13.4 `active_support/core_ext/date/zones`

in_time_zone

Converts `Date` object into a Ruby `Time` object in the current time zone. If `Time.zone` or `Time.zone_default` is not set, converts `Date` to a `Time` via `#to_time`.

```
>> Time.zone = "Eastern Time (US & Canada)"
=> "Eastern Time (US & Canada)"
>> Thu, 10 Oct 2013 00:00:00 EDT -04:00
```

B.13.5 `active_support/json/encoding`

as_json

Returns `self` as a JSON string. The `ActiveSupport.use_standard_json_time_format` configuration setting determines whether the date string is delimited with dashes or not.

```
>> Date.today.as_json
=> "2010-06-03"
```

B.14 DateTime

The following methods extend Ruby's built-in `DateTime` class.

B.14.1 `active_support/core_ext/date_time/acts_like`

Duck types a `DateTime`–like class. See `Object#acts_like?` for more explanation.

```
1 class DateTime
2   def acts_like_date?
3     true
4   end
5
6   def acts_like_time?
7     true
8   endd
9 end
```

B.14.2 `active_support/core_ext/date_time/calculations`

The following methods permit easier use of `DateTime` objects in date and time calculations.

<=> compare_with_coercion
Layers additional behavior on DateTime so that Time and ActiveSupport::TimeWithZone instances can be compared with DateTime instances.

advance(options)
Uses Date to provide precise Time calculations for years, months, and days. The options parameter takes a hash with any of the keys :months, :days, and :years.

ago(seconds)
Returns a new DateTime representing the time a number of seconds ago. The opposite of since.

at_beginning_of_day / at_midnight / beginning_of_day / midnight
Convenience method that represents the beginning of a day (00:00:00). Implemented simply as change(hour: 0).

at_beginning_of_hour / beginning_of_hour
Returns a new DateTime object representing the start of the hour (hh:00:00). Implemented simply as change(min: 0).

at_beginning_of_minute / beginning_of_minute
Returns a new DateTime object representing the start of the minute (hh:mm:00). Implemented simply as change(sec: 0).

at_end_of_day / end_of_day
Convenience method that represents the end of a day (23:59:59). Implemented simply as change(hour: 23, min: 59, sec: 59).

at_end_of_hour / end_of_hour
Returns a new DateTime object representing the end of the hour (hh:59:59). Implemented simply as change(min: 59, sec: 59).

at_end_of_minute / end_of_minute
Returns a new DateTime object representing the end of the minute (hh:mm:59). Implemented simply as change(sec: 59).

change(options)

Returns a new DateTime where one or more of the elements have been changed according to the options parameter. The valid date options are :year, :month, and :day. The valid time options are :hour, :min, :sec, :offset, and :start.

DateTime.current

Time zone–aware implementation of Time.now returns a DateTime instance.

future?

Tells whether the DateTime is in the future.

middle_of_day / noon

Returns a new DateTime object representing the middle of the day (12:00:00). Implemented simply as change(hour: 12).

past?

Tells whether the DateTime is in the past.

seconds_since_midnight

Returns how many seconds have passed since midnight.

seconds_until_end_of_day

Returns how many seconds left in the day until 23:59:59.

since(seconds) \ in(seconds)

Returns a new DateTime representing the time a number of seconds since the instance time (aliased as in). The opposite of ago.

utc

Returns a new DateTime with the offset set to 0 to represent UTC time.

utc?

Convenience method returns true if the offset is set to 0.

utc_offset

Returns the offset value in seconds.

B.14.3 `active_support/core_ext/date_time/conversions`

The following methods permit conversion of `DateTime` objects (and some of their attributes) into other types of data.

`formatted_offset(colon = true, alternate_utc_string = nil)`

Returns the `utc_offset` as an `HH:MM` formatted string.

```
datetime = DateTime.civil(2000, 1, 1, 0, 0, 0, Rational(-6, 24))

>> datetime.formatted_offset
=> "-06:00"
```

The options provide for tweaking the output of the method by doing things like omitting the colon character.

```
>> datetime.formatted_offset(false)
=> "-0600"
```

`nsec`

Returns the fraction of a second as nanoseconds.

`readable_inspect`

Overrides the default inspect method with a human-readable one that looks like this:

```
1 Mon, 21 Feb 2005 14:30:00 +0000
```

`to_date`

Converts `self` to a Ruby `Date` object, discarding time data.

`to_datetime`

Returns `self` to be able to keep `Time`, `Date`, and `DateTime` classes interchangeable on conversions.

`to_f`

Converts `self` to a floating-point number of seconds since the Unix epoch. Note the limitations of this methods with dates prior to 1970.

```
>> Date.new(2000, 4,4).to_datetime.to_f
=> 954806400.0
>> Date.new(1800, 4,4).to_datetime.to_f
=> -5356627200.0
```

`to_formatted_s(format=:default)`

See the options on `to_formatted_s` of the `Time` class. The primary difference is the appending of the time information.

```
>> datetime.to_formatted_s(:db)
=> "2007-12-04 00:00:00"
```

`to_i`

Converts self to an integer number of seconds since the Unix epoch. Note the limitations of this methods with dates prior to 1970.

```
>> Date.new(2000, 4,4).to_datetime.to_i
=> 954806400
>> Date.new(1800, 4,4).to_datetime.to_i
=> -5356627200
```

`usec`

Returns the fraction of a second as microseconds.

B.14.4 `active_support/core_ext/date_time/zones`

The following method allows conversion of a `DateTime` into a different time zone.

`in_time_zone(zone = ::Time.zone)`

Returns the simultaneous time in `Time.zone`.

```
>> Time.zone = 'Hawaii'
>> DateTime.new(2000).in_time_zone
=> Fri, 31 Dec 1999 14:00:00 HST -10:00
```

This method is similar to `Time#localtime` except that it uses the `Time.zone` argument as the local zone instead of the operating system's time zone. You can also pass it a string that identifies a TimeZone as an argument, and the conversion will be based on that zone instead. Allowable string parameters are operating-system dependent.

```
>> DateTime.new(2000).in_time_zone('Alaska')
=> Fri, 31 Dec 1999 15:00:00 AKST -09:00
```

B.14.5   `active_support/json/encoding`

`as_json`

Returns `self` as a JSON string. The `ActiveSupport.use_standard_json_time_format` configuration setting determines whether the output is formatted using `:xmlschema` or the following pattern:

```
strftime('%Y/%m/%d %H:%M:%S %z')
```

B.15   `ActiveSupport::Dependencies`

This module contains the logic for Rails' automatic class-loading mechanism, which is what makes it possible to reference any constant in the Rails varied load paths without ever needing to issue a `require` directive.

This module extends itself—a cool hack that you can use with modules that you want to use elsewhere in your codebase in a functional manner:

```
1 module Dependencies
2    extend self
3    ...
```

As a result, you can call methods directly on the module constant à la Java static class methods, like this:

```
>> ActiveSupport::Dependencies.search_for_file('person.rb')
=> "/Users/obie/work/time_and_expenses/app/models/person.rb"
```

You shouldn't need to use this module in day-to-day Rails coding—it's mostly for internal use by Rails and plugins. On occasion, it might also be useful to understand the workings of this module when debugging tricky class-loading problems.

B.15.1   `active_support/dependencies`

`autoload_once_paths`

The set of directories from which automatically loaded constants are loaded only once. Usually consists of your plugin `lib` directories. All directories in this set must also be present in `autoload_paths`.

`autoload_paths`

The set of directories from which Rails may automatically load files. Files under these directories will be reloaded on each request in development mode, unless the directory also appears in `load_once_paths`.

```
>> ActiveSupport::Dependencies.load_paths
=>  ["/Users/kfaustino/code/active/example_app/app/assets",
    "/Users/kfaustino/code/active/example_app/app/controllers",
    "/Users/kfaustino/code/active/example_app/app/helpers",
    "/Users/kfaustino/code/active/example_app/app/mailers",
    "/Users/kfaustino/code/active/example_app/app/models",
    "/Users/kfaustino/code/active/example_app/app/controllers/concerns",
    "/Users/kfaustino/code/active/example_app/app/models/concerns"]
```

constant_watch_stack

An internal stack used to record which constants are loaded by any block.

explicitly_unloadable_constants

An array of constant names that need to be unloaded on every request. Used to allow arbitrary constants to be marked for unloading.

history

The set of all files ever loaded.

loaded

The Set of all files currently loaded.

log_activity

Set this option to true to enable logging of const_missing and file loads. (Defaults to false.)

mechanism

A setting that determines whether files are loaded (default) or required. This attribute determines whether Rails reloads classes per request, as in development mode.

```
>> ActiveSupport::Dependencies.mechanism
=> :load
```

warnings_on_first_load

A setting that determines whether Ruby warnings should be activated on the first load of dependent files. Defaults to true.

associate_with(file_name)

Invokes depend_on with swallow_load_errors set to true. Wrapped by the require_association method of Object.

autoload_module!(into, const_name, qualified_name, path_suffix)

Attempts to autoload the provided module name by searching for a directory matching the expected `path suffix`. If found, the module is created and assigned to `into`'s constants with the name `+const_name+`. Provided that the directory was loaded from a reloadable base path, it is added to the set of constants that are to be unloaded.

autoloadable_module?(path_suffix)

Checks whether the provided `path_suffix` corresponds to an autoloadable module. Instead of returning a boolean, the autoload base for this module is returned.

autoloaded?(constant)

Determines if the specified `constant` has been automatically loaded.

clear

Clears all loaded items.

constantize(name)

Gets the reference for a specified class name. Raises an exception if the class does not exist.

depend_on(file_name, message = "No such file to load -- %s.rb")

Searches for the `file_name` specified and uses `require_or_load` to establish a new dependency. If the file fails to load, a `LoadError` is raised. Setting `message`, one can replace the error message set by `LoadError`.

hook!

Includes Rails-specific modules into some Ruby classes.

- `Object` includes `Loadable`.
- `Module` includes `ModuleConstMissing`.
- `Exception` includes `Blamable`.

load?

Returns `true` if `mechanism` is set to `:load`.

load_file(path, const_paths = loadable_constants_for_path(path))

Loads the file at the specified path. The const_paths is a set of fully qualified constant names to load. When the file is loading, Dependencies will watch for the addition of these constants. Each one that is defined will be marked as autoloaded and will be removed when Dependencies.clear is next called.

If the second parameter is left off, Dependencies will construct a set of names that the file at path may define. See loadable_constants_for_path for more details.

load_once_path?(path)

Returns true if the specified path appears in the load_once_path list.

load_missing_constant(from_mod, const_name)

Loads the constant named const_name, which is missing from from_mod. If it is not possible to load the constant from from_mod, try its parent module by calling const_missing on it.

loadable_constants_for_path(path, bases = autoload_paths)

Returns an array of constants based on a specified filesystem path to a Ruby file, which would cause Dependencies to attempt to load the file.

mark_for_unload(constant)

Marks the specified constant for unloading. The constant will be unloaded on each request, not just the next one.

new_constants_in(*descs, &block)

Runs the provided block and detects the new constants that were loaded during its execution. Constants may only be regarded as new once. If the block calls new_constants_in again, the constants defined within the inner call will not be reported in this one.

If the provided block does not run to completion and instead raises an exception, any new constants are regarded as only partially defined and will be removed immediately.

qualified_const_defined?(path)

Returns true if the provided constant path is defined?.

qualified_name_for(parent_module, constant_name)

Returns a qualified path for the specified parent_module and constant_name.

reference(klass)

Stores a reference to a class.

remove_constant(const)

Removes an explicit constant.

remove_unloadable_constants!

Removes the constants that have been autoloaded and those that have been marked for unloading.

require_or_load(file_name, const_path = nil)

Implements the main class-loading mechanism. Wrapped by the require_or_load method of Object.

safe_constantize(name)

Gets the reference for class named name if one exists.

search_for_file(path_suffix)

Searches for a file in the autoload paths matching the provided path_suffix.

to_constant_name(desc)

Converts the provided constant description to a qualified constant name.

will_unload?(constant)

Returns true if the specified constant is queued for unloading on the next request.

unhook!

Excludes module ModuleConstMissing from Module and Loadable from Object.

B.15.2 active_support/dependencies/autoload

This module allows you to define autoloads based on Rails conventions.

autoload(const_name, path = @_at_path)

Autoloads a constant.

```
1 autoload :Model
```

autoload_under(path)

Sets the name of a relative directory for all nested autoload declarations. For example, if the current file was action_controller.rb, and we call autoload_under ("metal"), the path used to autoload from is action_controller/metal.

```
1 module ActionController
2   extend ActiveSupport::Autoload
3
4   autoload_under "metal" do
5     autoload :Compatibility
6     ...
7   end
8   ...
9 end
```

autoload_at(path)

Sets an explicit path at which to autoload.

```
1 module ActionView
2   extend ActiveSupport::Autoload
3
4   autoload_at "action_view/template/resolver" do
5     autoload :Resolver
6     ...
7   end
8   ...
9 end
```

eager_autoload

Eager autoloads any nested autoload declarations.

```
1 module ActionMailer
2   extend ::ActiveSupport::Autoload
3
4   eager_autoload do
5     autoload :Collector
6   end
7   ...
8 end
```

eager_load!

Requires each file defined in autoloads.

autoloads

Collection of files to be autoloaded.

B.16 ActiveSupport::Deprecation

The deprecate method provides Rails core and application developers with a formal mechanism to be able to explicitly state what methods are deprecated. (Deprecation means to mark for future deletion.) Rails will helpfully log a warning message when deprecated methods are called.

B.16.1 active_support/deprecation

Deprecation.behavior

Returns the current behavior or, if one isn't set, defaults to :stderr.

Deprecation.behavior=(behavior)

Sets the behavior to the specified value. Can be a single value, array, or object that responds to call.

The following are available behaviors:

:stderr Log all deprecation warnings to $stderr.

:log Log all deprecation warnings to Rails.logger.

:notify Use ActiveSupport::Notifications to notify deprecation.rails.

:silence Do nothing.

Deprecation.deprecation_warning(deprecated_method _name, message = nil, caller_backtrace = nil)

Outputs a deprecating warning for a specific method.

```
>> ActiveSupport::Deprecation.
   deprecation_warning(:page_cache_extension, :default_static_extension)
=> "page_cache_extension is deprecated and will be removed from Rails 4.1
   (use default_static_extension instead)"
```

Deprecation.deprecate_methods(target_module, *method_names)

Pass the module and name(s) of the methods as symbols to deprecate.

Deprecation.silence(&block)

Silence deprecation warnings within the block.

Deprecation.warn(message = nil, callstack = nil)

Outputs a deprecation warning to the output configured by `ActiveSupport::Deprecation.behavior`.

```
1 ActiveSupport::Deprecation.warn('something broke!')
2 # => "DEPRECATION WARNING: something broke! (called from your_code.rb:1)"
```

B.17 ActiveSupport::DescendantsTracker

A module used internally by Rails to track descendants, which is faster than iterating through `ObjectSpace`.

B.17.1 active_support/descendants_tracker

DescendantsTracker.clear

Clears all descendants.

DescendantsTracker.descendants(klass)

Returns a set of all the descendants of a class.

descendants

A convenience method for returning the descendants of a class. Implemented simply as `DescendantsTracker.descendants(self)`.

DescendantsTracker.direct_descendants(klass)

Returns a set of the direct descendants of a class.

direct_descendants

A convenience method for returning the direct descendants of a class. Implemented simply as `DescendantsTracker.direct_descendants(self)`.

inherited(base)

Sets a class as a direct descendant of another base class. Implemented simply as `DescendantsTracker.store_inherited(base, self)`.

DescendantsTracker.store_inherited(klass, descendant)

Adds a direct descendant to a class. Warning: This method is not thread safe, but it is only called during the eager loading phase.

B.18 **ActiveSupport::Duration**

Provides accurate date and time measurements using the advance method of Date and Time. It mainly supports the methods on Numeric, such as in this example:

```
1.month.ago # equivalent to Time.now.advance(months: -1)
```

B.18.1 **active_support/duration**

+ **(other)**

Adds another Duration or a Numeric to this Duration. Numeric values are treated as seconds.

```
>> 2.hours + 2
=> 7202 seconds
```

- **(other)**

Subtracts another Duration or a Numeric to this Duration. Numeric values are treated as seconds.

```
>> 2.hours - 2
=> 7198 seconds
```

ago(time = Time.current)

Calculates a new Time or Date that is as far in the past as this Duration represents.

```
>> birth = 35.years.ago
=> Tue, 10 Oct 1978 16:21:34 EDT -04:00
```

from_now(time = Time.current)

Alias for since, which reads a little bit more naturally when using the default Time .current as the time argument.

```
>> expiration = 1.year.from_now
=> Fri, 10 Oct 2014 16:22:35 EDT -04:00
```

inspect

Calculates the time resulting from a Duration expression and formats it as a string appropriate for display in the console. (Remember that IRB and the Rails console automatically invoke inspect on objects returned to them. You can use that trick with your own objects.)

Active
Support

```
>> 10.years.ago
=> Fri, 10 Oct 2003 16:23:10 EDT -04:00
```

since(time = Time.current)

Calculates a new `Time` or `Date` that is as far in the future as this `Duration` represents.

```
expiration = 1.year.since(account.created_at)
```

until(time = Time.current)

Alias for `ago`. Reads a little more naturally when specifying a `time` argument instead of using the default value, `Time.current`.

```
membership_duration = created_at.until(expires_at)
```

B.19   Enumerable

Extensions to Ruby's built-in `Enumerable` module, which gives arrays and other types of collections iteration abilities.

B.19.1   active_support/core_ext/enumerable

The following methods are added to all `Enumerable` objects.

exclude?

The negative of the `Enumerable#include?`. Returns `true` if the collection does not include the object.

index_by(&block)

Converts an enumerable to a hash based on a block that identifies the keys. The most common usage is with a single attribute name:

```
>> people.index_by(&:login)
=> { "nextangle" => <Person ...>, "chad" => <Person ...>}
```

Use full block syntax (instead of the `to_proc` hack) to generate more complex keys:

```
>> people.index_by { |p| "#{p.first_name} #{p.last_name}" }
=> {"Chad Fowler" => <Person ...>, "David Hansson" => <Person ...>}
```

many?

Returns `true` if the enumerable has more than one element.

Use full block syntax to determine if there is more than one element based on a condition:

```
people.many? { |p| p.age > 26 }
```

sum(identity = 0, &block)

Calculates a sum from the elements of an enumerable based on a block.

```
payments.sum(&:price)
```

It's easier to understand than Ruby's clumsier `inject` method:

```
payments.inject { |sum, p| sum + p.price }
```

Use full block syntax (instead of the `to_proc` hack) to do more complicated calculations:

```
payments.sum { |p| p.price * p.tax_rate }
```

Also, `sum` can calculate results without the use of a block:

```
[5, 15, 10].sum # => 30
```

The default identity (a fancy way of saying "the sum of an empty list") is 0. However, you can override it with anything you want by passing a `default` argument:

```
[].sum(10) { |i| i.amount } # => 10
```

B.19.2   active_support/json/encoding

as_json

Returns `self.to_a`.

B.20   ERB::Util

B.20.1   active_support/core_ext/string/output_safety

html_escape(s)

A utility method for escaping HTML tag characters. This method is also aliased as h.

   In your templates, use this method to escape any unsafe (often, anything user submitted) content, like this:

```
= h @person.name
```

The method primarily escapes angle brackets and ampersands.

```
>> puts ERB::Util.html_escape("is a > 0 & a < 10?")
=> "is a &gt; 0 &amp; a &lt; 10?"
```

`html_escape_once(s)`

A utility method for escaping HTML without affecting existing escaped entities.

```
>> puts ERB::Util.html_escape_once('1 < 2 &amp; 3')
=> "1 &lt; 2 &amp; 3"
```

`json_escape(s)`

A utility method for escaping HTML entities in JSON strings.

In your ERb templates, use this method to escape any HTML entities:

```
= json_escape @person.to_json
```

The method primarily escapes angle brackets and ampersands.

```
>> puts ERB::Util.json_escape("is a > 0 & a < 10?")
=> "is a \\u003E 0 \\u0026 a \\u003C 10?"
```

B.21 FalseClass

B.21.1 `active_support/core_ext/object/blank`

blank?

Returns `true`.

B.21.2 `active_support/json/encoding`

as_json

Returns `false`.

B.22 File

B.22.1 `active_support/core_ext/file/atomic`

Provides an `atomic_write` method to Ruby's `File` class.

`atomic_write(file_name, temp_dir = Dir.tmpdir)`

Writes to a file atomically by writing to a temp file first and then renaming to the target `file_name`. Useful for situations where you need to absolutely prevent other processes or threads from seeing half-written files.

```
1 File.atomic_write("important.file") do |file|
2   file.write("hello")
3 end
```

If your `temp` directory is not on the same filesystem as the file you're trying to write, you can provide a different temporary directory with the `temp_dir` argument.

```
1 File.atomic_write("/data/something.important", "/data/tmp") do |f|
2   file.write("hello")
3 end
```

B.23 Hash

B.23.1 active_support/core_ext/hash/compact

compact
Returns a hash with non-`nil` values.

```
hash = { name: 'Marisa', email: nil  }

=> hash.compact
>> { name: 'Marisa' }
```

compact!
Replaces current hash with non-`nil` values.

B.23.2 active_support/core_ext/hash/conversions
Contains code that adds the ability to convert hashes to and from XML.

Hash.from_trusted_xml(xml)
Builds a hash from XML just like `Hash.from_xml` but also allows Symbol and YAML.

Hash.from_xml(xml)
Parses arbitrary strings of XML markup into nested Ruby arrays and hashes. Works great for quick-and-dirty integration of REST-style web services.

Here's a quick example in the console with some random XML content. The XML only has to be well-formed markup.

```
1 >> xml = %(<people>
2   <person id="1">
3     <name><family>Boss</family> <given>Big</given></name>
4     <email>chief@foo.com</email>
5   </person>
6   <person id="2">
7     <name>
8      <family>Worker</family>
9      <given>Two</given></name>
```

```
10       <email>two@foo.com</email>
11    </person>
12 </people>)
13 => "<people>...</people>"
14
15 >> h = Hash.from_xml(xml)
16 => {"people"=>{"person"=>[{"name"=>{"given"=>"Big", "family"=>"Boss"},
17 "id"=>"1", "email"=>"chief@foo.com"}, {"name"=>{"given"=>"Two",
18 "family"=>"Worker"}, "id"=>"2", "email"=>"two@foo.com"}]}}
```

Now you can easily access the data from the XML:

```
>> h["people"]["person"].first["name"]["given"]
=> "Big"
```

An exception `DisallowedType` is raised if the XML contains attributes with `type="yaml"` or `type="symbol"`.

to_xml(options={})

Collects the keys and values of a hash and composes a simple XML representation.

```
1 print ({greetings: {
2                english: "hello",
3                spanish: "hola"}}).to_xml
```

```
1 <?xml version="1.0" encoding="UTF-8"?>
2 <hash>
3   <greetings>
4     <english>hello</english>
5     <spanish>hola</spanish>
6   </greetings>
7 </hash>
```

B.23.3 `active_support/core_ext/hash/deep_merge`

deep_merge(other_hash)

Returns a new hash with `self` and `other_hash` merged recursively.

deep_merge!(other_hash)

Modifies `self` by merging in `other_hash` recursively.

B.23.4 `active_support/core_ext/hash/except`

except(*keys)

Returns a hash that includes everything but the given `keys`. This is useful for limiting a set of parameters to everything but a few known toggles.

```
1 person.update(params[:person].except(:admin))
```

If the receiver responds to `convert_key`, the method is called on each of the arguments. This allows `except` to play nice with hashes with indifferent access.

```
>> {a: 1}.with_indifferent_access.except(:a)
=> {}
```

```
>> {a: 1}.with_indifferent_access.except("a")
=> {}
```

except!(*keys)
Replaces the hash without the given keys.

B.23.5 `active_support/core_ext/hash/indifferent_access`

with_indifferent_access
Returns an `ActiveSupport::HashWithIndifferentAccess` out of its receiver.

```
>> {a: 1}.with_indifferent_access["a"]
=> 1
```

B.23.6 `active_support/core_ext/hash/keys`

Provides methods that operate on the keys of a hash. The `stringify` and `symbolize` methods are used liberally throughout the Rails codebase, which is why it generally doesn't matter if you pass option names as strings or symbols.

You can use `assert_valid_keys` method in your own application code, which takes Rails-style option hashes.

assert_valid_keys(*valid_keys)
Raises an `ArgumentError` if the hash contains any keys not specified in `valid_keys`.

```
1 def my_method(some_value, options={})
2   options.assert_valid_keys(:my_conditions, :my_order, ...)
3   ...
4 end
```

Note that keys are *not* treated indifferently, meaning if you use strings for keys but assert symbols as keys, this will fail.

```
>> { name: "Rob", years: "28" }.assert_valid_keys(:name, :age)
=> ArgumentError: Unknown key(s): years
>> { name: "Rob", age: "28" }.assert_valid_keys("name", "age")
=> ArgumentError: Unknown key(s): name, age
```

```
>> { name: "Rob", age: "28" }.assert_valid_keys(:name, :age)
=> {:name=>"Rob", :age=>"28"} # passes, returns hash
```

deep_stringify_keys

Returns a copy of the hash with all keys converted to strings. This includes the keys from the root hash and from all nested hashes.

deep_stringify_keys!

Destructively converts all keys in the hash to strings. This includes the keys from the root hash and from all nested hashes.

deep_symbolize_keys

Returns a new hash with all keys converted to symbols, as long as they respond to to_sym. This includes the keys from the root hash and from all nested hashes.

deep_symbolize_keys!

Destructively converts all keys in the hash to symbols, as long as they respond to to_sym. This includes the keys from the root hash and from all nested hashes.

deep_transform_keys(&block)

Returns a copy of the hash with all keys converted by the block operation. This includes the keys from the root hash and from all nested hashes.

deep_transform_keys!(&block)

Destructively converts all keys in the hash by the block operation. This includes the keys from the root hash and from all nested hashes.

stringify_keys

Returns a new copy of the hash with all keys converted to strings.

stringify_keys!

Destructively converts all keys in the hash to strings.

symbolize_keys and to_options

Returns a new hash with all keys converted to symbols, as long as they respond to to_sym.

symbolize_keys! and to_options!

Destructively converts all keys in the hash to symbols.

transform_keys(&block)

Returns a copy of the hash with all keys converted by the block operation.

transform_keys!(&block)

Destructively converts all keys in the hash by the block operation.

B.23.7   `active_support/core_ext/hash/reverse_merge`

Allows for reverse merging where the keys in the calling hash take precedence over those in the `other_hash`. This is particularly useful for initializing an incoming option hash with default values like this:

```
1 def setup(options = {})
2   options.reverse_merge! size: 25, velocity: 10
3 end
```

In the example, the default `:size` and `:velocity` are only set if the options passed in don't already have those keys set.

reverse_merge(other_hash)

Returns a merged version of two hashes, using key values in the `other_hash` as defaults, leaving the original hash unmodified.

reverse_merge!(other_hash) and **reverse_update**

Destructive versions of `reverse_merge`; both modify the original hash in place.

B.23.8   `active_support/core_ext/hash/slice`

extract!(*keys)

Removes and returns the key/value pairs matching the given keys.

```
>> { a: 1, b: 2 }.extract!(:a, :x)
=> {:a => 1}
```

slice(*keys)

Slice a hash to include only the given keys. This is useful for limiting an options hash to valid keys before passing to a method:

```
1 def search(criteria = {})
2   assert_valid_keys(:mass, :velocity, :time)
3 end
4
5 search(options.slice(:mass, :velocity, :time))
```

Active
Support

If you have an array of keys you want to limit to, you should splat them:

```
1 valid_keys = %i(mass velocity time)
2 search(options.slice(*valid_keys))
```

slice!(*keys)
Replaces the hash with only the given keys.

```
>> {a: 1, b: 2, c: 3, d: 4}.slice!(:a, :b)
=> {:c => 3, :d =>4}
```

B.23.9 active_support/core_ext/object/to_param

to_param(namespace = nil)
Converts a hash into a string suitable for use as a URL query string. An optional namespace can be passed to enclose the param names (see the following example).

```
>> { name: 'David', nationality: 'Danish' }.to_param
=> "name=David&nationality=Danish"
```

```
>> { name: 'David', nationality: 'Danish' }.to_param('user')
=> "user%5Bname%5D=David&user%5Bnationality%5D=Danish"
```

B.23.10 active_support/core_ext/object/to_query

to_query
Collects the keys and values of a hash and composes a URL-style query string using the ampersand and equals characters.

```
>> {foo: "hello", bar: "goodbye"}.to_query
=> "bar=goodbye&foo=hello"
```

B.23.11 active_support/json/encoding

as_json
Returns self as a string of JSON.

B.23.12 active_support/core_ext/object/blank

blank?
Alias for empty?.

B.24 ActiveSupport::Gzip
A wrapper for the zlib standard library that allows the compression/decompression of strings with gzip.

B.24.1 `active_support/gzip`

`Gzip.compress(source, level=Zlib::DEFAULT`
`_COMPRESSION, strategy=Zlib::DEFAULT_STRATEGY)`
Compresses a string with gzip.

```
>>   gzip = ActiveSupport::Gzip.compress('compress me!')
=>   "\x1F\x8B\b\x00\x9D\x18WR\x00\x03K\xCE\xCF-
     (J-.V\xC8MU\x04\x00R>n\x83\f\x00\x00\x00"
```

`Gzip.decompress(source)`
Decompresses a string that has been compressed with gzip.

```
>> ActiveSupport::Gzip.
   decompress("\x1F\x8B\b\x00\x9D\x18WR\x00\x03K\xCE\xCF-
   (J-.V\xC8MU\x04\x00R>n\x83\f\x00\x00\x00")
=> "compress me!"
```

B.25   ActiveSupport::HashWithIndifferentAccess
A subclass of `Hash` used internally by Rails.

B.25.1 `active_support/hash_with_indifferent_access`
Implements a hash where keys set as a string or symbol are considered to be the same.

```
>> hash = HashWithIndifferentAccess.new
=> {}
>> hash[:foo] = "bar"
=> "bar"
>> hash[:foo]
=> "bar"
>> hash["foo"]
=> "bar"
```

B.26   ActiveSupport::Inflector::Inflections
The `Inflections` class transforms words from singular to plural, class names to table names, modularized class names to ones without, and class names to foreign keys.

The default inflections for pluralization, singularization, and uncountable words are kept in `activesupport/lib/active_support/inflections.rb` and reproduced here for reference.

```
1  module ActiveSupport
2    Inflector.inflections(:en) do |inflect|
3      inflect.plural(/$/, 's')
4      inflect.plural(/s$/i, 's')
5      inflect.plural(/^(ax|test)is$/i, '\1es')
```

```
 6    inflect.plural(/(octop|vir)us$/i, '\1i')
 7    inflect.plural(/(octop|vir)i$/i, '\1i')
 8    inflect.plural(/(alias|status)$/i, '\1es')
 9    inflect.plural(/(bu)s$/i, '\1ses')
10    inflect.plural(/(buffal|tomat)o$/i, '\1oes')
11    inflect.plural(/([ti])um$/i, '\1a')
12    inflect.plural(/([ti])a$/i, '\1a')
13    inflect.plural(/sis$/i, 'ses')
14    inflect.plural(/(?:([^f])fe|([lr])f)$/i, '\1\2ves')
15    inflect.plural(/(hive)$/i, '\1s')
16    inflect.plural(/([^aeiouy]|qu)y$/i, '\1ies')
17    inflect.plural(/(x|ch|ss|sh)$/i, '\1es')
18    inflect.plural(/(matr|vert|ind)(?:ix|ex)$/i, '\1ices')
19    inflect.plural(/^(m|l)ouse$/i, '\1ice')
20    inflect.plural(/^(m|l)ice$/i, '\1ice')
21    inflect.plural(/^(ox)$/i, '\1en')
22    inflect.plural(/^(oxen)$/i, '\1')
23    inflect.plural(/(quiz)$/i, '\1zes')
24
25    inflect.singular(/s$/i, '')
26    inflect.singular(/(ss)$/i, '\1')
27    inflect.singular(/(n)ews$/i, '\1ews')
28    inflect.singular(/([ti])a$/i, '\1um')
29    inflect.singular(/((a)naly|(b)a|(d)iagno|(p)arenthe|
30        (p)rogno|(s)ynop|(t)he)(sis|ses)$/i, '\1sis')
31    inflect.singular(/(^analy)(sis|ses)$/i, '\1sis')
32    inflect.singular(/([^f])ves$/i, '\1fe')
33    inflect.singular(/(hive)s$/i, '\1')
34    inflect.singular(/(tive)s$/i, '\1')
35    inflect.singular(/([lr])ves$/i, '\1f')
36    inflect.singular(/([^aeiouy]|qu)ies$/i, '\1y')
37    inflect.singular(/(s)eries$/i, '\1eries')
38    inflect.singular(/(m)ovies$/i, '\1ovie')
39    inflect.singular(/(x|ch|ss|sh)es$/i, '\1')
40    inflect.singular(/^(m|l)ice$/i, '\1ouse')
41    inflect.singular(/(bus)(es)?$/i, '\1')
42    inflect.singular(/(o)es$/i, '\1')
43    inflect.singular(/(shoe)s$/i, '\1')
44    inflect.singular(/(cris|test)(is|es)$/i, '\1is')
45    inflect.singular(/^(a)x[that is]s$/i, '\1xis')
46    inflect.singular(/(octop|vir)(us|i)$/i, '\1us')
47    inflect.singular(/(alias|status)(es)?$/i, '\1')
48    inflect.singular(/^(ox)en/i, '\1')
49    inflect.singular(/(vert|ind)ices$/i, '\1ex')
50    inflect.singular(/(matr)ices$/i, '\1ix')
51    inflect.singular(/(quiz)zes$/i, '\1')
52    inflect.singular(/(database)s$/i, '\1')
53
54    inflect.irregular('person', 'people')
```

```
55    inflect.irregular('man', 'men')
56    inflect.irregular('child', 'children')
57    inflect.irregular('sex', 'sexes')
58    inflect.irregular('move', 'moves')
59    inflect.irregular('zombie', 'zombies')
60
61    inflect.uncountable(%w(equipment information rice money species
62       series fish sheep jeans police))
63  end
64 end
```

A singleton instance of `Inflections` is yielded by `Inflector.inflections`, which can then be used to specify additional inflection rules in an initializer.

```
1 ActiveSupport::Inflector.inflections(:en) do |inflect|
2   inflect.plural /^(ox)$/i, '\1en'
3   inflect.singular /^(ox)en/i, '\1'
4   inflect.irregular 'person', 'people'
5   inflect.uncountable %w( fish sheep )
6 end
```

New rules are added at the top. So in the example, the irregular rule for octopus will now be the first of the pluralization and singularization rules that are checked when an inflection happens. That way Rails can guarantee that your rules run before any of the rules that may already have been loaded.

B.26.1 `active_support/inflector/inflections`

This API reference lists the inflections methods themselves in the modules where they are actually used: `Numeric` and `String`. The `Inflections` module contains methods used for modifying the rules used by the inflector.

acronym(word)

Specifies a new acronym. An acronym must be specified as it will appear in a camelized string. An underscore string that contains the acronym will retain the acronym when passed to `camelize`, `humanize`, or `titleize`. A camelized string that contains the acronym will maintain the acronym when titleized or humanized and will convert the acronym into a nondelimited single lowercase word when passed to underscore. An acronym word *must* start with a capital letter.

```
1 ActiveSupport::Inflector.inflections(:en) do |inflect|
2   inflect.acronym 'HTML'
3 end
4
5 >> 'html'.titleize
```

Active
Support

```
 6 => "HTML"
 7
 8 >> 'html'.camelize
 9 => "HTML"
10
11 >> 'MyHTML'.underscore
12 => "my_html"
```

The acronym must occur as a delimited unit and not be part of another word for conversions to recognize it:

```
 1 ActiveSupport::Inflector.inflections(:en) do |inflect|
 2   inflect.acronym 'HTTP'
 3 end
 4
 5 >> 'HTTPS'.underscore
 6 => "http_s"                 # => 'http_s', not 'https'
 7
 8 # Alternatively
 9 ActiveSupport::Inflector.inflections(:en) do |inflect|
10   inflect.acronym 'HTTPS'
11 end
12
13 >> 'HTTPS'.underscore
14 => "https"
```

clear(scope = :all))

Clears the loaded inflections within a given scope. Give the scope as a symbol of the inflection type: :plurals, :singulars, :uncountables, or :humans.

```
1 ActiveSupport::Inflector.inflections.clear
2 ActiveSupport::Inflector.inflections.clear(:plurals)
```

human(rule, replacement)

Specifies a humanized form of a string by a regular expression rule or by a string mapping. When using a regular expression–based replacement, the normal humanize formatting is called after the replacement. When a string is used, the human form should be specified as desired (e.g., "The name," not "the_name")

```
1 ActiveSupport::Inflector.inflections(:en) do |inflect|
2   inflect.human /_cnt$/i, '\1_count'
3   inflect.human "legacy_col_person_name", "Name"
4 end
```

inflections(locale = :en)

Yields a singleton instance of ActiveSupport::Inflector::Inflections so you can specify additional inflector rules. If passed an optional locale, rules for other languages can be specified.

```
1 ActiveSupport::Inflector.inflections(:en) do |inflect|
2   inflect.uncountable "rails"
3 end
```

irregular(singular, plural)

Specifies a new irregular that applies to both pluralization and singularization at the same time. The singular and plural arguments must be strings, not regular expressions. Simply pass the irregular word in singular and plural form.

```
1 ActiveSupport::Inflector.inflections(:en) do |inflect|
2   inflect.irregular 'octopus', 'octopi'
3   inflect.irregular 'person', 'people'
4 end
```

plural(rule, replacement)

Specifies a new pluralization rule and its replacement. The rule can either be a string or a regular expression. The replacement should always be a string and may include references to the matched data from the rule by using backslash-number syntax, like this:

```
1 ActiveSupport::Inflector.inflections(:en) do |inflect|
2   inflect.plural /^(ox)$/i, '\1en'
3 end
```

singular(rule, replacement)

Specifies a new singularization rule and its replacement. The rule can either be a string or a regular expression. The replacement should always be a string and may include references to the matched data from the rule by using backslash-number syntax, like this:

```
1 ActiveSupport::Inflector.inflections(:en) do |inflect|
2   inflect.singular /^(ox)en/i, '\1'
3 end
```

uncountable(*words)

Adds uncountable words that should not be inflected to the list of inflection rules.

```
1 ActiveSupport::Inflector.inflections(:en) do |inflect|
2   inflect.uncountable "money"
3   inflect.uncountable "money", "information"
```

B.26.2 `active_support/inflector/transliterate`

`parameterize(string, sep = '-')`

Replaces special characters in a string so that it may be used as part of a "pretty" URL. This method replaces accented characters with their ASCII equivalents and discards all other non-ASCII characters by turning them into the string specified as `sep`. The method is smart enough to not double up separators. Leading and trailing separators are also removed.

```
1  class Person < ActiveRecord::Base
2    def to_param
3      "#{id}-#{name.parameterize}"
4    end
5  end
6
7  >> @person = Person.find(1)
8  => #<Person id: 1, name: "Donald E. Knuth">
9
10 >> helper.link_to(@person.name, person_path(@person))
11 => <a href="/person/1-donald-e-knuth">Donald E. Knuth</a>
```

`transliterate(string, replacement = "?")`

Replaces a non-ASCII character with an ASCII approximation or, if none exists, a replacement character that defaults to "?."

```
1 transliterate("Ærøskøbing")
2  # => "AEroskobing"
```

Default approximations are provided for Western/Latin characters—for example, "ø," "ñ," "é," "ß," and so on.

This method is I18n aware, so you can set up custom approximations for a locale. This can be useful, for example, to transliterate German's "ü" and "ö" to "ue" and "oe" or to add support for transliterating Russian to ASCII.

In order to make your custom transliterations available, you must set them as the `i18n.transliterate.rule` I18n key:

```
1 # Store the transliterations in locales/de.yml
2 i18n:
```

```
3    transliterate:
4      rule:
5        ü: "ue"
6        ö: "oe"
```

```
1  # Or set them using Ruby
2  I18n.backend.store_translations(:de, i18n: {
3    transliterate: {
4      rule: {
5        "ü" => "ue",
6        "ö" => "oe"
7      }
8    }
9  })
```

The value for i18n.transliterate.rule can be a simple hash that maps characters to ASCII approximations as shown earlier or, for more complex requirements, a proc:

```
1  I18n.backend.store_translations(:de, i18n: {
2    transliterate: {
3      rule: ->(string) { MyTransliterator.transliterate(string) }
4    }
5  })
```

Now you can have different transliterations for each locale:

```
1  I18n.locale = :en
2  transliterate("Jürgen")
3  # => "Jurgen"
```

```
1  I18n.locale = :de
2  transliterate("Jürgen")
3  # => "Juergen"
```

B.27 Integer
Extensions to Ruby's built-in Integer class.

B.27.1 active_support/core_ext/integer/ inflections

ordinal
Returns the suffix used to denote the position in an ordered sequence, such as 1st, 2nd, 3rd, 4th, and so on.

```
1 1.ordinal      # => "st"
2 2.ordinal      # => "nd"
3 1002.ordinal # => "nd"
4 1003.ordinal # => "rd"
```

ordinalize

Turns an integer into an ordinal string used to denote the position in an ordered sequence, such as 1st, 2nd, 3rd, 4th, and so on.

```
1 1.ordinalize      # => "1st"
2 2.ordinalize      # => "2nd"
3 1002.ordinalize # => "1002nd"
4 1003.ordinalize # => "1003rd"
```

B.27.2 `active_support/core_ext/integer/multiple`

`multiple_of?(number)`

Returns `true` if the integer is a multiple of `number`.

```
1 9.multiple_of? 3 # => true
```

B.28 `ActiveSupport::JSON`

The `JSON` module adds JSON decoding and encoding support to Rails, which takes advantage of the JSON gem.

B.28.1 `active_support/json/decoding`

`decode(json)`

Parses a JSON string or `IO` object and converts it into a hash.

B.28.2 `active_support/json/encoding`

`encode(value, options = nil)`

Dumps object in JSON.

```
>> ActiveSupport::JSON.encode({a: 1, b: 2})
=> "{\"a\":1,\"b\":2}"
```

B.29 `Kernel`

Methods added to Ruby's `Kernel` class are available in all contexts.

B.29.1 `active_support/core_ext/kernel/agnostics`

`` `(command)` ``

Makes backticks behave (somewhat more) similarly on all platforms. On win32 `nonexistent_command` raises `Errno::ENOENT`, but on Unix, the spawned shell prints a message to stderr and sets `$?`.

B.29.2 `active_support/core_ext/kernel/debugger`

debugger

Starts a debugging session if the `debugger` gem has been loaded. Use `rails server --debugger` to start Rails with the debugger enabled.

B.29.3 `active_support/core_ext/kernel/reporting`

capture(stream)

Captures the given stream and returns it.

```
1 stream = capture(:stdout) { puts 'notice' }
2 stream # => "notice\n"
```

enable_warnings

Sets `$VERBOSE` to true for the duration of the block provided and back to its original value afterward.

quietly(&block)

Silences both `STDOUT` and `STDERR`, even for subprocesses.

silence_stream(stream)

Silences any stream for the duration of the block provided.

```
1 silence_stream(STDOUT) do
2   puts 'This will never be seen'
3 end
4
5 puts 'But this will'
```

silence_warnings

Sets `$VERBOSE` to false for the duration of the block provided and back to its original value afterward.

suppress(*exception_classes)

A method that should be named `swallow`. Suppresses raising of any exception classes specified inside of the block provided. Use with caution.

B.29.4 **active_support/core_ext/kernel/singleton_class**

class_eval

Forces `class_eval` to behave like `singleton_class.class_eval`.

B.30 **ActiveSupport::KeyGenerator**

B.30.1 **active_support/key_generator**

initialize(secret, options = {})

Creates a new instance of `MessageEncryptor`.

generate_key(salt, key_size=64)

Returns a derived key suitable for use. The default key_size is chosen to be compatible with the default settings of `ActiveSupport::MessageVerifier`, such as `OpenSSL::Digest::SHA1#block_length`.

```
>> key_generator = ActiveSupport::KeyGenerator.new('my_secret_key')
=> #<ActiveSupport::KeyGenerator:0x007fde6788b5d8
   @secret="my_secret_key", @iterations=65536>
>> key_generator.generate_key('my_salt')
=> "\xB6o5\xB2v\xBA\x03\x8E\xE0\xA0\x06[7<>\x81\xBB\xD6B\xB6,
   \xF3@a\x153\xB5\xC1\x8C\x8B\xEF\x04\x1C\xB9\x8D\x93I~`\
   xCD\xCB\"IKw\\u\xE9v\x15\xEEl\x99\"\xBD\xC7a\x92Y\x1EY\x94d\xFB"
```

B.31 **ActiveSupport::Logger**

Accessible via the `logger` property in various Rails contexts such as Active Record models and controller classes. Always accessible via `Rails.logger`. Use of the logger is explained in Chapter 1, "Rails Environments and Configuration."

B.31.1 **active_support/logger**

Logger.broadcast(logger)

Generates an anonymous module that is used to extend an existing logger, which adds the behavior to broadcast to multiple loggers. For instance, when initializing a Rails console, `Rails.logger` is extended to broadcast to `STDERR`, causing Rails to log to both a log file and `STDERR`.

```
1 console = ActiveSupport::Logger.new(STDERR)
2 Rails.logger.extend ActiveSupport::Logger.broadcast(console)
```

B.31.2 `active_support/logger_silence`

`silence(temporary_level = Logger::ERROR, &block)`
Silences the logger for the duration of the block.

B.32 `ActiveSupport::MessageEncryptor`

`MessageEncryptor` is a simple way to encrypt values that get stored some-where you don't trust. The cipher text and initialization vector are base64 encoded and returned to you. This can be used in situations similar to the `Message Verifier` but where you don't want users to be able to determine the value of the payload.

B.32.1 `active_support/message_encryptor`

`initialize(secret, *signature_key_or_options)`
Creates a new instance of `MessageEncryptor`. The supplied `secret` must be at least as long as the cipher key size. By default, the cipher is `aes-256-cbc`, which would require a cipher key size of at least 256 bits. If you are using a user-entered secret, you can generate a suitable key with `OpenSSL::Digest::SHA256.new(user_secret).digest`.

The following are available options:

`:cipher` The cipher to use. Can be any cipher returned by `OpenSSL::Cipher` `.ciphers`.

`OpenSSL::Cipher.ciphers` Default is `aes-256-cbc`.

`:serializer` Object serializer to use. Default is Marshal.

`encrypt_and_sign(value)`
Encrypt and sign a `value`. The `value` needs to be signed to avoid padding attacks.

`decrypt_and_verify(value)`
Decrypts and verifies a `value`. The `value` needs to be verified to avoid padding attacks.

B.33 `ActiveSupport::MessageVerifier`

`MessageVerifier` makes it easy to generate and verify signed messages to prevent tampering.

```
>> v = ActiveSupport::MessageVerifier.new("A_SECRET_STRING")
=> #<ActiveSupport::MessageVerifier:0x007fde68036918
     @secret="A_SECRET_STRING", @digest="SHA1", @serializer=Marshal>

>> msg = v.generate([1, 2.weeks.from_now])
=> "BAhbB2kGVTogQWN0aXZlU3VwcG9ydDo..."

>> id, time = v.verify(msg)
=> [1, Fri, 25 Oct 2013 18:03:27 UTC +00:00]
```

This is useful for cases like remember-me tokens and autounsubscribe links where
the session store isn't suitable or available.

B.33.1 `active_support/message_verifier`

`initialize(secret, options = {})`
Creates a new `MessageVerifier` with the supplied `secret`.

The following are available options:

:digest Default is `SHA1`.

:serializer Object serializer to use. Default is Marshal.

`generate(value)`
Generate a signed message.

```
cookies[:remember_me] = verifier.generate([user.id, 2.weeks.from_now])
```

`verify(signed_message)`
Verify a signed message.

```
1 id, time = @verifier.verify(cookies[:remember_me])
2 if time < Time.now
3   self.current_user = User.find(id)
4 end
```

B.34 Module
Extensions to Ruby's `Module` class; it is available in all contexts.

B.34.1 `active_support/core_ext/module/aliasing`

`alias_attribute(new_name, old_name)`
This useful method allows you to easily make aliases for attributes, including their
reader, writer, and query methods.

In the following example, the `Content` class is serving as the base class for `Email` using STI, but emails should have a subject, not a title:

```
1 class Content < ActiveRecord::Base
2   # has column named 'title'
3 end
4
5 class Email < Content
6   alias_attribute :subject, :title
7 end
```

As a result of the `alias_attribute`, you can see in the following example that the `title` and `subject` attributes become interchangeable:

```
>> e = Email.find(:first)

>> e.title
=> "Superstars"

>> e.subject
=> "Superstars"

>> e.subject?
=> true

>> e.subject = "Megastars"
=> "Megastars"

>> e.title
=> "Megastars"
```

alias_method_chain(target, feature)

Encapsulates the following common pattern:

```
alias_method :foo_without_feature, :foo
alias_method :foo, :foo_with_feature
```

With `alias_method_chain`, you simply do one line of code and both aliases are set up for you:

```
alias_method_chain :foo, :feature
```

Query and bang methods keep the same punctuation. The following syntax

```
alias_method_chain :foo?, :feature
```

is equivalent to

Active
Support

```
alias_method :foo_without_feature?, :foo?
alias_method :foo?, :foo_with_feature?
```

so you can safely chain foo, foo?, and foo!.

B.34.2 `active_support/core_ext/module/anonymous`

anonymous?

Returns true if self does not have a name.

A module gets a name when it is first assigned to a constant, via the module or class keyword

```
 1 module M
 2 end
 3
 4 >> M.name
 5 => "M"
 6
 7 m = Module.new
 8
 9 >> m.name
10 => ""
```

or by an explicit assignment

```
1 m = Module.new
2
3 >> M = m    # m gets a name here as a side effect
4
5 >> m.name
6 => "M"
```

B.34.3 `active_support/core_ext/module/attr_internal`

attr_internal

Alias for attr_internal_accessor.

attr_internal_accessor(*attrs)

Declares attributes backed by internal instance variables names (using an @_naming convention). Basically just a mechanism to enhance controlled access to sensitive attributes.

For instance, Object's copy_instance_variables_from will not copy internal instance variables.

attr_internal_reader(*attrs)

Declares an attribute reader backed by an internally named instance variable.

attr_internal_writer(*attrs)

Declares an attribute writer backed by an internally named instance variable.

B.34.4 **active_support/core_ext/module/attribute_accessors**

mattr_accessor(*syms)

Defines one or more module attribute reader and writer methods in the style of the native `attr*` accessors—for instance, attributes.

mattr_reader(*syms)

Defines one or more module attribute reader methods.

mattr_writer(*syms)

Defines one or more module attribute writer methods.

B.34.5   **active_support/core_ext/module/concerning**

concerning(topic, &block)

Equivalent to defining an inline module within a class, having it extend `Active Support::Concern`, and then mixing it into the class.

```
1  class Foo < ActiveRecord::Base
2    concerning :Bar do
3      included do
4        has_many :things
5      end
6
7      private
8
9      def baz
10       ...
11     end
12   end
13 end
```

concern(topic, &module_definition)

Shorthand form of defining an `ActiveSupport::Concern`.

```
1  concern :Bar do
2    ...
3  end
4
5  # equivalent to
6
7  module Bar
```

```
 8    extend ActiveSupport::Concern
 9    ...
10 end
```

B.34.6 `active_support/core_ext/module/delegation`

`delegate(*methods)`

Provides a delegate class method to easily expose contained objects' methods as your own. Pass one or more methods (specified as symbols or strings) and the name of the target object via the :to option (also a symbol or string). At least one method name and the :to option are required.

Delegation is particularly useful with Active Record associations:

```
1 class Greeter < ActiveRecord::Base
2   def hello
3     "hello"
4   end
5
6   def goodbye
7     "goodbye"
8   end
9 end
```

```
1 class Foo < ActiveRecord::Base
2   belongs_to :greeter
3   delegate :hello, to: :greeter
4 end
```

```
1 Foo.new.hello   # => "hello"
2 Foo.new.goodbye # => NoMethodError: undefined method `goodbye' for #<Foo:0x1af30c>
```

Multiple delegates to the same target are allowed:

```
1 class Foo < ActiveRecord::Base
2   belongs_to :greeter
3   delegate :hello, :goodbye, to: :greeter
4 end
```

```
1 Foo.new.goodbye # => "goodbye"
```

Methods can be delegated to instance variables, class variables, or constants by providing them as a symbols:

```
1 class Foo
2   CONSTANT_ARRAY = [0,1,2,3]
3   @@class_array  = [4,5,6,7]
4
5   def initialize
```

```
 6      @instance_array = [8,9,10,11]
 7    end
 8    delegate :sum, to: :CONSTANT_ARRAY
 9    delegate :min, to: :@@class_array
10    delegate :max, to: :@instance_array
11 end
12
13 Foo.new.sum # => 6
14 Foo.new.min # => 4
15 Foo.new.max # => 11
```

Delegates can optionally be prefixed using the `:prefix` option. If the value is `true`, the delegate methods are prefixed with the name of the object being delegated to.

```
 1 Person = Struct.new(:name, :address)
 2
 3 class Invoice < Struct.new(:client)
 4    delegate :name, :address, to: :client, prefix: true
 5 end
 6
 7 john_doe = Person.new("John Doe", "Vimmersvej 13")
 8 invoice = Invoice.new(john_doe)
 9 invoice.client_name    # => "John Doe"
10 invoice.client_address # => "Vimmersvej 13"
```

It is also possible to supply a custom prefix.

```
1 class Invoice < Struct.new(:client)
2    delegate :name, :address, to: :client, prefix: :customer
3 end
4
5 invoice = Invoice.new(john_doe)
6 invoice.customer_name    # => "John Doe"
7 invoice.customer_address # => "Vimmersvej 13"
```

If the delegate object is `nil`, an exception is raised, and that happens no matter whether `nil` responds to the delegated method. You can get a `nil` instead with the `:allow_nil` option.

```
1 class Foo
2    attr_accessor :bar
3    def initialize(bar = nil)
4      @bar = bar
5    end
6    delegate :zoo, to: :bar
7 end
8
9 Foo.new.zoo   # raises NoMethodError exception (you called nil.zoo)
```

```
10
11 class Foo
12   attr_accessor :bar
13   def initialize(bar = nil)
14     @bar = bar
15   end
16   delegate :zoo, to: :bar, allow_nil: true
17 end
18
19 Foo.new.zoo   # returns nil
```

B.34.7 active_support/core_ext/module/deprecation

deprecate(*method_names)

Provides a deprecate class method to easily deprecate methods. Convenience wrapper for ActiveSupport::Deprecation.deprecate_methods(self, *method_names).

```
1 deprecate :foo
2 deprecate bar: 'message'
3 deprecate :foo, :bar, baz: 'warning!', qux: 'gone!'
```

B.34.8 active_support/core_ext/module/introspection

local_constants

Returns the constants that have been defined locally by this object and not in an ancestor.

parent

Returns the module that contains this one; if this is a root module, such as ::My Module, then Object is returned.

```
>> ActiveRecord::Validations.parent
=> ActiveRecord
```

parent_name

Returns the name of the module containing this one.

```
1 >> ActiveRecord::Validations.parent_name
2 => "ActiveRecord"
```

parents

Returns all the parents of this module according to its name, ordered from nested outward. The receiver is not contained within the result.

```
 1 module M
 2   module N
 3   end
 4 end
 5 X = M::N
 6
 7 >> M.parents
 8 => [Object]
 9
10 >> M::N.parents
11 => [M, Object]
12
13 >> X.parents
14 => [M, Object]
```

B.34.9 `active_support/core_ext/module/qualified_const`

Extends the API for constants to be able to deal with relative qualified constant names.

`qualified_const_defined?`

Returns `true` if the qualified constant is defined and `nil` otherwise.

```
Object.qualified_const_defined?("Math::PI")        # => true
>> Object.const_defined?("Math::PI")
NameError: wrong constant name Math::PI

>> Object.qualified_const_defined?("Math::PI")
=> true
```

`qualified_const_get(path)`

Returns the relative qualified constant given a `path`.

```
>> Object.qualified_const_get("Math::PI")
=> 3.141592653589793
```

`qualified_const_set(path, value)`

Sets a relative qualified constant.

```
>> Object.qualified_const_set("Math::Phi", 1.618034)
=> 1.618034
```

B.34.10 `active_support/core_ext/module/reachable`

`reachable?`

Returns `true` if a named module is reachable through its corresponding constant.

```
1 module M
2 end
3
4 M.reachable? # => true
```

However, since constants and modules are decoupled, modules can become unreachable.

```
>> orphan = Object.send(:remove_const, :M)
=> M
>> orphan.reachable?
=> false
```

B.34.11 **active_support/core_ext/module/remove_method**

remove_possible_method(method)
Removes a method definition if it exists.

redefine_method(method, &block)
The method define_method in Ruby allows the definition of methods dynamically.
However, define_method doesn't check for the existence of the method beforehand,
which issues a warning if it does exist. The method redefine_method resolves this by
first removing the method definition if it exists and internally calling define_method.

B.34.12 **active_support/dependencies**

const_missing(const_name)
The const_missing callback is invoked when Ruby can't find a specified constant
in the current scope, which is what makes Rails autoclass loading possible. See the
Dependencies module for more detail.

B.35 **ActiveSupport::Multibyte::Chars**
The chars proxy enables you to work transparently with multibyte encodings in the
Ruby String class without having extensive knowledge about encoding.

B.35.1 **active_support/multibyte/chars**
A Chars object accepts a string upon initialization and proxies String methods in
an encoding-safe manner. All the normal String methods are proxied through the
Chars object and can be accessed through the mb_chars method. Methods that
would normally return a String object now return a Chars object so that methods
can be chained together safely.

```
1 >> "The Perfect String".mb_chars.downcase.strip.normalize
2 => #<ActiveSupport::Multibyte::Chars:0x007ffdcac6f7d0
3     @wrapped_string="the perfect string">
```

Chars objects are perfectly interchangeable with String objects as long as no explicit class checks are made. If certain methods do explicitly check the class, call to_s before you pass Chars objects to them to go back to a normal String object:

```
1 bad.explicit_checking_method("T".chars.downcase.to_s)
```

The default Chars implementation assumes that the encoding of the string is UTF-8. If you want to handle different encodings, you can write your own multibyte string handler and configure it through ActiveSupport::Multibyte.proxy_class.

```
1 class CharsForUTF32
2   def size
3     @wrapped_string.size / 4
4   end
5
6   def self.accepts?(string)
7     string.length % 4 == 0
8   end
9 end
10
11 ActiveSupport::Multibyte.proxy_class = CharsForUTF32
```

Note that a few methods are defined on Chars instead of the handler because they are defined on Object or Kernel, and method_missing (the method used for delegation) can't catch them.

<=> (other)
Returns -1, 0, or +1, depending on whether the Chars object is to be sorted before, equal to, or after the object on the right side of the operation. In other words, it works exactly as you would expect it to.

capitalize
Converts the first character to uppercase and the remainder to lowercase.

```
>> 'über'.mb_chars.capitalize.to_s
=> "Über"
```

compose
Performs composition on all the characters.

decompose
Performs canonical decomposition on all the characters.

downcase

Converts characters in the string to lowercase.

```
>> 'VÉDA A VÝZKUM'.mb_chars.downcase.to_s
=> "véda a výzkum"
```

grapheme_length

Returns the number of grapheme clusters in the string.

limit(limit)

Limits the byte size of the string to a number of bytes without breaking characters.

method_missing(m, *a, &b)

Tries to forward all undefined methods to the enclosed string instance. Also responsible for making the bang (!) methods destructive, since a handler doesn't have access to change an enclosed string instance.

normalize(form = nil)

Returns the KC normalization of the string by default. NFKC is considered the best normalization form for passing strings to databases and validations.

A normalization form can be one of the following:

- :c
- :kc
- :d
- :kd

Default is `ActiveSupport::Multibyte::Unicode#default_normalization_form`.

reverse

Reverses all characters in the string.

```
>> 'Café'.mb_chars.reverse.to_s
=> 'éfaC'
```

slice!(*args)

Works like `String`'s `slice!`, with the exception that the items in the resulting list are `Char` instances instead of `String`.

split(*args)

Works just like the normal String's split method, with the exception that the items in the resulting list are Chars instances instead of String, which makes chaining calls easier.

```
>> 'Café périferôl'.mb_chars.split(/é/).map { |part| part.upcase.to_s }
=> ["CAF", " P", "RIFERÔL"]
```

swapcase

Converts characters in the string to the opposite case.

```
>> "El Cañón".mb_chars.swapcase.to_s
=> "eL cAÑÓN"
```

tidy_bytes(force = false)

Replaces all ISO-8859-1 or CP1252 characters by their UTF-8 equivalent, resulting in a valid UTF-8 string.

Passing true will forcibly tidy all bytes, assuming that the string's encoding is entirely CP1252 or ISO-8859-1.

```
> "obie".mb_chars.tidy_bytes
=> #<ActiveSupport::Multibyte::Chars:0x007ffdcb76ecf8
     @wrapped_string="obie">
```

B.35.2 active_support/multibyte/unicode

Contains methods handling Unicode strings.

Unicode.compose(codepoints)

Composes decomposed characters to the composed form.

Unicode.decompose(type, codepoints)

Decomposes composed characters to the decomposed form. The type argument accepts :canonical or :compatibility.

Unicode.downcase(string)

Converts a Unicode string to lowercase.

Unicode.in_char_class?(codepoint, classes)

Detects whether the codepoint is in a certain character class. Returns true when it's in the specified character class and false otherwise. Valid character classes are :cr, :lf, :l, :v, :lv, :lvt, and :t.

Unicode.normalize(string, form = nil)

Returns the KC normalization of the string by default. NFKC is considered the best normalization form for passing strings to databases and validations. The form specifies the form you want to normalize in and should be one of the following: :c, :kc, :d, or :kd. Default form is stored in the ActiveSupport ::Multibyte.default_normalization_form attribute and is overridable in an initializer.

Unicode.pack_graphemes(unpacked)

Reverses operation of unpack_graphemes.

Unicode.reorder_characters(codepoints)

Reorders codepoints so the string becomes canonical.

Unicode.swapcase(string)

Swapcase on a Unicode string.

Unicode.tidy_bytes(string, force = false)

Replaces all ISO-8859-1 or CP1252 characters by their UTF-8 equivalent, resulting in a valid UTF-8 string.

Unicode.unpack_graphemes(string)

Unpack the string at grapheme boundaries. Returns a list of character lists.

```
>> ActiveSupport::Multibyte::Unicode.unpack_graphemes('ffff')
=> [[102], [102], [102], [102]]

>> ActiveSupport::Multibyte::Unicode.unpack_graphemes('Café')
=> [[67], [97], [102], [233]]
```

Unicode.upcase(string)

Converts a Unicode string to uppercase.

B.36 **NilClass**

Remember that everything in Ruby is an object, even `nil`, which is a special reference to a singleton instance of the `NilClass`.

B.36.1 **active_support/core_ext/object/blank**

blank?
Returns `true`.

B.36.2 **active_support/json/encoding**

as_json
Returns `null`.

B.37 **ActiveSupport::Notifications**

Notifications provides an instrumentation API for Ruby. To instrument an action in Ruby, you just need to do the following:

```
1 ActiveSupport::Notifications.instrument(:render, extra: :information) do
2   render text: "Foo"
3 end
```

You can consume those events and the information they provide by registering a log subscriber. For instance, let's store all instrumented events in an array:

```
1 @events = []
2
3 ActiveSupport::Notifications.subscribe do |*args|
4   @events << ActiveSupport::Notifications::Event.new(*args)
5 end
6
7 ActiveSupport::Notifications.instrument(:render, extra: :information) do
8   render text: "Foo"
9 end
10
11 event = @events.first
12 event.name        # => :render
13 event.duration    # => 10 (in milliseconds)
14 event.result      # => "Foo"
15 event.payload     # => { :extra => :information }
```

When subscribing to `Notifications`, you can pass a pattern to only consume events that match the pattern:

```
1 ActiveSupport::Notifications.subscribe(/render/) do |event|
2   @render_events << event
3 end
```

Notifications ships with a queue implementation that consumes and publishes events to log subscribers in a thread. You can use any queue implementation you want.

Numeric

Extensions to Ruby's Numeric class.

B.37.1 active_support/core_ext/object/blank

blank?

Returns false.

B.37.2 active_support/json/encoding

as_json

Returns self.

encode_json

Returns self.to_s.

B.37.3 active_support/core_ext/numeric/bytes

Enables the use of byte calculations and declarations, like 45.bytes + 2.6.megabytes.

Constants

The following constants are defined in bytes.rb.

```
1 class Numeric
2   KILOBYTE = 1024
3   MEGABYTE = KILOBYTE * 1024
4   GIGABYTE = MEGABYTE * 1024
5   TERABYTE = GIGABYTE * 1024
6   PETABYTE = TERABYTE * 1024
7   EXABYTE  = PETABYTE * 1024
8   ...
9 end
```

byte / bytes

Returns the value of `self`. Enables the use of byte calculations and declarations, like `45.bytes + 2.6.megabytes`.

kilobyte / kilobytes

Returns `self * 1024`.

megabyte / megabytes

Returns `self * 1024.kilobytes`.

gigabyte / gigabytes

Returns `self * 1024.megabytes`.

terabyte / terabytes

Returns `self * 1024.gigabytes`.

petabyte / petabytes

Returns `self * 1024.terabytes`.

exabyte / exabytes2

Returns `self * 1024.petabytes`.

B.37.4 `active_support/core_ext/numeric/conversions`

to_formatted_s(format = :default, options = {})

Generates a formatted string representation of a number. Options are provided for phone numbers, currency, percentage, precision, positional notation, file size, and pretty printing.

Aliased as `to_s`.

:currency Formats a number into a currency string. The `:currency` formatting option can be combined with the following:

> **:delimiter** Sets the thousands delimiter. Defaults to `","`.

> **:format** Sets the format for nonnegative numbers. Defaults to `"%u%n"`.

> **:locale** Sets the locale to be used for formatting. Defaults to current locale.

> **:negative_format** Sets the format for negative numbers. Defaults to prepending a hyphen to the formatted number.

:precision Sets the level of precision. Defaults to 2.

:separator Sets the separator between the units. Defaults to ".".

:unit Sets the denomination of the currency. Defaults to "$".

```
>> 1234567890.50.to_s(:currency)
=> $1,234,567,890.50
```

```
>> 1234567890.506.to_s(:currency)
=> $1,234,567,890.51
```

```
>> 1234567890.506.to_s(:currency, precision: 3)
=> $1,234,567,890.506
```

```
>> 1234567890.506.to_s(:currency, locale: :fr)
=> 1 234 567 890,51
```

```
>> -1234567890.50.to_s(:currency, negative_format: '(%u%n)')
=> ($1,234,567,890.50)
```

```
>> 1234567890.50.to_s(:currency, unit: '&pound;', separator: ',',
     delimiter: '')
=> &pound;1234567890,50
```

:delimited Formats a number with grouped thousands using delimiter. The :delimited formatting option can be combined with the following:

:delimiter Sets the thousands delimiter. Defaults to ",".

:locale Sets the locale to be used for formatting. Defaults to current locale.

:separator Sets the separator between the units. Defaults to ".".

```
>> 12345678.to_s(:delimited)
=> 12,345,678
```

```
>> 12345678.05.to_s(:delimited)
=> 12,345,678.05
```

```
>> 12345678.to_s(:delimited, delimiter: '.')
=> 12.345.678
```

:human Formats a number that is more readable to humans. Useful for numbers that are extremely large. The :human formatting option can be combined with the following:

:delimiter Sets the thousands delimiter. Defaults to `" "`.

:format Sets the format for nonnegative numbers. Defaults to `"%n %u"`. The field types are the following:

- `%u` (the quantifier)
- `%n` (the number)

:locale Sets the locale to be used for formatting. Defaults to current locale.

:precision Sets the level of precision. Defaults to 3.

:separator Sets the separator between fractional and integer digits. Defaults to `"."`.

:significant If true, precision will be the number of significant_digits; otherwise, the number of fractional digits are used. Defaults to true.

:strip_insignificant_zeros Setting to true removes insignificant zeros after the decimal separator. Defaults to true.

:units A hash of unit quantifier names or a string containing an I18n scope where to find this hash. It might have the following keys:

- integers: `:unit, :ten, *:hundred, :thousand, :million, *:billion, :trillion, *:quadrillion`
- fractionals: `:deci, :centi, *:milli, :micro, :nano, *:pico, :femto`

```
>> 123.to_s(:human)
=> "123"

>> 1234.to_s(:human)
=> "1.23 Thousand"

>> 1234567.to_s(:human)
=> "1.23 Million"

>> 489939.to_s(:human, precision: 4)
=> "489.9 Thousand"
```

:human_size Formats the bytes in size into a more understandable representation. Useful for reporting file sizes to users. The `:human_size` formatting option can be combined with the following:

:delimiter Sets the thousands delimiter. Defaults to `""`.

:format Sets the format for nonnegative numbers. Defaults to `"%u%n"`.

:locale Sets the locale to be used for formatting. Defaults to current locale.

:precision Sets the level of precision. Defaults to 3.

:prefix Setting to `:si` formats the number using the SI prefix. Defaults to `:binary`.

:separator Sets the separator between fractional and integer digits. Defaults to `"."`.

:significant If true, precision will be the number of significant_digits; otherwise, the number of fractional digits are used. Defaults to true.

:strip_insignificant_zeros Setting to true removes insignificant zeros after the decimal separator. Defaults to true.

:raise Setting to `true` raises `InvalidNumberError` when the number is invalid.

```
1  >> 123.to_s(:human_size)
2  => 123 Bytes
3
4  >> 1234.to_s(:human_size)
5  => 1.21 KB
6
7  >> 12345.to_s(:human_size)
8  => 12.1 KB
9
10 >> 1234567.to_s(:human_size)
11 => 1.18 MB
12
13 >> 1234567.to_s(:human_size, precision: 2)
14 => 1.2 MB
```

:percentage Formats a number as a percentage string. The `:percentage` formatting option can be combined with the following:

:delimiter Sets the thousands delimiter. Defaults to `""`.

:format Sets the format of the percentage string. Defaults to `"%n%"`.

:locale Sets the locale to be used for formatting. Defaults to current locale.

:precision Sets the level of precision. Defaults to 3.

:separator Sets the separator between the units. Defaults to `"."`.

:significant If true, precision will be the number of significant_digits; otherwise, the number of fractional digits are used. Defaults to false.

:strip_insignificant_zeros Setting to true removes insignificant zeros after the decimal separator. Defaults to false.

```
>> 100.to_s(:percentage)
=> 100.000%

>> 100.to_s(:percentage, precision: 0)
=> 100%

>> 1000.to_s(:percentage, delimiter: '.', separator: ',')
=> 1.000,000%

>> 302.24398923423.to_s(:percentage, precision: 5)
=> 302.24399%

>> 1000.to_s(:percentage, locale: :fr)
=> 1 000,000%

>> 100.to_s(:percentage, format: '%n  %')
=> 100  %
```

:phone Formats a number into a US phone number. The `:phone` formatting option can be combined with the following:

:area_code Adds parentheses around the area code.

:country_code Sets the country code for the phone number.

:delimiter Specifies the delimiter to use. Defaults to `"-"`.

:extension Specifies an extension to add to the end of the generated number.

```
>> 5551234.to_s(:phone)
=> 555-1234

>> 1235551234.to_s(:phone)
=> 123-555-1234

>> 1235551234.to_s(:phone, area_code: true)
```

```
=> (123) 555-1234

>> 1235551234.to_s(:phone, delimiter: ' ')
=> 123 555 1234

>> 1235551234.to_s(:phone, area_code: true, extension: 555)
=> (123) 555-1234 x 555

>> 1235551234.to_s(:phone, country_code: 1)
=> +1-123-555-1234

>> 1235551234.to_s(:phone, country_code: 1, extension: 1343, de-
        limiter: '.')
=> +1.123.555.1234 x 1343
```

:round Formats a number with the specified level of precision. The :rounded formatting option can be combined with the following:

> **:delimiter** Sets the thousands delimiter. Defaults to " ".

> **:locale** Sets the locale to be used for formatting. Defaults to current locale.

> **:precision** Sets the level of precision. Defaults to 3.

> **:separator** Sets the separator between the units. Defaults to " . ".

> **:significant** If true, precision will be the number of significant_digits; otherwise, the number of fractional digits are used. Defaults to false.

> **:strip_insignificant_zeros** Setting to true removes insignificant zeros after the decimal separator. Defaults to false.

```
>> 111.2345.to_s(:rounded)
=> 111.235

>> 111.2345.to_s(:rounded, precision: 2)
=> 111.23

>> 13.to_s(:rounded, precision: 5)
=> 13.00000

>> 389.32314.to_s(:rounded, precision: 0)
=> 389

>> 111.2345.to_s(:rounded, significant: true)
=> 111
```

```
>> 111.2345.to_s(:rounded, precision: 1, significant: true)
=> 100
```

B.37.5 `active_support/core_ext/numeric/time`

Enables the use of time calculations and declarations, like `45.minutes + 2.hours + 4.years`.

These methods use `Time#advance` for precise date calculations when using `from_now`, `ago`, and so on, as well as adding or subtracting their results from a `Time` object. The following is an example:

```
1 # equivalent to Time.now.advance(months: 1)
2 1.month.from_now
3
4 # equivalent to Time.now.advance(years: 2)
5 2.years.from_now
6
7 # equivalent to Time.now.advance(months: 4, years: 5)
8 (4.months + 5.years).from_now
```

While these methods provide precise calculation when used as in the previous examples, care should be taken to note that this is not true if the result of "months," "years," and so on is converted before use:

```
1 # equivalent to 30.days.to_i.from_now
2 1.month.to_i.from_now
3
4 # equivalent to 365.25.days.to_f.from_now
5 1.year.to_f.from_now
```

In such cases, Ruby's core `Date` and `Time` should be used for precision date and time arithmetic.

`ago` and `until`

Append to a numeric time value to express a moment in the past.

```
1 10.minutes.ago
```

`day` / `days`

A duration equivalent to `self * 24.hours`.

`fortnight` / `fortnights`

A duration equivalent to `self * 2.weeks`.

from_now(time = Time.current) / since(time = Time .current)

An amount of time in the future from a specified time (which defaults to `Time .current`).

hour / hours

A duration equivalent to `self * 3600.seconds`.

in_milliseconds

An equivalent to `self * 1000`. This value can be set in JavaScript functions like `getTime()`.

minute / minutes

A duration equivalent to `self * 60.seconds`.

month / months

A duration equivalent to `self * 30.days`.

second / seconds

A duration in seconds equivalent to `self`.

week / weeks

A duration equivalent to `self * 7.days`.

year / years

A duration equivalent to `self * 365.25.days`.

B.38 Object

Rails mixes quite a few methods into the `Object` class, meaning they are available via every other object at runtime.

B.38.1 active_support/core_ext/object/acts_like

acts_like?(duck)

A duck-type assistant method. For example, Active Support extends `Date` to define an `acts_like_date?` method and extends `Time` to define `acts_like_time?`. As a result, we can do `x.acts_like?(:time)` and `x.acts_like?(:date)` to do duck-type safe comparisons, since classes that we want to act like `Time` simply need to define an `acts_like_time?` method.

B.38.2 `active_support/core_ext/object/blank`

blank?

An object is blank if it's `false`, empty, or a whitespace string. For example, `""`, `" "`, `nil`, `[]`, and `{}` are blank.

This simplifies

```
if !address.nil? && !address.empty?
```

to

```
unless address.blank?
```

presence

Returns object if it's `present?`; otherwise, returns `nil`. The expression `object.presence` is equivalent to `object.present? ? object : nil`.

This is handy for any representation of objects where blank is the same as not present at all. For example, this simplifies a common check for HTTP POST/query parameters:

```
state   = params[:state]   if params[:state].present?
country = params[:country] if params[:country].present?
region  = state || country || 'US'
```

becomes

```
region = params[:state].presence || params[:country].presence || 'US'
```

present?

An object is present if it's not blank.

B.38.3 `active_support/core_ext/object/deep_dup`

Returns a deep copy of object if it's duplicable. If it's not duplicable, returns `self`.

B.38.4 `active_support/core_ext/object/duplicable`

Most objects are cloneable, but not all. For example, you can't duplicate `nil`:

```
nil.dup # => TypeError: can't dup NilClass
```

Classes may signal their instances are not duplicable by removing `dup` and `clone` or raising exceptions from them. So to `dup` an arbitrary object, you normally use an optimistic approach and are ready to catch an exception, such as the following:

```
arbitrary_object.dup rescue object
```

Rails dups objects in a few critical spots where they are not that arbitrary. That `rescue` is very expensive (like 40 times slower than a predicate), and it is often triggered.

That's why we hard-code the following cases and check `duplicable?` instead of using the rescue idiom.

duplicable?

Is it possible to safely duplicate this object? Returns `false` for `nil`, `false`, `true`, symbols, numbers, class, and module objects, `true` otherwise.

B.38.5 active_support/core_ext/object/inclusion

in?(object)

Returns `true` if this object is included in the argument. The argument must respond to `include?`.

```
1 characters = %w(Hulk Thor Hawkeye)
2
3 >> "Thor".in?(characters)
4 => true
```

B.38.6 active_support/core_ext/object/instance
_variables

instance_values

Returns a hash that maps instance variable names without "@" to their corresponding values. Keys are strings in both Ruby 1.8 and 1.9.

```
1 class C
2   def initialize(x, y)
3     @x, @y = x, y
4   end
5 end
6
7 C.new(0, 1).instance_values # => {"x" => 0, "y" => 1}
```

instance_variable_names

Returns an array of instance variable names including "@."

```
1 class C
2   def initialize(x, y)
3     @x, @y = x, y
4   end
```

```
5 end
6
7 C.new(0, 1).instance_variable_names # => ["@y", "@x"]
```

B.38.7 `active_support/core_ext/object/json`

`to_json`

A basic definition of `to_json` that prevents calls to `to_json` from going directly to the `json` gem on the following core classes:

- `Object`
- `Array`
- `FalseClass`
- `Float`
- `Hash`
- `Integer`
- `NilClass`
- `String`
- `TrueClass`

B.38.8 `active_support/core_ext/object/to_param`

`to_param`

Alias of `to_s`.

B.38.9 `active_support/core_ext/object/to_query`

`to_query(key)`

Converts an object into a string suitable for use as a URL query string, using the given `key` as the param name.

B.38.10 `active_support/core_ext/object/try`

`try(*a, &block)`

Attempts to call a public method whose name is the first argument. Unlike `public_send`, if the object does not respond to the method, `nil` is returned rather than an exception being raised.

This simplifies

```
@person ? @person.name : nil
```

to

```
@person.try(:name)
```

If `try` is invoked without arguments, it yields the receiver unless it's `nil`.

```
@person.try do |p|
  ...
end
```

Arguments and blocks are forwarded to the method if invoked:

```
@posts.try(:each_slice, 2) do |a, b|
  ...
end
```

B.38.11 `active_support/core_ext/object/with_options`

`with_options(options)`

An elegant way to refactor out common options.

```
1 class Post < ActiveRecord::Base
2   with_options(dependent: :destroy) do |post|
3     post.has_many :comments
4     post.has_many :photos
5   end
6 end
```

B.38.12 `active_support/dependencies`

`load(file, *extras)`

Rails overrides Ruby's built-in `load` method to tie it into the `Dependencies` subsystem.

`require(file, *extras)`

Rails overrides Ruby's built-in `require` method to tie it into the `Dependencies` subsystem.

`require_dependency(file_name, file_name, message = "No such file to load -- %s")`

Used internally by Rails. Invokes `Dependencies.depend_on(file_name)`.

`require_or_load(file_name)`

Used internally by Rails. Invokes `Dependencies.require_or_load(file_name)`.

unloadable(const_desc)

Marks the specified constant as unloadable. Unloadable constants are removed each time dependencies are cleared.

Note that marking a constant for unloading needs to only be done once. Setup or init scripts may list each unloadable constant that will need unloading; constants marked in this way will be removed on every subsequent `Dependencies.clear`, as opposed to the first clear only.

The provided constant descriptor `const_desc` may be a (nonanonymous) module or class or a qualified constant name as a string or symbol.

Returns `true` if the constant was not previously marked for unloading and `false` otherwise.

B.39 ActiveSupport::OrderedHash

B.39.1 active_support/ordered_hash

A hash implementation that preserves the ordering of its elements. It's namespaced to prevent conflicts with other implementations, but you can assign it to a top-level namespace if you don't want to constantly use the fully qualified name:

```
>> oh = ActiveSupport::OrderedHash.new
=> []
>> oh[:one] = 1
=> 1
>> oh[:two] = 2
=> 2
>> oh[:three] = 3
=> 3
>> oh
=> [[:one, 1], [:two, 2], [:three, 3]]
```

Note that as of Ruby 1.9, hashes preserve their insertion order.

B.40 ActiveSupport::OrderedOptions

B.40.1 active_support/ordered_options

A subclass of `Hash` that adds a method-missing implementation so that hash elements can be accessed and modified using normal attribute semantics dot notation:

```
1 def method_missing(name, *args)
2   if name.to_s =~ /(.*)=$/
3     self[$1.to_sym] = args.first
4   else
5     self[name]
```

```
6    end
7  end
```

B.41 ActiveSupport::PerThreadRegistry
B.41.1 active_support/per_thread_registry

A module that encapsulates access to thread local variables, which prevents the polluting of the thread locals namespace. Instead of setting and getting variables via `Thread.current`, like this:

```
Thread.current[:handler]
```

you can define a class that extends `ActiveSupport::PerThreadRegistry`.

```
1  class Registry
2    extend ActiveSupport::PerThreadRegistry
3
4    attr_accessor :handler
5  end
```

This creates class-level methods to get/set attributes on the current thread based on the defined accessors.

```
>> Registry.handler
=> nil

>> Registry.handler = handler
=> #<Object:0x007fbeb326ea20>

>> Registry.handler
=> #<Object:0x007fbeb326ea20>
```

The key on `Thread.current` for the previous example would be the class name "Registry."

```
>> Thread.current["Registry"]
=> #<Registry:0x007fbeb3279880 @handler=#<Object:0x007fbeb326ea20>>
```

B.42 ActiveSupport::ProxyObject

A class with no predefined methods that behaves similarly to Builder's `BlankSlate`. Used for proxy classes and can come in handy when implementing domain-specific languages in your application code.

B.42.1 `active_support/proxy_object`

The implementation of ProxyObject inherits from BasicObject, undefines two methods, and allows exceptions to be raised. The implementation is reproduced here for your reference.

```
1 class ProxyObject < ::BasicObject
2   undef_method :==
3   undef_method :equal?
4
5   # Let ActiveSupport::ProxyObject at least raise exceptions.
6   def raise(*args)
7     ::Object.send(:raise, *args)
8   end
9 end
```

B.43   **ActiveSupport::Railtie**

B.43.1 `active_support/railtie`

Contains Active Support's initialization routine for itself and the I18n subsystem.

   If you're depending on Active Support outside of Rails, you should be aware of what happens in this Railtie in case you end up needing to replicate it in your code.

```
1 module ActiveSupport
2   class Railtie < Rails::Railtie # :nodoc:
3     config.active_support = ActiveSupport::OrderedOptions.new
4
5     config.eager_load_namespaces << ActiveSupport
6
7     initializer "active_support.deprecation_behavior" do |app|
8       if deprecation = app.config.active_support.deprecation
9         ActiveSupport::Deprecation.behavior = deprecation
10       end
11     end
12
13     # Sets the default value for Time.zone
14     # If assigned value cannot be matched to a TimeZone, an exception will be raised.
15     initializer "active_support.initialize_time_zone" do |app|
16       require 'active_support/core_ext/time/zones'
17       zone_default = Time.find_zone!(app.config.time_zone)
18
19       unless zone_default
20         raise 'Value assigned to config.time_zone not recognized. ' \
21           'Run "rake-D time" for a list of tasks for finding appropriate time zone names.'
22       end
23
```

Active
Support

```
24        Time.zone_default = zone_default
25    end
26
27    # Sets the default week start
28    # If assigned value is not a valid day symbol
29    # (e.g., :sunday, :monday, ...), an exception will be raised.
30    initializer "active_support.initialize_beginning_of_week" do |app|
31      require 'active_support/core_ext/date/calculations'
32      beginning_of_week_default = Date.
33        find_beginning_of_week!(app.config.beginning_of_week)
34
35      Date.beginning_of_week_default = beginning_of_week_default
36    end
37
38    initializer "active_support.set_configs" do |app|
39      app.config.active_support.each do |k, v|
40        k = "#{k}="
41        ActiveSupport.send(k, v) if ActiveSupport.respond_to? k
42      end
43    end
44  end
45 end
```

B.44   Range
Extensions to Ruby's Range class.

B.44.1   active_support/core_ext/range/conversions

to_formatted_s(format = :default)
Generates a formatted string representation of the range.

```
>> (20.days.ago..10.days.ago).to_formatted_s
=> "Fri Aug 10 22:12:33 -0400 2007..Mon Aug 20 22:12:33 -0400 2007"
>> (20.days.ago..10.days.ago).to_formatted_s(:db)
=> "BETWEEN '2007-08-10 22:12:36' AND '2007-08-20 22:12:36'"
```

B.44.2   active_support/core_ext/range/each
For internal use by Rails. Disables the ability to iterate over a range of Active Support::TimeWithZone due to significant performance issues.

B.44.3   active_support/core_ext/range/include_range

include?(value)
Extends the default Range#include? to support range comparisons.

```
>> (1..5).include?(1..5)
```

```
=> true

>> (1..5).include?(2..3)
=> true

>> (1..5).include?(2..6)
=> false
```

The native include? behavior is untouched.

```
>> ("a".."f").include?("c")
=> true

>> (5..9).include?(11)
=> false
```

B.44.4 `active_support/core_ext/range/overlaps`

`overlaps?(other)`

Compares two ranges and see if they overlap each other.

```
>> (1..5).overlaps?(4..6)
=> true

>> (1..5).overlaps?(7..9)
=> false
```

B.44.5 `active_support/core_ext/enumerable`

`sum(identity = 0)`

Optimize range sum to use arithmetic progression if a block is not given and we have a range of numeric values.

B.45 `Regexp`

Extensions to Ruby's Regexp class.

B.45.1 `active_support/core_ext/regexp`

`multiline?`

Returns true if a multiline regular expression.

B.45.2 `active_support/json/encoding`

`as_json`

Returns self.to_s.

B.46 `ActiveSupport::Rescuable`

The `Rescuable` module is a `Concern` that adds support for easier exception handling. Used within Rails primarily in controller actions, but potentially very useful in your own libraries too.

B.46.1 `active_support/rescuable`

`rescue_from(*klasses, &block)`

The `rescue_from` method receives a series of exception classes or class names and a trailing `:with` option with the name of a method or a `Proc` object to be called to handle them. Alternatively, a block can be given.

Handlers that take one argument will be called with the exception so that the exception can be inspected when dealing with it.

Handlers are inherited. They are searched from right to left, from bottom to top, and up the hierarchy. The handler of the first class for which `exception` `.is_a?(klass)` returns `true` is the one invoked, if any.

Here's some example code taken from Action Controller.

```
1 class ApplicationController < ActionController::Base
2   rescue_from User::NotAuthorized, with: :deny_access
3   rescue_from ActiveRecord::RecordInvalid, with: :show_errors
4
5   rescue_from 'MyAppError::Base' do |exception|
6     render xml: exception, status: 500
7   end
8
9   protected
10    def deny_access
11      ...
12    end
13
14    def show_errors(exception)
15      exception.record.new? ? ...
16    end
17 end
```

B.47 `String`

Extensions to Ruby's `String` class.

B.47.1 `active_support/json/encoding`

`as_json`

Returns `self`.

encode_json

Returns JSON-escaped version of `self`.

B.47.2 `active_support/core_ext/object/blank`

blank?

Returns `true` if the string consists of only whitespace.

```
1 class String
2   def blank?
3     self !~ /\S/
4   end
5 end
```

B.47.3 `active_support/core_ext/string/access`

at(position)

Returns the character at `position`, treating the string as an array (where 0 is the first character). Returns `nil` if the position exceeds the length of the string.

```
>> "hello".at(0)
=> "h"
```

```
>> "hello".at(4)
=> "o"
```

```
>> "hello".at(10)
=> nil
```

first(number)

Returns the first number of characters in a string.

```
1 "hello".first      # => "h"
2 "hello".first(2)   # => "he"
3 "hello".first(10)  # => "hello"
```

from(position)

Returns the remaining characters of a string from the `position`, treating the string as an array (where 0 is the first character). Returns `nil` if the position exceeds the length of the string.

```
1 "hello".at(0)   # => "hello"
2 "hello".at(2)   # => "llo"
3 "hello".at(10)  # => nil
```

last(number)

Returns the last number of characters in a string.

```
1 "hello".last      # => "o"
2 "hello".last(2)   # => "lo"
3 "hello".last(10)  # => "hello"
```

to(position)

Returns the beginning of the string up to the position, treating the string as an array (where 0 is the first character). Doesn't produce an error when the position exceeds the length of the string.

```
1 "hello".at(0) # => "h"
2 "hello".at(2)  # => "hel"
3 "hello".at(10) # => "hello"
```

B.47.4 active_support/core_ext/string/behavior

Duck types as a String-like class. See Object#acts_like? for more explanation.

```
1 class String
2   def acts_like_time?
3     true
4   end
5 end
```

B.47.5 active_support/core_ext/string/conversions

to_date

Uses Date.parse to turn a string into a Date.

to_datetime

Uses Date.parse to turn a string into a DateTime.

to_time(form = :local)

Uses Date.parse to turn a string into a Time, either using either :utc or :local (default).

B.47.6 active_support/core_ext/string/exclude

exclude?(other)

The inverse of include?. Returns true if self does not include the other string.

B.47.7 `active_support/core_ext/string/filters`

`remove(pattern)`

A convenience method for `gsub(pattern,  '')`. It returns a new string with all occurrences of the pattern removed.

`remove!(pattern)`

Performs a destructive `remove`. See `remove`.

`squish`

Returns the string, first removing all whitespace on both ends of the string and then changing remaining consecutive whitespace groups into one space each.

```
>> %{ Multi-line
   string }.squish
=> "Multi-line string"

>> " foo    bar   \n   \t   boo".squish
=> "foo bar boo"
```

`squish!`

Performs a destructive `squish`. See `squish`.

`truncate(length, options = )`

Truncates a given `text` after a given `length` if `text` is longer than `length`. The last characters will be replaced with the `:omission` (which defaults to "…") for a total length not exceeding `:length`.

Pass a `:separator` to truncate `text` at a natural break.

```
>> "Once upon a time in a world far far away".truncate(30)
=> "Once upon a time in a world..."

>> "Once upon a time in a world far far away".truncate(30, separator: ' ')
=> "Once upon a time in a world..."

>> "Once upon a time in a world far far away".truncate(14)
=> "Once upon a..."

>> "And they found that many people were sleeping better.".
     truncate(25, omission: "... (continued)")
=> "And they f... (continued)"
```

B.47.8 `active_support/core_ext/string/indent`

`indent(amount, indent_string=nil, indent_empty_lines=false)`

Indents a string by the given `amount`.

```
>> "foo".indent(2)
=> "  foo"

=> "foo\nbar"
>> "  foo\n  bar"
```

The second argument—`indent_string`—specifies what indent string to use. If no `indent_string` is specified, it will use the first indented line; otherwise, a space is used. If `indent_empty_lines` is set to `true`, empty lines will also be indented.

`indent!`

Performs a destructive indent. See `indent`.

B.47.9 `active_support/core_ext/string/inflections`

String inflections define new methods on the `String` class to transform names for different purposes.

For instance, you can figure out the name of a database from the name of a class:

```
>> "ScaleScore".tableize
=> "scale_scores"
```

If you get frustrated by the limitations of Rails inflections, try the most excellent linguistics library by Michael Granger at `https://github.com/ged/linguistics`. It doesn't do all the same inflections as Rails, but the ones that it does do, it does better. (See `titleize` for an example.)

`camelcase`

Alias for `camelize`.

`camelize(first_letter = :upper)`

By default, `camelize` converts strings to UpperCamelCase. If the argument to `camelize` is set to `:lower`, then `camelize` produces lowerCamelCase. Also converts "/" to "::," which is useful for converting paths to namespaces.

```
>> "active_record".camelize
=> "ActiveRecord"
```

```
>> "active_record".camelize(:lower)
=> "activeRecord"

>> "active_record/errors".camelize
=> "ActiveRecord::Errors"
>> "active_record/errors".camelize(:lower)
=> "activeRecord::Errors"
```

classify

Creates a class name from a table name; used by Active Record to turn table names
to model classes. Note that the classify method returns a string and not a Class.
(To convert to an actual class, follow classify with constantize.)

```
>> "egg_and_hams".classify
=> "EggAndHam"

>> "post".classify
=> "Post"
```

constantize

The constantize method tries to find a declared constant with the name specified
in the string. It raises a NameError if a matching constant is not located.

```
>> "Module".constantize
=> Module

>> "Class".constantize
=> Class
```

dasherize

Replaces underscores with dashes in the string.

```
>> "puni_puni"
=> "puni-puni"
```

demodulize

Removes the module prefixes from a fully qualified module or class name.

```
>> "ActiveRecord::CoreExtensions::String::Inflections".demodulize
=> "Inflections"

>> "Inflections".demodulize
=> "Inflections"
```

`foreign_key(separate_class_name_and_id_with_ underscore = true)`

Creates a foreign key name from a class name.

```
"Message".foreign_key # => "message_id"
"Message".foreign_key(false) # => "messageid"
"Admin::Post".foreign_key # => "post_id"
```

`humanize(options = {})`

Capitalizes the first word of a string, turns underscores into spaces, and strips `_id`. Similar to the `titleize` method in that it is intended for creating pretty output.

```
>> "employee_salary".humanize
=> "Employee salary"
>> "author_id".humanize
=> "Author"
```

Setting the `:capitalize` option to `false` results in the string being humanized without being capitalized.

```
>> "employee_salary".humanize(capitalize: false)
=> "employee salary"
```

`parameterize(sep = '-')`

Replaces special characters in a string with `sep` string so that it may be used as part of a *pretty* URL.

`pluralize`

Returns the plural form of the word in the string.

```
1 "post".pluralize # => "posts"
2 "octopus".pluralize # => "octopi"
3 "sheep".pluralize # => "sheep"
4 "words".pluralize # => "words"
5 "the blue mailman".pluralize # => "the blue mailmen"
6 "CamelOctopus".pluralize # => "CamelOctopi"
```

`safe_constantize`

The `safe_constantize` method tries to find a declared constant with the name specified in the string. It returns `nil` when the name is not in CamelCase or is not initialized.

singularize

The reverse of `pluralize`. Returns the singular form of a word in a string.

```
1  "posts".singularize # => "post"
2  "octopi".singularize # => "octopus"
3  "sheep".singluarize # => "sheep"
4  "word".singluarize # => "word"
5  "the blue mailmen".singularize # => "the blue mailman"
6  "CamelOctopi".singularize # => "CamelOctopus"
```

tableize

Creates a plural and underscored database table name based on Rails conventions. Used by Active Record to determine the proper table name for a model class. This method uses the `pluralize` method on the last word in the string.

```
1  "RawScaledScorer".tableize # => "raw_scaled_scorers"
2  "egg_and_ham".tableize # => "egg_and_hams"
3  "fancyCategory".tableize # => "fancy_categories"
```

titlecase

Alias for `titleize`.

titleize

Capitalizes all the words and replaces some characters in the string to create a nicer-looking title. The `titleize` method is meant for creating pretty output and is not used in the Rails internals.

```
>> "The light on the beach was like a sinus headache".titleize
=> "The Light On The Beach Was Like A Sinus Headache"
```

It's also not perfect. Among other things, it capitalizes words inside the sentence that it probably shouldn't, like "a" and "the."

underscore

The reverse of `camelize`. Makes an underscored form from the expression in the string. Changes "::" to "/" to convert namespaces to paths.

```
1  "ActiveRecord".underscore # => "active_record"
2  "ActiveRecord::Errors".underscore # => active_record/errors
```

Active
Support

B.47.10 `active_support/core_ext/string/inquiry`

inquiry

Wraps the current string in the `ActiveSupport::StringInquirer` class, providing an elegant way to test for equality.

```
1 env = 'production'.inquiry
2 env.production?  # => true
3 env.development? # => false
```

B.47.11 `active_support/core_ext/string/multibyte`

Defines a multibyte safe proxy for string methods.

mb_chars

The `mb_chars` method creates and returns an instance of `ActiveSupport::Multibyte::Chars`, encapsulating the original string. A Unicode-safe version of all the `String` methods are defined on the proxy class. If the proxy class doesn't respond to a certain method, it's forwarded to the encapsulated string.

```
>> name = 'Claus Müller'

>> name.reverse
=> "rell??M sualC"

>> name.length
=> 13

>> name.mb_chars.reverse.to_s
=> "rellüM sualC"
>> name.mb_chars.length
=> 12
```

All the methods on the `Chars` proxy that normally return a string will return a `Chars` object. This allows method chaining on the result of any of these methods.

```
>> name.mb_chars.reverse.length
=> 12
```

The `Chars` object tries to be as interchangeable with `String` objects as possible, sorting and comparing between `String` and `Char` work like expected. The bang! methods change the internal string representation in the `Chars` object. Interoperability problems can be resolved easily with a `to_s` call.

For more information about the methods defined on the Chars proxy, see ActiveSupport::Multibyte::Chars. For information about how to change the default Multibyte behavior, see ActiveSupport::Multibyte.

is_utf8?(suffix)
Returns true if the string has UTF-8 semantics versus strings that are simply being used as byte streams.

B.47.12 active_support/core_ext/string/output_safety

html_safe
Returns an HTML-escaped version of self. See ERB::Util#html_escape for more information.

B.47.13 active_support/core_ext/string/starts_ends_with
Provides String with additional condition methods.

starts_with?(prefix)
Alias for start_with?.

ends_with?(suffix)
Alias for end_with?.

B.47.14 active_support/core_ext/string/strip

strip_heredoc
Strips indentation in heredocs. For example,

```
1 if options[:usage]
2   puts <<-USAGE.strip_heredoc
3     This command does such and such.
4
5     Supported options are:
6       -h         This message
7       ...
8   USAGE
9 end
```

would cause the user to see the usage message aligned against the left margin.

B.47.15 `active_support/core_ext/string/in_time_zone`

`in_time_zone(zone = ::Time.zone)`

Converts the string to a `TimeWithZone` in the current zone if `Time.zone` or `Time.zone_default` are set. Otherwise, returns `String#to_time`.

B.48 `ActiveSupport::StringInquirer`

Wrapping a string in this class gives you a prettier way to test for equality. The value returned by `Rails.env` is wrapped in a `StringInquirer` object, so instead of calling

```
Rails.env == "production"
```

you can call

```
Rails.env.production?
```

This class is really simple, so you only really want to do this with strings that contain no whitespace or special characters.

```
>> s = ActiveSupport::StringInquirer.new("obie")
=> "obie"
>> s.obie?
=> true
```

B.49 `Struct`

Extensions to Ruby's `Struct` class.

B.49.1 `active_support/core_ext/struct`

`to_h`

Backports of `Struct#to_h` from Ruby 2.0 unless defined.

B.50 `ActiveSupport::Subscriber`

The `ActiveSupport::Subscriber` object is used to consume `ActiveSupport::Notifications`. The subscriber dispatches notifications to a registered object based on its given namespace.

For example, a subscriber could collect statistics about Active Record queries:

```
1 module ActiveRecord
2   class StatsSubscriber < ActiveSupport::Subscriber
```

```
3     def sql(event)
4       Statsd.timing("sql.#{event.payload[:name]}", event.
        duration)
5     end
6   end
7 end
```

To attach a subscriber to a namespace, use the `attach_to` method.

```
1 ActiveRecord::StatsSubscriber.attach_to :active_record
```

B.51   **Symbol**
Extensions to Ruby's `Symbol` class.

B.51.1   **active_support/json/encoding**

as_json
Returns `to_s` version of itself.

B.52   **ActiveSupport::TaggedLogging**
Wraps any standard `Logger` object to provide tagging capabilities.

B.52.1   **active_support/tagged_logger**

flush
Clears all tags and invoke the parent definition if it exists.

tagged(*tags, &block)
Prefixes `tags` to each log message in the yielded block.

```
1 logger = ActiveSupport::TaggedLogging.new(Logger.new(STDOUT))
2 logger.tagged("tr4w") { logger.info "Stuff" } # [tr4w] Stuff
```

B.53   **ActiveSupport::TestCase**
Inheriting from `MiniTest::Unit::TestCase`, adds Rails specific testing methods and behavior.

B.53.1   **active_support/test_case**

assert_no_match
Alias for `refute_match` for `Test::Unit` backward compatibility.

assert_not_empty

Alias for `refute_empty` for `Test::Unit` backward compatibility.

assert_not_equal

Alias for `refute_equal` for `Test::Unit` backward compatibility.

assert_not_in_delta

Alias for `refute_in_delta` for `Test::Unit` backward compatibility.

assert_not_in_epsilon

Alias for `refute_in_epsilon` for `Test::Unit` backward compatibility.

assert_not_includes

Alias for `refute_includes` for `Test::Unit` backward compatibility.

assert_not_instance_of

Alias for `refute_instance_of` for `Test::Unit` backward compatibility.

assert_not_kind_of

Alias for `refute_kind_of` for `Test::Unit` backward compatibility.

assert_not_nil

Alias for `refute_nil` for `Test::Unit` backward compatibility.

assert_not_operator

Alias for `refute_operator` for `Test::Unit` backward compatibility.

assert_not_predicate

Alias for `refute_predicate` for `Test::Unit` backward compatibility.

assert_not_respond_to

Alias for `refute_respond_to` for `Test::Unit` backward compatibility.

assert_not_same

Alias for `refute_same` for `Test::Unit` backward compatibility.

assert_nothing_raised(*args)

Tests if the block doesn't raise an exception.

assert_raise

Alias for `assert_raises` for `Test::Unit` backward compatibility.

B.54 **ActiveSupport::Testing::Assertions**
B.54.1 **active_support/testing/assertions**

Rails adds a number of assertions to the basic ones provided with `MiniTest`.

assert_difference(expressions, difference = 1, message = nil, &block)

Tests whether a numeric difference in the return value of an expression is a result of what is evaluated in the yielded block. (Easier to demonstrate than to explain!)

The following example evaluation's the expression `Article.count`, and it saves the result. Then it yields to the block, which will execute the `post :create` and return control to the `assert_difference` method. At that point, `Article.count` is evaluated again, and the difference is asserted to be 1 (the default difference).

```
1 assert_difference 'Article.count' do
2   post :create, article: {...}
3 end
```

Any arbitrary expression can be passed in and evaluated:

```
1 assert_difference 'assigns(:article).comments(:reload).size' do
2   post :create, comment: {...}
3 end
```

Arbitrary difference values may be specified. The default is 1, but negative numbers are OK too:

```
1 assert_difference 'Article.count', -1 do
2   post :delete, id: ...
3 end
```

An array of expressions can also be passed in—each will be evaluated:

```
1 assert_difference [ 'Article.count', 'Post.count' ], 2 do
2   post :create, article: {...}
3 end
```

A lambda or a list of lambdas can be passed in and evaluated:

```
1 assert_difference ->{ Article.count }, 2 do
2   post :create, article: {...}
3 end
```

```
4
5 assert_difference [->{ Article.count }, ->{ Post.count }], 2 do
6   post :create, article: {...}
7 end
```

A error message can be specified:

```
1 assert_difference 'Article.count', -1, "Article should be
        destroyed" do
2   post :delete, id: ...
3 end
```

assert_no_difference(expressions, message = nil, &block)

Tests that the return value of the supplied expression does not change as a result of what is evaluated in the yielded block.

```
1 assert_no_difference 'Article.count' do
2   post :create, article: invalid_attributes
3 end
```

assert_not(object, message = nil)

Assert that an expression is not true.

```
1 assert_not nil    # => true
2 assert_not false  # => true
3 assert_not 'foo'  # => 'foo' is not nil or false
```

B.54.2 active_support/testing/time_helpers

travel(duration, &block)

Changes the current time to the time in the future or in the past by a given time difference. This is accomplished by stubbing `Time.now` and `Date.today`.

```
1 Time.current # => Sat, 09 Nov 2013 15:34:49 EST -05:00
2 travel 1.day
3 Time.current # => Sun, 10 Nov 2013 15:34:49 EST -05:00
4 Date.current # => Sun, 10 Nov 2013
```

travel_to(date_or_time, &block)

Changes the current time to the supplied date or time. This is accomplished by stubbing `Time.now` and `Date.today`.

B.55 Thread

Extensions to Ruby's built-in `Thread` class.

B.55.1 `active_support/core_ext/thread`

freeze

Freeze thread local variables.

thread_variable?(key)

Returns `true` if the given string (or symbol) exists as a thread local variable.

```
>> current_thread = Thread.current
=> #<Thread:0x007fd2c08c0da8 run>

>> current_thread.thread_variable?(:tr4w)
=> false

>> current_thread.thread_variable_set(:tr4w, 'is awesome')
=> "is awesome"

>> current_thread.thread_variable?(:tr4w)
=> true
```

thread_variable_get(key)

Returns the value of a thread local variable that has been set.

thread_variable_set(key, value)

Set a thread local variable.

```
>> Thread.current.thread_variable_set(:tr4w, 'is awesome')
=> "is awesome"
```

thread_variables

Returns an array of thread local variables represented as symbols.

```
>> Thread.current.thread_variables
=> [:tr4w]
```

B.56 Time

Extensions to Ruby's built-in `Time` class.

B.56.1 `active_support/json/encoding`

as_json

Returns `self` as a JSON string. The `ActiveSupport.use_standard_json_time_format` configuration setting determines whether the output is formatted using `:xmlschema` or the following pattern:

Active Support

```
%(#{strftime("%Y/%m/%d %H:%M:%S")} #{formatted_offset(false)})
```

B.56.2 `active_support/core_ext/time/acts_like`

Duck types as a Time-like class. See `Object#acts_like?` for more explanation.

```
1 class Time
2   def acts_like_time?
3     true
4   end
5 end
```

B.56.3 `active_support/core_ext/time/calculations`

Contains methods that facilitate time calculations.

`===(other)`

Overriding case equality method so that it returns `true` for `ActiveSupport::TimeWithZone` instances.

`+ (other)`

Implemented by the `plus_with_duration` method. It allows addition of times like this:

```
expiration_time = Time.now + 3.days
```

`- (other)`

Implemented by the `minus_with_duration` method. It allows addition of times like this:

```
two_weeks_ago = Time.now - 2.weeks
```

`<=>`

Implemented by the `compare_with_coercion` method. Layers additional behavior on `Time#eql?` so that `ActiveSupport::TimeWithZone` instances can be compared with `Time` instances.

`advance(options)`

Provides precise `Time` calculations. The `options` parameter takes a hash with any of the following keys: `:months`, `:days`, `:years`, `:hours`, `:minutes`, and `:seconds`.

ago(seconds)

Returns a new Time representing the time a number of seconds into the past; this is basically a wrapper around the Numeric extension of the same name. For the best accuracy, do not use this method in combination with x.months; use months_ago instead!

all_day

Convenience method for beginning_of_day..end_of_day. Returns a range representing the whole day of the current time.

all_month

Convenience method for beginning_of_month..end_of_month. Returns a range representing the whole month of the current time.

all_quarter

Convenience method for beginning_of_quarter..end_of_quarter. Returns a range representing the whole quarter of the current time.

all_week(start_day = Date.beginning_of_week)

Convenience method for beginning_of_week(start_day)..end_of_week(start_day). Returns a range representing the whole week of the current time.

all_year

Convenience method for beginning_of_year..end_of_year. Returns a range representing the whole year of the current time.

at_beginning_of_day / at_midnight / beginning_of_day / midnight

Returns a new Time object representing the "start" of the current instance's day, hard-coded to 00:00 hours.

at_beginning_of_hour / beginning_of_hour

Returns a new Time object representing the start of the hour (hh:00:00). Implemented simply as change(min: 0).

at_beginning_of_minute / beginning_of_minute

Returns a new Time object representing the start of the minute (hh:mm:00). Implemented simply as change(sec: 0).

at_beginning_of_quarter / beginning_of_quarter

Returns a new Time object representing the start of the calendar quarter (first of January, April, July, October, 00:00 hours).

at_beginning_of_week

Alias for beginning_of_week.

at_beginning_of_year / beginning_of_year

Returns a new Time object representing the start of the year (first of January, 00:00 hours).

at_end_of_day / end_of_day

Returns a new Time object representing the end of a day (23:59:59). Implemented simply as change(hour: 23, min: 59, sec: 59).

at_end_of_hour / end_of_hour

Returns a new Time object representing the end of the hour (hh:59:59). Implemented simply as change(min: 59, sec: 59).

at_end_of_minute / end_of_minute

Returns a new Time object representing the end of the minute (hh:mm:59). Implemented simply as change(sec: 59).

at_end_of_month / end_of_month

Returns a new Time object representing the end of the month (last day of the month at 23:59:59 hours).

at_end_of_quarter / end_of_quarter

Returns a new Time object representing the end of the quarter (March 30, June 30, September 30, December 31, etc., at 23:59:59 hours).

at_end_of_week

Alias for end_of_week.

at_end_of_year / end_of_year

Returns a new Time object representing the end of the year (last day of the year at 23:59:59 hours).

beginning_of_week(start_day = Date.beginning _of_week)

Returns a new Time object representing the "start" of the current instance's week, defaulting to Date.beginning_of_week.

change(options)

Returns a new Time where one or more of the elements have been changed according to the options parameter. The valid date options are :year, :month, and :day. The valid time options are :hour, :min, :sec, :offset, and :start.

Time.current

Returns Time.zone.now when Time.zone or config.time_zone are set; otherwise, returns Time.now.

days_ago(days)

Returns a new Time object minus the specified number of days.

Time.days_in_month(month, year = nil)

Returns the number of days in the given month. If a year is given, February will return the correct number of days for leap years. Otherwise, this method will always report February as having 28 days.

```
>> Time.days_in_month(7, 1974)
=> 31
```

days_since(days)

Returns a new Time object representing the time a number of specified days into the future.

days_to_week_start(start_day = Date.beginning _of_week)

Returns the number of days to the start of the week.

end_of_week(start_day = Date.beginning_of_week)

Returns a new Time object representing the "end" of the current instance's week, with the week start_day defaulting to Date.beginning_of_week.

future?

Returns true if the Time instance is in the future.

middle_of_day / noon
Returns a new Time object representing the middle of the day (12:00:00). Implemented simply as change(hour: 12).

last_month / prev_month
Convenience method for months_ago(1).

last_quarter / prev_quarter
Convenience method for months_ago(3).

last_week(start_day = Date.beginning_of_week) / prev_week
Returns a new Time object representing the given day in the previous week, with the week start_day defaulting to Date.beginning_of_week.

last_year / prev_year
Convenience method for years_ago(1).

monday
Convenience method for beginning_of_week(:monday).

months_ago(months)
Returns a new Time object representing the time a number of specified months into the past.

months_since(months)
The opposite of months_ago. Returns a new Time object representing the time a number of specified months into the future.

next_month
Convenience method for months_since(1).

next_quarter
Convenience method for months_since(3).

next_week(given_day_in_next_week = Date.beginning _of_week)
Returns a new Time object representing the start of the given day in the following calendar week.

next_year
Convenience method for `years_since(1)`.

seconds_since_midnight
Returns the number of seconds that have transpired since midnight.

seconds_until_end_of_day
Returns how many seconds left in the day until 23:59:59.

since(seconds) / in(seconds)
Returns a new `Time` representing the time a number of `seconds` into the future starting from the instance time. This method is basically a wrapper around the `Numeric` extension of the same name. For best accuracy, do not use this method in combination with `x.months`; use `months_since` instead!

sunday
Convenience method for `end_of_week(:monday)`.

today?
Returns `true` if the `Time` is today.

tomorrow
Returns a new `Time` object advanced by one day.

weeks_ago(weeks)
Returns a new `Time` object representing the time a number of specified weeks ago.

weeks_since(weeks)
Returns a new `Time` object representing the time a number of specified weeks into the future.

years_ago(years)
Returns a new `Time` object representing the time a number of specified `years` into the past.

years_since(years)
The opposite of `years_ago`. Returns a new `Time` object representing the time a number of specified `years` into the future.

yesterday

Returns a new `Time` object subtracted by one day.

B.56.4 `active_support/core_ext/time/conversions`

Extensions to Ruby's `Time` class to convert time objects into different convenient string representations and other objects.

DATE_FORMATS

The `DATE_FORMATS` hash constant holds formatting patterns used by the `to_formatted_s` method to convert a `Time` object into a string representation:

```
1  DATE_FORMATS = {
2    :db            => '%Y-%m-%d %H:%M:%S',
3    :number        => '%Y%m%d%H%M%S',
4    :nsec          => '%Y%m%d%H%M%S%9N',
5    :time          => '%H:%M',
6    :short         => '%d %b %H:%M',
7    :long          => '%B %d, %Y %H:%M',
8    :long_ordinal => lambda { |time|
9      day_format = ActiveSupport::Inflector.ordinalize(time.day)
10     time.strftime("%B #{day_format}, %Y %H:%M")
11   },
12   :rfc822        => lambda { |time|
13     offset_format = time.formatted_offset(false)
14     time.strftime("%a, %d %b %Y %H:%M:%S #{offset_format}")
15   }
16 }
```

formatted_offset(colon = true, alternate_utc _string = nil)

Returns the UTC offset as an `HH:MM` formatted string.

```
1 Time.local(2000).formatted_offset         # => "-06:00"
2 Time.local(2000).formatted_offset(false)  # => "-0600"
```

to_formatted_s(format = :default)

Converts a `Time` object into a string representation. The `:default` option corresponds to the `Time` object's own `to_s` method.

```
>> time = Time.now
=> Thu Jan 18 06:10:17 CST 2007

>> time.to_formatted_s(:time)
=> "06:10"
```

```
>> time.to_formatted_s(:db)
=> "2007-01-18 06:10:17"

>> time.to_formatted_s(:number)
=> "20070118061017"

>> time.to_formatted_s(:short)
=> "18 Jan 06:10"

>> time.to_formatted_s(:long)
=> "January 18, 2007 06:10"

>> time.to_formatted_s(:long_ordinal)
=> "January 18th, 2007 06:10"

>> time.to_formatted_s(:rfc822)
=> "Thu, 18 Jan 2007 06:10:17 -0600"
```

to_s

Aliased to `to_formatted_s`.

B.56.5 `active_support/core_ext/time/marshal`

Rails layers behavior on the `_dump` and `_load` methods so that utc instances can be flagged on dump and coerced back to utc on load.

Ruby 1.9.2 adds `utc_offset` and zone to `Time`, but marshaling only preserves `utc_offset`. Rails preserves zone also, even though it may not work in some edge cases.

B.56.6 `active_support/core_ext/time/zones`

Extensions to `Time` having to do with support for time zones.

find_zone(time_zone)

Returns a `TimeZone` instance or `nil` if it does not exist.

```
>> Time.find_zone("Eastern Time (US & Canada)")
=> #<ActiveSupport::TimeZone:0x007fd2c0bc49c8
    @name="Eastern Time (US & Canada)", ...>
```

find_zone!(time_zone)

Same as `find_zone`, except it raises an `ArgumentError` if an invalid `time_zone` is provided.

in_time_zone(zone = ::Time.zone)

Returns the simultaneous time in the supplied `zone`.

```
>> Time.zone = 'Hawaii'
=> "Hawaii"
>> Time.utc(2000).in_time_zone
=> Fri, 31 Dec 1999 14:00:00 HST -10:00
```

use_zone(time_zone, &block)

Allows override of `Time.zone` locally inside supplied block; resets `Time.zone` to existing value when done.

```
>> Date.today
=> Wed, 02 Jun 2010

>> Time.use_zone(ActiveSupport::TimeZone['Hong Kong']) { Date.today }
=> Thu, 03 Jun 2010
```

zone

Returns the `TimeZone` for the current request if this has been set (via `Time.zone=`). If `Time.zone` has not been set for the current request, returns the `Time Zone` specified in `config.time_zone`.

zone=(time_zone)

Sets `Time.zone` to a `TimeZone` object for the current request/thread.

This method accepts any of the following:

- A Rails `TimeZone` object
- An identifier for a Rails `TimeZone` object (e.g., "Eastern Time (US & Canada)," `-5.hours`)
- A `TZInfo::TimeZone` object
- An identifier for a `TZInfo::TimeZone` object (e.g., "America/New_York")

Here's an example of how you might set `Time.zone` on a per request basis. The code assumes that `current_user.time_zone` returns a string identifying the user's preferred `TimeZone`:

```
1 class ApplicationController < ActionController::Base
2   before_action :set_time_zone
3
4   def set_time_zone
```

```
5      Time.zone = current_user.time_zone
6    end
7 end
```

B.57 `ActiveSupport::TimeWithZone`

A `Time`-like class that can represent a time in any time zone. Necessary because standard Ruby `Time` instances are limited to UTC and the system's ENV `['TZ']` zone.

You shouldn't ever need to create a `TimeWithZone` instance directly via new. Rails provides the methods `local`, `parse`, `at`, and `now` on `TimeZone` instances and `in_time_zone` on `Time` and `DateTime` instances for a more user-friendly syntax.

```
>> Time.zone = 'Eastern Time (US & Canada)'
=> 'Eastern Time (US & Canada)'

>> Time.zone.local(2007, 2, 10, 15, 30, 45)
=> Sat, 10 Feb 2007 15:30:45 EST -05:00

>> Time.zone.parse('2007-02-01 15:30:45')
=> Sat, 10 Feb 2007 15:30:45 EST -05:00

>> Time.zone.at(1170361845)
=> Sat, 10 Feb 2007 15:30:45 EST -05:00

>> Time.zone.now
=> Sun, 18 May 2008 13:07:55 EDT -04:00

>> Time.utc(2007, 2, 10, 20, 30, 45).in_time_zone
=> Sat, 10 Feb 2007 15:30:45 EST -05:00
```

See `Time` and `ActiveSupport::TimeZone` for further documentation of these methods.

`TimeWithZone` instances implement the same API as Ruby `Time` instances so that `Time` and `TimeWithZone` instances are interchangeable.

```
>> t = Time.zone.now
=> Sun, 18 May 2008 13:27:25 EDT -04:00

>> t.class
=> ActiveSupport::TimeWithZone

>> t.hour
=> 13
```

Active
Support

```
>> t.dst?
=> true

>> t.utc_offset
=> -14400

>> t.zone
=> "EDT"

>> t.to_s(:rfc822)
=> "Sun, 18 May 2008 13:27:25 -0400"

>> t + 1.day
=> Mon, 19 May 2008 13:27:25 EDT -04:00

>> t.beginning_of_year
=> Tue, 01 Jan 2008 00:00:00 EST -05:00

>> t > Time.utc(1999)
=> true

>> t.is_a?(Time)
=> true
```

B.58 `ActiveSupport::TimeZone`

The `TimeZone` class serves as a wrapper around `TZInfo::TimeZone` instances. It allows Rails to do the following:

- Limit the set of zones provided by `TZInfo` to a meaningful subset of 146 zones.

- Retrieve and display zones with a friendlier name (e.g., "Eastern Time (US & Canada)" instead of "America/New_York").

- Lazily load `TZInfo::TimeZone` instances only when they're needed.

- Create `ActiveSupport::TimeWithZone` instances via TimeZone's `local`, `parse`, `at`, and `now` methods.

If you set `config.time_zone` in an initializer, you can access this `TimeZone` object via `Time.zone`:

```
1 config.time_zone = "Eastern Time (US & Canada)"
2
3 Time.zone       # => #<TimeZone:0x514834...>
4 Time.zone.name  # => "Eastern Time (US & Canada)"
5 Time.zone.now   # => Sun, 18 May 2008 14:30:44 EDT -04:00
```

B.58.1   `active_support/values/time_zone`

The version of `TZInfo` bundled with Active Support only includes the definitions necessary to support the zones defined by the `TimeZone` class. If you need to use zones that aren't defined by `TimeZone`, you'll need to install the `TZInfo` gem. If a recent version of the gem is installed locally, this will be used instead of the bundled version.

`<=>` `(other)`

Compares this time zone to the parameter. The two are compared first based on their offsets and then by name.

`=~(re)`

Compare name and `TZInfo` identifier to a supplied regular expression. Returns `true` if a match is found.

`TimeZone[]` `(arg)`

Locates a specific time zone object. If the argument is a string, it is interpreted to mean the name of the time zone to locate.

```
>> ActiveSupport::TimeZone['Dublin']
=> #<TimeZone:0x3208390 @name="Dublin", @utc_offset=nil ...>
```

If it is a numeric value it is either the hour offset or the second offset of the time zone to find. (The first one with that offset will be returned.)

Returns `nil` if no such time zone is known to the system.

`TimeZone.all`

Returns an array of all 146 `TimeZone` objects. There are multiple `TimeZone` objects per time zone (in many cases) to make it easier for users to find their own time zone.

```
>> ActiveSupport::TimeZone.all
=> [#<ActiveSupport::TimeZone:0x551c34...
```

`at(seconds)`

Creates a new `ActiveSupport::TimeWithZone` instance in time zone of `self` from the number of seconds since the Unix epoch.

```
1 Time.zone = 'Hawaii'            # => "Hawaii"
2 Time.utc(2000).to_f            # => 946684800.0
3 Time.zone.at(946684800.0)      # => Fri, 31 Dec 1999 14:00:00 HST -10:00
```

TimeZone.create(name, offset)

Creates a new TimeZone instance with the given name and offset.

```
>> ActiveSupport::TimeZone.create("Atlanta", -5.hours)
=> #<ActiveSupport::TimeZone:0x007fd2c136b118 @name="Atlanta",
    @utc_offset=-18000 seconds, @tzinfo=#<TZInfo::TimeZoneProxy: Atlanta>,
    @current_period=nil>
```

TimeZone.find_tzinfo(name)

Returns a TZInfo instance matching the specified name.

formatted_offset(colon=true, alternate_utc_string = nil)

Returns the offset of this time zone as a formatted string in the format HH:MM. If the offset is zero, this method will return an empty string. If colon is false, a colon will not be inserted into the output.

initialize(name, utc_offset = nil, tzinfo = nil)

Create a new TimeZone object with the given name and offset. The offset is the number of seconds that this time zone is offset from UTC (GMT). Seconds were chosen as the offset unit because that is the unit that Ruby uses to represent time zone offsets (see Time#utc_offset). The tzinfo parameter can be explicitly passed in; otherwise, the name will be used to find it: TimeZone.find_tzinfo(name).

local(*args)

Creates a new ActiveSupport::TimeWithZone instance in time zone of self from given values.

local_to_utc(time, dst=true)

Adjust the given time to the simultaneous time in UTC. Returns a Time.utc() instance.

now

Returns Time.now adjusted to this time zone.

```
>> Time.now
=> 2013-10-16 17:45:49 -0400
>> ActiveSupport::TimeZone['Hawaii'].now
=> Wed, 16 Oct 2013 11:46:05 HST -10:00
```

parse(str, now=now)

Creates a new `ActiveSupport::TimeWithZone` instance in time zone of `self` from parsed string.

```
>> Time.zone = 'Hawaii'
=> "Hawaii"
>> Time.zone.parse('1999-12-31 14:00:00')
=> Fri, 31 Dec 1999 14:00:00 HST -10:00
```

period_for_local(time, dst=true)

Method exists so that `TimeZone` instances respond like `TZInfo::TimeZone`.

period_for_utf(time)

Method exists so that `TimeZone` instances respond like `TZInfo::TimeZone`.

TimeZone.seconds_to_utc_offset(seconds, colon = true)

Assumes `self` represents an offset from UTC in seconds (as returned from `Time#utc_offset`) and turns this into an +HH:MM formatted string.

```
1 ActiveSupport::TimeZone.seconds_to_utc_offset(-21_600) # => "-06:00"
```

to_s

Returns a textual representation of this time zone.

```
1 ActiveSupport::TimeZone['Dublin'].to_s   # => "(GMT+00:00) Dublin"
```

today

Returns the current date in this time zone.

```
>> Date.today
=> Wed, 16 Oct 2013
>> ActiveSupport::TimeZone['Darwin'].today
=> Thu, 17 Oct 2013
```

TimeZone.us_zones

A convenience method for returning a collection of `TimeZone` objects for time zones in the United States.

```
>> ActiveSupport::TimeZone.us_zones.map(&:name)
=> ["Hawaii", "Alaska", "Pacific Time (US & Canada)", "Arizona",
"Mountain Time (US & Canada)", "Central Time (US & Canada)", "Eastern
Time (US & Canada)", "Indiana (East)"]
```

utc_offset
Returns the offset of this time zone from UTC in seconds.

utc_to_local(time)
Adjust the given time to the simultaneous time in the time zone.

B.59 **TrueClass**

B.59.1 **active_support/core_ext/object/blank**

blank?
Returns `false`.

B.59.2 **active_support/json/encoding**

as_json
Returns `true`.

B.60 **ActiveSupport::XmlMini**

The `XmlMini` module contains code that allows Rails to serialize/deserialize and parse XML using a number of different libraries.

- JDOM (requires JRuby)
- LibXML (fast native XML parser)
- Nokogiri (requires `nokogiri` gem)

B.60.1 **active_support/xml_mini**

If you're doing anything of significance with XML in your application, you should definitely use the fast native `libxml` parser. Install the binaries (instructions vary depending on platform) and then the Ruby binding:

```
gem 'libxml-ruby', '=0.9.7'
```

Set `XmlMini` to use `libxml` in `application.rb` or an initializer.

```
XmlMini.backend = 'LibXML'
```

Constants
The `TYPE_NAMES` constant holds a mapping of Ruby types to their representation when serialized as XML.

```
1 TYPE_NAMES = {
2   "Symbol"     => "symbol",
```

```
3    "Fixnum"      => "integer",
4    "Bignum"      => "integer",
5    "BigDecimal"  => "decimal",
6    "Float"       => "float",
7    "TrueClass"   => "boolean",
8    "FalseClass"  => "boolean",
9    "Date"        => "date",
10   "DateTime"    => "dateTime",
11   "Time"        => "dateTime",
12   "Array"       => "array",
13   "Hash"        => "hash"
14 }
```

The FORMATTING constant holds a mapping of lambdas that define how Ruby values are serialized to strings for representation in XML.

```
1 FORMATTING = {
2   "symbol"   => Proc.new { |symbol| symbol.to_s },
3   "date"     => Proc.new { |date| date.to_s(:db) },
4   "dateTime" => Proc.new { |time| time.xmlschema },
5   "binary"   => Proc.new { |binary| ::Base64.encode64(binary) },
6   "yaml"     => Proc.new { |yaml| yaml.to_yaml }
7 }
```

The PARSING constant holds a mapping of lambdas used to deserialize values stored in XML back into Ruby objects.

```
1    PARSING = {
2      "symbol"        => Proc.new { |symbol| symbol.to_sym },
3      "date"          => Proc.new { |date| ::Date.parse(date) },
4      "datetime"      => Proc.new {
5        |time| Time.xmlschema(time).utc rescue ::DateTime.parse(time).utc },
6      "integer"       => Proc.new { |integer| integer.to_i },
7      "float"         => Proc.new { |float|   float.to_f },
8      "decimal"       => Proc.new { |number|  BigDecimal(number) },
9      "boolean"       => Proc.new {
10       |boolean| %w(1 true).include?(boolean.strip) },
11     "string"        => Proc.new { |string|  string.to_s },
12     "yaml"          => Proc.new { |yaml|   YAML::load(yaml) rescue yaml },
13     "base64Binary"  => Proc.new { |bin|    ::Base64.decode64(bin) },
14     "binary"        => Proc.new { |bin, entity| _parse_binary(bin, entity) },
15     "file"          => Proc.new { |file, entity| _parse_file(file, entity) }
16   }
```

```
1    PARSING.update(
2      "double"   => PARSING["float"],
3      "dateTime" => PARSING["datetime"]
4    )
```

Appendix C

Rails Essentials

Chances are you learned about Rails from watching beginner screencasts or studying our highly rated companion in the Professional Ruby Series, the excellent *Ruby on Rails Tutorial* by Michael Hartl. Those resources will get you through the initial slope of the learning curve and on a trajectory toward serious productivity. But to continue making progress, it helps to know the tools that real Rails masters use every day.

C.1 Environmental Concerns

No, I'm not about to go off on a tangent about carbon credits and global warming. As a Rails pro, you're going to spend a lot of time using the command line, so you might as well save yourself as much confusion and extra typing as possible. The following little tips and tricks should make your life easier and more enjoyable.

C.1.1 Operating System

While it is certainly possible to write Rails application on a Windows platform, and quite a few people do that, it is far from optimal.

The fact is, your application is most probably going to run on a Linux server in production, and so, being able to install all the essential pieces locally is very important. Many of the gems that you might want to use will simply refuse to compile in a non-Unix environment.

Note that while your server most probably runs Linux, you can quite easily use OS X as your development environment. At first glance this goes against the notion of running the same OS as the server, but fortunately, most Rails developers use Apple machines for development, and so, historically, they've made sure all relevant gems and software packages are available and compatible with those from the Linux environment. Practically all the gems that can be compiled on Linux will happily compile on OS X as well.

If you are stuck with Windows as your development machine, it is usually better to run a Linux virtual machine to host the Ruby environment. Check out Vagrant[1] for easy installation of development virtual machines.

C.1.2 Aliases

At minimum you should add aliases for starting your Rails server and console to your shell's execution environment. Geoffrey Grosenbach suggests `alias ss 'bundle exec rails server'` and `alias sc 'bundle exec rails console'`.

Vitaly Says ...

You might want to add –debugger to your aliases if you always include a debugger gem in your applications

---

C.2 Essential Gems

Some gems are so valuable that (arguably) they should be a part of the core Rails distribution. However, because of the "less is more" philosophy of the core team, the Rails core distribution is actually shrinking, not growing.

The following section contains an alphabetical list of essential gems for the Rails pro to be aware of and use regularly.

C.2.1 Better Errors

`https://github.com/charliesome/better_errors`

Better Errors replaces the standard Rails error page with a much better and more useful error page. It is also usable outside of Rails in any Rack app as Rack middleware.

Instead of a plain default error page, Better Errors will display a full interactive stack trace with source code inspection.

If you also include the companion `binding_of_caller`[2] gem in your application, Better Errors will be able to also let you inspect local and instance variables and even embed a full REPL into every stack frame of your error page backtrace. Of course, you should only ever do that in a development environment.

To use it simply add the following to your `Gemfile`:

---

1. `http://www.vagrantup.com`
2. `https://github.com/banister/binding_of_caller`

```
1 group :development do
2   gem "better_errors"
3   gem 'binding_of_caller'
4 end
```

C.2.2 Country Select

`https://github.com/stefanpenner/country_select`

This plugin, previously in Rails core, provides a simple way to get an HTML select tag with a list of countries. It lists countries as their full names and can optionally take a list of priority countries to display at the top of the options. It is English only and provides no I18n support.

C.2.3 Debugger

`https://github.com/cldwalker/debugger`

Debugger is a fork of a once-popular `ruby-debug` and `ruby-debug19` gems. It will work with Ruby `1.8.7` and `1.9.x` out of the box.

With the `ruby-debug` and `ruby-debug19` gems, you had to choose one of them according to your Ruby version, whereas `debugger` will just work. Debugger is usually added to the `:development` and `:test` groups of your `Gemfile`.

Once installed, you can simply add a call to `debugger` method in any place of your code to force the execution of the application to stop and start Debugger REPL.

C.2.4 Draper

`https://github.com/drapergem/draper`

As Rails applications grow, so can the complexity in the view layer. Some common symptoms for a complex view can include `if/else` conditions, multiple instance variables, and extensive chaining. The Draper gem provides an elegant solution to this problem by adding an object-oriented layer of presentation logic to your Rails application.

Instead of using a model instance variable directly in a view, using Draper, one can define a decorator instead. A decorator wraps an instance of a model with presentation-related logic. This allows you to encompass view-specific logic for a model in one place. Not only is this a cleaner solution, but it's also easier to test, as Draper supports `RSpec`, `MiniTest::Rails`, and `Test::Unit` out of the box.

To get started, add the `draper` gem to your `Gemfile` and run `bundle`.

```
# Gemfile
gem 'draper'
```

Essentials

To write a decorator for a model, create a new class in `app/decorators`, which inherits from `Draper::Decorator`. For the purposes of our examples, assume we have an Active Record model `Post` that we wish to decorate.

```
1 # app/decorators/post_decorator.rb
2 class PostDecorator < Draper::Decorator
3   ...
4 end
```

Draper also comes with a Rails generator to automatically create a decorator for a given model.

```
$ rails generate decorator Post
```

Within a decorator, you can access the underlying model via the `object` method. Draper also provides access to Rails helpers within your decorators via the h method. To demonstrate, the following method renders an avatar if the post author has one.

```
1 # app/decorators/post_decorator.rb
2 class PostDecorator < Draper::Decorator
3   ...
4   def author_avatar
5     return unless object.author.avatar?
6     h.image_tag(object.author.avatar, class: 'avatar')
7   end
8 end
```

To assign a decorator to an object, call the `decorate` method on a given object instance. This will automatically infer the decorator based on the object.

```
@post = Post.first.decorate
```

Alternatively, you can always explicitly instantiate a decorator yourself, supplying an instance of the decorated model as its argument.

```
@post = PostDecorator.new(Post.first)
```

Note that Draper also supports decoration on a collection. Each item in the collection will be decorated with the inferred decorator.

```
@posts = Posts.all.decorate
```

C.2.5 Kaminari

https://github.com/amatsuda/kaminari

One frequent need in a Rails application is paginating the database query results. For a long time, the number-one plugin to do it was `will_paginate`, but lately it is being replaced by a better alternative: Kaminari. Kaminari is "a Scope & Engine based, clean, powerful, customizable and sophisticated paginator for Rails." The interface is scope based. For example, to paginate a list of projects, you can do this:

```
@projects = Project.page(params[:page])
```

One area where Kaminari shines is customization. If you need a custom markup for your pagination links, you don't need to edit obscure configuration files. Instead, you just edit HTML templates. To get the templates to customize, run the following command:

```
$ rails g kaminari:views THEME
```

where THEME is "default" or one of the themes from `https://github.com/amatsuda/kaminari_themes`.

C.2.6   Nested Form Fields

`https://github.com/ncri/nested_form_fields`

It's common to want to edit records along with their has_many associations on a single page.

This Rails gem helps creating forms for models with nested has_many associations and relies on jQuery to dynamically add and remove nested form fields without a page reload. This gem has the following specifications:

- Works for arbitrarily deeply nested associations (tested up to four levels)
- Works with form builders like simple_form
- Requires at least Ruby 1.9 and the Rails Asset Pipeline

To install, add `nested_form_fields` to your application's `Gemfile`, run `bundle`, and in your application.js file, add the following:

```
//= require nested_form_fields
```

Usage is straightforward. The readme file uses the following example (assuming that you have a User model with nested videos):

```
1 class User < ActiveRecord::Base
2   has_many :videos
3   accepts_nested_attributes_for :videos, allow_destroy: true
4 end
```

Use the `nested_fields_for` helper inside your user form to add the video fields:

```
1  = form_for @user do |f|
2    = f.nested_fields_for :videos do |ff|
3      = ff.text_field :video_title
4      ..
```

Links to add and remove fields can be added using the `add_nested_fields` `_link` and `remove_nested_fields_link` helpers:

```
1  = form_for @user do |f|
2    = f.nested_fields_for :videos do |ff|
3      = ff.remove_nested_fields_link
4      = ff.text_field :video_title
5      ..
6    = f.add_nested_fields_link :videos
```

Note that `remove_nested_fields_link` needs to be called within the `nest-ed_fields_for` call and `add_nested_fields_link` outside of it via the parent builder.

C.2.7 Pry and Friends

Pry[3] is a powerful alternative to the standard IRB shell for Ruby. It features syntax highlighting, a flexible plugin architecture, runtime invocation, and source and documentation browsing.

The pry plugin `pry-debugger`[4] adds navigation commands via the debugger (formerly Ruby-debug) gem.

These two gems allow you to debug like a pro. Instead of `debugger`, you use `binding.pry` as your breakpoint command.

Once the execution stops you have all the power of Pry, including syntax highlighted source listing, variables inspections, shell access, and so on.

To use Pry, just add the following two gems to your `Gemfile` development and test groups:

```
1  group :development, :test do
2    gem 'pry-rails'
3    gem 'pry-debugger'
4  end
```

Note that the standard `debugger` commands won't work at a `Pry` prompt. Try `help` to see available commands.

---

3. http://pryrepl.org
4. https://github.com/nixme/pry-debugger

You add the following to ~/.pryrc file to make the n, c, s, f, and l work as before:

```
1 Pry.commands.alias_command 'l', 'whereami'
2 Pry.commands.alias_command 'c', 'continue'
3 Pry.commands.alias_command 'n', 'next'
4 Pry.commands.alias_command 's', 'step'
5 Pry.commands.alias_command 'f', 'finish'
```

Another useful pry plugin to be aware of is `pry-rescue`.[5] If an exception is raised and is not rescued, `pry-rescue` will automatically start a Pry session for you.

C.2.8   Rails Admin

`https://github.com/sferik/rails_admin`

Unlike some other frameworks—for example, Django—Rails doesn't come with a standard admin interface. Not to worry, though, as there is no shortage of gems that provide this functionality.

Rails Admin is one of the better looking and functional ones.

It will allow you to display, create, edit, and delete records in the database; export data to `CSV`, `JSON`, or `XML` formats; manage your record associations; and more.

To install it just add `rails_admin` gem to your `Gemfile`, run `bundle install`, and then run the provided generator:

```
$ rails g rails_admin:install
```

Rails Admin uses `devise` for authentication and will install it if it is not yet present in your project.

It is recommended to use a separate user model `Admin` in a separate table `admins` to authenticate access to the admin interface as it is less susceptible to accidental security exposure.

Remote Debugger

If you are using `Pow` or any other web server that runs in a background, you cannot directly use the debugger console. In this case, remote debugger can be used.

Add the following code to the bottom of `config/application.rb`:

```
1 if ENV['RUBY_DEBUG_PORT']
2   Debugger.start_remote nil, ENV['RUBY_DEBUG_PORT'].to_i
3 end
```

---

5. https://github.com/ConradIrwin/pry-rescue

Essentials

Now you just need to start your server with RUBY_DEBUG_PORT environment variable set to a port value, like 25001, to enable remote debugger.

To connect to this server, you use the `rdebug` command line:

```
$ rdebug -c -p 25001
```

C.2.9 Simple Form

`https://github.com/plataformatec/simple_form`

Generating complex forms by hand can be a very tedious and error-prone process. A number of gems are available to help. One of the most popular lately is SimpleForm. "SimpleForm aims to be as flexible as possible while helping you with powerful components to create your forms."

To add it to your project, first add the gem to your `Gemfile`:

```
gem 'simple_form'
```

Then run bundler to install it and a generator to install configuration file:

```
$ bundle install
$ rails g simple_form:install --bootstrap
```

The `--bootstrap` switch causes the generated markup to be Twitter Bootstrap compatible. Refer to the documentation for other markups supported out of the box.

C.2.10 State Machine

`https://github.com/pluginaweek/state_machine`

A state machine can be a very powerful tool to describe, validate, and use to maintain a complex object state. You can get by with using a couple of booleans for simple case, but it becomes too messy pretty soon. A proper state machine, on the other hand, can make even a complex case manageable.

The most popular state machine implementation at the time of writing is the `state_machine` gem. It has been described as the "gorilla of state machine gems" because it is packed with features like multiple state machines per class, event parallelization, and namespacing, plus it includes adapters for Active Record, DataMapper, Mongoid, MongoMapper, and Sequel.

Be sure to check its state machine drawing functionality:

```
$ rake state_machine:draw CLASS=Project,Issue
```

The Graphiz-based visualizations can be invaluable when you have complicated state transitions.

Some people think that it is overkill for simple uses. A popular alternative is the lighter-weight `Workflow` gem, which is fairly lightweight at only 500 lines of code and also features visualization capabilities. See `https://github.com/geekq/workflow`

The primary difference between the two libraries is that in `Workflow`, you define events inside of their related states. You possibility lose some reusability, but the definitions are somewhat easier to read and understand.

```
1  class Article
2    include Workflow
3
4    workflow do
5      state :new do
6        event :submit, :transitions_to => :awaiting_review
7      end
8
9      state :awaiting_review do
10       event :review, :transitions_to => :being_reviewed
11     end
12
13     state :being_reviewed do
14       event :accept, :transitions_to => :accepted
15       event :reject, :transitions_to => :rejected
16     end
17
18     state :accepted
19     state :rejected
20   end
21 end
```

C.3   Ruby Toolbox

`https://www.ruby-toolbox.com`

Didn't see what you're looking for in the previous list? This site lists and organizes a lot of Ruby and Rails gems by category and popularity. It's usually the first place to look if you're searching for third-party functionality to add to your Rails application.

C.4   Screencasts

Screencasts are videos distributed online that teach you a narrowly focused topic of interest by capturing actual screen output (hence the name) while the author explains concepts and writes code. The Rails community loves to create screencasts!

C.4.1   Railcasts

`http://railscasts.com/`

Short on cash? Host Ryan Bates posts a new screencast almost every two weeks for free. Episodes range between 5 to 15 minutes in length and are focused on Rails-specific topics.

Index

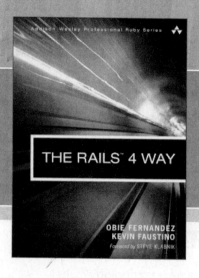

FREE
Online Edition

Your purchase of **The Rails™ 4 Way** includes access to a free online edition for 45 days through the **Safari Books Online** subscription service. Nearly every Addison-Wesley Professional book is available online through **Safari Books Online**, along with thousands of books and videos from publishers such as Cisco Press, Exam Cram, IBM Press, O'Reilly Media, Prentice Hall, Que, Sams, and VMware Press.

Safari Books Online is a digital library providing searchable, on-demand access to thousands of technology, digital media, and professional development books and videos from leading publishers. With one monthly or yearly subscription price, you get unlimited access to learning tools and information on topics including mobile app and software development, tips and tricks on using your favorite gadgets, networking, project management, graphic design, and much more.

Activate your FREE Online Edition at
informit.com/safarifree

STEP 1:   Enter the coupon code: WTVZGAA.

STEP 2:   New Safari users, complete the brief registration form.
Safari subscribers, just log in.

If you have difficulty registering on Safari or accessing the online edition,
please e-mail customer-service@safaribooksonline.com